NISSAN PICK-UPS AND PATHFINDER
1989-95 REPAIR MANUAL

CHILTON'S

Covers all U.S. and Canadian models of Nissan Pick-ups and Pathfinder; 2 and 4 wheel drive

by **Tony Tortorici,** A.S.E., S.A.E.

CHILTON *Automotive Books*

PUBLISHED BY **HAYNES NORTH AMERICA, Inc.**

Manufactured in USA
© 1995 Haynes North America, Inc.
ISBN 0-8019-8671-0
Library of Congress Catalog Card No. 94-069440
9012345678 9876543210

Haynes Publishing Group
Sparkford Nr Yeovil
Somerset BA22 7JJ England

Haynes North America, Inc
861 Lawrence Drive
Newbury Park
California 91320 USA

ABCDE
FG

9H1

Contents

Contents

DRIVE TRAIN **7**

SUSPENSION AND STEERING **8**

BRAKES **9**

BODY AND TRIM **10**

GLOSSARY

MASTER INDEX

SAFETY NOTICE

Proper service and repair procedures are vital to the safe, reliable operation of all motor vehicles, as well as the personal safety of those performing repairs. This manual outlines procedures for servicing and repairing vehicles using safe, effective methods. The procedures contain many NOTES, CAUTIONS and WARNINGS which should be followed, along with standard procedures to eliminate the possibility of personal injury or improper service which could damage the vehicle or compromise its safety.

It is important to note that repair procedures and techniques, tools and parts for servicing motor vehicles, as well as the skill and experience of the individual performing the work vary widely. It is not possible to anticipate all of the conceivable ways or conditions under which vehicles may be serviced, or to provide cautions as to all possible hazards that may result. Standard and accepted safety precautions and equipment should be used when handling toxic or flammable fluids, and safety goggles or other protection should be used during cutting, grinding, chiseling, prying, or any other process that can cause material removal or projectiles.

Some procedures require the use of tools specially designed for a specific purpose. Before substituting another tool or procedure, you must be completely satisfied that neither your personal safety, nor the performance of the vehicle will be endangered.

Although information in this manual is based on industry sources and is complete as possible at the time of publication, the possibility exists that some car manufacturers made later changes which could not be included here. While striving for total accuracy, the authors or publishers cannot assume responsibility for any errors, changes or omissions that may occur in the compilation of this data.

PART NUMBERS

Part numbers listed in this reference are not recommendations by Haynes North America, Inc. for any product brand name. They are references that can be used with interchange manuals and aftermarket supplier catalogs to locate each brand supplier's discrete part number.

SPECIAL TOOLS

Special tools are recommended by the vehicle manufacturer to perform their specific job. Use has been kept to a minimum, but where absolutely necessary, they are referred to in the text by the part number of the tool manufacturer. These tools can be purchased, under the appropriate part number, from your local dealer or regional distributor, or an equivalent tool can be purchased locally from a tool supplier or parts outlet. Before substituting any tool for the one recommended, read the SAFETY NOTICE at the top of this page.

ACKNOWLEDGMENTS

The publisher expresses appreciation to Nissan Motor Company for their generous assistance.

1

GENERAL INFORMATION AND MAINTENANCE

HOW TO USE THIS BOOK

This Chilton's Total Car Care manual for the 1989–95 Nissan Pick-up and Pathfinder is intended to help you learn more about the inner workings of your vehicle while saving you money on its upkeep and operation.

The beginning of the book will likely be referred to the most, since that is where you will find information for maintenance and tune-up. The other sections deal with the more complex systems of your vehicle. Systems (from engine through brakes) are covered to the extent that the average do-it-yourselfer can attempt. This book will not explain such things as rebuilding a differential because the expertise required and the special tools necessary make this uneconomical. It will, however, give you detailed instructions to help you change your own brake pads and shoes, replace spark plugs, and perform many more jobs that can save you money and help avoid expensive problems.

A secondary purpose of this book is a reference for owners who want to understand their vehicle and/or their mechanics better.

Where to Begin

Before removing any bolts, read through the entire procedure. This will give you the overall view of what tools and supplies will be required. So read ahead and plan ahead. Each operation should be approached logically and all procedures thoroughly understood before attempting any work.

If repair of a component is not considered practical, we tell you how to remove the part and then how to install the new or rebuilt replacement. In this way, you at least save labor costs.

Avoiding Trouble

Many procedures in this book require you to "label and disconnect . . ." a group of lines, hoses or wires. Don't be think you can remember where everything goes—you won't. If you hook up vacuum or fuel lines incorrectly, the vehicle may run poorly, if at all. If you hook up electrical wiring incorrectly, you may instantly learn a very expensive lesson.

You don't need to know the proper name for each hose or line. A piece of masking tape on the hose and a piece on its fitting will allow you to assign your own label. As long as you remember your own code, the lines can be reconnected by matching your tags. Remember that tape will dissolve in gasoline or solvents; if a part is to be washed or cleaned, use another method of identification. A permanent felt-tipped marker or a metal scribe can be very handy for marking metal parts. Remove any tape or paper labels after assembly.

Maintenance or Repair?

Maintenance includes routine inspections, adjustments, and replacement of parts which show signs of normal wear. Maintenance compensates for wear or deterioration. Repair implies that something has broken or is not working. A need for a repair is often caused by lack of maintenance. for example: draining and refilling automatic transmission fluid is maintenance recommended at specific intervals. Failure to do this can shorten the life of the transmission/transaxle, requiring very expensive repairs. While no maintenance program can prevent items from eventually breaking or wearing out, a general rule is true: MAINTENANCE IS CHEAPER THAN REPAIR.

TOOLS AND EQUIPMENT

▶See Figures 1 thru 15

Without the proper tools and equipment it is impossible to properly service your vehicle. It would be virtually impossible to catalog every tool that you would need to perform all of the operations in this book. It would be unwise for the amateur to rush out and buy an expensive set of tools on the theory that he/she may need one or more of them at some time.

The best approach is to proceed slowly, gathering a good quality set of those tools that are used most frequently. Don't be misled by the low cost of bargain tools. It is far better to spend a little more for better quality. Forged wrenches, 6 or 12-point sockets and fine tooth ratchets are by far preferable to their less expensive counterparts. As any good mechanic can tell you, there are few worse experiences than trying to work on a vehicle with bad tools. Your monetary savings will be far outweighed by frustration and mangled knuckles.

Two basic mechanic's rules should be mentioned here. First, whenever the left side of the vehicle or engine is referred to, it means the driver's side. Conversely, the right side of the vehicle means the passenger's side. Second, screws and bolts are removed by turning counterclockwise, and tightened by turning clockwise unless specifically noted.

Safety is always the most important rule. Constantly be aware of the dangers involved in working on an automobile and take the proper precautions. Please refer to the information in this section regarding SERVICING YOUR VEHICLE SAFELY and the SAFETY NOTICE on the acknowledgment page.

Avoiding the Most Common Mistakes

Pay attention to the instructions provided. There are 3 common mistakes in mechanical work:

1. Incorrect order of assembly, disassembly or adjustment. When taking something apart or putting it together, performing steps in the wrong order usually just costs you extra time; however, it CAN break something. Read the entire procedure before beginning. Perform everything in the order in which the instructions say you should, even if you can't see a reason for it. When you're taking apart something that is very intricate, you might want to draw a picture of how it looks when assembled in order to make sure you get everything back in its proper position. When making adjustments, perform them in the proper order. One adjustment possibly will affect another.

2. Overtorquing (or undertorquing). While it is more common for overtorquing to cause damage, undertorquing may allow a fastener to vibrate loose causing serious damage. Especially when dealing with aluminum parts, pay attention to torque specifications and utilize a torque wrench in assembly. If a torque figure is not available, remember that if you are using the right tool to perform the job, you will probably not have to strain yourself to get a fastener tight enough. The pitch of most threads is so slight that the tension you put on the wrench will be multiplied many times in actual force on what you are tightening.

There are many commercial products available for ensuring that fasteners won't come loose, even if they are not torqued just right (a very common brand is Loctite®. If you're worried about getting something together tight enough to hold, but loose enough to avoid mechanical damage during assembly, one of these products might offer substantial insurance. Before choosing a threadlocking compound, read the label on the package and make sure the product is compatible with the materials, fluids, etc. involved.

3. Crossthreading. This occurs when a part such as a bolt is screwed into a nut or casting at the wrong angle and forced. Crossthreading is more likely to occur if access is difficult. It helps to clean and lubricate fasteners, then to start threading the bolt, spark plug, etc. with your fingers. If you encounter resistance, unscrew the part and start over again at a different angle until it can be inserted and turned several times without much effort. Keep in mind that many parts have tapered threads, so that gentle turning will automatically bring the part you're threading to the proper angle. Don't put a wrench on the part until it's been tightened a couple of turns by hand. If you suddenly encounter resistance, and the part has not seated fully, don't force it. Pull it back out to make sure it's clean and threading properly.

Be sure to take your time and be patient, and always plan ahead. Allow yourself ample time to perform repairs and maintenance.

Begin accumulating those tools that are used most frequently: those associated with routine maintenance and tune-up. In addition to the normal assortment of screwdrivers and pliers, you should have the following tools:

• Wrenches/sockets and combination open end/box end wrenches in sizes from ⅛–¾ in. or 3–19mm, as well as a 13⁄16 in. or ⅝ in. spark plug socket (depending on plug type).

➡If possible, buy various length socket drive extensions. Universal-joint and wobble extensions can be extremely useful, but be careful when using them, as they can change the amount of torque applied to the socket.

• Jackstands for support.
• Oil filter wrench.

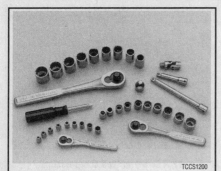

Fig. 1 All but the most basic procedures will require an assortment of ratchets and sockets

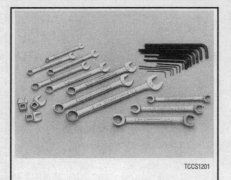

Fig. 2 In addition to ratchets, a good set of wrenches and hex keys will be necessary

Fig. 3 A hydraulic floor jack and a set of jackstands are essential for lifting and supporting the vehicle

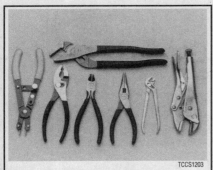

Fig. 4 An assortment of pliers, grippers and cutters will be handy for old rusted parts and stripped bolt heads

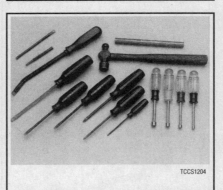

Fig. 5 Various drivers, chisels and prybars are great tools to have in your toolbox

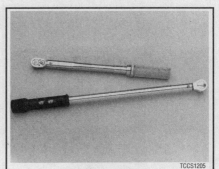

Fig. 6 Many repairs will require the use of a torque wrench to assure the components are properly fastened

Fig. 7 Although not always necessary, using specialized brake tools will save time

Fig. 8 A few inexpensive lubrication tools will make maintenance easier

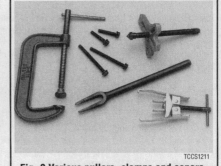

Fig. 9 Various pullers, clamps and separator tools are needed for many larger, more complicated repairs

- Spout or funnel for pouring fluids.
- Grease gun for chassis lubrication (unless your vehicle is not equipped with any grease fittings)
- Hydrometer for checking the battery (unless equipped with a sealed, maintenance-free battery).
- A container for draining oil and other fluids.
- Rags for wiping up the inevitable mess.

In addition to the above items there are several others that are not absolutely necessary, but handy to have around. These include an equivalent oil absorbent gravel, like cat litter, and the usual supply of lubricants, antifreeze and fluids. This is a basic list for routine maintenance, but only your personal needs and desire can accurately determine your list of tools.

After performing a few projects on the vehicle, you'll be amazed at the other tools and non-tools on your workbench. Some useful household items are: a large turkey baster or siphon, empty coffee cans and ice trays (to store parts), a ball of twine, electrical tape for wiring, small rolls of colored tape for tagging lines or hoses, markers and pens, a note pad, golf tees (for plugging vacuum lines), metal coat hangers or a roll of mechanic's wire (to hold things out of the way), dental pick or similar long, pointed probe, a strong magnet, and a small mirror (to see into recesses and under manifolds).

A more advanced set of tools, suitable for tune-up work, can be drawn up easily. While the tools are slightly more sophisticated, they need not be outrageously expensive. There are several inexpensive tach/dwell meters on the market that are every bit as good for the average mechanic as a professional model. Just be sure that it goes to a least 1200–1500 rpm on the tach scale and that it works on 4, 6 and 8-cylinder engines. The key to these purchases is to make them with an eye towards adaptability and wide range. A basic list of tune-up tools could include:

- Tach/dwell meter.
- Spark plug wrench and gapping tool.
- Feeler gauges for valve adjustment.
- Timing light.

The choice of a timing light should be made carefully. A light which works on the DC current supplied by the vehicle's battery is the best choice; it should

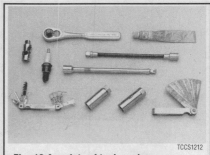

Fig. 10 A variety of tools and gauges should be used for spark plug gapping and installation

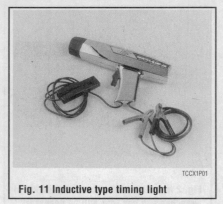

Fig. 11 Inductive type timing light

Fig. 12 A screw-in type compression gauge is recommended for compression testing

Fig. 13 A vacuum/pressure tester is necessary for many testing procedures

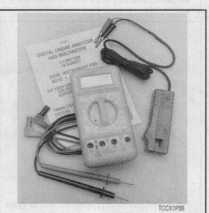

Fig. 14 Most modern automotive multimeters incorporate many helpful features

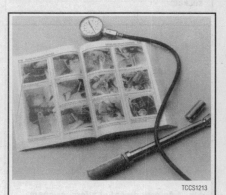

Fig. 15 Proper information is vital, so always have a Chilton Total Car Care manual handy

have a xenon tube for brightness. On any vehicle with an electronic ignition system, a timing light with an inductive pickup that clamps around the No. 1 spark plug cable is preferred.

In addition to these basic tools, there are several other tools and gauges you may find useful. These include:
- Compression gauge. The screw-in type is slower to use, but eliminates the possibility of a faulty reading due to escaping pressure.
- Manifold vacuum gauge.
- 12V test light.
- A combination volt/ohmmeter
- Induction Ammeter. This is used for determining whether or not there is current in a wire. These are handy for use if a wire is broken somewhere in a wiring harness.

As a final note, you will probably find a torque wrench necessary for all but the most basic work. The beam type models are perfectly adequate, although the newer click types (breakaway) are easier to use. The click type torque wrenches tend to be more expensive. Also keep in mind that all types of torque wrenches should be periodically checked and/or recalibrated. You will have to decide for yourself which better fits your pocketbook, and purpose.

Special Tools

Normally, the use of special factory tools is avoided for repair procedures, since these are not readily available for the do-it-yourself mechanic. When it is possible to perform the job with more commonly available tools, it will be pointed out, but occasionally, a special tool was designed to perform a specific function and should be used. Before substituting another tool, you should be convinced that neither your safety nor the performance of the vehicle will be compromised.

Special tools can usually be purchased from an automotive parts store or from your dealer. In some cases special tools may be available directly from the tool manufacturer.

SERVICING YOUR VEHICLE SAFELY

▶See Figures 16, 17 and 18

It is virtually impossible to anticipate all of the hazards involved with automotive maintenance and service, but care and common sense will prevent most accidents.

The rules of safety for mechanics range from "don't smoke around gasoline," to "use the proper tool(s) for the job." The trick to avoiding injuries is to develop safe work habits and to take every possible precaution.

Do's

- Do keep a fire extinguisher and first aid kit handy.
- Do wear safety glasses or goggles when cutting, drilling, grinding or prying, even if you have 20–20 vision. If you wear glasses for the sake of vision, wear safety goggles over your regular glasses.
- Do shield your eyes whenever you work around the battery. Batteries contain sulfuric acid. In case of contact with, flush the area with water or a mixture of water and baking soda, then seek immediate medical attention.
- Do use safety stands (jackstands) for any undervehicle service. Jacks are for raising vehicles; jackstands are for making sure the vehicle stays raised until you want it to come down.
- Do use adequate ventilation when working with any chemicals or hazardous materials. Like carbon monoxide, the asbestos dust resulting from some brake lining wear can be hazardous in sufficient quantities.
- Do disconnect the negative battery cable when working on the electrical system. The secondary ignition system contains EXTREMELY HIGH VOLTAGE. In some cases it can even exceed 50,000 volts.
- Do follow manufacturer's directions whenever working with potentially hazardous materials. Most chemicals and fluids are poisonous.
- Do properly maintain your tools. Loose hammerheads, mushroomed

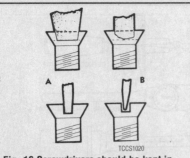

Fig. 16 Screwdrivers should be kept in good condition to prevent injury or damage which could result if the blade slips from the screw

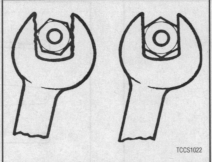

Fig. 17 Using the correct size wrench will help prevent the possibility of rounding off a nut

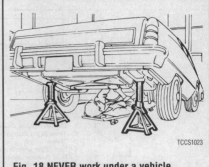

Fig. 18 NEVER work under a vehicle unless it is supported using safety stands (jackstands)

punches and chisels, frayed or poorly grounded electrical cords, excessively worn screwdrivers, spread wrenches (open end), cracked sockets, slipping ratchets, or faulty droplight sockets can cause accidents.

• Likewise, keep your tools clean; a greasy wrench can slip off a bolt head, ruining the bolt and often harming your knuckles in the process.

• Do use the proper size and type of tool for the job at hand. Do select a wrench or socket that fits the nut or bolt. The wrench or socket should sit straight, not cocked.

• Do, when possible, pull on a wrench handle rather than push on it, and adjust your stance to prevent a fall.

• Do be sure that adjustable wrenches are tightly closed on the nut or bolt and pulled so that the force is on the side of the fixed jaw.

• Do strike squarely with a hammer; avoid glancing blows.

• Do set the parking brake and block the drive wheels if the work requires a running engine.

Don'ts

• Don't run the engine in a garage or anywhere else without proper ventilation—EVER! Carbon monoxide is poisonous; it takes a long time to leave the human body and you can build up a deadly supply of it in your system by simply breathing in a little at a time. You may not realize you are slowly poisoning yourself. Always use power vents, windows, fans and/or open the garage door.

• Don't work around moving parts while wearing loose clothing. Short sleeves are much safer than long, loose sleeves. Hard-toed shoes with neoprene soles protect your toes and give a better grip on slippery surfaces. Watches and jewelry is not safe working around a vehicle. Long hair should be tied back under a hat or cap.

• Don't use pockets for toolboxes. A fall or bump can drive a screwdriver deep into your body. Even a rag hanging from your back pocket can wrap around a spinning shaft or fan.

• Don't smoke when working around gasoline, cleaning solvent or other flammable material.

• Don't smoke when working around the battery. When the battery is being charged, it gives off explosive hydrogen gas.

• Don't use gasoline to wash your hands; there are excellent soaps available. Gasoline contains dangerous additives which can enter the body through a cut or through your pores. Gasoline also removes all the natural oils from the skin so that bone dry hands will suck up oil and grease.

• Don't service the air conditioning system unless you are equipped with the necessary tools and training. When liquid or compressed gas refrigerant is released to atmospheric pressure it will absorb heat from whatever it contacts. This will chill or freeze anything it touches.

• Don't use screwdrivers for anything other than driving screws! A screwdriver used as an prying tool can snap when you least expect it, causing injuries. At the very least, you'll ruin a good screwdriver.

• Don't use an emergency jack (that little ratchet, scissors, or pantograph jack supplied with the vehicle) for anything other than changing a flat! These jacks are only intended for emergency use out on the road; they are NOT designed as a maintenance tool. If you are serious about maintaining your vehicle yourself, invest in a hydraulic floor jack of at least a 1½ ton capacity, and at least two sturdy jackstands.

FASTENERS, MEASUREMENTS AND CONVERSIONS

Bolts, Nuts and Other Threaded Retainers

▶**See Figures 19 and 20**

Although there are a great variety of fasteners found in the modern car or truck, the most commonly used retainer is the threaded fastener (nuts, bolts, screws, studs, etc.). Most threaded retainers may be reused, provided that they are not damaged in use or during the repair. Some retainers (such as stretch bolts or torque prevailing nuts) are designed to deform when tightened or in use and should not be reinstalled.

Whenever possible, we will note any special retainers which should be replaced during a procedure. But you should always inspect the condition of a retainer when it is removed and replace any that show signs of damage. Check all threads for rust or corrosion which can increase the torque necessary to achieve the desired clamp load for which that fastener was originally selected. Additionally, be sure that the driver surface of the fastener has not been compromised by rounding or other damage. In some cases a driver surface may become only partially rounded, allowing the driver to catch in only one direction. In many of these occurrences, a fastener may be installed and tightened, but the driver would not be able to grip and loosen the fastener again.

If you must replace a fastener, whether due to design or damage, you must ALWAYS be sure to use the proper replacement. In all cases, a retainer of the same design, material and strength should be used. Markings on the heads of

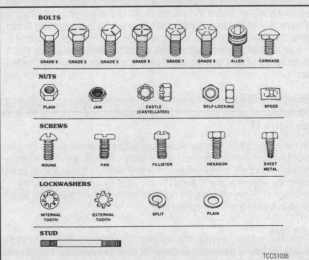

Fig. 19 There are many different types of threaded retainers found on vehicles

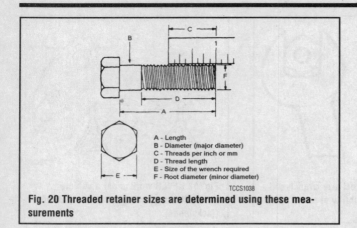

A - Length
B - Diameter (major diameter)
C - Threads per inch or mm
D - Thread length
E - Size of the wrench required
F - Root diameter (minor diameter)

TCCS1038

Fig. 20 Threaded retainer sizes are determined using these measurements

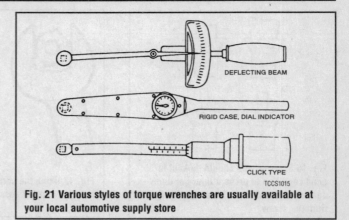

DEFLECTING BEAM

RIGID CASE, DIAL INDICATOR

CLICK TYPE

TCCS1015

Fig. 21 Various styles of torque wrenches are usually available at your local automotive supply store

most bolts will help determine the proper strength of the fastener. The same material, thread and pitch must be selected to assure proper installation and safe operation of the vehicle afterwards.

Thread gauges are available to help measure a bolt or stud's thread. Most automotive and hardware stores keep gauges available to help you select the proper size. In a pinch, you can use another nut or bolt for a thread gauge. If the bolt you are replacing is not too badly damaged, you can select a match by finding another bolt which will thread in its place. If you find a nut which threads properly onto the damaged bolt, then use that nut to help select the replacement bolt.

✳✳ WARNING

Be aware that when you find a bolt with damaged threads, you may also find the nut or drilled hole it was threaded into has also been damaged. If this is the case, you may have to drill and tap the hole, replace the nut or otherwise repair the threads. NEVER try to force a replacement bolt to fit into the damaged threads.

Torque

Torque is defined as the measurement of resistance to turning or rotating. It tends to twist a body about an axis of rotation. A common example of this would be tightening a threaded retainer such as a nut, bolt or screw. Measuring torque is one of the most common ways to help assure that a threaded retainer has been properly fastened.

When tightening a threaded fastener, torque is applied in three distinct areas, the head, the bearing surface and the clamp load. About 50 percent of the measured torque is used in overcoming bearing friction. This is the friction between the bearing surface of the bolt head, screw head or nut face and the base material or washer (the surface on which the fastener is rotating). Approximately 40 percent of the applied torque is used in overcoming thread friction. This leaves only about 10 percent of the applied torque to develop a useful clamp load (the force which holds a joint together). This means that friction can account for as much as 90 percent of the applied torque on a fastener.

TORQUE WRENCHES

♦See Figure 21

In most applications, a torque wrench can be used to assure proper installation of a fastener. Torque wrenches come in various designs and most automotive supply stores will carry a variety to suit your needs. A torque wrench should be used any time we supply a specific torque value for a fastener. Again, the general rule of "if you are using the right tool for the job, you should not have to strain to tighten a fastener" applies here.

Beam Type

The beam type torque wrench is one of the most popular types. It consists of a pointer attached to the head that runs the length of the flexible beam (shaft) to a scale located near the handle. As the wrench is pulled, the beam bends and the pointer indicates the torque using the scale.

Click (Breakaway) Type

Another popular design of torque wrench is the click type. To use the click type wrench you pre-adjust it to a torque setting. Once the torque is reached, the wrench has a reflex signaling feature that causes a momentary breakaway of the torque wrench body, sending an impulse to the operator's hand.

Pivot Head Type

♦See Figure 22

Some torque wrenches (usually of the click type) may be equipped with a pivot head which can allow it to be used in areas of limited access. BUT, it must be used properly. To hold a pivot head wrench, grasp the handle lightly, and as you pull on the handle, it should be floated on the pivot point. If the handle comes in contact with the yoke extension during the process of pulling, there is a very good chance the torque readings will be inaccurate because this could alter the wrench loading point. The design of the handle is usually such as to make it inconvenient to deliberately misuse the wrench.

➡ It should be mentioned that the use of any U-joint, wobble or extension will have an effect on the torque readings, no matter what type of wrench you are using. For the most accurate readings, install the socket directly on the wrench driver. If necessary, straight extensions (which hold a socket directly under the wrench driver) will have the least effect on the torque reading. Avoid any extension that alters the length of the wrench from the handle to the head/driving point (such as a crow's foot). U-joint or wobble extensions can greatly affect the readings; avoid their use at all times.

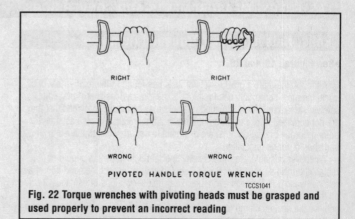

RIGHT

RIGHT

WRONG

WRONG

PIVOTED HANDLE TORQUE WRENCH

TCCS1041

Fig. 22 Torque wrenches with pivoting heads must be grasped and used properly to prevent an incorrect reading

Rigid Case (Direct Reading)

A rigid case or direct reading torque wrench is equipped with a dial indicator to show torque values. One advantage of these wrenches is that they can be held at any position on the wrench without affecting accuracy. These wrenches are often preferred because they tend to be compact, easy to read and have a great degree of accuracy.

TORQUE ANGLE METERS

Because the frictional characteristics of each fastener or threaded hole will vary, clamp loads which are based strictly on torque will vary as well. In most applications, this variance is not significant enough to cause worry. But, in certain applications, a manufacturer's engineers may determine that more precise clamp loads are necessary (such is the case with many aluminum cylinder heads). In these cases, a torque angle method of installation would be specified. When installing fasteners which are torque angle tightened, a predetermined seating torque and standard torque wrench are usually used first to remove any compliance from the joint. The fastener is then tightened the specified additional portion of a turn measured in degrees. A torque angle gauge (mechanical protractor) is used for these applications.

Standard and Metric Measurements

▶See Figure 23

Throughout this manual, specifications are given to help you determine the condition of various components on your vehicle, or to assist you in their installation. Some of the most common measurements include length (in. or cm/mm), torque (ft. lbs., inch lbs. or Nm) and pressure (psi, in. Hg, kPa or mm Hg). In most cases, we strive to provide the proper measurement as determined by the manufacturer's engineers.

Though, in some cases, that value may not be conveniently measured with what is available in your toolbox. Luckily, many of the measuring devices which are available today will have two scales so the Standard or Metric measurements may easily be taken. If any of the various measuring tools which are available to you do not contain the same scale as listed in the specifications, use the accompanying conversion factors to determine the proper value.

The conversion factor chart is used by taking the given specification and multiplying it by the necessary conversion factor. For instance, looking at the first line, if you have a measurement in inches such as "free-play should be 2 in." but your ruler reads only in millimeters, multiply 2 in. by the conversion factor of 25.4 to get the metric equivalent of 50.8mm. Likewise, if the specification was given only in a Metric measurement, for example in Newton Meters (Nm), then look at the center column first. If the measurement is 100 Nm, multiply it by the conversion factor of 0.738 to get 73.8 ft. lbs.

CONVERSION FACTORS

LENGTH–DISTANCE

Inches (in.)	x 25.4	= Millimeters (mm)	x .0394	= Inches
Feet (ft.)	x .305	= Meters (m)	x 3.281	= Feet
Miles	x 1.609	= Kilometers (km)	x .0621	= Miles

VOLUME

Cubic Inches (in3)	x 16.387	= Cubic Centimeters	x .061	= in3
IMP Pints (IMP pt.)	x .568	= Liters (L)	x 1.76	= IMP pt.
IMP Quarts (IMP qt.)	x 1.137	= Liters (L)	x .88	= IMP qt.
IMP Gallons (IMP gal.)	x 4.546	= Liters (L)	x .22	= IMP gal.
IMP Quarts (IMP qt.)	x 1.201	= US Quarts (US qt.)	x .833	= IMP qt.
IMP Gallons (IMP gal.)	x 1.201	= US Gallons (US gal.)	x .833	= IMP gal.
Fl. Ounces	x 29.573	= Milliliters	x .034	= Ounces
US Pints (US pt.)	x .473	= Liters (L)	x 2.113	= Pints
US Quarts (US qt.)	x .946	= Liters (L)	x 1.057	= Quarts
US Gallons (US gal.)	x 3.785	= Liters (L)	x .264	= Gallons

MASS–WEIGHT

Ounces (oz.)	x 28.35	= Grams (g)	x .035	= Ounces
Pounds (lb.)	x .454	= Kilograms (kg)	x 2.205	= Pounds

PRESSURE

Pounds Per Sq. In. (psi)	x 6.895	= Kilopascals (kPa)	x .145	= psi
Inches of Mercury (Hg)	x .4912	= psi	x 2.036	= Hg
Inches of Mercury (Hg)	x 3.377	= Kilopascals (kPa)	x .2961	= Hg
Inches of Water (H_2O)	x .07355	= Inches of Mercury	x 13.783	= H_2O
Inches of Water (H_2O)	x .03613	= psi	x 27.684	= H_2O
Inches of Water (H_2O)	x .248	= Kilopascals (kPa)	x 4.026	= H_2O

TORQUE

Pounds–Force Inches (in–lb)	x .113	= Newton Meters (N·m)	x 8.85	= in–lb
Pounds–Force Feet (ft–lb)	x 1.356	= Newton Meters (N·m)	x .738	= ft–lb

VELOCITY

Miles Per Hour (MPH)	x 1.609	= Kilometers Per Hour (KPH)	x .621	= MPH

POWER

Horsepower (Hp)	x .745	= Kilowatts	x 1.34	= Horsepower

FUEL CONSUMPTION*

Miles Per Gallon IMP (MPG)	x .354	= Kilometers Per Liter (Km/L)	
Kilometers Per Liter (Km/L)	x 2.352	= IMP MPG	
Miles Per Gallon US (MPG)	x .425	= Kilometers Per Liter (Km/L)	
Kilometers Per Liter (Km/L)	x 2.352	= US MPG	

*It is common to covert from miles per gallon (mpg) to liters/100 kilometers (1/100 km), where mpg (IMP) x 1/100 km = 282 and mpg (US) x 1/100 km = 235.

TEMPERATURE

Degree Fahrenheit (°F)	= (°C x 1.8) + 32
Degree Celsius (°C)	= (°F – 32) x .56

TCCS1044

Fig. 23 Standard and metric conversion factors chart

SERIAL NUMBER IDENTIFICATION

Vehicle Identification Number

▶ See Figures 24 thru 31

The vehicle serial number is stamped on a plate fastened to the driver's side door pillar.

The number is also located on the right front fender apron in the engine compartment (behind the wheel arch).

All models also have the vehicle identification number stamped on a plate attached to the left side of the instrument panel. The plate is visible through the windshield.

The vehicle identification (model variation codes) may be interpreted as follows:

All models use a four letter prefix followed by the model designation (D21), then a four letter suffix (five on 1991 and later models), as shown in the illustration.

The serial number on all models is the new 17-digit format. The first three digits are the World Manufacturer Identification number. The next five digits are the Vehicle Description Section (same as the series identification number). The remaining nine digits are the production numbers.

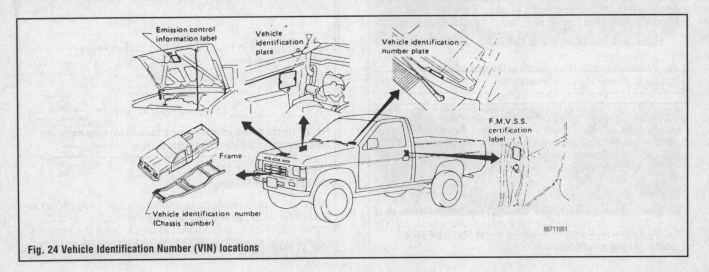

Fig. 24 Vehicle Identification Number (VIN) locations

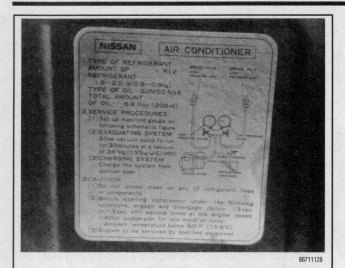

Fig. 25 A/C service label located in the engine compartment—R-12 refrigerant

Fig. 26 A/C service label located in the engine compartment—R-134a refrigerant

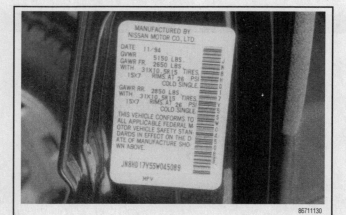

Fig. 27 Manufacturer's label located in the door pillar area—note that the build date of vehicle is at the top

Fig. 28 Vehicle identification number is on the firewall-mounted label in the engine compartment

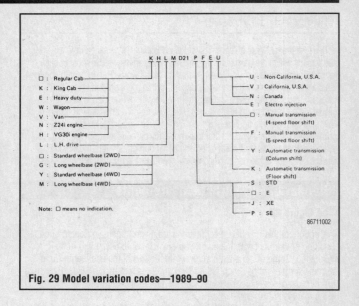

Fig. 29 Model variation codes—1989–90

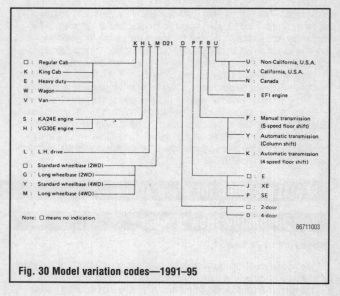

Fig. 30 Model variation codes—1991–95

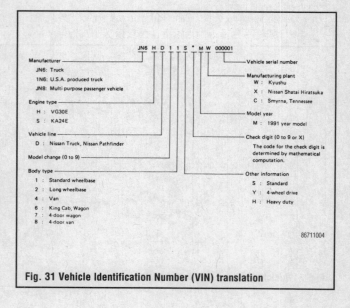

Fig. 31 Vehicle Identification Number (VIN) translation

ENGINE IDENTIFICATION

Year	Model	Actual Displacement cu. in.	cc	Liters	Engine Series Identification	Fuel System	No. of Cylinders	Engine Type
1989	Pick-Up	145.8	2389	2.4	Z24i	TBI	4	SOHC
		180.6	2960	3.0	VG30i	TBI	6	DOHC
	Pathfinder	180.6	2960	3.0	VG30i	TBI	6	DOHC
1990	Pick-Up	145.8	2389	2.4	KA24E	MFI	4	SOHC
		180.6	2960	3.0	VG30E	MFI	6	DOHC
	Pathfinder	180.6	2960	3.0	VG30E	MFI	6	DOHC
1991	Pick-Up	145.8	2389	2.4	KA24E	MFI	4	SOHC
		180.6	2960	3.0	VG30E	MFI	6	DOHC
	Pathfinder	180.6	2960	3.0	VG30E	MFI	6	DOHC
1992	Pick-Up	145.8	2389	2.4	KA24E	MFI	4	SOHC
		180.6	2960	3.0	VG30E	MFI	6	DOHC
	Pathfinder	180.6	2960	3.0	VG30E	MFI	6	DOHC
1993	Pick-Up	145.8	2389	2.4	KA24E	MFI	4	SOHC
		180.6	2960	3.0	VG30E	MFI	6	DOHC
	Pathfinder	180.6	2960	3.0	VG30E	MFI	6	DOHC
1994	Pick-Up	145.8	2389	2.4	KA24E	MFI	4	SOHC
		180.6	2960	3.0	VG30E	MFI	6	DOHC
	Pathfinder	180.6	2960	3.0	VG30E	MFI	6	DOHC
1995	Pick-Up	145.8	2389	2.4	KA24E	MFI	4	SOHC
		180.6	2960	3.0	VG30E	MFI	6	DOHC
	Pathfinder	180.6	2960	3.0	VG30E	MFI	6	DOHC

TBI: Throttle Body Fuel Injection
MFI: Multi-port Fuel Injection
SOHC: Single Overhead Camshaft
DOHC: Double Overhead Camshaft

86711C01

AUTOMATIC TRANSMISSION APPLICATION CHART

Year	Model	Engine	Transmission Type
1989	Pick-Up (2WD)	Z24i	L4N71B①
		VG30i	E4N71B①
	Pick-Up (4WD)	VG30i	RE4R01A
	Pathfinder	VG30i	RE4R01A
1990	Pick-Up (2WD)	KA24E	RL4R01A①
		VG30E	RE4R01A
	Pick-Up (4WD)	VG30E	RE4R01A
	Pathfinder	VG30E	RE4R01A
1991	Pick-Up (2WD)	KA24E	RL4R01A①
		VG30E	RE4R01A
	Pick-Up (4WD)	VG30E	RE4R01A
	Pathfinder	VG30E	RE4R01A
1992	Pick-Up (2WD)	KA24E	RL4R01A①
		VG30E	RE4R01A
	Pick-Up (4WD)	VG30E	RE4R01A
	Pathfinder	VG30E	RE4R01A
1993	Pick-Up (2WD)	KA24E	RL4R01A①
		VG30E	RE4R01A
	Pick-Up (4WD)	VG30E	RE4R01A
	Pathfinder	VG30E	RE4R01A
1994	Pick-Up (2WD)	KA24E	RL4R01A①
		VG30E	RE4R01A
	Pick-Up (4WD)	VG30E	RE4R01A
	Pathfinder	VG30E	RE4R01A
1995	Pick-Up (2WD)	KA24E	RL4R01A①
		VG30E	RE4R01A
	Pick-Up (4WD)	VG30E	RE4R01A
	Pathfinder	VG30E	RE4R01A

①- Floor shift or column shift

86711C03

TRANSFER CASE APPLICATION CHART

Transfer Case Types	Years	Models
TX10	1989–95	Pick-Up/Pathfinder

86711C04

MANUAL TRANSMISSION APPLICATION CHART

Year	Model	Engine	Transmission	Type
1989	Pick-Up (2WD)	Z24i	F4W71C	4 spd
			FS5W71C	5 spd
	Pick-Up (4WD)	Z24i	FS5W71C	5 spd
		VG30i	FS5R30A	5 spd
	Pathfinder	VG30i	FS5R30A	5 spd
1990	Pick-Up	KA24E	FS5W71C	5 spd
		VG30E	FS5R30A	5 spd
	Pathfinder	VG30E	FS5R30A	5 spd
1991	Pick-Up	KA24E	FS5W71C	5 spd
		VG30E	FS5R30A	5 spd
	Pathfinder	VG30E	FS5R30A	5 spd
1992	Pick-Up	KA24E	FS5W71C	5 spd
		VG30E	FS5R30A	5 spd
	Pathfinder	VG30E	FS5R30A	5 spd
1993	Pick-Up	KA24E	FS5W71C	5 spd
		VG30E	FS5R30A	5 spd
	Pathfinder	VG30E	FS5R30A	5 spd
1994	Pick-Up	KA24E	FS5W71C	5 spd
		VG30E	FS5R30A	5 spd
	Pathfinder	VG30E	FS5R30A	5 spd
1995	Pick-Up	KA24E	FS5W71C	5 spd
		VG30E	FS5R30A	5 spd
	Pathfinder	VG30E	FS5R30A	5 spd

86711C02

FRONT DRIVE AXLE APPLICATION CHART

Year	Model	Engine	Axle
1989	Pick-Up	Z24i	R180A
		VG30i	R200A
	Pathfinder	VG30i	R200A
1990	Pick-Up	KA24E	R180A
		VG30E	R200A
	Pathfinder	VG30E	R200A
1991	Pick-Up	KA24E	R180A
		VG30E	R200A
	Pathfinder	VG30E	R200A
1992	Pick-Up	KA24E	R180A
		VG30E	R200A
	Pathfinder	VG30E	R200A
1993	Pick-Up	KA24E	R180A
		VG30E	R200A
	Pathfinder	VG30E	R200A
1994	Pick-Up	KA24E	R180A
		VG30E	R200A
	Pathfinder	VG30E	R200A
1995	Pick-Up	KA24E	R180A
		VG30E	R200A
	Pathfinder	VG30E	R200A

86711C05

REAR DRIVE AXLE APPLICATION CHART

Year	Model	Engine	Axle
1989	Pick-Up (2WD)	Z24i	H190A
		VG30i	H233B
	Pick-Up (4WD)	Z24i	C200
		VG30i	H233B
	Pathfinder	VG30i	H233B
1990	Pick-Up (2WD)	KA24E	H190A
		VG30E	H233B
	Pick-Up (4WD)	KA24E	C200
		VG30E	H233B
	Pathfinder	VG30E	H233B
1991	Pick-Up (2WD)	KA24E	H190A
		VG30E	H233B
	Pick-Up (4WD)	KA24E	C200
		VG30E	H233B
	Pathfinder	VG30E	H233B
1992	Pick-Up (2WD)	KA24E	H190A
		VG30E	H233B
	Pick-Up (4WD)	KA24E	C200
		VG30E	H233B
	Pathfinder	VG30E	H233B
1993	Pick-Up (2WD)	KA24E	H190A
		VG30E	H233B
	Pick-Up (4WD)	KA24E	C200
		VG30E	H233B
	Pathfinder (2WD)	VG30E	H233B
	Pathfinder (4WD)	VG30E	H233B
1994	Pick-Up (2WD)	KA24E	H190A
		VG30E	H233B
	Pick-Up (4WD)	KA24E	C200
		VG30E	H233B
	Pathfinder	VG30E	H233B
1995	Pick-Up (2WD)	KA24E	H190A
		VG30E	H233B
	Pick-Up (4WD)	KA24E	C200
		VG30E	H233B
	Pathfinder (2WD)	VG30E	H233B
	Pathfinder (4WD)	VG30E	H233B

86711C06

Engine Serial Number

▶ **See Figures 32, 33 and 34**

The engine serial number consists of an engine series identification number followed by a six-digit production number. The number may be found in various places, depending upon the particular engine:

- Z24i Engine—the serial number is stamped on the left side of the cylinder block, below the No. 3 and No. 4 spark plugs.
- KA24E Engine—the serial number is stamped on the left side of the cylinder block, below the No. 2 and No. 3 spark plugs.
- VG30i and VG30E Engines—the serial number is stamped on the cylinder block, below the rear of the right side cylinder head.

Transmission Serial Number

▶ **See Figures 35, 36, 37 and 38**

The transmission serial number is stamped on the front upper face of the transmission case on manual transmissions, or on the right side of the transmission case on automatic transmissions.

Transfer Case Serial Number

▶ **See Figure 39**

The transfer case serial number is stamped on the front upper face of the transfer case.

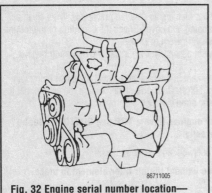

Fig. 32 Engine serial number location— Z24i engine

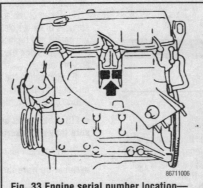

Fig. 33 Engine serial number location— KA24E engine

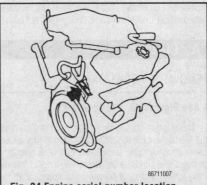

Fig. 34 Engine serial number location— VG30i and VG30E engines

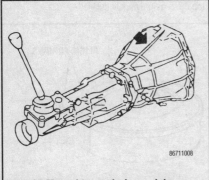

Fig. 35 Manual transmission serial number location

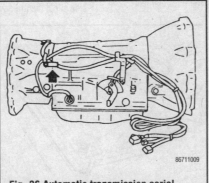

Fig. 36 Automatic transmission serial number location—RE4R01A

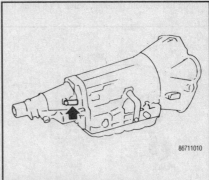

Fig. 37 Automatic transmission serial number location—RL4R01A

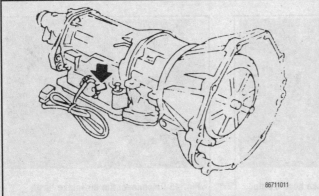

Fig. 38 Automatic transmission serial number location—L4N71B and E4N71B

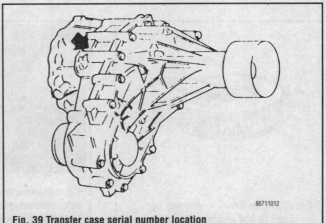

Fig. 39 Transfer case serial number location

ROUTINE MAINTENANCE

Proper maintenance and tune-up is the key to long and trouble-free vehicle life, and the work can yield its own rewards. Studies have shown that a properly tuned and maintained vehicle can achieve better gas mileage than an out-of-tune vehicle. As a conscientious owner and driver, set aside a Saturday morning, say once a month, to check or replace items which could cause major problems later. Keep your own personal log to jot down which services you performed, how much the parts cost you, the date, and the exact odometer reading at the time. Keep all receipts for such items as engine oil and filters, so that they may be referred to in case of related problems or to determine operating expenses. As a do-it-yourselfer, these receipts are the only proof you have that the required maintenance was performed. In the event of a warranty problem, these receipts will be invaluable.

The literature provided with your vehicle when it was originally delivered includes the factory recommended maintenance schedule. If you no longer have this literature, replacement copies are usually available from the dealer. A maintenance schedule is provided later in this section, in case you do not have the factory literature.

Air Cleaner

REMOVAL & INSTALLATION

▶ **See Figures 40, 41, 42 and 43**

The element should be replaced at the recommended intervals shown in the Maintenance Intervals charts later in this section. If your truck is operated under severely dusty conditions or severe operating conditions, more frequent changes will certainly be necessary. Inspect the element at least twice a year. Early spring and early fall are good times for an inspection. Remove the element and check for any perforations or tears in the filter. Check the cleaner housing for signs of dirt or dust that may have leaked through the filter element or in through the snorkel tube. Position a droplight on one side of the element and look through the filter at the light. If no glow of light can be seen through the element material, replace the filter. If holes in the filter element

are apparent, or signs of dirt seepage through the filter are evident, replace the filter.

Air Cleaner Assembly (Housing)

1. Disconnect all hoses, ducts and vacuum tubes from the air cleaner assembly.
2. On 1989 VG30i models and all 4 cylinder models, remove the two (2) top cover wing nuts and grommet (if so equipped). Most models also utilize four side clips (five on the VG30i) to further secure the top of the assembly. Simply pull the wire tab and release the clip. On the 1990 and later VG30E engine, air cleaners are secured solely by means of clips (air box-to-cleaner housing). Remove the cover and lift out the filter element.
3. Remove any side mount brackets and/or retaining bolts, then lift off the air cleaner assembly.
4. Clean or replace the filter element as detailed previously. Wipe clean all surfaces of the air cleaner housing and cover. Check the condition of the mounting gasket and replace if it appears worn or broken.
5. Reposition the air cleaner assembly, then install the mounting bracket and/or bolts.
6. Reposition the filter element in the case and install the cover being careful not to overtighten the wingnut(s). On round-style cleaners, be certain that the arrows on the cover lid and the snorkel match up properly.

➡**Filter elements on many engines have a TOP and BOTTOM side; be sure they are inserted correctly.**

7. Reconnect all hoses, ductwork and vacuum lines.

➡**Never operate the engine without the air filter element in place.**

Air Cleaner Element

▶ **See Figures 44, 45, 46, 47 and 48**

The air cleaner element can be replaced by removing the wingnut(s) and/or side clips, then removing the top cover as previously detailed.

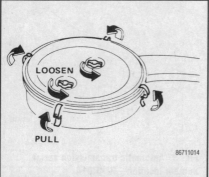

Fig. 40 The air cleaner can be mounted either on the carburetor/throttle body . . .

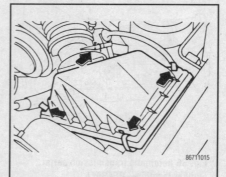

Fig. 41 . . . or remotely in the engine compartment

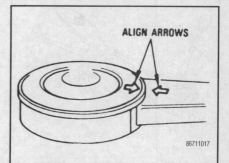

Fig. 42 Many air cleaner assemblies have arrows on the housing and lid—always make sure they align

Fig. 43 The air filter element may be cleaned with low pressure compressed air

Fig. 44 Loosen the air intake hose clamp before removing the filter element—VG30E engine shown

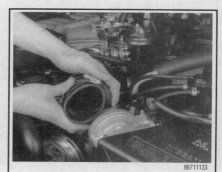

Fig. 45 Disconnect the air intake hose, being careful not to lose the retaining clamp

Fig. 46 Unfasten the side retaining clamps so that the air filter housing can be opened

Fig. 47 Remove the air filter element from the air filter housing

Fig. 48 View of the air filter element. Make sure that the element is installed in the housing properly before fastening the side clamps

Crankcase Ventilation Filter

▶ See Figure 49

Z24I, VG30I AND KA24E ENGINES

Certain models may also utilize an air cleaner-mounted crankcase ventilation filter. If so, it should also be cleaned or replaced at the same time as the regular air filter element. To replace the filter, remove the air cleaner top cover and pull the filter from its housing on the side of the cleaner assembly. Push a new filter into the housing and reinstall the cover. If the filter and plastic holder need replacement, remove the clip mounting the feeder tube to the cleaner housing, then remove the assembly from the air cleaner.

Fuel Filter

REMOVAL & INSTALLATION

▶ See Figures 50 thru 56

✳✳ CAUTION

NEVER SMOKE WHEN WORKING AROUND OR NEAR GASOLINE! MAKE SURE THAT THERE IS NO ACTIVE IGNITION SOURCE NEAR YOUR WORK AREA!

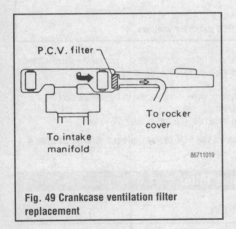

Fig. 49 Crankcase ventilation filter replacement

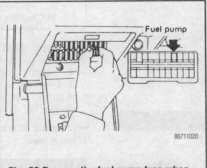

Fig. 50 Remove the fuel pump fuse when releasing the fuel pressure—the fuse's location may vary in the box

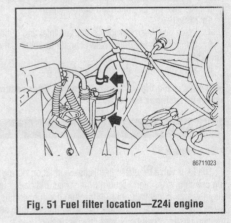

Fig. 51 Fuel filter location—Z24i engine

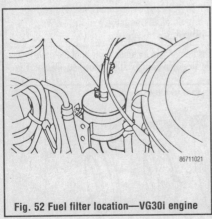

Fig. 52 Fuel filter location—VG30i engine

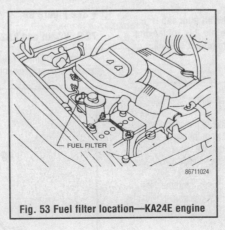

Fig. 53 Fuel filter location—KA24E engine

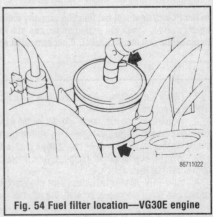

Fig. 54 Fuel filter location—VG30E engine

Fig. 55 Remove the fuel line hose clamp after releasing the fuel pressure

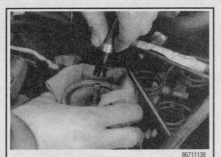

Fig. 56 When removing the fuel line from the fuel filter, have a shop towel in position to catch any fuel that may spill from the filter

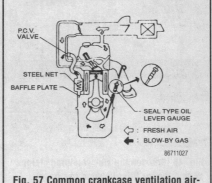

Fig. 57 Common crankcase ventilation airflow

☼ WARNING

Never attempt to remove the fuel filter without first relieving the fuel system pressure!

1. Release the fuel pressure from the fuel line as follows:
    a. Remove the fuel pump fuse at the fuse box.
    b. Start the engine.
    c. After the engine stalls, crank the engine two or three times to make sure that the fuel pressure is released.
    d. Turn the ignition switch **OFF** and reinstall the fuel pump fuse.
2. Loosen the hose clamps at the fuel inlet and outlet lines. Wrap a shop towel or absorbent rag around the filter, then slide each line off the filter nipples.
3. Remove the fuel filter and old hose clamps.

To install:
4. Place new hose clamps on the fuel inlet and outlet lines.
5. Connect the fuel filter, being careful to observe the correct direction of flow, then tighten the hose clamps.
6. Start the engine and check for fuel leaks.

➡ **Always use a high pressure-type fuel filter assembly. Do not use a synthetic resinous fuel filter.**

PCV Valve

▶ **See Figure 57**

The PCV valve regulates crankcase ventilation during various engine operating conditions. At high vacuum (idle speed and partial load range) it will open slightly, and at low vacuum (full throttle) it will open fully. This causes vapor to be removed from the crankcase by the engine vacuum and then be sucked into the combustion chamber where it is dissipated.

➡ **The PCV system will not function properly unless the oil filler cap is tightly sealed. Check the gasket on the cap and be certain it is not leaking. Replace the cap and/or gasket, if necessary, to ensure proper sealing.**

TESTING

1. Check the ventilation hoses and lines for leaks or clogging. Clean or replace as necessary.
2. With the engine running at idle, locate the PCV valve in the cylinder head cover or intake manifold and remove the ventilation hose from the valve; a strong hissing sound should be heard as air passes through the valve.
3. With the engine still idling, place your finger over the valve; a strong vacuum should be felt.
4. If the PCV valve failed either of the preceding two checks (and the ventilation hose is not clogged or broken), the valve will require replacement.

REMOVAL & INSTALLATION

▶ **See Figure 58**

1. If not already done, detach the ventilation hose from the PCV valve.

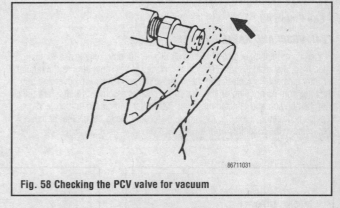

Fig. 58 Checking the PCV valve for vacuum

2. Remove the PCV valve. If its base is threaded, unscrew the valve; otherwise, simply pull the valve from its retaining grommet.

To install:
3. Depending on the type of valve, either screw in the replacement PCV valve or push it into its retaining grommet.
4. Slide the ventilation hose onto the end of the PCV valve.

➡ **For further information on the PCV system, please refer to Section 4 of this manual.**

Air Induction Valve Filter

REMOVAL & INSTALLATION

▶ **See Figure 59**

Z24i, VG30i and KA24E Engines

Regular maintenance for this component includes a check of the drive belt tension and replacement of the air pump air filter at the specified interval. The

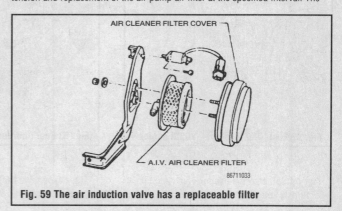

Fig. 59 The air induction valve has a replaceable filter

air filter case is located in the left front of the engine compartment on most models. To replace the air filter, simply unscrew the wing nut(s) securing the cover to the case, withdraw the old filter, install the new one, and reinstall the case. More information on the air pump system can be found in Section 4.

Evaporative Canister

SERVICING

▶ **See Figures 60, 61, 62, 63 and 64**

Check the evaporation control system, if so equipped, every 15,000 miles (24,000 km) or every 12 months. Check the fuel and vapor lines/hoses for proper connections, correct routing, and condition. Replace damaged or deteriorated parts as necessary.

To check the operation of the carbon canister purge control valve, disconnect the rubber hose between the canister control valve and the T-fitting at the T-fitting. Apply vacuum to the hose leading to the control valve. The vacuum condition should be maintained indefinitely. If the control valve leaks, remove the top cover of the valve and check for a dislocated or cracked diaphragm. If the diaphragm is damaged, a repair kit containing a new diaphragm, retainer, and spring is available and should be installed.

The carbon canister has a replaceable air filter in the bottom of the canister. The filter element should be checked once a year or every 15,000 miles (24,000 km); more frequently if the truck is operated in dusty areas. Replace the filter by pulling it out of the bottom of the canister and installing a new one.

Battery

PRECAUTIONS

Always use caution when working on or near the battery. Never allow a tool to bridge the gap between the negative and positive battery terminals. Also, be careful not to allow a tool to provide a ground between the positive cable/terminal and any metal component on the vehicle. Either of these conditions will cause a short circuit, leading to sparks and possible personal injury.

Do not smoke, have an open flame or create sparks near a battery; the gases contained in the battery are very explosive and, if ignited, could cause severe injury or death.

All batteries, regardless of type, should be carefully secured by a battery hold-down device. If this is not done, the battery terminals or casing may crack from stress applied to the battery during vehicle operation. A battery which is not secured may allow acid to leak out, making it discharge faster; such leaking corrosive acid can also eat away at components under the hood.

Always visually inspect the battery case for cracks, leakage and corrosion. A white corrosive substance on the battery case or on nearby components would indicate a leaking or cracked battery. If the battery is cracked, it should be replaced immediately.

GENERAL MAINTENANCE

▶ **See Figure 65**

A battery that is not sealed must be checked periodically for electrolyte level. You cannot add water to a sealed maintenance-free battery (though not all maintenance-free batteries are sealed); however, a sealed battery must also be checked for proper electrolyte level, as indicated by the color of the built-in hydrometer "eye."

Always keep the battery cables and terminals free of corrosion. Check these components about once a year. Refer to the removal, installation and cleaning procedures outlined in this section.

Keep the top of the battery clean, as a film of dirt can help completely discharge a battery that is not used for long periods. A solution of baking soda and water may be used for cleaning, but be careful to flush this off with clear water. DO NOT let any of the solution into the filler holes. Baking soda neutralizes battery acid and will de-activate a battery cell.

Batteries in vehicles which are not operated on a regular basis can fall victim to parasitic loads (small current drains which are constantly drawing current

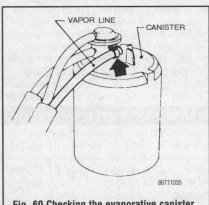

Fig. 60 Checking the evaporative canister

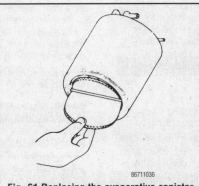

Fig. 61 Replacing the evaporative canister filter

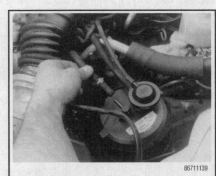

Fig. 62 Remove the lines to the evaporative canister assembly, before remove the canister

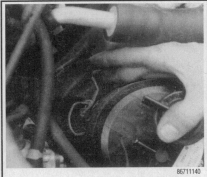

Fig. 63 Unfasten the evaporative canister assembly retaining clamp

Fig. 64 Remove the evaporative canister assembly from the vehicle

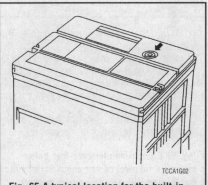

Fig. 65 A typical location for the built-in hydrometer on maintenance-free batteries

from the battery). Normal parasitic loads may drain a battery on a vehicle that is in storage and not used for 6–8 weeks. Vehicles that have additional accessories such as a cellular phone, an alarm system or other devices that increase parasitic load may discharge a battery sooner. If the vehicle is to be stored for 6–8 weeks in a secure area and the alarm system, if present, is not necessary, the negative battery cable should be disconnected at the onset of storage to protect the battery charge.

Remember that constantly discharging and recharging will shorten battery life. Take care not to allow a battery to be needlessly discharged.

BATTERY FLUID

Check the battery electrolyte level at least once a month, or more often in hot weather or during periods of extended vehicle operation. On non-sealed batteries, the level can be checked either through the case on translucent batteries or by removing the cell caps on opaque-cased types. The electrolyte level in each cell should be kept filled to the split ring inside each cell, or the line marked on the outside of the case.

If the level is low, add only distilled water through the opening until the level is correct. Each cell is separate from the others, so each must be checked and filled individually. Distilled water should be used, because the chemicals and minerals found in most drinking water are harmful to the battery and could significantly shorten its life.

If water is added in freezing weather, the vehicle should be driven several miles to allow the water to mix with the electrolyte. Otherwise, the battery could freeze.

Although some maintenance-free batteries have removable cell caps for access to the electrolyte, the electrolyte condition and level on all sealed maintenance-free batteries must be checked using the built-in hydrometer "eye." The exact type of eye varies between battery manufacturers, but most apply a sticker to the battery itself explaining the possible readings. When in doubt, refer to the battery manufacturer's instructions to interpret battery condition using the built-in hydrometer.

➡**Although the readings from built-in hydrometers found in sealed batteries may vary, a green eye usually indicates a properly charged battery with sufficient fluid level. A dark eye is normally an indicator of a battery with sufficient fluid, but one which may be low in charge. And a light or yellow eye is usually an indication that electrolyte supply has dropped below the necessary level for battery (and hydrometer) operation. In this last case, sealed batteries with an insufficient electrolyte level must usually be discarded.**

Checking the Specific Gravity

▶ See Figures 66, 67 and 68

A hydrometer is required to check the specific gravity on all batteries that are not maintenance-free. On batteries that are maintenance-free, the specific gravity is checked by observing the built-in hydrometer "eye" on the top of the battery case. Check with your battery's manufacturer for proper interpretation of its built-in hydrometer readings.

※ CAUTION

Battery electrolyte contains sulfuric acid. If you should splash any on your skin or in your eyes, flush the affected area with plenty of clear water. If it lands in your eyes, get medical help immediately.

The fluid (sulfuric acid solution) contained in the battery cells will tell you many things about the condition of the battery. Because the cell plates must be kept submerged below the fluid level in order to operate, maintaining the fluid level is extremely important. And, because the specific gravity of the acid is an indication of electrical charge, testing the fluid can be an aid in determining if the battery must be replaced. A battery in a vehicle with a properly operating charging system should require little maintenance, but careful, periodic inspection should reveal problems before they leave you stranded.

As stated earlier, the specific gravity of a battery's electrolyte level can be used as an indication of battery charge. At least once a year, check the specific gravity of the battery. It should be between 1.20 and 1.26 on the gravity scale. Most auto supply stores carry a variety of inexpensive battery testing hydrometers. These can be used on any non-sealed battery to test the specific gravity in each cell.

The battery testing hydrometer has a squeeze bulb at one end and a nozzle at the other. Battery electrolyte is sucked into the hydrometer until the float is lifted from its seat. The specific gravity is then read by noting the position of the float. If gravity is low in one or more cells, the battery should be slowly charged and checked again to see if the gravity has come up. Generally, if after charging, the specific gravity between any two cells varies more than 50 points (0.50), the battery should be replaced, as it can no longer produce sufficient voltage to guarantee proper operation.

CABLES

▶ See Figures 69, 70, 71, 72 and 73

Once a year (or as necessary), the battery terminals and the cable clamps should be cleaned. Loosen the clamps and remove the cables, negative cable first. On batteries with posts on top, the use of a puller specially made for this purpose is recommended. These are inexpensive and available in most auto parts stores. Side terminal battery cables are secured with a small bolt.

Clean the cable clamps and the battery terminal with a wire brush, until all corrosion, grease, etc., is removed and the metal is shiny. It is especially important to clean the inside of the clamp thoroughly (an old knife is useful here), since a small deposit of foreign material or oxidation there will prevent a sound electrical connection and inhibit either starting or charging. Special tools are available for cleaning these parts, one type for conventional top post batteries and another type for side terminal batteries. It is also a good idea to apply some dielectric grease to the terminal, as this will aid in the prevention of corrosion.

After the clamps and terminals are clean, reinstall the cables, negative cable last; DO NOT hammer the clamps onto battery posts. Tighten the clamps securely, but do not distort them. Give the clamps and terminals a thin external coating of grease after installation, to retard corrosion.

Check the cables at the same time that the terminals are cleaned. If the cable insulation is cracked or broken, or if the ends are frayed, the cable should be replaced with a new cable of the same length and gauge.

Fig. 66 On non-maintenance-free batteries, the fluid level can be checked through the case on translucent models; the cell caps must be removed on other models

TCCA1P07

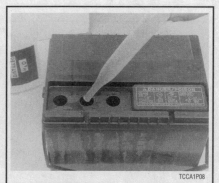

Fig. 67 If the fluid level is low, add only distilled water through the opening until the level is correct

TCCA1P08

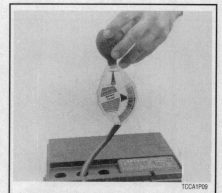

Fig. 68 Check the specific gravity of the battery's electrolyte with a hydrometer

TCCA1P09

Fig. 69 Maintenance is performed with household items and with special tools like this post cleaner

Fig. 70 The underside of this special battery tool has a wire brush to clean post terminals

Fig. 71 Place the tool over the battery posts and twist to clean until the metal is shiny

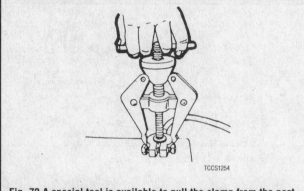

Fig. 72 A special tool is available to pull the clamp from the post

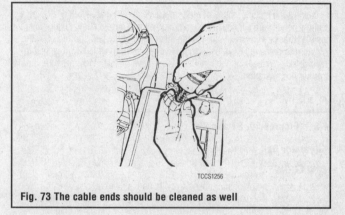

Fig. 73 The cable ends should be cleaned as well

CHARGING

> **⋇⋇ CAUTION**
>
> **The chemical reaction which takes place in all batteries generates explosive hydrogen gas. A spark can cause the battery to explode and splash acid. To avoid serious personal injury, be sure there is proper ventilation and take appropriate fire safety precautions when connecting, disconnecting, or charging a battery and when using jumper cables.**

A battery should be charged at a slow rate to keep the plates inside from getting too hot. However, if some maintenance-free batteries are allowed to discharge until they are almost "dead," they may have to be charged at a high rate to bring them back to "life." Always follow the charger manufacturer's instructions on charging the battery.

REPLACEMENT

When it becomes necessary to replace the battery, select one with an amperage rating equal to or greater than the battery originally installed. Deterioration and just plain aging of the battery cables, starter motor, and associated wires makes the battery's job harder in successive years. The slow increase in electrical resistance over time makes it prudent to install a new battery with a greater capacity than the old.

Belts

INSPECTION

▶ **See Figures 74 thru 79**

➡ **Check the condition of the drive belts, and check the belt tension at least every 30,000 miles (48,000 km) or every 24 months.**

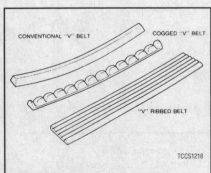

Fig. 74 There are typically 3 types of accessory drive belts found on vehicles today

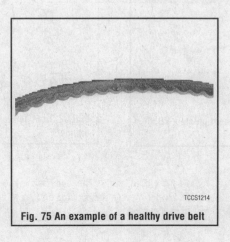

Fig. 75 An example of a healthy drive belt

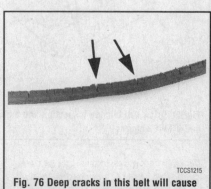

Fig. 76 Deep cracks in this belt will cause flex, building up heat that will eventually lead to belt failure

Fig. 77 The cover of this belt is worn, exposing the critical reinforcing cords to excessive wear

Fig. 78 Installing too wide a belt can result in serious belt wear and/or breakage

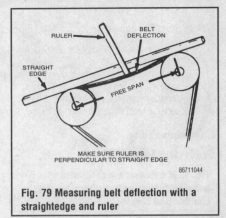

Fig. 79 Measuring belt deflection with a straightedge and ruler

Inspect the belts for signs of glazing or cracking. A glazed belt will be perfectly smooth from slippage, while a good belt will have a slight texture of fabric visible. Cracks will usually start at the inner edge of the belt and run outward. All worn or damaged drive belts should be replaced immediately. It is best to replace all drive belts at one time, as a preventive maintenance measure, during this service operation.

ADJUSTMENT

▶ See Figures 80, 81 and 82

Alternator Belt

Z24I ENGINE

1. Loosen the pivot and mounting bolts on the alternator.
2. Using a wooden hammer handle or broomstick (or even your hand if you're strong enough), move the alternator one way or the other until the tension is within acceptable limits.

➡**Never use a screwdriver or any other metal device, such as a prybar, as a lever when adjusting the alternator belt tension!**

3. Tighten the mounting bolts securely. If a new belt has been installed, always recheck the tension after a few hundred miles of driving.

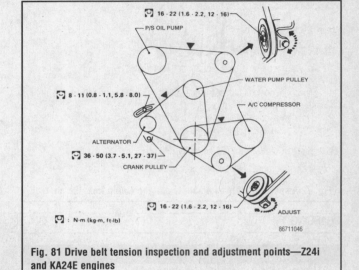

Fig. 81 Drive belt tension inspection and adjustment points—Z24i and KA24E engines

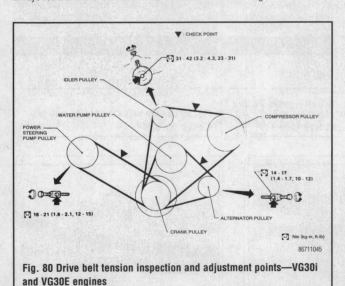

Fig. 80 Drive belt tension inspection and adjustment points—VG30i and VG30E engines

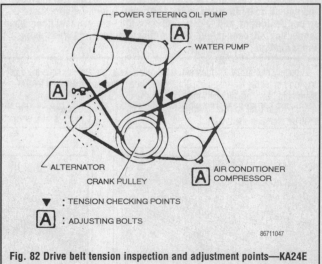

Fig. 82 Drive belt tension inspection and adjustment points—KA24E engine

VG30I, KA24E AND VG30E ENGINES

▶ See Figures 83, 84 and 85

Alternator belt tension is adjusted on these engines by means of a tension adjusting bolt.

1. Loosen the alternator pivot bolt, then turn the adjusting bolt until proper tension is achieved.

2. Tighten the mounting bolts securely. If a new belt has been installed, always recheck the tension after a few hundred miles of driving.

A/C Compressor Belt

▶ See Figures 86 and 87

Tension on the air conditioning compressor belt is adjusted by means of an idler pulley.

1. Loosen the lock-nut, then turn the adjusting bolt on the idler pulley until the desired tension is achieved.

2. Tighten the idler pulley lock-nut. If a new belt has been installed, always recheck the tension after a few hundred miles of driving.

Power Steering Pump

Z24I AND KA24E ENGINES

Tension on the power steering pump belt is adjusted by means of an idler pulley.

1. Loosen the lock-nut, then turn the adjusting bolt on the idler pulley until the desired tension is achieved.

2. Tighten the idler pulley lock-nut. If a new belt has been installed, always recheck the tension after a few hundred miles of driving.

VG30I AND VG30E ENGINES

Power steering pump belt tension is adjusted on these engines by means of a tension adjusting bolt.

1. Loosen the power steering pump pivot bolt, then turn the tension adjusting bolt until proper tension is achieved.

2. Tighten the mounting bolts securely. If a new belt has been installed, always recheck the tension after a few hundred miles of driving.

Timing Belt

INSPECTION

6-Cylinder Engines

➡Do not bend or twist the timing belt. If the timing belt breaks while driving, or the crankshaft and/or camshaft are turned separately after the timing belt is removed, valves may strike the piston heads, causing engine damage. Make sure the timing belt and tensioner are clean and free from oil and water.

On 1989–93 vehicles, replace the timing belt at 60,000 miles (96,000 km). On 1994–95 vehicles, replace the timing belt at 105,000 miles (168,000 km). Refer to Section 3 for removal and installation service procedures.

Hoses

INSPECTION

▶ See Figures 88, 89, 90 and 91

Upper and lower radiator hoses, along with the heater hoses, should be checked for deterioration, leaks and loose hose clamps at least every 15,000 miles (24,000 km). It is also wise to check the hoses periodically in early spring and at the beginning of the fall or winter when you are performing other maintenance. A quick visual inspection could discover a weakened hose which might have left you stranded if it had remained unrepaired.

Fig. 83 On some vehicles it is easier to access a component from underneath the truck

Fig. 84 Loosen the alternator pivot bolt with a box wrench or a ratchet and socket

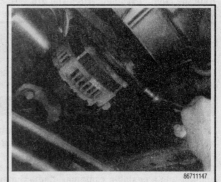
Fig. 85 Use the adjusting bolt to vary tension on the belt

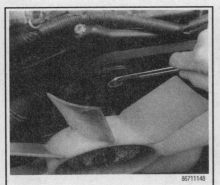
Fig. 86 Loosen the lock-nut on the idler pulley before adjusting the belt

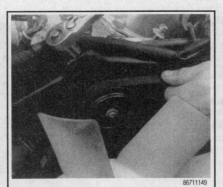
Fig. 87 Turn the adjusting bolt until the correct belt tension is achieved

Fig. 88 The cracks developing along this hose are a result of age-related hardening

Fig. 89 A hose clamp that is too tight can cause older hoses to separate and tear on either side of the clamp

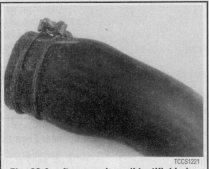

Fig. 90 A soft spongy hose (identifiable by the swollen section) will eventually burst and should be replaced

Fig. 91 Hoses are likely to deteriorate from the inside if the cooling system is not periodically flushed

Whenever you are checking the hoses, make sure the engine and cooling system are cold. Visually inspect for cracking, rotting or collapsed hoses, and replace as necessary. Run your hand along the length of the hose. If a weak or swollen spot is noted when squeezing the hose wall, the hose should be replaced.

REMOVAL & INSTALLATION

1. Remove the radiator pressure cap.

✻✻ CAUTION

Never remove the pressure cap while the engine is running, or personal injury from scalding hot coolant or steam may result. If possible, wait until the engine has cooled to remove the pressure cap. If this is not possible, wrap a thick cloth around the pressure cap and turn it slowly to the stop. Step back while the pressure is released from the cooling system. When you are sure all the pressure has been released, use the cloth to turn and remove the cap.

2. Position a clean container under the radiator and/or engine draincock or plug, then open the drain and allow the cooling system to drain to an appropriate level. For some upper hoses, only a little coolant must be drained. To remove hoses positioned lower on the engine, such as a lower radiator hose, the entire cooling system must be emptied.

✻✻ CAUTION

When draining coolant, keep in mind that cats and dogs are attracted by ethylene glycol antifreeze, and are quite likely to drink any that is left in an uncovered container or in puddles on the ground. This will prove fatal in sufficient quantity. Always drain coolant into a sealable container. Coolant may be reused unless it is contaminated or several years old.

3. Loosen the hose clamps at each end of the hose requiring replacement. Clamps are usually either of the spring tension type (which require pliers to squeeze the tabs and loosen) or of the screw tension type (which require screw or hex drivers to loosen). Pull the clamps back on the hose away from the connection.

4. Twist, pull and slide the hose off the fitting, taking care not to damage the neck of the component from which the hose is being removed.

➡ If the hose is stuck at the connection, do not try to insert a screwdriver or other sharp tool under the hose end in an effort to free it, as the connection and/or hose may become damaged. Heater connections especially may be easily damaged by such a procedure. If the hose is to be replaced, use a single-edged razor blade to make a slice along the portion of the hose which is stuck on the connection, perpendicular to the end of the hose. Do not cut deep so as to prevent damaging the connection. The hose can then be peeled from the connection and discarded.

5. Clean both hose mounting connections. Inspect the condition of the hose clamps and replace them, if necessary.

To install:

6. Dip the ends of the new hose into clean engine coolant to ease installation.

7. Slide the clamps over the replacement hose, then slide the hose ends over the connections into position.

8. Position and secure the clamps at least ¼ in. (6.35mm) from the ends of the hose. Make sure they are located beyond the raised bead of the connector.

9. Close the radiator or engine drains and properly refill the cooling system with the clean drained engine coolant or a suitable mixture of ethylene glycol coolant and water.

10. If available, install a pressure tester and check for leaks. If a pressure tester is not available, run the engine until normal operating temperature is reached (allowing the system to naturally pressurize), then check for leaks.

✻✻ CAUTION

If you are checking for leaks with the system at normal operating temperature, BE EXTREMELY CAREFUL not to touch any moving or hot engine parts. Once temperature has been reached, shut the engine OFF, and check for leaks around the hose fittings and connections which were removed earlier.

CV-Boots

INSPECTION

▶ **See Figures 92 and 93**

The CV (Constant Velocity) boots should be checked for damage each time the oil is changed and any other time the vehicle is raised for service. These boots keep water, grime, dirt and other damaging matter from entering the CV-joints. Any of these could cause early CV-joint failure which can be expensive to repair. Heavy grease thrown around the inside of the front wheel(s) and on the brake caliper/drum can be an indication of a torn boot. Thoroughly check the boots for missing clamps and tears. If the boot is damaged, it should be replaced immediately. Please refer to Section 7 for procedures.

Fig. 92 CV-boots must be inspected periodically for damage

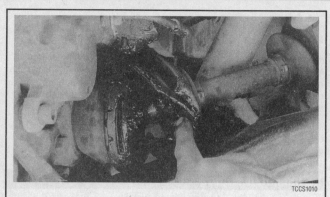

Fig. 93 A torn boot should be replaced immediately

Air Conditioning System

SYSTEM SERVICE & REPAIR

➡ **It is recommended that the A/C system be serviced by an EPA Section 609 certified automotive technician utilizing a refrigerant recovery/recycling machine.**

The do-it-yourselfer should not service his/her own vehicle's A/C system for many reasons, including legal concerns, personal injury, environmental damage and cost. The following are some of the reasons why you may decide not to service your own vehicle's A/C system.

According to the U.S. Clean Air Act, it is a federal crime to service or repair (involving the refrigerant) a Motor Vehicle Air Conditioning (MVAC) system for money without being EPA certified. It is also illegal to vent R-12 and R-134a refrigerants into the atmosphere. Selling or distributing A/C system refrigerant (in a container which contains less than 20 pounds of refrigerant) to any person who is not EPA 609 certified is also not allowed by law.

State and/or local laws may be more strict than the federal regulations, so be sure to check with your state and/or local authorities for further information. For further federal information on the legality of servicing your A/C system, call the EPA Stratospheric Ozone Hotline.

➡ **Federal law dictates that a fine of up to $25,000 may be levied on people convicted of venting refrigerant into the atmosphere. Additionally, the EPA may pay up to $10,000 for information or services leading to a criminal conviction of the violation of these laws.**

When servicing an A/C system you run the risk of handling or coming in contact with refrigerant, which may result in skin or eye irritation or frostbite. Although low in toxicity (due to chemical stability), inhalation of concentrated refrigerant fumes is dangerous and can result in death; cases of fatal cardiac arrhythmia have been reported in people accidentally subjected to high levels of refrigerant. Some early symptoms include loss of concentration and drowsiness.

➡ **Generally, the limit for exposure is lower for R-134a than it is for R-12. Exceptional care must be practiced when handling R-134a.**

Also, refrigerants can decompose at high temperatures (near gas heaters or open flame), which may result in hydrofluoric acid, hydrochloric acid and phosgene (a fatal nerve gas).

R-12 refrigerant can damage the environment because it is a Chlorofluorocarbon (CFC), which has been proven to add to ozone layer depletion, leading to increasing levels of UV radiation. UV radiation has been linked with an increase in skin cancer, suppression of the human immune system, an increase in cataracts, damage to crops, damage to aquatic organisms, an increase in ground-level ozone, and increased global warming.

R-134a refrigerant is a greenhouse gas which, if allowed to vent into the atmosphere, will contribute to global warming (the Greenhouse Effect).

It is usually more economically feasible to have a certified MVAC automotive technician perform A/C system service on your vehicle. Some possible reasons for this are as follows:

• While it is illegal to service an A/C system without the proper equipment, the home mechanic would have to purchase an expensive refrigerant recovery/recycling machine to service his/her own vehicle.

• Since only a certified person may purchase refrigerant—according to the Clean Air Act, there are specific restrictions on selling or distributing A/C system refrigerant—it is legally impossible (unless certified) for the home mechanic to service his/her own vehicle. Procuring refrigerant in an illegal fashion exposes one to the risk of paying a $25,000 fine to the EPA.

R-12 Refrigerant Conversion

If your vehicle still uses R-12 refrigerant, one way to save A/C system costs down the road is to investigate the possibility of having your system converted to R-134a. The older R-12 systems can be easily converted to R-134a refrigerant by a certified automotive technician by installing a few new components and changing the system oil.

The cost of R-12 is steadily rising and will continue to increase, because it is no longer imported or manufactured in the United States. Therefore, it is often possible to have an R-12 system converted to R-134a and recharged for less than it would cost to just charge the system with R-12.

If you are interested in having your system converted, contact local automotive service stations for more details and information.

PREVENTIVE MAINTENANCE

▶ **See Figures 94 and 95**

Although the A/C system should not be serviced by the do-it-yourselfer, preventive maintenance can be practiced and A/C system inspections can be performed to help maintain the efficiency of the vehicle's A/C system. For preventive maintenance, perform the following:

• The easiest and most important preventive maintenance for your A/C system is to be sure that it is used on a regular basis. Running the system for five minutes each month (no matter what the season) will help ensure that the seals and all internal components remain lubricated.

➡ **Some newer vehicles automatically operate the A/C system compressor whenever the windshield defroster is activated. When running, the compressor lubricates the A/C system components; therefore, the A/C system would not need to be operated each month.**

• In order to prevent heater core freeze-up during A/C operation, it is necessary to maintain proper antifreeze protection. Use a hand-held coolant tester (hydrometer) to periodically check the condition of the antifreeze in your engine's cooling system.

➡ **Antifreeze should not be used longer than the manufacturer specifies.**

• For efficient operation of an air conditioned vehicle's cooling system, the radiator cap should have a holding pressure which meets manufacturer's specifications. A cap which fails to hold these pressures should be replaced.

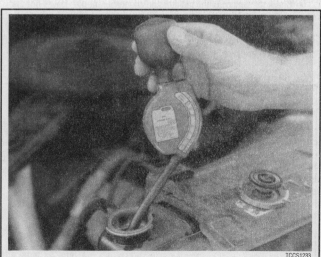

Fig. 94 A coolant tester can be used to determine the freezing and boiling levels of the coolant in your vehicle

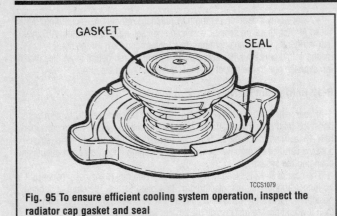

Fig. 95 To ensure efficient cooling system operation, inspect the radiator cap gasket and seal

• Any obstruction of or damage to the condenser configuration will restrict air flow which is essential to its efficient operation. It is, therefore, a good rule to keep this unit clean and in proper physical shape.

➡ **Bug screens which are mounted in front of the condenser (unless they are original equipment) are regarded as obstructions.**

• The condensation drain tube expels any water which accumulates on the bottom of the evaporator housing into the engine compartment. If this tube is obstructed, the air conditioning performance can be restricted and condensation buildup can spill over onto the vehicle's floor.

SYSTEM INSPECTION

▸ **See Figure 96**

Although the A/C system should not be serviced by the do-it-yourselfer, preventive maintenance can be practiced and A/C system inspections can be performed to help maintain the efficiency of the vehicle's A/C system. For A/C system inspection, perform the following:

The easiest and often most important check for the air conditioning system consists of a visual inspection of the system components. Visually inspect the air conditioning system for refrigerant leaks, damaged compressor clutch, abnormal compressor drive belt tension and/or condition, plugged evaporator drain tube, blocked condenser fins, disconnected or broken wires, blown fuses, corroded connections and poor insulation.

A refrigerant leak will usually appear as an oily residue at the leakage point in the system. The oily residue soon picks up dust or dirt particles from the surrounding air and appears greasy. Through time, this will build up and appear to be a heavy dirt impregnated grease.

For a thorough visual and operational inspection, check the following:
• Check the surface of the radiator and condenser for dirt, leaves or other material which might block air flow.
• Check for kinks in hoses and lines. Check the system for leaks.
• Make sure the drive belt is properly tensioned. When the air conditioning is operating, make sure the drive belt is free of noise or slippage.

• Make sure the blower motor operates at all appropriate positions, then check for distribution of the air from all outlets with the blower on **HIGH** or **MAX**.

➡ **Keep in mind that under conditions of high humidity, air discharged from the A/C vents may not feel as cold as expected, even if the system is working properly. This is because vaporized moisture in humid air retains heat more effectively than dry air, thereby making humid air more difficult to cool.**

• Make sure the air passage selection lever is operating correctly. Start the engine and warm it to normal operating temperature, then make sure the temperature selection lever is operating correctly.

Windshield Wipers

ELEMENT (REFILL) CARE & REPLACEMENT

▸ **See figures 97, 98 and 99**

For maximum effectiveness and longest element life, the windshield and wiper blades should be kept clean. Dirt, tree sap, road tar and so on will cause streaking, smearing and blade deterioration if left on the glass. It is advisable to wash the windshield carefully with a commercial glass cleaner at least once a month. Wipe off the rubber blades with the wet rag afterwards. Do not attempt to move wipers across the windshield by hand; damage to the motor and drive mechanism will result.

To inspect and/or replace the wiper blade elements, place the wiper switch in the **LOW** speed position and the ignition switch in the **ACC** position. When the wiper blades are approximately vertical on the windshield, turn the ignition switch to **OFF**.

Examine the wiper blade elements. If they are found to be cracked, broken or torn, they should be replaced immediately. Replacement intervals will vary with usage, although ozone deterioration usually limits element life to about one year. If the wiper pattern is smeared or streaked, or if the blade chatters across the glass, the elements should be replaced. It is easiest and most sensible to replace the elements in pairs.

If your vehicle is equipped with aftermarket blades, there are several different types of refills and your vehicle might have any kind. Aftermarket blades and arms rarely use the exact same type blade or refill as the original equipment.

Regardless of the type of refill used, be sure to follow the part manufacturer's instructions closely. Make sure that all of the frame jaws are engaged as the refill is pushed into place and locked. If the metal blade holder and frame are allowed to touch the glass during wiper operation, the glass will be scratched.

Tires and Wheels

Common sense and good driving habits will afford maximum tire life. Fast starts, sudden stops and hard cornering are hard on tires and will shorten their useful life span. Make sure that you don't overload the vehicle or run with incorrect pressure in the tires. Both of these practices will increase tread wear.

➡ **For optimum tire life, keep the tires properly inflated, rotate them often and have the wheel alignment checked periodically.**

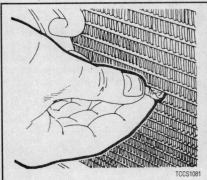

Fig. 96 Periodically remove any debris from the condenser and radiator fins

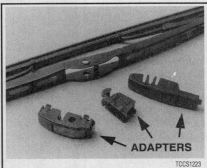

Fig. 97 Most aftermarket blades are available with multiple adapters to fit different vehicles

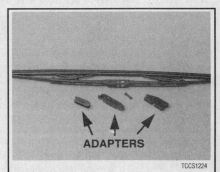

Fig. 98 Choose a blade which will fit your vehicle, and that will be readily available next time you need blades

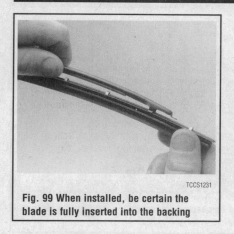

Fig. 99 When installed, be certain the blade is fully inserted into the backing

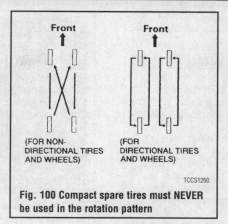

Fig. 100 Compact spare tires must NEVER be used in the rotation pattern

Fig. 101 Unidirectional tires are identifiable by sidewall arrows and/or the word "rotation"

Inspect your tires frequently. Be especially careful to watch for bubbles in the tread or sidewall, deep cuts or underinflation. Replace any tires with bubbles in the sidewall. If cuts are so deep that they penetrate to the cords, discard the tire. Any cut in the sidewall of a radial tire renders it unsafe. Also look for uneven tread wear patterns that may indicate the front end is out of alignment or that the tires are out of balance.

TIRE ROTATION

▶ See Figures 100 and 101

Tires must be rotated periodically to equalize wear patterns that vary with a tire's position on the vehicle. Tires will also wear in an uneven way as the front steering/suspension system wears to the point where the alignment should be reset.

Rotating the tires will ensure maximum life for the tires as a set, so you will not have to discard a tire early due to wear on only part of the tread. Regular rotation is required to equalize wear.

When rotating "unidirectional tires," make sure that they always roll in the same direction. This means that a tire used on the left side of the vehicle must not be switched to the right side and vice-versa. Such tires should only be rotated front-to-rear or rear-to-front, while always remaining on the same side of the vehicle. These tires are marked on the sidewall as to the direction of rotation; observe the marks when reinstalling the tire(s).

Some styled or "mag" wheels may have different offsets front to rear. In these cases, the rear wheels must not be used up front and vice-versa. Furthermore, if these wheels are equipped with unidirectional tires, they cannot be rotated unless the tire is remounted for the proper direction of rotation.

➡The compact or space-saver spare is strictly for emergency use. It must never be included in the tire rotation or placed on the vehicle for everyday use.

TIRE DESIGN

▶ See Figure 102

For maximum satisfaction, tires should be used in sets of four. Mixing of different types (radial, bias-belted, fiberglass belted) must be avoided. In most cases, the vehicle manufacturer has designated a type of tire on which the vehicle will perform best. Your first choice when replacing tires should be to use the same type of tire that the manufacturer recommends.

When radial tires are used, tire sizes and wheel diameters should be selected to maintain ground clearance and tire load capacity equivalent to the original specified tire. Radial tires should always be used in sets of four.

❊❊ CAUTION

Radial tires should never be used on only the front axle.

When selecting tires, pay attention to the original size as marked on the tire. Most tires are described using an industry size code sometimes referred to as P-Metric. This allows the exact identification of the tire specifications, regardless of the manufacturer. If selecting a different tire size or brand, remember to check the installed tire for any sign of interference with the body or suspension while the vehicle is stopping, turning sharply or heavily loaded.

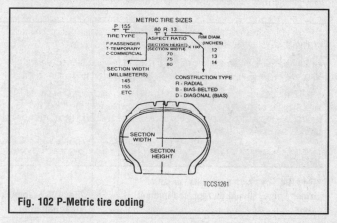

Fig. 102 P-Metric tire coding

Snow Tires

Good radial tires can produce a big advantage in slippery weather, but in snow, a street radial tire does not have sufficient tread to provide traction and control. The small grooves of a street tire quickly pack with snow and the tire behaves like a billiard ball on a marble floor. The more open, chunky tread of a snow tire will self-clean as the tire turns, providing much better grip on snowy surfaces.

To satisfy municipalities requiring snow tires during weather emergencies, most snow tires carry either an M + S designation after the tire size stamped on the sidewall, or the designation "all-season." In general, no change in tire size is necessary when buying snow tires.

Most manufacturers strongly recommend the use of 4 snow tires on their vehicles for reasons of stability. If snow tires are fitted only to the drive wheels, the opposite end of the vehicle may become very unstable when braking or turning on slippery surfaces. This instability can lead to unpleasant endings if the driver can't counteract the slide in time.

Note that snow tires, whether 2 or 4, will affect vehicle handling in all non-snow situations. The stiffer, heavier snow tires will noticeably change the turning and braking characteristics of the vehicle. Once the snow tires are installed, you must re-learn the behavior of the vehicle and drive accordingly.

➡Consider buying extra wheels on which to mount the snow tires. Once done, the "snow wheels" can be installed and removed as needed. This eliminates the potential damage to tires or wheels from seasonal removal and installation. Even if your vehicle has styled wheels, see if inexpensive steel wheels are available. Although the look of the vehicle will change, the expensive wheels will be protected from salt, curb hits and pothole damage.

TIRE STORAGE

If they are mounted on wheels, store the tires at proper inflation pressure. All tires should be kept in a cool, dry place. If they are stored in the garage or basement, do not let them stand on a concrete floor; set them on strips of wood, a mat or a large stack of newspaper. Keeping them away from direct moisture is of paramount importance. Tires should not be stored upright, but in a flat position.

INFLATION & INSPECTION

♦ **See Figures 103 thru 110**

The importance of proper tire inflation cannot be overemphasized. A tire employs air as part of its structure. It is designed around the supporting strength of the air at a specified pressure. For this reason, improper inflation drastically reduces the tire's ability to perform as intended. A tire will lose some air in day-to-day use; having to add a few pounds of air periodically is not necessarily a sign of a leaking tire.

Two items should be a permanent fixture in every glove compartment: an accurate tire pressure gauge and a tread depth gauge. Check the tire pressure (including the spare) regularly with a pocket type gauge. Too often, the gauge on the end of the air hose at your corner garage is not accurate because it suffers too much abuse. Always check tire pressure when the tires are cold, as pressure increases with temperature. If you must move the vehicle to check the tire inflation, do not drive more than a mile before checking. A cold tire is generally one that has not been driven for more than three hours.

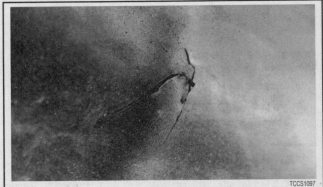

Fig. 103 Tires should be checked frequently for any sign of puncture or damage

Fig. 104 Tires with deep cuts, or cuts which bulge, should be replaced immediately

 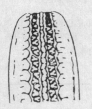

Fig. 105 Examples of inflation-related tire wear patterns

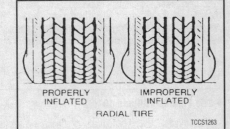

Fig. 106 Radial tires have a characteristic sidewall bulge; don't try to measure pressure by looking at the tire. Use a quality air pressure gauge

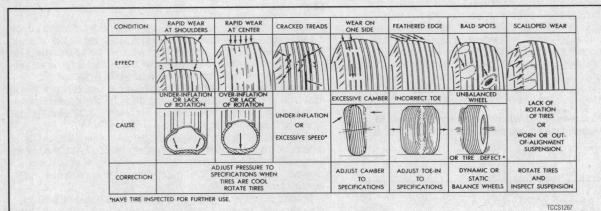

Fig. 107 Common tire wear patterns and causes

Fig. 108 Tread wear indicators will appear when the tire is worn

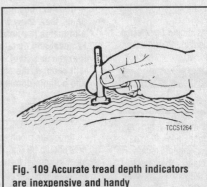

Fig. 109 Accurate tread depth indicators are inexpensive and handy

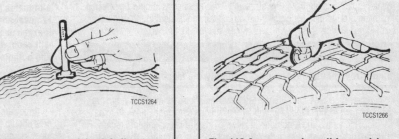

Fig. 110 A penny works well for a quick check of tread depth

A plate or sticker is normally provided somewhere in the vehicle (door post, hood, tailgate or trunk lid) which shows the proper pressure for the tires. Never counteract excessive pressure build-up by bleeding off air pressure (letting some air out). This will cause the tire to run hotter and wear quicker.

✳✳ CAUTION

Never exceed the maximum tire pressure embossed on the tire! This is the pressure to be used when the tire is at maximum loading, but it is rarely the correct pressure for everyday driving. Consult the owner's manual or the tire pressure sticker for the correct tire pressure.

Once you've maintained the correct tire pressures for several weeks, you'll be familiar with the vehicle's braking and handling personality. Slight adjustments in tire pressures can fine-tune these characteristics, but never change the cold pressure specification by more than 2 psi. A slightly softer tire pressure will give a softer ride but also yield lower fuel mileage. A slightly harder tire will give crisper dry road handling but can cause skidding on wet surfaces. Unless you're fully attuned to the vehicle, stick to the recommended inflation pressures.

All tires made since 1968 have built-in tread wear indicator bars that show up as ½ in. (13mm) wide smooth bands across the tire when ¹⁄₁₆ in. (1.5mm) of tread remains. The appearance of tread wear indicators means that the tires should be replaced. In fact, many states have laws prohibiting the use of tires with less than this amount of tread.

You can check your own tread depth with an inexpensive gauge or by using a Lincoln head penny. Slip the Lincoln penny (with Lincoln's head upside-down) into several tread grooves. If you can see the top of Lincoln's head in 2 adjacent grooves, the tire has less than ¹⁄₁₆ in. (1.5mm) tread left and should be replaced. You can measure snow tires in the same manner by using the "tails" side of the Lincoln penny. If you can see the top of the Lincoln memorial, it's time to replace the snow tire(s).

FLUIDS AND LUBRICANTS

♦ See Figure 111

Fluid Disposal

Used fluids such as engine oil, transmission fluid, antifreeze and brake fluid are hazardous wastes and must be disposed of properly. Before draining any fluids, consult with the local authorities; in many areas, waste oil, antifreeze, etc. are being accepted as a part of recycling programs. A number of service stations and auto parts stores are also accepting waste fluids for recycling.

Be sure of the recycling center's policies before draining any fluids, as many will not accept different fluids that have been mixed together, such as oil and antifreeze.

Oil and Fuel Recommendations

ENGINE OIL

♦ See Figures 112, 113 and 114

The SAE (Society of Automotive Engineers) grade number indicates the viscosity of the engine oil (its resistance to flow at a given temperature). The lower the SAE grade number, the lighter the oil. For example, the mono-grade oils begin with SAE 5 weight, which is a thin, light oil, and continue in viscosity up to SAE 80 or 90 weight, which are heavy gear lubricants. These oils are also

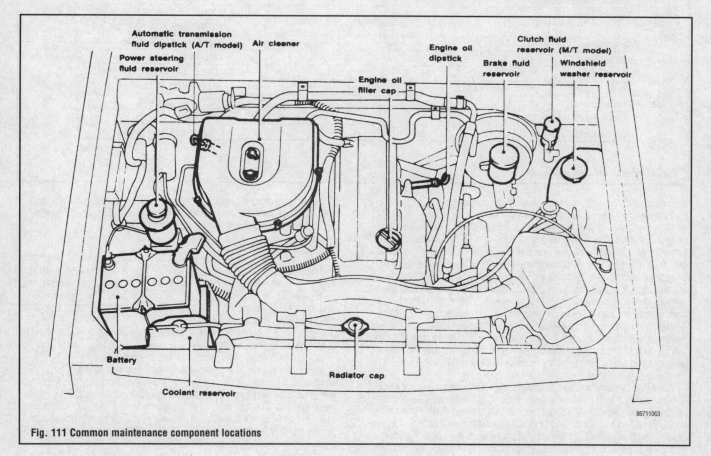

Fig. 111 Common maintenance component locations

86711063

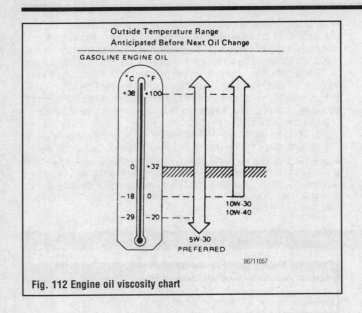

Fig. 112 Engine oil viscosity chart

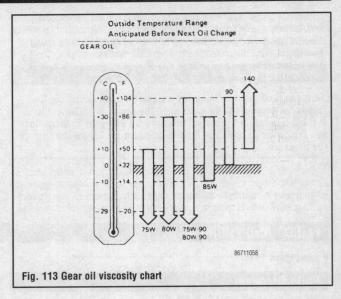

Fig. 113 Gear oil viscosity chart

RECOMMENDED LUBRICANTS

Component	Lubricant
Engine oil	API SG
Coolant	Ethylene Glycol-based Antifreeze
Manual Transmission	API GL-4, SAE 75W-90
Automatic Transmission	ATF DEXRON®
Transfer Case	1989: API GL-4, SAE 75W-90
	1990-95: ATF DEXRON®
Differentials	API GL-5, SAE 80W-90
Limited Slip	Nissan-approved LSD
Master Cylinder	DOT 3, SAE J1703
Power Steering	ATF DEXRON®
Manual Steering	API GL-4, SAE 90W
Multi-Purpose Grease	NLGI #2
Free-Running Hub	Nissan-approved grease

Fig. 114 Recommended lubricants

known as "straight weight," meaning they are of a single viscosity, and do not vary with engine temperature.

Multi-viscosity oils offer the important advantage of being adaptable to temperature extremes. These oils have designations such as 10W-40, 20W-50, etc. For example, 10W-40 means that in winter (the "W" in the designation) the oil acts like a thin 10 weight oil, allowing the engine to spin easily when cold and offering rapid lubrication. Once the engine has warmed up, however, the oil acts like a straight 40 weight, maintaining good lubrication and protection for the engine's internal components. A 20W-50 oil would therefore be slightly heavier than, and not as ideal, in cold weather as the 10W-40, but would offer better protection at higher rpm and temperatures because, when warm, it acts like a 50 weight oil. Whichever oil viscosity you choose when changing the oil and filter, you are anticipating the temperatures your engine will be operating in until the oil is changed again. Refer to the oil viscosity chart for oil recommendations according to temperature.

The API (American Petroleum Institute) designation indicates the classification of engine oil used under certain given operating conditions. Only oils designated for use "Service SG" should be used. Oils of the SG type perform a variety of functions inside the engine in addition to the basic function as a lubricant. Through a balanced system of metallic detergents and polymeric dispersants, the oil prevents the formation of high and low temperature deposits, and also keeps sludge and dirt particles in suspension. Acids, particularly sulfuric acid, as well as other by-products of combustion, are neutralized. Both the SAE grade number and the API designation can be found on the oil container.

For recommended oil viscosities, refer to the chart. Note that 10W-30 and 10W-40 grade oils are not recommended for sustained high speed driving when the temperature rises above the indicated limit.

Synthetic Oil

There are many excellent synthetic and fuel-efficient oils currently available that can provide better gas mileage, longer service life and, in some cases, better engine protection. These benefits do not come without a few hitches, however, the main one being the price of synthetic oils, which is three or four times the price per quart of conventional oil.

Synthetic oil is not for every truck and every type of driving, so you should consider your engine's condition and your type of driving. Also, check your truck's warranty conditions regarding the use of synthetic oils.

Brand new engines and older, high mileage engines are not good candidates for synthetic oil. The synthetic oils are so slippery that they can prevent the proper break-in of new engines; most manufacturers recommend that you wait until the engine is properly broken in (3000 miles) before using synthetic oil. Older engines with wear have a different problem with synthetics: they "use" (consume during operation) more oil as they age. Slippery synthetic oils get past these worn parts easily. If your engine is using conventional oil, it will use synthetics much faster. Also, if your truck is leaking oil past old seals, you'll have a much greater leak problem with synthetics.

Consider your type of driving. If most of your accumulated mileage is high speed, highway type driving, the more expensive synthetic oils may be a benefit. Extended highway driving gives the engine a chance to warm up, accumulating fewer acids in the oil, and putting less stress on the engine over the long run. Under these conditions, the oil change interval can be extended (as long as your oil filter can last the extended life of the oil) up to the advertised mileage claims of the synthetics. Trucks with synthetic oils may show increased fuel economy in highway driving, due to less internal friction. However, many automotive experts agree that 50,000 miles (80,000 km) is too long to keep any oil in your engine.

Trucks used under harsher circumstances, such as stop-and-go, city type driving, short trips, or extended idling, should be serviced more frequently. For the engines in these trucks, the much greater cost of synthetic or fuel-efficient oils may not be worth the investment. Internal wear increases much quicker on these trucks, causing greater oil consumption and leakage.

➡**The mixing of conventional and synthetic oils is possible but not recommended. Non-detergent or straight mineral oils must never be used in the engine.**

FUEL

It is important to use fuel of the proper octane rating in your truck. Octane rating is based on the quantity of anti-knock compounds added to the fuel, and also reflects the speed at which the gas will burn. The lower the octane rating, the faster it burns. The higher the octane, the slower the fuel will burn, and the greater the percentage of compounds in the fuel to prevent spark ping (knock), detonation and preignition (dieseling).

As the temperature of the engine increases, the air/fuel mixture exhibits a tendency to ignite before the spark plug is fired. If fuel of an octane rating too low for the engine is used, this will allow combustion to occur before the piston has completed its compression stroke, thereby creating a very high pressure very rapidly.

Fuel of the proper octane rating, for the compression ratio and ignition timing of your truck, will slow the combustion process sufficiently to allow the spark plug enough time to ignite the mixture completely and smoothly. The use of some super-premium fuel is no substitution for a properly tuned and maintained engine.

Light spark knock may be noticed when accelerating or driving up hills. The slight knocking may be considered normal (with 87 octane) because the maximum fuel economy is obtained under condition of occasional light spark knock. Gasoline with an octane rating higher than 87 may be used, but it is not necessary (in most cases) for proper operation.

➡**Your engine's fuel requirement can change with time, mainly due to carbon buildup, which changes the compression ratio. If your engine pings, knocks or runs on, switch to a higher grade of fuel. Sometimes just changing brands may cure the problem.**

Engine

✳✳ CAUTION

Prolonged and repeated skin contact with used engine oil, with no effort to remove the oil, may be harmful. Always follow these simple precautions when handling used motor oil:

- Avoid prolonged skin contact with used motor oil
- Remove oil from skin by washing thoroughly with soap and water, or waterless hand cleaner. Do not use gasoline, thinners or other solvents
- Avoid prolonged skin contact with oil-soaked clothing

OIL LEVEL CHECK

▶ **See Figures 115, 116, 117 and 118**

Every time you stop for fuel, check the engine oil as follows:
1. Park the truck on level ground.

➡**Although it is best for the engine to be at operating temperature, checking the oil immediately after stopping will lead to a false reading. Wait a few minutes after turning off the engine to allow the oil to drain back into the crankcase.**

2. Open the hood and locate the dipstick, which is on the left side of the engine. Pull the dipstick from its tube, wipe it clean and reinsert it.
3. Pull the dipstick out again and, holding it horizontally, read the oil level. The oil should be between the **H** and **L** marks on the dipstick. If the oil is below the **L** mark, add oil of the proper viscosity and classification through the capped opening on top of the cylinder head cover.
4. Insert the dipstick and check the oil level again after adding any oil. Be careful not to overfill the crankcase. Approximately one quart of oil will raise the level from the **L** mark to the **H** mark. Excess oil will generally be consumed at an accelerated rate.

OIL AND FILTER CHANGE

▶ **See Figures 119, 120, 121 and 122**

➡**It may be a good idea to look under the vehicle, before starting any service procedure, to orientate yourself with the necessary components and locations.**

The oil should be changed at least every 7500 miles (12,000 km) or every 6 months. Nissan recommends changing the oil filter with every other oil change; we suggest that the filter be changed with **every** oil change. There is approximately 1 quart of dirty oil remaining in the old oil filter if it is not changed! A few dollars more every year seems a small price to pay for extended engine life—so change the filter every time you change the oil!

✳✳ CAUTION

Prolonged and repeated skin contact with used engine oil, with no effort to remove the oil, may be harmful. Always follow these simple precautions when handling used motor oil.

- Avoid prolonged skin contact with used motor oil
- Remove oil from skin by washing thoroughly with soap and water, or waterless hand cleaner. Do not use gasoline, thinners or other solvents
- Avoid prolonged skin contact with oil-soaked clothing

The oil drain plug is located on the bottom, rear of the oil pan (bottom of the engine, underneath the truck). The oil filter is located on the right side of the engine on all models.

Fig. 115 Locate the oil dipstick in the engine compartment

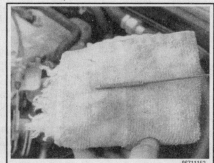

Fig. 116 Check the oil dipstick for the correct level of engine oil—never overfill the engine oil

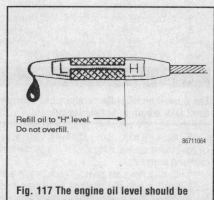

Refill oil to "H" level.
Do not overfill.

Fig. 117 The engine oil level should be maintained between the L and H marks

Fig. 118 If the engine oil level is low, add engine oil, but do not overfill

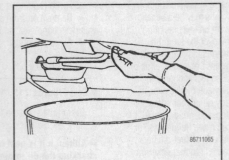

Fig. 119 By keeping inward pressure on the drain plug as you unscrew it, oil won't escape past the threads

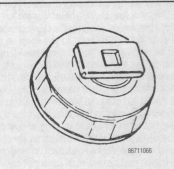

Fig. 120 On some models, a cap-type oil filter removal tool works best

Fig. 121 Lubricate the gasket on the new filter with clean engine oil. A dry gasket may not make as good a seal, and could allow the filter to leak

Fig. 122 Removing the oil drain plug—do not overtorque this drain plug upon installation

The mileage figures given are the Nissan recommended intervals assuming normal driving and conditions. If your truck is being used under dusty, polluted or off-road conditions, change the oil and filter more frequently than specified. The same goes for trucks driven in stop-and-go traffic or only for short distances. Always drain the oil after the engine has been running long enough to bring it to normal operating temperature. Hot oil will flow easier and more contaminants will be removed along with the oil than if it were drained cold. To change the oil and filter:

❊❊ CAUTION

The EPA warns that prolonged contact with used engine oil may cause a number of skin disorders, including cancer! You should make every effort to minimize your exposure to used engine oil. Protective gloves should be worn when changing the oil. Wash your hands and any other exposed skin areas as soon as possible after exposure to used engine oil. Soap and water, or waterless hand cleaner should be used.

1. Run the engine until it reaches normal operating temperature.
2. Jack up the front of the truck and support it on safety stands.
3. Slide a drain pan of at least 6 quarts capacity under the oil pan.
4. Loosen the drain plug. Turn the plug out by hand. By keeping inward pressure on the plug as you unscrew it, oil won't escape past the threads, and you can remove it without being burned by hot oil.

❊❊ CAUTION

The oil will be HOT! Be careful when removing the plug, so that you don't take a bath in hot engine oil.

5. Allow the oil to drain completely. Clean and inspect the drain plug and oil pan sealing surface. If the plug is equipped with a removable gasket, also clean and inspect it.
6. Using a new plug gasket, if necessary, install the drain plug and tighten to 22–29 ft. lbs. (29–39 Nm). Don't overtighten the plug; otherwise, you'll be buying a new pan or a replacement plug for stripped threads.

7. Using an oil filter strap wrench, remove the oil filter; on Z24i and VG30 engines, use a cap-type filter removal tool. Keep in mind that it's holding about one quart of dirty, hot oil.

➡ If the oil filter cannot be loosened by conventional methods, punch a hole through both sides near the mounting base of the filter and insert a punch, then turn to loosen the oil filter. After the oil filter is loosened, remove it from the engine with an oil filter wrench or equivalent.

8. Empty the old filter into the drain pan and dispose of the filter.
9. Using a clean rag, wipe off the filter adapter on the engine block. Be sure that the rag doesn't leave any lint which could clog an oil passage.
10. Coat the rubber gasket on the filter with fresh oil. Spin it onto the engine by hand; when the gasket touches the adapter surface, give it another ½–¾ turn. Do not overtighten, or you'll squash the gasket and it will leak.
11. Refill the engine with the correct amount of fresh oil. See the Capacities Chart later in this section.
12. Check the oil level on the dipstick. It is normal for the level to be a bit above the full mark. Start the engine and allow it to idle for a few minutes.

➡ Do not run the engine above idle speed until it has built up oil pressure, as indicated when the oil light goes out.

13. Shut off the engine and allow the oil to drain into the crankcase for a few minutes, then check the oil level. Check around the filter and drain plug for any leaks and correct as necessary.

Manual Transmission

FLUID RECOMMENDATIONS

All models: multipurpose gear oil API GL-4; SAE 75W-90 or 80W-90

FLUID LEVEL CHECK

▶ **See Figures 123 and 124**

The oil in the manual transmission should be checked at least every 15,000 miles (24,000 km) or every 12 months, and replaced every 25,000–30,000 miles (40,000–48,000 km) or every 24 months.

1. With the truck parked on a level surface, remove the filler plug from the side of the transmission housing.

2. If the lubricant begins to trickle out of the hole, there is enough. Otherwise, carefully insert your finger (watch out for sharp threads!) and check to see if the oil is up to the edge of the hole.

3. If the oil level is low, add oil through the hole until the level is at the edge of the hole. Most gear lubricants come in a plastic squeeze bottle with a nozzle that eases this process. You can also use a common everyday kitchen baster.

4. Install the filler plug and tighten it to 18–25 ft. lbs. (25–34 Nm). Run the engine and check for leaks.

DRAIN AND REFILL

▶ **See Figures 125, 126 and 127**

Once every 30,000 miles (48,000 km) or every 24 months, the oil in the manual transmission should be changed.

1. The transmission oil should be hot before it is drained. If the engine is at normal operating temperature, the transmission oil should be hot enough.

2. Raise the truck and support it properly on jackstands so that you can safely work underneath.

➡ **You will probably not have enough room to work if the truck is not raised.**

3. The drain plug is located on the bottom of the transmission. Place a pan under the drain plug and remove it. Keep a slight upward pressure on the plug while unscrewing it, as this will keep the oil from pouring out until the plug is removed.

✳✳ CAUTION

The oil will be HOT! Be careful when removing the plug, so that you don't take a bath in hot gear oil.

4. Allow the oil to drain completely. Clean off the plug, then install and tighten it to 18–25 ft. lbs. (25–34 Nm).

5. Remove the filler plug from the side of the transmission case. There is usually a gasket underneath this plug. Replace it if damaged.

6. Fill the transmission with gear oil through the filler plug hole. Refer to the Capacities Chart for the amount of oil needed to refill your transmission.

7. The oil level should come right up to the edge of the hole. You can stick your finger in to verify this. Watch out for sharp threads!

8. Install the filler plug and gasket, then lower the truck and check for leaks. Dispose of (recycle) the old oil in a proper manner.

CHECKING WATER ENTRY

4WD Models Only

▶ **See Figure 128**

After having driven in deep water or mud, the clutch housing should always be checked for water entry. There is a small rubber grommet at the bottom of the left-side leading edge of the transmission case where it mates with the rear of the engine block. Carefully pry it out and let any water that has collected in the clutch housing seep out. After all the water has drained, be sure to reinstall the grommet.

Automatic Transmission

FLUID RECOMMENDATIONS

All models use DEXRON®II or III ATF

➡ **If Dexron® II or III is not available, use genuine Nissan ATF or equivalent.**

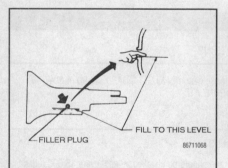

Fig. 123 Checking the manual transmission fluid

Fig. 124 Remove the plug on the side of the transmission to check the manual transmission fluid level

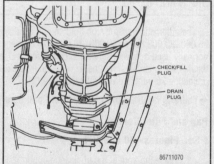

Fig. 125 Manual transmission fill and drain plug locations—Z24i and KA24E engines

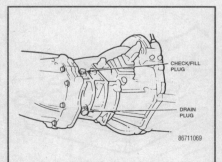

Fig. 126 Manual transmission fill and drain plug locations—VG30i and VG30E engines

Fig. 127 Remove the manual transmission drain plug using the proper tool

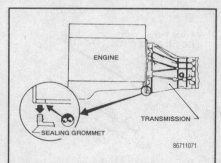

Fig. 128 After driving through high water, always drain any water from the clutch housing by removing the sealing grommet

FLUID LEVEL CHECK

▶ **See Figure 129**

Check the automatic transmission fluid level at least every 15,000 miles (24,000 km) or every 12 months. The dipstick is at the right rear of the engine compartment. The fluid level should be checked only when the transmission is hot (normal operating temperature). The transmission is considered hot after about 20 miles of highway driving.

1. Park the truck on a level surface with the engine idling. Shift the transmission into **P** and set the parking brake.

2. Remove the dipstick, wipe it clean and reinsert if firmly. Be sure that it has been pushed all the way in. Remove the dipstick and check the fluid level while holding it horizontally. All models have a HOT and a COLD side to the dipstick. On 2wd models, the fluid level should be between the two hash marks on the HOT side, or between the two notches on the COLD side. On 4wd models, the fluid level should be within the cross-hatched area on the HOT or COLD sides.

3. If the fluid level is below the lower hash mark (HOT) or lower notch (COLD) on 2wd models, or not within the cross-hatched area on either side of the dipstick on 4wd models, pour DEXRON® ATF into the dipstick tube. This is easily done with the aid of a funnel. Check the level often as you are filling the transmission. Be extremely careful not to overfill. Overfilling will cause slippage, seal damage and overheating. Approximately one pint of ATF will raise the level from one notch to the other.

➡ **Always use the proper transmission fluid when filling your truck's automatic transmission. All models use DEXRON type fluid. Always check with the owner's manual to be sure. NEVER use Type F in a transmission requiring DEXRON® or vice versa, as severe damage will result.**

✳✳ WARNING

The fluid on the dipstick should always be a bright red color. If it is discolored (brown or black) or smells burnt, serious transmission troubles, probably due to overheating, should be suspected. The transmission should be inspected by a qualified service technician to locate the cause of the burnt fluid.

DRAIN AND REFILL

The automatic transmission fluid should be changed at least every 25,000–30,000 miles (40,000–48,000 km) or every 24 months. If the truck is normally used in severe service, such as stop-and-go driving, trailer towing or the like, the interval should be halved. The fluid should be hot before it is drained; a 20 minute drive will accomplish this.

➡ **There is no drain plug, so the fluid pan must be removed.**

Pan and Filter Service

▶ **See Figures 130 and 131**

1. Raise the front of the truck and support it on jackstands.

➡ **It is a good idea to measure the amount of fluid drained from the transmission to determine the correct amount of fresh fluid to add. This** is because some parts of the transmission may not drain completely, and using the dry refill amount specified in the Capacities Chart could lead to overfilling.

2. Slide a drain pan under the transmission. Partially loosen the pan retaining screws and remove the rear oil pan bolts, then drop the rear of the pan slightly so as to allow most of the fluid to drain without making a mess on your garage floor.

✳✳ WARNING

Check the fluid in the drain pan, it should always be a bright red color. If it is discolored (brown or black) or smells burnt, serious transmission troubles, probably due to overheating, should be suspected. The transmission should be inspected by a qualified service technician to locate the cause of the burnt fluid.

3. After the pan has drained, remove the pan retaining screws along with the pan and gasket.

4. Clean the pan thoroughly and allow it to air dry. If you wipe it out with a rag, you run the risk of leaving bits of lint in the pan which will clog the tiny hydraulic passages in the transmission.

5. Replace the transmission filter or strainer at this time, if necessary.

To install:

6. If removed, install a new transmission filter or strainer.

7. Install the pan using a new gasket. If you decide to use sealer on the gasket, apply it only in a very thin bead running along the outside of the pan screw holes. Tighten the pan screws evenly in rotation from the center outwards, to 4–5 ft. lbs. (5–8 Nm). Lower the vehicle.

8. Remove the jackstands and carefully lower the truck.

9. Add the correct amount of the proper type automatic transmission fluid through the dipstick tube; DO NOT overfill.

10. Insert the dipstick after filling. Start the engine and allow it to idle. DO NOT race the engine.

11. After the engine has idled for a few minutes, shift the transmission slowly through the gears, then return it to **P**. With the engine still idling, check the fluid level on the dipstick. If necessary, add more fluid to raise the level to where it is supposed to be.

Transfer Case

FLUID RECOMMENDATIONS

1989 models: multipurpose gear oil API GL-4; SAE 75W-90 or 80W-90
1990–95 models: DEXRON® ATF

FLUID LEVEL CHECK

▶ **See Figures 132 and 133**

The oil in the transfer case should be checked at least every 15,000 miles (24,000 km) or every 12 months, and replaced every 25,000–30,000 miles (40,000–48,000 km) or every 24 months.

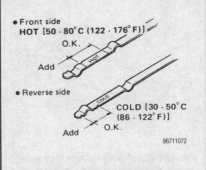

Fig. 129 Common automatic transmission dipstick marking

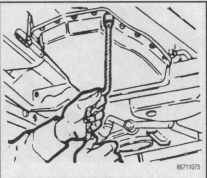

Fig. 130 Removing the fluid pan on an automatic transmission

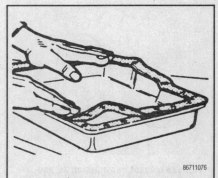

Fig. 131 Always replace the pan gasket when installing the fluid pan

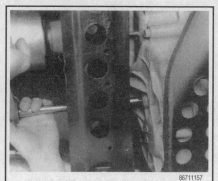

Fig. 132 Removing the filler plug with the proper tool

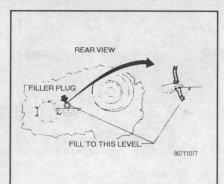

Fig. 133 Checking the fluid level in the transfer case

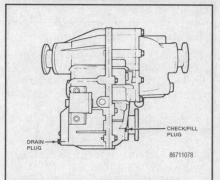

Fig. 134 Transfer case fill and drain plug locations

1. With the truck parked on a level surface, remove the filler plug from the rear of the housing.

2. If the lubricant begins to trickle out of the hole, there is enough. Otherwise, carefully insert your finger (watch out for sharp threads!) and check to see if the oil is up to the edge of the hole.

3. If not, add oil through the hole until the level is at the edge of the hole. Most gear lubricants come in a plastic squeeze bottle with a nozzle; making additions simple. You can also use a common everyday kitchen baster.

4. Replace the filler plug and tighten it to 18–25 ft. lbs. (25–34 Nm). Run the engine and check for leaks.

DRAIN AND REFILL

▶ **See Figures 134, 135 and 136**

Once every 30,000 miles (48,000 km) or every 24 months, the oil in the transfer case should be changed.

1. The transfer case oil should be hot before it is drained. If the engine is at normal operating temperature, the oil should be hot enough.

2. Raise the truck and support it properly on jackstands so that you can safely work underneath. You will probably not have enough room to work if the truck is not raised.

3. The drain plug is located near the bottom of the transfer case, toward the front. Place a pan under the drain plug and remove it. Keep a slight inward pressure on the plug while unscrewing it, as this will keep the oil from pouring out until the plug is removed.

✳✳ CAUTION

The oil will be HOT. Be careful when removing the plug, so that you don't take a bath in hot gear oil.

4. Allow the oil to drain completely. Clean off the plug, then reinstall and tighten it to 18–25 ft. lbs. (25–34 Nm).

5. Remove the filler plug from the side of the case. There will be a gasket underneath this plug. Replace it if damaged.

6. Fill the transfer case with gear oil through the filler plug hole. Refer to the Capacities Chart for the amount of oil needed to refill your transfer case.

7. The oil level should come right up to the edge of the hole. You can stick your finger in to verify this. Watch out for sharp threads.

8. Replace the filler plug and gasket, then lower the truck and check for leaks. Dispose of (recycle) the old oil in the proper manner.

Drive Axle (Differential)

FLUID RECOMMENDATIONS

All models without limited slip differential: Hypoid gear oil API GL-5
Limited Slip Differential: Nissan-approved limited slip differential fluid.

➡ **Raise the rear of the truck and spin one of the wheels by hand. If both wheels turn simultaneously, your truck is equipped with a limited slip differential.**

FLUID LEVEL CHECK

▶ **See Figures 137 and 138**

The oil in the front and/or rear differential should be checked at least every 15,000 miles (24,000 km) or every 12 months, and replaced every 25,000–30,000 miles (40,000–48,000 km) or every 24 months. If driven in deep water it should be replaced immediately.

1. With the truck parked on a level surface, remove the filler plug from the back of the differential.

➡ **The plug on the bottom is the drain plug on rear differentials. The lower of the two plugs on the back of the housing is the drain plug on front differentials.**

2. If the oil begins to trickle out of the hole, there is enough. Otherwise, carefully insert your finger (watch out for sharp threads!) into the hole and check to see if the oil is up to the bottom edge of the filler hole.

Fig. 135 Remove the drain plug with the proper tool, being careful not to round off the edges of the socket fitting

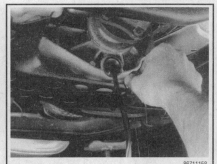

Fig. 136 After the drain plug is removed, the lubricant can be drained from the case assembly

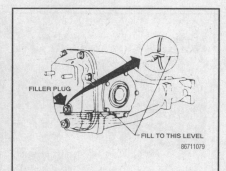

Fig. 137 Checking the fluid level in the front differential

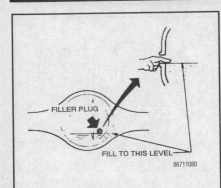

Fig. 138 Checking the fluid level in the rear differential

Fig. 139 View of the drain plug on the front differential assembly—do not round the edges of the drain plug

Fig. 140 Removing the drain plug on the front differential assembly

3. If not, add oil through the hole until the level is at the edge of the hole. Most gear oils come in a plastic squeeze bottle with a nozzle, making additions simple. You can also use a common kitchen baster. Use standard GL-5 hypoid type gear oil.

4. Replace the filler plug and drive the truck for a while. Stop the truck and check for leaks. Tighten the plug on the front differential to 29–43 ft. lbs. (39–59 Nm). On rear differentials, tighten the plug to 43–72 ft. lbs. (59–98 Nm) on the H190A and H233B; or 29–43 ft. lbs. (39–59 Nm) on the C200.

DRAIN AND REFILL

▸ See Figures 139 thru 145

The gear oil in the front or rear axle should be changed at least every 25,000–30,000 miles (40,000–48,000 km) or every 24 months; immediately if driven in deep water.

To drain and fill the differential, proceed as follows:

1. Park the vehicle on a level surface. Set the parking brake.

2. Remove the filler (upper) plug. Place a container which is large enough to catch all of the differential oil under the drain plug.

3. Remove the drain (lower) plug and gasket, if so equipped. Allow all of the oil to drain into the container.

4. Install the drain plug. On the front differential, tighten the drain plug to 29–43 ft. lbs. (39–59 Nm). On rear differentials, tighten the plug to 43–72 ft. lbs. (59–98 Nm) on the H190A and H233B; or 29–43 ft. lbs. (39–59 Nm) on the C200.

➡It's usually a good idea to replace the drain plug gasket at this time.

5. Refill with the proper axle lubricant (see the Recommended Lubricants chart). Be sure that the level reaches the bottom of the filler plug. DO NOT overfill.

6. Install the filler plug and check for leakage.

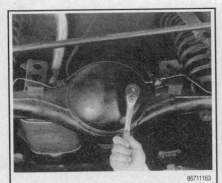

Fig. 141 Removing the filler plug on the rear differential assembly

Fig. 142 View of the filler plug on the rear differential assembly—do not round the edges of the drain plug

Fig. 143 View of the drain plug on the rear differential assembly—do not round the edges of the drain plug

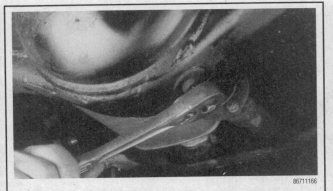

Fig. 144 Removing the drain plug on the rear differential assembly

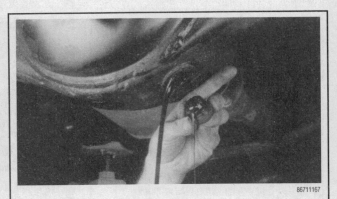

Fig. 145 Draining the oil from the rear differential assembly

Cooling System

FLUID RECOMMENDATIONS

When additional coolant is required to maintain the proper level, always add a mixture of aluminum-compatible antifreeze/coolant and water. Typically, a 50/50 mixture of antifreeze and water is recommended (even for vehicles which are not exposed to cold winter temperatures), since this mixture also imparts the necessary corrosion inhibition. A greater concentration of antifreeze may be used, but the coolant mixture's level of protection actually lessens if too much antifreeze is used. Unless you are simply topping off the cooling system, straight antifreeze should never be added without some water. For additional information on determining the optimum concentration for your vehicle, refer to the antifreeze manufacturer's labeling.

➡**Although Nissan recommends ethylene glycol-based antifreeze (which has long been the prevalent type on the market), other types (such as propylene glycol) may also be suitable for use in your vehicle. Be sure to thoroughly read the alternative product's labeling to ensure compatibility before switching to a different formula.**

FLUID LEVEL CHECK

▶ **See Figures 146, 147, 148, 149 and 150**

Dealing with the cooling system can be a tricky matter unless the proper precautions are observed. It is best to check the coolant level in the radiator when the engine is cold. This is done by checking the expansion tank. If coolant is visible above the **MIN** mark on the tank, the level is satisfactory. Always be certain that the filler caps on both the radiator and the reservoir are tightly closed.

In the event that the coolant level must be checked when the engine is warm or on engines without an expansion tank, place a thick rag over the radiator cap, then slowly turn the cap counterclockwise until it reaches the first detent. Allow all the hot steam to escape. This will allow the pressure in the system to drop gradually, preventing an explosion of hot coolant. When the hissing noise stops, remove the cap the rest of the way.

It's a good idea to check the coolant every time that you stop for fuel. If the coolant level is low, add equal amounts of suitable antifreeze and clean water. Fill the expansion tank to the **MAX** level. On models without an expansion tank, add coolant through the radiator filler neck.

➡**Never add cold coolant to a hot engine unless the engine is running, to avoid cracking the engine block.**

Avoid using water that is known to have a high alkaline content or is very hard, except in emergency situations. Drain and flush the cooling system as soon as possible after using such water.

The radiator hoses and clamps and the radiator cap should be checked at the same time as the coolant level. Hoses which are brittle, cracked, or swollen should be replaced. Clamps should be checked for tightness (screwdriver-tight only)! Do not allow the clamp to cut into the hose or crush the fitting. The radiator cap gasket should be checked for any tears, cracks, swelling, or any signs of incorrect seating in the radiator neck.

DRAIN, REFILL AND FLUSH

▶ **See Figures 151 thru 157**

❋❋ CAUTION

When draining the coolant, keep in mind that cats and dogs are attracted by ethylene glycol antifreeze, and are quite likely to drink any that is left in an uncovered container or in puddles on the ground. This will prove fatal in sufficient quantity. Always drain the coolant into a sealable container. Coolant should be reused unless it is contaminated or several years old.

Complete draining and refilling of the cooling system at least once every two years will remove accumulated rust, scale and other deposits.

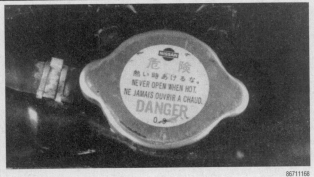

Fig. 146 View of the radiator cap installed—never open when the engine is hot!

Fig. 147 Add engine coolant to the radiator with a funnel to avoid spills

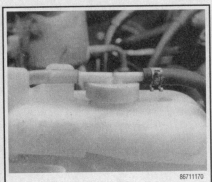

Fig. 148 View of the coolant expansion tank

Fig. 149 Remove the cap on the coolant expansion tank and add coolant to the proper level

Fig. 150 Add engine coolant to the expansion tank with a funnel to avoid spills

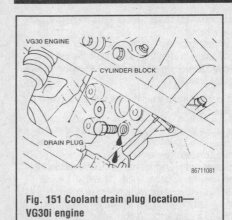

Fig. 151 Coolant drain plug location—VG30i engine

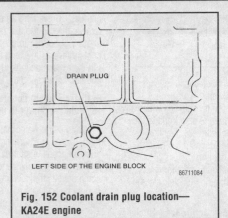

Fig. 152 Coolant drain plug location—KA24E engine

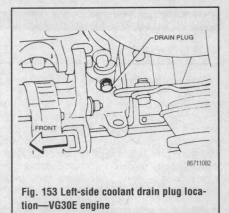

Fig. 153 Left-side coolant drain plug location—VG30E engine

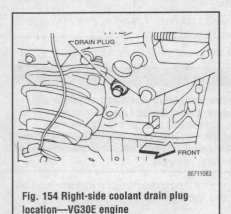

Fig. 154 Right-side coolant drain plug location—VG30E engine

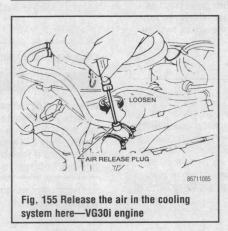

Fig. 155 Release the air in the cooling system here—VG30i engine

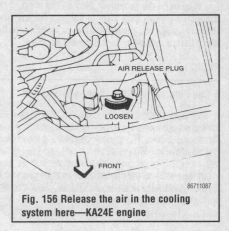

Fig. 156 Release the air in the cooling system here—KA24E engine

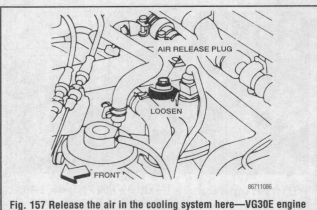

Fig. 157 Release the air in the cooling system here—VG30E engine

➡️**Use a good quality antifreeze with water pump lubricants, rust inhibitors and other corrosion inhibitors along with acid neutralizers. Use a permanent-type coolant that meets specification ESE M97B44A or the equivalent.**

1. Drain the existing coolant as follows: Position suitable drain pans beneath the radiator and engine block. Open the radiator petcock and engine drain plug(s)—2 on the V6 engine; 1 on the 4-cylinder engine—or disconnect the bottom radiator hose at the radiator outlet.

➡️**If it is rusted or difficult to open, spray the radiator petcock with some penetrating lubricant.**

2. Set the heater temperature controls to the full HOT position.

3. Close the petcock and tighten the drain plug(s) to 25–33 ft. lbs. (34–44 Nm), or reconnect the lower hose. Open the air relief plug (except on the Z24i engine), then fill the system with water.

4. Add a can of quality radiator flush. Be sure the flush is safe to use in engines having aluminum components.

5. Idle the engine until the upper radiator hose gets hot. Race it 2 or 3 times, then shut it **OFF**. Let the engine cool down.

6. Drain the system again.

7. Repeat this process until the drained water is clear and free of scale.

8. Close the petcock and drain plug(s) or, if applicable, connect the radiator hose.

9. If equipped with a coolant recovery system, flush the reservoir with water and leave empty.

➡️**Always open the air relief plug before filling the cooling system, in order to bleed the trapped air. Only when the cooling system is bled properly can the correct amount of coolant be added to the system.**

10. Determine the capacity of your cooling system (see the Capacities Chart, later in this section). Add the appropriate ratio of quality aluminum-compatible antifreeze and water (normally a 50/50 mix) to provide the desired protection. With the air relief plug open, add the coolant mixture through the radiator filler neck until full, then close the bleeder plug and radiator cap.

11. Using the same concentration of clean antifreeze and water, fill the expansion tank to the **MAX** line, then cap the tank.

SYSTEM INSPECTION

Most permanent antifreeze/coolants have a colored dye added which makes the solution an excellent leak detector. When servicing the cooling system, check for leakage at:

- All hoses and hose connections
- Radiator seams, radiator core, and radiator draincock
- All engine block and cylinder head freeze (core) plugs, and drain plugs
- Edges of all cooling system gaskets (head gaskets, thermostat gasket)
- Transmission fluid cooler
- Heating system components
- Water pump

In addition, check the engine oil dipstick for signs of coolant in the oil; also, check the coolant in the radiator for signs of oil. Investigate and correct any indication of coolant leakage.

Check the Radiator Cap

▶ See Figure 158

While you are checking the coolant level, check the radiator cap for a worn or cracked gasket. If the cap doesn't seal properly, fluid will be lost and the engine will overheat. A worn cap should be replaced with a new one.

Clean Radiator of Debris

▶ See Figure 159

Periodically clean any debris such as leaves, paper, insects, etc. from the radiator fins. Pick the large pieces off by hand. The smaller pieces can be washed away with water pressure from a hose.

Carefully straighten any bent radiator fins with a pair of needlenose pliers. Be careful, the fins are very soft. Don't wiggle the fins back and forth too much. Straighten them once and try not to move them again.

CHECKING SYSTEM PROTECTION

▶ See Figure 160

A 50/50 mix of antifreeze/coolant concentrate and water will usually provide the necessary protection. Freeze protection may be checked by using a cooling system hydrometer. Inexpensive hydrometers (floating ball types) may be obtained from a local department store (automotive section) or an auto supply store. Follow the directions packaged with the coolant hydrometer when checking protection.

Master Cylinders

All models are equipped with a brake master cylinder. In addition, those models equipped with a manual transmission also utilize a separate clutch mas-

ter cylinder. Both master cylinders are located above the brake booster unit at the driver's side firewall.

FLUID RECOMMENDATIONS

Use only Heavy Duty Brake fluid meeting DOT 3 or SAE J1703 specifications.

FLUID LEVEL CHECK

▶ See Figures 161, 162 and 163

➥The clutch master cylinder uses the same fluid as the brake system, and should be checked at the same time as the brake master cylinder.

The fluid in the brake and/or clutch master cylinders should be checked every 6 months or 6000 miles (9600 km). Check the fluid level on the side of the reservoir. If fluid is required, clean the area around the cap (to prevent the entry of dirt), then unscrew and remove the filler cap and gasket from the master cylinder. Fill the reservoir to the **MAX** line on the reservoir. Install the filler cap, making sure the gasket is properly seated in the cap.

➥It is normal for the fluid level in the brake master cylinder to fall as the disc brake pads wear. However, if the master cylinder requires filling frequently, you should check the system for leaks in the hoses, master cylinder, or wheel cylinders. Brake fluid dissolves paint. It also absorbs moisture from the air; never leave a container of fluid or either master cylinder uncovered any longer than necessary.

Power Steering Pump

FLUID RECOMMENDATIONS

Use only DEXRON® ATF in the power steering system.

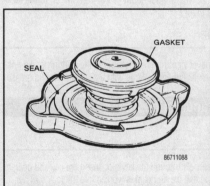

Fig. 158 Check the radiator cap seal and gasket condition

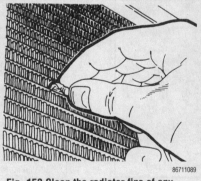

Fig. 159 Clean the radiator fins of any debris which impedes air flow

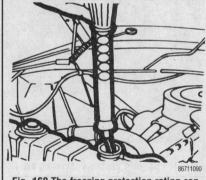

Fig. 160 The freezing protection rating can be checked with an antifreeze tester

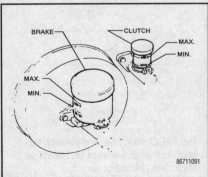

Fig. 161 Check the master cylinder fluid levels here

Fig. 162 Adding brake fluid to the brake master cylinder reservoir

Fig. 163 Adding brake fluid to the clutch master cylinder reservoir

FLUID LEVEL CHECK

▶ **See Figures 164, 165 and 166**

Check the power steering fluid level every 6 months or 6000 miles (9600 km).

1. Park the vehicle on a level surface. Run the engine until normal operating temperature is reached.

2. Turn the steering all the way to the left and then all the way to the right several times. Center the steering wheel and shut off the engine.

3. Open the hood and check the power steering reservoir fluid level.

4. Remove the filler cap and wipe the attached dipstick clean.

5. Reinsert the dipstick and tighten the cap. Remove the dipstick and note the fluid level indicated on the dipstick.

6. The level should be at any point below the upper hash mark, but not below the lower hash mark (in the HOT or COLD ranges).

7. Add fluid as necessary, but do not overfill.

Steering Gear

FLUID RECOMMENDATIONS

Use standard hypoid-type gear oil API GL-4, SAE 90W when refilling the steering gear.

FLUID LEVEL CHECK

▶ **See Figure 167**

Check the steering gear housing lubricating oil every 15,000 miles (24,000 km) or 12 months. Unscrew the filler plug on top of the housing. The level should be at or near the top of the housing. If necessary, add the recommended fluid. When finished, be sure to reinstall the filler plug.

Fig. 164 Remove the power steering cap to check the fluid level

Chassis Greasing

▶ **See Figures 168, 169 and 170**

➡ **If the vehicle is driven in extremely sandy conditions, lubricating the driveshaft assembly is a must!**

Complete chassis greasing should include an inspection of all rubber suspension bushings and lubrication of all body hinges, as well as proper greasing of the front suspension upper and lower ball joints and control arm bushings. To provide correct operation, the chassis should be greased every 7500 miles (12,000 km) or every 6 months.

If you wish to perform this operation yourself, you should purchase a cartridge-type grease gun and several cartridges of multipurpose lithium base grease. You will also need to purchase grease fittings from your Nissan dealer, as certain front end components are fitted with screw-in plugs to prevent entry of foreign material.

Remove the plug and install the grease fitting (if necessary). Push the nozzle of the grease gun down firmly onto the fitting and, while applying pressure, force the new grease into the boot. Force sufficient grease into the fitting to cause the old grease to be expelled. When this has been accomplished, remove the fitting and install the plug. Follow this procedure on each front suspension lubrication point.

Certain models have a two-piece driveshaft which must be greased at the same 6 month/7,500 mile (12,000 km) interval. The driveshaft is equipped with a grease fitting, located on the shaft just behind the center support bearing. Simply wipe off the fitting and pump in two or three shots of grease. There is no built in escape hole for the old grease to exit, so don't keep pumping in grease until the seal gives way.

MANUAL TRANSMISSION AND CLUTCH LINKAGE

On models so equipped, apply a small amount of chassis grease to the pivot points of the transmission and clutch linkage as per the chassis lubrication diagram.

AUTOMATIC TRANSMISSION LINKAGE

On models so equipped, apply a small amount of 10W engine oil to the kickdown and shift linkage at the pivot points.

PARKING BRAKE LINKAGE

At yearly intervals or whenever binding is noticeable in the parking brake linkage, lubricate the cable guides, levers and linkage with a suitable chassis grease.

Body Lubrication and Maintenance

LOCK CYLINDERS

Apply graphite lubricant sparingly through the key slot. Insert the key and operate the lock several times to be sure that the lubricant is worked into the lock cylinder.

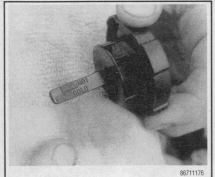

Fig. 165 View of the power steering cap dipstick—note the hot and cold marks

Fig. 166 Adding power steering fluid—use a funnel to avoid spills

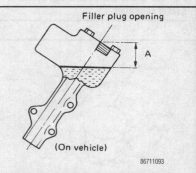

Fig. 167 Checking the manual steering gear fluid level. Distance (A) should be 1½ inches (38mm) or less

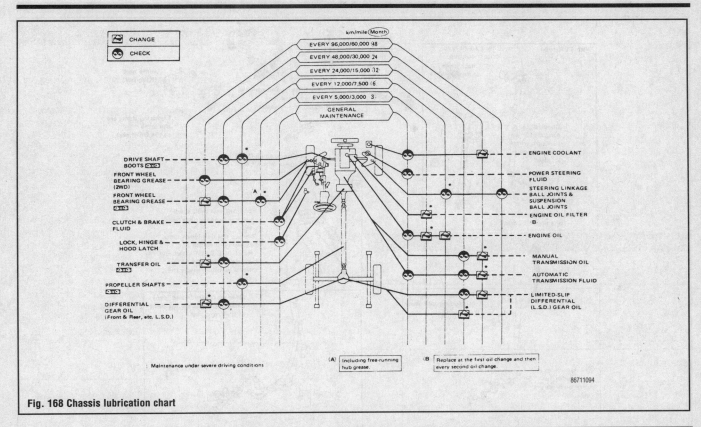

Fig. 168 Chassis lubrication chart

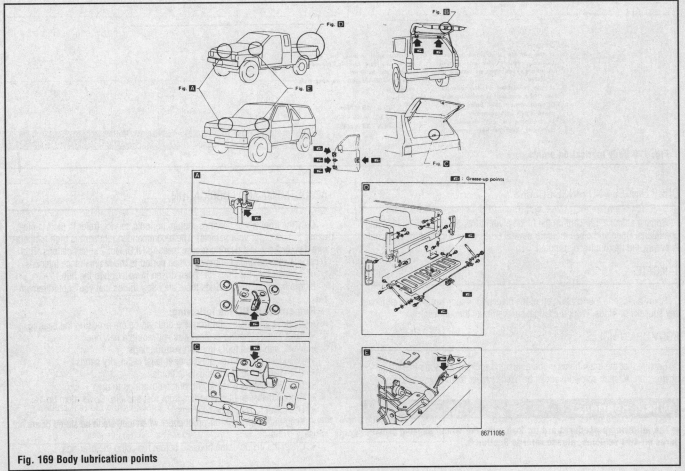

Fig. 169 Body lubrication points

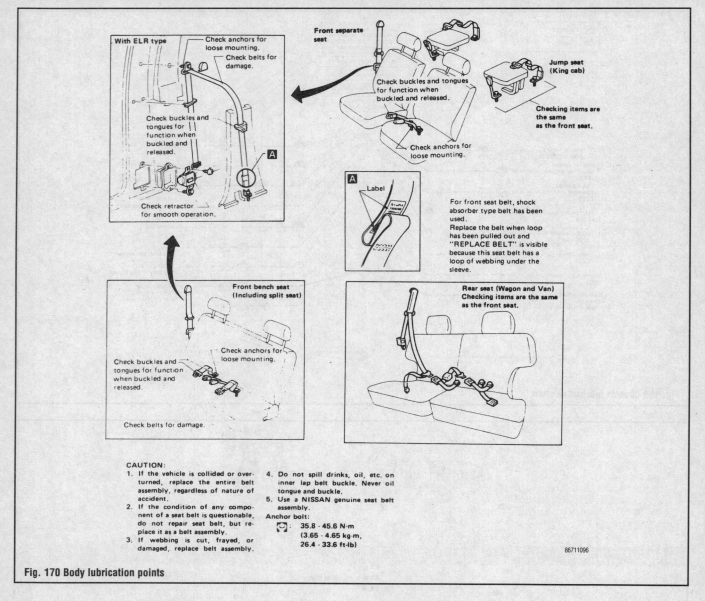

Fig. 170 Body lubrication points

DOOR HINGES AND HINGE CHECKS

Spray a silicone lubricant on the hinge pivot points to eliminate any binding conditions. Open and close the door several times to be sure that the lubricant is evenly and thoroughly distributed.

TAILGATE

Spray a silicone lubricant on all of the pivot and friction surfaces to eliminate any squeaks or binds. Work the tailgate to distribute the lubricant.

BODY DRAIN HOLES

Be sure that the drain holes in the doors and rocker panels are free of obstruction. A small screwdriver can be used to clear them of any debris.

Wheel Bearings

➡ **The following procedures are for 2wd only. For wheel bearing procedures on 4wd vehicles, please refer to Section 8.**

ADJUSTMENT AND LUBRICATION

Only the front wheel bearings require periodic service (refer to the Maintenance Schedule for your vehicle). The recommended lubricant is high temperature disc brake wheel bearing grease meeting NLGI No. 2 specifications. This service is recommended at the specified period in the Maintenance Intervals chart, or whenever the truck has been driven in water up to the hub.

Before handling the bearings there are a few things that you should remember:

Remember to DO the following:

- Remove all outside dirt from the housing before exposing the bearing.
- Treat a used bearing as gently as you would a new one.
- Work with clean tools in clean surroundings.
- Use clean, dry canvas gloves, or at least clean, dry hands.
- Use clean solvents and flushing fluids.
- Use clean paper when laying out the bearings to dry.
- Protect disassembled bearings from rust and dirt. Cover them up.
- Use clean rags to wipe bearings.
- Keep the bearings in oil-proof paper when they are to be stored or are not in use.
- Clean the inside of the housing before replacing the bearings.

Do NOT do the following:
- Don't work in dirty surroundings.
- Don't use dirty, chipped, or damaged tools.
- Do not use gasoline for cleaning; use a safe solvent.
- Do not spin wheel bearings with compressed air.
- Avoid using cotton waste or dirty cloths to wipe bearings.
- Try not to scratch or nick bearing surfaces.
- Do not allow the bearing to come in contact with dirt or rust at any time.

2-Wheel Drive

1. Remove the brake caliper, following the procedure outlined in Section 9.
2. The outer wheel bearing will come off with the hub. Simply pull the hub/disc assembly towards you off the spindle. Be sure to catch the inner bearing before it falls to the ground.
3. The inner bearing will have to be driven from the hub along with the oil seal. Use only a brass rod as a drift and carefully drive the inner bearing out. Remove the bearing and the oil seal. Discard the seal.
4. Clean the bearings in solvent and allow to air dry. You risk leaving bits of lint if you dry them with a rag. Clean the bearing cups in the hub.
5. Inspect the bearings carefully. If they are worn, pitted, burned, or scored, they should be replaced, along with the bearing cups in which they run.
6. If necessary, drive the inner and outer bearings cups from the hub using a brass rod as a drift, or a large socket or piece of pipe.
7. Install the new inner cup, and then the outer cup, into the hub using either the brass drift or a large socket.

➡**Use care not to cock the bearing cups in the hub. If they are not fully seated, the bearings will be impossible to adjust properly.**

8. Place a large glob of grease into one palm and force the edge of the inner bearing into it so that the grease fills the bearing. Do this until the whole bearing is packed. Coat the inner bearing cup with grease. Install the inner bearing into the cup. Press a new oil seal into place on top of the hub assembly. You may have to give the seal a few gentle raps with a soft drift to get it to seat properly.
9. Install the hub assembly onto the spindle.
10. Coat the outer bearing cup with grease. Pack the outer bearing with grease and install into the cup.
11. Pack the grease cap with grease and set it aside. It will be installed last, after the preload adjustment. You can put the grease away now.
12. Install the lock washer, nut, and adjusting castle nut loosely, and go on to the preload adjustment.

BEARING PRELOAD ADJUSTMENT

▶ **See Figure 171**

1. While turning the hub forward, tighten the adjusting nut to 25–29 ft. lbs. (34–39 Nm).
2. Rotate the hub in both directions a few times to seat the bearings.
3. Retighten the nut to the above specification.
4. Loosen the wheel bearing lock-nut 45 degrees. Fit the adjusting cap (castle nut) and a new cotter pin. Align the cotter pin slot by loosening the nut 15 degrees or less.
5. Install the grease cap, and wipe off any grease that oozes out.
6. Check the axial play of the wheel by shaking it back and forth; the bearing free-play should be close to zero, but the wheel should spin freely.

➡**If you measure wheel bearing preload with a spring-type gauge, measure it at the wheel hub bolt, with the tire removed. The hub assembly (with new grease seal installed) should rotate with 2.2–6.4 lbs. (1–3 kg) of pressure.**

7. Install the brake caliper assembly.

4-Wheel Drive

For wheel bearing procedures on 4wd vehicles, please refer to Section 8 of this manual.

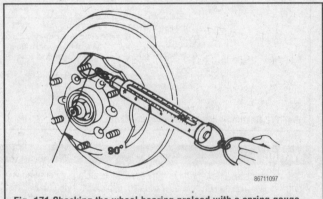

86711097

Fig. 171 Checking the wheel bearing preload with a spring gauge

TRAILER TOWING

Factory trailer towing packages are available on most Nissan trucks. However, if you are installing a trailer hitch and wiring on your truck, there are a few thing that you ought to know.

Trailer Weight

Trailer weight is the first, and most important, factor in determining whether or not your vehicle is suitable for towing the trailer you have in mind. The horsepower-to-weight ratio should be calculated. The basic standard is a ratio of 35:1. That is, 35 pounds of GVW for every horsepower.

To calculate this ratio, multiply you engine's rated horsepower by 35, then subtract the weight of the vehicle, including passengers and luggage. The resulting figure is the ideal maximum trailer weight that you can tow. One point to consider: a numerically higher axle ratio can offset what appears to be a low trailer weight. If the weight of the trailer that you have in mind is somewhat higher than the weight you just calculated, you might consider changing your rear axle ratio to compensate.

Hitch Weight

▶ **See Figure 172**

There are three kinds of hitches: bumper mounted, frame mounted, and load equalizing.

Bumper mounted hitches are those which attach solely to the vehicle's bumper. Many states prohibit towing with this type of hitch, when it attaches to the vehicle's stock bumper, since it subjects the bumper to stresses for which it was not designed. Aftermarket rear step bumpers, designed for trailer towing, are acceptable for use with bumper mounted hitches.

Frame mounted hitches can be of the type which bolts to two or more points on the frame, plus the bumper, or just to several points on the frame. Frame mounted hitches can also be of the tongue type, for Class I towing, or, of the receiver type, for Classes II and III.

Load equalizing hitches are usually used for large trailers. Most equalizing hitches are welded in place and use equalizing bars and chains to level the vehicle after the trailer is hooked up.

The bolt-on hitches are the most common, since they are relatively easy to install.

Check the gross weight rating of your trailer. Tongue weight is usually figured as 10% of gross trailer weight. Therefore, a trailer with a maximum gross weight of 2000 lbs. will have a maximum tongue weight of 200 lb. Class I trailers fall into this category. Class II trailers are those with a gross weight rating of 2000–3500 lbs., while Class III trailers fall into the 3500–6000 lb. category. Class IV trailers are those over 6000 lbs. and are for use with fifth wheel trucks, only.

When you've determined the hitch that you'll need, follow the manufacturer's installation instructions, exactly, especially when it comes to fastener torques. The hitch will subjected to a lot of stress and good hitches come with hardened bolts. Never substitute an inferior bolt for a hardened bolt.

Recommended Equipment Checklist

Equipment	Class I Trailers Under 2,000 pounds	Class II Trailers 2,000-3,500 pounds	Class III Trailers 3,500-6,000 pounds	Class IV Trailers 6,000 pounds and up
Hitch	Frame or Equalizing	Equalizing	Equalizing	Fifth wheel Pick-up truck only
Tongue Load Limit**	Up to 200 pounds	200-350 pounds	350-600 pounds	600 pounds and up
Trailer Brakes	Not Required	Required	Required	Required
Safety Chain	3/16" diameter links	1/4" diameter links	5/16" diameter links	—
Fender Mounted Mirrors	Useful, but not necessary	Recommended	Recommended	Recommended
Turn Signal Flasher	Standard	Constant Rate or heavy duty	Constant Rate or heavy duty	Constant Rate or heavy duty
Coolant Recovery System	Recommended	Required	Required	Required
Transmission Oil Cooler	Recommended	Recommended	Recommended	Recommended
Engine Oil Cooler	Recommended	Recommended	Recommended	Recommended
Air Adjustable Shock Absorbers	Recommended	Recommended	Recommended	Recommended
Flex or Clutch Fan	Recommended	Recommended	Recommended	Recommended
Tires	***	***	***	***

NOTE The information in this chart is a guide. Check the manufacturer's recommendations for your car if in doubt

*Local laws may require specific equipment such as trailer brakes or fender mounted mirrors. Check your local laws Hitch weight is usually 10-15% of trailer gross weight and should be measured with trailer loaded

**Most manufacturer's do not recommend towing trailers of over 1,000 pounds with compacts. Some intermediates cannot tow Class III trailers

***Check manufacturer's recommendations for your specific car trailer combination

—Does not apply

86711098

Fig. 172 Recommended equipment checklist

Wiring

Wiring your Nissan for towing is fairly easy. There are a number of good wiring kits available and these should be used, rather than trying to design your own. All trailers will need brake lights and turn signals, as well as tail lights and side marker lights. Most states require extra marker lights for overly wide trailers. Also, most states have recently required back-up lights for trailers, and most trailer manufacturers have been building trailers with back-up lights for several years.

Additionally, some Class I, most Class II, and just about all Class III trailers will have electric brakes.

Add to this number an accessories wire, to operate trailer internal equipment or to charge the trailer's battery, and you can have as many as seven wires in the harness.

Determine the equipment on your trailer and buy the wiring kit necessary. The kit will contain all the wires needed, plus a plug adapter set which includes the female plug, mounted on the bumper or hitch, and the male plug, wired into, or plugged into the trailer harness.

When installing the kit, follow the manufacturer's instructions. The color coding of the wires is standard throughout the industry.

One point to note is that most imported vehicles do not have separate turn signals. On most of these vehicles, the brake lights and rear turn signals operate with the same bulb. For those vehicles without separate turn signals, you can purchase an isolation unit so that the brake lights won't blink whenever the turn signals are operated, or, you can go to your local electronics supply house and buy four diodes to wire in series with the brake and turn signal bulbs. Diodes will isolate the brake and turn signals. The choice is yours. The isolation units are simple and quick to install, but far more expensive than the diodes. The diodes, however, require more work to install properly, since they require the cutting of each bulb's wire and soldering in place of the diode.

One final point, the best kits are those with a spring loaded cover on the vehicle mounted socket. This cover prevents dirt and moisture from corroding the terminals. Never let the vehicle socket hang loosely. Always mount it securely to the bumper or hitch.

Cooling

ENGINE

One of the most common, if not THE most common, problem associated with trailer towing is engine overheating.

With factory installed trailer towing packages, a heavy duty cooling system is usually included. Heavy duty cooling systems are available as optional equipment on most Nissans, with or without a trailer package. If you have one of these extra-capacity systems, you shouldn't have any overheating problems.

If you have a standard cooling system, without an expansion tank, you'll definitely need to get an aftermarket expansion tank kit, preferably one with at least a 2 quart capacity. These kits are easily installed on the radiator's overflow hose, and come with a pressure cap designed for expansion tanks.

Another helpful accessory is a flex fan. These fan are large diameter units are designed to provide more airflow at low speeds, with blades that have deeply cupped surfaces. The blades then flex, or flatten out, at high speed, when less cooling air is needed. These fans are far lighter in weight than stock fans, requiring less horsepower to drive them. Also, they are far quieter than stock fans.

If you do decide to replace your stock fan with a flex fan, note that if your truck has a fan clutch, a spacer between the flex fan and water pump hub will be needed.

Aftermarket engine oil coolers are helpful for prolonging engine oil life and reducing overall engine temperatures. Both of these factors increase engine life.

While not absolutely necessary in towing Class I and some Class II trailers, they are recommended for heavier Class II and all Class III towing.

Engine oil cooler systems consist of an adapter, screwed on in place of the oil filter, a remote filter mounting and a multi-tube, finned heat exchanger, which is mounted in front of the radiator or air conditioning condenser.

TRANSMISSION

An automatic transmission is usually recommended for trailer towing. Modern automatics have proven reliable and, of course, easy to operate, in trailer towing.

The increased load of a trailer, however, causes an increase in the temperature of the automatic transmission fluid. Heat is the worst enemy of an automatic transmission. As the temperature of the fluid increases, the life of the fluid decreases.

It is essential, therefore, that you install an automatic transmission cooler.

The cooler, which consists of a multi-tube, finned heat exchanger, is usually installed in front of the radiator or air conditioning compressor, and hooked inline with the transmission cooler tank inlet line. Follow the cooler manufacturer's installation instructions.

Select a cooler of at least adequate capacity, based upon the combined gross weights of the truck and trailer.

Cooler manufacturers recommend that you use an aftermarket cooler in addition to, and not instead of, the present cooling tank in your radiator. If you do want to use it in place of the radiator cooling tank, get a cooler at least two sizes larger than normally necessary.

➡A transmission cooler can, sometimes, cause slow or harsh shifting in the transmission during cold weather, until the fluid has a chance to come up to normal operating temperature. Some coolers can be purchased with (or retrofitted with) a temperature bypass valve, which will allow fluid flow through the cooler only when the fluid has reached operating temperature, or above.

TOWING THE VEHICLE

♦ **See Figures 173, 174, 175 and 176**

➡Push-starting is not recommended. If equipped with manual locking hubs, set the free-running hubs to the FREE position. Set the gearshift and transfer lever to the NEUTRAL position before towing. When towing, make sure the transmission, axles, steering system and powertrain are in good condition. If any unit is damaged, a dolly should be used.

The truck can be towed with the rear wheels on the ground for distances under 15 miles at speeds no greater then 30 mph. If the truck has to be towed over 15 miles or over 30 mph the truck must be dollied or towed with the rear wheels raised and the steering wheel secured so that the front wheels remain in the straight-ahead position. The steering wheel must be clamped with a special clamping device designed for towing service. If the key controlled lock is used damage to the lock and steering column may occur.

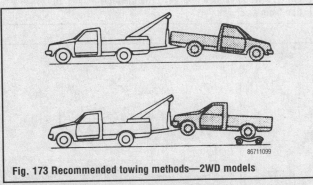

Fig. 173 Recommended towing methods—2WD models

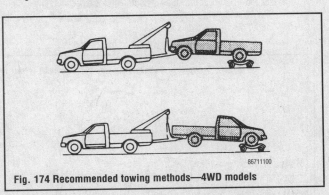

Fig. 174 Recommended towing methods—4WD models

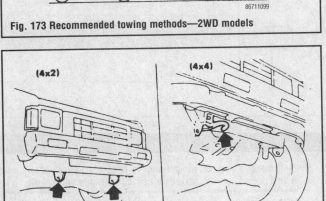

Fig. 175 Towing points—front

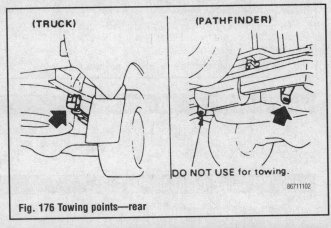

Fig. 176 Towing points—rear

JACKING

♦ **See Figures 177 and 178**

➡Refer to the illustration for correct placement of a floor jack or safety stands. A good hydraulic floor jack is worth the investment when working on your vehicle.

Your truck is equipped with either a pantograph-type (scissors) jack, or a screw-type (bottle) jack. The jack should be placed under the side of the truck so that it fits into the notch in the vertical rocker panel flange nearest the wheel to be changed. These jacking notches are located approximately 8 in. (20cm) from the wheel opening on the rocker panel flanges.

On 4wd models equipped with a bottle jack, be sure to put the adapter on the jack when raising the front of the vehicle. However, do not use the adapter when raising the rear of the vehicle.

When raising the truck with a scissors or bottle jack, follow these precautions:

• Never crawl under the vehicle while it is supported only by the jack
• Use the jack provided with the vehicle; DO NOT attempt to raise the vehicle using a bumper jack
• Use only the designated jacking points
• Never jack up the vehicle more than necessary
• Never use blocks on or under the jack
• Do not start or run the engine while the vehicle is on the jack
• Do not allow passengers to stay in the truck while it is on the jack
• On models equipped with a limited slip differential, NEVER run the engine with one rear wheel off the ground; this may cause the vehicle to move.

❄❄ CAUTION

If you're going to work beneath the vehicle, always support it on safety stands. NEVER use cinder blocks, as they could crumble, causing personal injury or death.

1. Park the truck on a firm, level spot. Put the gear selector in **P** (PARK) for an automatic transmission, or in Reverse for a manual transmission.
2. Apply the parking brake, then block the front and rear of the wheel that is diagonally opposite the wheel being changed.
3. If applicable, position the adapter on the bottle jack.
4. Place the jack directly beneath the designated jacking point.
5. Loosen each wheel lug nut one or two turns with the wheel nut wrench.

➡**Do not remove the wheel nuts until the tire is off the ground.**

6. Carefully raise the vehicle until the tire clears the ground.
7. Remove the wheel nuts, then remove the wheel. Do not remove the brake drum with the wheel.

To install the wheel:

8. Clean any mud or dirt from the surface between the wheel and hub.
9. Place the wheel over the studs, then tighten the wheel nuts finger-tight.
10. Using the wheel nut wrench, turn the wheel nuts alternately and evenly until they are tight.

11. Lower the vehicle slowly until the tire touches the ground. Again tighten the wheel nuts securely in a crisscross pattern. As soon as possible, retighten the wheel nuts to their specified torque with a torque wrench.

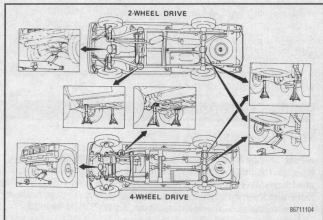

Fig. 177 When using a floor jack and/or safety stands, always position them as shown

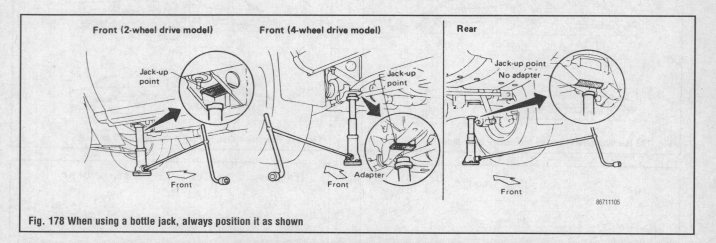

Fig. 178 When using a bottle jack, always position it as shown

JUMP STARTING A DEAD BATTERY

Except for replacing the dead battery, jump starting is the only way to start vehicles equipped with an automatic transmission, and is the preferred method for vehicles equipped with a manual transmission.

Jump Starting Precautions

1. Be sure that both batteries are of the same voltage. All vehicles covered by this manual and most vehicles on the road today utilize a 12 volt charging system.
2. Be sure that both batteries are of the same polarity (have the same terminal, in most cases NEGATIVE grounded).
3. Be sure that the vehicles are not touching or a short could occur.
4. On serviceable batteries, be sure the vent cap holes are not obstructed.
5. Do not smoke or allow sparks anywhere near the batteries.
6. In cold weather, make sure the battery electrolyte is not frozen. This can occur more readily in a battery that has been in a state of discharge.
7. Do not allow electrolyte to contact your skin or clothing.

Jump Starting Procedure

❄❄ CAUTION

Do not attempt this procedure on a frozen battery, it will probably explode. The battery in the other vehicle must be a 12 volt, nega-

tively grounded one. Do not attempt to jump start your vehicle with a 24 volt power source; serious electrical damage will result.

1. Make sure that the voltages of the 2 batteries are the same. Most batteries and charging systems are of the 12 volt variety.
2. Pull the jumping vehicle (with the good battery) into a position so the jumper cables can reach the dead battery and that vehicle's engine. Make sure that the vehicles do NOT touch.
3. Place the transmissions of both vehicles in **Neutral** or **Park**, as applicable, then firmly set their parking brakes.

➡**If necessary for safety reasons, both vehicle's hazard lights may be operated throughout the entire procedure without significantly increasing the difficulty of jumping the dead battery.**

4. Turn all lights and accessories off on both vehicles. Make sure the ignition switches on both vehicles are turned to the **OFF** position.
5. Cover the battery cell caps with a rag, but do not cover the terminals.
6. Make sure the terminals on both batteries are clean and free of corrosion or proper electrical connection will be impeded. If necessary, clean the battery terminals before proceeding.
7. Identify the positive (+) and negative (−) terminals on both battery posts.
8. Connect the first jumper cable to the positive (+) terminal of the dead battery, then connect the other end of that cable to the positive (+) terminal of the booster (good) battery.

9. Connect one end of the other jumper cable to the negative (−) terminal of the booster battery and the other cable clamp to an engine bolt head, alternator bracket or other solid, metallic point on the dead battery's engine. Try to select a ground on the engine that is positioned away from the battery, in order to minimize the possibility of the 2 clamps touching should one loosen during the procedure. DO NOT connect this clamp to the negative (−) terminal of the bad battery.

❊❊ CAUTION

Be very careful to keep the jumper cables away from moving parts (cooling fan, belts, etc.) on both engines.

10. Check to make sure that the cables are routed away from any moving parts, then start the donor vehicle's engine. Run the engine at moderate speed for several minutes to allow the dead battery a chance to receive some initial charge.

11. With the donor vehicle's engine still running slightly above idle, try to start the vehicle with the dead battery. Crank the engine for no more than 10 seconds at a time and let the starter cool for at least 20 seconds between tries.

If the vehicle does not start in 3 tries, it is likely that something else is also wrong or that the battery needs additional time to charge.

12. Once the vehicle is started, allow it to run at idle for a few seconds to make sure that it is properly operating.

13. Turn on the headlights, heater blower and, if equipped, the rear defroster of both vehicles in order to reduce the severity of voltage spikes and subsequent risk of damage to the vehicles' electrical systems when the cables are disconnected.

14. Carefully disconnect the cables in the reverse order of connection. Start with the negative cable that is attached to the engine ground, then the negative cable on the donor battery. Disconnect the positive cable from the donor battery and, finally, disconnect the positive cable from the formerly dead battery. Be careful when disconnecting the cables from the positive terminals not to allow the alligator clips to touch any metal on either vehicle or a short and sparks will occur.

➡ **It is recognized that some of the precautions outlined in this procedure are often ignored without harmful results. However, the procedure outlined is the safest and we DO NOT recommend any shortcuts.**

MAINTENANCE SCHEDULES

The following charts show the normal maintenance schedule. Under severe driving conditions, additional or more frequent maintenance will be required. Refer to "Maintenance under severe driving conditions".
The periodic maintenance schedule is repeated beyond the last mileage and period shown by returning to the first 15,000 miles (24,000 km) or 12 months.

Emission control system maintenance

MAINTENANCE OPERATION		MAINTENANCE INTERVAL								
Perform at number of miles,	Miles x 1,000	7.5	15	30	45	60	75	90	105	120
kilometers or months,	(km x 1,000)	(12)	(24)	(48)	(72)	(96)	(121)	(145)	(169)	(193)
whichever comes first.	Months	6	12	24	36	48	60	72	84	96
Drive belts					I*		I*		I*	I*
Air cleaner filter			Replace every 30,000 miles (48,000 km).							
Positive crankcase ventilation (P.C.V.) filter	See NOTE (1).		Replace every 30,000 miles (48,000 km).							
Vapor lines					I*		I*		I*	I*
Fuel lines (hoses, piping, connections, etc.)					I*		I*		I*	I*
Fuel filter			See NOTE (1).*							
Engine coolant				R		R		R		R
Engine oil		R	Then replace every 7,500 miles (12,000 km) or 6 months.							
Engine oil filter (Use Nissan PREMIUM type or equivalent.)		R	Then replace every second oil change.							
Spark plugs			Replace every 30,000 miles (48,000 km).							
Ignition wires			Inspect every 3 years.*							
Intake & exhaust valve clearance (Z24i engine only)		A	A	A	A	A	A	A	A
Idle rpm	Except the below				I*		A		I*	A
	For California models				I*		I*		I*	I*
Timing belt (VG30i engine only)			Replace every 60,000 miles (96,000 km).							

Chassis and body maintenance

MAINTENANCE OPERATION		MAINTENANCE INTERVAL							
Perform at number of miles,	Miles x 1,000	15	30	45	60	75	90	105	120
kilometers or months,	(km x 1,000)	(24)	(48)	(72)	(96)	(121)	(145)	(169)	(193)
whichever comes first.	Months	12	24	36	48	60	72	84	96
Brake lines & hoses		I	I	I	I	I	I	I	I
Brake pads, discs, drums & linings		I	I	I	I	I	I	I	I
Manual and automatic transmission, transfer & differential gear oil (exc. L.S.D.)		I	I	I	I	I	I	I	I
Limited-slip differential (L.S.D.) gear oil		I	R	I	R	I	R	I	R
Steering gear (box) & linkage, (steering damper 4x4), axle & suspension parts			I		I		I		I
Front drive shaft boots (4x4)		I	I	I	I	I	I	I	I
Steering linkage ball joints & front suspension ball joints					I				I
Front wheel bearing grease (4x2)			I		I		I		I
Front wheel bearing grease (4x4)		I	R	I	R	I	R	I	R
Exhaust system		I	I	I	I	I	I	I	I

NOTE: (1) If vehicle is operated under extremely adverse weather conditions or in areas where ambient temperatures are either extremely low or extremely high, the filters might become clogged. In such an event, replace them immediately.

(2) Maintenance items and intervals with "*" are recommended by NISSAN for reliable vehicle operation. The owner need not perform such maintenance in order to maintain the emission warranty or manufacturer recall liability. Other maintenance items and intervals are required.

Abbreviations: A = Adjust   R = Replace   I = Inspect. Correct or replace if necessary.

86711106

Fig. 179 Normal conditions recommended maintenance schedule—1989 models

MAINTENANCE UNDER SEVERE DRIVING CONDITIONS

The maintenance intervals shown on the preceding pages are for normal operating conditions. If the vehicle is mainly operated under severe driving conditions as shown below, more frequent maintenance is required to be performed on the following items as shown in the table.

Severe driving conditions

A — Repeated short trips less than 5 miles (8 km) and outside temperatures remain below freezing

B — Extensive idling and/or low speed driving for a long distance such as police, taxi or door-to-door delivery use

C — Driving in dusty conditions

D — Driving on rough, muddy, or salt spread roads

E — Towing a trailer, using a camper or a car-top carrier

F — Frequent driving in water

Driving condition	Maintenance item	Maintenance operation	Maintenance interval
. . C . . .	Air cleaner filter	R	More frequently
	Air induction valve filter	R	Every 30,000 miles (48,000 km)
A B C D E .	Engine oil & oil filter	R	Every 3,000 miles (5,000 km) or 3 months
A . C D E .	Brake pads, discs, drums & lining	I	Every 7,500 miles (12,000 km)
. . . D E .	Manual and automatic transmission, transfer & differential gear oil (exc. L.S.D.)	R	Every 30,000 miles (48,000 km) or 24 months
	Limited-slip differential (L.S.D.) gear oil	R	Every 15,000 miles (24,000 km) or 12 months
. . . D . .	Steering gear (box) & linkage, (steering damper 4×4), axle & suspension parts, & (front drive shaft boots 4×4)	I	Every 7,500 miles (12,000 km) or 6 months
. . C D . .	Steering linkage ball joints & front suspension ball joints	I	
. . . D E .	Propeller shaft(s) (4×4)	I	
A . . D E .	Exhaust system	I	
. . . . . F	Front wheel bearing grease & free-running hub grease (4×4)	I	Every 3,000 miles (5,000 km) or 3 months

Maintenance operations: I = Inspect. Correct or replace if necessary   R = Replace

Maintenance for off-road driving (4×4 only)

Whenever you drive off-road through sand, mud or water as deep as the wheel hub, more frequent maintenance may be required of the following items:

▲ Brake pads and discs
▲ Brake lining and drums
▲ Brake lines and hoses
▲ Wheel bearing grease and free-running hub grease
▲ Differential, transmission and transfer oil

▲ Steering linkage
▲ Propeller shafts and front drive shafts
▲ Air cleaner filter
▲ Clutch housing

86711107

Fig. 180 Severe conditions recommended maintenance schedule—1989 models

Abbreviations: R = Replace   I = Inspect. Correct or replace if necessary.

MAINTENANCE OPERATION		MAINTENANCE INTERVAL							
Perform at number of miles, kilometers or months, whichever comes first. Miles x 1,000		7.5	15	22.5	30	37.5	45	52.5	60
(km x 1,000)		(12)	(24)	(36)	(48)	(60)	(72)	(84)	(96)
Months		6	12	18	24	30	36	42	48
Emission control system maintenance									
Drive belts					I*				I*
Air cleaner filter					[R]				[R]
Positive crankcase ventilation (P.C.V.) filter (KA24E engine only)	See NOTE (1)				[R]				[R]
Vapor lines					I*				I*
Fuel lines					I*				I*
Fuel filter	See NOTE (1)*								
Engine coolant					R*				R*
Engine oil		R	R	R	R	R	R	R	R
Engine oil filter (Use Nissan PREMIUM type or equivalent.)		R		R		R		R	
Spark plugs					[R]				[R]
Timing belt (VG30E engine only)									[R]
Chassis and body maintenance									
Brake lines & cables			I		I		I		I
Brake pads, discs, drums & linings			I		I		I		I
Manual and automatic transmission, transfer & differential gear oil (exc. L.S.D.)			I		I		I		I
Limited-slip differential (L.S.D.) gear oil			I		R		I		R
Steering gear (box) & linkage, (steering damper 4x4), axle & suspension parts					I				I
Drive shaft boots (4x4)			I		I		I		I
Steering linkage ball joints & front suspension ball joints									I
Front wheel bearing grease (4x2)					I				I
Front wheel bearing grease & free-running hub grease (4x4)			I		R		I		R
Exhaust system			I		I		I		I

NOTE: (1) If vehicle is operated under extremely adverse weather conditions or in areas where ambient temperatures are either extremely low or extremely high, the filters might become clogged. In such an event, replace them immediately.

(2) Maintenance items and intervals with "*" are recommended by NISSAN for reliable vehicle operation. The owner need not perform such maintenance in order to maintain the emission warranty or manufacturer recall liability. Other maintenance items and intervals are required.

86711109

Fig. 181 Normal conditions recommended maintenance schedule—1990 models

---

Abbreviations: R = Replace   I = Inspect. Correct or replace if necessary.

MAINTENANCE OPERATION		MAINTENANCE INTERVAL															
Perform at number of miles, kilometers or months, whichever comes first. Miles x 1,000		3.75	7.5	11.25	15	18.75	22.5	26.25	30	33.75	37.5	41.25	45	48.75	52.5	56.25	60
(km x 1,000)		(6)	(12)	(18)	(24)	(30)	(36)	(42)	(48)	(54)	(60)	(66)	(72)	(78)	(84)	(90)	(96)
Months		3	6	9	12	15	18	21	24	27	30	33	36	39	42	45	48
Emission control system maintenance																	
Drive belts									I*								I*
Air cleaner filter	See NOTE (1)								[R]								[R]
Positive crankcase ventilation (P.C.V.) filter (KA24E engine only)	See NOTE (3)								[R]								[R]
Air induction valve filter (KA24E engine only)	See NOTE (2)																
Vapor lines									I*								I*
Fuel lines									I*								I*
Fuel filter	See NOTE (3)*																
Engine coolant									R*								R*
Engine oil		R	R	R	R	R	R	R	R	R	R	R	R	R	R	R	R
Engine oil filter (Use Nissan PREMIUM type or equivalent.)		R	R	R	R	R	R	R	R	R	R	R	R	R	R	R	R
Spark plugs									[R]								[R]
Timing belt (VG30E engine only)																	[R]
Chassis and body maintenance																	
Brake lines & cables					I				I				I				I
Brake pads, discs, drums & linings			I		I		I		I		I		I		I		I
Manual and automatic transmission, transfer & differential gear oil (exc. L.S.D.)	See NOTE (4)				I				I				I				I
Limited-slip differential (L.S.D.) gear oil	See NOTE (4)								R				I				R
Steering gear (box) & linkage, (steering damper 4x4), axle & suspension parts			I		I		I		I		I		I		I		I
Drive shaft boots & propeller shaft (4x4)			I		I		I		I		I		I		I		I
Steering linkage ball joints & front suspension ball joints			I		I		I		I		I		I		I		I
Front wheel bearing grease (4x2)																	
Front wheel bearing grease & free-running hub grease (4x4)	See NOTE (5)		I						R								R
Exhaust system			I		I		I		I		I		I		I		I

NOTE: (1) If operating mainly in dusty conditions, more frequent maintenance may be required.

(2) If operating mainly in dusty conditions, replace every 30,000 miles (48,000 km).

(3) If vehicle is operated under extremely adverse weather conditions or in areas where ambient temperatures are either extremely low or extremely high, the filters might become clogged. In such an event, replace them immediately.

(4) If towing a trailer, using a camper or a car-top carrier, or driving on rough or muddy roads, change (not just inspect) oil at every 30,000 miles (48,000 km) or 24 months except for L.S.D. Change L.S.D. gear oil every 15,000 miles (24,000 km) or 12 months.

(5) If operating frequently in water, replace grease every 3,750 miles (6,000 km) or 3 months.

(6) Maintenance items and intervals with "*" are recommended by NISSAN for reliable vehicle operation. The owner need not perform such maintenance in order to maintain the emission warranty or manufacturer recall liability. Other maintenance items and intervals are required.

86711108

Fig. 182 Severe conditions recommended maintenance schedule—1990 models

Abbreviations: R = Replace   I = Inspect. Correct or replace if necessary.

MAINTENANCE OPERATION		MAINTENANCE INTERVAL							
Perform at number of miles, kilometers or months, whichever comes first.	Miles x 1,000	7.5	15	22.5	30	37.5	45	52.5	60
	(km x 1,000)	(12)	(24)	(36)	(48)	(60)	(72)	(84)	(96)
	Months	6	12	18	24	30	36	42	48
Emission control system maintenance									
Drive belts					I*				I*
Air cleaner filter					[R]				[R]
Positive crankcase ventilation (P.C.V.) filter (KA24E engine only)	See NOTE (1)				[R]				[R]
Vapor lines					I*				I*
Fuel lines					I*				I*
Fuel filter	See NOTE (1)*								
Engine coolant	See NOTE (2)								R*
Engine oil		R	R	R	R	R	R	R	R
Engine oil filter (Use Nissan PREMIUM type or equivalent.)		R		R		R		R	
Spark plugs					[R]				[R]
Timing belt (VG30E engine only)									[R]
Chassis and body maintenance									
Brake lines & cables				I		I		I		I
Brake pads, discs, drums & linings				I		I		I		I
Manual and automatic transmission, transfer & differential gear oil (exc. L.S.D.)				I		I		I		I
Limited-slip differential (L.S.D.) gear oil				I		R		I		R
Steering gear (box) & linkage, (steering damper 4x4), axle & suspension parts						I				I
Drive shaft boots (4x4)				I		I		I		I
Steering linkage ball joints & front suspension ball joints										I
Front wheel bearing grease (4x2)						I				I
Front wheel bearing grease & free-running hub grease (4x4)				I		R		I		R
Exhaust system				I		I		I		I

NOTE: (1) If vehicle is operated under extremely adverse weather conditions or in areas where ambient temperatures are either extremely low or extremely high, the filters might become clogged. In such an event, replace them immediately.

(2) After 60,000 miles (96,000 km) or 48 months, replace every 30,000 miles (48,000 km) or 24 months.

(3) Maintenance items and intervals with "*" are recommended by NISSAN for reliable vehicle operation. The owner need not perform such maintenance in order to maintain the emission warranty or manufacturer recall liability. Other maintenance items and intervals are required.

86711111

Fig. 183 Normal conditions recommended maintenance schedule—1991–93 models

---

Abbreviations: R = Replace   I = Inspect. Correct or replace if necessary.

MAINTENANCE OPERATION		MAINTENANCE INTERVAL															
Perform at number of miles, kilometers or months, whichever comes first.	Miles x 1,000	3.75	7.5	11.25	15	18.75	22.5	26.25	30	33.75	37.5	41.25	45	48.75	52.5	56.25	60
	(km x 1,000)	(6)	(12)	(18)	(24)	(30)	(36)	(42)	(48)	(54)	(60)	(66)	(72)	(78)	(84)	(90)	(96)
	Months	3	6	9	12	15	18	21	24	27	30	33	36	39	42	45	48
Emission control system maintenance																	
Drive belts									I*								I*
Air cleaner filter	See NOTE (1)								[R]								[R]
Positive crankcase ventilation (P.C.V.) filter (KA24E engine only)	See NOTE (3)								[R]								[R]
Air induction valve filter (KA24E engine only)	See NOTE (2)																
Vapor lines									I*								I*
Fuel lines									I*								I*
Fuel filter	See NOTE (3)*																
Engine coolant	See NOTE (4)																R*
Engine oil		R	R	R	R	R	R	R	R	R	R	R	R	R	R	R	R
Engine oil filter (Use Nissan PREMIUM type or equivalent.)		R	R	R	R	R	R	R	R	R	R	R	R	R	R	R	R
Spark plugs									[R]								[R]
Timing belt (VG30E engine only)																	[R]
Chassis and body maintenance																	
Brake lines & cables					I				I				I				I
Brake pads, discs, drums & linings		I			I				I				I				I
Manual and automatic transmission, transfer & differential gear oil (exc. L.S.D.)	See NOTE (5)				I				I				I				I
Limited-slip differential (L.S.D.) gear oil	See NOTE (5)				I				R				I				R
Steering gear (box) & linkage, (steering damper 4x4), axle & suspension parts		I			I				I				I				I
Drive shaft boots & propeller shaft (4x4)		I			I				I				I				I
Steering linkage ball joints & front suspension ball joints		I			I				I				I				I
Front wheel bearing grease (4x2)																	
Front wheel bearing grease & free-running hub grease (4x4)	See NOTE (6)				I				R				I				R
Exhaust system		I			I				I				I				I

NOTE: (1) If operating mainly in dusty conditions, more frequent maintenance may be required.

(2) If operating mainly in dusty conditions, replace every 30,000 miles (48,000 km).

(3) If vehicle is operated under extremely adverse weather conditions or in areas where ambient temperatures are either extremely low or extremely high, the filters might become clogged. In such an event, replace them immediately.

(4) After 60,000 miles (96,000 km) or 48 months, replace every 30,000 miles (48,000 km) or 24 months.

(5) If towing a trailer, using a camper or a car-top carrier, or driving on rough or muddy roads, change (not just inspect) oil at every 30,000 miles (48,000 km) or 24 months except for L.S.D. Change L.S.D. gear oil every 15,000 miles (24,000 km) or 12 months.

(6) If operating frequently in water, replace grease every 3,750 miles (6,000 km) or 3 months.

(7) Maintenance items and intervals with "*" are recommended by NISSAN for reliable vehicle operation. The owner need not perform such maintenance in order to maintain the emission warranty or manufacturer recall liability. Other maintenance items and intervals are required.

86711110

Fig. 184 Severe conditions recommended maintenance schedule—1991–93 models

SCHEDULE 1

Abbreviations: R = Replace   I = Inspect. Correct or replace if necessary.   [ ]: At the mileage intervals only

MAINTENANCE OPERATION							MAINTENANCE INTERVAL									
Perform at number of miles, kilometers or months, whichever comes first.	Miles × 1,000	3.75	7.5	11.25	15	18.75	22.5	26.25	30	33.75	37.5	41.25	45	48.75	52.5	56.25	60
	(km × 1,000)	(6)	(12)	(18)	(24)	(30)	(36)	(42)	(48)	(54)	(60)	(66)	(72)	(78)	(84)	(90)	(96)
	Months	3	6	9	12	15	18	21	24	27	30	33	36	39	42	45	48
Emission control system maintenance																
Air cleaner filter	See NOTE (3)																[R]
Positive crankcase ventilation (PCV) filter (KA24E engine only)	See NOTE (3)								[R]								[R]
Pulsed secondary air filter (KA24E engine only)	See NOTE (2)																
Vapor lines									I*								I*
Fuel lines									I*								I*
Fuel filter	See NOTE (3)*																I*
Engine coolant	See NOTE (4)																R*
Engine oil		R	R	R	R	R	R	R	R	R	R	R	R	R	R	R	R
Engine oil filter (Use Nissan PREMIUM type or equivalent.)		R	R	R	R	R	R	R	R	R	R	R	R	R	R	R	R
Spark plugs									[R]								[R]
Timing belt (VG30E engine only)						Replace every 105,000 miles (168,000 km)											

NOTE: (1) If operating mainly in dusty conditions, more frequent maintenance may be required.
(2) If operating mainly in dusty conditions, replace every 30,000 miles (48,000 km).
(3) If vehicle is operated under extremely adverse weather conditions or in areas where ambient temperatures are either extremely low or extremely high, the filters might become clogged. In such an event, replace them immediately.
(4) After 60,000 miles (96,000 km) or 48 months, replace every 30,000 miles (48,000 km) or 24 months.
(5) Maintenance items and intervals with "****" are recommended by NISSAN for reliable vehicle operation. The owner need not perform such maintenance in order to maintain the emission warranty or manufacturer recall liability. Other maintenance items and intervals are required.

SCHEDULE 1

Abbreviations: R = Replace   I = Inspect. Correct or replace if necessary.   [ ]: At the mileage intervals only

MAINTENANCE OPERATION							MAINTENANCE INTERVAL									
Perform at number of miles, kilometers or months, whichever comes first.	Miles × 1,000	3.75	7.5	11.25	15	18.75	22.5	26.25	30	33.75	37.5	41.25	45	48.75	52.5	56.25	60
	(km × 1,000)	(6)	(12)	(18)	(24)	(30)	(36)	(42)	(48)	(54)	(60)	(66)	(72)	(78)	(84)	(90)	(96)
	Months	3	6	9	12	15	18	21	24	27	30	33	36	39	42	45	48
Chassis and body maintenance																
Brake lines & cables									I								I
Brake pads, discs, drums & linings									I								I
Manual & automatic transmission, transfer & differential gear oil (exc. LSD)	See NOTE (1)																
Limited-slip differential (LSD) gear oil									R								R
Steering gear (box) & linkage, (steering damper [4WD]), axle & suspension parts									I								I
Drive shaft boots & propeller shaft ([4WD])									I								I
Steering linkage ball joints & front suspension ball joints									I								I
Front wheel bearing grease & free-running hub grease ([4WD])	See NOTE (2)																
Exhaust system									I								I

NOTE: (1) If towing a trailer, using a camper or a car-top carrier, or driving on rough or muddy roads, change (not just inspect) oil at every 30,000 miles (48,000 km) or 24 months except for LSD. Change LSD gear oil every 15,000 miles (24,000 km) or 12 months.
(2) If operating frequently in water, replace grease every 3,750 miles (6,000 km) or 3 months.

86711112

Fig. 186 Severe conditions recommended maintenance schedule—1993–95 models

SCHEDULE 2

Abbreviations: R = Replace   I = Inspect. Correct or replace if necessary.   [ ]: At the mileage intervals only

MAINTENANCE OPERATION					MAINTENANCE INTERVAL			
Perform at number of miles, kilometers or months, whichever comes first.	Miles × 1,000	7.5	15	22.5	30	37.5	45	52.5	60
	(km × 1,000)	(12)	(24)	(36)	(48)	(60)	(72)	(84)	(96)
	Months	6	12	18	24	30	36	42	48
Emission control system maintenance									
Air cleaner filter					[R]				[R]
Positive crankcase ventilation (PCV) filter (KA24E engine only)	See NOTE (1)								
Vapor lines					I*				I*
Fuel filter	See NOTE (1)*								I*
Engine coolant	See NOTE (2)								R*
Engine oil		R	R	R	R	R	R	R	R
Engine oil filter (Use Nissan PREMIUM type or equivalent.)		R	R	R	R	R	R	R	R
Spark plugs									[R]
Timing belt (VG30E engine only)			Replace every 105,000 miles (168,000 km)						

NOTE: (1) If vehicle is operated under extremely adverse weather conditions or in areas where ambient temperatures are either extremely low or extremely high, the filters might become clogged. In such an event, replace them immediately.
(2) After 60,000 miles (96,000 km) or 48 months, replace every 30,000 miles (48,000 km) or 24 months.
(3) Maintenance items and intervals with "****" are recommended by NISSAN for reliable vehicle operation. The owner need not perform such maintenance in order to maintain the emission warranty or manufacturer recall liability. Other maintenance items and intervals are required.

SCHEDULE 2

Abbreviations: R = Replace   I = Inspect. Correct or replace if necessary.   [ ]: At the mileage intervals only

MAINTENANCE OPERATION					MAINTENANCE INTERVAL			
Perform at number of miles, kilometers or months, whichever comes first.	Miles × 1,000	7.5	15	22.5	30	37.5	45	52.5	60
	(km × 1,000)	(12)	(24)	(36)	(48)	(60)	(72)	(84)	(96)
	Months	6	12	18	24	30	36	42	48
Chassis and body maintenance									
Brake lines & cables		—	—	—	I	—	—	—	I
Brake pads, discs, drums & linings		—	—	—	I	—	—	—	I
Manual & automatic transmission, transfer & differential gear oil (exc. LSD)	See NOTE (1)								
Limited-slip differential (LSD) gear oil		—	—	—	R	—	—	—	R
Steering gear (box) & linkage, (steering damper [4WD]), axle & suspension parts		—	—	—	I	—	—	—	I
Drive shaft boots (4x2)		—	—	—	I	—	—	—	I
Steering linkage ball joints & front suspension ball joints		—	—	—	I	—	—	—	I
Front wheel bearing grease & free-running hub grease ([4WD])		—	—	—	R	—	—	—	R
Exhaust system		—	—	—	I	—	—	—	I

86711113

Fig. 185 Normal conditions recommended maintenance schedule—1993–95 models

CAPACITIES

Years	Model	Engine Displacement cu. in. (cc)	Crankcase Includes Filter (qt.)	Transmission (pts.)			Transfer Case (pts.)	Drive Axle (pts.)		Fuel Tank (gal.)	Cooling System (qt.)	
				4-sp	5-sp	Auto①		Front	Rear		w/AC	wo/AC
1989	Pick-Up (2WD)	145.8 (2389)	4	3.75	4.25	7.25	—	—	3.25	15.9	8.75	8.75
		180.6 (2960)	4.25	—	5.1	7.25	—	—	5.9	15.9	10.5	10.5
	Pick-Up (4WD)	145.8 (2389)	4.5	—	8.5	—	2.4	2.75	2.75	15.9	8.75	8.75
		180.6 (2960)	3.75	—	7.9	7.25	2.4	3.1	5.9	15.9	10.5	10.5
	Pathfinder	180.6 (2960)	3.75	—	7.9	7.25	2.4	3.1	5.9	15.9	10.5	10.5
1990	Pick-Up (2WD)	145.8 (2389)	4.1	—	4.25	8.25	—	—	3.1	15.9	8.75	8.75
		180.6 (2960)	4.25	—	5.1	8.25	—	—	5.9	15.9	11.25	11.25
	Pick-Up (4WD)	145.8 (2389)	3.5	—	8.5	—	2.4	2.75	2.75	15.9	9.5	9.5
		180.6 (2960)	3.75	—	7.75	9.0	2.4	3.1	5.9	15.9	12.4	12.4
	Pathfinder	180.6 (2960)	3.75	—	7.75	9.0	2.4	3.1	5.9	15.9	12.4	12.4
1991	Pick-Up (2WD)	145.8 (2389)	4.1	—	4.25	8.25	—	—	3.1	15.9	8.75	8.75
		180.6 (2960)	4.25	—	5.1	8.25	—	—	5.9	15.9	11.25	11.25
	Pick-Up (4WD)	145.8 (2389)	3.5	—	8.5	—	2.4	2.75	2.75	15.9	9.5	9.5
		180.6 (2960)	3.5	—	7.75	9.0	2.4	3.1	5.9	15.9	12.4	12.4
	Pathfinder (2WD)	180.6 (2960)	4.25	—	5.1	8.25	—	—	5.9	15.9	11.25	11.25
	Pathfinder (4WD)	180.6 (2960)	3.5	—	7.75	9.0	2.4	3.1	5.9	15.9	12.4	12.4
1992	Pick-Up (2WD)	145.8 (2389)	4.1	—	4.25	8.25	—	—	3.1	15.9	8.75	8.75
		180.6 (2960)	4.25	—	5.1	8.25	—	—	5.9	15.9	11.25	11.25
	Pick-Up (4WD)	145.8 (2389)	3.5	—	8.5	—	2.4	2.75	2.75	15.9	9.5	9.5
		180.6 (2960)	3.75	—	7.75	9.0	2.4	3.1	5.9	15.9	12.4	12.4
	Pathfinder	180.6 (2960)	3.75	—	7.75	9.0	2.4	3.1	5.9	15.9	12.4	12.4
1993	Pick-Up (2WD)	145.8 (2389)	4.1	—	4.25	8.25	—	—	3.1	15.9	8.75	8.75
		180.6 (2960)	4.25	—	5.1	8.25	—	—	5.9	15.9	11.25	11.25
	Pick-Up (4WD)	145.8 (2389)	3.5	—	8.5	—	2.4	2.75	2.75	15.9	9.5	9.5
		180.6 (2960)	3.5	—	7.75	9.0	2.4	3.1	5.9	15.9	12.4	12.4
	Pathfinder (2WD)	180.6 (2960)	4.25	—	5.1	8.25	—	—	5.9	15.9	11.25	11.25
	Pathfinder (4WD)	180.6 (2960)	3.5	—	7.75	9.0	2.4	3.1	5.9	15.9	12.4	12.4
1994	Pick-Up (2WD)	145.8 (2389)	4.1	—	4.25	8.25	—	—	3.1	15.9	8.75	8.75
		180.6 (2960)	4.25	—	5.1	8.25	—	—	5.9	15.9	11.25	11.25
	Pick-Up (4WD)	145.8 (2389)	3.5	—	8.5	—	2.4	2.75	2.75	15.9	9.5	9.5
		180.6 (2960)	3.75	—	7.75	9.0	2.4	3.1	5.9	15.9	12.4	12.4
	Pathfinder	180.6 (2960)	3.75	—	7.75	9.0	2.4	3.1	5.9	15.9	12.4	12.4
1995	Pick-Up (2WD)	145.8 (2389)	4.1	—	4.25	8.25	—	—	3.1	15.9	8.75	8.75
		180.6 (2960)	4.25	—	5.1	8.25	—	—	5.9	15.9	11.25	11.25
	Pick-Up (4WD)	145.8 (2389)	3.5	—	8.5	—	2.4	2.75	2.75	15.9	9.5	9.5
		180.6 (2960)	3.5	—	7.75	9.0	2.4	3.1	5.9	15.9	12.4	12.4
	Pathfinder (2WD)	180.6 (2960)	4.25	—	5.1	8.25	—	—	5.9	15.9	11.25	11.25
	Pathfinder (4WD)	180.6 (2960)	3.5	—	7.75	9.0	2.4	3.1	5.9	15.9	12.4	12.4

① AT capacity is measured in quarts

86711C07

ENGLISH TO METRIC CONVERSION: MASS (WEIGHT)

Current **mass** measurement is expressed in pounds and ounces (lbs. & ozs.). The metric unit of mass (or weight) is the kilogram (kg). Even although this table does not show conversion of masses (weights) larger than 15 lbs, it is easy to calculate larger units by following the data immediately below.

To convert ounces (oz.) to grams (g): multiply th number of ozs. by 28
To convert grams (g) to ounces (oz.): multiply the number of grams by .035

To convert pounds (lbs.) to kilograms (kg): multiply the number of lbs. by .45
To convert kilograms (kg) to pounds (lbs.): multiply the number of kilograms by 2.2

lbs	kg	lbs	kg	oz	kg	oz	kg
0.1	0.04	0.9	0.41	0.1	0.003	0.9	0.024
0.2	0.09	1	0.4	0.2	0.005	1	0.03
0.3	0.14	2	0.9	0.3	0.008	2	0.06
0.4	0.18	3	1.4	0.4	0.011	3	0.08
0.5	0.23	4	1.8	0.5	0.014	4	0.11
0.6	0.27	5	2.3	0.6	0.017	5	0.14
0.7	0.32	10	4.5	0.7	0.020	10	0.28
0.8	0.36	15	6.8	0.8	0.023	15	0.42

ENGLISH TO METRIC CONVERSION: TEMPERATURE

To convert Fahrenheit (°F) to Celsius (°C): take number of °F and subtract 32; multiply result by 5; divide result by 9

To convert Celsius (°C) to Fahrenheit (°F): take number of °C and multiply by 9; divide result by 5; add 32 to total

Fahrenheit (F)		Celsius (C)		Fahrenheit (F)		Celsius (C)		Fahrenheit (F)		Celsius (C)	
°F	°C	°C	°F	°F	°C	°C	°F	°F	°C	°C	°F
−40	−40	−38	−36.4	80	26.7	18	64.4	215	101.7	80	176
−35	−37.2	−36	−32.8	85	29.4	20	68	220	104.4	85	185
−30	−34.4	−34	−29.2	90	32.2	22	71.6	225	107.2	90	194
−25	−31.7	−32	−25.6	95	35.0	24	75.2	230	110.0	95	202
−20	−28.9	−30	−22	100	37.8	26	78.8	235	112.8	100	212
−15	−26.1	−28	−18.4	105	40.6	28	82.4	240	115.6	105	221
−10	−23.3	−26	−14.8	110	43.3	30	86	245	118.3	110	230
−5	−20.6	−24	−11.2	115	46.1	32	89.6	250	121.1	115	239
0	−17.8	−22	−7.6	120	48.9	34	93.2	255	123.9	120	248
1	−17.2	−20	−4	125	51.7	36	96.8	260	126.6	125	257
2	−16.7	−18	−0.4	130	54.4	38	100.4	265	129.4	130	266
3	−16.1	−16	3.2	135	57.2	40	104	270	132.2	135	275
4	−15.6	−14	6.8	140	60.0	42	107.6	275	135.0	140	284
5	−15.0	−12	10.4	145	62.8	44	112.2	280	137.8	145	293
10	−12.2	−10	14	150	65.6	46	114.8	285	140.6	150	302
15	−9.4	−8	17.6	155	68.3	48	118.4	290	143.3	155	311
20	−6.7	−6	21.2	160	71.1	50	122	295	146.1	160	320
25	−3.9	−4	24.8	165	73.9	52	125.6	300	148.9	165	329
30	−1.1	−2	28.4	170	76.7	54	129.2	305	151.7	170	338
35	1.7	0	32	175	79.4	56	132.8	310	154.4	175	347
40	4.4	2	35.6	180	82.2	58	136.4	315	157.2	180	356
45	7.2	4	39.2	185	85.0	60	140	320	160.0	185	365
50	10.0	6	42.8	190	87.8	62	143.6	325	162.8	190	374
55	12.8	8	46.4	195	90.6	64	147.2	330	165.6	195	383
60	15.6	10	50	200	93.3	66	150.8	335	168.3	200	392
65	18.3	12	53.6	205	96.1	68	154.4	340	171.1	205	401
70	21.1	14	57.2	210	98.9	70	158	345	173.9	210	410
75	23.9	16	60.8	212	100.0	75	167	350	176.7	215	414

ENGLISH TO METRIC CONVERSION: LENGTH

To convert inches (ins.) to millimeters (mm): multiply number of inches by 25.4

To convert millimeters (mm) to inches (ins.): multiply number of millimeters by .04

Inches		Decimals	Milli-meters	Inches to millimeters			Inches		Decimals	Milli-meters	Inches to millimeters	
				inches	mm						inches	mm
	1/64	0.051625	0.3969	0.0001	0.00254			33/64	0.515625	13.0969	0.6	15.24
1/32		0.03125	0.7937	0.0002	0.00508		17/32		0.53125	13.4937	0.7	17.78
	3/64	0.046875	1.1906	0.0003	0.00762			35/64	0.546875	13.8906	0.8	20.32
1/16		0.0625	1.5875	0.0004	0.01016		9/16		0.5625	14.2875	0.9	22.86
	5/64	0.078125	1.9844	0.0005	0.01270			37/64	0.578125	14.6844	1	25.4
3/32		0.09375	2.3812	0.0006	0.01524		19/32		0.59375	15.0812	2	50.8
	7/64	0.109375	2.7781	0.0007	0.01778			39/64	0.609375	15.4781	3	76.2
1/8		0.125	3.1750	0.0008	0.02032		5/8		0.625	15.8750	4	101.6
	9/64	0.140625	3.5719	0.0009	0.02286			41/64	0.640625	16.2719	5	127.0
5/32		0.15625	3.9687	0.001	0.0254		21/32		0.65625	16.6687	6	152.4
	11/64	0.171875	4.3656	0.002	0.0508			43/64	0.671875	17.0656	7	177.8
3/16		0.1875	4.7625	0.003	0.0762		11/16		0.6875	17.4625	8	203.2
	13/64	0.203125	5.1594	0.004	0.1016			45/64	0.703125	17.8594	9	228.6
7/32		0.21875	5.5562	0.005	0.1270		23/32		0.71875	18.2562	10	254.0
	15/64	0.234375	5.9531	0.006	0.1524			47/64	0.734375	18.6531	11	279.4
1/4		0.25	6.3500	0.007	0.1778		3/4		0.75	19.0500	12	304.8
	17/64	0.265625	6.7469	0.008	0.2032			49/64	0.765625	19.4469	13	330.2
9/32		0.28125	7.1437	0.009	0.2286		25/32		0.78125	19.8437	14	355.6
	19/64	0.296875	7.5406	0.01	0.254			51/64	0.796875	20.2406	15	381.0
5/16		0.3125	7.9375	0.02	0.508		13/16		0.8125	20.6375	16	406.4
	21/64	0.328125	8.3344	0.03	0.762			53/64	0.828125	21.0344	17	431.8
11/32		0.34375	8.7312	0.04	1.016		27/32		0.84375	21.4312	18	457.2
	23/64	0.359375	9.1281	0.05	1.270			55/64	0.859375	21.8281	19	482.6
3/8		0.375	9.5250	0.06	1.524		7/8		0.875	22.2250	20	508.0
	25/64	0.390625	9.9219	0.07	1.778			57/64	0.890625	22.6219	21	533.4
13/32		0.40625	10.3187	0.08	2.032		29/32		0.90625	23.0187	22	558.8
	27/64	0.421875	10.7156	0.09	2.286			59/64	0.921875	23.4156	23	584.2
7/16		0.4375	11.1125	0.1	2.54		15/16		0.9375	23.8125	24	609.6
	29/64	0.453125	11.5094	0.2	5.08			61/64	0.953125	24.2094	25	635.0
15/32		0.46875	11.9062	0.3	7.62		31/32		0.96875	24.6062	26	660.4
	31/64	0.484375	12.3031	0.4	10.16			63/64	0.984375	25.0031	27	690.6
1/2		0.5	12.7000	0.5	12.70							

ENGLISH TO METRIC CONVERSION: TORQUE

To convert foot-pounds (ft. lbs.) to Newton-meters: multiply the number of ft. lbs. by 1.3

To convert inch-pounds (in. lbs.) to Newton-meters: multiply the number of in. lbs. by .11

in lbs	N-m	in lbs	N-m	in lbs	N-m	in lbs	N-m	in lbs	N-m
0.1	0.01	1	0.11	10	1.13	19	2.15	28	3.16
0.2	0.02	2	0.23	11	1.24	20	2.26	29	3.28
0.3	0.03	3	0.34	12	1.36	21	2.37	30	3.39
0.4	0.04	4	0.45	13	1.47	22	2.49	31	3.50
0.5	0.06	5	0.56	14	1.58	23	2.60	32	3.62
0.6	0.07	6	0.68	15	1.70	24	2.71	33	3.73
0.7	0.08	7	0.78	16	1.81	25	2.82	34	3.84
0.8	0.09	8	0.90	17	1.92	26	2.94	35	3.95
0.9	0.10	9	1.02	18	2.03	27	3.05	36	4.0

ENGLISH TO METRIC CONVERSION: TORQUE

Torque is now expressed as either foot-pounds (ft./lbs.) or inch-pounds (in./lbs.). The metric measurement unit for torque is the Newton-meter (Nm). This unit—the Nm—will be used for all SI metric torque references, both the present ft./lbs. and in./lbs.

ft lbs	N-m	ft lbs	N-m	ft lbs	N-m	ft lbs	N-m
0.1	0.1	33	44.7	74	100.3	115	155.9
0.2	0.3	34	46.1	75	101.7	116	157.3
0.3	0.4	35	47.4	76	103.0	117	158.6
0.4	0.5	36	48.8	77	104.4	118	160.0
0.5	0.7	37	50.7	78	105.8	119	161.3
0.6	0.8	38	51.5	79	107.1	120	162.7
0.7	1.0	39	52.9	80	108.5	121	164.0
0.8	1.1	40	54.2	81	109.8	122	165.4
0.9	1.2	41	55.6	82	111.2	123	166.8
1	1.3	42	56.9	83	112.5	124	168.1
2	2.7	43	58.3	84	113.9	125	169.5
3	4.1	44	59.7	85	115.2	126	170.8
4	5.4	45	61.0	86	116.6	127	172.2
5	6.8	46	62.4	87	118.0	128	173.5
6	8.1	47	63.7	88	119.3	129	174.9
7	9.5	48	65.1	89	120.7	130	176.2
8	10.8	49	66.4	90	122.0	131	177.6
9	12.2	50	67.8	91	123.4	132	179.0
10	13.6	51	69.2	92	124.7	133	180.3
11	14.9	52	70.5	93	126.1	134	181.7
12	16.3	53	71.9	94	127.4	135	183.0
13	17.6	54	73.2	95	128.8	136	184.4
14	18.9	55	74.6	96	130.2	137	185.7
15	20.3	56	75.9	97	131.5	138	187.1
16	21.7	57	77.3	98	132.9	139	188.5
17	23.0	58	78.6	99	134.2	140	189.8
18	24.4	59	80.0	100	135.6	141	191.2
19	25.8	60	81.4	101	136.9	142	192.5
20	27.1	61	82.7	102	138.3	143	193.9
21	28.5	62	84.1	103	139.6	144	195.2
22	29.8	63	85.4	104	141.0	145	196.6
23	31.2	64	86.8	105	142.4	146	198.0
24	32.5	65	88.1	106	143.7	147	199.3
25	33.9	66	89.5	107	145.1	148	200.7
26	35.2	67	90.8	108	146.4	149	202.0
27	36.6	68	92.2	109	147.8	150	203.4
28	38.0	69	93.6	110	149.1	151	204.7
29	39.3	70	94.9	111	150.5	152	206.1
30	40.7	71	96.3	112	151.8	153	207.4
31	42.0	72	97.6	113	153.2	154	208.8
32	43.4	73	99.0	114	154.6	155	210.2

TCCS1C03

ENGLISH TO METRIC CONVERSION: FORCE

Force is presently measured in pounds (lbs.). This type of measurement is used to measure spring pressure, specifically how many pounds it takes to compress a spring. Our present force unit (the pound) will be replaced in SI metric measurements by the Newton (N). This term will eventually see use in specifications for electric motor brush spring pressures, valve spring pressures, etc.

To convert pounds (lbs.) to Newton (N): multiply the number of lbs. by 4.45

lbs	N	lbs	N	lbs	N	oz	N
0.01	0.04	21	93.4	59	262.4	1	0.3
0.02	0.09	22	97.9	60	266.9	2	0.6
0.03	0.13	23	102.3	61	271.3	3	0.8
0.04	0.18	24	106.8	62	275.8	4	1.1
0.05	0.22	25	111.2	63	280.2	5	1.4
0.06	0.27	26	115.6	64	284.6	6	1.7
0.07	0.31	27	120.1	65	289.1	7	2.0
0.08	0.36	28	124.6	66	293.6	8	2.2
0.09	0.40	29	129.0	67	298.0	9	2.5
0.1	0.4	30	133.4	68	302.5	10	2.8
0.2	0.9	31	137.9	69	306.9	11	3.1
0.3	1.3	32	142.3	70	311.4	12	3.3
0.4	1.8	33	146.8	71	315.8	13	3.6
0.5	2.2	34	151.2	72	320.3	14	3.9
0.6	2.7	35	155.7	73	324.7	15	4.2
0.7	3.1	36	160.1	74	329.2	16	4.4
0.8	3.6	37	164.6	75	333.6	17	4.7
0.9	4.0	38	169.0	76	338.1	18	5.0
1	4.4	39	173.5	77	342.5	19	5.3
2	8.9	40	177.9	78	347.0	20	5.6
3	13.4	41	182.4	79	351.4	21	5.8
4	17.8	42	186.8	80	355.9	22	6.1
5	22.2	43	191.3	81	360.3	23	6.4
6	26.7	44	195.7	82	364.8	24	6.7
7	31.1	45	200.2	83	369.2	25	7.0
8	35.6	46	204.6	84	373.6	26	7.2
9	40.0	47	209.1	85	378.1	27	7.5
10	44.5	48	213.5	86	382.6	28	7.8
11	48.9	49	218.0	87	387.0	29	8.1
12	53.4	50	224.4	88	391.4	30	8.3
13	57.8	51	226.9	89	395.9	31	8.6
14	62.3	52	231.3	90	400.3	32	8.9
15	66.7	53	235.8	91	404.8	33	9.2
16	71.2	54	240.2	92	409.2	34	9.4
17	75.6	55	244.6	93	413.7	35	9.7
18	80.1	56	249.1	94	418.1	36	10.0
19	84.5	57	253.6	95	422.6	37	10.3
20	89.0	58	258.0	96	427.0	38	10.6

TCCS1C04

2

ENGINE
PERFORMANCE
AND
TUNE-UP

TUNE-UP PROCEDURES

◆ See Figures 1 and 2

In order to extract the best performance and economy from your engine it is essential that it be properly tuned at regular intervals. A regular tune-up/inspection will keep your Nissan's engine running smoothly and will prevent the annoying minor breakdowns and poor performance associated with an untuned engine.

A complete tune-up/inspection should be performed every 30,000 miles (48,000 km) or 24 months, whichever comes first. This interval should be halved (as a general rule of thumb) if the truck is operated under severe conditions, such as trailer towing, prolonged idling, continual stop and start driving, or if starting or running problems are noticed. It is assumed that the routine maintenance described in Section 1 has been kept up, as this will have a decided effect on the results of a tune-up.

A tune-up/inspection for models covered in this manual should consists of the following items, but always refer to the Maintenance Interval Chart for additional service information.

- Inspect the drive belts.
- If necessary, check and adjust valve clearance
- Clean the air filter housing and replacing the air filter element.
- If equipped, replace the PCV filter and Pulsed secondary air injection filter.
- Inspect or replace the fuel filter assembly.
- Inspect all fuel and vapor lines.
- Check or replace the distributor cap, rotor and ignition wires.
- Replace the spark plugs and make all necessary engine adjustments.
- Always refer to the Maintenance Interval Chart for additional service information.

➥If the tune-up specifications on the Vehicle Emission Control Information sticker in the engine compartment of your Nissan disagree with the Tune-Up Specifications chart in this section, the figures on the sticker must be used. The sticker often reflects changes made during the production run.

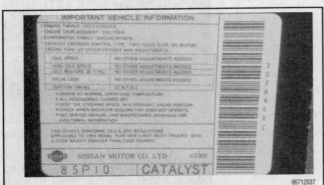

Fig. 1 Vehicle Emission Control Information (VECI) label located in the engine compartment

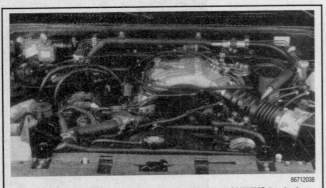

Fig. 2 Because of the tangle of underhood wiring ALWAYS tag/note wire locations before removal

Spark Plugs

◆ See Figure 3

A typical spark plug consists of a metal shell surrounding a ceramic insulator. A metal electrode extends downward through the center of the insulator and protrudes a small distance. Located at the end of the plug and attached to the side of the outer metal shell is the side electrode. The side electrode bends in at a 90° angle so that its tip is just past and parallel to the tip of the center electrode. The distance between these two electrodes (measured in thousandths of an inch or hundredths of a millimeter) is called the spark plug gap.

The spark plug does not produce a spark, but instead provides a gap across which the current can arc. The coil produces anywhere from 20,000 to 50,000 volts (depending on the type and application) which travels through the wires to the spark plugs. The current passes along the center electrode and jumps the gap to the side electrode, and in doing so, ignites the air/fuel mixture in the combustion chamber.

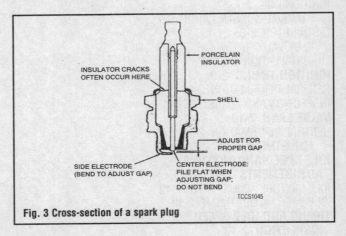

Fig. 3 Cross-section of a spark plug

SPARK PLUG HEAT RANGE

◆ See Figure 4

Spark plug heat range is the ability of the plug to dissipate heat. The longer the insulator (or the farther it extends into the engine), the hotter the plug will operate; the shorter the insulator (the closer the electrode is to the block's cooling passages) the cooler it will operate. A plug that absorbs little heat and remains too cool will quickly accumulate deposits of oil and carbon since it is not hot enough to burn them off. This leads to plug fouling and consequently to misfiring. A plug that absorbs too much heat will have no deposits but, due to the excessive heat, the electrodes will burn away quickly and might possibly lead to preignition or other ignition problems. Preignition takes place when plug

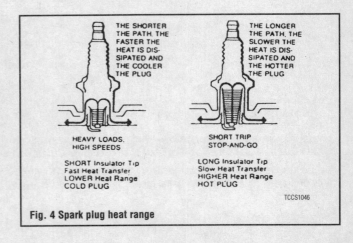

Fig. 4 Spark plug heat range

tips get so hot that they glow sufficiently to ignite the air/fuel mixture before the actual spark occurs. This early ignition will usually cause a pinging during low speeds and heavy loads.

The general rule of thumb for choosing the correct heat range when picking a spark plug is: if most of your driving is long distance, high speed travel, use a colder plug; if most of your driving is stop and go, use a hotter plug. Original equipment plugs are generally a good compromise between the 2 styles and most people never have the need to change their plugs from the factory-recommended heat range.

REMOVAL & INSTALLATION

A set of spark plugs usually requires replacement after about 20,000–30,000 miles (32,000–48,000 km), depending on your style of driving. In normal operation plug gap increases about 0.001 in. (0.025mm) for every 2500 miles (4000 km). As the gap increases, the plug's voltage requirement also increases. It requires a greater voltage to jump the wider gap and about two to three times as much voltage to fire the plug at high speeds than at idle. The improved air/fuel ratio control of modern fuel injection combined with the higher voltage output of modern ignition systems will often allow an engine to run significantly longer on a set of standard spark plugs, but keep in mind that efficiency will drop as the gap widens (along with fuel economy and power).

When you're removing spark plugs, work on one at a time. Don't start by removing the plug wires all at once, because, unless you number them, they may become mixed up. Take a minute before you begin and number the wires with tape.

1. Disconnect the negative battery cable, and if the vehicle has been run recently, allow the engine to thoroughly cool.

2. Carefully twist the spark plug wire boot to loosen it, then pull upward and remove the boot from the plug. Be sure to pull on the boot and not on the wire, otherwise the connector located inside the boot may become separated.

3. Using compressed air, blow any water or debris from the spark plug well to assure that no harmful contaminants are allowed to enter the combustion chamber when the spark plug is removed. If compressed air is not available, use a rag or a brush to clean the area.

➡**Remove the spark plugs when the engine is cold, if possible, to prevent damage to the threads. If removal of the plugs is difficult, apply a few drops of penetrating oil or silicone spray to the area around the base of the plug, and allow it a few minutes to work.**

4. Using a spark plug socket that is equipped with a rubber insert to properly hold the plug, turn the spark plug counterclockwise to loosen and remove the spark plug from the bore.

❊❊ WARNING

Be sure not to use a flexible extension on the socket. Use of a flexible extension may allow a shear force to be applied to the plug. A shear force could break the plug off in the cylinder head, leading to costly and frustrating repairs.

To install:
5. Inspect the spark plug boot for tears or damage. If a damaged boot is found, the spark plug wire must be replaced.

6. Using a wire feeler gauge, check and adjust the spark plug gap. When using a gauge, the proper size should pass between the electrodes with a slight drag. The next larger size should not be able to pass while the next smaller size should pass freely.

7. Carefully thread the plug into the bore by hand. If resistance is felt before the plug is almost completely threaded, back the plug out and begin threading again. In small, hard to reach areas, an old spark plug wire and boot could be used as a threading tool. The boot will hold the plug while you twist the end of the wire and the wire is supple enough to twist before it would allow the plug to crossthread.

❊❊ WARNING

Do not use the spark plug socket to thread the plugs. Always carefully thread the plug by hand or using an old plug wire to prevent the possibility of crossthreading and damaging the cylinder head bore.

8. Carefully tighten the spark plug. If the plug you are installing is equipped with a crush washer, seat the plug, then tighten about ¼ turn to crush the washer. If you are installing a tapered seat plug, tighten the plug to specifications provided by the vehicle or plug manufacturer.

9. Apply a small amount of silicone dielectric compound to the end of the spark plug lead or inside the spark plug boot to prevent sticking, then install the boot to the spark plug and push until it clicks into place. The click may be felt or heard, then gently pull back on the boot to assure proper contact.

INSPECTION & GAPPING

▶ **See Figures 5, 6, 7, 8 and 9**

Check the plugs for deposits and wear. If they are not going to be replaced, clean the plugs thoroughly. Remember that any kind of deposit will decrease the efficiency of the plug. Plugs can be cleaned on a spark plug cleaning machine, which can sometimes be found in service stations, or you can do an acceptable job of cleaning with a stiff brush. If the plugs are cleaned, the electrodes must be filed flat. Use an ignition points file, not an emery board or the like, which will leave deposits. The electrodes must be filed perfectly flat with sharp edges; rounded edges reduce the spark plug voltage by as much as 50%.

Check spark plug gap before installation. The ground electrode (the L-shaped one connected to the body of the plug) must be parallel to the center electrode and the specified size wire gauge (please refer to the Tune-Up Specifications chart for details) must pass between the electrodes with a slight drag.

➡**NEVER adjust the gap on a used platinum type spark plug.**

Always check the gap on new plugs as they are not always set correctly at the factory. Do not use a flat feeler gauge when measuring the gap on a used plug, because the reading may be inaccurate. A round-wire type gapping tool is the best way to check the gap. The correct gauge should pass through the electrode gap with a slight drag. If you're in doubt, try one size smaller and one larger. The smaller gauge should go through easily, while the larger one shouldn't go through at all. Wire gapping tools usually have a bending tool attached. Use that to adjust the side electrode until the proper distance is obtained. Absolutely never attempt to bend the center electrode. Also, be careful not to bend the side electrode too far or too often as it may weaken and break off within the engine, requiring removal of the cylinder head to retrieve it.

Spark Plug Wires

CHECKING & REPLACEMENT

▶ **See Figures 10 and 11**

At every tune-up/inspection, visually inspect the spark plug cables for burns cuts, or breaks in the insulation. Check the boots and the nipples on the distributor cap and coil. Replace any damaged wiring.

Every 50,000 miles (80,000 Km) or 60 months, the resistance of the wires should be checked with an ohmmeter. Wires with excessive resistance will cause misfiring, and may make the engine difficult to start in damp weather.

To check resistance, remove the distributor cap, leaving the wires attached. Connect one lead of an ohmmeter to an electrode within the cap; connect the other lead to the corresponding spark plug terminal (remove it from the plug for this test). Replace any wire which shows a resistance over 30,000 ohms. Test the high tension lead from the coil by connecting the ohmmeter between the center contact in the distributor cap and either of the primary terminals of the coil. If resistance is more than 25,000 ohms, remove the cable from the coil and check the resistance of the cable alone. Anything over 15,000 ohms is cause for replacement. It should be remembered that resistance is also a function of length; the longer the cable, the greater the resistance. Thus, if the cables on your truck are longer than the factory originals, resistance will be higher, and quite possibly outside these limits.

When installing new cables, replace them one at a time to avoid mix-ups. Start by replacing the longest one first. Install the boot firmly over the spark

A **normally worn** spark plug should have light tan or gray deposits on the firing tip.

A **carbon fouled** plug, identified by soft, sooty, black deposits, may indicate an improperly tuned vehicle. Check the air cleaner, ignition components and engine control system.

This spark plug has been **left in the engine too long,** as evidenced by the extreme gap- Plugs with such an extreme gap can cause misfiring and stumbling accompanied by a noticeable lack of power.

An **oil fouled** spark plug indicates an engine with worn poston rings and/or bad valve seals allowing excessive oil to enter the chamber.

A **physically damaged** spark plug may be evidence of severe detonation in that cylinder. Watch that cylinder carefully between services, as a continued detonation will not only damage the plug, but could also damage the engine.

A **bridged or almost bridged** spark plug, identified by a build-up between the electrodes caused by excessive carbon or oil build-up on the plug.

TCCA1P40

Fig. 5 Inspect the spark plug to determine engine running conditions

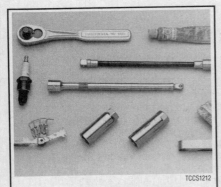
TCCS1212
Fig. 6 A variety of tools and gauges are needed for spark plug service

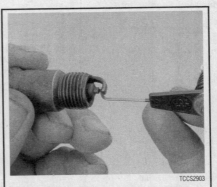
TCCS2903
Fig. 7 Checking the spark plug gap with a feeler gauge

TCCS2904
Fig. 8 Adjusting the spark plug gap

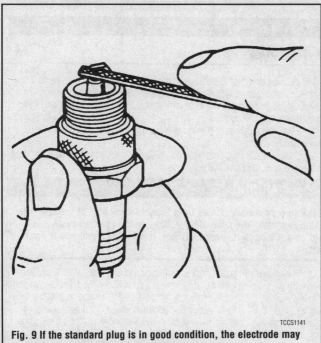

Fig. 9 If the standard plug is in good condition, the electrode may be filed flat—WARNING: do not file platinum plugs

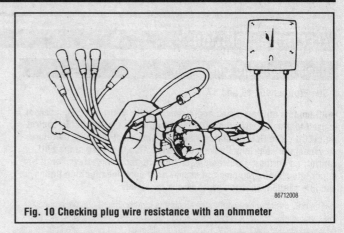

Fig. 10 Checking plug wire resistance with an ohmmeter

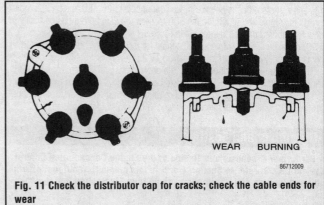

Fig. 11 Check the distributor cap for cracks; check the cable ends for wear

plug. Route the wire over the same path as the original. Insert the nipple firmly into the tower on the cap or the coil. Check the spark plug cable routing and always make sure the plug wires are in the correct plug wire bracket.

FIRING ORDERS

▶ See Figures 12, 13 and 14

➡ To avoid confusion, remove and tag the spark plug wires one at a time, for replacement.

If a distributor is not keyed for installation with only one orientation, it could have been removed previously and rewired. The resultant wiring would hold the correct firing order, but could change the relative placement of the plug towers in relation to the engine. For his reason it is imperative that you label all wires before disconnecting any of them. Also, before removal, compare the current wiring with the accompanying illustrations. If the current wiring does not match, make notes in your book to reflect how your engine is wired.

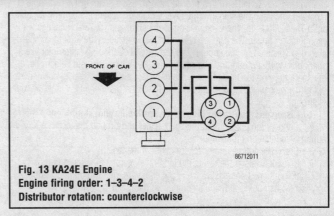

Fig. 13 KA24E Engine
Engine firing order: 1–3–4–2
Distributor rotation: counterclockwise

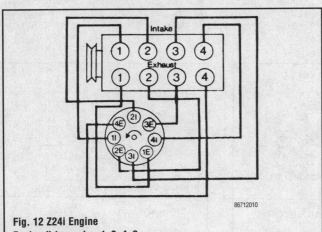

Fig. 12 Z24i Engine
Engine firing order: 1–3–4–2
Distributor rotation: counterclockwise

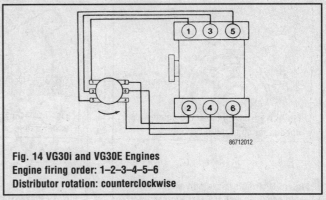

Fig. 14 VG30i and VG30E Engines
Engine firing order: 1–2–3–4–5–6
Distributor rotation: counterclockwise

ELECTRONIC IGNITION

Description and Operation

♦ **See Figures 15, 16 and 17**

➥ **All models utilize a crank angle sensor in the distributor. This sensor is used to provide engine position information to the Electronic Control Unit (ECU). The ECU regulates ignition timing electronically, therefore no vacuum or centrifugal advance is used. Also, because of the ECU control, no periodic service adjustments are necessary. However, if timing or idle speed problems are suspected a combined ignition timing and idle speed inspection procedure is provided.**

The only major component in the electronic ignition distributor assembly is the crank angle sensor. It is basically a rotor plate wheel with 360 slits, one per degree of crankshaft rotation. A Light Emitting Diode (LED) is mounted above the slits and a photo diode is below. As each slit uncovers the LED, the photo diode detects the signal and reports to the ECU. A second LED/photo diode pair is mounted inboard of the 1 degree set to read slits indicating Top Dead Center (TDC) of each cylinder, with a special signal for the No. 1 cylinder. On all engines, the assembly is in the distributor (retained by 2 screws), just below the rotor.

The ECU sends an ignition signal to a power transistor, which turns the coil primary circuit on and off. The primary circuit current is amplified by a resistor. The ignition system is a standard configuration: one power transistor firing one ignition coil, which sends the high voltage to the distributor cap.

Diagnosis and Testing

➥ **For further Diagnosis and Testing of the Engine Concentrated Control System (ECCS) refer to Section 4 or 5 in this manual. Additional distributor and ignition coil information can be found in Section 3 of this manual.**

SECONDARY SPARK TEST

The best way to perform this procedure is to use a spark tester (available at most automotive parts stores). Three types of spark testers are commonly available. The Neon Bulb type is connected to the spark plug wire and flashes with each ignition pulse. The Air Gap type must be adjusted to the individual spark plug gap specified for the engine. The last type of spark plug tester loks like a spark plug with a grounding clip on the side, but there is no side electrode for the spark to jump to.The last two types of testers allows the user to not only detect the presence of spark, but also the intensity (orange/yellow is weak, blue is strong).

1. Disconnect a spark plug wire at the spark plug end.
2. Connect the plug wire to the spark tester and ground the tester to an appropriate location on the engine.
3. Crank the engine and check for spark at the tester.
4. If spark exists at the tester, the ignition system is functioning properly.
5. If spark does not exist at the spark plug wire, perform diagnosis of the ignition system using individual component diagnosis procedures.

CYLINDER DROP TEST

The cylinder drop test is performed when an engine misfire is evident. This test helps determine which cylinder is not contributing the proper power. The easiest way to perform this test is to remove the plug wires one at a time from the cylinders with the engine running.

1. Place the transaxle in **P**, engage the emergency brake, and start the engine and let it idle.
2. Using a spark plug wire removing tool, preferably, the plier type, carefully remove the boot from one of the cylinders.

✸✸ WARNING

Make sure your body is free from touching any part of the car which is metal. The secondary voltage in the ignition system is high and although it cannot kill you, it will shoch you and it does hurt.

3. The engine will sputter, run worse, and possibly nearly stall. If this happens reinstall the plug wire and move to the next cylinder. If the engine runs no differently, or the difference is minimal, shut the engine off and inspect the spark plug wire, spark plug, and if necessary, perform component diagnostics as covered in this section. Perform the test on all cylinders to verify the which cylinders are suspect.

IGNITION COIL

♦ **See Figures 18 thru 23**

Primary Resistance Check

In order to check the coil primary resistance, you must first disconnect all wires from the ignition coil terminals. Using an ohmmeter, check the resistance between the positive and the negative terminals on the coil. The resistance should be:

- Z24i—0.80–1.00 ohms
- VG30i—0.80–1.00 ohms
- KA24E—0.80–1.00 ohms
- VG30E—0.80–1.00 ohms

➥ **Remember that all Z24i engines have 2 ignition coils; check them both!**

If the resistance is not within these tolerances, the coil will require replacement.

Secondary Resistance Check

In order to check the coil secondary resistance, you must first disconnect all wires from the ignition coil terminals. Using an ohmmeter, check the resistance between the positive terminal and the coil wire terminal. The resistance should be:

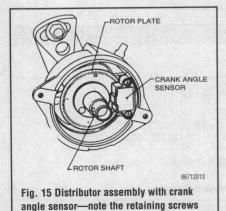

Fig. 15 Distributor assembly with crank angle sensor—note the retaining screws

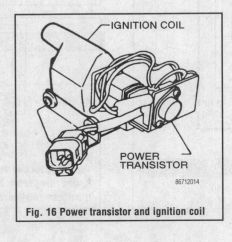

Fig. 16 Power transistor and ignition coil

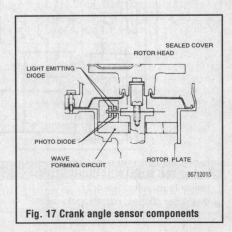

Fig. 17 Crank angle sensor components

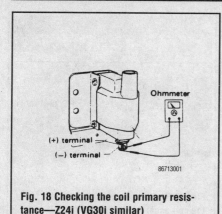

Fig. 18 Checking the coil primary resistance—Z24i (VG30i similar)

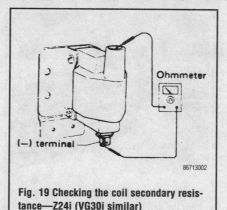

Fig. 19 Checking the coil secondary resistance—Z24i (VG30i similar)

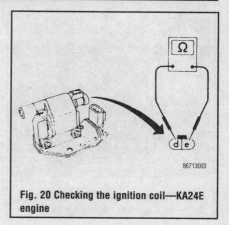

Fig. 20 Checking the ignition coil—KA24E engine

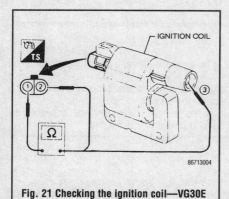

Fig. 21 Checking the ignition coil—VG30E engine

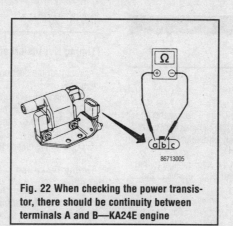

Fig. 22 When checking the power transistor, there should be continuity between terminals A and B—KA24E engine

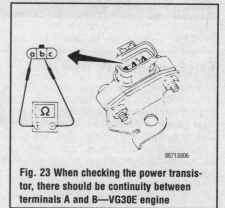

Fig. 23 When checking the power transistor, there should be continuity between terminals A and B—VG30E engine

- Z24i—7600–11,400 ohms
- VG30i—7600–11,400 ohms
- KA24E—7600–11,400 ohms
- VG30E—7600–11,400 ohms

➡ **Remember that all Z24i engines have 2 ignition coils; check them both!**

If the resistance is not within these tolerances, the coil will require replacement.

CRANK ANGLE SENSOR

When the ignition is **ON** and the main ECCS relay is activated, 12 volts is sent to the crank angle sensor LED. When a slit uncovers the photo diode and it detects the light, a 5 volt signal is sent to the ECU. The unit is easy to test but it must be removed from the engine. Refer to test procedure below.

1. First test the circuit to the sensor. Unplug the sensor connector, turn the ignition **ON** and check for 12 volts between one of the terminals and ground. The other terminals are return signals to the ECU, do not use them for voltmeter ground.

2. Turn the ignition **OFF**, remove the distributor assembly and reconnect the plug to the crank angle sensor. Peel back the insulation sufficiently to connect a voltmeter to the wires. Ground the coil high tension wire.

3. With the voltmeter connected to a good chassis ground, turn the ignition **ON** and slowly rotate the distributor. One of the return signal wires should have 5 volts off and on with each degree of rotation. The other should have 5 volts off and on with each 180 degrees (4 cyl.) or 120 degrees (6 cyl.) of rotation.

4. Visually check the rotor plate for rust or damage.

Service Parts Replacement

Service consists of inspection or replacement of the distributor cap, rotor and spark plug wires.

1. Disconnect the negative battery cable.

2. The distributor cap is held on by two screws. Release them with a screwdriver and lift the cap straight up and off, with the wires attached. Inspect the cap for cracks, carbon tracks, or a worn center contact.

3. Pull the ignition rotor straight up to remove. Replace it if its contacts are worn, burned, or pitted. Do not file the contacts.

To install:

4. If removed, press the rotor firmly onto the shaft. It only goes on one way, so be sure it is fully seated.

5. Inspect the plug wires for cracks or brittleness. Replace them one at a time to prevent crosswiring, carefully pressing the replacement wires into place. The cores of electronic wires are more susceptible to breakage than those of standard wires, so treat them gently.

➡ **Check the spark plug cable routing and always make sure the plug wires are in the correct plug wire bracket.**

6. Install the distributor cap and tighten the two screws.

7. Disconnect the negative battery cable.

Ignition Coil

REMOVAL & INSTALLATION

◆ **See Figures 24, 25 and 26**

1. Disconnect the negative battery cable.

2. Tag and disconnect all electrical leads at the coil.

3. Remove the two mounting bolts and lift off the ignition coil.

To install:

4. Install the coil in position and tighten the mounting bolts.

5. Connect all wires.

6. Connect the negative battery cable.

Fig. 24 Remove the coil assembly mounting bolts—all 6-cylinder engines are similar

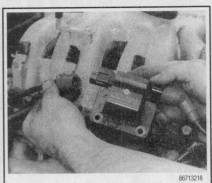

Fig. 25 Remove the electrical connection from the coil assembly

Fig. 26 Remove the coil ignition wire from the coil assembly

Distributor

REMOVAL

◆ See Figures 27, 28, 29, 30 and 31

1. Disconnect the negative battery cable.
2. Unfasten the retaining clips (only remove the coil wire if necessary) and lift the distributor cap straight off. It will be easier to install the distributor if the spark plug wiring is left connected to the cap. If the plug wires must be removed from the cap, mark their positions to aid in installation.
3. Remove the dust cover and mark the position of the rotor relative to the distributor body; then mark the position of the distributor body relative to the engine block.
4. Detach the harness assembly connector.
5. Remove the pinch-bolt and lift the distributor straight out, away from the engine. The rotor and body are marked so that they can be returned to the position from which they were removed. Do not turn or disturb the engine (unless absolutely necessary) after the distributor assembly has been removed.

INSTALLATION

Timing Not Disturbed

1. Insert the distributor in the block and align ALL matchmarks made during removal.
2. Engage the distributor driven gear with the distributor drive.
3. Install the distributor clamp and secure it with the pinch-bolt.
4. Install the distributor cap and fasten the harness electrical connector.
5. If necessary, install the spark plug wires and coil wire.
6. Start the engine. Check the timing and adjust it if necessary.

Timing Disturbed

1. It is necessary to place the No. 1 cylinder in the firing position to correctly install the distributor. To locate this position, the ignition timing marks on the crankshaft front pulley can be used.
2. Remove the No. 1 cylinder spark plug. Turn the crankshaft until the piston in the No. 1 cylinder is moving up on the compression stroke. This can be determined by placing your thumb over the spark plug hole and feeling the air

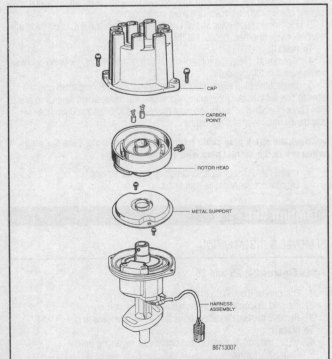

Fig. 27 Exploded view of the distributor assembly—4-cylinder engine

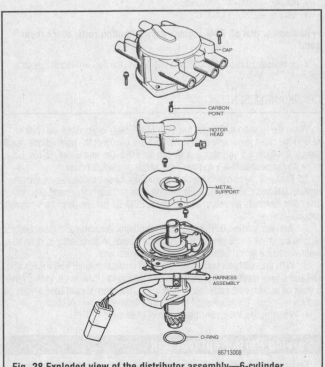

Fig. 28 Exploded view of the distributor assembly—6-cylinder engine

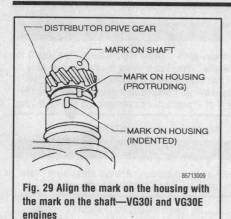

Fig. 29 Align the mark on the housing with the mark on the shaft—VG30i and VG30E engines

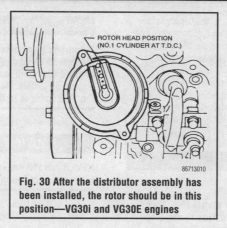

Fig. 30 After the distributor assembly has been installed, the rotor should be in this position—VG30i and VG30E engines

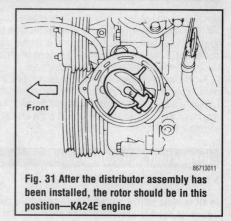

Fig. 31 After the distributor assembly has been installed, the rotor should be in this position—KA24E engine

being forced out of the cylinder. Stop turning the crankshaft when the timing marks indicate **TDC** or **0**.

3. Oil the distributor housing lightly where the distributor bears on the cylinder block.

4. Install the distributor so that the rotor, which is mounted on the shaft, points toward the No. 1 spark plug terminal tower position when the cap is installed. Of course, you won't be able to see the direction in which the rotor is pointing if the cap is installed, so lay the cap on the top of the distributor and make a mark on the side of the distributor housing just below the No. 1 spark plug terminal. Make sure that the rotor points toward that mark when you install the distributor.

➡**On the VG30i and VG30E engines, align the mark on the distributor shaft with the protruding mark on the housing.**

5. When the distributor shaft has reached the bottom of the hole, gently move the rotor back and forth slightly until the driving lug on the end of the shaft enter the slots cut in the end of the oil pump shaft and the distributor assembly slides down into place.

➡**On the VG30i and VG30E engines, the distributor rotor tip should be in the 11 o'clock position.**

6. Fasten the distributor hold-down bolt.
7. Install the spark plug into the No. 1 spark plug hole.
8. Install the distributor cap and engage the harness electrical connector.
9. If necessary, attach the spark plug wires and coil wire.
10. Start the engine. Check the timing and adjust it if necessary.

IGNITION TIMING

General Information

▶ See Figure 32

Ignition timing is the measurement in degrees of crankshaft rotation of the instant the spark plug fires, in relation to the location of the piston (while the piston is on its compression stroke).

Although no periodic service is necessary, ignition timing can be adjusted by loosening the distributor locking device and turning the distributor in the engine.

Ideally, the air/fuel mixture in the cylinder will be ignited (by the spark plug) and just begin its rapid expansion as the piston passes top dead center (TDC) of the compression stroke. If this happens, the piston will be beginning the power stroke just as the compressed (by the movement of the piston) air/fuel mixture starts to expand. The expansion of the air/fuel mixture will then force the piston down on the power stroke and turn the crankshaft.

It takes a fraction of a second for the spark from the plug to completely ignite the mixture in the cylinder. Because of this, the spark plug must fire before the piston reaches TDC, if the mixture is to be completely ignited as the piston passes TDC. This measurement is given in degrees (of crankshaft rotation) Before the piston reaches Top Dead Center (BTDC). If the ignition timing setting for your engine is seven (7°) BTDC, this means that the spark plug must fire at a time when the piston for that cylinder is 7° before top dead center of its compression stroke. However, this only holds true while your engine is at idle speed.

As you accelerate from idle, the speed of your engine (rpm) increases. The increase in rpm means that the pistons are now traveling up and down much faster. Because of this, the spark plugs will have to fire even sooner if the mixture is to be completely ignited as the piston passes TDC. To accomplish this, the ECU unit incorporates means to advance the timing of the spark as engine speed increases.

If ignition timing is set too far advanced (too far BTDC), the ignition and expansion of the air/fuel mixture in the cylinder will try to force the piston down the cylinder while it is still traveling upward. This causes engine "ping", a sound which resembles marbles being dropped into an empty tin can. If the ignition timing is too far retarded (after, or ATDC), the piston will have already started down on the power stroke when the air/fuel mixture ignites and expands. This will cause the piston to be forced down only a portion of its travel, resulting in poor engine performance and lack of power.

Ignition timing adjustment is checked with a timing light. This instrument is

connected to the Number One (No. 1) spark plug of the engine. The timing light flashes every time an electrical current is sent from the distributor, through the No. 1 spark plug wire, to the spark plug. The crankshaft pulley and the front cover of the engine are marked with a timing pointer and a timing scale. When the timing pointer is aligned with the **0** mark on the timing scale, the piston for the No. 1 cylinder is at TDC of its compression stroke. With the engine running, and the timing light aimed at the timing pointer/scale, the flashes from the timing light will allow you to check the ignition timing. The timing light flashes every time the spark plug in the No. 1 cylinder of the engine fires. Since the flash from the timing light makes the crankshaft pulley seem stationary for a moment you will be able to read the exact position of the piston in the No. 1 cylinder on the timing scale.

There are three basic types of timing lights available. The first is a simple neon bulb with two wire connections (one for the spark plug and one for the plug wire, connecting the light in series). This type of light is quite dim, and must be held closely to the marks to be seen, but it is inexpensive. The second type of light operates from the battery. Two alligator clips connect to the battery terminals, while a third wire connects to the spark plug with an adapter. This type of light is more expensive, but the xenon bulb provides a nice bright flash

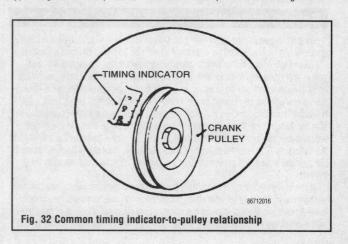

Fig. 32 Common timing indicator-to-pulley relationship

which can even be seen in sunlight. The third type replaces the battery source with 110 volt house current. Some timing lights have other functions built into them, such as dwell meters, tachometers, or remote starting switches. These are convenient, in that they reduce the tangle of wires under the hood, but may duplicate the functions of tools you already have.

For the vehicles covered by this manual, it is best to use a timing light with an inductive pickup. This pickup simply clamps onto the No. 1 plug wire, eliminating the adapter. It is not susceptible to crossfiring or false triggering, which may occur with a conventional light, due to the greater voltages produced by electronic ignition.

Inspection and Adjustment

▶ **See Figures 33, 34 and 35**

➡**All models utilize a crank angle sensor in the distributor. This sensor is used to provide engine position information to the Electronic Control Unit (ECU). The ECU regulates ignition timing electronically, therefore no vacuum or centrifugal advance is used. Also, because of the ECU control, no periodic service adjustments are necessary. However, if timing or idle speed problems are suspected a combined ignition timing and idle speed inspection procedure is provided.**

The following procedure should only be used as part of the timing and idle speed inspection found on the flow charts at the end of the section. No periodic timing settings should be required by these vehicles. ALSO, always refer to the instructions or specifications found on the Vehicle Emission Control Information (VECI) label found underhood for additional or updated information which is applicable to your particular vehicle.

✳✳ CAUTION

Automatic transmission equipped models should be shifted into D for idle speed checks. When in Drive, the parking brake must be fully applied with both front and rear wheels chocked. When racing the engine on automatic transmission equipped models, make sure that the shift lever is in the N or P position and remove the wheel chocks.

1. Run the engine until it reaches normal operating temperature.

✳✳ CAUTION

NEVER run the engine in a closed garage. Always make sure there is proper ventilation to prevent carbon monoxide poisoning.

2. Open the hood, and race the engine at 2000 rpm for about 2 minutes under no-load (all accessories must be OFF, including the air conditioner).
3. Run the engine at idle speed.
4. Race the engine two or three times under no-load, then run the engine for one minute at idle.
5. Check the idle speed. If necessary, adjust the idle speed to specifications by turning the idle speed adjusting screw. For details please refer to the Tune-Up Specifications Chart.
6. Connect a timing light according to the light manufacturer's instructions. Adjust the timing by loosening the distributor hold-down bolt(s) and turning the distributor clockwise to advance and counterclockwise to retard.
7. Once the proper timing setting is reached, hold the distributor steady and tighten the hold-down bolt(s). After the distributor is secured, recheck the timing to verify it did not move while tightening the retainer(s).
8. Once the inspection is finished, stop the engine, then remove the timing light and tachometer.

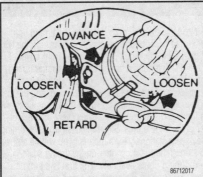

Fig. 33 Adjust the ignition timing by rotating the distributor

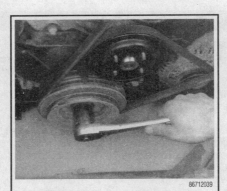

Fig. 34 Timing marks 6 cylinder engine—note the fan was removed for a better view

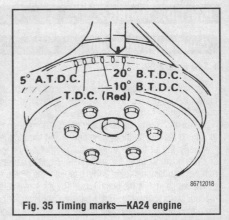

Fig. 35 Timing marks—KA24 engine

VALVE LASH

General Information

As part of every tune-up or every 15,000 miles (24,000 km) the valve clearance should be checked. The clearance should be adjusted ONLY if necessary.

Valve lash is one factor which determines how far the intake and exhaust valves will open into the cylinder. If the valve clearance is too large, part of the lift of the camshaft will be used up in removing the excessive clearance, thus the valves will not be opened far enough. This condition has two effects; one, the valve train components will emit a tapping noise as they take up the excessive clearance. Two, the engine will perform poorly, since the less the intake valves open, the smaller the amount of air/fuel mixture which can be admitted to the cylinders. The less the exhaust valves open, the greater the back-pressure in the cylinder which will prevent the proper air/fuel mixture from entering the cylinder.

If the valve clearance is too small, the intake and exhaust valves will not fully seat on the cylinder head when they close. When a valve seats on the cylinder head it does two things; it seals the combustion chamber so none of the gases in the cylinder can escape and it cools itself by transferring some of the heat it

absorbed from the combustion process through the cylinder head and into the engine cooling system. Therefore, if the valve clearance is too small, the engine will run poorly (due to gases escaping from the combustion chamber), and the valves will overheat and warp (since they cannot transfer heat unless they are touching the seat in the cylinder head).

➡**While all valve adjustments must be as accurate as possible, it is better to have the valve adjustment slightly loose than slightly tight, as burnt valves may result from overly tight adjustments.**

ADJUSTMENT

Although it is sometimes possible to reuse an old cylinder head cover gasket, in most cases it makes more sense to purchase a new one before beginning the procedure. Some vehicles may require the use of silicone sealant either with or without a new cover gasket. For more details, please refer to the cylinder head cover procedures in Section 3 of this manual and refer to the gasket manufacturer's instructions.

Z24i Engine

▶ **See Figures 36, 37 and 38**

➡For the intake valves: 1–4–5–8 valve clearance is 0.012 in. (0.30mm). For the exhaust valves: 2–3–6–7 valve clearance is 0.012 in. (0.30mm). The pivot lock-nut torque specification is 12–16 ft. lbs. (16–22 Nm).

1. The valves must be adjusted with the engine warm, so start the truck and run the engine until the needle on the temperature gauge reaches the middle setting. After the engine is warm, shut it off.

2. Note the location of any wires and hoses which may interfere with cylinder head cover removal, disconnect them and move them to one side. Remove the bolts holding the cylinder head cover in place and remove the cover. Remember, the engine will be hot, so be careful!

3. Rotate the crankshaft until the timing marks indicate that the No. 1 piston is at TDC of the compression stroke. If you're not sure of which stroke you're on, remove the No. 1 spark plug and hold your thumb over the hole. Pressure will be felt as the piston starts up on the compression stroke.

4. Refer to the accompanying illustration (upper part), then check valves (1), (2), (4) and (6) using a flat bladed feeler gauge. The feeler gauge should pass between the valve stem end and the rocker arm screw with a very slight drag. Insert the feeler gauge straight, not at an angle.

5. If the clearance is not within the specified value, loosen the rocker arm lock nut and turn the rocker arm screw to obtain the proper clearance. After correct clearance is obtained, tighten the lock-nut.

6. Rotate the crankshaft until the timing marks indicate that the No. 4 piston is at TDC of the compression stroke. If you're not sure of which stroke you're on, remove the No. 4 spark plug and hold your thumb over the hole. Pressure will be felt as the piston starts up on the compression stroke.

7. See the illustration (lower part), then check valves (3), (5), (7) and (8). Check and adjust valve clearance as necessary.

8. Install the cylinder head cover gasket, the cover itself and any wires or hoses which were removed. Check the engine oil level.

Fig. 36 Check the valve clearance with a flat feeler gauge—Z24i engine

Fig. 37 Loosen the lock-nut and turn the adjusting screw to adjust the valve clearance—Z24i engine

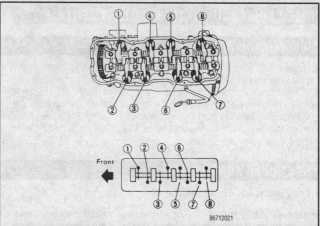

Fig. 38 With the No. 1 piston at TDC, adjust the top set of valves FIRST; with the No. 4 piston at TDC, adjust the bottom set of valves SECOND—Z24i engine

KA24E, VG30i and VG30E Engines

▶ **See Figures 39 and 40**

These models utilize hydraulic valve lifters. Periodic adjustment is neither necessary or possible. There is however a bleed down procedure that is necessary when the valve train has been disassembled.

HYDRAULIC LIFTER BLEED DOWN

1. Remove the cylinder head cover.
2. Check the lifters for proper operation by pushing hard on each lifter with fingertip pressure.
3. If the valve lifter moves more than 0.04 in. (1mm), air may be inside it. Make sure the rocker arm is not on the cam lobe when making this check.
4. Install the cylinder head cover.
5. If there was air in the lifters, bleed the air by running the engine at 1000 rpm for 10 minutes.

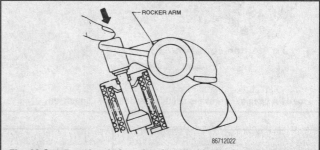

Fig. 39 Cross-sectional view of an installed hydraulic valve lifter—4 cylinder engine

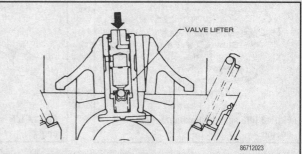

Fig. 40 Cross-sectional view of an installed hydraulic valve lifter—6 cylinder engine

IDLE SPEED AND MIXTURE ADJUSTMENTS

Idle Mixture Adjustment

These trucks use a rather complex electronic fuel injection system which is regulated by a series of temperature, altitude (for California) and air flow sensors which feed information into an Electronic Control Unit (ECU). The control unit then relays an electronic signal to the injector nozzle(s), which allow(s) a predetermined amount of fuel into the combustion chamber. In this way all mixture control adjustments are regulated by the ECU, therefore no manual adjustments are necessary or possible.

Idle Speed Adjustment

▶ **See Figures 41, 42, 43, 44 and 45**

➡Because of ECU control, no periodic service adjustments are necessary. However, if timing or idle speed problems are suspected a combined ignition timing and idle speed inspection procedure is provided.

The following procedure should only be used as part of the timing and idle speed inspection found on the flow charts at the end of the section. No periodic idle speed adjustments should be required by these vehicles. ALSO, always refer to the instructions or specifications found on the Vehicle Emission Control Information (VECI) label found underhood for additional or updated information which is applicable to your particular vehicle.

✳✳ CAUTION

For manual transmission models, set parking brake and check idle speed in N position. For automatic transmission equipped models, shifted into D for idle speed checks. When in Drive, the parking brake must be fully applied with both front and rear wheels chocked.

1. Turn off the: headlights, heater blower, air conditioning, and rear window defogger. If the truck has power steering, make sure the wheels are in the straight ahead position. The ignition timing must be correct to get an effective idle speed adjustment. Connect a tachometer (a special adapter harness may be needed, SST# EG11170000) according to the instrument manufacturer's directions.
2. Start the engine and warm the engine so it reaches normal operating temperature. The water temperature indicator should be in the middle of the gauge.

✳✳ CAUTION

NEVER run the engine in a closed garage. Always make sure there is proper ventilation to prevent carbon monoxide poisoning.

3. Run engine at 2000 rpm for about 2 minutes under no load.
4. Race the engine to 2000–3000 rpm a few times under no load and then allow it to return to idle speed.
5. Apply the parking brake securely. If equipped with an automatic, put the transmission into **D**.
6. Adjust the idle speed to the figure shown in the Tune-Up Specifications Chart by turning the idle speed adjusting screw.
7. Turn the engine **OFF** and remove the tachometer. Road test for proper operation.

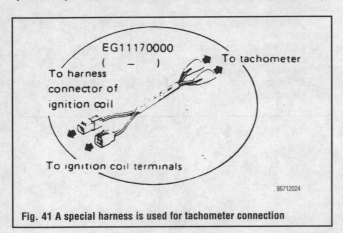

Fig. 41 A special harness is used for tachometer connection

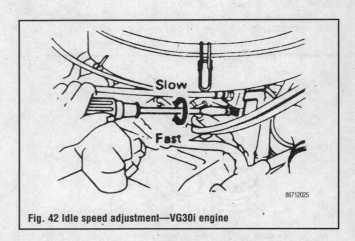

Fig. 42 Idle speed adjustment—VG30i engine

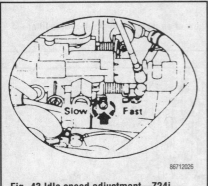

Fig. 43 Idle speed adjustment—Z24i engine

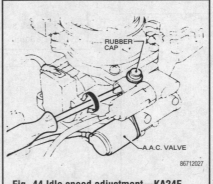

Fig. 44 Idle speed adjustment—KA24E engine

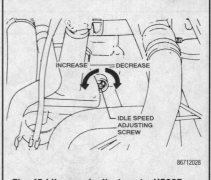

Fig. 45 Idle speed adjustment—VG30E engine

TIMING AND IDLE SPEED INSPECTION

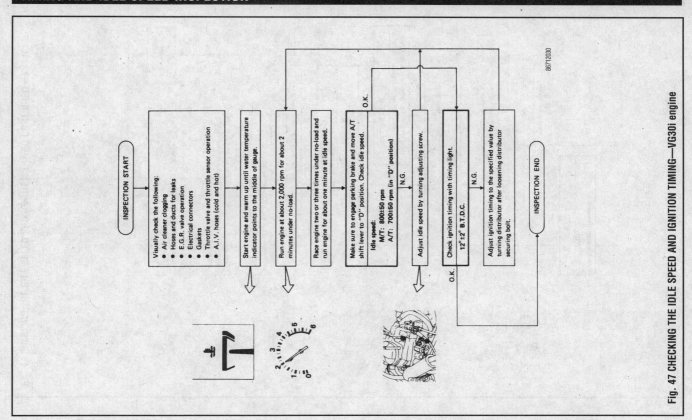

Fig. 47 CHECKING THE IDLE SPEED AND IGNITION TIMING—VG30i engine

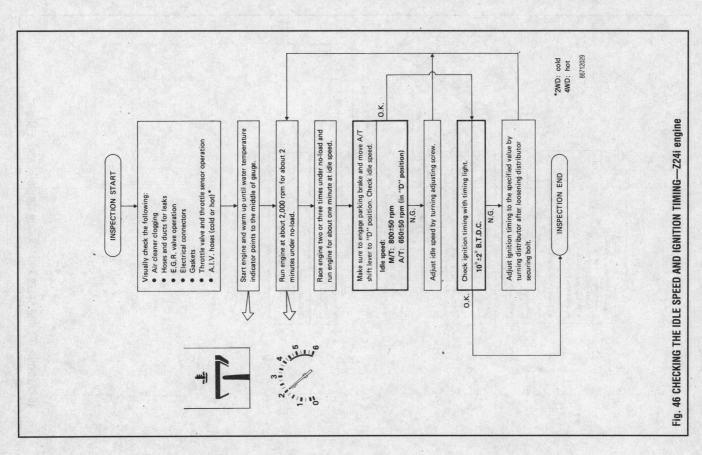

Fig. 46 CHECKING THE IDLE SPEED AND IGNITION TIMING—Z24i engine

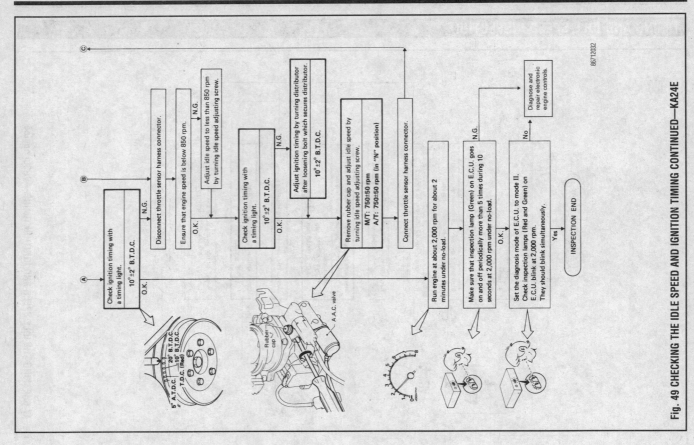

Fig. 49 CHECKING THE IDLE SPEED AND IGNITION TIMING CONTINUED—KA24E

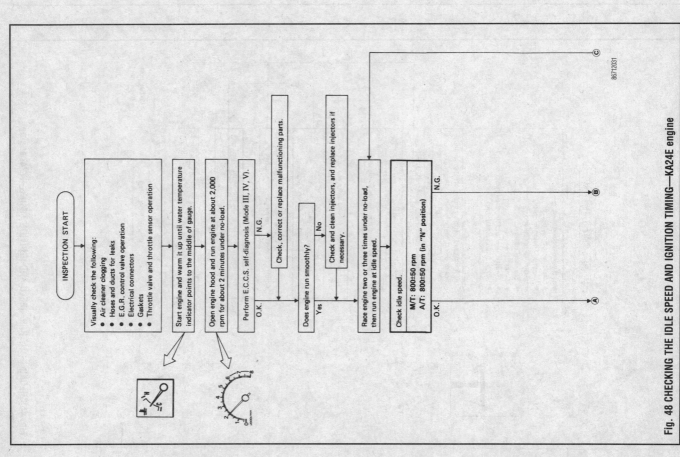

Fig. 48 CHECKING THE IDLE SPEED AND IGNITION TIMING—KA24E engine

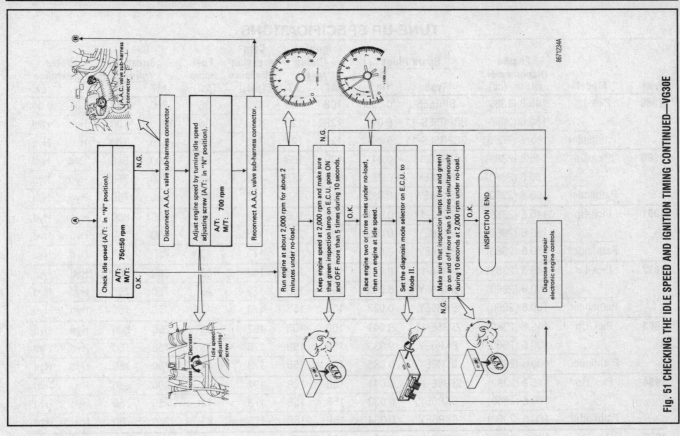

Fig. 51 CHECKING THE IDLE SPEED AND IGNITION TIMING CONTINUED—VG30E

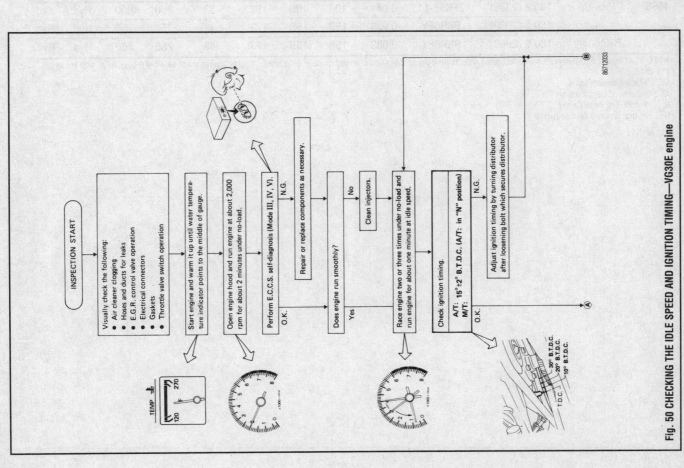

Fig. 50 CHECKING THE IDLE SPEED AND IGNITION TIMING—VG30E engine

TUNE-UP SPECIFICATIONS

Year	Model	Engine Displacement cu. in. (cc)	Spark Plugs Type	Gap (in.)	Ignition Timing (deg.) MT	AT	Com-pression Pressure (psi)	Fuel Pump (psi)	Idle Speed (rpm) MT	AT	Valve Clearance In.	Ex.
1989	Pick-Up	145.8 (2389)	BPR5ES	0.033	10B	10B	173	36	800	650	0.012	0.012
		180.6 (2960)	BCPR5ES-11	0.041	12B	12B	173	36	800	700	Hyd.	Hyd.
	Pathfinder	180.6 (2960)	BCPR5ES-11	0.041	12B	12B	173	36	800	700	Hyd.	Hyd.
1990	Pick-Up	145.8 (2389)	ZFR5E-11	0.041	10B	10B	192	33	800	800	Hyd.	Hyd.
		180.6 (2960)	BKR6EY	0.033	15B	15B	173	43	750	750	Hyd.	Hyd.
	Pathfinder	180.6 (2960)	BKR6EY	0.033	15B	15B	173	43	750	750	Hyd.	Hyd.
1991	Pick-Up	145.8 (2389)	ZFR5E-11	0.041	10B	10B	192	33	800	800	Hyd.	Hyd.
		180.6 (2960)	BKR6EY	0.033	15B	15B	173	43	750	750	Hyd.	Hyd.
	Pathfinder	180.6 (2960)	BKR6EY	0.033	15B	15B	173	43	750	750	Hyd.	Hyd.
1992	Pick-Up	145.8 (2389)	ZFR5E-11	0.041	10B	10B	192	33	800	800	Hyd.	Hyd.
		180.6 (2960)	BKR6EY	0.033	15B	15B	173	43	750	750	Hyd.	Hyd.
	Pathfinder	180.6 (2960)	BKR6EY	0.033	15B	15B	173	43	750	750	Hyd.	Hyd.
1993	Pick-Up	145.8 (2389)	ZFR5E-11	0.041	10B	10B	192	33	800	800	Hyd.	Hyd.
		180.6 (2960)	BKR6EY	0.033	15B	15B	173	43	750	750	Hyd.	Hyd.
	Pathfinder	180.6 (2960)	BKR6EY	0.033	15B	15B	173	43	750	750	Hyd.	Hyd.
1994	Pick-Up	145.8 (2389)	ZFR5E-11	0.041	10B	10B	192	33	800	800	Hyd.	Hyd.
		180.6 (2960)	BKR6EY	0.033	15B	15B	173	43	750	750	Hyd.	Hyd.
	Pathfinder	180.6 (2960)	BKR6EY	0.033	15B	15B	173	43	750	750	Hyd.	Hyd.
1995	Pick-Up	145.8 (2389)	ZFR5E-11	0.041	10B	10B	192	33	800	800	Hyd.	Hyd.
		180.6 (2960)	BKR6EY	0.033	15B	15B	173	43	750	750	Hyd.	Hyd.
	Pathfinder	180.6 (2960)	BKR6EY	0.033	15B	15B	173	43	750	750	Hyd.	Hyd.

NOTE: The Underhood Specifications sticker often reflects tune-up specification changes made in production. Sticker figures must be used if they differ with those in this chart.

MT   Manual transmission
AT   Automatic transmission
B   Before Top Dead Center
Hyd. Hydraulic valve lash adjusters

86712C01

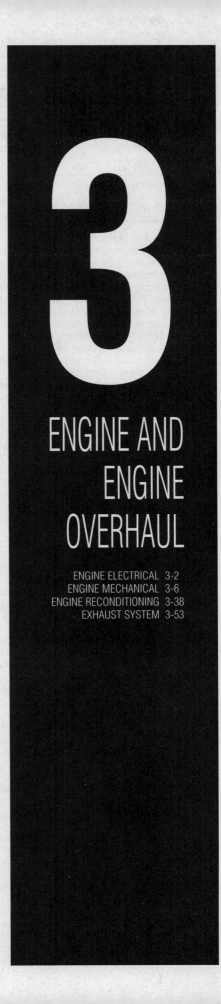

3

ENGINE AND ENGINE OVERHAUL

ENGINE ELECTRICAL

Description and Operation

The engine electrical system can be broken down into three sub-systems:
1. The starting system
2. The charging system
3. The ignition system

THE BATTERY AND STARTING SYSTEM

The battery is the first link in the chain of mechanisms which work together to provide cranking of the automobile engine. In most modern trucks, the battery is a lead/acid electro-chemical device consisting of six two-volt (2V) subsections connected in series, so the unit is capable of producing approximately 12V of electrical pressure. Each subsection, or cell, consists of a series of positive and negative plates held a short distance apart in a solution of sulfuric acid and water. The two types of plates are of dissimilar metals. This causes a chemical reaction to be set up; it is this reaction which produces current flow from the battery when its positive and negative terminals are connected to an electrical appliance such as a lamp or a motor. The continued transfer of electrons would eventually convert sulfuric acid in the electrolyte to water, and make the two plates identical in chemical composition. As electrical energy is removed from the battery, its voltage output tends to drop. Thus, measuring battery voltage and battery electrolyte composition are two ways of checking the ability of the unit to supply power. During engine starting, electrical energy is removed from the battery. However, if the charging circuit is in good condition and the operating conditions are normal, the power removed from the battery will be replaced by the alternator, which will force electrons back through the battery, thereby reversing the normal flow and restoring the battery to its original chemical state.

The battery and starting motor are linked by very heavy electrical cables designed to minimize resistance to the flow of current. Generally, the major power supply cable that leaves the battery goes directly to the starter, while other electrical needs are supplied by a smaller cable. During starter operation, power flows from the battery to the starter, and is grounded through the truck's frame and the battery's negative ground strap.

The starting motor is a specially designed, direct current electric motor capable of producing a very great amount of power for its size. One thing that allows the motor to produce a great deal of power is its tremendous rotating speed. It drives the engine through a tiny pinion gear (attached to the starter's armature), which drives the very large flywheel ring gear at a greatly reduced speed. Another factor allowing it to produce so much power is that only intermittent operation is required of it. Thus, little allowance for air circulation is required, and the windings can be built into a very small space.

The starter solenoid is a magnetic device which employs the small current supplied by the starting switch circuit of the ignition switch. The magnetic action moves a plunger which mechanically engages the starter and electrically closes the heavy switch which connects it to the battery. The starting switch circuit consists of the starting switch contained within the ignition switch, a transmission neutral safety switch or clutch pedal switch, and the wiring necessary to connect these with the starter solenoid or relay.

A pinion, which is a small gear, is mounted to a one-way drive clutch. This clutch is splined to the starter armature shaft. When the ignition switch is moved to the **START** position, the solenoid plunger slides the pinion toward the flywheel ring gear via a collar and spring. If the teeth on the pinion and flywheel match properly, the pinion will engage the flywheel immediately. If the gear teeth butt one another, the spring will be compressed and will force the gears to mesh as soon as the starter turns far enough to allow them to do so. As the solenoid plunger reaches the end of its travel, it closes the contacts that connect the battery and starter, then the engine is cranked.

As soon as the engine starts, the flywheel ring gear begins turning fast enough to drive the pinion at an extremely high rate of speed. At this point, the one-way clutch begins allowing the pinion to spin faster than the starter shaft, so that the starter will not operate at excessive speed. When the ignition switch is released from the **START** position, the solenoid is de-energized; a spring contained within the solenoid assembly then pulls the gear out of mesh and interrupts the current flow to the starter.

Some starters employ a separate relay, mounted away from the starter, to switch the motor and solenoid current on and off. The relay thus replaces the solenoid electrical switch, but does not eliminate the need for a solenoid mounted on the starter used to mechanically engage the starter drive gears. The relay is used to reduce the amount of current which the starting switch must carry.

THE CHARGING SYSTEM

The automobile charging system provides electrical power for operation of the vehicle's ignition and starting systems, along with all electrical accessories. The battery serves as an electrical surge or storage tank, storing (in chemical form) the energy originally produced by the engine-driven generator. The system also provides a means of regulating generator output to protect the battery from being overcharged and to avoid excessive voltage to the accessories.

The storage battery is a chemical device incorporating parallel lead plates in a tank containing a sulfuric acid/water solution. Adjacent plates are slightly dissimilar, and the chemical reaction of the two dissimilar plates produces electrical energy when the battery is connected to a load such as the starter motor. The chemical reaction is reversible, so that when the generator is producing a voltage (electrical pressure) greater than that produced by the battery, electricity is forced into the battery, and the battery is returned to its fully charged state.

The vehicle's generator is driven mechanically, through V-belts, by the engine crankshaft. It consists of two coils of fine wire, one stationary (the stator), and one moveable (the rotor). The rotor, also known as the armature, consists of fine wire wrapped around an iron core which is mounted on the shaft. The electricity which flows through the two coils of wire (provided initially by the battery in some cases) creates an intense magnetic field around both the rotor and stator, and the interaction between the two fields creates voltage, allowing the generator to power the accessories and charge the battery.

There are two types of generators; the earlier is the direct current (DC) type. The current produced by the DC generator is generated in the armature and carried off the spinning armature by stationary brushes contacting the commutator. The commutator plates, which are separated by a very short gap, are connected to the armature circuits so that the current will flow in one direction only in the wires carrying the generator output. The generator stator consists of two stationary coils of wire which draw some of the output current of the generator to form a powerful magnetic field and create the interaction of fields which generates the voltage. The generator field is wired in series with the regulator.

Newer vehicles use Alternating Current (AC) generators because they are more efficient, can be rotated at higher speeds, and have fewer brush problems. In an alternator, the field rotates while all the current produced passes only through the stator windings. The brushes bear against continuous slip rings rather than a commutator. This causes the current produced to periodically reverse the direction of its flow. Diodes (electrical one-way switches) block the flow of current from traveling in the wrong direction. A series of diodes is wired together to permit the alternating flow of the stator to be converted to a pulsating, but unidirectional flow at the alternator output. The alternator's field is wired in series with the voltage regulator.

The regulator consists of several circuits. Each circuit has a core, or magnetic coil of wire, which operates a switch. Each switch connects to ground through one or more resistors. The coil of wire responds directly to system voltage. When the voltage reaches the required level, the magnetic field created by the winding of wire closes the switch and inserts a resistance into the generator field circuit, thus reducing the output. The contacts of the switch cycle open and close many times each second to precisely control voltage.

While alternators are self-limiting as far as maximum current is concerned, DC generators employ a current regulating circuit which responds directly to the total amount of current flowing through the generator circuit rather than to the output voltage. The current regulator is similar to the voltage regulator except that all system current must flow through the energizing coil on its way to the various accessories.

SAFETY PRECAUTIONS

Observing these precautions will ensure safe handling of the electrical systems components and will avoid damage to the vehicle's electrical system:
• Be absolutely sure of the polarity of a booster battery before making connections. Connect the cables positive-to-positive, and negative-to-negative. Connect positive cables first, then make the last connection to a ground on the body of the booster vehicle so that arcing cannot ignite hydrogen gas that may have accumulated near the battery. Even momentary connection of a booster battery with the polarity reversed will damage alternator diodes.

- Disconnect both vehicle battery cables before attempting to charge a battery.
- Never ground the alternator/generator output or battery terminal. Be cautious when using metal tools around a battery to avoid creating a short circuit between the terminals.
- Never ground the field circuit between the alternator and regulator.
- Never attempt to polarize an alternator.
- Keep the regulator cover (if so equipped) in place when taking voltage and current limiter readings.

IGNITION SYSTEM

The ignition system is covered in Section 2. Please refer to that Section for operation, diagnosis, and removal and installation procedures.

Alternator

GENERAL INFORMATION

The alternator converts the mechanical energy supplied by the drive belt into electrical energy by a process of electromagnetic induction. When the ignition switch is turned **ON**, current flows from the battery through the charging system light (or ammeter) to the voltage regulator, and finally to the alternator. When the engine is started, the drive belt turns the rotating field (rotor) in the stationary windings (stator), inducing alternating current. This alternating current is converted into usable direct current by the diode rectifier. Most of this current is used to charge the battery and to supply power for the vehicle's electrical accessories. A small part of this current is returned to the field windings of the alternator, enabling it to increase its power output. When the current in the field windings reaches a predetermined level, the voltage regulator grounds the circuit preventing any further increase. The cycle is continued so that the voltage supply remains constant.

All models use a 12-volt alternator. Amperage ratings vary according to the year and model. All models have an electronic, nonadjustable regulator, integral with the alternator.

ALTERNATOR PRECAUTIONS

Several precautions must be observed when performing work on alternator equipment.

- If the battery is removed for any reason, make sure that it is reconnected with the correct polarity. Reversing the battery connections may result in damage to the one-way rectifiers.
- Never operate the alternator with the main circuit broken. Make sure that the battery, alternator, and regulator leads are not disconnected while the engine is running.
- Never attempt to polarize an alternator.
- When charging a battery that is installed in the vehicle, disconnect the negative battery cable.
- When utilizing a booster battery as a starting aid, always connect it in parallel; negative to negative, and positive to positive.
- When arc (electric) welding is to be performed on any part of the vehicle, disconnect the negative battery cable and alternator leads.
- Never unplug the PCM while the engine is running or with the ignition in the **ON** position. Severe and expensive damage may result within the solid state equipment.

TESTING

Voltage Test

1. Make sure the engine is **OFF**, and turn the headlights on for 15–20 seconds to remove any surface charge from the battery.
2. Using a DVOM set to volts DC, probe across the battery terminals.
3. Measure the battery voltage.
4. Write down the voltage reading and proceed to the next test.

No-Load Test

1. Connect a tachometer to the engine.

✳✳ CAUTION

Ensure that the transmission is in PARK and the emergency brake is set. Blocking a wheel is optional and an added safety measure.

2. Turn off all electrical loads (radio, blower motor, wipers, etc.)
3. Start the engine and increase engine speed to approximately 1500 rpm.
4. Measure the voltage reading at the battery with the engine holding a steady 1500 rpm. Voltage should have raised at least 0.5 volts, but no more than 2.5 volts.
5. If the voltage does not go up more than 0.5 volts, the alternator is not charging. If the voltage goes up more than 2.5 volts, the alternator is overcharging.

➡️**Usually under and overcharging is caused by a defective alternator, or its related parts (regulator), and replacement will fix the problem; however, faulty wiring and other problems can cause the charging system to malfunction. Further testing, which is not covered by this book, will reveal the exact component failure. Many automotive parts stores have alternator bench testers available for use by customers. An alternator bench test is the most definitive way to determine the condition of your alternator.**

6. If the voltage is within specifications, proceed to the next test.

Load Test

1. With the engine running, turn on the blower motor and the high beams (or other electrical accessories to place a load on the charging system).
2. Increase and hold engine speed to 2000 rpm.
3. Measure the voltage reading at the battery.
4. The voltage should increase at least 0.5 volts from the voltage test. If the voltage does not meet specifications, the charging system is malfunctioning.

➡️**Usually under and overcharging is caused by a defective alternator, or its related parts (regulator), and replacement will fix the problem; however, faulty wiring and other problems can cause the charging system to malfunction. Further testing, which is not covered by this book, will reveal the exact component failure. Many automotive parts stores have alternator bench testers available for use by customers. An alternator bench test is the most definitive way to determine the condition of your alternator.**

REMOVAL & INSTALLATION

➡️**On some models, the alternator is mounted very low on the engine. On these models, it may be necessary to remove the gravel shield and work from beneath the truck in order to gain access to the alternator.**

1. Disconnect the negative battery cable.
2. Remove the alternator pivot bolt. Push the alternator inward and remove the drive belt.
3. Pull back the rubber boots and disconnect the wiring from the back of the alternator.
4. Remove the alternator mounting bolt, then withdraw the alternator from its bracket.

To install:

5. Position the alternator in its mounting bracket, then lightly tighten the mounting and adjusting bolts.
6. Connect the electrical leads at the rear of the alternator.
7. Adjust the belt tension.
8. Connect the negative battery cable.
9. Start the engine and check the charging system for proper operation.

Regulator

All models are equipped with an electronic regulator which is attached to the brush assembly internally in the alternator housing. If faulty, it must be replaced; there are no adjustments which can be made.

REMOVAL & INSTALLATION

The electronic regulator is soldered to the brush assembly inside the alternator. It is non-adjustable, and must be replaced together with the brush assembly, if faulty.

1. Remove the alternator.

2. Remove the through-bolts and separate the front cover from the stator housing.

3. Unsolder the wire connecting the diode plate to the brush at the brush terminal.

4. Remove the bolt retaining the diode plate to the rear cover.

5. Remove the nut securing the battery terminal bolt.

6. Lift the stator slightly, together with the diode plate, to gain access to the diode plate screw. Remove the screw.

7. Separate the stator and diode, then remove the brush and regulator assembly.

8. On assembly, apply soldering heat sparingly, carrying out the operation as quickly as possible, to avoid damage to the transistors and diodes. Before assembling the alternator halves, bend a piece of wire into an L-shape and slip it through the rear cover, next to the brushes. Use the wire to hold the brushes in a retracted position until the case halves are assembled. Remove the wire carefully, to prevent damage to the slip rings.

9. Install the alternator.

ADJUSTMENT

Regulators on these models are not adjustable.

Battery

Refer to Section 1 for details on battery maintenance.

REMOVAL & INSTALLATION

1. Disconnect the negative battery cable from the terminal, then disconnect the positive cable. Special pullers are available to remove the clamps.

➡ **To avoid sparks, always disconnect the negative cable first and reconnect it last.**

2. Unscrew and remove the battery hold-down clamp.

3. Remove the battery, being careful not to spill any of the acid.

➡ **Spilled acid can be neutralized with a baking soda and water solution. If you somehow get acid into your eyes, flush it out with lots of clean water and get to a doctor as quickly as possible.**

To install:

4. Clean the battery posts thoroughly.

5. Clean the cable clamps using the special tools or a wire brush, both inside and out.

6. Install the battery, then fasten the hold-down clamp.

7. Connect the positive and then the negative cable. Do not hammer them into place. Coat the terminals with grease to prevent corrosion.

✳✳ CAUTION

Make absolutely sure that the battery is connected properly before you turn on the ignition switch. Reversed polarity can burn out the alternator and regulator in a matter of seconds.

Starter

TESTING

Voltage Drop Test

➡ **The battery must be in good condition and fully charged prior to performing this test.**

1. Disable the ignition system by unplugging the coil pack. Verify that the vehicle will not start.

2. Connect a voltmeter between the positive terminal of the battery and the starter **B+** circuit.

3. Turn the ignition key to the **START** position and note the voltage on the meter.

4. If voltage reads 0.5 volts or more, there is high resistance in the starter cables or the cable ground, repair as necessary. If the voltage reading is ok proceed to the next step.

5. Connect a voltmeter between the positive terminal of the battery and the starter **M** circuit.

6. Turn the ignition key to the **START** position and note the voltage on the meter.

7. If voltage reads 0.5 volts or more, there is high resistance in the starter. Repair or replace the starter as necessary.

➡ **Many automotive parts stores have starter bench testers available for use by customers. A starter bench test is the most definitive way to determine the condition of your starter.**

REMOVAL & INSTALLATION

▸ **See Figures 1 and 2**

1. Disconnect the negative battery cable at the battery, then disconnect the positive battery cable at the starter.

2. On 4wd models with the 6-cylinder engine:
   a. Remove the front gravel shield.
   b. Detach the oil pressure switch connector.
   c. Drain the engine oil and remove the oil filter.

✳✳ CAUTION

The EPA warns that prolonged contact with used engine oil may cause a number of skin disorders, including cancer! You should make every effort to minimize your exposure to used engine oil. Protective gloves should be worn when changing the oil. Wash your hands and any other exposed skin areas as soon as possible after exposure to used engine oil. Soap and water, or waterless hand cleaner should be used.

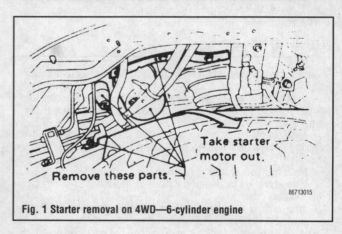

Fig. 1 Starter removal on 4WD—6-cylinder engine

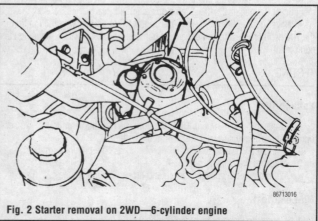

Fig. 2 Starter removal on 2WD—6-cylinder engine

d. Remove the exhaust manifold heat insulator.

e. Remove the fuel tube retainer bolt.

3. On 2wd models with the 6-cylinder engine:

a. Remove the front right wheel.

b. Remove the front gravel shield.

c. Remove the exhaust manifold heat insulator.

d. Remove the exhaust manifold.

e. Detach the oil pressure switch connector.

4. Unfasten the remaining electrical connections at the starter solenoid.

5. Remove the two nuts holding the starter to the bell housing, then pull the starter toward the front of the vehicle and out.

To install:

6. Insert the starter into the bell housing, being sure that the starter drive is not jammed against the flywheel.

7. Tighten the attaching nuts and secure all electrical connections to the starter assembly.

8. Install all remaining components in reverse order of removal.

9. Reconnect the battery cables. If applicable, refill and check the oil level. Check the starter assembly for proper operation.

OVERHAUL

Solenoid Replacement

1. Remove the starter.

2. Unscrew the two solenoid switch (magnetic switch) retaining screws.

3. Remove the solenoid. In order to unhook the solenoid from the starter drive lever, lift it up at the same time that you are pulling it out of the starter housing.

4. Installation is in the reverse order of removal. Make sure that the solenoid switch is properly engaged with the drive lever before tightening the mounting screws.

Sending Units and Sensors

REMOVAL & INSTALLATION

Engine Coolant Temperature Sensor

1. Disconnect the negative battery cable.

2. Drain the cooling system into a suitable container.

➡The system does not have to be drained completely on all engines, but the level must be dropped below the point where the sensor enters the coolant passage.

3. Detach the electrical connector from the sensor.

4. Remove the sensor from the engine or thermostat housing.

5. Installation is the reverse of the removal. Connect the negative battery cable and properly refill the cooling system.

Power Steering Oil Pressure Sensor

1. Disconnect the negative battery cable.

2. Detach the electrical connector from the sensor.

3. Remove the sensor.

4. Installation is the reverse of the removal procedure. Check the power steering fluid level and add, as necessary.

Oil Pressure Sender

1. Disconnect the negative battery cable.

2. Disengage the connector from the pressure sender.

3. Remove the oil pressure sender from the engine.

4. Installation is the reverse of the removal procedure. Check the engine oil level and add, as necessary

STARTER SPECIFICATIONS

Year	Engine Displacement cu. in. (cc)	Country	Model	Starter Type	No-Load Test			Brush Spring Tension (lb.)
					Amps	Volts	RPM	
1989	145.8 (2389)	U.S.	2WD/MT	①	60	11.5	7000	4.0–4.9
				②	100	11.5	7000	4.0–4.9
				③	60	11.5	6500	3.1–5.7
			2WD/AT	N	60	11.5	6000	4.0–4.9
			4WD	R	100	11.0	3900	3.5–4.4
		Canada	All	R	100	11.0	3900	3.5–4.4
	180.6 (2960)	All	All	R	90	11.0	2650	4.0–4.9
1990	145.8 (2389)	U.S.	2WD/MT	②	100	11.5	7000	4.0–4.9
				③	60	11.5	6500	3.1–5.7
			2WD/AT	④	90	11.0	2950	4.0–4.9
				⑤	50–75	11.0	3000–4000	3.1–5.7
			4WD	④	90	11.0	2950	4.0–4.9
				⑤	50–75	11.0	3000–4000	3.1–5.7
		Canada	All	R	50–75	11.0	3000–4000	3.1–5.7
	180.6 (2960)	All	All	R	90	11.0	2650	4.0–4.9
1991	145.8 (2389)	U.S.	2WD/MT	②	100	11.5	7000	4.0–4.9
				③	60	11.5	6500	3.1–5.7
			2WD/AT	④	90	11.0	2950	4.0–4.9
				⑤	50–75	11.0	3000–4000	3.1–5.7
			4WD	⑤	50–75	11.0	3000–4000	3.1–5.7
				⑥	90	11.0	2950	4.0–4.9
		Canada	All	⑤	50–75	11.0	3000–4000	3.1–5.7
				⑥	90	11.0	2950	4.0–4.9
	180.6 (2960)	All	All	R	90	11.0	2650	4.0–4.9
1992	145.8 (2389)	U.S.	2WD/MT	②	100	11.5	7000	4.0–4.9
				③	60	11.5	6500	3.1–5.7
			2WD/AT	④	90	11.0	2950	4.0–4.9
				⑤	50–75	11.0	3000–4000	3.1–5.7
			4WD	④	90	11.0	2950	4.0–4.9
				⑤	50–75	11.0	3000–4000	3.1–5.7
		Canada	All	R	50–75	11.0	3000–4000	3.1–5.7
	180.6 (2960)	All	All	R	90	11.0	2650	4.0–4.9

86713C01

STARTER SPECIFICATIONS

Year	Engine Displacement cu. in. (cc)	Country	Model	Starter Type	No-Load Test Amps	No-Load Test Volts	No-Load Test RPM	Brush Spring Tension (lb.)
1993	145.8 (2389)	U.S.	2WD/MT	②	100	11.5	7000	4.0–4.9
				③	60	11.5	6500	3.1–5.7
			2WD/AT	④	90	11.0	2950	4.0–4.9
				⑤	50–75	11.0	3000–4000	3.1–5.7
			4WD	⑤	50–75	11.0	3000–4000	3.1–5.7
				⑥	90	11.0	2950	4.0–4.9
		Canada	All	⑤	50–75	11.0	3000–4000	3.1–5.7
				⑥	90	11.0	2950	4.0–4.9
	180.6 (2960)	All	All	R	90	11.0	2650	4.0–4.9
1994	145.8 (2389)	U.S.	2WD/MT	②	100	11.5	7000	4.0–4.9
				③	60	11.5	6500	3.1–5.7
			2WD/AT	④	90	11.0	2950	4.0–4.9
				⑤	50–75	11.0	3000–4000	3.1–5.7
			4WD	④	90	11.0	2950	4.0–4.9
				⑤	50–75	11.0	3000–4000	3.1–5.7
		Canada	All	R	50–75	11.0	3000–4000	3.1–5.7
	180.6 (2960)	All	All	R	90	11.0	2650	4.0–4.9
1995	145.8 (2389)	U.S.	2WD/MT	②	100	11.5	7000	4.0–4.9
				③	60	11.5	6500	3.1–5.7
			2WD/AT	④	90	11.0	2950	4.0–4.9
or S114-607B or S114-528				⑤	50–75	11.0	3000–4000	3.1–5.7
			4WD	⑤	50–75	11.0	3000–4000	3.1–5.7
				⑥	90	11.0	2950	4.0–4.9
		Canada	All	⑤	50–75	11.0	3000–4000	3.1–5.7
				⑥	90	11.0	2950	4.0–4.9
	180.6 (2960)	All	All	R	90	11.0	2650	4.0–4.9

N Non-reduction starter
R Reduction starter
① Hitachi, non-reduction, # S114-605
② Hitachi, non-reduction, # S114-607 or S114-607B
③ Mitsubishi, non-reduction, # M3T38482
④ Hitachi, reduction, # S114-527A or S114-528
⑤ Mitsubishi, reduction, #M1T60281
⑥ Hitachi, reduction, # S114-703A

86713C1B

ENGINE MECHANICAL

GENERAL ENGINE SPECIFICATIONS

Year	Engine Displacement cu. in. (cc)	Fuel System Type	SAE net Horsepower @ rpm	SAE net Torque ft. lb. @ rpm	Bore x Stroke	Comp. Ratio	Oil Pressure (psi) @ 2000 rpm
1989	145.8 (2389)	TBI	106 @ 4800	137 @ 2400	3.50 x 3.78	8.3:1	47–67
	180.6 (2960)	TBI	145 @ 4800	166 @ 2800	3.43 x 3.27	9.0:1	53–67
1990	145.8 (2389)	MFI	134 @ 5200	154 @ 3600	3.50 x 3.78	8.6:1	60–70
	180.6 (2960)	MFI	153 @ 4800	180 @ 4000	3.43 x 3.27	9.0:1	53–65
1991	145.8 (2389)	MFI	134 @ 5200	154 @ 3600	3.50 x 3.78	8.6:1	60–70
	180.6 (2960)	MFI	153 @ 4800	180 @ 4000	3.43 x 3.27	9.0:1	53–65
1992	145.8 (2389)	MFI	134 @ 5200	154 @ 3600	3.50 x 3.78	8.6:1	60–70
	180.6 (2960)	MFI	153 @ 4800	180 @ 4000	3.43 x 3.27	9.0:1	53–65
1993	145.8 (2389)	MFI	134 @ 5200	154 @ 3600	3.50 x 3.78	8.6:1	60–70
	180.6 (2960)	MFI	153 @ 4800	180 @ 4000	3.43 x 3.27	9.0:1	53–65
1994	145.8 (2389)	MFI	134 @ 5200	154 @ 3600	3.50 x 3.78	8.6:1	60–70
	180.6 (2960)	MFI	153 @ 4800	180 @ 4000	3.43 x 3.27	9.0:1	53–65
1995	145.8 (2389)	MFI	134 @ 5200	154 @ 3600	3.50 x 3.78	8.6:1	60–70
	180.6 (2960)	MFI	153 @ 4800	180 @ 4000	3.43 x 3.27	9.0:1	53–65

TBI - THROTTLE BODY FUEL INJECTION
MFI - MULTI-PORT FUEL INJECTION

86713C02

CAMSHAFT SPECIFICATIONS
(All specifications in inches)

Year	Engine Displacement cu. in. (cc)	Journal Diameter					Bearing Clearance	Elevation		End-Play
		1	2	3	4	5		In.	Ex.	
1989	145.8 (2389)	1.2961-1.2968	1.2961-1.2968	1.2961-1.2968	1.2961-1.2968	1.2961-1.2968	0.0024-0.0041	1.5148-1.5168	1.5150-1.5170	0.008
	180.6 (2960)	1.8866-1.8874①	1.8472-1.8480	1.8472-1.8480	1.8472-1.8480	1.6701-1.6709	0.0018-0.0035	1.5566-1.5641	1.5566-1.5641	0.0012-0.0024
1990	145.8 (2389)	1.2967-1.2974	1.2967-1.2974	1.2967-1.2974	1.2967-1.2974	1.2967-1.2974	0.0018-0.0035	1.7653-1.7728	1.7653-1.7728	0.0028-0.0059
	180.6 (2960)	1.8866-1.8874①	1.8472-1.8480	1.8472-1.8480	1.8472-1.8480	1.6701-1.6709	0.0024-0.0041	1.5566-1.5641	1.5566-1.5641	0.0012-0.0024
1991	145.8 (2389)	1.2967-1.2974	1.2967-1.2974	1.2967-1.2974	1.2967-1.2974	1.2967-1.2974	0.0018-0.0035	1.7653-1.7728	1.7653-1.7728	0.0028-0.0059
	180.6 (2960)	1.8866-1.8874①	1.8472-1.8480	1.8472-1.8480	1.8472-1.8480	1.6701-1.6709	0.0018-0.0035	1.5566-1.5641	1.5566-1.5641	0.0012-0.0024
1992	145.8 (2389)	1.2967-1.2974	1.2967-1.2974	1.2967-1.2974	1.2967-1.2974	1.2967-1.2974	0.0018-0.0035	1.7653-1.7728	1.7653-1.7728	0.0028-0.0059
	180.6 (2960)	1.8866-1.8874①	1.8472-1.8480	1.8472-1.8480	1.8472-1.8480	1.6701-1.6709	0.0024-0.0041	1.5566-1.5641	1.5566-1.5641	0.0012-0.0024
1993	145.8 (2389)	1.2967-1.2974	1.2967-1.2974	1.2967-1.2974	1.2967-1.2974	1.2967-1.2974	0.0018-0.0035	1.7653-1.7728	1.7653-1.7728	0.0028-0.0059
	180.6 (2960)	1.8866-1.8874①	1.8472-1.8480	1.8472-1.8480	1.8472-1.8480	1.6701-1.6709	0.0018-0.0035	1.5566-1.5641	1.5566-1.5641	0.0012-0.0024
1994	145.8 (2389)	1.2967-1.2974	1.2967-1.2974	1.2967-1.2974	1.2967-1.2974	1.2967-1.2974	0.0018-0.0035	1.7653-1.7728	1.7653-1.7728	0.0028-0.0059
	180.6 (2960)	1.8866-1.8874①	1.8472-1.8480	1.8472-1.8480	1.8472-1.8480	1.6701-1.6709	0.0024-0.0041	1.5566-1.5641	1.5566-1.5641	0.0012-0.0024
1995	145.8 (2389)	1.2967-1.2974	1.2967-1.2974	1.2967-1.2974	1.2967-1.2974	1.2967-1.2974	0.0018-0.0035	1.7653-1.7728	1.7653-1.7728	0.0028-0.0059
	180.6 (2960)	1.8866-1.8874①	1.8472-1.8480	1.8472-1.8480	1.8472-1.8480	1.6701-1.6709	0.0018-0.0035	1.5566-1.5641	1.5566-1.5641	0.0012-0.0024

① Left-hand camshaft only

VALVE SPECIFICATIONS

Year	Engine Displacement cu. in. (cc)	Seat Angle (deg.)	Face Angle (deg.)	Spring Test Pressure (lbs. @ in.)	Spring Free Height (in.)	Stem-to-Guide Clearance (in.)		Stem Diameter (in.)	
						Intake	Exhaust	Intake	Exhaust
1989	145.8 (2389)	45	45.5	①	②	0.0008-0.0021	0.0016-0.0029	0.3136-0.3142	0.3128-0.3134
	180.6 (2960)	45.5	45	③	④	0.0008-0.0021	0.0016-0.0029	0.2742-0.2748	0.3128-0.3134
1990	145.8 (2389)	45	45.5	⑤	⑥	0.0008-0.0021	0.0016-0.0029	0.2742-0.2748	0.3129-0.3134
	180.6 (2960)	45.5	45	③	④	0.0008-0.0021	0.0012-0.0021	0.2742-0.2748	0.3136-0.3138
1991	145.8 (2389)	45	45.5	⑤	⑥	0.0008-0.0021	0.0016-0.0028	0.2742-0.2748	0.3129-0.3134
	180.6 (2960)	45.5	45	③	④	0.0008-0.0021	0.0016-0.0029	0.2742-0.2748	0.3136-0.3138
1992	145.8 (2389)	45	45.5	⑤	⑥	0.0008-0.0021	0.0016-0.0029	0.2742-0.2748	0.3129-0.3134
	180.6 (2960)	45.5	45	③	④	0.0008-0.0021	0.0012-0.0021	0.2742-0.2748	0.3136-0.3138
1993	145.8 (2389)	45	45.5	⑤	⑥	0.0008-0.0021	0.0016-0.0028	0.2742-0.2748	0.3129-0.3134
	180.6 (2960)	45.5	45	③	④	0.0008-0.0021	0.0016-0.0029	0.2742-0.2748	0.3136-0.3138
1994	145.8 (2389)	45	45.5	⑤	⑥	0.0008-0.0021	0.0016-0.0029	0.2742-0.2748	0.3129-0.3134
	180.6 (2960)	45.5	45	③	④	0.0008-0.0021	0.0012-0.0021	0.2742-0.2748	0.3136-0.3138
1995	145.8 (2389)	45	45.5	⑤	⑥	0.0008-0.0021	0.0016-0.0028	0.2742-0.2748	0.3129-0.3134
	180.6 (2960)	45.5	45	③	④	0.0008-0.0021	0.0016-0.0029	0.2742-0.2748	0.3136-0.3138

① Outer: 50.7 @ 1.575
Inner: 24.3 @ 1.378
② Outer: 1.9594
Inner: 1.7362
③ Outer: 117.7 @ 1.181
Inner: 57.3 @ 0.984
④ Outer: 2.016
Inner: 1.736
⑤ Intake
Outer: 135.8 @ 1.480
Inner: 63.9 @ 1.283
Exhaust
Outer: 144.0 @ 1.343
Inner: 73.9 @ 1.146
⑥ Intake
Outer: 2.2614
Inner: 2.1000
Exhaust
Outer: 2.0949
Inner: 1.8878

86713C04

86713C03

CRANKSHAFT AND CONNECTING ROD SPECIFICATIONS
(All specifications in inches)

Year	Engine Displacement cu. in. (cc)	Crankshaft Main Brg. Journal Dia.	Crankshaft Main Brg. Oil Clearance	Crankshaft Shaft End-Play	Thrust on No.	Connecting Rod Journal Diameter	Connecting Rod Oil Clearance	Connecting Rod Side Clearance
1989	145.8 (2389)	2.3599-2.3604	①	0.0020-0.0071	3	1.9670-1.9675	0.0006-0.0019	0.008-0.012
	180.6 (2960)	2.4790-2.4793	0.0011-0.0022	0.0020-0.0067	4	1.9667-1.9675	0.0006-0.0021	0.0079-0.0138
1990	145.8 (2389)	2.5057-2.5060	0.0008-0.0019	0.0020-0.0071	3	1.7701-1.7706	0.0004-0.0014	0.008-0.016
	180.6 (2960)	2.4790-2.4793	0.0011-0.0022	0.0020-0.0067	4	1.9667-1.9675	0.0006-0.0021	0.0079-0.0138
1991	145.8 (2389)	2.5057-2.5060	0.0008-0.0019	0.0020-0.0071	3	1.7701-1.7706	0.0004-0.0014	0.008-0.016
	180.6 (2960)	2.4790-2.4793	0.0011-0.0022	0.0020-0.0067	4	1.9667-1.9675	0.0006-0.0021	0.0079-0.0138
1992	145.8 (2389)	2.5057-2.5060	0.0008-0.0019	0.0020-0.0071	3	1.7701-1.7706	0.0004-0.0014	0.008-0.016
	180.6 (2960)	2.4790-2.4793	0.0011-0.0022	0.0020-0.0067	4	1.9667-1.9675	0.0006-0.0021	0.0079-0.0138
1993	145.8 (2389)	2.5057-2.5060	0.0008-0.0019	0.0020-0.0071	3	1.7701-1.7706	0.0004-0.0014	0.008-0.016
	180.6 (2960)	2.4790-2.4793	0.0011-0.0022	0.0020-0.0067	4	1.9667-1.9675	0.0006-0.0021	0.0079-0.0138
1994	145.8 (2389)	2.5057-2.5060	0.0008-0.0019	0.0020-0.0071	3	1.7701-1.7706	0.0004-0.0014	0.008-0.016
	180.6 (2960)	2.4790-2.4793	0.0011-0.0022	0.0020-0.0067	4	1.9667-1.9675	0.0006-0.0021	0.0079-0.0138
1995	145.8 (2389)	2.5057-2.5060	0.0008-0.0019	0.0020-0.0071	3	1.7701-1.7706	0.0004-0.0014	0.008-0.016
	180.6 (2960)	2.4790-2.4793	0.0011-0.0022	0.0020-0.0067	4	1.9667-1.9675	0.0006-0.0021	0.0079-0.0138

① No. 1 & 5: 0.0008-0.0024
No. 2, 3 & 4: 0.0008-0.0030

86713C05

PISTON AND RING SPECIFICATIONS
(All specifications in inches)

Year	Engine Displacement cu. in. (cc)	Ring Gap #1 Compr.	Ring Gap #2 Compr.	Ring Gap Oil Control	Ring Side Clearance #1 Compr.	Ring Side Clearance #2 Compr.	Ring Side Clearance Oil Control	Piston Clearance
1989	145.8 (2389)	0.0110-0.0150	0.0098-0.0138	0.0079-0.0236	0.0016-0.0029	0.0012-0.0025	—	0.0010-0.0018
	180.6 (2960)	0.0083-0.0173	0.0071-0.0173	0.0079-0.0299	0.0016-0.0029	0.0012-0.0025	0.0006-0.0075	0.0010-0.0018
1990	145.8 (2389)	0.0118-0.0205	0.0177-0.0272	0.0079-0.0272	0.0016-0.0031	0.0012-0.0028	0.0026-0.0053	0.0008-0.0016
	180.6 (2960)	0.0083-0.0173	0.0071-0.0173	0.0079-0.0299	0.0016-0.0029	0.0012-0.0025	0.0006-0.0075	0.0010-0.0018
1991	145.8 (2389)	0.0118-0.0205	0.0177-0.0272	0.0079-0.0272	0.0016-0.0031	0.0012-0.0028	—	0.0008-0.0016
	180.6 (2960)	0.0083-0.0173	0.0071-0.0173	0.0079-0.0299	0.0016-0.0031	0.0012-0.0028	0.0026-0.0053	0.0008-0.0016
1992	145.8 (2389)	0.0118-0.0205	0.0177-0.0272	0.0079-0.0272	0.0016-0.0031	0.0012-0.0028	0.0006-0.0075	0.0006-0.0014
	180.6 (2960)	0.0083-0.0173	0.0071-0.0173	0.0079-0.0299	0.0016-0.0031	0.0012-0.0028	0.0026-0.0053	0.0008-0.0016
1993	145.8 (2389)	0.0118-0.0205	0.0177-0.0272	0.0079-0.0272	0.0016-0.0031	0.0012-0.0028	—	0.0008-0.0016
	180.6 (2960)	0.0083-0.0173	0.0071-0.0173	0.0079-0.0299	0.0016-0.0031	0.0012-0.0028	0.0026-0.0053	0.0006-0.0014
1994	145.8 (2389)	0.0118-0.0205	0.0177-0.0272	0.0079-0.0272	0.0016-0.0031	0.0012-0.0028	0.0026-0.0053	0.0008-0.0016
	180.6 (2960)	0.0083-0.0173	0.0071-0.0173	0.0079-0.0299	0.0016-0.0031	0.0012-0.0028	0.0026-0.0053	0.0010-0.0018
1995	145.8 (2389)	0.0118-0.0205	0.0177-0.0272	0.0079-0.0272	0.0016-0.0031	0.0012-0.0028	—	0.0008-0.0016
	180.6 (2960)	0.0083-0.0173	0.0071-0.0173	0.0079-0.0299	0.0016-0.0029	0.0012-0.0025	0.0006-0.0075	0.0006-0.0014

86713C06

TORQUE SPECIFICATIONS
(All specifications in ft. lbs.)

Year	Engine Displacement cu. in. (cc)	Cyl. Head	Conn. Rod	Main Bearing	Crankshaft Damper	Flywheel	Manifold Intake	Manifold Exhaust
1989	145.8 (2389)	54-61	①	33-40	87-116	101-116	12-15	12-15
	180.6 (2960)	②	①	67-74	90-98	72-80	12-14③	13-16
1990	145.8 (2389)	④	①	34-38	87-116	72-80	12-15	12-15
	180.6 (2960)	④	①	67-74	90-98	72-80	12-14③	13-16
1991	145.8 (2389)	④	①	34-38	87-116	⑤	12-15	12-15
	180.6 (2960)	②	①	67-74	90-98	72-80	12-14③	13-16
1992	145.8 (2389)	④	①	34-38	87-116	⑤	12-15	12-15
	180.6 (2960)	④	①	67-74	90-98	72-80	12-14③	13-16
1993	145.8 (2389)	④	①	34-38	87-116	⑤	12-15	12-15
	180.6 (2960)	④	①	67-74	90-98	72-80	12-14③	13-16
1994	145.8 (2389)	④	①	34-38	87-116	⑤	12-15	12-15
	180.6 (2960)	②	①	67-74	90-98	72-80	12-14③	13-16
1995	145.8 (2389)	②	①	34-38	87-116	⑤	12-15	12-15
	180.6 (2960)	②	①	67-74	90-98	72-80	12-14③	13-16

① 1st step: 10-12 ft. lbs.
2nd step: 28-33 ft. lbs.
② 1st step: 22 ft. lbs.
2nd step: 43 ft. lbs.
3rd step: loosen completely
4th step: 22 ft. lbs.
5th step: 54-61 ft. lbs.
③ Figure is for bolts.
tighten nut to 17-20 ft. lbs.
④ 1st step: 22 ft. lbs.
2nd step: 58 ft. lbs.
3rd step: loosen completely
4th step: 22 ft. lbs.
5th step: 54-61 ft. lbs.
⑤ MT flywheel: 105-112 ft. lbs.
AT driveplate: 69-76 ft. lbs.

86713C07

Engine

REMOVAL & INSTALLATION

♦ **See Figures 3 and 4**

1. Disconnect the negative battery cable.
2. Remove the engine under cover.
3. Disconnect the windshield washer hose. Scribe matchmarks around the hinges (for easy installation) and remove the hood.

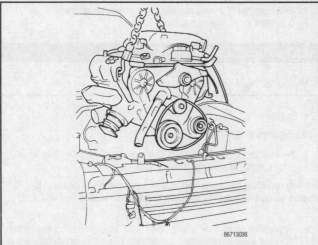

Fig. 3 Removing the engine from the vehicle—6-cylinder shown (most engines similar)

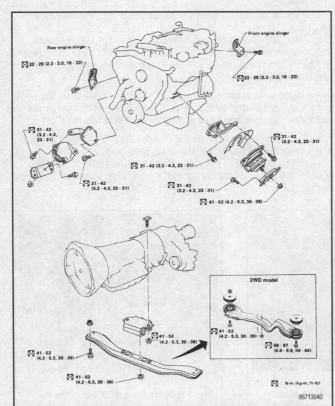

Fig. 4 The engine is secured in the vehicle through the use of motor mounts and a crossmember

⁂ CAUTION

The EPA warns that prolonged contact with used engine oil may cause a number of skin disorders, including cancer! You should make every effort to minimize your exposure to used engine oil. Protective gloves should be worn when changing the oil. Wash your hands and any other exposed skin areas as soon as possible after exposure to used engine oil. Soap and water, or waterless hand cleaner should be used.

4. Drain the engine oil. Drain the engine coolant from the radiator and the cylinder block.

⁂ CAUTION

When draining the coolant, keep in mind that cats and dogs are attracted by ethylene glycol antifreeze, and are quite likely to drink any that is left in an uncovered container or in puddles on the ground. This will prove fatal in sufficient quantity. Always drain the coolant into a sealable container. Coolant should be reused unless it is contaminated or several years old.

5. If equipped, drain the automatic transmission fluid.
6. Disconnect the air cleaner hose, then remove the air cleaner.
7. Relieve the fuel pressure as described in Section 5. Disconnect and plug all fuel lines.
8. Remove the radiator and shroud as detailed later in this section. On models with an automatic transmission oil cooler, disconnect and plug the oil lines at the radiator.
9. Remove the coupling fan.
10. Disconnect the two heater hoses at the engine.
11. Remove the drive belts.
12. Remove the power steering pump from its bracket (if equipped). Disconnect the ground strap from the bracket.
13. On models with air conditioning, loosen the drive belt and remove the air conditioning compressor. Position it out of the way with the refrigerant lines still attached.
14. Disconnect the transmission control linkage.
15. On 4wd models, disconnect the starter leads and remove the starter. On 2wd models, disconnect the starter motor leads.
16. Disconnect the speedometer cable. Tag and disconnect any electrical leads at the transmission.
17. On models with a manual transmission, remove the clutch release cylinder and its bracket from the transmission. Position it aside without disconnecting the hydraulic lines.
18. Remove the bolts and disconnect the exhaust pipe at the manifold.
19. On 4wd models, matchmark the front driveshaft to the transfer case flange, then remove the front driveshaft.
20. On 4wd models, carefully slide a floor jack underneath the front differential carrier and remove the front mounting bolt. Remove the rear mounting bolts and crossmember, then slowly lower the carrier.
21. On 4wd models, remove the transmission-to-engine bracket mounting nuts.
22. On 4wd models, remove the mounting bolts for the front engine mounts.
23. Attach an engine hoist chain to the lifting brackets on the engine, then raise the engine just enough to ease the weight on the front and rear engine mount insulators.
24. On 4wd models, remove the front differential carrier.
25. On 2wd models, matchmark the rear driveshaft to the transmission flange, then remove the driveshaft. Be sure to plug the hole in the extension housing.
26. On 2wd models, remove the transmission-to-rear engine mount bracket bolts.
27. On 2wd models, remove the transmission member.
28. On 4wd models, remove the transmission-to-engine mounting bolts.
29. Tighten the engine hoist chain and carefully lift the engine (4wd) or engine/transmission (2wd) assembly up and out of the truck. Be very careful not to bump into anything as the engine assembly comes out of the engine compartment.

To install:
30. Slowly lower the engine or engine/transmission assembly into the engine compartment.

31. Raise the transmission onto the crossmember with a floor jack.

32. Align the holes in the engine mounts and the frame, install the bolts, then remove the engine hoist chain.

33. On 4wd models, install the transmission-to-engine mounting bolts. Tighten the 16mm and 25mm bolts to 22–29 ft. lbs. (29–39 Nm).

34. On 2wd models, install the transmission member.

35. On 2wd models, install the transmission-to-rear engine mount bracket bolts and tighten to 30–38 ft. lbs. (41–52 Nm).

36. On 2wd models, install the rear driveshaft to the transmission flange.

37. On 4wd models, install the front differential carrier.

38. Install the mounting bolts for the front engine mounts and tighten to 23–31 ft. lbs. (31–42 Nm).

39. On 4wd models, install the transmission-to-engine bracket mounting nuts and tighten to 30–38 ft. lbs. (41–52 Nm).

40. On 4wd models, align the matchmarks on the front driveshaft with those on the transfer case flange, then install the front driveshaft.

41. Connect the exhaust pipe to the manifold.

42. Install the clutch release cylinder and its bracket to the transmission.

43. Connect the speedometer cable. Connect any electrical leads at the transmission.

44. On 4wd models, connect the starter leads and install the starter. On 2wd models, connect the starter motor leads.

45. Install the air conditioning compressor and drive belt.

46. Install the power steering pump and its bracket (if equipped). Be sure to connect the ground strap to the bracket.

47. Install and adjust the drive belts.

48. Connect the heater hoses.

49. Install the coupling fan.

50. Install the radiator and shroud. If so equipped, unplug and connect the automatic transmission oil cooler lines.

51. Install all fuel lines and the air cleaner assembly.

52. Refill the engine, cooling system and, if applicable, the automatic transmission.

53. Install and adjust the hood.

54. Install the engine under cover.

55. Connect the negative battery cable, then start the truck and road test it for proper operation. Recheck all fluid levels and add, as necessary.

Cylinder Head Cover

REMOVAL & INSTALLATION

♦ See Figures 5, 6 and 7

1. Disconnect the negative battery cable. Remove the air cleaner assembly.

2. Disconnect the PCV hose from the cylinder head cover. Mark and reposition the spark plug wires, if necessary.

3. Remove the nuts and washers, then lift the cover off the cylinder head. Cover the oil return hole in the head to prevent dirt or objects from falling in. Remove the gasket.

To install:

4. Replace or reinstall the cover gasket, as necessary. Be sure to clean the mating surfaces. If the old gasket shows any signs of damage, breaks or cracks, it should be replaced.

➡ **When installing the cylinder head cover (valve cover), always torque the 2 center retaining bolts to half their specified torque first; then, working towards the ends, torque the retaining bolts in equal steps to their final torque.**

5. On all 1989 models, tighten the nuts evenly to 0.7–2.2 ft. lbs. (1–3 Nm).

6. On 1990–95 models, tighten the nuts evenly to 0.7–2.2 ft. lbs. (1–3 Nm) on 6-cylinder models or to 5–8 ft. lbs. (7–11 Nm) on 4-cylinder engines.

7. Reconnect the PCV hose and install the air cleaner assembly.

8. Connect the negative battery cable.

Rocker Arm/Shaft Assembly

REMOVAL & INSTALLATION

Z24i Engine

♦ See Figures 8, 9, 10, 11 and 12

1. Remove the cylinder head cover. The rocker shaft assembly can be removed by simply unthreading its retaining bolts.

➡ **When removing the bolts, DO NOT remove the No. 1 and No. 5 bracket bolts, since the rocker shaft bracket and rocker arm will spring out.**

2. Remove the rocker shaft bracket, then slide the valve rockers and springs off of the rocker shaft. Be absolutely sure to keep all parts in the order in which they were removed; they must be reassembled in the same position and location.

3. Inspect the rocker arms and shaft for damage; replace as necessary.

To install:

4. Slide the springs and rockers onto the shafts in the order that they were removed.

5. The intake rocker shaft has a slit on its leading edge, but the exhaust shaft does not. Additionally, each shaft has one punch mark on its leading edge. The shafts should be assembled with these marks facing upward, as they are used for oil hole identification.

➡ **The intake and exhaust rockers for Cylinders No. 1 and 3 are the same and are identified by the mark "1". The same holds true for the rockers on Cylinders No. 2 and 4; they are identified with a "2".**

6. The rocker shaft brackets are also marked as to their original location; simply match them to the like marks on the cylinder head.

7. At this point, reinsert a bracket bolt into holes for the No. 1 and No. 5 brackets. This will insure that the assembly stays together while you mount it on the head.

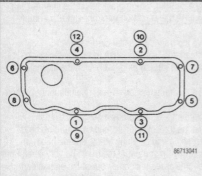

Fig. 5 Cylinder head cover torque sequence—KA24E engine

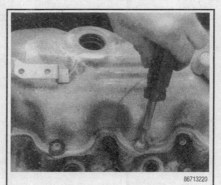

Fig. 6 Remove the cylinder head cover retaining screws—do not lose the washers

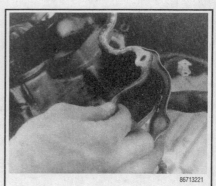

Fig. 7 Remove the gasket and clean the cylinder head cover

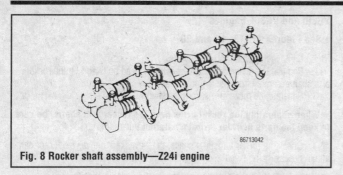

Fig. 8 Rocker shaft assembly—Z24i engine

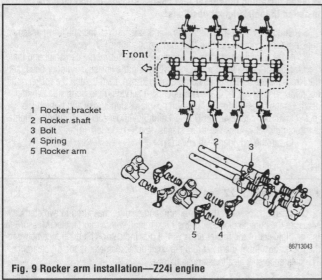

1 Rocker bracket
2 Rocker shaft
3 Bolt
4 Spring
5 Rocker arm

Fig. 9 Rocker arm installation—Z24i engine

8. Mount the rocker shaft assembly on the cylinder head in a manner that accommodates the camshaft knock pin, then tighten the retaining bolts gradually, in two or three stages, to 11–18 ft. lbs. (15–25 Nm).

9. Before installing the cylinder head cover, please refer to Section 2 for valve lash adjustment.

KA24E Engine

▶ **See Figures 13, 14, 15 and 16**

➡ **The KA24E engine is unique in that its hydraulic lifters are installed inside the rocker arm assemblies. If a hydraulic lifter is kept on its side, even when installed in the rocker arm assembly, there is the possibility of air entering it. After removal, always set rocker arm assembly straight up.**

1. Remove the cylinder head cover. The rocker shaft assembly can be removed by simply removing its retaining bolts.

➡ **When removing the bolts, loosen them in two or three stages, from the outside to the inside, in the proper sequence.**

2. Remove the rocker shaft retainers, then slide the valve rockers and springs off of the rocker shaft. Be absolutely sure to keep all parts in the order in which they were removed; they must be reassembled in the same position and location.

3. Inspect the rocker arms and shaft for damage; and replace as necessary.

To install:

4. Slide the springs and rockers onto the shafts in the order that they were removed.

5. Install the rocker retainers so that the cutouts are facing in the direction shown in the illustration.

6. The intake rocker shaft has a single punch mark on its leading edge, but the exhaust shaft has two punch marks. The shafts should be assembled with these marks facing upward, as they are used for oil hole identification.

7. The rocker shaft brackets are also marked as to their original location; simply match them to the like marks on the cylinder head.

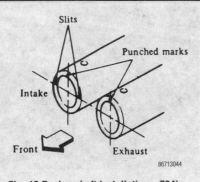

Fig. 10 Rocker shaft installation—Z24i engine

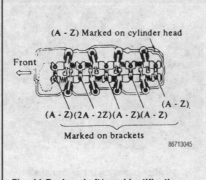

Fig. 11 Rocker shaft/arm identification—Z24i engine

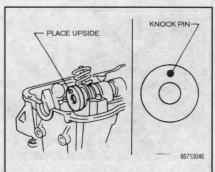

Fig. 12 Make sure that the camshaft knockpin is in the UP position—Z24i engine

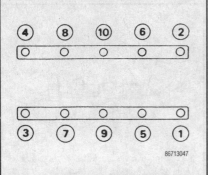

Fig. 13 Rocker shaft assembly loosening sequence—KA24E engine

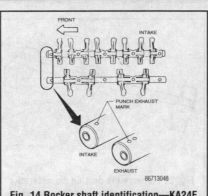

Fig. 14 Rocker shaft identification—KA24E engine

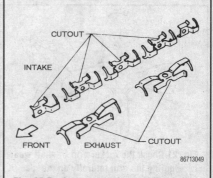

Fig. 15 Rocker arm retainer positioning—KA24E engine

8. Mount the rocker shaft assembly on the cylinder head in a manner that accommodates the camshaft knock pin, then tighten the retaining bolts gradually, in two or three stages to 27–30 ft. lbs. (37–41 Nm). Follow the tightening sequence shown in the illustration.

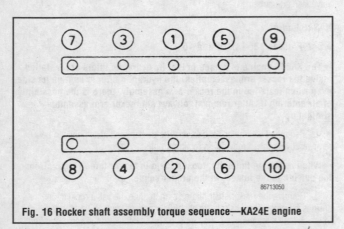

Fig. 16 Rocker shaft assembly torque sequence—KA24E engine

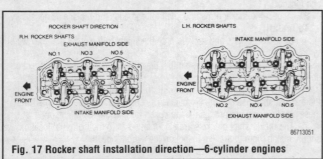

Fig. 17 Rocker shaft installation direction—6-cylinder engines

VG30i and VG30E Engines

♦ **See Figures 17, 18, 19 and 20**

1. Remove the cylinder head cover(s).
2. Remove the rocker arm shaft-to-cylinder head bolts and lift the rocker arm/shaft assembly from the cylinder head.
3. Separate the rocker arms from the shaft.

➡ **When separating the rocker arms from the rocker arm shafts, be sure to keep the parts in order for reinstallation purposes.**

4. Check the rocker arms, the shafts, the valves and the valve lifter for damage. If necessary, replace the damaged components.

➡ **When installing the rocker arm shafts, be certain that they are installed in their original positions.**

5. Slide the rocker arms onto the shafts, then install the shaft/arm assemblies onto the cylinder head in their proper positions.
6. Make sure the camshaft knock pin is at the top of the camshaft and that the lobe is not in the lifted position. If servicing the left-side cylinder head, set the No. 1 piston at TDC of its compression stroke, then tighten the rocker shaft bolts for cylinder No. 2, 4 and 6 cylinders. If servicing the right-side cylinder head, set the No. 4 piston at TDC of its compression stroke and tighten the rocker shaft bolts for cylinder No. 1, 3 and 5 cylinder rocker shaft bolts. Tighten all bolts gradually, in two or three stages, to 13–16 ft. lbs. (18–22 Nm).
7. Install the cylinder head cover(s).

INSPECTION

♦ **See Figures 21, 22 and 23**

Oil clearance between the rocker arm and shaft is measured in two steps. Measure the outside diameter of the rocker shaft with a micrometer. Measure the inside diameter of the rocker arms with a dial indicator. The difference between the rocker arm inner diameter and the shaft outer diameter is the oil clearance. The clearance specifications are as follows:

Fig. 18 View of the rocker shaft installed—all 6-cylinder engines are similar

Fig. 19 After removing the rocker shaft assembly, keep all bolts in the proper order if possible

Fig. 20 Use a torque wrench when installing the rocker shaft assembly

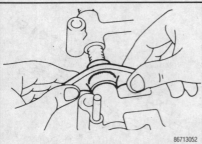

Fig. 21 Check the rocker arm-to-shaft wear by wiggling the arm laterally on the shaft—little or no movement should be felt

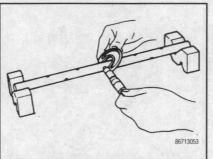

Fig. 22 Measure the outside diameter of the rocker shaft with an outside micrometer

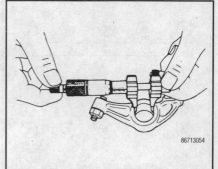

Fig. 23 Measure the inside diameter of the rocker shaft with an inside micrometer

- Z24i: 0.0003–0.0019 in. (0.008–0.050mm)
- VG30i: 0.0003–0.0019 in. (0.008–0.050mm)
- KA24E: 0.0005–0.0020 in. (0.012–0.050mm)
- VG30E: 0.0003–0.0019 in. (0.008–0.050mm)

If specifications are not within these ranges, replace either the rocker shaft or rocker arm. Clearance can also be checked by moving the rocker arm laterally on the shaft when assembled. **There should be little or no movement.**

While disassembled, check the cam follower end (the flat end that contacts the camshaft) of the rocker arm for excess wear. The surface should be smooth and shiny. If excess wear is evident, check the lobe of the camshaft, since it may also be worn.

Reassemble the rocker shaft assemblies in the exact opposite order of removal. Accelerated camshaft wear and/or sloppy valve action will result if rocker arms are mixed and operate against the wrong cam lobes.

Thermostat

REMOVAL & INSTALLATION

▶ **See Figures 24, 25, 26 and 27**

1. Drain the engine coolant into a clean container, so that the level is below the thermostat housing.

✳✳ CAUTION

When draining the coolant, keep in mind that cats and dogs are attracted by ethylene glycol antifreeze, and are quite likely to drink any that is left in an uncovered container or in puddles on the ground. This will prove fatal in sufficient quantity. Always drain the coolant into a sealable container. Coolant should be reused unless it is contaminated or several years old.

2. If necessary, disconnect the upper radiator hose at the water outlet.
3. Loosen the securing nuts, then remove the water outlet, gasket, and thermostat from the thermostat housing.
4. When installing the thermostat, always use a new gasket with sealer and make sure the thermostat spring is facing the inside of the engine. The water outlet housing on VG30i and VG30E engines has the letters **UPR** and an arrow embossed on the flange edge; they should always be pointing up. The KA24E, VG30i and VG30E engines have a jiggle valve on the thermostat which should always be facing up. Water outlet mounting screws should be tightened to 12–15 ft. lbs. (16–21 Nm) on all engines but the KA24E, which should be tightened to 5–6 ft. lbs. (7–8 Nm). Refill and check the coolant level.

Intake Manifold

REMOVAL & INSTALLATION

Z24i and KA24E Engines

▶ **See Figures 28 and 29**

➡ **Always relieve the fuel pressure before removing any fuel system component.**

1. Relieve the fuel system pressure, as described in Section 5.
2. Drain the coolant and disconnect the negative battery cable.

✳✳ CAUTION

When draining the coolant, keep in mind that cats and dogs are attracted by ethylene glycol antifreeze, and are quite likely to drink any that is left in an uncovered container or in puddles on the ground. This will prove fatal in sufficient quantity. Always drain the coolant into a sealable container. Coolant should be reused unless it is contaminated or several years old.

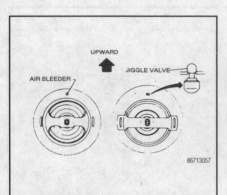

Fig. 24 The jiggle valve should always face upward

Fig. 25 Remove the thermostat assembly retaining bolts

Fig. 26 In some cases the hose may be left attached to the housing

Fig. 27 Remove the thermostat from the engine—other models similar

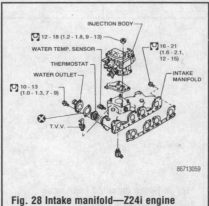

Fig. 28 Intake manifold—Z24i engine

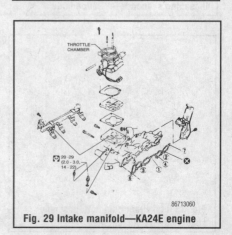

Fig. 29 Intake manifold—KA24E engine

3. Remove the air cleaner hoses.
4. Disconnect the radiator hoses from the intake manifold.
5. Remove the throttle cable, then disconnect the fuel pipe and the return fuel line. Plug the fuel pipe to prevent fuel spillage.

➡Before unplugging wires and hoses, mark each wire or hose and its connection with a piece of masking tape, then mark the two pieces of tape with the numbers 1, 2, 3, etc. When assembling, simply match the pieces of tape.

6. Remove all remaining wires and tubes, including the EGR and PCV tubes, from the rear of the intake manifold. Remove the manifold supports.
7. Unbolt the intake manifold. Remove the manifold with injectors.

To install:
8. Clean the gasket mounting surfaces, then install the intake manifold on the engine. Always use a new intake manifold gasket. Tighten the mounting bolts outward from the center (using multiple passes) to 12–15 ft. lbs. (16–21 Nm).
9. Fasten all electrical connections and tubes, including the EGR and PCV tubes, to the rear of the intake manifold. Install the manifold supports.
10. Reconnect the fuel pipe and the return fuel line, then install the throttle cable.
11. Connect the radiator hoses to the intake manifold.
12. Install the air cleaner hoses.
13. Refill the coolant level and connect the battery cable. Start the engine and check for leaks.

VG30i Engine

▶ See Figures 30, 31 and 32

1. Relieve the fuel system pressure (refer to Section 5), then disconnect the negative battery cable.
2. Drain the engine coolant.

✳✳ CAUTION

When draining the coolant, keep in mind that cats and dogs are attracted by ethylene glycol antifreeze, and are quite likely to drink

any that is left in an uncovered container or in puddles on the ground. This will prove fatal in sufficient quantity. Always drain the coolant into a sealable container. Coolant should be reused unless it is contaminated or several years old.

3. Disconnect all valves, lines, hoses, cables and or brackets to gain access to the intake manifold assembly retaining bolts.
4. Remove the intake manifold and injection unit assembly. Loosen the intake manifold bolts (in steps) in the sequence shown.

To install:
5. Install the intake manifold and injection unit assembly with a new gasket to the engine. Tighten the manifold bolts and nuts in two or three stages, to 12–14 ft. lbs. (16–20 Nm) in the order shown.
6. Connect all valves, lines, hoses, cables and or brackets to the intake manifold assembly.
7. Refill the cooling system. Reconnect the battery cables.
8. Check fluid levels, then start the engine and check for leaks.

VG30E Engine

▶ See Figures 33, 34, 35 and 36

1. Relieve the fuel system pressure (refer to Section 5), then disconnect the negative battery cable.
2. Drain the coolant by removing drain plugs from both sides of the cylinder block.

✳✳ CAUTION

When draining the coolant, keep in mind that cats and dogs are attracted by ethylene glycol antifreeze, and are quite likely to drink any that is left in an uncovered container or in puddles on the ground. This will prove fatal in sufficient quantity. Always drain the coolant into a sealable container. Coolant should be reused unless it is contaminated or several years old.

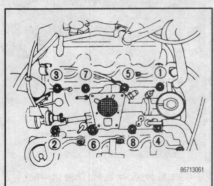

Fig. 30 Intake manifold assembly bolt loosening sequence—VG30i engine

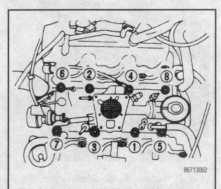

Fig. 31 Intake manifold assembly bolt torque sequence—VG30i engine

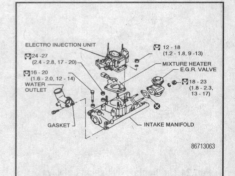

Fig. 32 Intake manifold assembly—VG30i engine

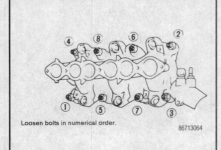

Loosen bolts in numerical order.

Fig. 33 Intake manifold bolt loosening sequence—VG30E engine

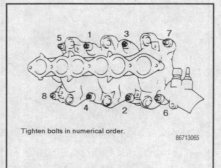

Tighten bolts in numerical order.

Fig. 34 Intake manifold bolt torque sequence—VG30E engine

Fig. 35 Removing the intake manifold assembly—read the entire service procedure before beginning this repair

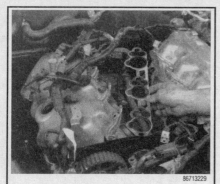

Fig. 36 ALWAYS replace the intake manifold gasket upon installation

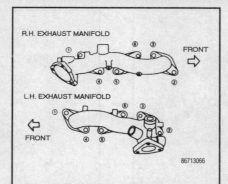

Fig. 37 Exhaust manifold bolt loosening sequence—VG30i and VG30E engines

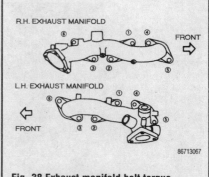

Fig. 38 Exhaust manifold bolt torque sequence—VG30i and VG30E engines

3. Disconnect all valves, lines, hoses, cables and or brackets to gain access to the collector assembly retaining bolts.

4. Remove the collector-to-intake manifold bolts (working from the end bolts to the center bolts).

5. Disconnect the fuel feed and return lines from the injector fuel tube assembly.

6. Detach all fuel injector harness connectors.

7. Remove the injector fuel tube assembly.

8. Tag and separate the engine temperature switch harness connector as well as the thermal transmitter harness connector. Disconnect the coolant line at the thermostat housing.

9. Loosen the intake manifold bolts using multiple passes of the sequence shown, then remove the manifold from the engine.

To install:

10. Install the intake manifold and a new gasket to the engine. Tighten the manifold bolts and nuts (in two or three stages) to 2.2–3.6 ft. lbs. (3–5 Nm), then tighten all bolts to 12–14 ft. lbs. (16–20 Nm) and all nuts to 17–20 ft. lbs. (24–27 Nm), in the order shown.

11. Fasten the engine temperature switch harness connector and the thermal transmitter harness connector. Install the coolant line at the thermostat housing.

12. Install the injector fuel tube assembly.

13. Secure all fuel injector harness connectors.

14. Connect the fuel feed and fuel return lines to the injector fuel tube assembly.

15. Install the collector assembly with a new gasket. Tighten the collector-to-intake manifold bolts in two or three stages (working from the center bolts outward) to 13–16 ft. lbs. (18–22 Nm).

16. Connect all valves, lines, hoses, cables and or brackets to the collector assembly.

17. Refill the cooling system. Reconnect the battery cable.

18. Check all fluid levels and add, as necessary, then start the engine and check for leaks.

Exhaust Manifold

REMOVAL & INSTALLATION

Z24i and KA24E Engines

1. Disconnect the negative battery cable.

2. Remove the air cleaner assembly. Remove the heat shield.

3. Tag and disconnect the high tension wires from the spark plugs on the exhaust side of the engine.

4. Detach the oxygen sensor connector.

5. Disconnect the exhaust pipe from the exhaust manifold.

➡ Soak the exhaust pipe retaining bolts with penetrating oil, if necessary, to loosen them.

6. Remove the exhaust manifold mounting nuts, then remove the manifold from the cylinder head.

To install:

7. Clean the exhaust gasket mounting surfaces.

8. Using new gaskets, install the manifold onto the engine and, working from the center outward, tighten the exhaust manifold nuts/bolts to 12–15 ft. lbs. (16–21 Nm).

9. Reconnect the exhaust pipe to the manifold with a new gasket. Attach the oxygen sensor connector.

10. Connect the spark plug wires, then install the air cleaner and any related hoses. Install the heat shield.

11. Connect the negative battery cable.

12. Start the engine and check for exhaust leaks.

VG30i and VG30E Engines

▶ See Figures 37 thru 42

1. Disconnect the negative battery cable.

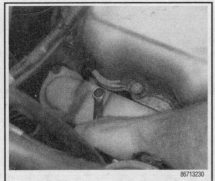

Fig. 39 Remove the exhaust manifold cover bolts

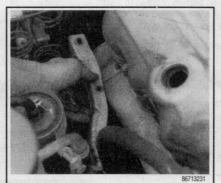

Fig. 40 Remove the exhaust manifold cover

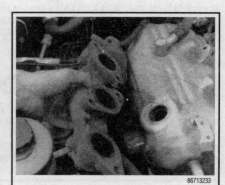

Fig. 41 After removing the retaining bolts, lift out the manifold assembly

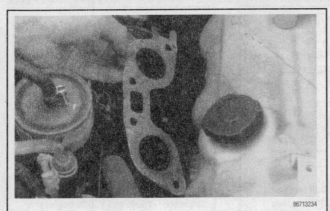

Fig. 42 Always replace the exhaust manifold gasket—note the location of the gasket for correct installation

2. Remove the exhaust manifold sub-cover and manifold cover. Separate the EGR tube from the right-side exhaust manifold. Remove the exhaust manifold stay.

3. Disconnect the left-side exhaust manifold at the exhaust pipe after removing the retaining nuts, then disconnect the right-side manifold from the connecting pipe.

➡Soak the exhaust pipe retaining bolts with penetrating oil, if necessary, to loosen them.

4. Remove the bolts for each manifold in the order shown.

To install:

5. Clean all gasket surfaces, then position new gaskets.

6. Install the manifold to the engine, tightening the mounting bolts alternately, in two stages, in the order shown. Tighten the left-side bolts to 13–16 ft. lbs. (18–22 Nm); tighten the right-side bolts to 16–20 ft. lbs. (22–27 Nm).

7. Reconnect the exhaust pipe and the connecting pipe. Be careful not to break the bolts.

8. Install the exhaust manifold stay and the EGR tube to the right-side manifold.

9. Install the exhaust manifold covers.

10. Connect the negative battery cable.

11. Start the engine and check for exhaust leaks.

Radiator

REMOVAL & INSTALLATION

♦ **See Figures 43**

➡The cooling system can be drained by opening the draincock at the bottom of the radiator or by disconnecting the lower radiator hose. Be careful not to damage the fins or core tubes when removing and installing the radiator. Always open the air relief plug before filling the cooling system, in order to bleed any trapped air. Only when the cooling system is bled properly can the correct amount of coolant be added to the system. NEVER OPEN THE RADIATOR CAP WHEN THE ENGINE IS HOT!

1. Drain the engine coolant into a clean container. Remove the air cleaner inlet pipe.

✳✳ CAUTION

When draining the coolant, keep in mind that cats and dogs are attracted by ethylene glycol antifreeze, and are quite likely to drink any that is left in an uncovered container or in puddles on the ground. This will prove fatal in sufficient quantity. Always drain the coolant into a sealable container. Coolant should be reused unless it is contaminated or several years old.

2. Disconnect the upper and lower radiator hoses, as well as the coolant reserve tank hose.

3. Disconnect the automatic transmission oil cooler lines, if so equipped. Plug the lines to keep dirt from entering them.

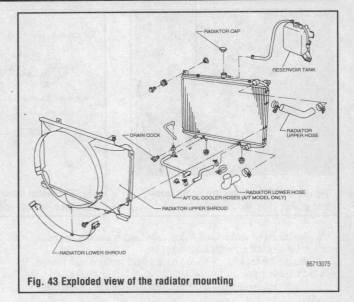

Fig. 43 Exploded view of the radiator mounting

4. Unbolt the fan shroud and move it back. Hang it over the fan assembly.

5. Remove the radiator mounting bolts and the radiator.

To install:

6. Install the radiator in the vehicle and tighten the mounting bolts evenly.

7. Check that the rubber mounting legs are in good shape.

8. If equipped with an automatic transmission, unplug and connect the cooling lines at the radiator.

9. Connect the upper and lower hoses (use new hose clamps if necessary) and the coolant reserve tank hose.

10. Refill and bleed the cooling system, as described in Section 1. Operate the engine until warm, then check the coolant level. Check also for any coolant leaks.

11. On automatic transmission vehicles, check the fluid level and add, as necessary.

Engine Fan

REMOVAL & INSTALLATION

♦ **See Figures 44, 45 and 46**

1. Disconnect the negative battery cable.

2. Remove all drive belts.

3. Unfasten the fan shroud securing bolts, then remove the fan shroud.

➡Removing the radiator and/or A/C condenser may facilitate fan removal.

4. Loosen the fan-to-fluid coupling bolts, then remove the fan.

To install:

5. Position the fan on the fluid coupling and tighten the bolts evenly to 4–7 ft. lbs. (6–10 Nm).

6. Install the fan shroud.

7. Install all drive belts and adjust them as described in Section 1.

8. Check the cooling system level and add as necessary. Start the engine and check for proper operation.

Water Pump

REMOVAL & INSTALLATION

♦ **See Figures 47, 48 and 49**

1. Drain the cooling system.

✳✳ CAUTION

When draining the coolant, keep in mind that cats and dogs are attracted by ethylene glycol antifreeze, and are quite likely to drink

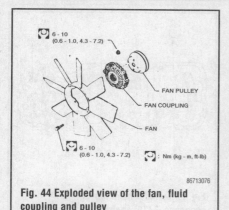

Fig. 44 Exploded view of the fan, fluid coupling and pulley

Fig. 45 Remove the fan retaining nuts, then lift the fan assembly from the engine—6-cylinder engine

Fig. 46 After removing the drive belt and fan assembly, lift off the pulley—6-cylinder engines

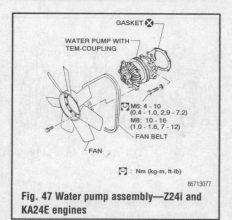

Fig. 47 Water pump assembly—Z24i and KA24E engines

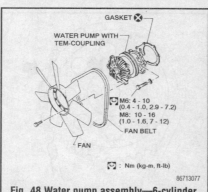

Fig. 48 Water pump assembly—6-cylinder engines

Fig. 49 View of the water pump assembly—VG30E engine

any that is left in an uncovered container or in puddles on the ground. This will prove fatal in sufficient quantity. Always drain the coolant into a sealable container. Coolant should be reused unless it is contaminated or several years old.

2. Remove all drive belts.
3. Unfasten the fan shroud securing bolts and remove the fan shroud assembly.
4. Unfasten the water pump retaining bolts (note the different size bolts on the VG30i and VG30E engines), then remove the water pump and fan assembly, using care not to damage the radiator with the fan.

➡If the fan is equipped with a fluid coupling, do not tip the fan/pump assembly on its side, as the fluid will run out.

To install:
5. Remove all traces of gasket and/or sealant from the pump-to-cover mounting surfaces. Install the water pump and tighten the M6-size mounting bolts to 3–7 ft. lbs. (4–10 Nm). Tighten the M8-size bolts to 7–12 ft. lbs. (10–16 Nm) on Z24i engines, or 12–15 ft. lbs. (16–21 Nm) on KA24E, VG30i and VG30E engines. Always use a new gasket between the pump body and its mounting.

➡The KA24E engine uses a liquid gasket. Carefully scrape any old gasket material from the mounting surfaces, then apply a 0.079–0.118 in. (2–3mm) continuous bead of liquid gasket around the entire mounting surface.

6. Install the fan shroud assembly.
7. Install the drive belt and adjust the tension.
8. Refill and bleed the cooling system (refer to Section 1), then start the engine and check for coolant leaks.

Cylinder Head

REMOVAL & INSTALLATION

➡When installing sliding parts such as rocker arms, camshafts and oil seals, be sure to apply clean engine oil on their friction surfaces. When tightening the cylinder head or rocker shaft bolts, apply clean engine oil to the bolt threads and seat surfaces.

Z24i Engine

◢ **See Figures 50 thru 56**

1. Relieve the fuel system pressure, as described in Section 5.
2. Crank the engine until the No. 1 piston is at TDC of the compression stroke.
3. Disconnect the negative battery cable and drain the cooling system.
4. Remove the air cleaner and attending hoses.
5. Remove all drive belts. Remove the alternator and power steering pump.
6. Remove the radiator and heater hoses.
7. If equipped with air conditioning, unbolt the compressor and move it aside onto the fender.

✳✳ WARNING

Do not detach any of the compressor lines; the escaping refrigerant will freeze any surface it contacts, including your skin.

8. Disconnect the exhaust pipe from the exhaust manifold.
9. Remove the fan and fan pulley.
10. Disconnect the fuel line, the return fuel line and any other vacuum lines or electrical leads.

➡A good rule of thumb when disconnecting the rather complex engine wiring of today's vehicles is to put a piece of masking tape on the wire or hose and on the corresponding connection, then mark both pieces of tape 1, 2, 3, etc. When reattaching the wiring, simply match the pieces of tape.

11. Remove the EGR tube from around the rear of the engine.
12. Remove the intake manifold supports from under the manifold. Remove the PCV valve from the rear of the engine, if necessary.
13. Remove the spark plugs to protect them from damage. Remove the cylinder head cover.

Fig. 50 Removing the camshaft sprocket—
4-cylinder engines

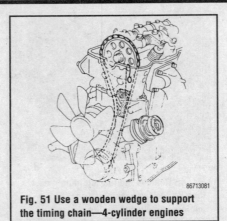

Fig. 51 Use a wooden wedge to support
the timing chain—4-cylinder engines

Fig. 52 Cylinder head loosening
sequence—Z24i engine

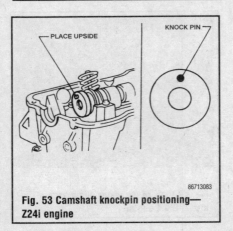

Fig. 53 Camshaft knockpin positioning—
Z24i engine

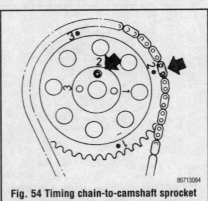

Fig. 54 Timing chain-to-camshaft sprocket
alignment—Z24i engine

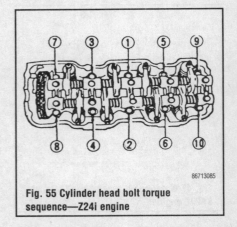

Fig. 55 Cylinder head bolt torque
sequence—Z24i engine

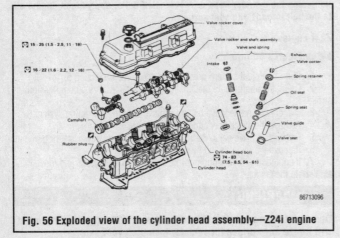

Fig. 56 Exploded view of the cylinder head assembly—Z24i engine

➡ **The spark plug leads may already be marked; however, it would be wise to mark them yourself.**

14. Mark the relationship of the camshaft sprocket to the timing chain with paint or chalk. If this is done, it will not be necessary to locate the factory timing marks. Before removing the camshaft sprocket, it will be necessary to wedge the chain in place so that it will not fall down into the front cover. The factory procedure is to wedge the timing chain in place with a wooden wedge, as illustrated. The problem with this procedure is that it may allow the chain tensioner to move out far enough to cock itself against the chain. If this happens, you'll find that the chain won't go back over the sprocket after you've reinstalled the sprocket. In this case, you'll have to remove the front cover and push the tensioner back. After you've wedged the chain, unbolt the camshaft sprocket and remove it.

15. Working from both ends in, loosen the cylinder head bolts a little at a time and remove them. Remove the bolts securing the cylinder head to the front cover assembly.

16. Lift the cylinder head (with manifolds attached) off the engine block. It may be necessary to tap the head lightly with a rubber mallet to loosen it.

To install:

17. Thoroughly clean the cylinder block and head surfaces, then check both for warpage.

18. Fit the new head gasket. Don't use sealant. Install the cylinder head assembly. Make sure that no open valves are in the way of raised pistons, and never rotate the crankshaft or camshaft separately because of possible damage which might occur to the valves.

19. Temporarily tighten the two center right and left cylinder head bolts to 14 ft. lbs. (19 Nm).

20. Install the camshaft sprocket together with the timing chain (remove the wooden wedge) to the camshaft. Make sure the marks you made earlier line up with each other. If necessary, see the Timing Chain removal and installation procedures, later in this section.

21. Confirm that the No. 1 cylinder is set at TDC on its compression stroke. Make sure that the front knock pin is positioned at the upper surface of the camshaft. Set the chain on the camshaft sprocket by aligning each mating mark. Then, install the camshaft sprocket to the camshaft and tighten to 87–116 ft. lbs. (118–157 Nm). The camshaft sprocket should be installed by fitting the knock pin of the camshaft into its No. 2 hole—and the No. 2 timing mark must be used.

➡ **Allow the rocker cover-to-cylinder head rubber plug to dry for 30 minutes before starting the engine. This will allow the liquid gasket sealer to cure properly.**

22. Apply sealant to the sealant point of the cylinder head and install the rubber plug.

23. Install the cylinder head bolts and torque them to 22 ft. lbs. (29 Nm), then 40 ft. lbs., and then 58 ft. lbs. (78 Nm). Loosen all bolts completely and retighten to 22 ft. lbs. (29 Nm), and then to 54–61 ft. lbs. (74–83 Nm); or, if you have an angle torque wrench, give all bolts a final turn of 90–95 degrees. Tighten all bolts gradually, in the order shown.

24. Clean and regap the spark plugs then install them in the cylinder head. Do not overtorque the spark plugs.

25. Temporarily install the cylinder head cover with a new gasket. Keep in mind that the cover will have to be removed to adjust valves later in the procedure.

26. Install the intake manifold supports to the manifold. Install the PCV valve if it was removed.

27. Connect the exhaust pipe to exhaust manifold.

28. Install the EGR tube from around the rear of the engine.

29. Connect the throttle linkage, the air cleaner or its intake hose assembly. Reconnect the fuel line, the return fuel line and any other vacuum lines or electrical leads.

30. Install the power steering pump and correctly adjust the drive belt.

31. Install the air conditioning compressor and correctly adjust the drive belt.

32. Install the alternator mounting bracket and alternator. Fasten the electrical connections to the alternator and adjust the drive belt.

33. Reconnect the heater and radiator hoses, then refill the cooling system.

34. Start the engine and run it until it reaches normal operating temperature. Stop the engine, then check for the correct coolant level and adjust as necessary.

35. Adjust the valves (adjustment should be made while engine is warm but not running), as described in Section 2.

➡ It is advisable to drain the crankcase oil and change the oil filter after the cylinder head assembly has been installed.

36. Check for leaks and road test the vehicle for proper operation.

KA24E Engine

▶ See Figures 57 thru 63

➡ After completing this procedure, allow the rocker cover-to-cylinder head rubber plugs to dry for 30 minutes before starting the engine. This will allow the liquid gasket sealer to cure properly.

1. Relieve the fuel system pressure, as described in Section 5.
2. Disconnect the negative battery cable and drain the cooling system.

3. Remove the power steering drive belt, power steering pump, idler pulley and power steering brackets.

4. Tag and disconnect all vacuum hoses, water hoses, fuel tubes and wiring harnesses necessary to gain access to the cylinder head.

5. Disconnect the EGR tube at the exhaust manifold.

6. Disconnect the air induction hose.

7. Detach the accelerator bracket. If necessary, mark the position and remove the accelerator cable wire end from the throttle drum.

8. Remove the intake manifold.

9. Unplug the exhaust gas sensor, then remove the exhaust cover and exhaust pipe at the exhaust manifold connection. Remove the exhaust manifold from the cylinder head.

10. Remove the rocker cover. If it sticks to the cylinder head, tap the cover with a rubber mallet. Be careful not to strike the rocker arms when removing the rocker arm cover.

➡ After removing the rocker cover, matchmark the timing chain and the camshaft sprocket with paint or chalk. If this is done, it will not be necessary to locate the factory timing marks.

11. Remove the spark plugs to protect them from damage. Remove the cylinder head cover.

➡ The spark plug leads may already be marked; however, it would be wise to mark them yourself.

12. Set the No. 1 cylinder piston at TDC on its compression stroke. This piston will be at TDC when the timing pointer is aligned with the red timing mark on the crankshaft pulley.

13. Before removing the camshaft sprocket, it will be necessary to wedge the chain in place so that it will not fall down into the front cover. The factory procedure is to wedge the timing chain in place with a wooden wedge, as illustrated. The problem with this procedure is that it may allow the chain tensioner to move out far enough to cock itself against the chain. If this happens, you'll find that the chain won't go back over the sprocket after you've reinstalled the sprocket. In this case, you'll have to remove the front cover and push the ten-

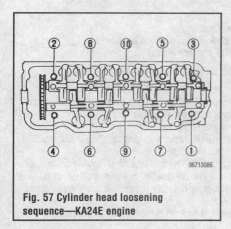

Fig. 57 Cylinder head loosening sequence—KA24E engine

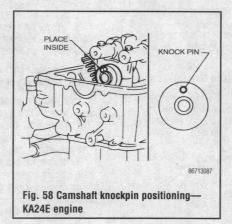

Fig. 58 Camshaft knockpin positioning—KA24E engine

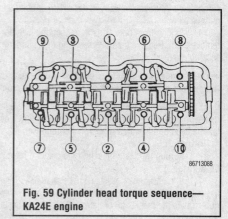

Fig. 59 Cylinder head torque sequence—KA24E engine

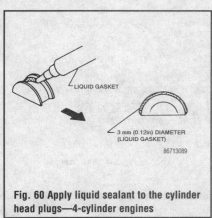

Fig. 60 Apply liquid sealant to the cylinder head plugs—4-cylinder engines

Fig. 61 Press the rubber plug into the cylinder head—4-cylinder engines

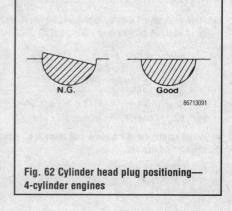

Fig. 62 Cylinder head plug positioning—4-cylinder engines

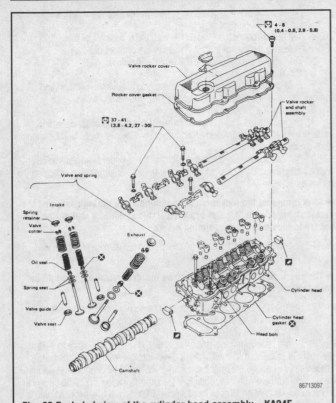

Fig. 63 Exploded view of the cylinder head assembly—KA24E engine

sioner back. After you've wedged the chain, unbolt the camshaft sprocket and remove it.

14. Working from both ends in, loosen the cylinder head bolts in steps and remove them. Remove the bolts securing the cylinder head to the front cover assembly.

➡ **The cylinder head bolts should be loosened in two or three steps in the correct order to prevent head warpage or cracking.**

15. Loosen and remove the cylinder head bolts a little at a time in the correct sequence. Lift the cylinder head off the engine block. It may be necessary to tap the head lightly with a rubber mallet to loosen it.

To install:

16. Thoroughly clean the cylinder block and head surfaces, and check both for warpage.

17. Fit the new head gasket. Don't use sealant. Install the cylinder head assembly. Make sure that no open valves are in the way of raised pistons, and never rotate the crankshaft or camshaft separately because of possible damage which might occur to the valves.

18. Confirm that the No. 1 piston is at TDC on its compression stroke as follows: Align the timing mark with the red (0 degree) mark on the crankshaft pulley. Make sure the distributor rotor head is set at No. 1 on the distributor cap. Confirm that the knock pin on the camshaft is set at the top position.

19. Install the cylinder head and torque the head bolts in numerical order using the following 5-step procedure:
   a. Torque all bolts to 22 ft. lbs. (29 Nm).
   b. Torque all bolts to 58 ft. lbs. (78 Nm).
   c. Loosen all bolts completely.
   d. Torque all bolts to 22 ft. lbs. (29 Nm).
   e. Torque all bolts to 54–61 ft. lbs. (74–83 Nm), or if an angle wrench is used, turn all bolts 80–85 degrees clockwise.

➡ **Do not rotate the crankshaft and camshaft separately, or valves will hit the tops of the pistons.**

20. Remove the wedge from the timing chain. Position the timing chain on the camshaft sprocket by aligning each matchmark. Install the camshaft sprocket to the camshaft.

21. Hold the camshaft sprocket stationary, and tighten the sprocket bolt to 87–116 ft. lbs. (118–157 Nm).

22. Install the front cover-to-cylinder head retaining bolts. Torque the 6mm bolts to 5–6 ft. lbs. (7–8 Nm) and the 8mm bolts to 12–15 ft. lbs. (16–21 Nm).

23. Clean and regap the spark plugs, then install them in the cylinder head. Do not overtorque the spark plugs.

24. Install the intake manifold and collector assembly with new gaskets.

25. Install the exhaust manifold with new gaskets.

26. Apply liquid gasket to the rubber plugs, then install the plugs in their correct location in the cylinder head. The seating surface of the rubber plugs must be clean and dry, and the plugs should be installed within 5 minutes of the sealant application. After the sealant is applied and the rubber plugs are in place, rock the plugs back and forth a few times to distribute the sealant evenly. Wipe the excess sealant from the cylinder head with a clean rag.

27. Install the rocker cover with a new gasket.

28. Attach the accelerator bracket and cable, if removed.

29. Attach all vacuum hoses, water hoses, fuel tubes and electrical connections that were removed to gain access to the cylinder head.

30. Reconnect the air induction hose.

31. Install the spark plugs wires in their correct location.

32. Install the power steering brackets, idler pulley, and power steering pump.

33. Install and adjust the drive belts.

➡ **It is advisable to drain the crankcase oil and change the oil filter after the cylinder head assembly has been installed.**

34. Fill and bleed the cooling system, and connect the negative battery cable.

35. Make all the necessary engine adjustments.

VG30i Engine

▶ **See Figures 64, 65, 66, 67 and 68**

➡ **To remove or install the cylinder head, you'll need a special hex head wrench ST10120000 (J24239 01) or equivalent. The distributor assembly is located in the left cylinder head; mark and remove it if necessary.**

1. Relieve the fuel system pressure, as described in Section 5.
2. Disconnect the negative battery cable.
3. Remove the cylinder head covers.
4. Remove the front upper and lower timing belt covers.
5. Set the engine to TDC and then remove the timing belt.

➡ **Do not rotate either the crankshaft or camshaft from this point onward, or the valves could be bent by hitting the pistons.**

6. Drain the coolant from the engine. Tag and disconnect all the vacuum hoses and water hoses connected to the intake manifold.

7. Remove the intake manifold and fuel tube assembly.

8. Remove the exhaust manifold covers. Disconnect the exhaust manifold where it attaches to the exhaust pipe (three bolts).

9. Remove the camshaft pulleys and the rear timing cover securing bolts.

10. Loosen and remove the cylinder head bolts a little at a time, in the order shown. When removing the cylinder head bolts, note their location for correct installation.

11. Remove the cylinder head with the exhaust manifold attached.

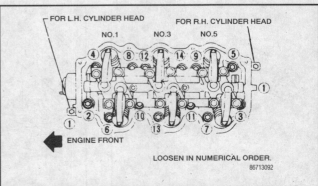

Fig. 64 Cylinder head loosening sequence—VG30i and VG30E engines

To install:

12. Check the positions of the timing marks and camshaft sprockets to make sure they have not shifted. The mark on the crankshaft should be aligned with the one on the oil pump body, and the camshaft knockpin should be at the top.

13. Install the cylinder head with a new gasket. Apply clean engine oil to the threads and seats of the bolts, then install the bolts with washers (beveled edges up) in the correct position. Note that bolts 4, 5, 12 and 13 measure 5.00 in. (127mm), and are longer than the others. Other bolts are 4.17 in. (106mm) long.

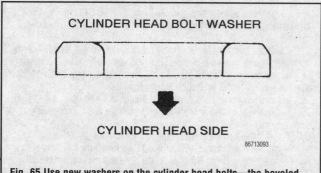

Fig. 65 Use new washers on the cylinder head bolts—the beveled side should face upward—VG30i and VG30E engines

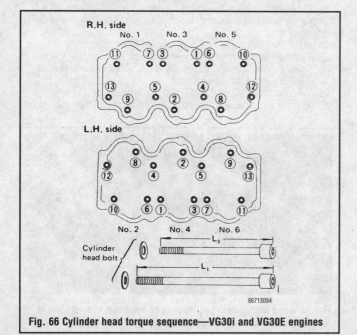

Fig. 66 Cylinder head torque sequence—VG30i and VG30E engines

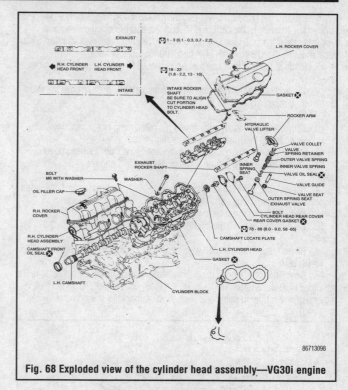

Fig. 67 Camshaft sprocket positioning and alignment—VG30i and VG30E engines

Fig. 68 Exploded view of the cylinder head assembly—VG30i engine

14. Tighten the bolts in the proper sequence, in the following stages:
   a. Tighten all bolts, in order, to 22 ft. lbs. (29 Nm).
   b. Tighten all bolts, in order, to 43 ft. lbs. (59 Nm).
   c. Loosen all bolts completely.
   d. Tighten all bolts, in order, to 22 ft. lbs. (29 Nm).
   e. Tighten all bolts, in order, to 40–47 ft. lbs. (54–64 Nm). Or, if you have an angle torque wrench available, tighten them an additional 60–65 degrees.

15. Install the rear timing cover bolts and the camshaft pulleys. Make sure the pulley marked **R3** goes on the right and the one marked **L3** goes on the left.

16. Align the timing marks, if necessary, then install the timing belt and adjust the belt tension.

17. Install the front upper and lower belt covers.

18. Make sure that the cylinder head cover bolts, trays and washers are free of oil. Then, install the cylinder head covers.

19. Install the intake manifold and fuel tube. Tighten manifold bolts and nuts in two or three stages in reverse order of removal.

20. Install the exhaust manifold if removed from the cylinder head.

21. Attach the exhaust manifold to the exhaust pipe connection. Install the exhaust manifold cover.

22. Connect all the vacuum hoses and water hoses.

➡ **It is advisable to drain the crankcase oil and change the oil filter after the cylinder head assembly has been installed.**

23. Refill and bleed the cooling system. Start the engine, then check the engine timing. After the engine reaches the normal operating temperature, check for the correct coolant level.

24. Road test the vehicle for proper operation.

VG30E Engine

▸ **See Figures 66, 67, 69 thru 73**

1. Relieve the fuel system pressure, as described in Section 5.
2. Disconnect the negative battery cable.
3. Set the engine to TDC and then remove the timing belt.

➡ **Do not rotate either the crankshaft or camshaft from this point onward, or the valves could be bent by hitting the pistons.**

4. Drain the coolant from the engine.
5. Tag and separate the Automatic Speed Control Device (ASCD) and accelerator control wire from the intake manifold collector.

6. Remove the collector cover and the collector. Tag and detach all harness connectors attached to the collector. Disconnect and remove the water and heater hoses at the collector. Disconnect the PCV line. Tag and disconnect all vacuum lines, then remove the EGR tube and the air duct hose.

7. Remove the fuel feed and fuel return hoses from the injector fuel tube assembly.

8. Tag and separate all injector harness connectors, then remove the injector fuel tube assembly.

9. Remove the intake manifold.

10. Remove the camshaft pulleys and the rear timing cover securing bolts.

11. Remove the distributor and the ignition wires.

12. Remove the harness clamp from the right-side cylinder head cover.

13. Unbolt the forward exhaust pipe at the manifold and move it out of the way.

14. Remove the drive belts, then remove the A/C compressor and alternator. Remove the mounting bolts and then remove the compressor bracket.

15. Remove the cylinder head covers.

16. Loosen and remove the cylinder head bolts a little at a time, in the order shown.

17. Remove the cylinder head with the exhaust manifold attached.

To install:

18. Check the positions of the timing marks and camshaft sprockets to make sure they have not shifted. The mark on the crankshaft should be aligned with the one on the oil pump body, and the camshaft knockpin should be at the top.

19. Install the cylinder head with a new gasket. Apply clean engine oil to the bolt threads and seats, then install the bolts with washers (beveled edges up) in the correct position. Note that bolts 4, 5, 12 and 13 measure 5.00 in. (127mm), and are longer than the others. The other bolts are 4.17 in. (106mm) long.

20. Tighten the bolts in the proper sequence, in the following stages:
   a. Tighten all bolts, in order, to 22 ft. lbs. (29 Nm).
   b. Tighten all bolts, in order, to 43 ft. lbs. (59 Nm).
   c. Loosen all bolts completely.
   d. Tighten all bolts, in order, to 22 ft. lbs. (29 Nm).
   e. Tighten all bolts, in order, to 40–47 ft. lbs. (54–64 Nm). Or, if you have an angle torque wrench available, tighten them an additional 60–65 degrees.

21. Check the hydraulic valve lifter by pushing the plunger forcefully with your finger (be sure that the rocker arm is in the free position, NOT on the lobe). If the lifter moves more than 0.04 in. (1mm), it must be bled, as described at the end of this procedure and in Section 2 of this manual.

22. Install the cylinder head covers and tighten to 1–2 ft. lbs. (1.4–3 Nm).

23. Fasten the compressor bracket, then install the A/C compressor and alternator.

24. Connect the forward exhaust pipe to the manifold.

25. Install the rear timing cover bolts and then install the camshaft pulleys. Make sure the pulley marked **R3** goes on the right and the one marked **L3** goes on the left.

26. Align the timing marks, if necessary, then install the timing belt and adjust the belt tension.

27. Install the distributor by aligning the mark on the distributor shaft with the protruding mark on the housing. The distributor rotor tip should be at the 11 o'clock position.

28. Install the intake manifold and injector fuel tube assembly.

29. Fasten the injector harness connectors.

30. Install the fuel feed and return hoses to the injector fuel tube assembly.

31. Install the intake manifold collector.

32. Reconnect the ASCD and accelerator control wire.

33. Connect all the vacuum hoses and water hoses to the intake collector.

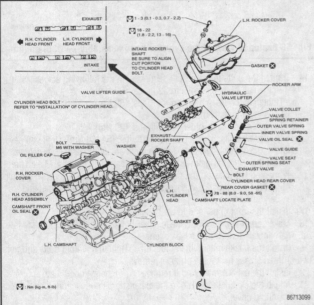

Fig. 69 Exploded view of the cylinder head assembly—VG30E engine

Fig. 70 When removing the cylinder head bolts use a proper tool to loosen the bolts evenly—VG30E engine

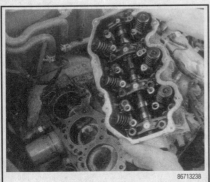

Fig. 71 Remove the cylinder head assembly—VG30E engine

Fig. 72 The cylinder head gasket must be replaced upon installation—VG30E engine

Fig. 73 Always use a torque wrench when installing cylinder head bolts, and follow the designated service procedure—VG30E engine

➡️It is advisable to drain the crankcase oil and change the oil filter after the cylinder head assembly has been installed.

34. Connect the negative battery cable and refill the cooling system. Start the engine and check the engine timing. After the engine reaches the normal operating temperature, check for the correct coolant level.

35. If the hydraulic valve lifters require bleeding, run the engine at about 1000 rpm, under no load, for about 10 minutes. If the lifter is still noisy after bleeding, replace it and bleed it again.

36. Road test the vehicle for proper operation.

Hydraulic Valve Lifters

REMOVAL & INSTALLATION

▶ **See Figure 74**

Although cylinder head removal is not usually necessary in order to remove only the lifters from these engines, other problems may necessitate the heads removal. If a lifter becomes stuck in the bore, or if the camshaft must be replaced, it may then become necessary to remove the cylinder head. For more details, please refer to the cylinder and camshaft procedures found in this section.

The KA24E engine is unique in that the hydraulic lifters are installed inside the rocker arm assemblies and retained by a snapring. Lifter and camshaft service on this engine should NOT require cylinder head removal.

1. Disconnect the negative battery cable.
2. Remove the cylinder head cover.
3. Remove the rocker arms and shafts.
4. Withdraw each lifter from its cylinder head bore (VG30i and VG30E engines) or from the bore in the rocker arm assembly (KA24E engines). In order to remove a lifter which is installed in the rocker arm, be sure to remove the snapring first, but be careful not to bend or break the snapring during removal.

➡️If lifters are to be reused, they must be tagged to ensure installation in the original locations.

❊❊ WARNING

Do not lay the lifters on their sides because air will be allowed to enter the lifter. When storing lifters (or rocker arm assemblies with lifters in them such as on the KA24E engines), set them straight upward. To store lifters on their sides, they must be soaked in a bath of clean engine oil.

To install:

5. Install the lifters in their original locations. Use new lifter snaprings as needed. New lifters should be soaked in a bath of clean engine oil prior to installation to remove the air.

Fig. 74 Removing the hydraulic lifter from the valve lifter guide assembly—6-cylinder engines

6. Install the rocker arms and shafts.
7. If removed, install the cylinder head and leave the valve cover off.
8. Check the lifters for proper operation by pushing hard on each lifter with fingertip pressure. If the valve lifter moves more than 0.04 in. (1mm), air may be inside it. Make sure the rocker arm is not on the cam lobe when making this check.
9. Install the cylinder head cover and connect the negative battery cable. If air was found in the lifters during the previous step, bleed the air by running the engine at 1000 rpm (with no-load) for 10 minutes.

Oil Pan

REMOVAL & INSTALLATION

Z24i Engine

1. Remove the engine under cover and drain the engine oil.

❊❊ CAUTION

The EPA warns that prolonged contact with used engine oil may cause a number of skin disorders, including cancer! You should make every effort to minimize your exposure to used engine oil. Protective gloves should be worn when changing the oil. Wash your hands and any other exposed skin areas as soon as possible after exposure to used engine oil. Soap and water, or waterless hand cleaner should be used.

2. On 2wd models, remove the front crossmember.
3. On 4wd models:
   a. Remove the bolt from the front differential carrier member on 4wd models.
   b. Position a floor jack under the front differential carrier and remove the mounting bolts.
   c. Remove the transmission-to-rear engine mount bracket nuts.
   d. Remove the engine mount nuts and bolts.
   e. Attach an engine hoist and raise the engine slightly.
4. Remove the oil pan mounting bolts. Insert a seal cutter tool between the cylinder block and the oil pan, then tap it around the circumference of the pan with a hammer. Remove the oil pan.

➡️Be careful not to drive the seal cutter into the oil pump or rear oil seal retainer as you will damage the aluminum mating surface.

To install:

5. Remove all traces of gasket material from the pan and block mating surfaces.
6. Apply a continuous 0.14–0.18 in. (3.5–4.5mm) thick bead of sealant to the oil pan mating surface. Be sure to run the sealant bead to the inside of the bolt holes where there is no groove.
7. Install the pan and tighten all bolts to 4–5 ft. lbs. (6–7 Nm).
8. On 2wd models, install the crossmember.
9. On 4wd models, lower the engine and fasten the engine mount nuts/bolts. Then, install the transmission-to-rear engine mount bracket nuts and differential carrier mounting bolts. Remove the floor jack.
10. Wait at least 30 minutes, then refill the engine with oil. Run the engine until it reaches normal operating temperature, then check for leaks.
11. Once you are sure there are no leaks, install the engine under cover.

KA24E Engine

▶ **See Figure 75**

1. Raise the front of the vehicle and support it with safety stands.
2. Drain the engine oil into a suitable container.

❊❊ CAUTION

The EPA warns that prolonged contact with used engine oil may cause a number of skin disorders, including cancer! You should make every effort to minimize your exposure to used engine oil. Protective gloves should be worn when changing the oil. Wash your hands and any other exposed skin areas as soon as possible after exposure to used engine oil. Soap and water, or waterless hand cleaner should be used.

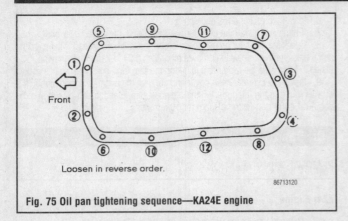

Fig. 75 Oil pan tightening sequence—KA24E engine

3. Remove the front stabilizer bar mounting nuts and bolts from the side member.

4. Carefully position a floor jack and a piece of wood under the engine, then raise the engine in its mounts.

5. Loosen the oil pan bolts in the illustrated sequence. Insert a seal cutter tool between the cylinder block and oil pan, then tap it around the circumference of the pan with a hammer. Remove the oil pan, pulling it out from the front side.

➤Be careful not to drive the seal cutter into the oil pump or rear oil seal retainer, as this would damage the aluminum mating surface.

To install:

6. Remove all traces of gasket material from the pan and block mating surfaces.

7. Apply a continuous 0.14–0.18 in. (3.5–4.5mm) thick bead of sealant to the oil pan mating surface. Be sure to run the sealant bead to the inside of the bolt holes where there is no groove.

8. Install the pan and tighten all bolts to 4–5 ft. lbs. (6–7 Nm) in the reverse order of removal.

9. Lower the engine to its normal position, then remove the floor jack and piece of wood.

10. Attach the front stabilizer bar mounting nuts and bolts to the side member.

11. Remove the jackstands and lower the front of the vehicle.

12. Wait at least 30 minutes, then refill the engine with oil. Run the engine until it reaches normal operating temperature, then check for leaks.

VG30i and VG30E Engines

▶ See Figures 76 thru 81

1. Remove the engine under cover and drain the engine oil.

✳✳ CAUTION

The EPA warns that prolonged contact with used engine oil may cause a number of skin disorders, including cancer! You should make every effort to minimize your exposure to used engine oil. Protective gloves should be worn when changing the oil. Wash your hands and any other exposed skin areas as soon as possible after exposure to used engine oil. Soap and water, or waterless hand cleaner should be used.

2. On 2wd models, remove the stabilizer bar bracket bolts, then remove the front crossmember.

3. On 4wd models, remove the front driveshaft and disconnect the half-shafts at the transfer case. Position a floor jack under the front differential carrier and remove the mounting bolts.

4. Remove the idler arm.

5. Remove the starter motor.

6. On 4wd models, remove the transmission-to-rear engine mount bracket nuts. Then, remove the engine mount nuts and bolts.

7. Remove the engine gussets.

8. On 4wd models, attach an engine hoist and raise the engine slightly.

9. Remove the oil pan mounting bolts in the order shown. Insert a seal cutter tool between the cylinder block and the oil pan, then tap it around the circumference of the pan with a hammer. Remove the oil pan.

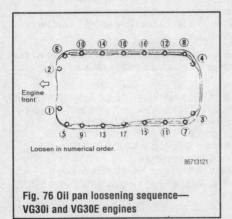

Fig. 76 Oil pan loosening sequence—VG30i and VG30E engines

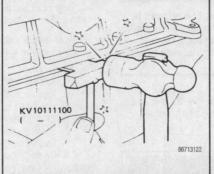

Fig. 77 Carefully install the seal cutter like this

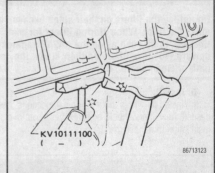

Fig. 78 Slide the cutter by tapping its side with a hammer

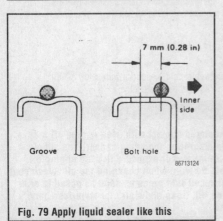

Fig. 79 Apply liquid sealer like this

Fig. 80 Removing the oil pan retaining bolts evenly

Fig. 81 Removing the oil pan from the engine

➡️Be careful not to drive the seal cutter into the oil pump or rear oil seal retainer as this would damage the aluminum mating surface.

To install:

10. Remove all traces of gasket material from the pan and block mating surfaces.

11. Apply sealant to the oil pump and oil seal retainer gasket.

12. Apply a continuous 0.14–0.18 in. (3.5–4.5mm) thick bead of sealant to the oil pan mating surface. Be sure to run the sealant bead to the inside of the bolt holes where there is no groove.

13. Install the pan and tighten all bolts to 4–5 ft. lbs. (6–7 Nm). Lower the engine assembly.

14. Install the engine gussets.

15. On 4wd models, install the engine mounts nuts and bolts. Install the transmission-to-rear engine mount bracket nuts.

16. Install the starter motor and engage all electrical connections.

17. Install the idler arm with a new cotter pin.

18. On 2wd models, install the front crossmember and stabilizer bar bracket bolts (reposition stabilizer bar if necessary).

19. On 4wd models, position a floor jack under the front differential carrier and install the mounting bolts. Reconnect the halfshafts at the transfer case. Install the front driveshaft. Remember to remove the floor jack.

20. Wait at least 30 minutes and then refill the engine with oil. Run the engine until it reaches normal operating temperature and then check for leaks.

Oil Pump

REMOVAL & INSTALLATION

Z24i and KA24E Engines

◆ **See Figures 82 and 83**

➡️The oil pump is mounted externally on the engine, eliminating the need to remove the oil pan in order to remove the oil pump.

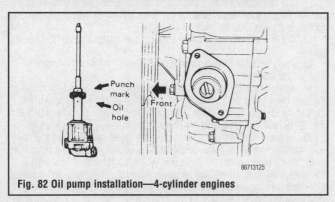

Fig. 82 Oil pump installation—4-cylinder engines

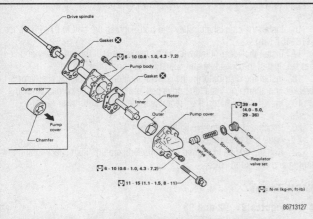

Fig. 83 Exploded view of the oil pump assembly—4-cylinder engines

1. Matchmark and remove the distributor, as detailed earlier in this section.

2. Drain the engine oil.

3. Remove the front stabilizer bar.

4. Remove the splash shield board.

5. Loosen the mounting bolts and remove the oil pump body with the drive spindle assembly.

To install:

6. Before installing the oil pump in the engine, turn the crankshaft so that the No. 1 piston is at TDC of the compression stroke.

7. Fill the pump housing with engine oil, then align the punch mark on the spindle with the hole in the oil pump.

8. With a new gasket placed over the drive spindle, install the oil pump and drive spindle assembly so that the projection on the top of the drive spindle is located at the 11 o'clock position.

9. Install the distributor with the metal tip of the rotor pointing toward the No. 1 spark plug tower of the distributor cap.

10. Install the splash shield and front stabilizer bar.

11. Refill the engine with oil, then start and run the engine to normal operating temperature.

12. Check ignition timing and adjust, as necessary, then check for oil leaks.

VG30i and VG30E Engines

◆ **See Figures 84 thru 89**

1. Remove the timing belt. For details, please refer to the procedure in this section.

2. Remove the oil pan. For details, please refer to the procedure in this section.

3. Remove the crankshaft timing sprocket (it may be necessary to use a puller) and the timing belt plate.

4. Remove the oil pump strainer and pick-up tube.

5. Loosen the oil pump retaining bolts, then remove the oil pump.

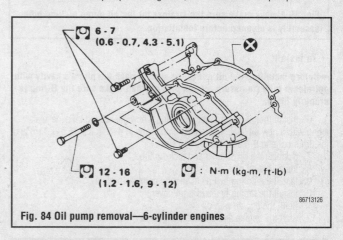

Fig. 84 Oil pump removal—6-cylinder engines

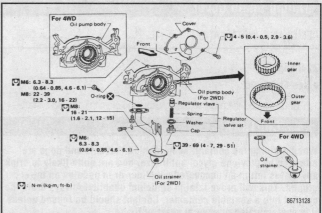

Fig. 85 Exploded view of the oil pump assembly—6-cylinder engines

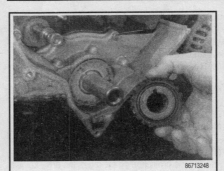

Fig. 86 Remove the crankshaft sprocket before removing the oil pump assembly—6-cylinder engines

Fig. 87 Remove the oil pump cover to gain access to oil pump body—6-cylinder engines

Fig. 88 Remove the oil pump pick-up tube assembly mounting bolts—6-cylinder engines

Fig. 89 Always make sure the strainer for the oil pump pick-up tube assembly is cleaned before installation

To install:

➡Before installing the oil pump, be sure to pack the pump's cavity with petroleum jelly (to assure a good prime), then make sure the O-ring is properly fitted.

6. Install the oil pump assembly using a new gasket and silicone sealant, along with a new oil seal. Tighten the 6mm bolts to 4–5 ft. lbs. (5.5–7 Nm) and the 8mm bolts to 9–12 ft. lbs. (12–16 Nm).
7. Connect the oil strainer and pick-up tube.
8. Install the oil pan.
9. Install the timing belt plate and the crankshaft pulley.
10. Install the timing belt and front cover.
11. Refill the engine with oil.
12. Start the engine and check for any leaks.

Timing Chain Cover

REMOVAL & INSTALLATION

Z24i Engine

▶ See Figure 90

1. Disconnect the negative battery cable and drain the cooling system.

☀☀☀ CAUTION

When draining the coolant, keep in mind that cats and dogs are attracted by ethylene glycol antifreeze, and are quite likely to drink any that is left in an uncovered container or in puddles on the ground. This will prove fatal in sufficient quantity. Always drain the coolant into a sealable container. Coolant should be reused unless it is contaminated or several years old.

2. Remove the radiator, along with the upper and lower radiator hoses.

3. Loosen the alternator drive belt adjusting screw and remove the drive belt. Remove the bolts which attach the alternator bracket to the engine and position the alternator aside, out of the way.
4. Remove the distributor.
5. Unthread the oil pump attaching screws, then remove the pump and its drive spindle.
6. Remove the cooling fan and the fan pulley, along with the drive belt.
7. Remove the water pump.
8. Unfasten and remove the crankshaft pulley.
9. Remove the bolts holding the front cover to the front of the cylinder block, the bolts which retain the front of the oil pan to the bottom of the front cover, and the bolts which are screwed down through the front of the cylinder head into the top of the front cover.
10. With a suitable drain pan in place, carefully pry the front cover off the engine assembly.

To install:

11. Cut the exposed front section of the oil pan gasket away from the oil pan. Do the same to the gasket at the top of the front cover. Remove the two side gaskets and clean all of the mating surfaces.
12. Cut the portions needed from a new oil pan gasket and top front cover gasket.
13. Apply sealer to all of the gaskets and position them on the engine in their proper locations.
14. Apply a light coating of oil to the crankshaft oil seal. Carefully mount in the front cover to the front of the engine and install all of the mounting bolts. Tighten the 8mm bolts to 7–12 ft. lbs. (10–16 Nm) and the 6mm bolts to 3–7 ft. lbs. (4–10 Nm). Tighten the oil pan attaching bolts to 4–7 ft. lbs. (6–8 Nm).
15. Before installing the oil pump, place the gasket over the shaft and make sure that the mark on the drive spindle faces (is aligned with) the oil pump hole. Install the oil pump so that the projection on the top of the shaft is located in the exact position as when it was removed. However, if the engine was disturbed since disassembly, place the projection on top of the shaft at the 11 o'clock position when the piston when the No. 1 cylinder is placed at TDC on the compression stroke. Tighten the oil pump attaching screws to 8–10 ft. lbs. (11–15 Nm).
16. Install the crankshaft pulley and bolt. Tighten the bolt to 87–116 ft. lbs. (118–157 Nm).
17. Install the water pump with a new gasket. Install the fan pulley and cooling fan. Install the drive belt and adjust to the correct tension.
18. Install the distributor in the correct position. Reattach the alternator bracket and alternator. Install the drive belt and adjust to the correct tension.
19. Install the radiator, then reconnect the upper and lower radiator hoses.
20. Reconnect the negative battery cable.
21. Refill and bleed the cooling system.
22. Run the engine to normal operating temperature, then check ignition timing and check for leaks.

KA24E Engine

▶ See Figures 91, 92 and 93

1. Disconnect the negative battery cable from the battery and drain the cooling system.

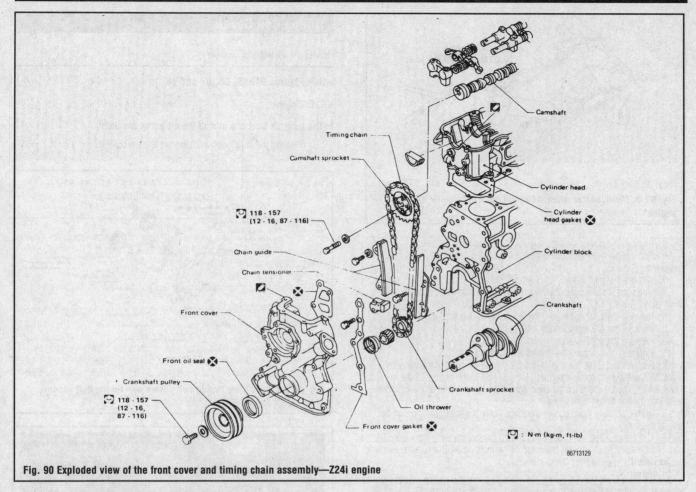

Fig. 90 Exploded view of the front cover and timing chain assembly—Z24i engine

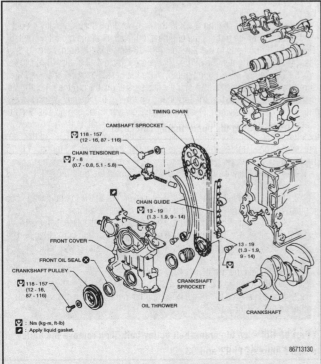

Fig. 91 Exploded view of the front cover and timing chain assembly—KA24E engine

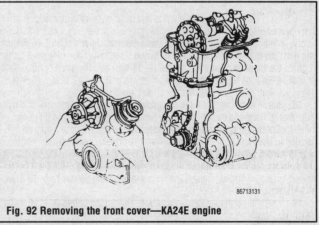

Fig. 92 Removing the front cover—KA24E engine

✳✳ CAUTION

When draining the coolant, keep in mind that cats and dogs are attracted by ethylene glycol antifreeze, and are quite likely to drink any that is left in an uncovered container or in puddles on the ground. This will prove fatal in sufficient quantity. Always drain the coolant into a sealable container. Coolant should be reused unless it is contaminated or several years old.

2. Remove the radiator. along with the upper and lower radiator hoses.

3. Loosen the alternator drive belt adjusting screw and remove the drive belt. Remove the bolts which attach the alternator bracket to the engine and position the alternator aside, out of the way.

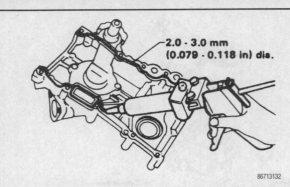

Fig. 93 Us liquid sealer when installing the front cover—KA24E engine

4. Remove the power steering and A/C compressor drive belts.

5. Remove all spark plugs and then set the No. 1 cylinder to TDC of its compression stroke.

6. Remove the distributor.

7. Unthread the oil pump attaching screws, then remove the pump and its drive spindle.

8. Remove the cooling fan and the fan pulley, along with the drive belt.

9. Remove the A/C compressor idler pulley.

10. Remove the water pump.

11. Unfasten and remove the crankshaft pulley.

12. Remove the bolts holding the front cover to the front of the cylinder block, the bolts which retain the front of the oil pan to the bottom of the front cover, and the bolts which are screwed down through the front of the cylinder head into the top of the front cover.

13. With a suitable drain pan in place, carefully pry the front cover off the engine assembly.

14. Cut the exposed front section of the oil pan gasket away from the oil pan. Do the same to the gasket at the top of the front cover. Remove the two side gaskets and clean all of the mating surfaces.

To install:

15. Cut the portions needed from a new oil pan gasket and top front cover gasket.

16. Apply sealer to all of the gaskets and position them on the engine in their proper places.

17. Apply a light coating of oil to the crankshaft oil seal. Carefully mount the front cover to the front of the engine and install all of the mounting bolts. Tighten the 8mm bolts to 7–12 ft. lbs. (9–16 Nm) and the 6mm bolts to 3–7 ft. lbs. (4–9 Nm). Tighten the oil pan attaching bolts to 4–7 ft. lbs. (5.5–9 Nm).

18. Before installing the oil pump, place the gasket over the shaft and make sure that the mark on the drive spindle faces (is aligned with) the oil pump hole. Install the oil pump so that the projection on the top of the shaft is located in the exact position as when it was removed. However, if the engine was disturbed since disassembly, place the projection on top of the shaft at the 11 o'clock position when the piston in the No. 1 cylinder is placed at TDC on the compression stroke. Tighten the oil pump attaching screws to 8–10 ft. lbs. (11–15 Nm).

19. Install the crankshaft pulley and bolt. Tighten the bolt to 87–116 ft. lbs. (118–157 Nm).

20. Install the water pump with a new gasket. Install the fan pulley and cooling fan. Install the drive belt and adjust to the correct tension.

21. Install the distributor in the correct position. Reconnect the alternator bracket and alternator. Install the drive belt and adjust the tension.

22. Install the A/C compressor idler pulley.

23. Install all spark plugs.

24. Install the radiator, then reconnect the upper and lower radiator hoses.

25. Reconnect the negative battery cable.

26. Refill and bleed the cooling system.

27. Check the ignition timing and check for leaks.

Timing Belt Cover

REMOVAL & INSTALLATION

◆ **See Figures 94, 95, 96, 97 and 98**

VG30i Engine

➡ **The front oil seal is a part of the oil pump assembly.**

1. Remove the radiator shroud, the fan and the pulleys.

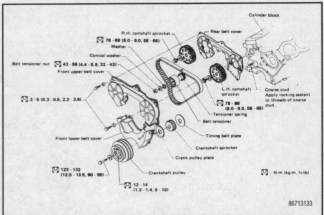

Fig. 94 Exploded view timing belt covers and timing belt assembly—VG30i and VG30E engines

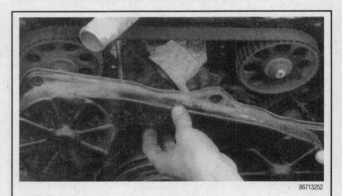

Fig. 95 Removing the upper timing belt cover

Fig. 96 Unfasten the crankshaft pulley bolt, then remove the pulley with a suitable puller

Fig. 97 View of the crankshaft pulley—
note the pulley is keyed for correct installation

Fig. 98 Removing the lower timing belt
cover

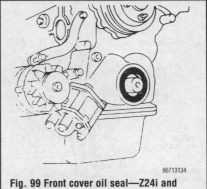

Fig. 99 Front cover oil seal—Z24i and
KA24E engines

2. Drain the coolant from the radiator and disconnect the water pump hose.
3. Remove the power steering, A/C compressor and alternator drive belts.
4. Remove the suction pipe bracket, then remove the lower hose from the suction pipe.
5. Remove the spark plugs.
6. Set the No. 1 piston at TDC of its compression stroke, then remove the idler bracket for the compressor drive belt.
7. Remove the crankshaft pulley.
8. Loosen all bolts and remove the upper and lower timing belt covers.

To install:
9. Install the two timing belt covers and tighten the mounting bolts to 2–4 ft. lbs. (3–5 Nm).
10. Press the crankshaft pulley onto the crankshaft and tighten the bolt to 90–98 ft. lbs. (123–132 Nm). Install the spark plugs.
11. Install the A/C compressor idler bracket.
12. Install the suction pipe bracket and connect the lower hose. Install all drive belts and adjust their tension.
13. Reconnect the water pump hose.
14. Install the fan, shroud and pulleys.
15. Refill the engine with coolant and bleed the cooling system of air.
16. Run the engine and check for any leaks.

VG30E Engine

➡The front oil seal is a part of the oil pump assembly.

1. Remove the engine under cover.
2. Remove the radiator shroud, the fan and the pulleys.
3. Drain the coolant from the radiator and disconnect the water pump hose.
4. Remove the radiator.
5. Remove the power steering, A/C compressor and alternator drive belts.
6. Remove the spark plugs.
7. Remove the distributor protector (dust shield).
8. Remove the A/C compressor drive belt idler pulley and bracket.
9. Remove the fresh air intake tube at the cylinder head cover.
10. Disconnect the radiator hose at the thermostat housing.
11. Unfasten the crankshaft pulley bolt, then remove the pulley with a suitable puller.
12. Unfasten the bolts, then remove the front upper and lower timing belt covers.

To install:
13. Position the two timing belt covers on the block and then tighten the mounting bolts to 2–4 ft. lbs. (3–5 Nm).
14. Press the crankshaft pulley onto the shaft, then thread and tighten the bolt to 90–98 ft. lbs. (123–132 Nm).
15. Connect the radiator hose to the thermostat housing.
16. Reconnect the fresh air intake tube at the cylinder head cover.
17. Install the A/C compressor drive belt idler pulley and bracket.
18. Install the distributor protector (dust shield).
19. Install the spark plugs.
20. Install the power steering, A/C compressor and alternator drive belts.
21. Install the radiator.
22. Reconnect the water pump hose, then install the fan, shroud and pulleys.

23. Fill the engine with coolant (bleed the cooling system).
24. Start the engine and check for any leaks.
25. Install the engine under cover.

Front Oil Seal

REMOVAL & INSTALLATION

Z24i and KA24E Engines

◗ See Figure 99

1. Remove the front cover.
2. Pry the old seal from the cover with a pointed piece of plastic or wood. Do not use a screwdriver to avoid scratching the seal surface.
3. Oil the lip of the new seal. Do not use grease. Press it into place, making sure the flat side faces forward and the lip faces the engine.
4. Install the front cover.

VG30i and VG30E Engines

The front oil seal is a part of the oil pump assembly. To replace the oil pump seal, please refer to the Oil Pump service procedures, earlier in this section.

Timing Chain and Tensioner

REMOVAL & INSTALLATION

➡After this service procedure is finished, changing the engine oil and oil filter is good preventive maintenance due to contamination of old gasket material.

Z24i and KA24E Engines

◗ See Figures 100 thru 112

1. Before beginning any disassembly procedures, position the No. 1 piston at TDC on the compression stroke.
2. Disconnect the negative battery cable.
3. Remove the timing chain cover (place a suitable drain pan under cover assembly).
4. Remove the cylinder head cover.
5. With the No. 1 piston at TDC, the timing marks on the camshaft sprocket and the timing chain should be visible. Mark both of them with paint. Also mark the relationship of the camshaft sprocket to the camshaft. There are three sets of timing marks and locating holes in the sprocket; they are for making adjustments to compensate for timing chain stretch.
6. With the timing marks on the camshaft sprocket clearly indicated, locate and label (for easier reference) the timing marks on the crankshaft sprocket. Also label the chain timing mark. Of course, if the chain is not to be reused, marking it is useless.
7. Unbolt and remove the sprocket, along with the chain. As you remove the chain, hold it where the chain tensioner contacts it. When the chain is

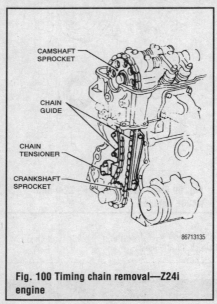

Fig. 100 Timing chain removal—Z24i engine

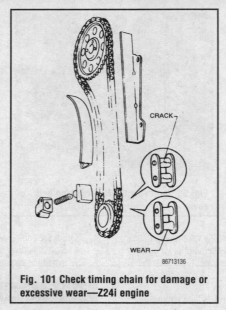

Fig. 101 Check timing chain for damage or excessive wear—Z24i engine

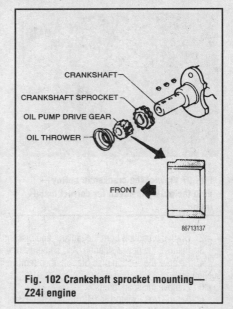

Fig. 102 Crankshaft sprocket mounting—Z24i engine

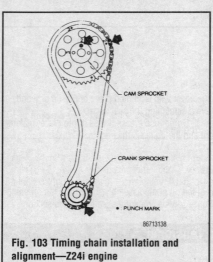

Fig. 103 Timing chain installation and alignment—Z24i engine

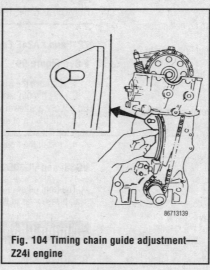

Fig. 104 Timing chain guide adjustment—Z24i engine

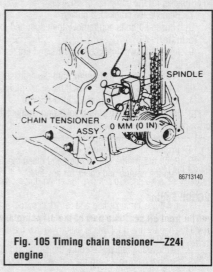

Fig. 105 Timing chain tensioner—Z24i engine

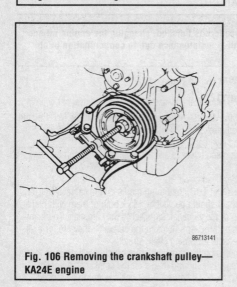

Fig. 106 Removing the crankshaft pulley—KA24E engine

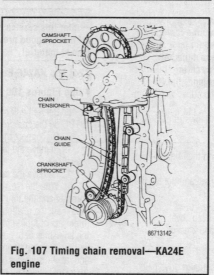

Fig. 107 Timing chain removal—KA24E engine

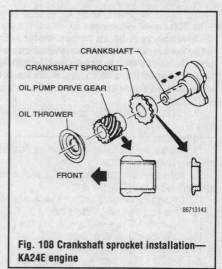

Fig. 108 Crankshaft sprocket installation—KA24E engine

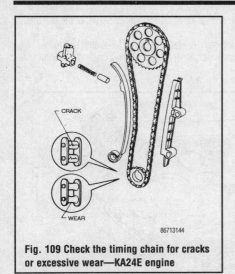

Fig. 109 Check the timing chain for cracks or excessive wear—KA24E engine

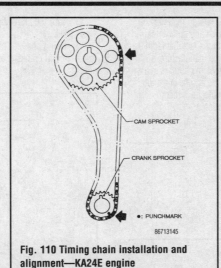

Fig. 110 Timing chain installation and alignment—KA24E engine

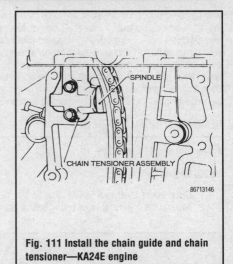

Fig. 111 Install the chain guide and chain tensioner—KA24E engine

Fig. 112 Don't forget the oil seals—KA24E engine

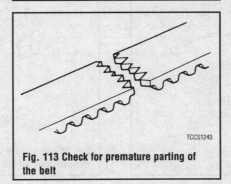

Fig. 113 Check for premature parting of the belt

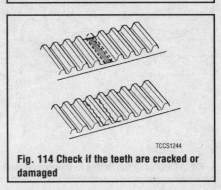

Fig. 114 Check if the teeth are cracked or damaged

removed, the tensioner is going to come apart. Hold on to it and you won't lose any of the parts. The crankshaft sprocket can be removed with a puller, if necessary. There is no need to remove the chain guide unless it is being replaced.

To install:

8. Install the timing chain and camshaft sprocket together after first positioning the chain over the crankshaft sprocket. Position the sprocket so that the marks made previously line up. (This is assuming that the engine has not been disturbed.) The camshaft and crankshaft keys should both be pointing upward. If a new chain and/or gear is being installed, position the sprocket so that the timing marks on the chain align with the marks on the sprocket (with both keys pointing up). The marks are on the right-hand side of the sprockets as you face the engine.

➡The Z24i and KA24E engines do not use the pin counting method for finding correct valve timing. Instead, set the timing chain by aligning its mating marks with those of the crankshaft sprocket and camshaft sprocket. The camshaft sprocket should be installed by fitting the knock pin of the camshaft into its No. 2 hole. On the Z24i engine, the No. 2 timing mark must also be used.

9. Install the camshaft sprocket bolt and tighten it to 87–116 ft. lbs. (118–157 Nm).

10. Install the chain guide and tensioner. Adjust the protrusion of the chain tensioner spindle to zero clearance. Tighten the bolts to 4–7 ft. lbs. (6–10 Nm).

11. With a new seal installed in the timing chain cover and a light coat of oil applied to the seal, install the cover.

12. Install the cylinder head cover.

13. Connect the negative battery.

14. Check all fluids and add, as necessary.

15. Start the engine and check for any leaks. Check the ignition timing and adjust, as necessary.

Timing Belt

INSPECTION

▸ See Figures 113, 114, 115, 116 and 117

The timing belt should be periodically inspected for wear. Removal of the timing cover is necessary to visually check the belt for signs of wear or contamination. The belt should show no signs of wear such as cracked teeth, wear on the belt face,

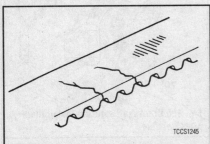

Fig. 115 Look for noticeable cracks or wear on the belt face

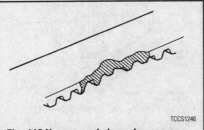

Fig. 116 You may only have damage on one side of the belt; if so, the guide could be the culprit

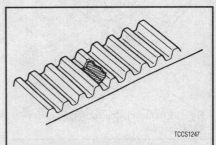

Fig. 117 Foreign materials can get in between the teeth and cause damage

wear on one or both sides of the belt, and there should be no foreign materials on the belt or between the teeth. If there is oil, coolant, lubricant, or any other foreign material on the belt, it is a good idea to replace the belt due to the fact that rapid wear can result from this contamination. Usually sticking to the manufacturer's guide for timing belt replacement interval will ensure little problems but it is still a good idea to periodically inspect your belt. If the belt breaks the engine will shut down and serious engine damage can occur. The proper manufacturer recommended timing belt replacement interval can be found in Section 1.

REMOVAL & INSTALLATION

♦ See Figures 118 thru 129

VG30i Engine

1. Disconnect the negative battery cable.
2. Remove the upper and lower timing belt covers.

3. Turn the crankshaft so that the No. 1 cylinder is at TDC of the compression stroke.
4. Using chalk or paint, mark the relationship of the timing belt to the camshaft and crankshaft sprockets; also, mark the timing belt's direction of rotation.

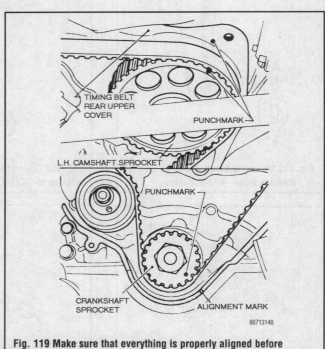

Fig. 119 Make sure that everything is properly aligned before removing the timing belt—6-cylinder engines

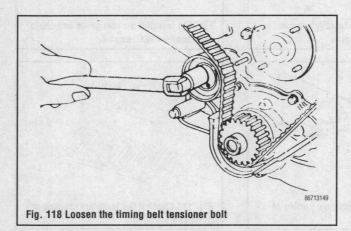

Fig. 118 Loosen the timing belt tensioner bolt

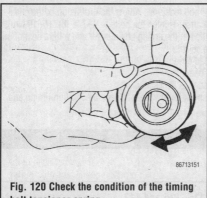

Fig. 120 Check the condition of the timing belt tensioner spring

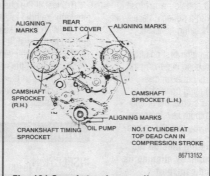

Fig. 121 Sprocket and cover alignment marks prior to installation

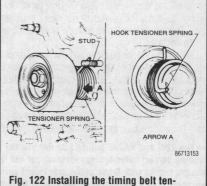

Fig. 122 Installing the timing belt tensioner and spring

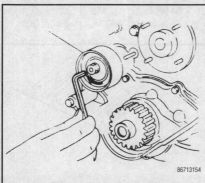

Fig. 123 Turn the tensioner clockwise and tighten the lock-nut

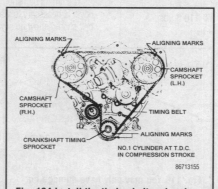

Fig. 124 Install the timing belt and make sure everything is in alignment

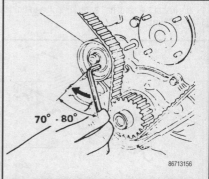

Fig. 125 Turn the tensioner 70–80° clockwise and then tighten it again

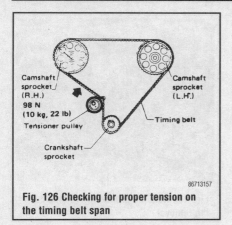

Fig. 126 Checking for proper tension on the timing belt span

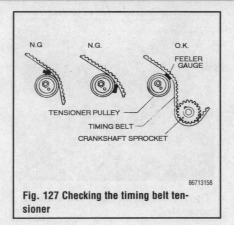

Fig. 127 Checking the timing belt tensioner

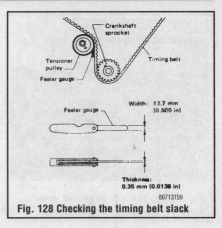

Fig. 128 Checking the timing belt slack

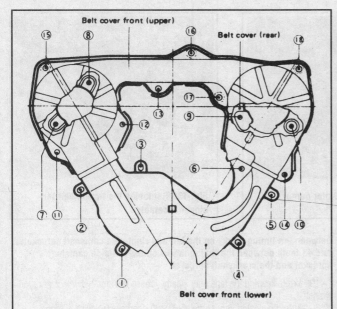

Tightened parts	Section	Parts tightened with bolts
Bolt A (6 pcs.) Rubber washer Belt cover front (lower)	①, ②, ③, ④ ⑤, 14	①, ②, ③, ④, ⑤: Cylinder block 14: Compressor bracket
Bolt B (1 pc.) Rubber washer Belt cover front (lower) Water pump mounting bolt	⑥	Water pump mounting bolt
Bolt C (4 pcs.) Belt cover (rear)	⑦, ⑧, ⑨, 10	Cylinder head
Bolt A (7 pcs.) Rubber washer Belt cover front (upper) Belt cover (rear) Welded nut (4 pcs.)	15, 16, 17, 18 11, 12 13	15, 16, 17, 18: Welded nuts 11, 12: Cylinder head 13: Water outlet

Fig. 129 Installing the front upper and lower covers

5. Loosen the timing belt tensioner and return spring, then remove the timing belt.

➡ **Before installing the timing belt, confirm that the No. 1 cylinder is set at TDC of the compression stroke.**

To install:

6. Remove both cylinder head covers and loosen all rocker arm shaft retaining bolts.

➡ **The rocker arm shaft bolts MUST be loosened so that the correct belt tension can be obtained.**

7. Install the tensioner and the return spring. Using a hexagon wrench, turn the tensioner clockwise, then temporarily tighten the lock-nut.

8. Make sure that the timing belt is clean and free from oil or water, before installation.

9. Install the timing belt. Align the white lines on the belt with the punch-marks on the camshaft and crankshaft sprockets. Be sure to have the arrow on the timing belt pointing toward the front belt covers.

➡ **A good way (although rather tedious) to check for proper timing belt installation is to count the number of belt teeth between the timing marks. There are 133 teeth on the belt; there should be 40 teeth between the timing marks on the left and right-side camshaft sprockets, and 43 teeth between the timing marks on the left-side camshaft sprocket and the crankshaft sprocket.**

10. While keeping the tensioner steady, loosen the lock-nut with a hexagon wrench.

11. Turn the tension approximately 70–80 degrees clockwise with the wrench, then tighten the lock-nut.

12. Turn the crankshaft in a clockwise direction several times, then slowly set the No. 1 piston to TDC of the compression stroke.

13. Apply 22 lbs. (10 kg) of pressure (push it in) to the center span of the timing belt between the right-side camshaft sprocket and the tensioner pulley, then loosen the tensioner lock-nut.

14. Using a 0.0138 in. (0.35mm) feeler gauge (the actual width of the blade must be 1/2 in. or 12.7mm thick), positioned as shown in the illustration, slowly turn the crankshaft clockwise. The timing belt should move approximately 2 1/2 teeth. Tighten the tensioner lock-nut, then turn the crankshaft slightly and remove the feeler gauge.

15. Slowly rotate the crankshaft clockwise several more times , then set the No. 1 piston to TDC of the compression stroke; recheck all alignment marks.

16. Install the upper and lower timing belt covers.

17. Connect the negative battery cable.

VG30E Engine

◆ **See Figures 130 thru 135**

1. Disconnect the negative battery cable. Remove the engine under cover.
2. Remove the radiator shroud, the fan and the pulleys.
3. Drain the coolant from the radiator and disconnect the water pump hose.
4. Remove the radiator.

Fig. 130 If a belt is to be reused, match-mark it to the pulleys before removal

Fig. 131 Release the timing belt tensioner assembly

Fig. 132 Note the proper belt routing during removal

Fig. 133 Removing the water pump mounting bolts

Fig. 134 Removing the water pump assembly

Fig. 135 Removing the timing belt tensioner assembly

5. Remove the power steering, A/C compressor and alternator drive belts.

6. Remove the spark plugs.

7. Remove the distributor protector (dust shield).

8. Remove the A/C compressor drive belt idler pulley and bracket.

9. Remove the fresh air intake tube at the cylinder head cover.

10. Disconnect the radiator hose at the thermostat housing.

11. Unfasten the crankshaft pulley bolt, then remove the pulley with a suitable puller.

12. Unfasten the bolts, then remove the front upper and lower timing belt covers.

13. Set the No. 1 piston at TDC of its compression stroke. Align the punchmark on the left camshaft sprocket with the punchmark on the timing belt upper rear cover. Align the punchmark on the crankshaft sprocket with the notch on the oil pump housing. Temporarily install the crank pulley bolt so the crankshaft can be rotated if necessary.

14. Loosen the timing belt tensioner and return spring, then remove the timing belt.

To install:

➡Before installing the timing belt, confirm that the No. 1 cylinder is set at TDC of the compression stroke.

15. Remove both cylinder head covers and loosen all rocker arm shaft retaining bolts.

➡The rocker arm shaft bolts MUST be loosened so that the correct belt tension can be obtained.

16. Install the tensioner and the return spring. Using a hexagon wrench, turn the tensioner clockwise, then temporarily tighten the lock-nut.

17. Make sure that the timing belt is clean and free from oil or water.

18. When installing the timing belt, align the white lines on the belt with the punchmarks on the camshaft and crankshaft sprockets. Be sure to have the arrow on the timing belt pointing toward the front belt covers.

➡A good way (although rather tedious) to check for proper timing belt installation is to count the number of belt teeth between the timing marks. There are 133 teeth on the belt; there should be 40 teeth between the timing marks on the left and right-side camshaft sprockets, and 43 teeth between the timing marks on the left-side camshaft sprocket and the crankshaft sprocket.

19. While keeping the tensioner steady, loosen the lock-nut with a hexagon wrench.

20. Turn the tension approximately 70–80 degrees clockwise with the wrench, then tighten the lock-nut.

21. Turn the crankshaft in a clockwise direction several times, then slowly set the No. 1 piston to TDC of the compression stroke.

22. Apply 22 lbs. (10 kg) of pressure (push it in) to the center span of the timing belt between the right-side camshaft sprocket and the tensioner pulley, then loosen the tensioner lock-nut.

23. Using a 0.0138 in. (0.35mm) feeler gauge (the actual width of the blade must be 1/2 in. or 12.7mm thick) positioned as shown in the illustration, turn the crankshaft clockwise slowly. The timing belt should move approximately 2 1/2 teeth. Tighten the tensioner lock-nut, then turn the crankshaft slightly and remove the feeler gauge.

24. Slowly rotate the crankshaft clockwise several more times, then set the No. 1 piston to TDC of the compression stroke; recheck all alignment marks.

25. Position the two timing covers on the block and then tighten the mounting bolts to 2–4 ft. lbs. (3–5 Nm).

26. Press the crankshaft pulley onto the shaft, then tighten the bolt to 90–98 ft. lbs. (123–132 Nm).

27. Connect the radiator hose to the thermostat housing.

28. Reconnect the fresh air intake tube at the cylinder head cover.

29. Install the A/C compressor drive belt idler pulley and bracket.

30. Install the distributor protector (dust shield).

31. Install the spark plugs.

32. Install the power steering, A/C compressor and alternator drive belts.

33. Install the radiator.

34. Reconnect the water pump hose.

35. Install the fan shroud and pulleys.

36. Connect the negative battery cable and refill the engine with coolant (bleed the cooling system).

37. Run the engine and check for any leaks.
38. Install the engine under cover.

Camshaft Sprocket/Pulleys

REMOVAL & INSTALLATION

▶ See Figure 136

Z24i and KA24E Engines

1. Remove the timing chain with the camshaft sprocket.

➡The engines are designed so that the camshaft sprocket MUST be removed at the same time that the timing chain is removed.

2. To install, use new gaskets and reverse the removal procedures.

VG30i and VG30E Engines

▶ See Figures 137, 138, 139 and 140

1. Remove the timing belt.
2. Using an adjustable spanner wrench (to hold the camshaft pulley) and a socket wrench, remove the camshaft pulley bolt and washer.
3. Remove the camshaft pulley(s) from the camshaft(s). Be careful not to lose the Woodruff keys.

➡The right and left camshaft pulleys are different parts. Install them in their correct positions. The right pulley has an R3 identification mark and the left pulley has an L3.

To install:
4. To install the camshaft pulleys, perform the following:
   a. Remove the cylinder head covers.
   b. Loosen the rocker arm shaft assembly bolts.
   c. Remove the spark plugs.

d. Make sure the Woodruff keys are in position, then install the camshaft pulleys.
5. Install and adjust the timing belt.
6. Install the timing belt covers.

Camshaft

REMOVAL & INSTALLATION

Z24i and KA24E Engines

▶ See Figures 141 and 142

➡Removal of the cylinder head from the engine is optional. Mark and keep all parts in order for correct installation.

1. Disconnect the negative battery cable.
2. Either remove the cylinder head from the vehicle, or if the job is to be attempted with the cylinder head installed, remove the necessary components for access to the camshaft. Begin by removing the cylinder head cover.
3. Set the No. 1 piston at TDC on its compression stroke, then remove the camshaft sprocket from the camshaft together with the timing chain.

➡The KA24E engine is unique in that its hydraulic lifters are installed inside the rocker arm assemblies. If a hydraulic lifter is kept on its side, even when installed in the rocker arm assembly, there is the possibility of air entering it. After removal, always set rocker arm assembly straight up.

4. Loosen the bolts holding the rocker shaft assembly in place, then remove the six center bolts. Do not pull the four end bolts out of the rocker assembly because they hold the unit together.

➡When loosening the bolts, work from the ends inward and loosen all of the bolts a little at a time, so that you do not strain the camshaft or the rocker assembly. Remember, the camshaft is under pressure from the valve springs.

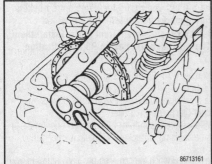

Fig. 136 Tightening the camshaft sprocket bolt with a spanner-type wrench—4-cylinder engines

Fig. 137 Loosen the camshaft pulley retaining bolt

Fig. 138 Remove the camshaft pulley retaining bolt

Fig. 139 View of the camshaft pulley—note the timing mark on top of the pulley

Fig. 140 Tighten the camshaft pulley retaining bolt—note the tool to hold the pulley in place

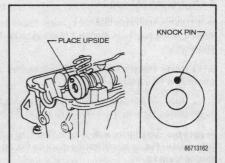

Fig. 141 Make sure that the camshaft is installed with the knockpin UP—Z24i and KA24E engines

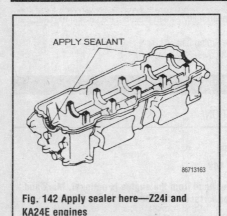

Fig. 142 Apply sealer here—Z24i and KA24E engines

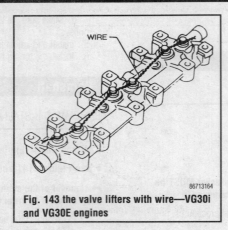

Fig. 143 the valve lifters with wire—VG30i and VG30E engines

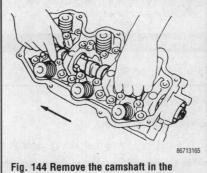

Fig. 144 Remove the camshaft in the direction of the arrow—VG30i and VG30E engines

5. After removing the rocker assembly, remove the camshaft. Slide the camshaft carefully out of the front of the vehicle.

➡**Mark and keep the disassembled parts in order.**

If you disassembled the rocker unit, assemble as follows:

6. Position the mounting brackets, valve rockers and springs, observing the following considerations:

a. The two rocker shafts are different. Both have punch marks in the ends that face the front of the engine. The rocker shaft that goes on the side of the intake manifold has two slits in its end just below the punch mark. The exhaust side rocker shaft does not have slits.

b. The rocker arms for the intake and exhaust valves are interchangeable between cylinders one and three and are identified by the mark **1**. Similarly, the rockers for cylinders two and four are interchangeable and are identified by the mark **2**.

c. The rocker shaft mounting brackets are also coded for correct placement with either an **A** or a **Z** plus a number code.

7. Check camshaft run-out, end-play, wear, and journal clearance.

To install:

8. Apply sealant to the end camshaft saddles, as shown in the accompanying illustration. Place the camshaft on the head with its knockpin pointing up.

9. Fit the rocker assembly on the head, making sure you mount it on its knock pin.

10. Tighten the bolts to 11–18 ft. lbs. (15–25 Nm) on the Z24i engine or to 27–30 ft. lbs. (37–41 Nm) on the KA24E engine, in several stages working from the middle bolts and moving outwards on both sides.

➡**Make sure that the engine is at TDC of the compression stroke for the No. 1 piston or you may damage some valves.**

11. On the Z24i engine, check and adjust the valves, as necessary.
12. If removed, install the cylinder head.
13. Install the cylinder head cover.

VG30i and VG30E Engines

▶ **See Figures 143 and 144**

➡**Nissan recommends that the cylinder heads be removed from the engine, if the engine is mounted in the vehicle, before removing the camshafts.**

1. Disconnect the negative battery cable.
2. Remove the timing belt.
3. Remove the cylinder head.
4. With cylinder head mounted on a suitable workbench, remove the rocker shafts with rocker arms. Bolts should be loosened in two or three stages.

➡**Hold the valve lifters with wire so that they will not drop from the lifter guide. Put an identification mark on the lifters or guide to avoid mixing them up.**

5. At the rear of the cylinder head, remove the cylinder head rear cover, the camshaft bolt and the locating plate.
6. Remove the camshaft front oil seal and then slide the camshaft out the front of the cylinder head assembly.

To install:

7. Install the camshaft, locator plate, cylinder head rear cover and front oil seal. Set the camshaft knock pin at the 12:00 o'clock position (straight up).
8. Install cylinder head with new gasket to engine.
9. Install valve lifter guide assembly, being sure that the valve lifters are retained in their original positions. After installing them in the correct location, remove the wire holding them in lifter guide.
10. Install the rocker shafts in position with their rocker arms. Tighten the bolts in two or three stages to 13–16 ft. lbs. (18–22 Nm). Before tightening, be sure to set the camshaft lobe in a position where the lobe is not lifted or the valve closed. You can set each cylinder one at a time or follow the procedure below (the timing belt must be installed in the correct position):

a. Set the No. 1 piston at TDC of its compression stroke, then tighten the rocker shaft bolts for the No. 2, No. 4 and No. 6 cylinders.
b. Set the No. 4 piston at TDC of its compression stroke, then tighten the rocker shaft bolts for the No. 1, No. 3 and No. 5 cylinders.
c. Tighten the rocker shaft retaining bolts to 13–16 ft. lbs. (18–22 Nm).

11. Install the rear timing belt cover and camshaft sprocket. The left and right camshaft sprockets are different parts. Install the correct sprocket in the correct position.

➡**The right and left camshaft sprockets are different parts. Install them in their correct positions. The right sprocket has an R3 identification mark and the left has an L3.**

12. Install the timing belt.
13. Connect the negative battery cable.

CHECKING CAMSHAFT RUN-OUT

▶ **See Figure 145**

Camshaft run-out should be checked when the camshaft has been removed from the engine. An accurate dial indicator is needed for this procedure; engine specialists and most machine shops have this equipment. If you have access to a dial indicator, or can take your camshaft to someone who does, measure the camshaft bearing journal run-out. The maximum (limit) run-out on the Z24i camshafts is 0.0008 in. (0.2mm). The run-out limit on the KA24E camshafts is 0.0047 in. (0.12mm). The maximum (limit) run-out on the VG30i and VG30E camshaft is 0.0039 in. (0.1mm) If the run-out exceeds the service limit, it should be replaced.

CHECKING CAMSHAFT LOBE HEIGHT

▶ **See Figure 146**

Use a micrometer to check camshaft lobe height, making sure the anvil and the spindle of the micrometer are positioned directly on the heel and tip of the camshaft lobe.

CHECKING CAMSHAFT JOURNALS & BEARINGS

▶ **See Figures 147 and 148**

While the camshaft is still removed from the cylinder head, the camshaft bearing journals should be measured with a micrometer. Compare the measure-

Fig. 145 Camshaft run-out must be measured with a dial indicator

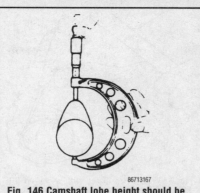

Fig. 146 Camshaft lobe height should be measured with a micrometer

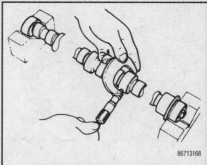

Fig. 147 Measuring the outside diameter of the camshaft journals to determine journal clearance

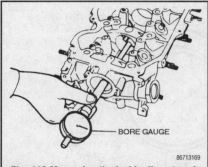

Fig. 148 Measuring the inside diameter of the camshaft saddles to determine journal clearance

Fig. 149 Measuring the camshaft end-play—4-cylinder engines

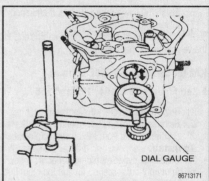

Fig. 150 Measuring the camshaft end-play—6-cylinder engines

ments with those listed in the Camshaft Specifications chart. If the measurements are less than the limits listed in the chart, the camshaft will require replacement, since the camshafts in all of the engines covered in this manual run directly on the cylinder head surface; no actual bearings or bushings are used, so no oversize bearings or bushings are available.

Using an inside dial gauge or inside micrometer, measure the inside diameter of the camshaft saddles. The camshaft journal oil clearances are listed in the Camshaft Specifications chart. If the saddle inside diameters are worn, the cylinder head must be replaced (again, because oversize bearings or bushings are not available).

CHECKING CAMSHAFT END-PLAY

▶ **See Figures 149 and 150**

After the camshaft has been installed, end-play should be checked. Use a dial gauge to check the end-play, by moving the camshaft forward and backward in the cylinder head. End-play specifications should be as noted in the Camshaft Specifications chart.

Rear Main Oil Seal

REMOVAL & INSTALLATION

Z24i Engine

▶ **See Figures 151 and 152**

1. Remove the transmission assembly.
2. If equipped, remove the clutch assembly from the flywheel.
3. Remove the flywheel or flexplate.
4. Remove the rear main oil seal from around the crankshaft.

To install:

5. Apply lithium grease around the sealing lip of the oil seal, then install the seal around the crankshaft using a suitable tool.

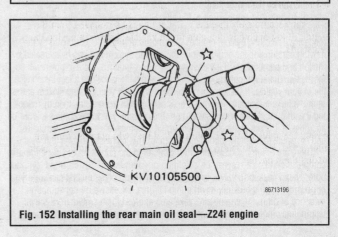

Fig. 151 Removing the rear main oil seal—Z24i engine

Fig. 152 Installing the rear main oil seal—Z24i engine

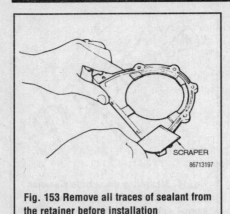

Fig. 153 Remove all traces of sealant from the retainer before installation

Fig. 154 Removing the oil seal from retainer

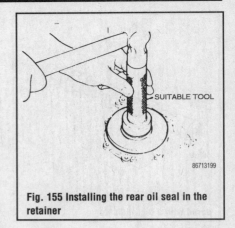

Fig. 155 Installing the rear oil seal in the retainer

6. Install the flywheel or flexplate. If equipped, install the clutch assembly.
7. Install the transmission assembly.
8. Check all fluid levels, start the engine and check for any leaks. Road test the vehicle for proper operation.

KA24E, VG30i and VG30E Engines

♦ **See Figures 153, 154, 155 and 156**

1. Remove the flywheel or flexplate.
2. Remove the rear oil seal retainer from the rear of the engine.
3. Pry the oil seal from the oil seal retainer, using a small prybar.
To install:
4. Clean the gasket mounting surfaces.
5. Apply oil to the sealing lip and the mounting surface of the new oil seal, then press the seal into the oil seal retainer. Install the oil seal retainer/seal.
6. Install the flywheel or flexplate.

Flywheel and Ring Gear

REMOVAL & INSTALLATION

➡ **The clutch cover and pressure plate are balanced as an assembly; if replacement of either part becomes necessary, replace both parts as an assembly.**

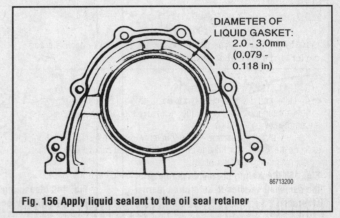

Fig. 156 Apply liquid sealant to the oil seal retainer

1. Remove the transmission as described in Section 7 of this manual.
2. Remove the clutch assembly, if equipped.
3. Remove the flywheel or flexplate.
To install:
4. Position the flywheel or flexplate and secure using new retaining bolts.
5. Torque the bolts in a crisscross pattern to specification.
6. If applicable, install the clutch assembly.
7. Install the transmission.

ENGINE RECONDITIONING

Determining Engine Condition

Anything that generates heat and/or friction will eventually burn or wear out (for example, a light bulb generates heat, therefore its life span is limited). With this in mind, a running engine generates tremendous amounts of both; friction is encountered by the moving and rotating parts inside the engine and heat is created by friction and combustion of the fuel. However, the engine has systems designed to help reduce the effects of heat and friction and provide added longevity. The oiling system reduces the amount of friction encountered by the moving parts inside the engine, while the cooling system reduces heat created by friction and combustion. If either system is not maintained, a break-down will be inevitable. Therefore, you can see how regular maintenance can affect the service life of your vehicle. If you do not drain, flush and refill your cooling system at the proper intervals, deposits will begin to accumulate in the radiator, thereby reducing the amount of heat it can extract from the coolant. The same applies to your oil and filter; if it is not changed often enough it becomes laden with contaminates and is unable to properly lubricate the engine. This increases friction and wear.

There are a number of methods for evaluating the condition of your engine. A compression test can reveal the condition of your pistons, piston rings, cylinder bores, head gasket(s), valves and valve seats. An oil pressure test can warn you of possible engine bearing, or oil pump failures. Excessive oil consumption, evidence of oil in the engine air intake area and/or bluish smoke from the tailpipe may indicate worn piston rings, worn valve guides and/or valve seals.

As a general rule, an engine that uses no more than one quart of oil every 1000 miles is in good condition. Engines that use one quart of oil or more in less than 1000 miles should first be checked for oil leaks. If any oil leaks are present, have them fixed before determining how much oil is consumed by the engine, especially if blue smoke is not visible at the tailpipe.

COMPRESSION TEST

♦ **See Figure 157**

A noticeable lack of engine power, excessive oil consumption and/or poor fuel mileage measured over an extended period are all indicators of internal engine wear. Worn piston rings, scored or worn cylinder bores, blown head gaskets, sticking or burnt valves, and worn valve seats are all possible culprits. A check of each cylinder's compression will help locate the problem.

➡ **A screw-in type compression gauge is more accurate than the type you simply hold against the spark plug hole. Although it takes slightly longer to use, it's worth the effort to obtain a more accurate reading.**

1. Make sure that the proper amount and viscosity of engine oil is in the crankcase, then ensure the battery is fully charged.
2. Warm-up the engine to normal operating temperature, then shut the engine **OFF**.

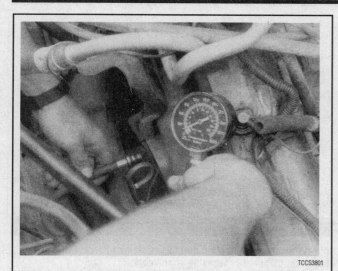

Fig. 157 A screw-in type compression gauge is more accurate and easier to use without an assistant

3. Disable the ignition system.

4. Label and disconnect all of the spark plug wires from the plugs.

5. Thoroughly clean the cylinder head area around the spark plug ports, then remove the spark plugs.

6. Set the throttle plate to the fully open (wide-open throttle) position. You can block the accelerator linkage open for this, or you can have an assistant fully depress the accelerator pedal.

7. Install a screw-in type compression gauge into the No. 1 spark plug hole until the fitting is snug.

✳✳ WARNING

Be careful not to crossthread the spark plug hole.

8. According to the tool manufacturer's instructions, connect a remote starting switch to the starting circuit.

9. With the ignition switch in the **OFF** position, use the remote starting switch to crank the engine through at least five compression strokes (approximately 5 seconds of cranking) and record the highest reading on the gauge.

10. Repeat the test on each cylinder, cranking the engine approximately the same number of compression strokes and/or time as the first.

11. Compare the highest readings from each cylinder to that of the others. The indicated compression pressures are considered within specifications if the lowest reading cylinder is within 75 percent of the pressure recorded for the highest reading cylinder. For example, if your highest reading cylinder pressure was 150 psi (1034 kPa), then 75 percent of that would be 113 psi (779 kPa). So the lowest reading cylinder should be no less than 113 psi (779 kPa).

12. If a cylinder exhibits an unusually low compression reading, pour a tablespoon of clean engine oil into the cylinder through the spark plug hole and repeat the compression test. If the compression rises after adding oil, it means that the cylinder's piston rings and/or cylinder bore are damaged or worn. If the pressure remains low, the valves may not be seating properly (a valve job is needed), or the head gasket may be blown near that cylinder. If compression in any two adjacent cylinders is low, and if the addition of oil doesn't help raise compression, there is leakage past the head gasket. Oil and coolant in the combustion chamber, combined with blue or constant white smoke from the tailpipe, are symptoms of this problem. However, don't be alarmed by the normal white smoke emitted from the tailpipe during engine warm-up or from cold weather driving. There may be evidence of water droplets on the engine dipstick and/or oil droplets in the cooling system if a head gasket is blown.

OIL PRESSURE TEST

Check for proper oil pressure at the sending unit passage with an externally mounted mechanical oil pressure gauge (as opposed to relying on a factory installed dash-mounted gauge). A tachometer may also be needed, as some specifications may require running the engine at a specific rpm.

1. With the engine cold, locate and remove the oil pressure sending unit.

2. Following the manufacturer's instructions, connect a mechanical oil pressure gauge and, if necessary, a tachometer to the engine.

3. Start the engine and allow it to idle.

4. Check the oil pressure reading when cold and record the number. You may need to run the engine at a specified rpm, so check the specifications.

5. Run the engine until normal operating temperature is reached (upper radiator hose will feel warm).

6. Check the oil pressure reading again with the engine hot and record the number. Turn the engine **OFF**.

7. Compare your hot oil pressure reading to that given in the chart. If the reading is low, check the cold pressure reading against the chart. If the cold pressure is well above the specification, and the hot reading was lower than the specification, you may have the wrong viscosity oil in the engine. Change the oil, making sure to use the proper grade and quantity, then repeat the test.

Low oil pressure readings could be attributed to internal component wear, pump related problems, a low oil level, or oil viscosity that is too low. High oil pressure readings could be caused by an overfilled crankcase, too high of an oil viscosity or a faulty pressure relief valve.

Buy or Rebuild?

Now that you have determined that your engine is worn out, you must make some decisions. The question of whether or not an engine is worth rebuilding is largely a subjective matter and one of personal worth. Is the engine a popular one, or is it an obsolete model? Are parts available? Will it get acceptable gas mileage once it is rebuilt? Is the car it's being put into worth keeping? Would it be less expensive to buy a new engine, have your engine rebuilt by a pro, rebuild it yourself or buy a used engine from a salvage yard? Or would it be simpler and less expensive to buy another car? If you have considered all these matters and more, and have still decided to rebuild the engine, then it is time to decide how you will rebuild it.

➡**The editors at Chilton feel that most engine machining should be performed by a professional machine shop. Don't think of it as wasting money, rather, as an assurance that the job has been done right the first time. There are many expensive and specialized tools required to perform such tasks as boring and honing an engine block or having a valve job done on a cylinder head. Even inspecting the parts requires expensive micrometers and gauges to properly measure wear and clearances. Also, a machine shop can deliver to you clean, and ready to assemble parts, saving you time and aggravation. Your maximum savings will come from performing the removal, disassembly, assembly and installation of the engine and purchasing or renting only the tools required to perform the above tasks. Depending on the particular circumstances, you may save 40 to 60 percent of the cost doing these yourself.**

A complete rebuild or overhaul of an engine involves replacing all of the moving parts (pistons, rods, crankshaft, camshaft, etc.) with new ones and machining the non-moving wearing surfaces of the block and heads. Unfortunately, this may not be cost effective. For instance, your crankshaft may have been damaged or worn, but it can be machined undersize for a minimal fee.

So, as you can see, you can replace everything inside the engine, but, it is wiser to replace only those parts which are really needed, and, if possible, repair the more expensive ones. Later in this section, we will break the engine down into its two main components: the cylinder head and the engine block. We will discuss each component, and the recommended parts to replace during a rebuild on each.

Engine Overhaul Tips

Most engine overhaul procedures are fairly standard. In addition to specific parts replacement procedures and specifications for your individual engine, this section is also a guide to acceptable rebuilding procedures. Examples of standard rebuilding practice are given and should be used along with specific details concerning your particular engine.

Competent and accurate machine shop services will ensure maximum performance, reliability and engine life. In most instances it is more profitable for the do-it-yourself mechanic to remove, clean and inspect the component, buy the necessary parts and deliver these to a shop for actual machine work.

Much of the assembly work (crankshaft, bearings, piston rods, and other components) is well within the scope of the do-it-yourself mechanic's tools and abilities. You will have to decide for yourself the depth of involvement you desire in an engine repair or rebuild.

TOOLS

The tools required for an engine overhaul or parts replacement will depend on the depth of your involvement. With a few exceptions, they will be the tools found in a mechanic's tool kit (see Section 1 of this manual). More in-depth work will require some or all of the following:
- A dial indicator (reading in thousandths) mounted on a universal base
- Micrometers and telescope gauges
- Jaw and screw-type pullers
- Scraper
- Valve spring compressor
- Ring groove cleaner
- Piston ring expander and compressor
- Ridge reamer
- Cylinder hone or glaze breaker
- Plastigage®
- Engine stand

The use of most of these tools is illustrated in this section. Many can be rented for a one-time use from a local parts jobber or tool supply house specializing in automotive work.

Occasionally, the use of special tools is called for. See the information on Special Tools and the Safety Notice in the front of this book before substituting another tool.

OVERHAUL TIPS

Aluminum has become extremely popular for use in engines, due to its low weight. Observe the following precautions when handling aluminum parts:
- Never hot tank aluminum parts (the caustic hot tank solution will eat the aluminum.
- Remove all aluminum parts (identification tag, etc.) from engine parts prior to the tanking.
- Always coat threads lightly with engine oil or anti-seize compounds before installation, to prevent seizure.
- Never overtighten bolts or spark plugs especially in aluminum threads.

When assembling the engine, any parts that will be exposed to frictional contact must be prelubed to provide lubrication at initial start-up. Any product specifically formulated for this purpose can be used, but engine oil is not recommended as a prelube in most cases.

When semi-permanent (locked, but removable) installation of bolts or nuts is desired, threads should be cleaned and coated with Loctite® or another similar, commercial non-hardening sealant.

CLEANING

▶ **See Figures 158, 159, 160 and 161**

Before the engine and its components are inspected, they must be thoroughly cleaned. You will need to remove any engine varnish, oil sludge and/or carbon deposits from all of the components to insure an accurate inspection. A crack in the engine block or cylinder head can easily become overlooked if hidden by a layer of sludge or carbon.

Most of the cleaning process can be carried out with common hand tools and readily available solvents or solutions. Carbon deposits can be chipped away using a hammer and a hard wooden chisel. Old gasket material and varnish or sludge can usually be removed using a scraper and/or cleaning solvent. Extremely stubborn deposits may require the use of a power drill with a wire brush. If using a wire brush, use extreme care around any critical machined surfaces (such as the gasket surfaces, bearing saddles, cylinder bores, etc.). USE OF A WIRE BRUSH IS NOT RECOMMENDED ON ANY ALUMINUM COMPONENTS. Always follow any safety recommendations given by the manufacturer of the tool and/or solvent. You should always wear eye protection during any cleaning process involving scraping, chipping or spraying of solvents.

An alternative to the mess and hassle of cleaning the parts yourself is to drop them off at a local garage or machine shop. They will, more than likely, have the necessary equipment to properly clean all of the parts for a nominal fee.

> ※ **CAUTION**
>
> **Always wear eye protection during any cleaning process involving scraping, chipping or spraying of solvents.**

Remove any oil galley plugs, freeze plugs and/or pressed-in bearings and carefully wash and degrease all of the engine components including the fasteners and bolts. Small parts such as the valves, springs, etc., should be placed in a metal basket and allowed to soak. Use pipe cleaner type brushes, and clean all passageways in the components. Use a ring expander and remove the rings from the pistons. Clean the piston ring grooves with a special tool or a piece of broken ring. Scrape the carbon off of the top of the piston. You should never use a wire brush on the pistons. After preparing all of the piston assemblies in this manner, wash and degrease them again.

> ※ **WARNING**
>
> **Use extreme care when cleaning around the cylinder head valve seats. A mistake or slip may cost you a new seat.**

When cleaning the cylinder head, remove carbon from the combustion chamber with the valves installed. This will avoid damaging the valve seats.

REPAIRING DAMAGED THREADS

▶ **See Figures 162, 163, 164, 165 and 166**

Several methods of repairing damaged threads are available. Heli-Coil® (shown here), Keenserts® and Microdot® are among the most widely used. All involve basically the same principle—drilling out stripped threads, tapping the hole and installing a prewound insert—making welding, plugging and oversize fasteners unnecessary.

Two types of thread repair inserts are usually supplied: a standard type for most inch coarse, inch fine, metric course and metric fine thread sizes and a spark lug type to fit most spark plug port sizes. Consult the individual tool manufacturer's catalog to determine exact applications. Typical thread repair kits will contain a selection of prewound threaded inserts, a tap (corresponding to the

Fig. 158 Use a gasket scraper to remove the old gasket material from the mating surfaces

TCCS3132

Fig. 159 Use a ring expander tool to remove the piston rings

TCCS3211

Fig. 160 Clean the piston ring grooves using a ring groove cleaner tool, or . . .

TCCS3208

Fig. 161 . . . use a piece of an old ring to clean the grooves. Be careful, the ring can be quite sharp

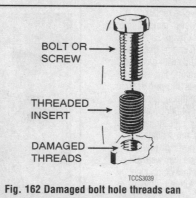
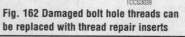

BOLT OR SCREW

THREADED INSERT

DAMAGED THREADS

Fig. 162 Damaged bolt hole threads can be replaced with thread repair inserts

TANG

NOTCH

Fig. 163 Standard thread repair insert (left), and spark plug thread insert

Fig. 164 Drill out the damaged threads with the specified size bit. Be sure to drill completely through the hole or to the bottom of a blind hole

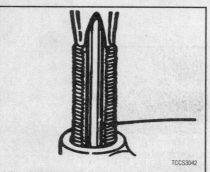

Fig. 165 Using the kit, tap the hole in order to receive the thread insert. Keep the tap well oiled and back it out frequently to avoid clogging the threads

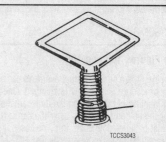

Fig. 166 Screw the insert onto the installer tool until the tang engages the slot. Thread the insert into the hole until it is 1/4–1/2 turn below the top surface, then remove the tool and break off the tang using a punch

outside diameter threads of the insert) and an installation tool. Spark plug inserts usually differ because they require a tap equipped with pilot threads and a combined reamer/tap section. Most manufacturers also supply blister-packed thread repair inserts separately in addition to a master kit containing a variety of taps and inserts plus installation tools.

Before attempting to repair a threaded hole, remove any snapped, broken or damaged bolts or studs. Penetrating oil can be used to free frozen threads. The offending item can usually be removed with locking pliers or using a screw/stud extractor. After the hole is clear, the thread can be repaired, as shown in the series of accompanying illustrations and in the kit manufacturer's instructions.

Engine Preparation

To properly rebuild an engine, you must first remove it from the vehicle, then disassemble and diagnose it. Ideally you should place your engine on an engine stand. This affords you the best access to the engine components. Follow the manufacturer's directions for using the stand with your particular engine. Remove the flywheel or flexplate before installing the engine to the stand.

Now that you have the engine on a stand, and assuming that you have drained the oil and coolant from the engine, it's time to strip it of all but the necessary components. Before you start disassembling the engine, you may want to take a moment to draw some pictures, or fabricate some labels or containers to mark the locations of various components and the bolts and/or studs which fasten them. Modern day engines use a lot of little brackets and clips which hold wiring harnesses and such, and these holders are often mounted on studs and/or bolts that can be easily mixed up. The manufacturer spent a lot of time and money designing your vehicle, and they wouldn't have wasted any of it by haphazardly placing brackets, clips or fasteners on the vehicle. If it's present when you disassemble it, put it back when you assemble, you will regret not remembering that little bracket which holds a wire harness out of the path of a rotating part.

You should begin by unbolting any accessories still attached to the engine, such as the water pump, power steering pump, alternator, etc. Then, unfasten any manifolds (intake or exhaust) which were not removed during the engine removal procedure. Finally, remove any covers remaining on the engine such as

the rocker arm, front or timing cover and oil pan. Some front covers may require the vibration damper and/or crank pulley to be removed beforehand. The idea is to reduce the engine to the bare necessities (cylinder head(s), valve train, engine block, crankshaft, pistons and connecting rods), plus any other `in block' components such as oil pumps, balance shafts and auxiliary shafts.

Finally, remove the cylinder head(s) from the engine block and carefully place on a bench. Disassembly instructions for each component follow later in this section.

Cylinder Head

There are two basic types of cylinder heads used on today's automobiles: the Overhead Valve (OHV) and the Overhead Camshaft (OHC). The latter can also be broken down into two subgroups: the Single Overhead Camshaft (SOHC) and the Dual Overhead Camshaft (DOHC). Generally, if there is only a single camshaft on a head, it is just referred to as an OHC head. Also, an engine with an OHV cylinder head is also known as a pushrod engine.

Most cylinder heads these days are made of an aluminum alloy due to its light weight, durability and heat transfer qualities. However, cast iron was the material of choice in the past, and is still used on many vehicles today. Whether made from aluminum or iron, all cylinder heads have valves and seats. Some use two valves per cylinder, while the more hi-tech engines will utilize a multi-valve configuration using 3, 4 and even 5 valves per cylinder. When the valve contacts the seat, it does so on precision machined surfaces, which seals the combustion chamber. All cylinder heads have a valve guide for each valve. The guide centers the valve to the seat and allows it to move up and down within it. The clearance between the valve and guide can be critical. Too much clearance and the engine may consume oil, lose vacuum and/or damage the seat. Too little, and the valve can stick in the guide causing the engine to run poorly if at all, and possibly causing severe damage. The last component all cylinder heads have are valve springs. The spring holds the valve against its seat. It also returns the valve to this position when the valve has been opened by the valve train or camshaft. The spring is fastened to the valve by a retainer and valve locks (sometimes called keepers). Aluminum heads will also have a valve spring shim to keep the spring from wearing away the aluminum.

An ideal method of rebuilding the cylinder head would involve replacing all of the valves, guides, seats, springs, etc. with new ones. However, depending on how the engine was maintained, often this is not necessary. A major cause of valve, guide and seat wear is an improperly tuned engine. An engine that is running too rich, will often wash the lubricating oil out of the guide with gasoline, causing it to wear rapidly. Conversely, an engine which is running too lean will place higher combustion temperatures on the valves and seats allowing them to wear or even burn. Springs fall victim to the driving habits of the individual. A driver who often runs the engine rpm to the redline will wear out or break the springs faster then one that stays well below it. Unfortunately, mileage takes it toll on all of the parts. Generally, the valves, guides, springs and seats in a cylinder head can be machined and re-used, saving you money. However, if a valve is burnt, it may be wise to replace all of the valves, since they were all operating in the same environment. The same goes for any other component on the cylinder head. Think of it as an insurance policy against future problems related to that component.

Unfortunately, the only way to find out which components need replacing, is to disassemble and carefully check each piece. After the cylinder head(s) are disassembled, thoroughly clean all of the components.

DISASSEMBLY

▶ See Figures 167 and 168

Whether it is a single or dual overhead camshaft cylinder head, the disassembly procedure is relatively unchanged. One aspect to pay attention to is careful labeling of the parts on the dual camshaft cylinder head. There will be an intake camshaft and followers as well as an exhaust camshaft and followers and they must be labeled as such. In some cases, the components are identical and could easily be installed incorrectly. DO NOT MIX THEM UP! Determining which is which is very simple; the intake camshaft and components are on the same side of the head as was the intake manifold. Conversely, the exhaust camshaft and components are on the same side of the head as was the exhaust manifold.

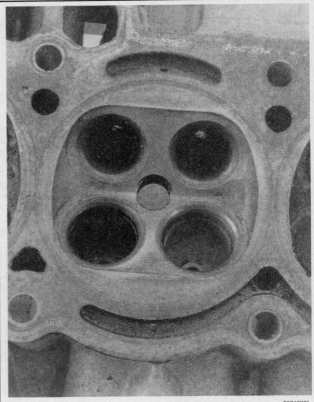

Fig. 168 Example of a multi-valve cylinder head. Note how it has 2 intake and 2 exhaust valve ports

Cup Type Camshaft Followers

▶ See Figures 169, 170 and 171

Most cylinder heads with cup type camshaft followers will have the valve spring, retainer and locks recessed within the follower's bore. You will need a C-clamp style valve spring compressor tool, an OHC spring removal tool (or equivalent) and a small magnet to disassemble the head.

1. If not already removed, remove the camshaft(s) and/or followers. Mark their positions for assembly.

2. Position the cylinder head to allow use of a C-clamp style valve spring compressor tool.

Fig. 167 Exploded view of a valve, seal, spring, retainer and locks from an OHC cylinder head

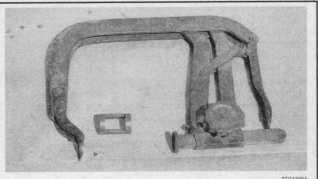

Fig. 169 C-clamp type spring compressor and an OHC spring removal tool (center) for cup type followers

TCCA3P63

Fig. 170 Most cup type follower cylinder heads retain the camshaft using bolt-on bearing caps

TCCA3P65

Fig. 171 Position the OHC spring tool in the follower bore, then compress the spring with a C-clamp type tool

➡It is preferred to position the cylinder head gasket surface facing you with the valve springs facing the opposite direction and the head laying horizontal.

3. With the OHC spring removal adapter tool positioned inside of the follower bore, compress the valve spring using the C-clamp style valve spring compressor.
4. Remove the valve locks. A small magnetic tool or screwdriver will aid in removal.
5. Release the compressor tool and remove the spring assembly.
6. Withdraw the valve from the cylinder head.
7. If equipped, remove the valve seal.

➡Special valve seal removal tools are available. Regular or needlenose type pliers, if used with care, will work just as well. If using ordinary pliers, be sure not to damage the follower bore. The follower and its bore are machined to close tolerances and any damage to the bore will effect this relationship.

8. If equipped, remove the valve spring shim. A small magnetic tool or screwdriver will aid in removal.
9. Repeat Steps 3 through 8 until all of the valves have been removed.

Rocker Arm Type Camshaft Followers

◗ **See Figures 172 thru 180**

Most cylinder heads with rocker arm-type camshaft followers are easily disassembled using a standard valve spring compressor. However, certain models may not have enough open space around the spring for the standard tool and may require you to use a C-clamp style compressor tool instead.

1. If not already removed, remove the rocker arms and/or shafts and the camshaft. If applicable, also remove the hydraulic lash adjusters. Mark their positions for assembly.
2. Position the cylinder head to allow access to the valve spring.
3. Use a valve spring compressor tool to relieve the spring tension from the retainer.

➡Due to engine varnish, the retainer may stick to the valve locks. A gentle tap with a hammer may help to break it loose.

4. Remove the valve locks from the valve tip and/or retainer. A small magnet may help in removing the small locks.
5. Lift the valve spring, tool and all, off of the valve stem.
6. If equipped, remove the valve seal. If the seal is difficult to remove with the valve in place, try removing the valve first, then the seal. Follow the steps below for valve removal.
7. Position the head to allow access for withdrawing the valve.

➡Cylinder heads that have seen a lot of miles and/or abuse may have mushroomed the valve lock grove and/or tip, causing difficulty in removal of the valve. If this has happened, use a metal file to carefully remove the high spots around the lock grooves and/or tip. Only file it enough to allow removal.

8. Remove the valve from the cylinder head.
9. If equipped, remove the valve spring shim. A small magnetic tool or screwdriver will aid in removal.
10. Repeat Steps 3 though 9 until all of the valves have been removed.

INSPECTION

Now that all of the cylinder head components are clean, it's time to inspect them for wear and/or damage. To accurately inspect them, you will need some specialized tools:

- A 0–1 in. micrometer for the valves
- A dial indicator or inside diameter gauge for the valve guides
- A spring pressure test gauge

If you do not have access to the proper tools, you may want to bring the components to a shop that does.

Fig. 172 Example of the shaft mounted rocker arms on some OHC heads

Fig. 173 Another example of the rocker arm type OHC head. This model uses a follower under the camshaft

Fig. 174 Before the camshaft can be removed, all of the followers must first be removed . . .

Fig. 175 . . . then the camshaft can be removed by sliding it out (shown), or unbolting a bearing cap (not shown)

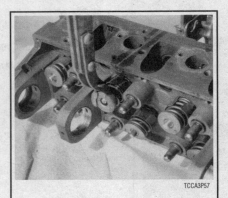

Fig. 176 Compress the valve spring . . .

Fig. 177 . . . then remove the valve locks from the valve stem and spring retainer

Fig. 178 Remove the valve spring and retainer from the cylinder head

Fig. 179 Remove the valve seal from the guide. Some gentle prying or pliers may help to remove stubborn ones

Fig. 180 All aluminum and some cast iron heads will have these valve spring shims. Remove all of them as well

Valves

♦ See Figures 181 and 182

The first thing to inspect are the valve heads. Look closely at the head, margin and face for any cracks, excessive wear or burning. The margin is the best place to look for burning. It should have a squared edge with an even width all around the diameter. When a valve burns, the margin will look melted and the edges rounded. Also inspect the valve head for any signs of tulipping. This will show as a lifting of the edges or dishing in the center of the head and will usually not occur to all of the valves. All of the heads should look the same, any that seem dished more than others are probably bad. Next, inspect the valve lock grooves and valve tips. Check for any burrs around the lock grooves, especially if you had to file them to remove the valve. Valve tips should appear flat, although slight rounding with high mileage engines is normal. Slightly worn valve tips will need to be machined flat. Last, measure the valve stem diameter with the micrometer. Measure the area that rides within the guide, especially towards the tip where

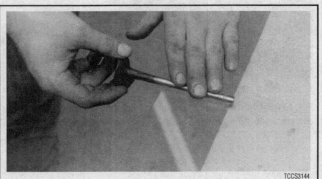

Fig. 181 Valve stems may be rolled on a flat surface to check for bends

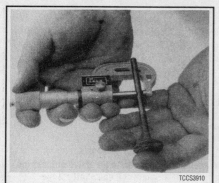

Fig. 182 Use a micrometer to check the valve stem diameter

TCCS3910

Fig. 183 Use a caliper to check the valve spring free-length

TCCS3907

Fig. 184 Check the valve spring for squareness on a flat surface; a carpenter's square can be used

TCCS3908

most of the wear occurs. Take several measurements along its length and compare them to each other. Wear should be even along the length with little to no taper. If no minimum diameter is given in the specifications, then the stem should not read more than 0.001 in. (0.025mm) below the unworn area of the valve stem. Any valves that fail these inspections should be replaced.

Springs, Retainers and Valve Locks

▶ **See Figures 183 and 184**

The first thing to check is the most obvious, broken springs. Next check the free length and squareness of each spring. If applicable, insure to distinguish between intake and exhaust springs. Use a ruler and/or carpenter's square to measure the length. A carpenter's square should be used to check the springs for squareness. If a spring pressure test gauge is available, check each springs rating and compare to the specifications chart. Check the readings against the specifications given. Any springs that fail these inspections should be replaced.

The spring retainers rarely need replacing, however they should still be checked as a precaution. Inspect the spring mating surface and the valve lock retention area for any signs of excessive wear. Also check for any signs of cracking. Replace any retainers that are questionable.

Valve locks should be inspected for excessive wear on the outside contact area as well as on the inner notched surface. Any locks which appear worn or broken and its respective valve should be replaced.

Cylinder Head

There are several things to check on the cylinder head: valve guides, seats, cylinder head surface flatness, cracks and physical damage.

VALVE GUIDES

▶ **See Figure 185**

Now that you know the valves are good, you can use them to check the guides, although a new valve, if available, is preferred. Before you measure any-

thing, look at the guides carefully and inspect them for any cracks, chips or breakage. Also if the guide is a removable style (as in most aluminum heads), check them for any looseness or evidence of movement. All of the guides should appear to be at the same height from the spring seat. If any seem lower (or higher) from another, the guide has moved. Mount a dial indicator onto the spring side of the cylinder head. Lightly oil the valve stem and insert it into the cylinder head. Position the dial indicator against the valve stem near the tip and zero the gauge. Grasp the valve stem and wiggle towards and away from the dial indicator and observe the readings. Mount the dial indicator 90 degrees from the initial point and zero the gauge and again take a reading. Compare the two readings for a out of round condition. Check the readings against the specifications given. An Inside Diameter (I.D.) gauge designed for valve guides will give you an accurate valve guide bore measurement. If the I.D. gauge is used, compare the readings with the specifications given. Any guides that fail these inspections should be replaced or machined.

VALVE SEATS

A visual inspection of the valve seats should show a slightly worn and pitted surface where the valve face contacts the seat. Inspect the seat carefully for severe pitting or cracks. Also, a seat that is badly worn will be recessed into the cylinder head. A severely worn or recessed seat may need to be replaced. All cracked seats must be replaced. A seat concentricity gauge, if available, should be used to check the seat run-out. If run-out exceeds specifications the seat must be machined (if no specification is given use 0.002 in. or 0.051mm).

CYLINDER HEAD SURFACE FLATNESS

▶ **See Figures 186 and 187**

After you have cleaned the gasket surface of the cylinder head of any old gasket material, check the head for flatness.

Place a straightedge across the gasket surface. Using feeler gauges, determine the clearance at the center of the straightedge and across the cylinder head at several points. Check along the centerline and diagonally on the head sur-

TCCS3142

Fig. 185 A dial gauge may be used to check valve stem-to-guide clearance; read the gauge while moving the valve stem

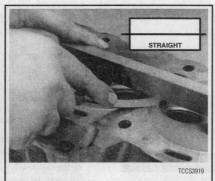

TCCS3919

Fig. 186 Check the head for flatness across the center of the head surface using a straightedge and feeler gauge

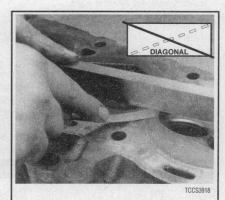

TCCS3918

Fig. 187 Checks should also be made along both diagonals of the head surface

face. If the warpage exceeds 0.003 in. (0.076mm) within a 6.0 in. (15.2cm) span, or 0.006 in. (0.152mm) over the total length of the head, the cylinder head must be resurfaced. After resurfacing the heads of a V-type engine, the intake manifold flange surface should be checked, and if necessary, milled proportionally to allow for the change in its mounting position.

CRACKS AND PHYSICAL DAMAGE

Generally, cracks are limited to the combustion chamber, however, it is not uncommon for the head to crack in a spark plug hole, port, outside of the head or in the valve spring/rocker arm area. The first area to inspect is always the hottest: the exhaust seat/port area.

A visual inspection should be performed, but just because you don't see a crack does not mean it is not there. Some more reliable methods for inspecting for cracks include Magnaflux®, a magnetic process or Zyglo®, a dye penetrant. Magnaflux® is used only on ferrous metal (cast iron) heads. Zyglo® uses a spray on fluorescent mixture along with a black light to reveal the cracks. It is strongly recommended to have your cylinder head checked professionally for cracks, especially if the engine was known to have overheated and/or leaked or consumed coolant. Contact a local shop for availability and pricing of these services.

Physical damage is usually very evident. For example, a broken mounting ear from dropping the head or a bent or broken stud and/or bolt. All of these defects should be fixed or, if unrepairable, the head should be replaced.

Camshaft and Followers

Inspect the camshaft(s) and followers as described earlier in this section.

REFINISHING & REPAIRING

Many of the procedures given for refinishing and repairing the cylinder head components must be performed by a machine shop. Certain steps, if the inspected part is not worn, can be performed yourself inexpensively. However, you spent a lot of time and effort so far, why risk trying to save a couple bucks if you might have to do it all over again?

Valves

Any valves that were not replaced should be refaced and the tips ground flat. Unless you have access to a valve grinding machine, this should be done by a machine shop. If the valves are in extremely good condition, as well as the valve seats and guides, they may be lapped in without performing machine work.

It is a recommended practice to lap the valves even after machine work has been performed and/or new valves have been purchased. This insures a positive seal between the valve and seat.

LAPPING THE VALVES

➡**Before lapping the valves to the seats, read the rest of the cylinder head section to insure that any related parts are in acceptable enough condition to continue.**

➡**Before any valve seat machining and/or lapping can be performed, the guides must be within factory recommended specifications.**

1. Invert the cylinder head.
2. Lightly lubricate the valve stems and insert them into the cylinder head in their numbered order.
3. Raise the valve from the seat and apply a small amount of fine lapping compound to the seat.
4. Moisten the suction head of a hand-lapping tool and attach it to the head of the valve.
5. Rotate the tool between the palms of both hands, changing the position of the valve on the valve seat and lifting the tool often to prevent grooving.
6. Lap the valve until a smooth, polished circle is evident on the valve and seat.
7. Remove the tool and the valve. Wipe away all traces of the grinding compound and store the valve to maintain its lapped location.

✳✳ WARNING

Do not get the valves out of order after they have been lapped. They must be put back with the same valve seat with which they were lapped.

Springs, Retainers and Valve Locks

There is no repair or refinishing possible with the springs, retainers and valve locks. If they are found to be worn or defective, they must be replaced with new (or known good) parts.

Cylinder Head

Most refinishing procedures dealing with the cylinder head must be performed by a machine shop. Read the sections below and review your inspection data to determine whether or not machining is necessary.

VALVE GUIDE

➡**If any machining or replacements are made to the valve guides, the seats must be machined.**

Unless the valve guides need machining or replacing, the only service to perform is to thoroughly clean them of any dirt or oil residue.

There are only two types of valve guides used on automobile engines: the replaceable-type (all aluminum heads) and the cast-in integral-type (most cast iron heads). There are four recommended methods for repairing worn guides.
- Knurling
- Inserts
- Reaming oversize
- Replacing

Knurling is a process in which metal is displaced and raised, thereby reducing clearance, giving a true center, and providing oil control. It is the least expensive way of repairing the valve guides. However, it is not necessarily the best, and in some cases, a knurled valve guide will not stand up for more than a short time. It requires a special knurlizer and precision reaming tools to obtain proper clearances. It would not be cost effective to purchase these tools, unless you plan on rebuilding several of the same cylinder head.

Installing a guide insert involves machining the guide to accept a bronze insert. One style is the coil-type which is installed into a threaded guide. Another is the thin-walled insert where the guide is reamed oversize to accept a split-sleeve insert. After the insert is installed, a special tool is then run through the guide to expand the insert, locking it to the guide. The insert is then reamed to the standard size for proper valve clearance.

Reaming for oversize valves restores normal clearances and provides a true valve seat. Most cast-in type guides can be reamed to accept an valve with an oversize stem. The cost factor for this can become quite high as you will need to purchase the reamer and new, oversize stem valves for all guides which were reamed. Oversizes are generally 0.003 to 0.030 in. (0.076 to 0.762mm), with 0.015 in. (0.381mm) being the most common.

To replace cast-in type valve guides, they must be drilled out, then reamed to accept replacement guides. This must be done on a fixture which will allow centering and leveling off of the original valve seat or guide, otherwise a serious guide-to-seat misalignment may occur making it impossible to properly machine the seat.

Replaceable-type guides are pressed into the cylinder head. A hammer and a stepped drift or punch may be used to install and remove the guides. Before removing the guides, measure the protrusion on the spring side of the head and record it for installation. Use the stepped drift to hammer out the old guide from the combustion chamber side of the head. When installing, determine whether or not the guide also seals a water jacket in the head, and if it does, use the recommended sealing agent. If there is no water jacket, grease the valve guide and its bore. Use the stepped drift, and hammer the new guide into the cylinder head from the spring side of the cylinder head. A stack of washers the same thickness as the measured protrusion may help the installation process.

VALVE SEATS

➡**Before any valve seat machining can be performed, the guides must be within factory recommended specifications.**

➡**If any machining or replacements were made to the valve guides, the seats must be machined.**

If the seats are in good condition, the valves can be lapped to the seats, and the cylinder head assembled. See the valves section for instructions on lapping.

If the valve seats are worn, cracked or damaged, they must be serviced by a machine shop. The valve seat must be perfectly centered to the valve guide, which requires very accurate machining.

CYLINDER HEAD SURFACE

If the cylinder head is warped, it must be machined flat. If the warpage is extremely severe, the head may need to be replaced. In some instances, it may be possible to straighten a warped head enough to allow machining. In either case, contact a professional machine shop for service.

➡**Any OHC cylinder head that shows excessive warpage should have the camshaft bearing journals align bored after the cylinder head has been resurfaced.**

❊❊ WARNING

Failure to align bore the camshaft bearing journals could result in severe engine damage including but not limited to: valve and piston damage, connecting rod damage, camshaft and/or crankshaft breakage.

CRACKS AND PHYSICAL DAMAGE

Certain cracks can be repaired in both cast iron and aluminum heads. For cast iron, a tapered threaded insert is installed along the length of the crack. Aluminum can also use the tapered inserts, however welding is the preferred method. Some physical damage can be repaired through brazing or welding. Contact a machine shop to get expert advice for your particular dilemma.

ASSEMBLY

◆ **See Figure 188**

The first step for any assembly job is to have a clean area in which to work. Next, thoroughly clean all of the parts and components that are to be assembled. Finally, place all of the components onto a suitable work space and, if necessary, arrange the parts to their respective positions.

Cup Type Camshaft Followers

To install the springs, retainers and valve locks on heads which have these components recessed into the camshaft follower's bore, you will need a small screwdriver-type tool, some clean white grease and a lot of patience. You will also need the C-clamp style spring compressor and the OHC tool used to disassemble the head.

1. Lightly lubricate the valve stems and insert all of the valves into the cylinder head. If possible, maintain their original locations.
2. If equipped, install any valve spring shims which were removed.
3. If equipped, install the new valve seals, keeping the following in mind:
 • If the valve seal presses over the guide, lightly lubricate the outer guide surfaces.

Fig. 188 Once assembled, check the valve clearance and correct as needed

TCCA3P64

 • If the seal is an O-ring type, it is installed just after compressing the spring but before the valve locks.
4. Place the valve spring and retainer over the stem.
5. Position the spring compressor and the OHC tool, then compress the spring.
6. Using a small screwdriver as a spatula, fill the valve stem side of the lock with white grease. Use the excess grease on the screwdriver to fasten the lock to the driver.
7. Carefully install the valve lock, which is stuck to the end of the screwdriver, to the valve stem then press on it with the screwdriver until the grease squeezes out. The valve lock should now be stuck to the stem.
8. Repeat Steps 6 and 7 for the remaining valve lock.
9. Relieve the spring pressure slowly and insure that neither valve lock becomes dislodged by the retainer.
10. Remove the spring compressor tool.
11. Repeat Steps 2 through 10 until all of the springs have been installed.
12. Install the followers, camshaft(s) and any other components that were removed for disassembly.

Rocker Arm Type Camshaft Followers

1. Lightly lubricate the valve stems and insert all of the valves into the cylinder head. If possible, maintain their original locations.
2. If equipped, install any valve spring shims which were removed.
3. If equipped, install the new valve seals, keeping the following in mind:
 • If the valve seal presses over the guide, lightly lubricate the outer guide surfaces.
 • If the seal is an O-ring type, it is installed just after compressing the spring but before the valve locks.
4. Place the valve spring and retainer over the stem.
5. Position the spring compressor tool and compress the spring.
6. Assemble the valve locks to the stem.
7. Relieve the spring pressure slowly and insure that neither valve lock becomes dislodged by the retainer.
8. Remove the spring compressor tool.
9. Repeat Steps 2 through 8 until all of the springs have been installed.
10. Install the camshaft(s), rockers, shafts and any other components that were removed for disassembly.

Engine Block

GENERAL INFORMATION

A thorough overhaul or rebuild of an engine block would include replacing the pistons, rings, bearings, timing belt/chain assembly and oil pump. For OHV engines also include a new camshaft and lifters. The block would then have the cylinders bored and honed oversize (or if using removable cylinder sleeves, new sleeves installed) and the crankshaft would be cut undersize to provide new wearing surfaces and perfect clearances. However, your particular engine may not have everything worn out. What if only the piston rings have worn out and the clearances on everything else are still within factory specifications? Well, you could just replace the rings and put it back together, but this would be a very rare example. Chances are, if one component in your engine is worn, other components are sure to follow, and soon. At the very least, you should always replace the rings, bearings and oil pump. This is what is commonly called a "freshen up".

Cylinder Ridge Removal

Because the top piston ring does not travel to the very top of the cylinder, a ridge is built up between the end of the travel and the top of the cylinder bore.

Pushing the piston and connecting rod assembly past the ridge can be difficult, and damage to the piston ring lands could occur. If the ridge is not removed before installing a new piston or not removed at all, piston ring breakage and piston damage may occur.

➡**It is always recommended that you remove any cylinder ridges before removing the piston and connecting rod assemblies. If you know that new pistons are going to be installed and the engine block will be bored oversize, you may be able to forego this step. However, some ridges may actually prevent the assemblies from being removed, necessitating its removal.**

There are several different types of ridge reamers on the market, none of which are inexpensive. Unless a great deal of engine rebuilding is anticipated, borrow or rent a reamer.

1. Turn the crankshaft until the piston is at the bottom of its travel.
2. Cover the head of the piston with a rag.
3. Follow the tool manufacturers instructions and cut away the ridge, exercising extreme care to avoid cutting too deeply.
4. Remove the ridge reamer, the rag and as many of the cuttings as possible. Continue until all of the cylinder ridges have been removed.

DISASSEMBLY

▶ **See Figures 189 and 190**

The engine disassembly instructions following assume that you have the engine mounted on an engine stand. If not, it is easiest to disassemble the engine on a bench or the floor with it resting on the bell housing or transmission mounting surface. You must be able to access the connecting rod fasteners and turn the crankshaft during disassembly. Also, all engine covers (timing, front, side, oil pan, whatever) should have already been removed. Engines which are seized or locked up may not be able to be completely disassembled, and a core (salvage yard) engine should be purchased.

If not done during the cylinder head removal, remove the timing chain/belt and/or gear/sprocket assembly. Remove the oil pick-up and pump assembly and, if necessary, the pump drive. If equipped, remove any balance or auxiliary shafts. If necessary, remove the cylinder ridge from the top of the bore. See the cylinder ridge removal procedure earlier in this section.

Rotate the engine over so that the crankshaft is exposed. Use a number punch or scribe and mark each connecting rod with its respective cylinder number. The cylinder closest to the front of the engine is always number 1. However, depending on the engine placement, the front of the engine could either be the flywheel or damper/pulley end. Generally the front of the engine faces the front of the vehicle. Use a number punch or scribe and also mark the main bearing caps from front to rear with the front most cap being number 1 (if there are five caps, mark them 1 through 5, front to rear).

✳✳ WARNING

Take special care when pushing the connecting rod up from the crankshaft because the sharp threads of the rod bolts/studs will score the crankshaft journal. Insure that special plastic caps are installed over them, or cut two pieces of rubber hose to do the same.

Again, rotate the engine, this time to position the number one cylinder bore (head surface) up. Turn the crankshaft until the number one piston is at the bottom of its travel, this should allow the maximum access to its connecting rod. Remove the number one connecting rods fasteners and cap and place two lengths of rubber hose over the rod bolts/studs to protect the crankshaft from damage. Using a sturdy wooden dowel and a hammer, push the connecting rod up about 1 in. (25mm) from the crankshaft and remove the upper bearing insert. Continue pushing or tapping the connecting rod up until the piston rings are

Fig. 189 Place rubber hose over the connecting rod studs to protect the crankshaft and cylinder bores from damage

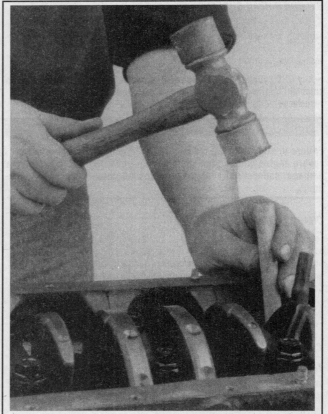

Fig. 190 Carefully tap the piston out of the bore using a wooden dowel

out of the cylinder bore. Remove the piston and rod by hand, put the upper half of the bearing insert back into the rod, install the cap with its bearing insert installed, and hand-tighten the cap fasteners. If the parts are kept in order in this manner, they will not get lost and you will be able to tell which bearings came form what cylinder if any problems are discovered and diagnosis is necessary. Remove all the other piston assemblies in the same manner. On V-style engines, remove all of the pistons from one bank, then reposition the engine with the other cylinder bank head surface up, and remove that banks piston assemblies.

The only remaining component in the engine block should now be the crankshaft. Loosen the main bearing caps evenly until the fasteners can be turned by hand, then remove them and the caps. Remove the crankshaft from the engine block. Thoroughly clean all of the components.

INSPECTION

Now that the engine block and all of its components are clean, it's time to inspect them for wear and/or damage. To accurately inspect them, you will need some specialized tools:

• Two or three separate micrometers to measure the pistons and crankshaft journals
• A dial indicator
• Telescoping gauges for the cylinder bores
• A rod alignment fixture to check for bent connecting rods

If you do not have access to the proper tools, you may want to bring the components to a shop that does.

Generally, you shouldn't expect cracks in the engine block or its components unless it was known to leak, consume or mix engine fluids, it was severely overheated, or there was evidence of bad bearings and/or crankshaft damage. A visual inspection should be performed on all of the components, but just because you don't see a crack does not mean it is not there. Some more reliable methods for inspecting for cracks include Magnaflux®, a magnetic process or Zyglo®, a dye penetrant. Magnaflux® is used only on ferrous metal (cast iron). Zyglo® uses a spray on fluorescent mixture along with a black light to reveal the cracks. It is strongly recommended to have your engine block checked professionally for cracks, especially if the engine was known to have overheated and/or leaked or consumed coolant. Contact a local shop for availability and pricing of these services.

Engine Block

ENGINE BLOCK BEARING ALIGNMENT

Remove the main bearing caps and, if still installed, the main bearing inserts. Inspect all of the main bearing saddles and caps for damage, burrs or high spots. If damage is found, and it is caused from a spun main bearing, the block will need to be align-bored or, if severe enough, replacement. Any burrs or high spots should be carefully removed with a metal file.

Place a straightedge on the bearing saddles, in the engine block, along the centerline of the crankshaft. If any clearance exists between the straightedge and the saddles, the block must be align-bored.

Align-boring consists of machining the main bearing saddles and caps by means of a flycutter that runs through the bearing saddles.

DECK FLATNESS

The top of the engine block where the cylinder head mounts is called the deck. Insure that the deck surface is clean of dirt, carbon deposits and old gasket material. Place a straightedge across the surface of the deck along its centerline and, using feeler gauges, check the clearance along several points. Repeat the checking procedure with the straightedge placed along both diagonals of the deck surface. If the reading exceeds 0.003 in. (0.076mm) within a 6.0 in. (15.2cm) span, or 0.006 in. (0.152mm) over the total length of the deck, it must be machined.

CYLINDER BORES

▶ See Figure 191

The cylinder bores house the pistons and are slightly larger than the pistons themselves. A common piston-to-bore clearance is 0.0015–0.0025 in. (0.0381mm–0.0635mm). Inspect and measure the cylinder bores. The bore should be checked for out-of-roundness, taper and size. The results of this inspection will determine whether the cylinder can be used in its existing size and condition, or a rebore to the next oversize is required (or in the case of removable sleeves, have replacements installed).

The amount of cylinder wall wear is always greater at the top of the cylinder than at the bottom. This wear is known as taper. Any cylinder that has a taper of 0.0012 in. (0.305mm) or more, must be rebored. Measurements are taken at a number of positions in each cylinder: at the top, middle and bottom and at two points at each position; that is, at a point 90 degrees from the crankshaft centerline, as well as a point parallel to the crankshaft centerline. The measurements are made with either a special dial indicator or a telescopic gauge and micrometer. If the necessary precision tools to check the bore are not available, take the block to a machine shop and have them mike it. Also if you don't have the tools

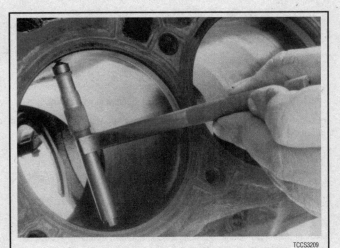

Fig. 191 Use a telescoping gauge to measure the cylinder bore diameter—take several readings within the same bore

to check the cylinder bores, chances are you will not have the necessary devices to check the pistons, connecting rods and crankshaft. Take these components with you and save yourself an extra trip.

For our procedures, we will use a telescopic gauge and a micrometer. You will need one of each, with a measuring range which covers your cylinder bore size.

1. Position the telescopic gauge in the cylinder bore, loosen the gauges lock and allow it to expand.

➡**Your first two readings will be at the top of the cylinder bore, then proceed to the middle and finally the bottom, making a total of six measurements.**

2. Hold the gauge square in the bore, 90 degrees from the crankshaft centerline, and gently tighten the lock. Tilt the gauge back to remove it from the bore.
3. Measure the gauge with the micrometer and record the reading.
4. Again, hold the gauge square in the bore, this time parallel to the crankshaft centerline, and gently tighten the lock. Again, you will tilt the gauge back to remove it from the bore.
5. Measure the gauge with the micrometer and record this reading. The difference between these two readings is the out-of-round measurement of the cylinder.
6. Repeat steps 1 through 5, each time going to the next lower position, until you reach the bottom of the cylinder. Then go to the next cylinder, and continue until all of the cylinders have been measured.

The difference between these measurements will tell you all about the wear in your cylinders. The measurements which were taken 90 degrees from the crankshaft centerline will always reflect the most wear. That is because at this position is where the engine power presses the piston against the cylinder bore the hardest. This is known as thrust wear. Take your top, 90 degree measurement and compare it to your bottom, 90 degree measurement. The difference between them is the taper. When you measure your pistons, you will compare these readings to your piston sizes and determine piston-to-wall clearance.

Crankshaft

Inspect the crankshaft for visible signs of wear or damage. All of the journals should be perfectly round and smooth. Slight scores are normal for a used crankshaft, but you should hardly feel them with your fingernail. When measuring the crankshaft with a micrometer, you will take readings at the front and rear of each journal, then turn the micrometer 90 degrees and take two more readings, front and rear. The difference between the front-to-rear readings is the journal taper and the first-to-90 degree reading is the out-of-round measurement. Generally, there should be no taper or out-of-roundness found, however, up to 0.0005 in. (0.0127mm) for either can be overlooked. Also, the readings should fall within the factory specifications for journal diameters.

If the crankshaft journals fall within specifications, it is recommended that it be polished before being returned to service. Polishing the crankshaft insures that any minor burrs or high spots are smoothed, thereby reducing the chance of scoring the new bearings.

Pistons and Connecting Rods

PISTONS

▶ See Figure 192

The piston should be visually inspected for any signs of cracking or burning (caused by hot spots or detonation), and scuffing or excessive wear on the skirts. The wrist pin attaches the piston to the connecting rod. The piston should move freely on the wrist pin, both sliding and pivoting. Grasp the connecting rod securely, or mount it in a vise, and try to rock the piston back and forth along the centerline of the wrist pin. There should not be any excessive play evident between the piston and the pin. If there are C-clips retaining the pin in the piston then you have wrist pin bushings in the rods. There should not be any excessive play between the wrist pin and the rod bushing. Normal clearance for the wrist pin is approx. 0.001–0.002 in. (0.025mm–0.051mm).

Use a micrometer and measure the diameter of the piston, perpendicular to the wrist pin, on the skirt. Compare the reading to its original cylinder measurement obtained earlier. The difference between the two readings is the piston-to-wall clearance. If the clearance is within specifications, the piston may be used as is. If the piston is out of specification, but the bore is not, you will need a new piston. If both are out of specification, you will need the cylinder rebored and oversize pistons installed. Generally if two or more pistons/bores are out of specification, it is best to rebore the entire block and purchase a complete set of oversize pistons.

TCCS3209

Fig. 192 Measure the piston's outer diameter, perpendicular to the wrist pin, with a micrometer

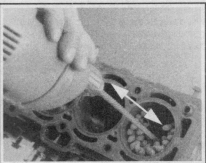

Fig. 193 Use a ball type cylinder hone to remove any glaze and provide a new surface for seating the piston rings

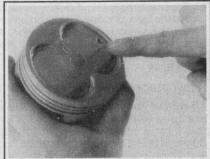

Fig. 194 Most pistons are marked to indicate positioning in the engine (usually a mark means the side facing the front)

CONNECTING ROD

You should have the connecting rod checked for straightness at a machine shop. If the connecting rod is bent, it will unevenly wear the bearing and piston, as well as place greater stress on these components. Any bent or twisted connecting rods must be replaced. If the rods are straight and the wrist pin clearance is within specifications, then only the bearing end of the rod need be checked. Place the connecting rod into a vice, with the bearing inserts in place, install the cap to the rod and torque the fasteners to specifications. Use a telescoping gauge and carefully measure the inside diameter of the bearings. Compare this reading to the rods original crankshaft journal diameter measurement. The difference is the oil clearance. If the oil clearance is not within specifications, install new bearings in the rod and take another measurement. If the clearance is still out of specifications, and the crankshaft is not, the rod will need to be reconditioned by a machine shop.

➡You can also use Plastigage® to check the bearing clearances. The assembling section has complete instructions on its use.

Camshaft

Inspect the camshaft and lifters/followers as described earlier in this section.

Bearings

All of the engine bearings should be visually inspected for wear and/or damage. The bearing should look evenly worn all around with no deep scores or pits. If the bearing is severely worn, scored, pitted or heat blued, then the bearing, and the components that use it, should be brought to a machine shop for inspection. Full-circle bearings (used on most camshafts, auxiliary shafts, balance shafts, etc.) require specialized tools for removal and installation, and should be brought to a machine shop for service.

Oil Pump

➡The oil pump is responsible for providing constant lubrication to the whole engine and so it is recommended that a new oil pump be installed when rebuilding the engine.

Completely disassemble the oil pump and thoroughly clean all of the components. Inspect the oil pump gears and housing for wear and/or damage. Insure that the pressure relief valve operates properly and there is no binding or sticking due to varnish or debris. If all of the parts are in proper working condition, lubricate the gears and relief valve, and assemble the pump.

REFINISHING

▶ See Figure 193

Almost all engine block refinishing must be performed by a machine shop. If the cylinders are not to be rebored, then the cylinder glaze can be removed with a ball hone. When removing cylinder glaze with a ball hone, use a light or penetrating type oil to lubricate the hone. Do not allow the hone to run dry as this may cause excessive scoring of the cylinder bores and wear on the hone. If new pistons are required, they will need to be installed to the connecting rods. This should be performed by a machine shop as the pistons must be installed in the correct relationship to the rod or engine damage can occur.

Pistons and Connecting Rods

▶ See Figure 194

Only pistons with the wrist pin retained by C-clips are serviceable by the home-mechanic. Press fit pistons require special presses and/or heaters to remove/install the connecting rod and should only be performed by a machine shop.

All pistons will have a mark indicating the direction to the front of the engine and the must be installed into the engine in that manner. Usually it is a notch or arrow on the top of the piston, or it may be the letter F cast or stamped into the piston.

ASSEMBLY

Before you begin assembling the engine, first give yourself a clean, dirt free work area. Next, clean every engine component again. The key to a good assembly is cleanliness.

Mount the engine block into the engine stand and wash it one last time using water and detergent (dishwashing detergent works well). While washing it, scrub the cylinder bores with a soft bristle brush and thoroughly clean all of the oil passages. Completely dry the engine and spray the entire assembly down with an anti-rust solution such as WD-40® or similar product. Take a clean lint-free rag and wipe up any excess anti-rust solution from the bores, bearing saddles, etc. Repeat the final cleaning process on the crankshaft. Replace any freeze or oil galley plugs which were removed during disassembly.

Crankshaft

▶ See Figures 195, 196, 197 and 198

1. Remove the main bearing inserts from the block and bearing caps.
2. If the crankshaft main bearing journals have been refinished to a definite undersize, install the correct undersize bearing. Be sure that the bearing inserts and bearing bores are clean. Foreign material under inserts will distort bearing and cause failure.
3. Place the upper main bearing inserts in bores with tang in slot.

➡The oil holes in the bearing inserts must be aligned with the oil holes in the cylinder block.

4. Install the lower main bearing inserts in bearing caps.
5. Clean the mating surfaces of block and rear main bearing cap.
6. Carefully lower the crankshaft into place. Be careful not to damage bearing surfaces.
7. Check the clearance of each main bearing by using the following procedure:
   a. Place a piece of Plastigage® or its equivalent, on bearing surface across full width of bearing cap and about ¼ in. off center.
   b. Install cap and tighten bolts to specifications. Do not turn crankshaft while Plastigage® is in place.
   c. Remove the cap. Using the supplied Plastigage® scale, check width of Plastigage® at widest point to get maximum clearance. Difference between readings is taper of journal.

d. If clearance exceeds specified limits, try a 0.001 in. or 0.002 in. undersize bearing in combination with the standard bearing. Bearing clearance must be within specified limits. If standard and 0.002 in. undersize bearing does not bring clearance within desired limits, refinish crankshaft journal, then install undersize bearings.

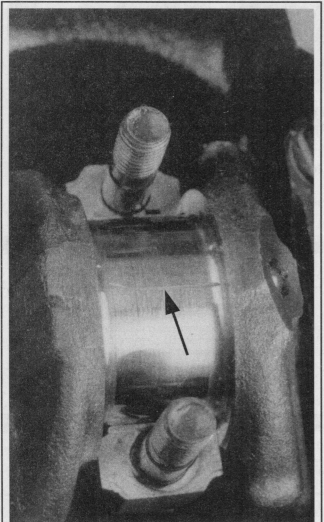

Fig. 195 Apply a strip of gauging material to the bearing journal, then install and torque the cap

8. Install the rear main seal.

9. After the bearings have been fitted, apply a light coat of engine oil to the journals and bearings. Install the rear main bearing cap. Install all bearing caps except the thrust bearing cap. Be sure that main bearing caps are installed in original locations. Tighten the bearing cap bolts to specifications.

10. Install the thrust bearing cap with bolts finger-tight.

11. Pry the crankshaft forward against the thrust surface of upper half of bearing.

12. Hold the crankshaft forward and pry the thrust bearing cap to the rear. This aligns the thrust surfaces of both halves of the bearing.

13. Retain the forward pressure on the crankshaft. Tighten the cap bolts to specifications.

14. Measure the crankshaft end-play as follows:

a. Mount a dial gauge to the engine block and position the tip of the gauge to read from the crankshaft end.

b. Carefully pry the crankshaft toward the rear of the engine and hold it there while you zero the gauge.

c. Carefully pry the crankshaft toward the front of the engine and read the gauge.

d. Confirm that the reading is within specifications. If not, install a new thrust bearing and repeat the procedure. If the reading is still out of specifications with a new bearing, have a machine shop inspect the thrust surfaces of the crankshaft, and if possible, repair it.

15. Rotate the crankshaft so as to position the first rod journal to the bottom of its stroke.

Pistons and Connecting Rods

▶ See Figures 199, 200, 201 and 202

1. Before installing the piston/connecting rod assembly, oil the pistons, piston rings and the cylinder walls with light engine oil. Install connecting rod bolt protectors or rubber hose onto the connecting rod bolts/studs. Also perform the following:

a. Select the proper ring set for the size cylinder bore.

b. Position the ring in the bore in which it is going to be used.

c. Push the ring down into the bore area where normal ring wear is not encountered.

d. Use the head of the piston to position the ring in the bore so that the ring is square with the cylinder wall. Use caution to avoid damage to the ring or cylinder bore.

e. Measure the gap between the ends of the ring with a feeler gauge. Ring gap in a worn cylinder is normally greater than specification. If the ring gap is greater than the specified limits, try an oversize ring set.

f. Check the ring side clearance of the compression rings with a feeler gauge inserted between the ring and its lower land according to specification. The gauge should slide freely around the entire ring circumference without binding. Any wear that occurs will form a step at the inner portion of the lower land. If the lower lands have high steps, the piston should be replaced.

2. Unless new pistons are installed, be sure to install the pistons in the cylinders from which they were removed. The numbers on the connecting rod and bearing cap must be on the same side when installed in the cylinder bore. If a connecting rod is ever transposed from one engine or cylinder to another, new bearings should be fitted and the connecting rod should be numbered to corre-

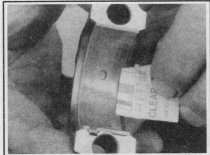

Fig. 196 After the cap is removed again, use the scale supplied with the gauging material to check the clearance

Fig. 197 A dial gauge may be used to check crankshaft end-play

Fig. 198 Carefully pry the crankshaft back and forth while reading the dial gauge for end-play

Fig. 199 Checking the piston ring-to-ring groove side clearance using the ring and a feeler gauge

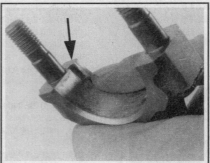

Fig. 200 The notch on the side of the bearing cap matches the tang on the bearing insert

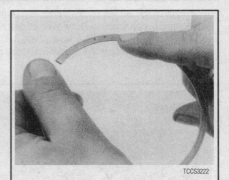

Fig. 201 Most rings are marked to show which side of the ring should face up when installed to the piston

Fig. 202 Install the piston and rod assembly into the block using a ring compressor and the handle of a hammer

spond with the new cylinder number. The notch on the piston head goes toward the front of the engine.

3. Install all of the rod bearing inserts into the rods and caps.

4. Install the rings to the pistons. Install the oil control ring first, then the second compression ring and finally the top compression ring. Use a piston ring expander tool to aid in installation and to help reduce the chance of breakage.

5. Make sure the ring gaps are properly spaced around the circumference of the piston. Fit a piston ring compressor around the piston and slide the piston and connecting rod assembly down into the cylinder bore, pushing it in with the wooden hammer handle. Push the piston down until it is only slightly below the top of the cylinder bore. Guide the connecting rod onto the crankshaft bearing journal carefully, to avoid damaging the crankshaft.

6. Check the bearing clearance of all the rod bearings, fitting them to the crankshaft bearing journals. Follow the procedure in the crankshaft installation above.

7. After the bearings have been fitted, apply a light coating of assembly oil to the journals and bearings.

8. Turn the crankshaft until the appropriate bearing journal is at the bottom of its stroke, then push the piston assembly all the way down until the connecting rod bearing seats on the crankshaft journal. Be careful not to allow the bearing cap screws to strike the crankshaft bearing journals and damage them.

9. After the piston and connecting rod assemblies have been installed, check the connecting rod side clearance on each crankshaft journal.

10. Prime and install the oil pump and the oil pump intake tube.

Cylinder Head(S)

1. Install the cylinder head(s) using new gaskets.
2. Install the timing sprockets/gears and the belt/chain assemblies.

Engine Covers and Components

Install the timing cover(s) and oil pan. Refer to your notes and drawings made prior to disassembly and install all of the components that were removed. Install the engine into the vehicle.

Engine Start-up and Break-in

STARTING THE ENGINE

Now that the engine is installed and every wire and hose is properly connected, go back and double check that all coolant and vacuum hoses are connected. Check that your oil drain plug is installed and properly tightened. If not already done, install a new oil filter onto the engine. Fill the crankcase with the proper amount and grade of engine oil. Fill the cooling system with a 50/50 mixture of coolant/water.

1. Connect the vehicle battery.
2. Start the engine. Keep your eye on your oil pressure indicator; if it does not indicate oil pressure within 10 seconds of starting, turn the vehicle off.

✳✳ WARNING

Damage to the engine can result if it is allowed to run with no oil pressure. Check the engine oil level to make sure that it is full. Check for any leaks and if found, repair the leaks before continuing. If there is still no indication of oil pressure, you may need to prime the system.

3. Confirm that there are no fluid leaks (oil or other).
4. Allow the engine to reach normal operating temperature (the upper radiator hose will be hot to the touch).
5. At this point you can perform any necessary checks or adjustments, such as checking the ignition timing.
6. Install any remaining components or body panels which were removed.

BREAKING IT IN

Make the first miles on the new engine, easy ones. Vary the speed but do not accelerate hard. Most importantly, do not lug the engine, and avoid sustained high speeds until at least 100 miles. Check the engine oil and coolant levels frequently. Expect the engine to use a little oil until the rings seat. Change the oil and filter at 500 miles, 1500 miles, then every 3000 miles past that.

KEEP IT MAINTAINED

Now that you have just gone through all of that hard work, keep yourself from doing it all over again by thoroughly maintaining it. Not that you may not have maintained it before, heck you could have had one to two hundred thousand miles on it before doing this. However, you may have bought the vehicle used, and the previous owner did not keep up on maintenance. Which is why you just went through all of that hard work. See?

EXHAUST SYSTEM

Safety Precautions

For a number of reasons, exhaust system work can be dangerous. Always observe the following precautions:
- Support the vehicle securely by using jackstands or equivalent under the frame of the vehicle.
- Wear safety goggles to protect your eyes from metal chips that may fly free while working on the exhaust system.
- When using a torch, be careful not to come close to any fuel lines.
- Always use the proper tool for the job.
- NEVER WORK ON A HOT EXHAUST SYSTEM!

Special Tools

A number of special exhaust tools can be rented or bought from a local auto parts store. It may also be quite helpful to use solvents designed to loosen rusted nuts or bolts. Remember that these products are often flammable, so apply only to parts after they are cool.

Front Pipe

REMOVAL & INSTALLATION

◢ See Figures 203, 204 and 205

1. Support the vehicle securely by using jackstands or equivalent under the frame of the vehicle.
2. Remove the exhaust pipe clamps and, if equipped, the front exhaust pipe shield.
3. Soak the exhaust manifold front pipe mounting studs with penetrating oil. Remove the attaching nuts and gasket from the manifold.

Fig. 203 Removing the exhaust pipe connection—most models are similar

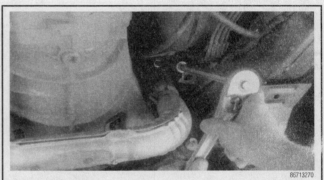

Fig. 204 Removing the front pipe from the manifold—note the tools used for this job

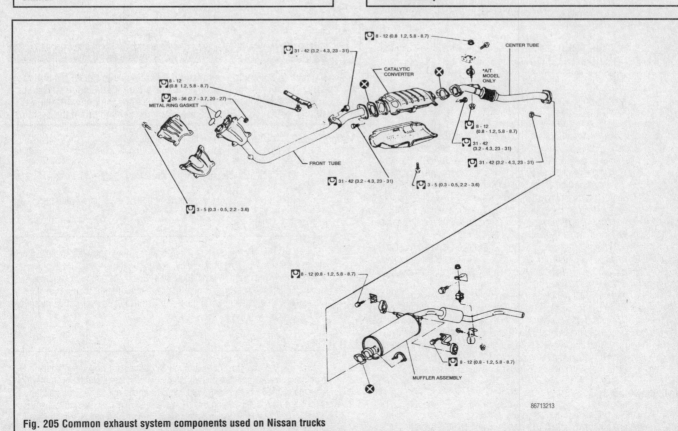

Fig. 205 Common exhaust system components used on Nissan trucks

➡**If these studs snap off while removing the front pipe, remove the manifold then drill out the stud and tap the hole.**

4. If equipped, remove the exhaust pipe mounting hanger or bracket.
5. Remove the front pipe from the muffler/catalytic converter.

To install:

6. Install the front pipe on the manifold with seal, if so equipped.
7. Connect the pipe to the muffler/catalytic converter. Assemble all parts loosely and position the pipe to insure proper clearance from vehicle body.
8. Tighten mounting studs, bracket bolts and exhaust clamps.
9. If equipped, install exhaust pipe shield.
10. Start the engine and check for exhaust leaks.

Catalytic Converter

▸ **See Figure 205**

REMOVAL & INSTALLATION

1. Remove the converter lower shield.
2. Disconnect the converter from the front pipe.
3. Disconnect the converter from the center pipe or tailpipe assembly.
4. Remove the catalytic converter.

➡**Assemble all parts loosely and position the converter before tightening the exhaust clamps.**

5. To install, reverse the removal procedures. Always use new clamps and exhaust seals, then start the engine and check for leaks.

Center Pipe

▸ **See Figure 205**

REMOVAL & INSTALLATION

1. Raise the vehicle and support it with safety stands.
2. Soak all nuts and bolts at the converter and muffler connections with penetrating oil.
3. Disconnect the pipe at the catalytic converter.
4. While supporting the pipe, disconnect it at the muffler, then remove the pipe from the vehicle.
5. Position the pipe and connect it to the muffler.
6. Connect the pipe to the converter, then install all applicable mounting brackets and hardware.

Tailpipe and Muffler

▸ **See Figure 205**

REMOVAL & INSTALLATION

1. Disconnect the tailpipe at the catalytic converter assembly.
2. Remove all brackets and exhaust clamps.
3. Remove the tailpipe from the muffler. On some models, the tailpipe and muffler are one piece.
4. To install, reverse the removal procedure. Always use new clamps and exhaust seals. When finished, start the engine and check for leaks.

Z24i ENGINE REBUILDING SPECIFICATIONS

	U.S.	Metric
Camshaft run-out	0.0008 in.	0.02 mm
Camshaft lobe height		
Intake	1.5148-1.5168 in.	38.477-38.527 mm
Exhaust	1.5150-1.5170 in.	38.481-38.531 mm
Camshaft sprocket run-out (less than)	0.004 in.	0.10 mm
Connecting rod center distance	6.4949-6.4972 in.	164.97-165.03 mm
Crankshaft center distance	1.8886-1.8909 in.	47.97-48.03 mm
Crankshaft out-of-round (less than)	0.0002 in.	0.005 mm
Crankshaft taper (less than)	0.0002 in.	0.005 mm
Crankshaft run-out	0.0010 in.	0.025 mm
Cylinder head surface distortion		
Limit	0.004 in.	0.10 mm
Cylinder block surface flatness		
Limit	0.004 in.	0.10 mm
Cylinder out-of-round (less than)	0.0006 in.	0.015 mm
Cylinder taper (less than)	0.0004 in.	0.010 mm
Flywheel run-out (less than)	0.0039 in.	0.10 mm
Piston pin hole diameter	0.8268-0.8271 in.	21.001-21.008 mm
Piston-to-cylinder block clearance	0.0010-0.0018 in.	0.025-0.045 mm
Piston pin-to-piston clearance	0.0003-0.0005 in.	0.008-0.012 mm
Rocker arm-to-shaft clearance	0.0003-0.0019 in.	0.007-0.049 mm
Rocker shaft diameter	0.7866-0.7874 in.	19.979-20.000 mm
Rocker arm rocker shaft hole diameter	0.7877-0.7885 in.	20.007-20.028 mm
Valve head diameter		
Intake	1.654-1.661 in.	42.0-42.2 mm
Exhaust	1.496-1.504 in.	38.0-38.2 mm
Valve length		
Intake	4.835-4.846 in.	122.8-123.1 mm
Exhaust	4.866-4.878 in.	123.6-123.9 mm
Valve margin		
Intake	0.0051 in.	1.3 mm
Exhaust	0.0059 in.	1.5 mm
Valve clearance		
Intake		
Cold	0.008 in.	0.21 mm
Hot	0.012 in.	0.30 mm
Exhaust		
Cold	0.009 in.	0.23 mm
Hot	0.012 in.	0.30 mm
Valve spring out-of-square		
Outer	0.087 in.	2.2 mm
Inner	0.075 in.	1.9 mm
Valve deflection		
Limit	0.008 in.	0.20 mm

86713C08

KA24E ENGINE REBUILDING SPECIFICATIONS

	U.S.	Metric
Camshaft run-out	0.0008 in.	0.02 mm
Camshaft lobe height	1.7653-1.7728 in.	44.839-45.029 mm
Camshaft sprocket run-out (less than)	0.0047 in.	0.12 mm
Connecting rod center distance	6.4941-6.4980 in.	164.95-165.05 mm
Crankshaft center distance	1.8886-1.8909 in.	47.97-48.03 mm
Crankshaft out-of-round (less than)	0.0002 in.	0.005 mm
Crankshaft taper (less than)	0.0002 in.	0.005 mm
Crankshaft run-out	0.0010 in.	0.0039 mm
Cylinder head surface distortion		
Limit	0.004 in.	0.10 mm
Cylinder block surface flatness		
Limit	0.004 in.	0.10 mm
Cylinder out-of-round (less than)	0.0006 in.	0.015 mm
Cylinder taper (less than)	0.0004 in.	0.010 mm
Flywheel run-out (less than)	0.004 in.	0.10 mm
Piston pin hole diameter	0.8268-0.8271 in.	21.001-21.008 mm
Piston-to-cylinder block clearance	0.0008-0.0016 in.	0.020-0.040 mm
Piston pin-to-piston clearance	0.0003-0.0005 in.	0.008-0.012 mm
Rocker arm-to-shaft clearance	0.0005-0.0020 in.	0.012-0.050 mm
Rocker shaft diameter	0.8653-0.8661 in.	21.979-22.000 mm
Rocker arm rocker shaft hole diameter	0.8666-0.8673 in.	22.012-22.029 mm
Valve head diameter		
Intake	1.339-1.346 in.	34.0-34.2 mm
Exhaust	1.575-1.583 in.	40.0-40.2 mm
Valve length		
Intake	4.720-4.732 in.	119.9-120.2 mm
Exhaust	4.7508-4.7626 in.	120.67-120.97 mm
Valve margin		
Intake	0.0453 in.	1.15 mm
Exhaust	0.0531 in.	1.35 mm
Valve clearance	0.0 in.	0.0 mm
Valve spring out-of-square		
Outer	0.091 in.	2.3 mm
Inner	0.083 in.	2.1 mm

86713C09

VG30i AND VG30E ENGINE REBUILDING SPECIFICATIONS

	U.S.	Metric
Camshaft run-out		
Standard	0.0016 in.	0.04 mm
Limit	0.004 in.	0.1 mm
Camshaft lobe height	1.5566-1.5641 in.	39.537-39.727 mm
Camshaft height wear limit	0.0059 in.	0.15 mm
Camshaft sprocket run-out (less than)	0.004 in.	0.1 mm
Connecting rod center distance	6.0669-6.0709 in.	154.10-154.20 mm
Crankshaft center distance	1.634 in.	41.5 mm
Crankshaft out-of-round (less than)	0.0002 in.	0.005 mm
Crankshaft taper (less than)	0.0002 in.	0.005 mm
Crankshaft run-out	0.0039 in.	0.10 mm
Cylinder head surface distortion		
Standard (less than)	0.002 in.	0.05 mm
Limit	0.004 in.	0.10 mm
Cylinder block surface flatness		
Standard (less than)	0.0012 in.	0.03 mm
Limit	0.0039 in.	0.10 mm
Cylinder bore wear limit	0.0079 in.	0.20 mm
Cylinder out-of-round (less than)	0.0006 in.	0.015 mm
Cylinder taper (less than)	0.0006 in.	0.015 mm
Flywheel run-out (less than)	0.0059 in.	0.15 mm
Hydraulic valve lifter		
(clearance between lifter and lifter guide)	0.0017-0.0026 in.	0.0043-0.066 mm
Piston pin hole diameter	0.8255-0.8260 in.	20.969-20.981 mm
Piston-to-cylinder block clearance		
VG30i	0.0010-0.0018 in.	0.025-0.045 mm
VG30E	0.0006-0.0014 in.	0.015-0.035 mm
Piston pin bushing inner diameter		
(after installing the connecting rod)	0.8261-0.8265 in.	20.982-20.994 mm
Rocker shaft		
Outer diameter	0.7078-0.7087 in.	17.979-18.000 mm
Rocker shaft		
Inner diameter	0.7089-0.7098 in.	18.007-18.028 mm
Rocker arm and rocker shaft clearance	0.0003-0.0019 in.	0.007-0.049 mm
Valve clearance		
Intake	0.0 in.	0.0 mm
Exhaust	0.0 in.	0.0 mm
Valve deflection		
Limit	0.0079 in.	0.20 mm
Valve head diameter		
Intake	1.654-1.661 in.	42.0-42.2 mm
Exhaust	1.378-1.386 in.	35.0-35.2 mm

86713C10

TORQUE SPECIFICATIONS—Z24i AND KA24E ENGINES

Component	U.S.	Metric
Camshaft sprocket bolt	87-116 ft. lbs.	118-157 Nm
Chain guide bolt	5-8 ft. lbs.	6-10 Nm
Chain tensioner bolt	5-8 ft. lbs.	6-10 Nm
Crankshaft pulley bolt	87-116 ft. lbs.	118-157 Nm
Cylinder head-to-front cover	3-8 ft. lbs.	4-10 Nm
Flywheel bolt	101-116 ft. lbs.	137-157 Nm
Front cover bolt		
M8 type	7-12 ft. lbs.	10-16 Nm
M6 type	3-8 ft. lbs.	4-10 Nm
Injection body nut	9-13 ft. lbs.	12-18 Nm
Oil pan drain plug	22-29 ft. lbs.	29-39 Nm
Oil strainer bolt	12-15 ft. lbs.	16-21 Nm
Rocker cover bolt	1-3 ft. lbs.	2-4 Nm
Rocker shaft bracket bolt	11-18 ft. lbs.	15-25 Nm
Spark plug	14-22 ft. lbs.	20-29 Nm
Starter motor bolt	22-29 ft. lbs.	29-39 Nm
Thermostat housing bolt	7-9 ft. lbs.	10-13 Nm
Transmission-to-block bolt	29-36 ft. lbs.	39-49 Nm
Valve clearance adjusting nut	12-16 ft. lbs.	16-22 Nm
Water pump bolt		
M8 type	7-12 ft. lbs.	10-16 Nm
M6 type	3-8 ft. lbs.	4-10 Nm

86713C11

TORQUE SPECIFICATIONS—VG30i AND VG30E ENGINES

Component	U.S.	Metric
Camshaft pulley bolt	58-65 ft. lbs.	78-88 Nm
Crankshaft pulley	90-98 ft. lbs.	123-132 Nm
Flywheel bolts	72-80 ft. lbs.	98-108 Nm
Oil pan bolts	6 ft. lbs.	8 Nm
Oil pan drain plug	22-29 ft. lbs.	29-39 Nm
Rear oil seal retainer	5 ft. lbs.	7 Nm
Rocker cover bolts	1-3 ft. lbs.	2-4 Nm
Rocker shaft bolts	13-16 ft. lbs.	18-22 Nm
Spark plugs	14-22 ft. lbs.	20-29 Nm
Starter motor	22-27 ft. lbs.	30-36 Nm
Timing belt tensioner	3-4 ft. lbs.	4-6 Nm
Timing belt cover bolts	32-43 ft. lbs.	43-58 Nm
Water inlet	12-15 ft. lbs.	16-21 Nm
Water pump bolts	12-15 ft. lbs.	16-21 Nm

86713C12

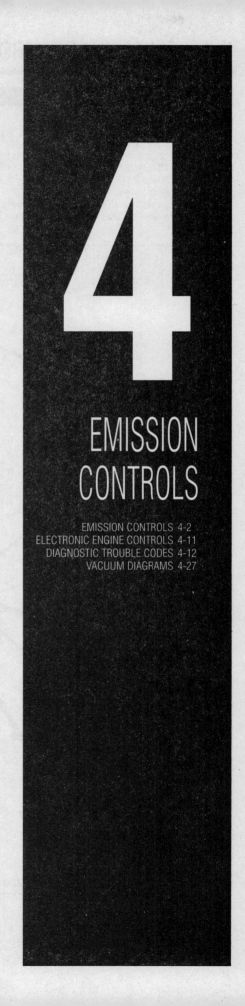

4

EMISSION
CONTROLS

EMISSION CONTROLS

♦ **See Figures 1 thru 6**

There are basically three sources of automotive pollutants; crankcase fumes, exhaust gases, and gasoline evaporation. The pollutants formed from these sources fall into three categories: unburnt hydrocarbons (HC), carbon monoxide (C), and oxides of nitrogen (NOx). The equipment used to limit these pollutants is called emission control equipment.

Due to varying state, federal, and provincial regulations, specific emission control equipment will vary. The U.S. emission equipment is divided into two categories: California and Federal. Some equipment installed on trucks designed to meet California emissions standards is generally not shared with equipment installed on trucks built to be sold in other states (Federal). Though, changes in legislation may lead to California emissions equipped vehicles in other states with standards which are tighter than the Federal emission requirement. In any case, the improvements which have been made over the years with emissions equipment has led to a closing of the gap between the two standards and vehicles built to meet the two standards are often quite similar to one another.

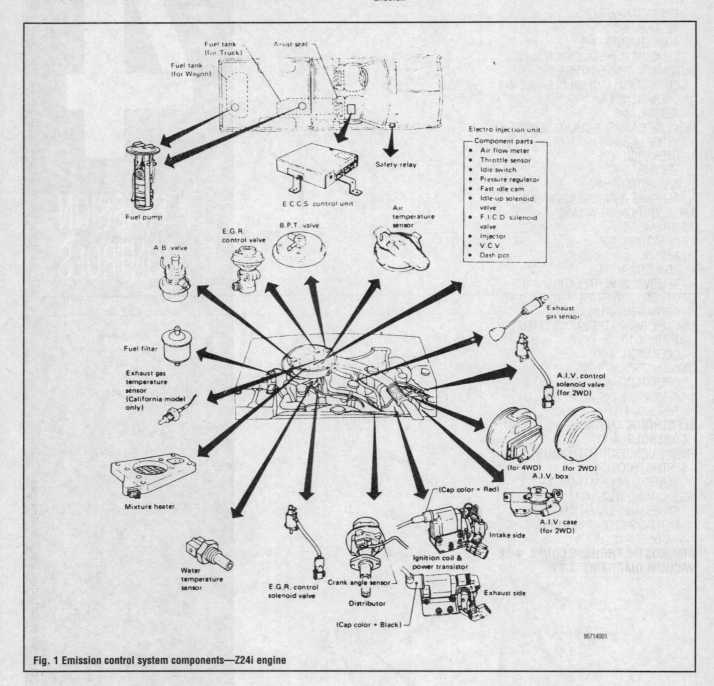

Fig. 1 Emission control system components—Z24i engine

86714001

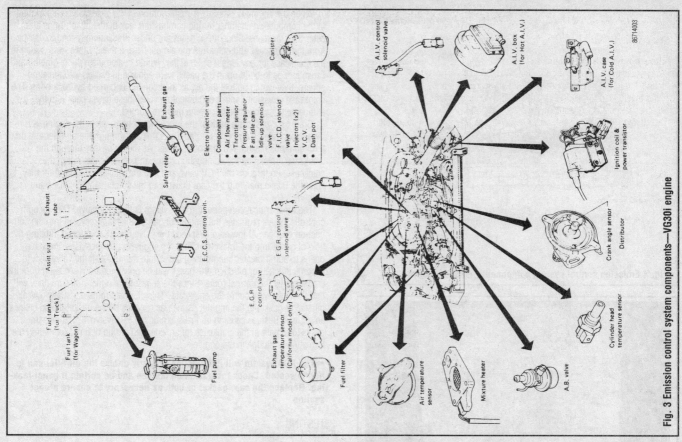

Fig. 3 Emission control system components—VG30i engine

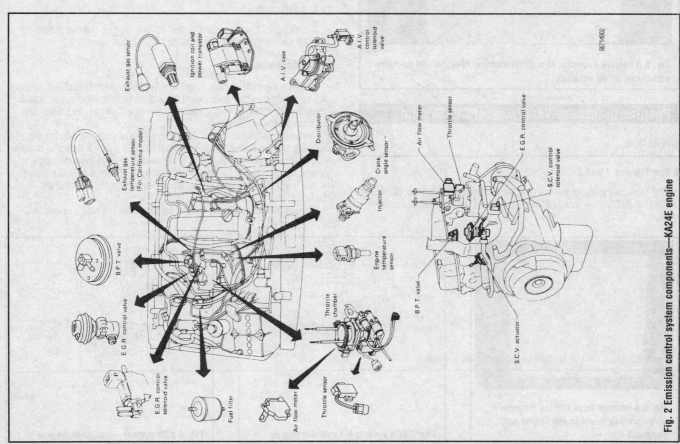

Fig. 2 Emission control system components—KA24E engine

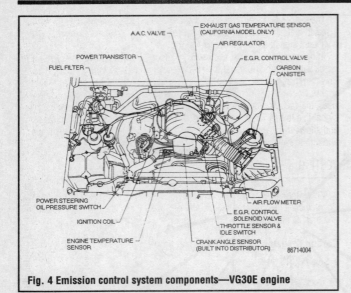

Fig. 4 Emission control system components—VG30E engine

Fig. 5 A vehicle emission control information label should be found underhood on all vehicles

Positive Crankcase Ventilation (PCV) System

OPERATION

♦ See Figures 7 and 8

The crankcase emission control equipment consists of a Positive Crankcase Ventilation (PCV) valve, a closed filler cap and hoses to connect this equipment.

When the engine is running, a small portion of the gases which are formed in the combustion chamber during combustion leak by the piston rings and enter the crankcase. Since these gases are under pressure they tend to escape from the crankcase and enter into the atmosphere. If these gases were sealed in the crankcase for any length of time, they would contaminate the engine oil and cause sludge to build up. If the gases were allowed to escape into the atmosphere, they would pollute the air, as they contain unburned hydrocarbons. The crankcase emission control equipment recycles these gases back into the engine combustion chamber where they are burned.

Crankcase gases are used in the following manner: while the engine is running, clean filtered air is drawn into the crankcase through the air filter and then through a hose leading to the rocker cover. As the air passes through the crankcase it picks up the combustion gases and carries them out of the crankcase, up through the PCV valve and into the intake manifold. After they enter the intake manifold they are drawn into the combustion chamber and burned.

The most critical component in the system is the PCV valve. This vacuum controlled valve regulates the amount of gases which are recycled into the combustion changer. At low engine speeds the valve is partially closed, limiting the flow of gases into the intake manifold. As engine speed increases, the valve opens to admit greater quantities of gases into the intake. If the valve should become blocked or plugged, the gases will be prevented from escaping from the crankcase by the normal route. Since these gases are under pressure, they will find their own way out of the crankcase. This alternate route is usually a weak oil seal or gasket in the engine. As the gas escapes by the gasket it also creates an oil leak. Besides causing oil leaks, a clogged PCV valve also allows these gases to remain in the crankcase for an extended period of time, promoting the formation of sludge in the engine.

➡ The PCV system will not function properly unless the oil filler cap is tightly sealed. Check the gasket on the cap and be certain it is not leaking. Replace the cap, gasket or both as necessary to ensure proper sealing.

TESTING

♦ See Figure 9

Check the PCV valve, system hoses, retaining clamps and connections, to see that there are no leaks. Then replace or tighten, as necessary.

Valve Assembly

To check the valve, remove it and blow through both of its ends. When blowing from the side which goes toward the intake manifold, very little air should pass through it. When blowing from the crankcase (cylinder head cover) side, air should pass through freely.

An additional check without removing the valve could be with the engine running, remove the ventilator hose from the PCV valve. If the valve is working, a hissing noise will be heard as air passes through the valve and a strong vacuum should be felt immediately when the valve inlet is blocked with a finger. If the valve is suspected of being plugged, it should be replaced.

Replace the valve with a new one if the valve fails to function as outlined.

Fig. 6 A vacuum hose routing diagram is also normally found in the engine compartment

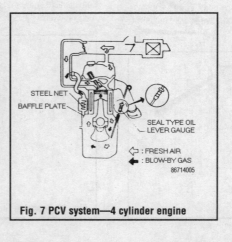

Fig. 7 PCV system—4 cylinder engine

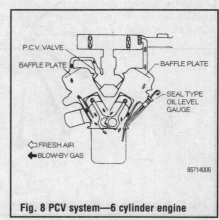

Fig. 8 PCV system—6 cylinder engine

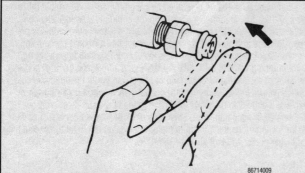

Fig. 9 A strong vacuum should be felt when testing the PCV valve attached to the system hose with engine running

→After removing the PCV valve shake it end to end, listening for the rattle of the needle inside the valve. If no rattle is heard, the needle and valve is jammed. Do not attempt to clean or adjust the valve, replace it.

System Hoses

Check all hoses and connections for leaks. Disconnect all hoses and clean them with compressed air. If the hose cannot be freed of its obstruction with the force of air, replace the hose.

ADJUSTMENTS

No adjustments are either necessary or possible on the PCV system.

REMOVAL & INSTALLATION

Valve Assembly

To remove the PCV valve, simply loosen the hose clamp and remove the valve from the manifold-to-crankcase hose and intake manifold. Most valves pull right out, although some may require unscrewing.

PCV Filter

Z24I ENGINES ONLY

Remove the air cleaner housing lid. Unclip the PCV filter from the side of the housing and then replace it with a new one. Install the housing lid.

Evaporative Emission Control System

OPERATION

▶ See Figure 10

When raw fuel evaporates, the vapors contain hydrocarbons. To prevent these fumes from escaping into the atmosphere, the fuel evaporative emission control system was developed.

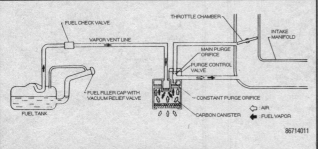

Fig. 10 Evaporative emission control system

The evaporative emission control systems used on Nissan trucks consists of a sealed fuel tank, a vapor/liquid separator, a vapor vent line, a carbon canister, a vacuum signal line and a canister purge line.

In operation, fuel (vapor and liquid) is routed to the liquid/vapor separator or check valve where liquid fuel is directed back into the fuel tank as fuel vapors flow into the charcoal filled canister. The charcoal absorbs and stores the fuel vapors when the engine is not running or is at idle. When the throttle vacuum rises, the vacuum from above the throttle valves is routed through a vacuum signal line to the purge control valve on the canister. The control valve opens and allows the fuel vapors to be drawn from the canister through a purge line and into the intake manifold and the combustion chambers.

TESTING

Check the hoses for proper connections and damage. Replace as necessary. Check the vapor separator tank assembly for fuel leaks, distortion and dents, and then as necessary.

Carbon Canister and Purge Control Valve

▶ See Figure 11

To check the operation of the carbon canister purge control valve, disconnect the rubber hose between the valve and the T-fitting, at the T-fitting. Apply vacuum to the hose leading to the control valve. The vacuum condition should be maintained indefinitely. If the control valve leaks, remove the top cover of the valve and check for a dislocated or cracked diaphragm. If the diaphragm is damaged, a repair kit containing a new diaphragm, retainer, and spring is available and should be installed.

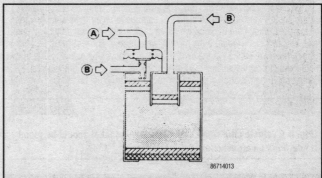

Fig. 11 The evaporative emissions canister should be checked using its vacuum/vapor ports

Fuel Check Valve

▶ See Figure 12

1. Locate the valve in the fuel line and remove it.
2. Blow air though the connector on the fuel tank side. You should notice a considerable amount of resistance and some of the air should be deflected to the evaporative canister.

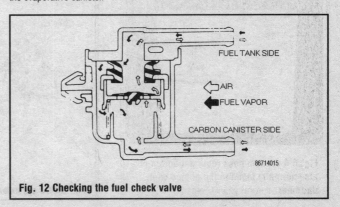

Fig. 12 Checking the fuel check valve

3. Now blow air through the connector on the canister side. There should be no obstructions and the air should flow toward the fuel tank.
4. If the valve does not work properly in both tests, it should be replaced.
5. Install the valve in the fuel line.

ADJUSTMENTS

No adjustment are either necessary or possible

REMOVAL & INSTALLATION

Removal and installation of the various evaporative emission control system components consists of disconnecting the hoses, loosening any retaining screws, and removing the part which is to be replaced or checked. Installation should then be obvious. When replacing hoses, make sure that they are fuel and vapor resistant.

Automatic Temperature Controlled (ATC) Air Cleaner

OPERATION

▶ **See Figures 13 and 14**

Z24i and VG30i Engines Only

The rate of fuel atomization is dependent upon the temperature of the air being taken into the engine and the temperature of the engine itself (which can have the effect of heating intake air). The air/fuel ratio cannot be held constant (during engine warm-up) for efficient fuel combustion if air temperatures vary. For example, when cold air is drawn into a cold engine, the fuel does not atomize as efficiently as it would if the mixture were heated. The end result is more hydrocarbons are emitted in the exhaust gas. In contrast, as warmer air is drawn into a cold engine, the air/fuel mixture undergoes a more efficient atomization, creating better combustion and less hydrocarbons from the exhaust.

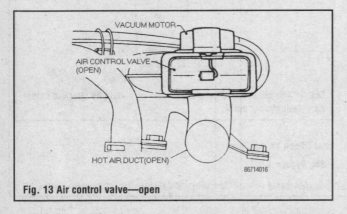

Fig. 13 Air control valve—open

The automatic temperature controlled air cleaner is designed so that the temperature of the ambient air being drawn into the engine is automatically controlled during cold engine operation. This holds the temperature of the air and consequently, the air/fuel ratio, at a more constant rate for better combustion.

A temperature sensing switch controls the vacuum applied to a vacuum motor operating a valve in the intake snorkel of the air cleaner. This valve determines whether the engine receives cold or heated air. When the engine is cold, the switch causes the vacuum motor to open the valve, allowing air heated by the exhaust manifold to be drawn into the engine. As the engine approaches normal operating temperature (and the supplemental heat is no longer necessary), the switch triggers the vacuum motor to close, shutting off the heated air and allowing cooler ambient air to be drawn in.

TESTING

▶ **See Figures 15 and 16**

Vacuum Motor

When the air temperature around the sensor is below 100°F (38°C), the sensor should allow vacuum to pass through the air valve vacuum motor, thus blocking off the air cleaner snorkel, making the engine take in heated air from the exhaust manifold. When the air temperature around the sensor reaches 100°F (38°C), the sensor should trigger the blockage of vacuum to the air control valve vacuum motor. This will allow the engine to take in cooler unheated air, through the air snorkel.

When the air temperature around the sensor is about 118°F (48°C), the air control valve should be completely open to unheated air.

When the engine is operating under a heavy load (wide open throttle acceleration), the air control valve fully opens to underhood air to obtain full power no matter what the temperature is around the temperature sensor.

If the air cleaner fails to operate correctly, check for loose or broken vacuum hoses. If the hoses are not the cause, replace the vacuum motor in the air cleaner.

Temperature Sensor

While the engine is cool and at idle, disconnect the hose at the vacuum motor and check that there is vacuum present at the end of the hose. If there is little or no vacuum, check the condition of the hose. If its good, replace the temperature sensor.

After the engine has warmed up, check the hose again. There should be no vacuum felt; if there is vacuum, replace the sensor.

Exhaust Gas Recirculation (EGR) System

OPERATION

▶ **See Figures 17 and 18**

Exhaust gas recirculation is used to reduce combustion temperatures in the engine, thereby reducing the oxides of nitrogen (NOx) emissions. An EGR valve assembly with a gasket is mounted on the intake manifold. An EGR valve vacuum diaphragm is connected to a timed signal port at the intake manifold.

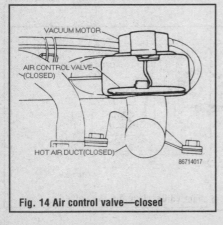

Fig. 14 Air control valve—closed

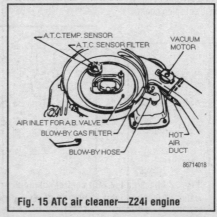

Fig. 15 ATC air cleaner—Z24i engine

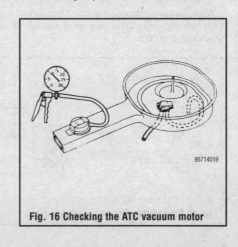

Fig. 16 Checking the ATC vacuum motor

As the throttle valve is opened, vacuum is applied to the EGR valve vacuum diaphragm. When the vacuum reaches about 2.0 in. Hg (6.7 kPa), the diaphragm moves against spring pressure and is in a fully up position at 8 in. Hg (27.0 kPa) of vacuum. As the diaphragm moves up, it opens the exhaust gas metering valve which allows exhaust gas to be pulled into the engine intake manifold. The system does not operate when the engine is idling because the exhaust gas recirculation would cause a rough idle.

Some models have a Back Pressure Transducer (BPT) valve installed between the EGR valve and the thermal vacuum valve. The BPT valve has a diaphragm raised or lowered by exhaust back pressure. The diaphragm opens or closes an air bleed, which is connected into the EGR vacuum line. High pressure results in higher levels of EGR, because the diaphragm is raised, closing off the air bleed, which allows more vacuum to reach and open the EGR valve. Thus, the amount of recirculated exhaust gas varies with exhaust pressure.

All models utilize an EGR control solenoid valve. At both low and high engine rpm, the solenoid valve turns on and causes the EGR control valve to cut the flow of gases leading to the intake manifold.

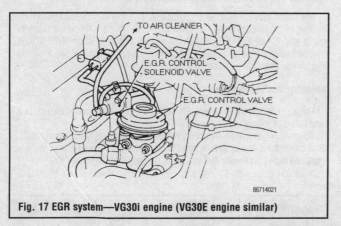

Fig. 17 EGR system—VG30i engine (VG30E engine similar)

TESTING

EGR Control Valve

▸ **See Figures 19 and 20**

1. Remove the EGR valve and apply enough vacuum to the diaphragm to open the valve.
2. The valve should remain open for over 30 seconds after the vacuum is removed.
3. Check the valve for damage, such as warpage, cracks, and excessive wear around the valve and seat.
4. Clean the seat with a brush and compressed air and remove any deposits from around the valve and port (seat).

EGR Control Solenoid Valve

▸ **See Figures 21 and 22**

Disconnect the solenoid valve harness connector and then apply battery voltage (12V) to terminals 1 and 2. There should be continuity between ports **A** and **B**. There should be NO continuity between ports **B** and **C**. If your readings do not agree with these, replace the solenoid valve.

Thermal Vacuum Valve (TVV)

▸ **See Figure 23**

To check the operation of the thermal vacuum valve, remove the valve from the engine and apply vacuum to the ports of the valve. The valve should not allow vacuum to pass.

Place the valve in a container of water with a thermometer and heat the water. When the temperature of the water reaches 134–145°F (57–63°C), remove the valve and apply vacuum to the ports; the valve should allow vacuum to pass through it.

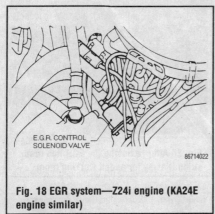

Fig. 18 EGR system—Z24i engine (KA24E engine similar)

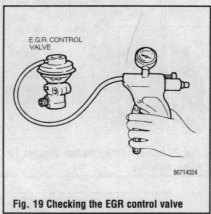

Fig. 19 Checking the EGR control valve

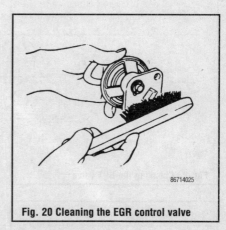

Fig. 20 Cleaning the EGR control valve

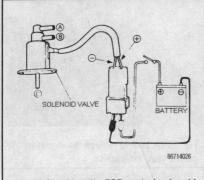

Fig. 21 Checking the EGR control solenoid valve—1989

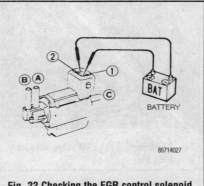

Fig. 22 Checking the EGR control solenoid valve—1990 and later

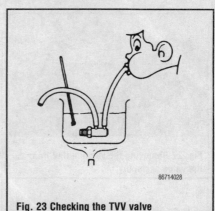

Fig. 23 Checking the TVV valve

Back Pressure Transducer (BPT) Valve

♦ See Figure 24

To test the BPT valve, disconnect the two vacuum hoses from the valve. Plug one of the ports. While applying pressure to the bottom of the valve, apply vacuum to the unplugged port and check for leakage. If any exists, replace the valve.

ADJUSTMENT

No adjustments are either necessary or possible to this system.

REMOVAL & INSTALLATION

♦ See Figures 25, 26, 27, 28 and 29

1. Remove the nut which attaches the EGR tube and/or the back pressure tube to the EGR valve (if so equipped).
2. Unscrew the mounting bolts and remove the heat shield between the EGR control valve (if equipped with a heat shield), and the intake manifold.
3. Tag and disconnect the EGR vacuum hose(s).
4. Unscrew the mounting bolts and remove the EGR control valve.
To install:
5. Install the EGR valve assembly (using a new gasket) with mounting bolts to the intake manifold location.
6. Connect all vacuum hoses, and install the heat shield between the EGR control valve and the intake manifold, if equipped with a heat shield.
7. Connect the EGR tube and/or the back pressure tube to the EGR valve, if so equipped.

➡️**If replacing the EGR valve, always be sure that the new valve is identical to the old one.**

Air Induction Valve (AIV) System

OPERATION

The air induction system is designed to send secondary air to the exhaust manifold, utilizing a vacuum caused by exhaust pulsation in the exhaust manifold. The exhaust pressure in the exhaust manifold usually pulsates in response to the opening and closing of the exhaust valve and it decreases below atmospheric pressure periodically. If a secondary air intake pipe is opened to the atmosphere under vacuum conditions, secondary air can be drawn into the exhaust manifold in proportion to the vacuum.

➡️**On some applications, the Air Induction Valve (AIV) control solenoid and the Swirl Control Valve (SCV) solenoid cuts the intake manifold vacuum signal. These solenoids have an electrical connection and vacuum lines. If equipped in your vehicle, make sure the unit is properly mounted and all connections are properly installed.**

The introduction of fresh air (oxygen) into the exhaust stream allows a further burning of the exhaust gases even after they have left the combustion chamber. In this way, the air induction system contributes to the reduction of CO and HC emissions in the exhaust gasses. The system usually consists of two air induction valves, filter hoses and routing cables.

Air Induction Valve Case

The air induction valve case is attached to the air cleaner, and consists of 2 reed valves, a rubber seal and a filter.

There are 2 types of air induction valve cases. One type is equipped with 2 hose connectors, and is installed on California models. The other type is equipped with 1 connector and is installed on non-California models.

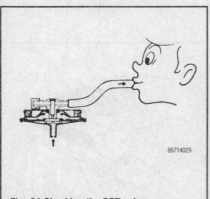

Fig. 24 Checking the BPT valve

Fig. 25 Removing the EGR line from the valve assembly

Fig. 26 After removing the EGR line reposition it away for added working room

Fig. 27 Removing the vacuum line from the valve assembly

Fig. 28 Removing the EGR valve assembly mounting bolt

Fig. 29 Be sure to replace the mounting gasket upon installation

Air Induction Valve

Two reed type check valves are installed in the air cleaner. When the exhaust pressure is below atmospheric pressure (negative vacuum), secondary air is sent to the exhaust manifold.

When the exhaust pressure is above atmospheric pressure, the reed valves prevent secondary air from being sent back to the air cleaner.

Air Induction Valve Filter

The air induction valve filter is installed at the dust side of the air cleaner. It purifies secondary air to be sent to the exhaust manifold.

Air Induction Pipe

The secondary air fed from the air induction valve goes through the routing pipe to the exhaust manifold.

Anti-Backfire (AB) Valve

The AB valve provides air from the air cleaner to the intake manifold to prevent backfiring during deceleration.

TESTING

Air Induction Valve (AIV) Case

▶ **See Figures 30, 31 and 32**

Before proceeding with any extensive testing, check the condition of the hoses and lines used. If any hoses are cracked, torn or fit loosely, replace with a new piece.

To check the AIV system, start the engine and allow it to reach a normal operating temperature. Open the hood and try to listen to the AIV unit. If it is functioning correctly, it will be emitting a low pitched buzzing sound at idle. There should be no sound above idle. Also, remove the vacuum line from the top of the AIV assembly, and check for vacuum during idle. If you place a finger over the line, you should feel a sucking motion on your finger. As noted earlier, this condition exists only at idle, not under throttle conditions.

Turn the engine **OFF**. With the vacuum line removed from the AIV unit, connect a vacuum pump. Remove one end of the remaining hoses from the AIV unit. Apply vacuum to the unit, while at the same time blowing into the hose. With vacuum applied, you should be able to blow through the hose without any difficulty.

One final condition to check is the voltage level. Unplug the wire harness connector from the AIV unit, and check for voltage during idle, and under throttle. At idle, there should be no voltage, while at throttle, there should be battery voltage.

Anti-Backfire (AB) Valve

▶ **See Figures 33, 34 and 35**

To check the AB valve, Open the engine hood, and remove the air cleaner cover. With the filter out, and the engine running at idle, place your finger over the opening in the base of the cleaner. If the valve function correctly, there should be a sucking action under all conditions, except under throttle.

ADJUSTMENT

No adjustments are either necessary or possible to this system.

REMOVAL & INSTALLATION

Air Induction Valve and Filter

1. Remove the valve and filter cover on the air cleaner, by removing the retaining nuts securing the assembly.
2. With the cover removed, the valve and parts can be accessed easily.
To install:
3. Check the filter housing and make sure if is free of dirt and debris.
4. Position the filter and valve in place, then install the cover and secure with the retaining nuts.

Fig. 30 Exploded view of the AIV canister assembly

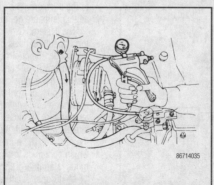

Fig. 31 Checking the AIV case assembly—6 cylinder engine

Fig. 32 Checking the AIV case assembly—4 cylinder engine

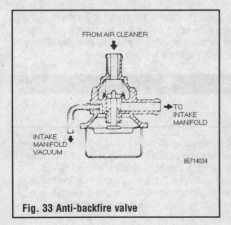

Fig. 33 Anti-backfire valve

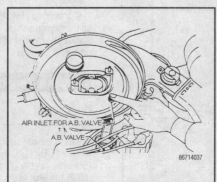

Fig. 34 Checking the AB valve—6 cylinder engine

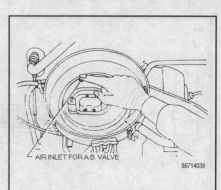

Fig. 35 Checking the AB valve—4 cylinder engine

Anti-backfire (AB) Valve

1. Remove air cleaner cover, followed by the filter.
2. Disconnect the air hoses and vacuum tube, being careful to mark them before disassembly. Remove the AB valve from air cleaner housing assembly, by unfastening the retaining hardware.

To install:

3. Position the AB valve to the air cleaner, and secure using the retaining hardware.
4. Attach the hoses and vacuum line to the valve. Make sure the order is correct.
5. Install the filter and air cleaner cover.

Catalytic Converter

OPERATION

◆ See Figures 36 and 37

The catalytic converter is a muffler like container built into the exhaust system to aid in the reduction of exhaust emissions. The catalyst element consists of individual pellets or a honeycomb monolithic substrate coated with a noble metal such as platinum, palladium, rhodium or a combination. When the exhaust gases come into contact with the catalyst, a chemical reaction occurs which will reduce the pollutants into harmless substances like water and carbon dioxide.

There are essentially two types of catalytic converters: an oxidizing type is used on some models. It requires the addition of oxygen to spur the catalyst into reducing the engine's HC and CO emissions into H_2O and CO_2. Because of this need for oxygen, the Air Injection system is used with all these models.

The oxidizing catalytic converter, while effectively reducing HC and CO emissions, does little, if anything in the way of reducing NOx emissions. For this reason, the three way catalytic converter was developed.

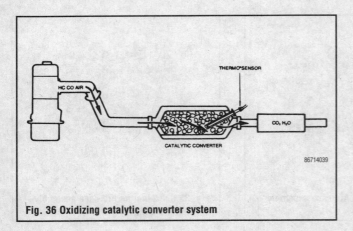

Fig. 36 Oxidizing catalytic converter system

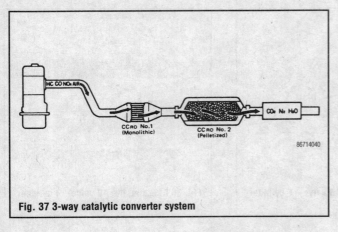

Fig. 37 3-way catalytic converter system

The three way converter, unlike the oxidizing type, is capable of reducing HC, CO and NOx emissions; all at the same time. In theory, it seems impossible to reduce all three pollutants in one system since the reduction of HC and CO requires the addition of oxygen, while the reduction of NOx calls for the removal of oxygen. In actuality, the three way system really can reduce all three pollutants, but only if the amount of oxygen in the exhaust system is precisely controlled.

➥**The catalytic converter and related parts should be inspected periodically for mechanical damage. The air injection system should be checked at the same time, and maintained in proper working at all times.**

Mixture Ratio Feedback System (MRFS)

OPERATION

The need for better fuel economy coupled to increasingly strict emission control regulations dictates a more exact control of the engine air/fuel mixture. Nissan has developed a Mixture Ratio Feedback System (MRFS) in response to these needs.

The main function of the system is to control the air/fuel mixture exactly, so that more complete combustion can occur in the engine, and a more thorough oxidation and reduction of the exhaust gases can occur in the catalytic converter. The object is to maintain a stoichiometric air/fuel mixture, which is chemically correct for theoretically complete combustion. The stoichiometric ratio is 14.7:1 (air to fuel). At that point, the converter's efficiency is greatest in oxidizing and reducing HC, CO, and NOx into CO_2, H_2O, O_2, and N_2.

Components used in the system include an oxygen sensor, installed in the exhaust manifold (upstream of the converter), a catalytic converter, an electronic control unit, and the fuel injection system itself.

The oxygen sensor reads the oxygen content of the exhaust gases. It generates an electric signal which is sent to the control unit. The control unit then decides how to adjust the mixture to keep it at the correct air/fuel ratio. For example, if the mixture is too lean, the control unit increases the fuel metering to the injectors. The monitoring process is a continual one, so that fine mixture adjustments are going on at all times.

The system has two modes of operation: open loop and closed loop. Open loop operation takes place when the engine is first started, and is still cold. In this mode, the control unit ignores any signals from the oxygen sensor (because will not send reliable information until it is at operating temperature. Instead, the engine control computer calculates air/fuel mixture requirements based on input from other engine control sensors. Closed loop operation takes place when the engine and catalytic converter have warmed to normal operating temperature. In closed loop operation, the control unit uses the oxygen sensor signals (along with the data from other engine sensors) to more precisely adjust the mixture. The burned mixture's oxygen content is read by the oxygen sensor, which continues to signal the control unit, and so on. Thus, the closed loop mode is an interdependent system of information feedback.

Mixture is, of course, not readily adjustable in this system. All system adjustments require the use of special diagnostic equipment. Thus, they should be entrusted to a qualified dealer or Automotive Service Excellence (ASE) certified technician with access to the equipment and special training in this system's repair.

It should be noted that proper operation of the system is entirely dependent on the oxygen sensor. Thus, if the sensor fails during normal operation, the engine fuel mixture will be incorrect, resulting in poor fuel economy, starting problems, or stumbling and stalling of the engine when warm.

Oxygen Sensor

OPERATION

The three-way catalytic converter, which is capable of reducing HC, CO and NOx into CO_2, H_2O, O_2 and N_2 can only function as long as the air/fuel mixture is kept within a critically precise range. The Mixture Ratio Feedback System (MRFS) is what keeps the oxygen range in control. By receiving feedback from the oxygen sensor, the control unit can determine how well the air/fuel mixture is burning and signal the engine to adjust for different driving situations.

The sensor, located in the exhaust manifold, or other part of the exhaust system, senses the oxygen content present in the exhaust gases. Basically, the oxygen sensor system works like this: When the sensor reaches a predetermined temperature, (usually around same time that the engine reaches normal operating temperature), the signal should fall within certain parameters. At this point, the computer begins to accept information from the oxygen sensor. Up to this point, the computer had ignored oxygen sensor signals, favoring instead the information from other sensors in the engine compartment. The O_2 sensor produces a small voltage level, between 0 and 1 volt, that varies depending on the amount of oxygen in the exhaust. This voltage read by the computer as oxygen content in the exhaust stream, which is an indication of combustion. The computer works together with the fuel injectors to vary the air/fuel mixture based upon this information.

If the amount of oxygen in the exhaust system is low, the mixture is said to be rich, and the sensor voltage will be high, somewhere around 1 volt. The higher the voltage signal sent to the computer, the more the computer will attempt to reduce the amount of fuel available to the engine. The amount of fuel is controlled until the amount of oxygen in the exhaust system increases, indicating a more lean mixture. When the mixture is lean, around 0 volts, the sensor will send a low voltage signal to the computer. The computer will then increase the availability of fuel until the sensor voltage increases again and then the cycle will start all over. The computer will continue this cycle in an attempt to maintain the stoichiometric air/fuel ratio of 14.7:1 which results in the most efficient catalytic converter operation.

REMOVAL & INSTALLATION

The oxygen sensor is installed in the exhaust system between the exhaust valves and the catalytic converter. It is often placed close to the engine for quick and efficient warm-up.

The oxygen sensor is removed in the same manner as a spark plug. Exercise care when handling the sensor. Do not drop or handle the sensor roughly. When installing a new oxygen sensor, use care not to get the anti-seize compound (which is normally found on the sensor's threads) on your fingers. More importantly, make sure you do NOT get any on the probe end of the sensor. If reinstalling an old oxygen sensor, you must reapply the anti-seize compound to the sensor.

1. Disconnect the negative battery cable.
2. Unplug the wiring connector leading from the O_2 sensor.
3. Unscrew the sensor from the exhaust manifold.
To install:
4. If not already on the sensor, coat the threads of the replacement sensor with a nickel base anti-seize compound. Do not use other types of compounds, since they may electrically insulate the sensor.
5. Install the sensor into the exhaust system. Torque the sensor to 18–25 ft. lbs. (24–34 Nm). Connect the electrical lead. Be careful handling the electrical lead as it is easily damaged.
6. Reconnect the battery cable.

TESTING

1. Locate the sensor in or near the exhaust manifold and access the wire harness.
2. With the engine running at normal operating temperature, unplug the connector and see if the engine idles at a different rate. If the sensor is functioning correctly, the idle should change.
3. With the engine still running, and the oxygen sensor connected, use a multimeter and check the voltage level between the control unit and the sensor. The correct voltage should fluctuate rapidly between 0 and 1.0 volts.

ELECTRONIC ENGINE CONTROLS

Engine Concentrated Control System (ECCS)

GENERAL INFORMATION

➡The engine management system has 2 main functions, to optimize engine performance under ANY given condition, and to control engine emissions under ALL conditions.

All vehicles use a very sophisticated engine management system called Engine Concentrated Control System (ECCS). The basic control functions are fuel injection, ignition timing, idle speed, various solenoid valves and the fuel pump relay. Other functions of the ECCS include operating a heating circuit for the exhaust gas oxygen sensor, a cold start mixture heater on throttle body injection systems and turning off the air conditioner compressor under full throttle. Inputs to the ECU come from a variety of temperature and pressure sensors, position sensors and switches, a detonation sensor, a speed sensor and an air flow meter. The ECU is capable of storing and reporting trouble codes and on some vehicles, can also operate the engine in a Fail Safe or "limp home" mode.

Electric fuel injectors are used, either two in the throttle body or one per cylinder injecting into the intake port just upstream of the intake valve. The ECU controls the length of time each injector is open, based both on information from sensors and switches and according to programmed maps in the ECU's permanent memory. On engines with port injection, when the ignition switch is in the **START** position, all the injectors are opened at the same time twice each engine revolution. Once the engine is running and the ignition switch is in the **RUN** position, each injector is operated sequentially according to firing order. When the throttle is closed to decelerate engine rpm, the injectors are shut off until a programmed condition is met and injection is turned on again. On some vehicles this fuel cut-off is also used to prevent engine overspeed.

The air/fuel mixture control strategy is called "closed loop". The oxygen sensor detects the concentration of oxygen in the exhaust and reports this to the ECU, which then adjusts the fuel injection to maintain the air/fuel mixture within very narrow limits. What comes out of the combustion chamber is used as data, to determine what will go back into the chamber, thereby closing the loop of information. Under specific conditions, the ECU will switch to open loop control. In this mode, injection quantity and timing are according to internal programming regardless of exhaust gas oxygen content, or other sensor parameters. In this mode the computer choices to ignore the input from the oxygen sensor. Conditions where an open loop system occur include, full load, deceleration, initial engine starting and certain system malfunction conditions. On some vehicles this last condition will cause the ECU to go into what the manufacturer calls a Fail-Safe system or a "limp home" mode. Fuel injection is controlled the same way as in engine starting and, the fuel pump, ignition timing and idle speed are all controlled by other internal programs. Engine power is greatly reduced, engine speed is limited and the CHECK ENGINE light will come on.

The Fail-Safe system is canceled each time the ignition switch is turned **OFF** but will be reactivated as long as the malfunction exists. The Fail-Safe can be activated each time an intermittent fault occurs.

The fuel injection system consists of the injectors, ECU, fuel pressure regulator, air flow meter, throttle position sensor, exhaust oxygen sensor, various inlet air control devices and a power steering hydraulic pressure switch. The ECU also uses the crankangle sensor in the distributor for computing injection timing and duration.

➡Before connecting or disconnecting the ECU wiring, disconnect the negative battery cable. The ECU receives power at all times through this connector and can be permanently damaged if improperly powered up or down. Never connect or disconnect any wiring with the ignition switch ON. When using an ohmmeter, make sure the voltage from the meter does not find a path back to the ECU. Improper test methods can instantly and permanently damage the ECU or other components.

Self-Diagnostics

GENERAL INFORMATION

The Electronic Control Unit (ECU) in all vehicles will store and report fault codes. If a malfunction is detected only one time, the CHECK ENGINE light may not stay lit. However the fault code will remain in memory for the next 50 ignition cycles when the starter is operated. If the fault occurs again, the counter will reset to 0 and the code will be in memory for 50 ignition cycles from that point. The fault code can be erased manually and is erased any time the vehicle battery is disconnected. If the ignition switch is turned **OFF** when in diagnostic mode, the ECU automatically defaults to Mode 1.

There are two diagnostic programs used by Nissan, a four mode and a five mode. All vehicles covered here use the five mode program. Modes 1 and 2 monitor mixture ratio feedback control. Mode 3 reports trouble codes and is the mode used for clearing the stored codes. Mode 4 monitors various switches in the engine management system. Mode 5 displays faults occurring at the moment of operation and can be used while driving the vehicle.

As useful as these diagnostic tests are, the first step in repair or service to engine management systems is still to gain and evaluate as much information as possible regarding intermittent problems and to repair the obvious. Before checking fault codes, it is absolutely essential to check for any obvious mechanical faults or failures. Remember, a trouble code only indicates which sensor or circuit is effected by the problem. Simple mechanical faults such as a vacuum leak or poor electrical connection can cause a fault code.

➡**The Electronic Control Unit (ECU) for all models is located under the front passenger seat. If equipped, the ECCS check connector is located in the instrument panel to the rear of the hood opener assembly.**

ENTERING SELF-DIAGNOSTIC MODE

1. Locate the ECU and remove it from its bracket to gain access to the mode select switch. Do not disconnect the wiring.
2. With the ignition switch **ON**, turn the diagnostic mode selector switch (a small slotted screwdriver is usually necessary to reach the 3 position knob) to the ECU diagnostic position (fully clockwise), hold it in this position and wait for the inspection lamp to flash.
3. Count the number of flashes, and after the inspection lamp has flashed the number of the required mode, immediately turn the diagnostic mode selector fully counterclockwise.
4. When the ignition switch is turned **OFF**, the ECU automatically returns to Mode 1. When the battery is disconnected, or when manually leaving Mode 3 or 4, the stored fault codes will be automatically cleared.

Mode 1: Exhaust Oxygen Sensor Monitor

1. With the ignition **ON**, engine not running, both the green and red LEDs will be lit.
2. With the engine running, the green LED will stay on or off until the engine and oxygen sensor are warm enough to go into closed loop operation. At that point the green LED will blink on and off.
3. The red LED will be off unless the vehicle is a California model and has stored fault codes.

Mode 2: Mixture Ratio Control Monitor

1. With the engine running in closed loop operation, the green LED will blink on and off.
2. If the red LED blinks with the green one, the air/fuel ratio is cycling correctly.
3. If the red LED stays off, the mixture is more than 5 percent rich.
4. If the red LED stays on, the mixture is more than 5 percent lean.
5. If the red LED stays on or off during closed loop operation, complete the diagnostics before beginning repairs.

Mode 3: Stored Fault Code Reporting

All fault codes are two digits and both LEDs are used to report the fault codes. The red LED is the first digit, the green is the second digit. If the red LED flashes 2 times, then the green flashes 4 times, this indicates code No. 24.

1. With the engine running in closed loop operation, operate the Mode select switch to enter Mode 3. The red LED will flash first, then the green one.
2. Count the flashes and write them down. Allow the cycle to repeat a number of times to make sure they have been correctly read.
3. If code 55 is the only code displayed, no faults are in memory.
4. When the ECU is switched to any other mode from Mode 3, the stored fault codes are automatically erased, including intermittent faults. This can be avoided by turning the ignition switch **OFF**. The ECU will automatically leave diagnostic mode without loosing the stored fault codes.

Mode 4: Switch Operation Monitor

These switches are monitored by the ECU: the throttle and idle switch, starter switch and the reed switch for the speed sensor. In Mode 4, each switch that is turned on or off will cause an LED to flash. If no LED flashes when the switch is operated, the switch circuit, the ECU, or switch itself is faulty. When the ECU is moved out of Mode 4, the fault codes are automatically erased. To leave Mode 4 without loosing the codes, turn the ignition **OFF**, then the ECU will default to Mode 1.

1. With the ECU in Mode 4, turn the ignition switch to **START**. The red LED should flash when the starter switch is turned on and again when the starter switch is released.
2. With the ignition **ON**, with or without the engine running, the red LED should flash whenever the throttle switch is turned on or off. The throttle switch signals the ECU that the throttle is in the idle position.
3. When the vehicle is moving at more than 12 mph (20 km/h), the green LED should flash or stay on.

Mode 5: Real Time Diagnostic Function

In Mode 5, the ECU will report one of 3 fault codes while the engine is running: malfunction of the crankangle sensor, the ignition signal, or the air flow meter. These codes are not stored, but can be reported while the engine is running or while vehicle is being driven, if desired. Should the ECU detect a malfunction, an LED will flash on and off at different rates for each sensor. The codes are reported differently from Mode 3. If no fault is detected, no LEDs will flash.

1. With the engine running, put the ECU into Mode 5.
2. Watch the LEDs for more than 5 minutes while the engine is operated at different rpm. If any LEDs flash, write down the number of flashes and note the time between groups of flashes.
3. Compare the notes to the diagnostic codes to find which of the sensors (or circuits) is faulty.

➡**This diagnosis procedure is a very effective measure to diagnose whether the above systems cause the malfunction or not, during a road test.**

DIAGNOSTIC TROUBLE CODES

When using these charts along with the ECU self-diagnostic system, remember that a code only points to a faulty circuit not necessary to a faulty component. Loose, damaged or corroded connections may contribute to a fault code on a circuit when the sensor or component is operating properly. Be sure that the components are faulty before replacing them, especially the expensive ones.

MODE III SELF-DIAGNOSTIC SYSTEM — Z24I AND VG30I ENGINES

Modes I & II — Mixture Ratio Feedback Control Monitors A & B

In these modes, the control unit provides the Air-fuel ratio monitor presentation and the Air-fuel ratio feedback coefficient monitor presentation.

Mode	LED	Engine stopped (Ignition switch "ON")	Engine running	
			Open loop condition	Closed loop condition
Mode I (Monitor A)	Green	ON	*Remains ON or OFF	Blinks
	Red	ON	Except for California model • OFF	For California model • ON: when CHECK ENGINE LIGHT ITEMS are stored in the E.C.U. • OFF: except for the above condition
Mode II (Monitor B)	Green	ON	*Remains ON or OFF	Blinks
	Red	OFF	*Remains ON or OFF (synchronous with green LED)	Compensating mixture ratio

	More than 5% rich	Between 5% lean and 5% rich	More
	OFF	Synchronized with green LED	Remains ON

*: Maintains conditions just before switching to open loop

Mode III — Self-Diagnostic System

The E.C.U. constantly monitors the function of these sensors and actuators, regardless of ignition key position. If a malfunction occurs, the information is stored in the E.C.U. and can be retrieved from the memory by turning on the diagnostic mode selector, located on the side of the E.C.U. When activated, the malfunction is indicated by flashing a red and a green L.E.D. (Light Emitting Diode), also located on the E.C.U. Since all the self-diagnostic results are stored in the E.C.U.'s memory even intermittent malfunctions can be diagnosed.

A malfunctioning part's group is indicated by the number of both the red and the green L.E.D.s flashing. First, the red L.E.D. flashes and the green flashes follow. The red L.E.D. refers to the number of tens while the green one refers to the number of units. For example, when the red L.E.D. flashes once and then the green one flashes twice, this means the number "12" showing the air flow meter signal is malfunctioning. In this way, all the problems are classified by the code numbers.

• When engine fails to start, crank engine more than two seconds before starting self-diagnosis.

• Before starting self-diagnosis, do not erase stored memory. If doing so, self-diagnosis function for intermittent malfunctions would be lost.

The stored memory would be lost if:
1. Battery terminal is disconnected.
2. After selecting Mode III, Mode IV is selected.

DISPLAY CODE TABLE

X: Available
—: Not available
*: Check engine light item

Code No.	Detected items	California	Non-California
11	Crank angle sensor circuit	X	X
12	Air flow meter circuit	X*	X
13	Cylinder head/Water temperature sensor circuit	X*	X
21	Ignition signal missing in primary coil	X*	X
31	E.C.U. (E.C.C.S. control unit)	X*	X
32	E.G.R. circuit	X*	—
33	Exhaust gas sensor circuit	X*	—
35	Exhaust gas temperature sensor circuit	X*	—
43	Throttle sensor circuit	X*	X
45	Injector leak	X*	—
51	Injector (VG30i model only)	X	X
55	No malfunction in the above circuit	X	X

86714801-

MODE III SELF-DIAGNOSTIC SYSTEM — Z24I AND VG30I ENGINES

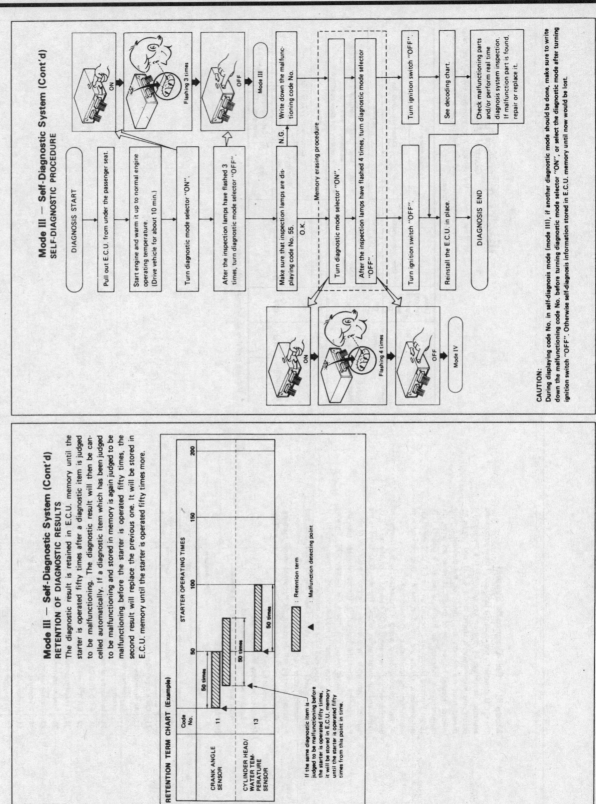

Mode III — Self-Diagnostic System (Cont'd)
RETENTION OF DIAGNOSTIC RESULTS

The diagnostic result is retained in E.C.U. memory until the starter is operated fifty times after a diagnostic item is judged to be malfunctioning. The diagnostic result will then be cancelled automatically. If a diagnostic result which has been judged to be malfunctioning and stored in memory is again judged to be malfunctioning before the starter is operated fifty times, the second result will replace the previous one. It will be stored in E.C.U. memory until the starter is operated fifty times more.

RETENTION TERM CHART (Example)

	Code No.	STARTER OPERATING TIMES
CRANK ANGLE SENSOR	11	50 times
CYLINDER HEAD/WATER TEMPERATURE SENSOR	13	50 times / 50 times

[hatched] : Retention term
▲ : Malfunction detecting point

If the same diagnostic item is judged to be malfunctioning before the starter is operated fifty times, it will be stored in E.C.U. memory until the starter is operated fifty times from this point in time.

Mode III — Self-Diagnostic System (Cont'd)
SELF-DIAGNOSTIC PROCEDURE

DIAGNOSIS START

Pull out E.C.U. from under the passenger seat.

Start engine and warm it up to normal engine operating temperature. (Drive vehicle for about 10 min.)

Turn diagnostic mode selector "ON".

After the inspection lamps have flashed 3 times, turn diagnostic mode selector "OFF".

Flashing 3 times → Mode III

Make sure that inspection lamps are displaying code No. 55.

N.G. → Write down the malfunctioning code No.

O.K. → Memory erasing procedure

Turn diagnostic mode selector "ON".

After the inspection lamps have flashed 4 times, turn diagnostic mode selector "OFF".

Flashing 4 times → Mode IV

Turn ignition switch "OFF".

Reinstall the E.C.U. in place.

DIAGNOSIS END

Write down the malfunctioning code No.

Turn ignition switch "OFF".

See decoding chart.

Check malfunctioning parts and/or perform real time diagnosis system inspection. If malfunction part is found, repair or replace it.

CAUTION:
During displaying code No. in self-diagnosis mode (mode III), if another diagnostic mode should be done, make sure to write down the malfunctioning code No. before turning diagnostic mode selector "ON", or select the diagnostic mode after turning ignition switch "OFF". Otherwise self-diagnosis information stored in E.C.U. memory until now would be lost.

86714802

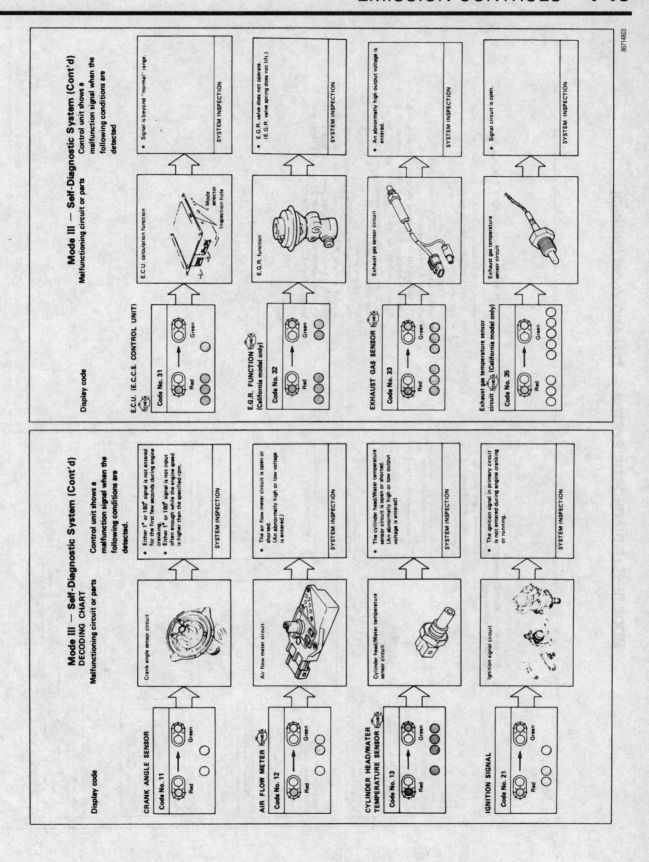

MODE III SELF-DIAGNOSTIC SYSTEM — Z24I AND VG30I ENGINES

Mode IV — Switches ON/OFF Diagnostic System

In switches ON/OFF diagnosis system, ON/OFF operation of the following switches can be detected continuously.

- Idle switch
- Starter switch
- Vehicle speed sensor (VG30i A/T model only)

(1) Idle switch & Starter switch

The switches ON/OFF status at the point when mode IV is selected is stored in E.C.U. memory. When either switch is turned from "ON" to "OFF" or "OFF" to "ON", the red L.E.D. on E.C.U. alternately comes on and goes off each time switching is detected.

(2) Vehicle Speed Sensor

The switches ON/OFF status at the point when mode IV is selected is stored in E.C.U. memory. When vehicle speed is 20 km/h (12 MPH) or slower, the green L.E.D. on E.C.U. is off. When vehicle speed exceeds 20 km/h (12 MPH), the green L.E.D. on E.C.U. comes "ON".

Mode III — Self-Diagnostic System (Cont'd)

Malfunctioning circuit or parts

Control unit shows a malfunction signal when the following conditions are detected

Display code

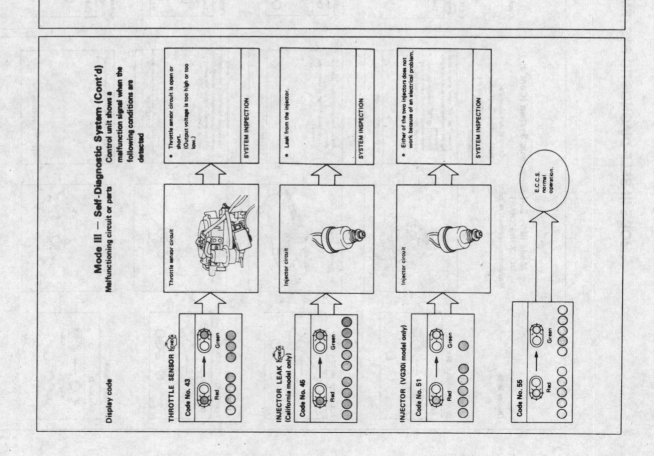

THROTTLE SENSOR (ECCS)

Code No. 43

Throttle sensor circuit

- Throttle sensor circuit is open or short.
  (Output voltage is too high or too low.)

SYSTEM INSPECTION

INJECTOR LEAK (ECCS)
(California model only)

Code No. 45

Injector circuit

- Leak from the injector.

SYSTEM INSPECTION

INJECTOR (VG30i model only)

Code No. 51

Injector circuit

- Either of the two injectors does not work because of an electrical problem.

SYSTEM INSPECTION

Code No. 55

E.C.C.S. normal operation.

MODE III SELF-DIAGNOSTIC SYSTEM — KA24E ENGINES

Self-diagnosis — Mode III (Self-diagnostic system)

The E.C.U. constantly monitors the function of these sensors and actuators, regardless of ignition key position. If a malfunction occurs, the information is stored in the E.C.U. and can be retrieved from the memory by turning on the diagnostic mode selector, located on the side of the E.C.U. When activated, the malfunction is indicated by flashing a red and a green L.E.D. (Light Emitting Diode), also located on the E.C.U. Since all the self-diagnostic results are stored in the E.C.U.'s memory even intermittent malfunctions can be diagnosed.

A malfunction is indicated by the number of both red and green flashing L.E.D.s. First, the red L.E.D. flashes and the green flashes follow. The red L.E.D. corresponds to units of ten and the green L.E.D. corresponds to units of one. For example, when the red L.E.D. flashes once and the green L.E.D. flashes twice, this signifies the number "12", showing that the air flow meter signal is malfunctioning. All problems are classified by code numbers in this way.

- When the engine fails to start, crank it two or more seconds before beginning self-diagnosis.
- Before starting self-diagnosis, do not erase the stored memory before beginning self-diagnosis. If it is erased, the self-diagnosis function for intermittent malfunctions will be lost.

DISPLAY CODE TABLE

Code No.	Detected items	California	Non-California
11	Crank angle sensor circuit	X	X
12	Air flow meter circuit	X	X
13	Engine temperature sensor circuit	X	X
14	Vehicle speed sensor circuit	X	X
21	Ignition signal missing in primary coil	X	X
31	E.C.U. (E.C.C.S. control unit)	X	X
32	E.G.R. function	X	—
33	Exhaust gas sensor circuit	X	X
35	Exhaust gas temperature sensor circuit	X	—
41	Air temperature sensor circuit	X	X
43	Throttle sensor circuit	X	X
45	Injector leak	X	—
55	No malfunction in the above circuits	X	X

X: Available   —: Not available

MODE III SELF-DIAGNOSTIC SYSTEM — KA24E ENGINES

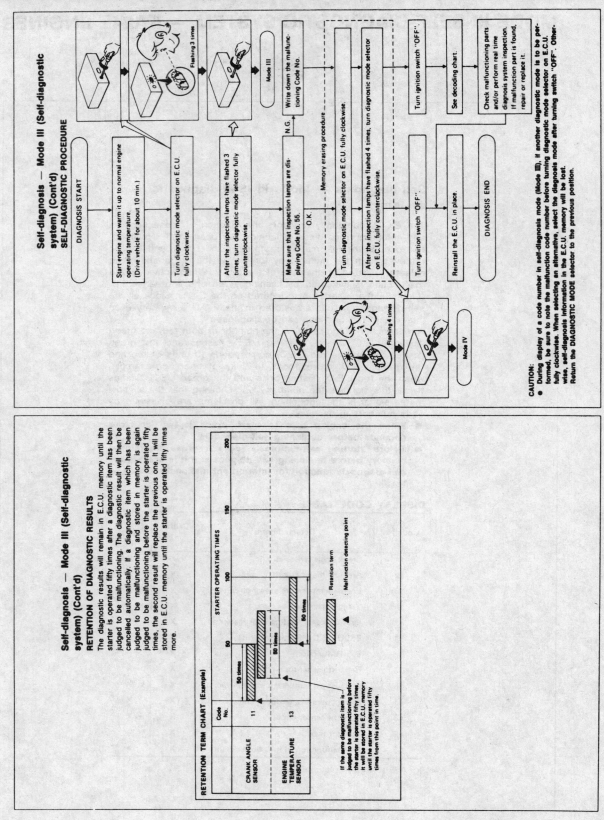

Self-diagnosis — Mode III (Self-diagnostic system) (Cont'd)
SELF-DIAGNOSTIC PROCEDURE

DIAGNOSIS START

Start engine and warm it up to normal engine operating temperature. (Drive vehicle for about 10 min.)

Turn diagnostic mode selector on E.C.U. fully clockwise.

After the inspection lamps have flashed 3 times, turn diagnostic mode selector fully counterclockwise.

Make sure that inspection lamps are displaying Code No. 55.

N.G. → Write down the malfunctioning Code No.

Mode III

Flashing 3 times

O.K.

Memory erasing procedure

Turn diagnostic mode selector on E.C.U. fully clockwise.

After the inspection lamps have flashed 4 times, turn diagnostic mode selector on E.C.U. fully counterclockwise.

Mode IV

Flashing 4 times

Turn ignition switch "OFF".

Reinstall the E.C.U. in place.

DIAGNOSIS END

Turn ignition switch "OFF".

See decoding chart.

Check malfunctioning parts and/or perform real time diagnosis system inspection. If malfunction part is found, repair or replace it.

CAUTION:
● During display of a code number in self-diagnosis mode (Mode III), if another diagnostic mode is to be performed, be sure to note the malfunction code number before turning diagnostic mode selector on E.C.U. fully clockwise. When selecting an alternative, select the diagnosis mode after turning switch "OFF". Otherwise, self-diagnosis information in the E.C.U. memory will be lost. Return the DIAGNOSTIC MODE selector to the previous position.

Self-diagnosis — Mode III (Self-diagnostic system) (Cont'd)
RETENTION OF DIAGNOSTIC RESULTS

The diagnostic results will remain in E.C.U. memory until the starter is operated fifty times after a diagnostic item has been judged to be malfunctioning. The diagnostic result will then be cancelled automatically. If a diagnostic item which has been judged to be malfunctioning and stored in memory is again judged to be malfunctioning before the starter is operated fifty times, the second result will replace the previous one. It will be stored in E.C.U. memory until the starter is operated fifty times more.

RETENTION TERM CHART (Example)

	Code No.	STARTER OPERATING TIMES
		50 100 150 200
CRANK ANGLE SENSOR	11	
ENGINE TEMPERATURE SENSOR	13	

50 times
50 times
50 times

: Retention term
▲ : Malfunction detecting point

If the same diagnostic item is judged to be malfunctioning before the starter is operated fifty times, it will be stored in E.C.U. memory until the starter is operated fifty times from this point in time.

86714831

MODE III SELF-DIAGNOSTIC SYSTEM — KA24E ENGINES

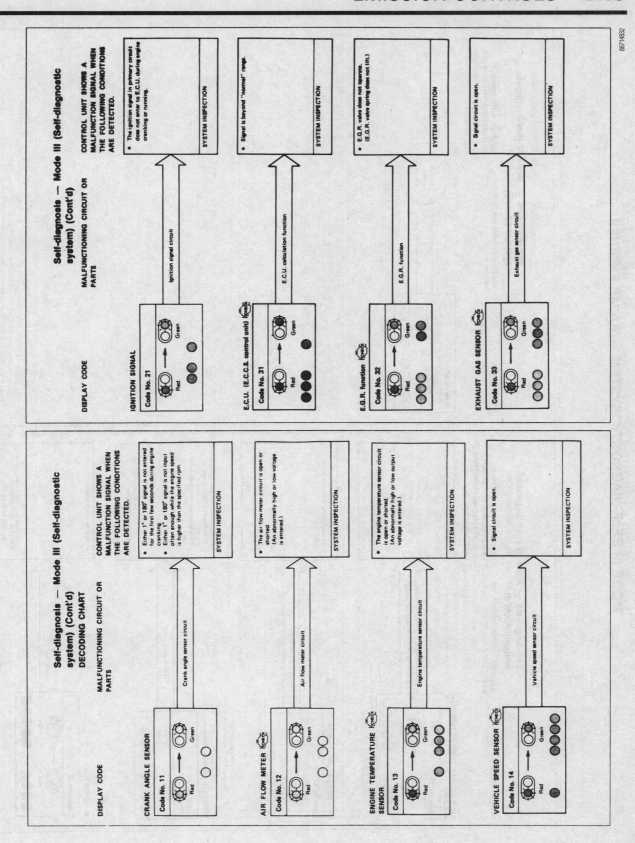

Self-diagnosis — Mode III (Self-diagnostic system) DECODING CHART

DISPLAY CODE	MALFUNCTIONING CIRCUIT OR PARTS
CRANK ANGLE SENSOR Code No. 11	Crank angle sensor circuit
AIR FLOW METER Code No. 12	Air flow meter circuit
ENGINE TEMPERATURE SENSOR Code No. 13	Engine temperature sensor circuit
VEHICLE SPEED SENSOR Code No. 14	Vehicle speed sensor circuit

CONTROL UNIT SHOWS A MALFUNCTION SIGNAL WHEN THE FOLLOWING CONDITIONS ARE DETECTED.

- Either 1° or 180° signal is not entered for the first few seconds during engine cranking.
- Either 1° or 180° signal is not input often enough while the engine speed is higher than the specified rpm.

SYSTEM INSPECTION

- The air flow meter circuit is open or shorted. (An abnormally high or low voltage is entered.)

SYSTEM INSPECTION

- The engine temperature sensor circuit is open or shorted. (An abnormally high or low output voltage is entered.)

SYSTEM INSPECTION

- Signal circuit is open.

SYSTEM INSPECTION

Self-diagnosis — Mode III (Self-diagnostic system) (Cont'd)

DISPLAY CODE	MALFUNCTIONING CIRCUIT OR PARTS
IGNITION SIGNAL Code No. 21	Ignition signal circuit
E.C.U. (E.C.C.S. control unit) Code No. 31	E.C.U. calculation function
E.G.R. function Code No. 32	E.G.R. function
EXHAUST GAS SENSOR Code No. 33	Exhaust gas sensor circuit

CONTROL UNIT SHOWS A MALFUNCTION SIGNAL WHEN THE FOLLOWING CONDITIONS ARE DETECTED.

- The ignition signal in primary circuit does not enter to E.C.U. during engine cranking or running.

SYSTEM INSPECTION

- Signal is beyond "normal" range.

SYSTEM INSPECTION

- E.G.R. valve does not operate. (E.G.R. valve spring does not lift.)

SYSTEM INSPECTION

- Signal circuit is open.

SYSTEM INSPECTION

8671432

MODE III SELF-DIAGNOSTIC SYSTEM – KA24E ENGINES

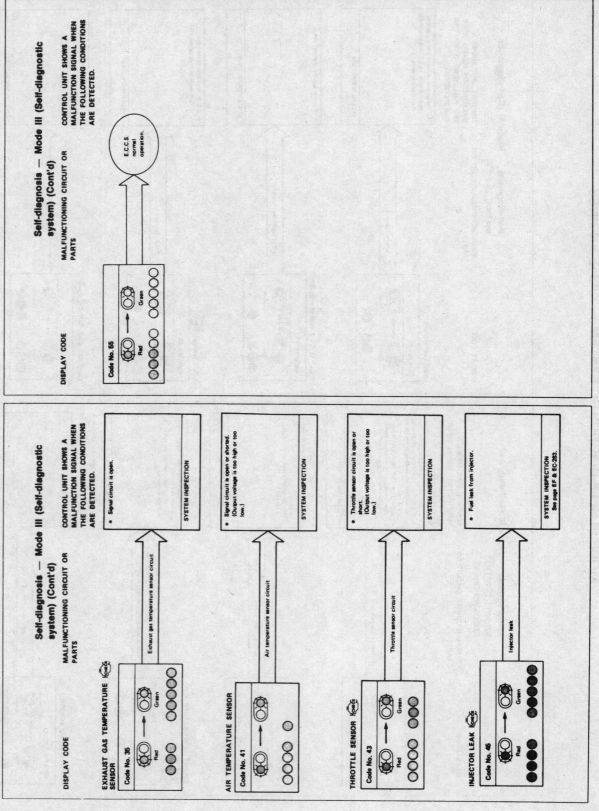

MODE III SELF-DIAGNOSTIC SYSTEM
KA24E ENGINES

Self-diagnosis — Mode IV (Switches ON/OFF diagnostic system)

In switches ON/OFF diagnosis system, ON/OFF operation of the following switches can be detected continuously.

- Soft idle switch
- Starter switch
- Vehicle speed sensor

(1) Soft idle switch & Starter switch

The switches ON/OFF status in mode IV is stored in E.C.U. memory. When either switch is turned from "ON" to "OFF" or "OFF" to "ON", the red L.E.D. on E.C.U. alternately comes on and goes off each time switching is performed.

(2) Vehicle Speed Sensor

The switches ON/OFF status in mode IV is selected is stored in E.C.U. memory. The green L.E.D. on E.C.U. remains off when vehicle speed is 20 km/h (12 MPH) or below, and comes ON at higher speeds.

MODE III SELF-DIAGNOSTIC SYSTEM — VG30E ENGINES

Self-diagnosis — Mode III (Self-diagnostic system)

The E.C.U. constantly monitors the function of these sensors and actuators, regardless of ignition key position. If a malfunction occurs, the information is stored in the E.C.U. and can be retrieved from the memory by turning on the diagnostic mode selector, located on the side of the E.C.U. When activated, the malfunction is indicated by flashing a red and a green L.E.D. (Light Emitting Diode), also located on the E.C.U. Since all the self-diagnostic results are stored in the E.C.U.'s memory even intermittent malfunctions can be diagnosed.

A malfunction is indicated by the number of both red and green flashing L.E.D.s. First, the red L.E.D. flashes and the green flashes follow. The red L.E.D. corresponds to units of ten and the green L.E.D. corresponds to units of one. For example, when the red L.E.D. flashes once and the green L.E.D. flashes twice, this signifies the number "12", showing that the air flow meter signal is malfunctioning. All problems are classified by code numbers in this way.

- When the engine fails to start, crank it two or more seconds before beginning self-diagnosis.
- Before starting self-diagnosis, do not erase the stored memory before beginning self-diagnosis. If it is erased, the self-diagnosis function for intermittent malfunctions will be lost.

The stored memory would be lost if:
1. Battery terminal is disconnected.
2. After selecting Mode III, Mode IV is selected.

DISPLAY CODE TABLE

Code No.	Detected items	California	Non-California
11	Crank angle sensor circuit	X	X
12	Air flow meter circuit	X	X
13	Engine temperature sensor circuit	X	X
14	Vehicle speed sensor circuit	X	X
21	Ignition signal missing in primary coil	X	X
31	E.C.U. (E.C.C.S. control unit)	X	X
32	E.G.R. function	X	–
33	Exhaust gas sensor circuit	X	X
34	Detonation sensor circuit	X	X
35	Exhaust gas temperature sensor circuit	X	–
43	Throttle sensor circuit	X	X
45	Injector leak	X	–
51	Injector circuit	X	–
55	No malfunction in the above circuit	X	X

X: Available   –: Not available

Self-diagnosis — Mode III (Self-diagnostic system) (Cont'd)
RETENTION OF DIAGNOSTIC RESULTS

The diagnostic results will remain in E.C.U. memory until the starter is operated fifty times after a diagnostic item has been judged to be malfunctioning. The diagnostic result will then be cancelled automatically. If a diagnostic item which has been judged to be malfunctioning and stored in memory is again judged to be malfunctioning before the starter is operated fifty times, the second result will replace the previous one. It will be stored in E.C.U. memory until the starter is operated fifty times more.

RETENTION TERM CHART (Example)

	Code No.				
CRANK ANGLE SENSOR	11				
ENGINE TEMPERATURE SENSOR	13				

STARTER OPERATING TIMES
50   100   150   200

50 times
50 times
50 times

🔲 : Retention term
▲ : Malfunction detecting point

If the same diagnostic item is judged to be malfunctioning before the starter is operated fifty times, it will be stored in E.C.U. memory until the starter is operated fifty times from this point in time.

MODE III SELF-DIAGNOSTIC SYSTEM — VG30E ENGINES

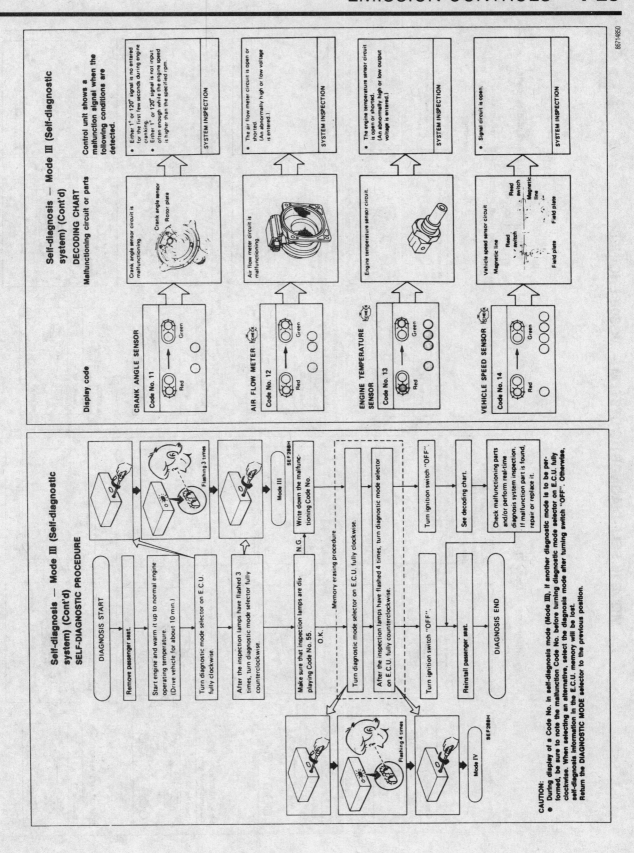

MODE III SELF-DIAGNOSTIC SYSTEM — VG30E ENGINES

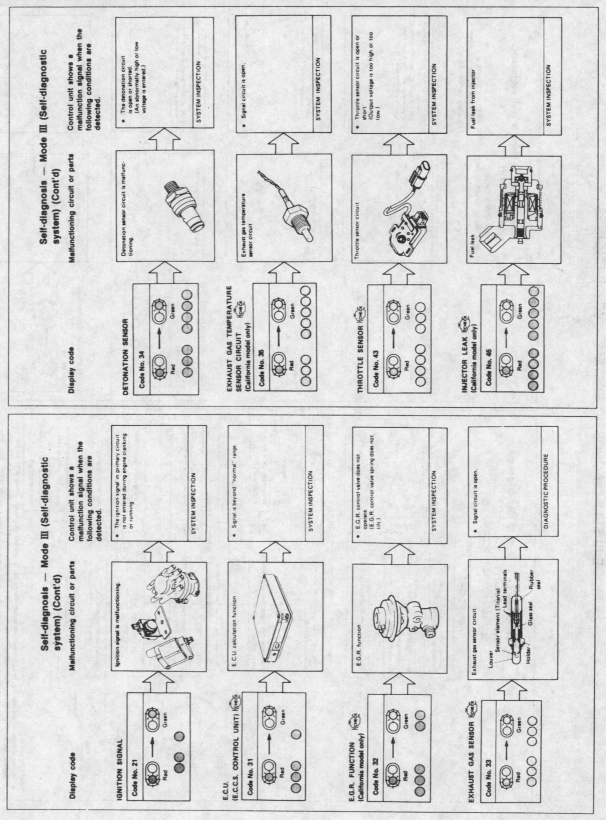

Self-diagnosis — Mode III (Self-diagnostic system) (Cont'd)

Display code | **Malfunctioning circuit or parts** | Control unit shows a malfunction signal when the following conditions are detected.

IGNITION SIGNAL
Code No. 21
Red / Green

Ignition signal is malfunctioning.

- The ignition signal in primary circuit is not entered during engine cranking or running

SYSTEM INSPECTION

E.C.U.
(E.C.C.S. CONTROL UNIT)
Code No. 31
Red / Green

E.C.U. calculation function

- Signal is beyond "normal" range

SYSTEM INSPECTION

E.G.R. FUNCTION
(California model only)
Code No. 32
Red / Green

E.G.R. function

- E.G.R. control valve does not operate.
  (E.G.R. control valve spring does not lift.)

SYSTEM INSPECTION

EXHAUST GAS SENSOR
Code No. 33
Red / Green

Exhaust gas sensor circuit

Louver / Sensor element (Titania) / Lead terminals / Rubber seal / Holder / Glass seal

- Signal circuit is open.

DIAGNOSTIC PROCEDURE

Self-diagnosis — Mode III (Self-diagnostic system) (Cont'd)

Display code | **Malfunctioning circuit or parts** | Control unit shows a malfunction signal when the following conditions are detected.

DETONATION SENSOR
Code No. 34
Red / Green

Detonation sensor circuit is malfunctioning.

- The detonation circuit is open or shorted.
  (An abnormally high or low voltage is entered.)

SYSTEM INSPECTION

EXHAUST GAS TEMPERATURE SENSOR CIRCUIT
(California model only)
Code No. 35
Red / Green

Exhaust gas temperature sensor circuit

- Signal circuit is open.

SYSTEM INSPECTION

THROTTLE SENSOR
Code No. 43
Red / Green

Throttle sensor circuit

- Throttle sensor circuit is open or short.
  (Output voltage is too high or too low.)

SYSTEM INSPECTION

INJECTOR LEAK
(California model only)
Code No. 45
Red / Green

Fuel leak

Fuel leak from injector

SYSTEM INSPECTION

8674851

MODE III SELF-DIAGNOSTIC SYSTEM — VG30E ENGINES

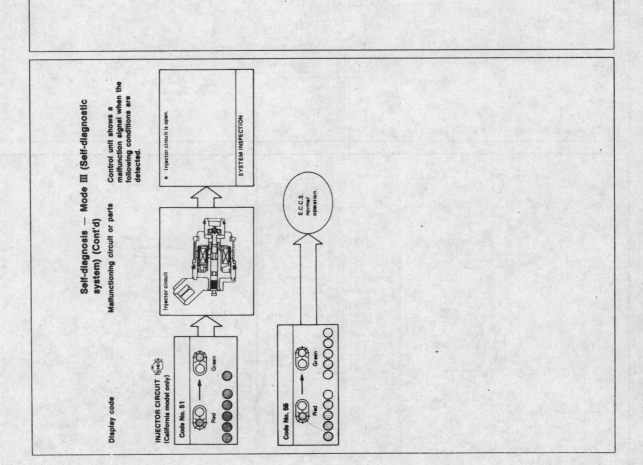

Self-diagnosis — Mode III (Self-diagnostic system) (Cont'd)

Display code	Malfunctioning circuit or parts	Control unit shows a malfunction signal when the following conditions are detected.
INJECTOR CIRCUIT (California model only) Code No. 51 Red → Green	Injector circuit	• Injector circuit is open.
Code No. 55 Red → Green		E.C.C.S. normal operation.

SYSTEM INSPECTION

Self-diagnosis — Mode IV (Switches ON/OFF diagnostic system)

In switches ON/OFF diagnostic system, ON/OFF operation of the following switches can be detected continuously.
- Soft idle switch
- Starter switch
- Vehicle speed sensor

(1) Throttle valve switch & Starter switch

The switches ON/OFF status in Mode IV is stored in E.C.U. memory. When either switch is turned from "ON" to "OFF" or "OFF" to "ON", the red L.E.D. on E.C.U. alternately comes on and goes off each time switching is performed.

(2) Vehicle speed sensor

The switches ON/OFF status in Mode IV is selected is stored in E.C.U. memory. The green L.E.D. on E.C.U. remains off when vehicle speed is 20 km/h (12 MPH) or below, and comes ON at higher speeds.

VACUUM DIAGRAMS

Following is a listing of vacuum diagrams for most of the engine and emissions package combinations covered by this manual. Because vacuum circuits will vary based on various engine and vehicle options, always refer first to the vehicle emission control information label, if present. Should the label be missing, or should vehicle be equipped with a different engine from the truck's original equipment, refer to the diagrams below for the same or similar configuration.

If you wish to obtain a replacement emissions label, most manufacturers make the labels available for purchase. The labels can usually be ordered from a local dealer. Speak to the dealership's parts department first to make sure you copy down all the identification codes they will need to order the replacement label.

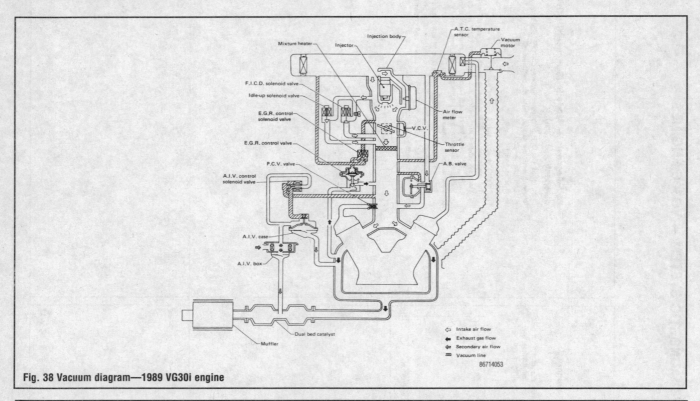

Fig. 38 Vacuum diagram—1989 VG30i engine

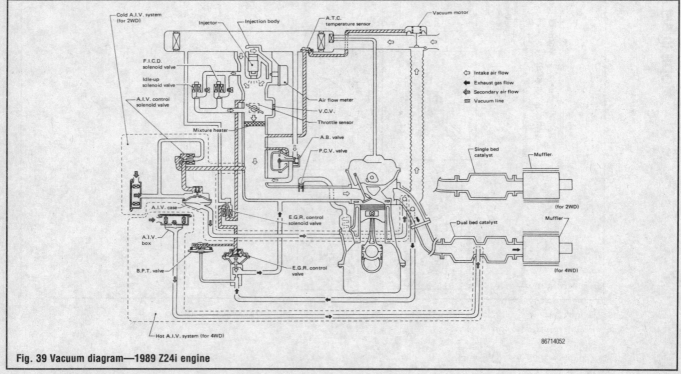

Fig. 39 Vacuum diagram—1989 Z24i engine

Vacuum Hose Drawing

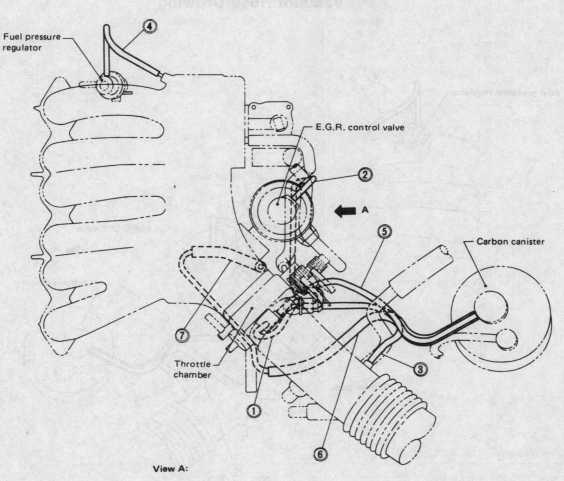

View A:

① E.G.R. control solenoid valve to Throttle chamber
② E.G.R. control solenoid valve to E.G.R. control valve
③ E.G.R. control solenoid valve to Air duct
④ Fuel pressure regulator to Intake manifold collector
⑤ Carbon canister vacuum port to Throttle chamber
⑥ Carbon canister purge port to Vapor purge tube
⑦ Vapor purge tube to Throttle chamber

86714054

Fig. 40 Vacuum diagram—1990–93 VG30E engine

Vacuum Hose Drawing

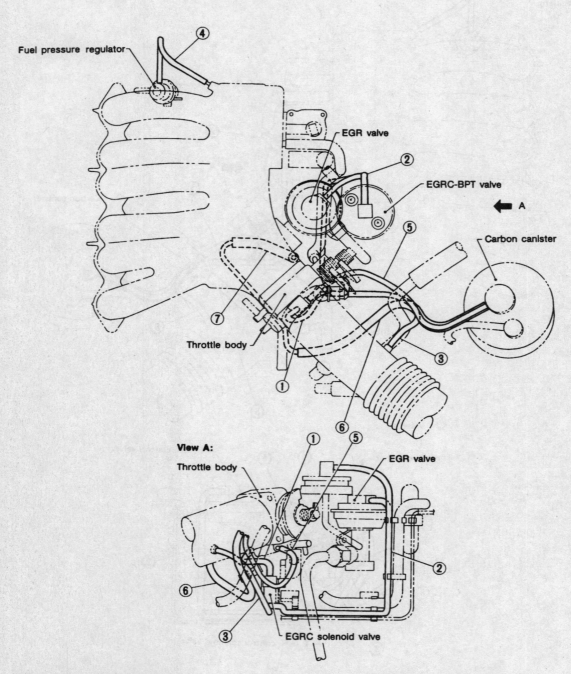

Fuel pressure regulator

EGR valve

EGRC-BPT valve

A

Carbon canister

Throttle body

View A:

Throttle body

EGR valve

EGRC solenoid valve

① EGRC solenoid valve to Throttle body
② EGRC solenoid valve to EGR valve
③ EGRC solenoid valve to Air duct
④ Fuel pressure regulator to Intake
   manifold collector

⑤ Carbon canister vacuum port to Throttle
   body
⑥ Carbon canister purge port to Vapor
   purge tube
⑦ Vapor purge tube to Throttle body

86714055

Fig. 41 Vacuum diagram—1994–95 VG30E engine

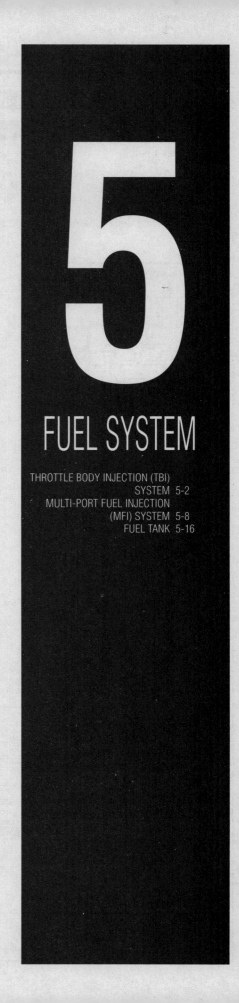

5

FUEL SYSTEM

THROTTLE BODY INJECTION (TBI) SYSTEM

General Information

♦ See Figures 1 thru 7

The Nissan Electro Injection System is a throttle body fuel injection system used on 1989 models equipped with the VG30i or Z24i engines. This system is part of Electronic Concentrated Control System (ECCS). The ECCS utilizes a computerized brain center known as the Electronic Control Unit (ECU), along with various sensors and solenoids/regulators to precisely control fuel delivery to the injectors.

SYSTEM COMPONENTS

Crank Angle Sensor

The crank angle sensor is a basic component of the entire system. It monitors engine speed/piston position and sends signals which the control unit uses to calculate ignition timing and fuel delivery functions.

The crank angle sensor has a rotor plate and a wave forming circuit. On all models, the signal rotor plate has 360 slits for 1 degree signals (crank angle). On models equipped with VG30i engines, the rotor plate also consists of 6 slits for 120

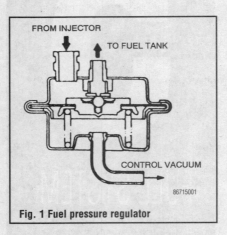

Fig. 1 Fuel pressure regulator

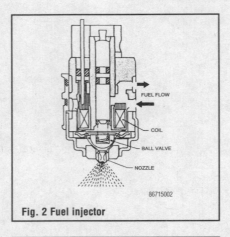

Fig. 2 Fuel injector

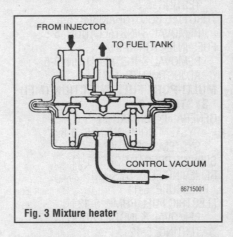

Fig. 3 Mixture heater

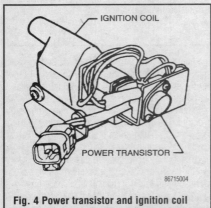

Fig. 4 Power transistor and ignition coil

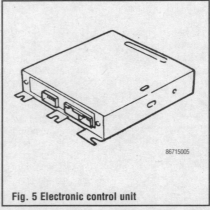

Fig. 5 Electronic control unit

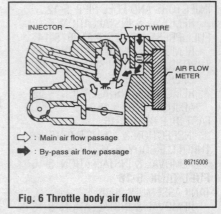

Fig. 6 Throttle body air flow

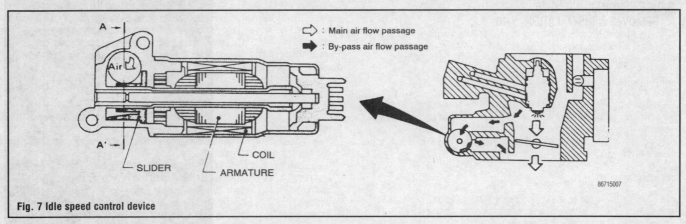

Fig. 7 Idle speed control device

degree signals (engine speed). On models equipped with Z24i engines, the rotor plate also consists of 4 slits for 180 degree signals (engine speed). Light emitting diodes (LED's) and photo diodes are built into the wave forming circuit. When the rotor plate passes the space between the LED and the photo diode, the slits of the rotor plate continually cut the light which is sent to the photo diode from the LED, causing rough shaped pulses. These pulses are converted into on-off signals by the wave forming circuit and sent to the control unit as input signals.

Air Flow Meter

The air flow meter measures the intake air flow rate by taking a part of the entire flow. Measurements are made in such a manner that the control unit receives electrical output signals which vary by the amount of heat emitted from a hot wire placed in the stream of intake are. When intake are flows into the intake manifold through a route around the hot wire, the heat generated by the wire is taken away by the passing air. The amount of heat removed depends on the air flow, but the maximum temperature of the hot wire is automatically controlled, requiring more electrical current to maintain the controlled temperature in the wire as the amount of intake air increases. By measuring the amount of current necessary to maintain the hot wire temperature, the control unit measures the amount of intake air passing the wire and, therefore, knows the volume of air entering the engine.

Water and Air Temperature Sensors

The water temperature sensor, located on the front side of the intake manifold, detects engine coolant temperature and sends signals to the control unit. The air temperature sensor, installed in the air cleaner, monitors the intake air temperature. Both of these sensors employ a thermistor (temperature dependant resistor) which is sensitive to changes in temperature. The electrical resistance of these thermistors decreases as temperature rises.

Exhaust Gas Sensor

The exhaust gas sensor, which is placed in the exhaust pipe, monitors the amount of oxygen in the exhaust gas. The sensor is made of ceramic titania which changes electrical resistance at the ideal air/fuel ratio (14.7:1). The control unit supplies the sensor with approximately 1 volt and reads the varying output voltage of the sensor, depending on its resistance. The oxygen sensor is equipped with a heater to bring it to operating temperature quickly.

Throttle Sensor/Idle Switch

The throttle sensor/idle switch is attached to the throttle body and operates in response to accelerator pedal movement. This sensor has 2 functions: it contains an idle switch and throttle position sensor. The idle switch closes when the throttle valve is positioned at idle, and opens when it is in any other position. The throttle sensor is a potentiometer which transforms the throttle valve position into output voltage and feeds the voltage signal to the control unit. In addition, the throttle sensor detects the opening or closing speed of the throttle valve and feeds the rate of voltage change to the control unit.

Power Steering Oil Pressure Switch

A power steering oil pressure switch is attached to the power steering high pressure line and detects the power steering load, sending a load signal to the control unit which then sends the idle-up signal to the Idle Speed Control (ISC) valve.

Fuel Pressure Regulator

A fuel pressure regulator is built into the side of the throttle body. It maintains fuel pressure at a constant value. Since the injected fuel amount depends on injection pulse duration, it is necessary to keep the fuel pressure constant. A fuel pump with a fuel damper is located in the fuel tank. The pump is an electric, vane roller type.

Fuel Injector

The fuel injector is basically a small solenoid valve. The control unit sends electrical signals to the injector in order to actuate a coil which pulls back a ball from the injector check valve. High pressure fuel, which is constantly supplied to the injector (from the fuel pump and lines), then forces past the tiny opening in the nozzle, spraying into the intake. The amount of injected fuel is controlled by the computer through longer or shorter control signals (pulse duration)

which simply have the effect of opening the injector valve for a longer or shorter period of time. A mixture heater is located between the throttle valve and the intake manifold. This is designed and operated for atomizing fuel in the cold engine start condition. The heater is also controlled by the computer.

Mixture Heater

The mixture heater is located between the throttle valve and the intake manifold. This is designed and operated for atomizing fuel in the cold engine start condition. The ECU regulates the heater.

Idle Speed Control (ISC) Valve

The Idle Speed Control (ISC) valve is a rotary solenoid valve that receives a pulse signal from the control unit. This pulse signal determines the position of the slider, thereby varying bypass air quantity which raises or lowers the idle speed. The ISC valve has additional functions which include idle-up after cold start (fast idle), idle speed feedback control, idle-up for air conditioner and power steering (fast idle control device) and deceleration vacuum control.

Power Transistor and Ignition Coil

The ignition signal from the ECU is amplified by the power transistor, which turns the ignition coil primary circuit on and off, inducing the proper high voltage in the secondary circuit. The ignition coil is a small, molded type.

Electronic Control Unit (ECU)

In conjunction with its sensors and related components, the ECU basically controls engine operation from ignition to fuel delivery. The ECU consists of a microcomputer, inspection lamps, and a diagnostic mode selector, as well as connectors for signal input/output and for power supply. The unit regulates the ignition timing, idle speed, fuel mixture (based on ratio feedback), fuel pump operation, mixture heating, Air Injection Valve (AIV) operation, Exhaust Gas Recirculation (EGR), and vapor canister purge operation.

SYSTEM OPERATION

In operation, the on-board computer (control unit) calculates the basic injection pulse width by processing signals from the crank angle sensor and air flow meter. Receiving signals from each sensor which detects various engine operating conditions, the computer adds various enrichments (which are preprogrammed) to the basic injection amount. In this manner, the optimum amount of fuel is delivered through the injectors. The fuel is enriched when starting, during warm-up, when accelerating and when operating under a heavy load. The fuel is leaned during deceleration according to the closing rate of the throttle valve.

The mixture ratio feedback system (closed loop control) is designed to control the air/fuel mixture precisely to the stoichiometric, or optimum point, so that the 3-way catalytic converter can minimize CO, HC and NOx emissions simultaneously. The optimum air/fuel mixture is 14.7:1. This system uses an exhaust gas (oxygen) sensor located in the exhaust manifold to give an indication of whether the fuel mixture is richer or leaner than the stoichiometric point. The control unit adjusts the injection pulse width according to the sensor voltage so the mixture ratio will be within the narrow window around the stoichiometric fuel ratio. The system goes into closed loop as soon as the oxygen sensor heats up enough to register. The system will operate under open loop under any of these conditions:
- Starting the engine
- Engine temperature is cold
- Exhaust gas sensor temperature is cold
- Driving at high speeds or under heavy load, at idle (after mixture ratio learning is completed)
- When the exhaust gas sensor monitors a rich condition for more than 10 seconds and during deceleration.

Ignition timing is controlled in response to engine operating conditions. The optimum ignition timing in each driving condition is preprogrammed in the computer. The signal from the control unit is transmitted to the power transistor and controls ignition timing. The idle speed is also controlled according to engine operating conditions, temperature and gear position. On manual transmission models, if battery voltage is less than 12 volts for a few seconds, a higher idle speed will be maintained by the control unit to improve battery charging.

The control unit energizes the mixture heating relay when the engine is running and the water temperature is below 122°F (50°C). The mixture heating relay will be shut off after several minutes when the water temperature exceeds 122°F (50°C). In addition, the Air Injection Valve (AIV), which supplies secondary air to the exhaust manifold, is controlled by the computer according to engine temperature. When the engine is cold, the AIV system operates to reduce HC and CO emissions. In extremely cold conditions, the AIV control system does not operate to reduce afterburning.

A signal from the control unit is also sent to the EGR and fuel vapor canister purge cut solenoid valve, which cuts the vacuum for the EGR and canister control valve. The EGR and canister purge activates when the vehicle speed is above 6 mph, the water temperature is above 140°F (60°C) and the engine is under light load or low rpm. The vacuum will be interrupted unless all of the conditions are met.

Finally, the control unit operates the air flow meter self-cleaning system. After the engine is stopped, the control unit heats up the hot wire to approximately 1832°F (1000°C) to burn off dust adhering to the wire. The self-cleaning function will activate if the engine speed has exceeded 2000 rpm before the key is turned **OFF**, vehicle speed has exceeded 12 mph before the key is turned **OFF**, water temperature is 140–203°F (60–95°C), or the engine has been stopped by turning the ignition key **OFF**. Self-cleaning will be activated only if all of the above conditions are met. The hot wire will be heated for 0.3 seconds, 5 seconds after the ignition is switched **OFF**.

There is a fail-safe system built into the control unit should the air flow meter malfunction. If the air flow meter output voltage is higher or lower than the specified value, the control unit senses an air flow meter malfunction and substitutes the throttle sensor signal for the air flow meter input. It is possible to start the engine and drive the vehicle, but the engine speed will not rise more than 2400 rpm, in order to inform the driver of fail-safe system operation while driving.

Service Precautions

- Do not operate the fuel pump when the fuel lines are empty.
- Do not reuse fuel hose clamps.
- Do not disengage the ECCS harness connectors before the battery ground cable has been disconnected.
- Make sure all ECCS connectors are fastened securely. A poor connection can cause an extremely high voltage surge and result in damage to integrated circuits.
- Keep the ECCS harness at least 6 in. (15 cm) away from adjacent harnesses to prevent an ECCS system malfunction due to external electronic "noise."
- Keep all parts and harnesses dry during service.
- Before attempting to remove any parts, turn the ignition switch **OFF** and disconnect the battery ground cable.
- Always use a 12 volt battery as a power source.
- Do not attempt to disconnect the battery cables with the engine running.
- Do not depress the accelerator pedal when starting.
- Do not rev up the engine immediately after starting or just prior to shutdown.
- Do not attempt to disassemble the ECCS control unit under any circumstances.
- If a battery cable is disconnected, the memory will return to the ROM (programmed) values. Engine operation may vary slightly, but this is not an indication of a problem. Do not replace parts because of a slight variation.
- If installing a 2-way or CB radio, keep the antenna as far away as possible from the electronic control unit. Keep the antenna feeder line at least 12 in. (30 cm) away from the ECCS harness and to not let the 2 run parallel for a long distance. Be sure to ground the radio to the vehicle body.

Relieving Fuel System Pressure

♦ See Figure 8

✷✷ CAUTION

Never smoke when working around gasoline! Avoid all sources of sparks or ignition. Gasoline vapors are EXTREMELY volatile! Whenever you are working on or around the fuel system you should ALWAYS keep a dry chemical (Class B) fire extinguisher handy.

Fig. 8 One method of releasing fuel pressure is to remove the fuel pump fuse with the engine running

1. There are various methods of relieving the fuel system pressure. All cause the engine fuel delivery system to purge itself while the engine is running by stopping the flow of additional fuel before stopping the engine. This may be accomplished in one or more of 3 possible methods, depending upon your vehicle. Perform one of the following while your engine is running:
- Remove the fuel pump fuse from the fuse block.
- Disconnect the fuel pump relay.
- Detach the wiring harness connector at the fuel tank.
2. The vehicle should run and then stall when the fuel in the lines is exhausted. When the engine stops, crank the starter a few times for about 5 seconds to make sure all pressure in the fuel lines is released.
3. Install or engage the fuel pump fuse, relay or harness connector (as applicable) after the repair/replacement is made.
4. The "Check Engine Light" may stay on after the test has been completed. The trouble code in the control unit's memory must be erased. This may be done by disconnecting the battery cable for 10 seconds, then reconnecting it and verifying that the light has extinguished.

Electric Fuel Pump

The fuel pump assembly is located in the fuel tank. Refer to the fuel tank assembly illustrations in this section. On most applications, the fuel tank must be lowered to remove the fuel pump assembly. The fuel pump assembly is cooled by the fuel in the tank.

REMOVAL & INSTALLATION

♦ See Figure 9

1. Before disconnecting the fuel lines or any of the fuel system components, release the fuel system pressure as described previously in this section. Releasing system pressure is a very important step for the correct removal of the electric fuel pump.
2. Disconnect the negative battery cable. Unfasten the fuel pump assembly electrical connector and remove the fuel tank inspection cover.

➡**If the truck has no fuel tank inspection cover, the fuel tank must be lowered or removed to gain access to the in-tank fuel pump.**

3. Disconnect the fuel outlet and return hoses. Remove the fuel tank assembly, if necessary.
4. Remove the ring retaining bolts and the O-ring, then lift the fuel pump assembly from the fuel tank. Plug the opening with a clean rag to prevent dirt from entering the system.

➡**When removing or installing the fuel pump assembly, be careful not to damage or deform it. Always install a new O-ring.**

To install:
5. Install the fuel pump assembly in the fuel tank with a new O-ring. Install the ring retaining bolts. Install the fuel tank if removed.
6. Reconnect the fuel lines and fasten the electrical connection.
7. Connect the battery cable, then start the engine and check for fuel leaks.

➡**The "Check Engine Light" may stay on after installation is completed. If so, the trouble code in the control unit's memory must be erased. To**

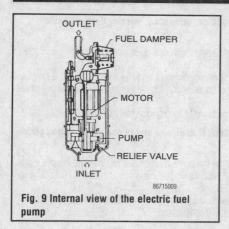

Fig. 9 Internal view of the electric fuel pump

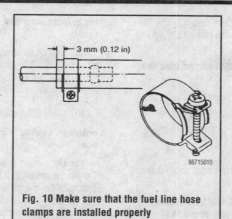

Fig. 10 Make sure that the fuel line hose clamps are installed properly

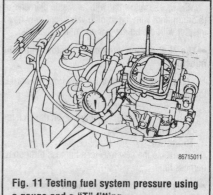

Fig. 11 Testing fuel system pressure using a gauge and a "T" fitting

erase the code, disconnect the battery cable for 10 seconds, then reconnect it a verify that the light is extinguished.

TESTING

▶ **See Figures 10 and 11**

1. Relieve the fuel system pressure, as described previously in this section.
2. Disconnect the fuel inlet hose at the electro injection unit.
3. Install a fuel pressure gauge.
4. Start the engine and check the fuel line for leakage.
5. Read the pressure on the pressure gauge. The gauge should read approximately 36.3 psi (250 kPa).
6. Relieve the fuel system pressure again.
7. Remove the pressure gauge from the fuel line and reconnect the fuel inlet hose.

➥When reconnecting a fuel line, always use a new clamp. Make sure that the screw of the clamp does not contact any adjacent parts and tighten the hose clamp to 1 ft. lb. (1.4 Nm)

Throttle Body/Chamber

REMOVAL & INSTALLATION

❉❉ CAUTION

Never smoke when working around gasoline! Avoid all sources of sparks or ignition. Gasoline vapors are EXTREMELY volatile!

1. Release the fuel system pressure, as described previously in this section.
2. Disconnect the negative battery cable and remove the intake duct from the throttle chamber.

3. Drain about 1½ quarts (1.43 liters) of engine coolant. Remove the coolant hose.
4. Detach the vacuum hoses and the electrical harness connector from the throttle chamber. Disconnect the accelerator cable from the throttle chamber.
5. Remove the mounting bolts and the throttle chamber from the intake manifold.
6. To install, use a new gasket and reverse the removal procedures. Torque the throttle chamber bolts to 9–13 ft. lbs. (12–18 Nm). Refill the cooling system.
7. Check the throttle for smooth operation and make sure that the bypass port is clean and free of obstacles. Check to make sure the idle speed adjusting screw moves smoothly. Make all necessary adjustments.

Do not touch the EGR vacuum port screw or, on some later models, the throttle valve stopper screw, as they are factory adjusted.

➥**Because of the sensitivity of the air flow meter, there cannot be any air leaks in the fuel system. Even the smallest leak could unbalance the system and affect the performance of the vehicle.**

During every check, pay attention to hose connections, as well as the dipstick and oil filler cap for evidence of air leaks. Should you encounter any, take steps to correct the problem.

Fuel Injector

REMOVAL & INSTALLATION

▶ **See Figures 12 thru 24**

1. Release the fuel system pressure, as described previously in this section.
2. Disconnect the negative battery cable.
3. Remove the throttle body assembly, as previously outlined.
4. Remove the rubber seal and the injector harness grommet from the top of the throttle body. Remove the injector cover.

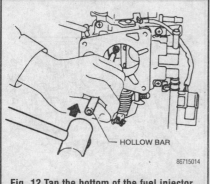

Fig. 12 Tap the bottom of the fuel injector to remove the assembly

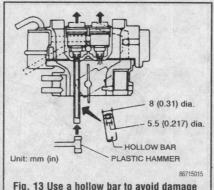

Fig. 13 Use a hollow bar to avoid damage to the injector assembly

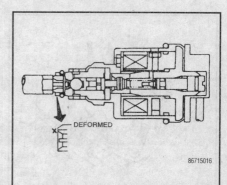

Fig. 14 Check the fuel injector for deformities

5. Use a hollow bar with an inside diameter of not less than 0.217 in. (5.5mm) and, with the throttle valve kept fully open, tap the bottom of the fuel injector with the hollow bar and plastic hammer.

➡**The Z24i engine uses one injector, while the VG30i engine uses two injectors.**

6. Detach the injector harness from the harness connector using the following procedure:

    a. Remove the terminal retainer.

    b. Using a small screwdriver, tilt the lock tongue and, at the same time, push out the terminal.

To install:

7. Route the new injector's harness through a new grommet and into the harness tube.

➡**Every time a harness grommet is removed, it should be replaced with a new one. When assembling the connector, pay attention to** the harness color and position; otherwise, injector damage could occur.

8. Replace all injector O-rings with new ones coated with some silicone oil.

9. Push the injector(s) into the injector body by hand, until the O-rings are fully seated. Invert the injection body and insure that the injector tips are properly seated.

10. Apply some silicone bond to the injector harness grommet.

➡**Airtight sealing is essential to ensure stable and proper idling condition.**

11. Use locking sealer on the screw threads and reinstall the injector cover. Tighten the screws to 2.5 ft. lbs. (3 Nm) in a crisscross pattern to ensure proper seating of the injector and cover.

12. Apply some silicone bond to the bottom of the rubber seal and attach the seal to the top face of the throttle body.

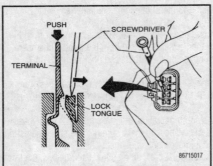

Fig. 15 Tilt the lock tongue with a small screwdriver in order to separate the terminal

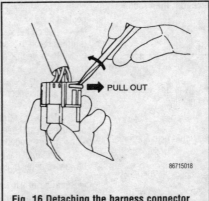

Fig. 16 Detaching the harness connector

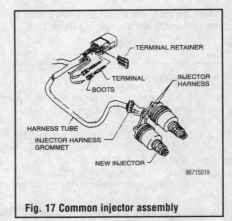

Fig. 17 Common injector assembly

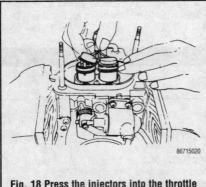

Fig. 18 Press the injectors into the throttle body

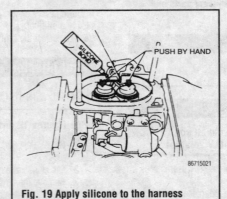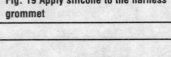

Fig. 19 Apply silicone to the harness grommet

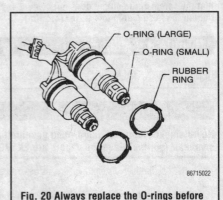

Fig. 20 Always replace the O-rings before installing the fuel injectors

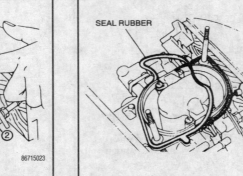

Fig. 21 Tighten the injector cover screws in a crisscross pattern

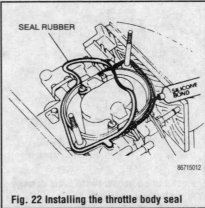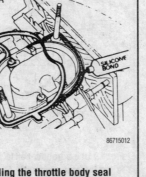

Fig. 22 Installing the throttle body seal

Fig. 23 Checking the throttle body for leaks

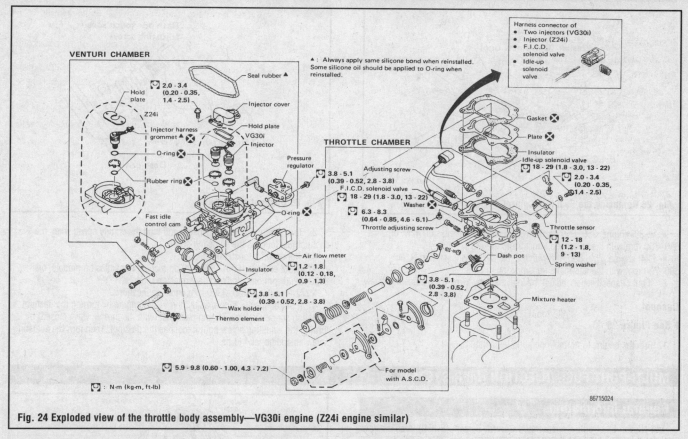

Fig. 24 Exploded view of the throttle body assembly—VG30i engine (Z24i engine similar)

➡ **Do not reinstall the air cleaner until the silicone bond has hardened.**

13. Install the injection unit to the intake manifold and tighten the bolts evenly to 9–13 ft. lbs. (12–18 Nm). Install/connect all components which were disturbed during throttle body removal.

14. Connect the negative battery cable and make all necessary fuel system adjustments.

ADJUSTMENTS

Fast Idle Speed

◆ **See Figures 25 and 26**

1. Start the engine and run it until it reaches normal operating temperature.
2. Make sure that the aligning mark stamped on the fast idle cam meets the center of the roller installed on the cam follow lever. If not, correct the location of the fast idle cam by turning the adjusting screw (**S1**).

➡ **If it is not adjustable, replace the thermo element.**

3. Measure the clearance **G** between the roller and the fast idle cam. The clearance should be 0.020–0.118 in. (0.51–3.00mm) for the VG30i engine or 0.028–0.118 in. (0.71–2.99mm) for the Z24i engine.
4. If not correct, adjust clearance **G** by turning the adjusting screw (**S2**). Make sure the engine is warmed up sufficiently and adjust to 0.031–0.047 in. (0.787–1.194mm) for the VG30i engine or 0.047–0.063 in. (1.194–1.600mm) for the Z24i engine.

FICD Solenoid

◆ **See Figures 27 and 28**

1. With the engine at normal operating temperature, check the idle speed and adjust, as necessary. For details and specifications, please refer to Section 2 of this manual.
2. Turn the air conditioner switch **ON**. With the A/C is on, the idle speed should be:

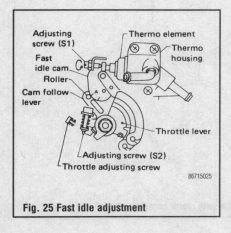

Fig. 25 Fast idle adjustment

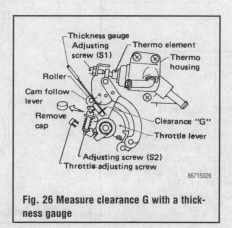

Fig. 26 Measure clearance G with a thickness gauge

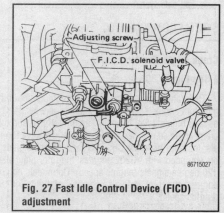

Fig. 27 Fast Idle Control Device (FICD) adjustment

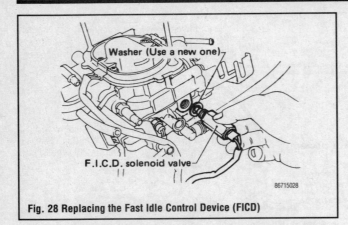

Fig. 28 Replacing the Fast Idle Control Device (FICD)

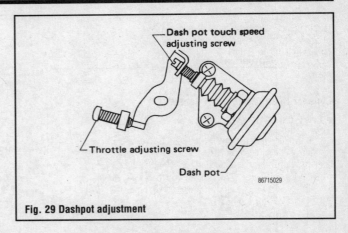

Fig. 29 Dashpot adjustment

- VG30i engine: 750–850 rpm with the manual transmission in N, or 650–700 rpm with the automatic transmission in D.
- Z24i engine: 750–850 rpm with the manual transmission in N, or 600–700 rpm with the automatic transmission in D.

3. If out of specification, adjust the idle speed by turning the adjusting screw.

Dashpot

▶ **See Figure 29**

1. Run the engine to normal operating temperature.

2. Turn the throttle valve by hand, and read the engine speed when the dashpot just touches the adjusting screw.

3. The dashpot touch speed is:
- VG30i engine: 1600–1800 rpm on manual transmission models, or 2000–2200 rpm on automatic transmission models.
- Z24i engine: 2700–3300 rpm on all applications.

4. If out of specifications, adjust the VG30i engine by turning the dashpot adjusting screw. On the Z24i engine adjust (with the throttle valve closed) by turning the adjusting screw until it touches the dashpot. Then turn the adjusting screw an additional 4 turns.

MULTI-PORT FUEL INJECTION (MFI) SYSTEM

General Information

The Nissan Electronic Concentrated Control System (ECCS) is an air flow regulated, port fuel injection and engine control system. It is used on 1990–95 models equipped with VG30E and KA24E engines. The KA24E engines use 4 fuel injectors, while the VG30E engines use 6 injectors to spray fuel into the intake manifold near the cylinders' intake valves. The ECCS Electronic Control Unit (ECU) consists of a microcomputer, inspection lamps, a diagnostic mode selector and connectors for signal input and output as well as for power supply. The system's ECU regulates the following functions:
- Amount of injected fuel
- Ignition timing
- Mixture ratio feedback
- Pressure regulator control
- Exhaust Gas Recirculation (EGR) operation
- Idle speed control
- Fuel pump operation
- Air regulator control
- Air Injection Valve (AIV) operation
- Self-diagnostics
- Air flow meter self-cleaning control
- Fail-safe system

SYSTEM COMPONENTS

Crank Angle Sensor

▶ **See Figure 30**

The crank angle sensor is a basic component of the ECCS system. It monitors engine speed/piston position and sends signals which the ECU uses to regulate fuel injection, ignition timing and other functions. The crank angle sensor has a rotor plate and a wave forming circuit. On all models, the rotor plate has 360 slits for 1 degree signals (crank angle). On models equipped with VG30E engines, the rotor plate also consists of 6 slits for 120 degree signals (engine speed). On models equipped with KA24E engines, the rotor plate also consists of 4 slits for 180 degree signals (engine speed).

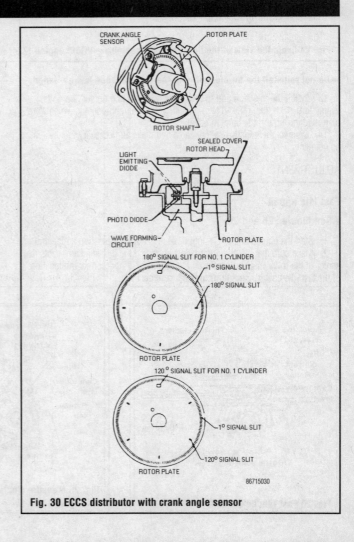

Fig. 30 ECCS distributor with crank angle sensor

The Light Emitting Diodes (LED's) and photo diodes are built into the wave forming circuit. When the rotor plate passes the space between the LED and the photo diode, the slits of the rotor plate continually cut the light which is sent to the photo diode from the LED. This generates rough shaped pulses which are converted into ON/OFF pulses by the wave forming circuit and are then sent to the ECU.

Cylinder Head Temperature Sensor

▶ See Figure 31

The cylinder head temperature sensor monitors changes in cylinder head temperature and transmits a signal to the ECU. The temperature sensing unit employs a thermistor (temperature variable resistor) which is sensitive to changes in temperature, with electrical resistance decreasing as temperature rises.

Air Flow Meter

▶ See Figure 32

The air flow meter measures the mass flow rate of intake air. The volume of air entering the engine is measured by the use of a hot wire placed in the intake air stream. The control unit sends current to the wire to maintain it at a preset temperature. As the intake air moves past the wire, it removes heat, so the control unit must increase the voltage to the wire to maintain it at the preset temperature. By measuring the amount of current necessary to maintain the temperature of the wire in the air stream, the ECU determines exactly how much air is entering the engine. A self-cleaning system briefly heats the hot air wire to approximately 1832°F (1000°C) after engine shutdown to burn off any dust or contaminants on the wire.

Exhaust Gas Sensor

▶ See Figures 33 and 34

The exhaust gas sensor, which is placed in the exhaust pipe, monitors the amount of oxygen in the exhaust gas. The sensor is made of ceramic titania which changes electrical resistance at the ideal air/fuel ratio (14.7:1). The control unit supplies the sensor with approximately 1 volt and reads the varying output voltage of the sensor, depending on its resistance. The oxygen sensor is equipped with a heater to bring it to operating temperature quickly.

Throttle Valve Switch

▶ See Figure 35

A throttle valve switch is attached to the throttle chamber and operates in response to accelerator pedal movement. The switch has an idle contact and a full throttle contact. The idle contact closes when the throttle valve is positioned at idle and opens when it is in any other position.

Fuel Injector

▶ See Figure 36

The fuel injector is a small, precision solenoid valve. As the ECU sends a signal to each injector, the coil built into the injector pulls the needle valve back allowing pressurized fuel to be sprayed through the nozzle and into the intake manifold. The amount of fuel injected is dependent on the length of the signal (pulse duration); the longer the signal, the more fuel delivered.

Fuel Temperature Sensor

▶ See Figure 37

A fuel temperature sensor is built into the fuel pressure regulator. When the fuel temperature is higher than the preprogrammed level, the ECU will enrich the fuel injected to compensate for temperature expansion. The temperature sensor and pressure regulator should be replaced as an assembly if either malfunctions. The electric fuel pump with an integral damper is installed in the fuel tank. It is a vane roller type with the electric motor cooled by the fuel itself. The fuel filter is of metal construction, in order to withstand the high fuel system pressure.

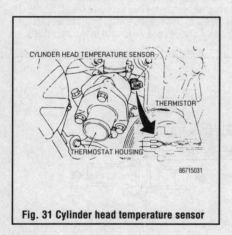

Fig. 31 Cylinder head temperature sensor

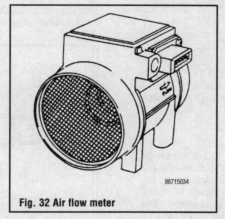

Fig. 32 Air flow meter

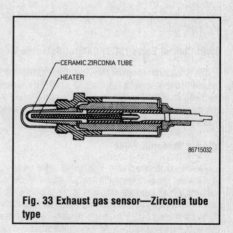

Fig. 33 Exhaust gas sensor—Zirconia tube type

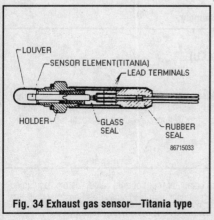

Fig. 34 Exhaust gas sensor—Titania type

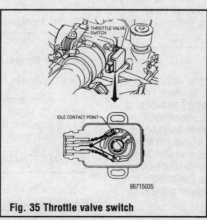

Fig. 35 Throttle valve switch

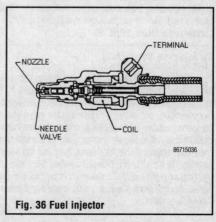

Fig. 36 Fuel injector

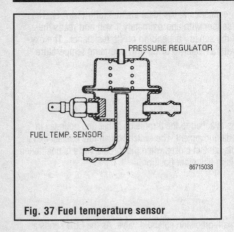

Fig. 37 Fuel temperature sensor

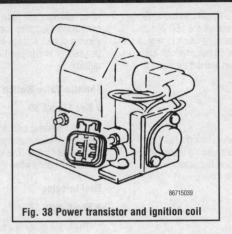

Fig. 38 Power transistor and ignition coil

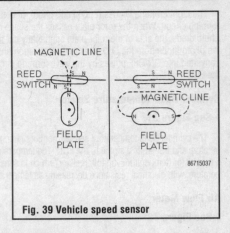

Fig. 39 Vehicle speed sensor

Power Transistor

▶ See Figure 38

The ignition signal from the ECU is amplified by the power transistor, which turns the ignition coil primary circuit on and off, indicating the necessary high voltage in the secondary circuit to fire the spark plugs. Ignition timing is controlled according to engine operating conditions, with the optimum timing advance for each driving condition preprogrammed into the ECU memory.

Vehicle Speed Sensor

▶ See Figure 39

The vehicle speed sensor provides a vehicle speed signal to the ECU. On conventional speedometers, the speed sensor consists of a reed switch which transforms vehicle speed into a pulse signal. On digital electronic speedometers, the speed sensor consists of an LED, photo diode, shutter and wave forming circuit. It operates on the same principle as the crank angle sensor.

Swirl Control Valve (SCV) Control Solenoid Valve

The SCV control solenoid valve cuts the intake manifold vacuum signal for the swirl control valve. It responds to an ON/OFF signal from the ECU. When the solenoid is off, the vacuum signal from the intake manifold is cut. When the control unit sends an ON signal, the coil pulls the plunger and feeds the vacuum signal to the swirl control valve actuator.

Idle-Up Solenoid Valve

An idle-up solenoid valve is attached to the intake collector to stabilize idle speed when the engine load is heavy because of electrical load, power steering load, etc. An air regulator provides an air bypass when the engine is cold in order to increase idle speed during warm-up (fast idle). A bimetal, heater and rotary shutter are built into the air regulator. When bimetal temperature is low, the air bypass port is open. As the engine starts and electric current flows through a heater, the bimetal begins to rotate the shutter to close off the air bypass port. The air passage remains closed until the engine is stopped and the bimetal temperature drops.

Air Injection Valve (AIV)

Under certain conditions, the Air Injection Valve (AIV) sends secondary air to the exhaust manifold, by utilizing vacuum caused by exhaust pulsation in the exhaust manifold. When exhaust pressure is below atmospheric pressure (negative pressure), secondary air is sent to the exhaust manifold; when exhaust pressure is above atmospheric pressure, the reed valves prevent secondary air from being sent to the air cleaner. The AIV control solenoid valve cuts the intake manifold vacuum signal for AIV control, and the solenoid valve actuates in response to the ON/OFF signal from the ECU. When the solenoid is off, the vacuum signal from the intake manifold is cut. As the control unit outputs an ON signal, the coil pulls the plunger downward and feeds the vacuum signal to the AIV control valve.

Exhaust Gas Recirculation (EGR) Vacuum Cut Solenoid Valve

The EGR vacuum cut solenoid valve is the same type as that of the AIV. The EGR system is controlled by the ECU; at both low and high engine speed (rpm), the solenoid valve turns on and the EGR valve cuts the exhaust gas recirculation into the intake manifold. The pressure regulator control solenoid valve also actuates in response to the ON/OFF signal from the ECU. When it is off, a vacuum signal from the intake manifold is fed into the pressure regulator. As the control unit outputs an ON signal, the coil pulls the plunger downward and cuts the vacuum signal.

Air Regulator

▶ See Figure 40

The air regulator provides an air bypass when the engine is cold for the purpose of a fast idle during warm-up. A bimetal heater and rotary shutter are built into the air regulator. When the bimetal temperature is low, the air bypass port is open. As the engine starts and electric current flows through a heater, the bimetal begins to rotate the shutter to close off the bypass port. The air passage remains closed until the engine is stopped and the bimetal temperature drops.

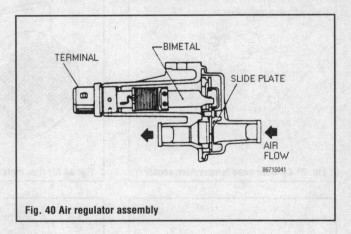

Fig. 40 Air regulator assembly

Electronic Control Unit (ECU)

▶ See Figure 41

In conjunction with its sensors and related components, the ECU basically regulates the engine. The ECU consists of a microcomputer, inspection lamps, and a diagnostic mode selector, as well as connectors for signal input/output and for power supply.

SYSTEM OPERATION

In operation, the on-board computer (control unit) calculates the basic injection pulse width by processing signals from the crank angle sensor and air flow

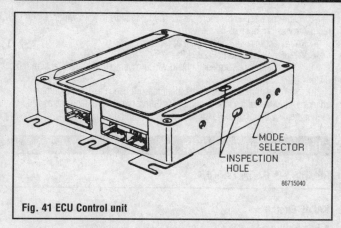

Fig. 41 ECU Control unit

MODE SELECTOR

INSPECTION HOLE

meter. Receiving signals from each sensor which detects various engine operating conditions, the computer adds various enrichments (which are preprogrammed) to the basic injection amount. In this manner, the optimum amount of fuel is delivered through the injectors (4 injectors on the KA24E engine and 6 injectors on the VG30E engine). The fuel is enriched during starting, warm-up, and acceleration, as well as when cylinder head temperature is high or when operating under a heavy load. The fuel is leaned during deceleration, according to the closing rate of the throttle valve. Fuel shut-off is accomplished during deceleration, when vehicle speed exceeds 130 mph, or when engine speed exceeds 6400 rpm for about 500 revolutions.

The mixture ratio feedback system (closed loop control) is designed to control the air/fuel mixture precisely to the stoichiometric, or optimum point, so that the 3-way catalytic converter can minimize CO, HC and NOx emissions simultaneously. The optimum air/fuel fuel mixture is 14.7:1. This system uses an exhaust gas (oxygen) sensor located in the exhaust manifold to give an indication of whether the fuel mixture is richer or leaner than the stoichiometric point. The control unit adjusts the injection pulse width according to the sensor voltage so that the mixture ratio will be within the narrow window around the stoichiometric fuel ratio. The system goes into closed loop operation as soon as the oxygen sensor heats up enough to register. However, there are several different conditions under which the system will operate in the open loop mode. These include when starting the engine, when the engine temperature is cold, and when the exhaust gas sensor temperature is cold. The system also operates in open loop mode when:

• Driving at high speeds or under heavy load, at idle (after mixture ratio learning is completed)
• During deceleration
• When the exhaust gas sensor monitors a rich condition for more than 10 seconds.
• Should the exhaust gas sensor malfunction, the system would also operate in open loop mode.

Ignition timing is controlled in response to engine operating conditions. The optimum ignition timing in each driving condition is preprogrammed in the computer. The signal from the control unit is transmitted to the power transistor and controls ignition timing. The idle speed is also controlled according to engine operating conditions, temperature and gear position. On manual transmission models, if battery voltage is less than 12 volts for a few seconds, a higher idle speed will be maintained by the control unit to improve charging.

There is a fail-safe system built into the ECCS control unit. If the output voltage of the air flow meter is extremely low, the ECU will substitute a preprogrammed value for the air flow meter signal and allow the vehicle to be driven as long as the engine speed is kept below 2000 rpm. If the cylinder head temperature sensor circuit is open, the control unit clamps the warm-up enrichment at a certain amount. This amount is almost the same as that when the cylinder head temperature is 68–176°F (20–80°C). If the fuel pump circuit malfunctions, the fuel pump relay comes on until the engine stops. This allows the fuel pump to receive power from the relay.

Service Precautions

• Do not operate the fuel pump when the fuel lines are empty.
• Do not reuse fuel hose clamps.
• Do not disconnect the ECCS harness connectors before the battery ground cable has been disconnected.

• Make sure all ECCS connectors are fastened securely. A poor connection can cause an extremely high surge voltage and result in damage to integrated circuits.
• Keep the ECCS harness at least 6 in. (15 cm) away from adjacent harnesses to prevent an ECCS system malfunction due to external electronic "noise."
• Keep all parts and harnesses dry during service.
• Before attempting to remove any parts, turn the ignition switch **OFF** and disconnect the battery ground cable.
• Always use a 12 volt battery as a power source.
• Do not attempt to disconnect the battery cables with the engine running.
• Do not depress the accelerator pedal when starting.
• Do not rev up the engine immediately after starting or just prior to shut-down.
• Do not attempt to disassemble the ECCS control unit under any circumstances.
• If a battery cable is disconnected, the memory will return to the ROM (programmed) values. Engine operation may vary slightly, but this is not an indication of a problem. Do not replace parts because of a slight variation.
• If installing a 2-way or CB radio, keep the antenna as far as possible away from the electronic control unit. Keep the antenna feeder line at least 12 in. (30 cm) away from the ECCS harness and do not let the two run parallel for a long distance. Be sure to ground the radio to the vehicle body.

Relieving Fuel System Pressure

▶ See Figure 42

❄❄ CAUTION

Never smoke when working around gasoline! Avoid all sources of sparks or ignition. Gasoline vapors are EXTREMELY volatile! Any time the fuel system is being worked on always keep a dry chemical (Class B) fire extinguisher near the work area.

1. There are various methods of relieving the fuel system pressure. All cause the engine fuel delivery system to purge itself while the engine is running by stopping the flow of additional fuel before stopping the engine. This may be accomplished in one or more of 3 possible methods, depending upon your vehicle. Perform one of the following while your engine is running:
• Remove the fuel pump fuse from the fuse block.
• Disconnect the fuel pump relay.
• Detach the wiring harness connector at the fuel tank.

2. The vehicle should run and then stall when the fuel in the lines is exhausted. When the engine stops, crank the starter a few times for about 5 seconds to make sure all pressure in the fuel lines is released.

3. Install or engage the fuel pump fuse, relay or harness connector (as applicable) after the repair/replacement is made.

4. The "Check Engine Light" may stay on after the test has been completed. The trouble code in the control unit's memory must be erased. This may be done by disconnecting the battery cable for 10 seconds, then reconnecting it and verifying that the light has extinguished.

FUEL PUMP

Fig. 42 One method of releasing fuel pressure is to remove the fuel pump fuse with the engine running

Electric Fuel Pump

The fuel pump assembly is located in the fuel tank. Refer to the fuel tank assembly illustrations in this section. On most applications, the fuel tank must be lowered to remove the fuel pump assembly. The fuel pump assembly is cooled by the fuel in the tank.

REMOVAL & INSTALLATION

1. Before disconnecting the fuel lines or any of the fuel system components, release the fuel pressure, as previously described in this section. Reducing the fuel pressure is a very important step for correct removal of the electric fuel pump.
2. Disconnect the negative battery cable.
3. Unfasten the fuel pump assembly electrical connector and remove the fuel tank inspection cover.

➡ If the truck has no fuel tank inspection cover, the fuel tank must be lowered or removed to gain access to the in-tank fuel pump.

4. Disconnect the fuel outlet and return hoses. Remove the fuel tank assembly, if necessary.
5. Remove the ring retaining bolts and the O-ring, then lift the fuel pump assembly from the fuel tank. Plug the opening with a clean rag to prevent dirt from entering the system.

➡ When removing or installing the fuel pump assembly, be careful not to damage or deform it. Always install a new O-ring.

To install:
6. Install the fuel pump assembly in the fuel tank with a new O-ring. Install the ring retaining bolts. Install the fuel tank if removed.
7. Reconnect the fuel lines and fasten the electrical connection.
8. Connect the battery cable, start the engine and check for fuel leaks.

➡ The "Check Engine Light" may stay on after installation is completed. If so, the trouble code in the control unit's memory must be erased. To erase the code; disconnect the battery cable for 10 seconds, then reconnect it a verify that the light is extinguished.

TESTING

♦ **See Figure 43**

1. Relieve the fuel system pressure, described previously in this section.
2. Disconnect the fuel inlet hose between the fuel filter and fuel line on the engine side.
3. Install a fuel pressure gauge.
4. Start the engine and check the fuel line for leakage.
5. Read the pressure on the pressure gauge.
6. Pressure gauge should read as follows with pressure regulator vacuum hose connected:
   • KA24E engine—33 psi (228 kPa)
   • VG30E engine—34 psi (234 kPa)
7. Stop the engine and disconnect the fuel pressure regulator vacuum hose from the intake manifold. Plug the intake manifold with a rubber cap.

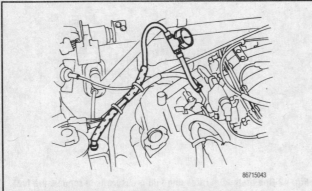

Fig. 43 Checking fuel pressure with a pressure gauge

8. Start the engine. Pressure gauge should read as follows with pressure regulator vacuum hose disconnected:
   • KA24E engine—43 psi (296 kPa)
   • VG30E engine—43 psi (296 kPa)
9. Stop the engine. Connect a hand vacuum pump to the fuel pressure regulator.
10. Start the engine and read the fuel pressure gauge as the vacuum is changed with the hand vacuum pump. Fuel pressure should decrease as vacuum increases. If not, replace the fuel pressure regulator.

Injectors and Fuel Pipe

REMOVAL & INSTALLATION

KA24E Engine

♦ **See Figure 44**

1. Relieve the fuel pressure from the system. Disconnect the negative battery cable.
2. Remove the BPT valve and the bolts securing the fuel tube.
3. Remove the bolts securing the injectors, then take out the fuel tube and injector as an assembly.
4. Remove the injectors from the fuel tube.
To install:
5. Install the injectors to the fuel tube. Always use new O-rings. Lubricate O-rings with a small amount of silicone oil.
6. Install the injector/fuel tube assembly. Tighten the fuel tube bolts evenly to 12–15 ft. lbs. (16–21 Nm) and install the BPT valve.
7. Start the engine, then check for fuel leaks around the injectors and fuel tube.

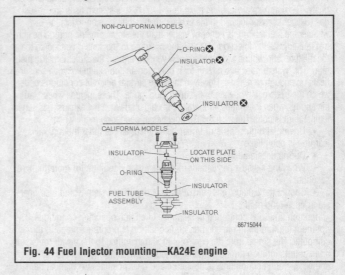

Fig. 44 Fuel Injector mounting—KA24E engine

VG30E Engine

♦ **See Figures 45 thru 62**

1. Relive the fuel pressure from the system. Disconnect the negative battery cable.
2. Remove the 2 drain plugs (from both sides of the cylinder block) and drain the engine coolant into a suitable container.
3. Disconnect the Automatic Speed Control Device (ASCD) and accelerator control wire from the intake manifold collector.
4. Disconnect the following from the intake manifold collector:
   a. Auxiliary Air Control (AAC) valve
   b. Throttle sensor and throttle valve switch
   c. Ignition coil
   d. EGR control solenoid
   e. Air regulator
   f. Exhaust gas temperature sensor (California models)
   g. PCV hose from the right-hand rocker cover

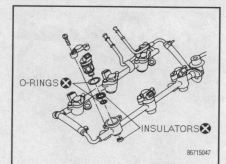

Fig. 45 Fuel injector mounting on the VG30E engine—Be sure to always replace the O-rings and insulators

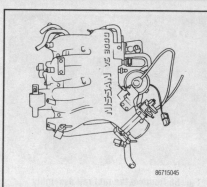

Fig. 46 Intake manifold collector assembly—VG30E engine

Fig. 47 Remove the throttle cable from the drum assembly using needlenose pliers

Fig. 48 Remove the throttle cable mounting bracket bolts before removing the intake manifold collector

Fig. 49 Use a socket to remove the intake manifold collector mounting bolts

Fig. 50 Remove all necessary brackets from the intake manifold collector

Fig. 51 Using a hex-type socket, remove the intake manifold collector mounting bolts

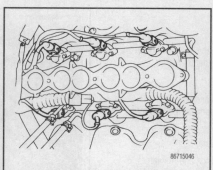

Fig. 52 Once the collector is removed, the fuel injector harness connectors are accessible

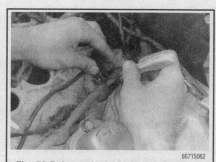

Fig. 53 Release the locktabs in order to unfasten the fuel injector electrical connection—be careful not damage the connectors

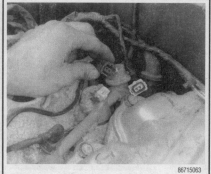

Fig. 54 Once the locktabs are released, carefully separate the connectors

Fig. 55 Remove the fuel lines from the fuel rail—always use new fuel injection hose retaining clamps upon assembly

Fig. 56 View of the fuel rail installed—note the location of the pressure regulator assembly

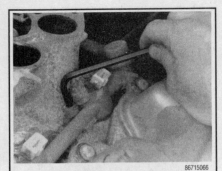

Fig. 57 Remove the fuel rail retaining bolts—use a hex-type socket or Allen key for this job

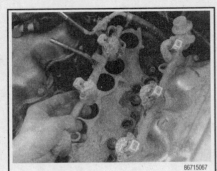

Fig. 58 Remove the fuel rail assembly from the engine with the injectors installed

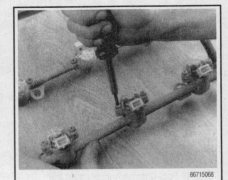

Fig. 59 In order to remove the injectors, loosen and remove the cover retainers

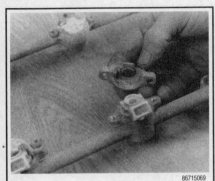

Fig. 60 Once the retainers are unthreaded, lift the injector cover from the fuel rail

Fig. 61 Separate the injector from the fuel rail assembly

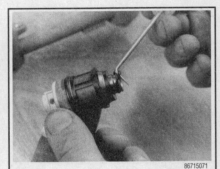

Fig. 62 Always replace and lubricate the O-rings upon installation of the fuel injector

 h. Air duct hose
 i. Ground wire
 j. EGR Tube
 k. Purge hose from the evaporative canister

 5. Disconnect the brake master cylinder, pressure regulator and the remaining carbon canister vacuum hoses.

 6. Remove the intake collector.

 7. Remove the fuel hoses from the injector fuel tube assembly.

 8. Disengage the injector electrical connectors, then remove the injectors with the fuel tube assembly.

To install:

 9. Replace or clean the injectors, as necessary.

 10. Install the injectors to the fuel tube using new O-rings and insulators.

 11. Install all parts which were disconnected from the intake manifold collector, in the reverse order of removal.

 12. Connect the negative battery cable.

 13. Verify that the drain plugs are installed in the cylinder block, then refill and bleed the cooling system.

 14. Run the engine, then check for fuel leaks around injectors and fuel tube.

Fuel Pressure Regulator

REMOVAL & INSTALLATION

▸ **See Figures 63 and 64**

 1. Relieve the fuel pressure from the system. Disconnect the negative battery cable.

 2. Disengage the intake manifold vacuum hose from the pressure regulator.

 3. Remove the screws securing the pressure regulator assembly to the fuel tube.

 4. Unfasten the hose clamps, then disconnect the pressure regulator from the fuel hose.

➡ Place a rag under the fuel pipe to absorb any remaining fuel.

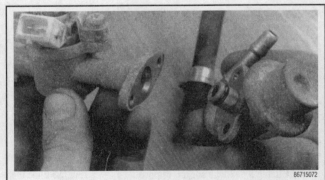

Fig. 63 The pressure regulator is easily removed from the fuel rail—note that the rail usually does not have to be removed for this

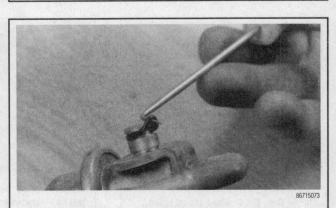

Fig. 64 Always replace the O-ring for the fuel pressure regulator

5. Installation is the reverse of the removal procedure.
6. Start the engine, then check for fuel leaks around the pressure regulator mounting and fuel tube area.

Throttle Position Sensor

OPERATION

This sensor is a potentiometer directly attached to the throttle plate shaft. It signals not only throttle position but also opening and closing speed. The ECU uses this information for controlling injection and ignition. Normally, the ECU relays on a switch built into the sensor to read throttle-closed position. If this hard idle switch fails, the potentiometer signal is used and a trouble code will be set. If the unit is removed, it must be adjusted so that the idle switch is closed when the throttle is closed.

REMOVAL & INSTALLATION

1. Disconnect the negative battery cable.
2. Remove the throttle sensor mounting screws, then remove the sensor from the engine.
3. If the throttle sensor is replaced or removed, it will be necessary to install it in the correct position and adjust it, for proper operation. Refer to the adjustment procedure later in this section.

ADJUSTMENT

▶ **See Figures 65 and 66**

KA24E Engine

1. When the throttle sensor has been removed or replaced, reinstall it in the throttle chamber, but do not tighten the bolts.

2. Engage the sensor harness connector, then start the engine. Run the engine until it is warm.
3. Measure the output voltage of the sensor using a voltmeter. Connect the voltmeter to the TPS sensor harness connector. Rotate the body of the sensor until the voltage is 0.4–0.6 volts, then tighten the bolts.
4. Separate the harness connector for a few seconds, then reconnect it.
5. Start engine and check for proper operation.

VG30E Engine

1. When the throttle sensor has been removed or replaced, reinstall it in throttle chamber, but do not tighten the bolts.
2. Connect the throttle sensor and throttle wire switch harnesses.
3. Disengage the Auxiliary Air Control (AAC) valve sub-harness connector.
4. Disconnect the throttle valve switch harness.
5. While closing the valve manually, check the OFF–ON speed with a circuit tester. The throttle valve switch OFF–ON speed specifications are as follows:
  * Manual transmission idle speed—100–400 rpm
  * Automatic transmission idle speed (in N position)—100–400 rpm
6. If not within specifications, rotate the sensor body to achieve the proper speed.
7. Tighten the sensor bolts so that the sensor does not move.

Fast Idle Cam

INSPECTION & ADJUSTMENT

▶ **See Figures 67, 68, 69 and 70**

1. Start the engine and warm it up until the coolant temperature indicator points to the normal operating temperature.
2. Stop the engine and remove the air cleaner assembly.
3. Set the alignment mark to point to the roller center. A mark is impressed on the fast idle cam so that the top of the cam may be faced in the correct direction.

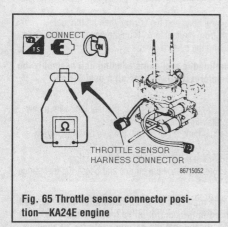

Fig. 65 Throttle sensor connector position—KA24E engine

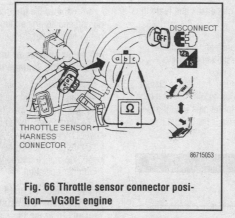

Fig. 66 Throttle sensor connector position—VG30E engine

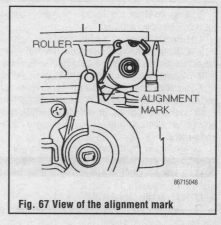

Fig. 67 View of the alignment mark

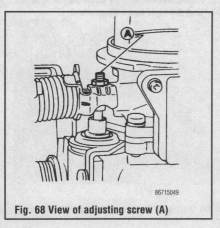

Fig. 68 View of adjusting screw (A)

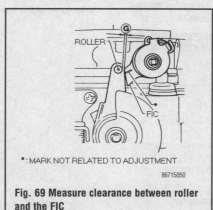

Fig. 69 Measure clearance between roller and the FIC

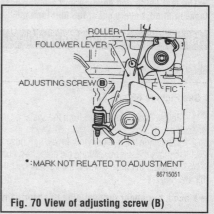

Fig. 70 View of adjusting screw (B)

4. If necessary, turn the adjusting screw (A) until the top of the cam faces the center of the lever roller.

5. Measure clearance (G) between the roller and the top of the Fast Idle Cam (FIC) using a feeler gauge. The clearance specification (G) value is 0.079–0.102 in. (2.0–2.6 mm) on manual transmission models. The clearance specification (G) value is 0.071–0.094 in. (1.8–2.4 mm) on automatic transmission models.

6. If clearance (G) is out of specification, adjust clearance (G) using adjusting screw (B) to 0.091 in. (2.3 mm) on manual transmission models, or 0.083 in. (2.1 mm) on automatic transmission models.

Throttle Body

REMOVAL & INSTALLATION

1. Disconnect the negative battery cable.
2. Disconnect the accelerator cable.
3. Tag and disconnect all necessary hoses, cables and brackets.

FUEL TANK

Tank Assembly

REMOVAL & INSTALLATION

◆ See Figures 71, 72 and 73

1. Disconnect the negative cable from the battery.
2. Remove the fuel tank protector cover.

✳✳ CAUTION

Never smoke when working around gasoline! Avoid all sources of sparks or ignition. Gasoline vapors are EXTREMELY volatile!

3. If equipped, remove the drain plug at the bottom of the tank and drain the fuel into a suitable container.

4. Disconnect the filler tube from the filler hose.

5. Disconnect the ventilation hoses, the fuel return hose and fuel outlet hose from the tank. Detach the gauge unit wires at the electrical connector.

6. Unfasten the mounting bolts and remove the fuel tank.

7. Installation is the reverse of removal. When installing, tighten the clamps securely, but do not crimp any of the lines. Install the clips holding the fuel tube to the underbody securely. Do not attach the filler hose to the tube until the tank is in place; attaching the filler hose prematurely may cause leaks around the connection.

Gauge Sending Unit

REMOVAL & INSTALLATION

➡The fuel pump and sending unit are one assembly, located in the fuel tank. In almost every case, the fuel tank must be removed in order to

4. Disengage the throttle position (TP) sensor electrical connector.
5. Unbolt and remove the throttle body assembly.

To install:

6. Install the throttle body to the intake using a new gasket. Tighten the bolts to 14 ft. lbs. (19 Nm).

7. Engage the TP sensor electrical connector.

8. Reconnect all necessary hoses, cables and brackets as tagged during removal.

9. Connect the throttle cable.
10. Connect the negative battery cable.
11. Start the engine and check for leaks.

➡To properly position the TP sensor, start the engine and allow to warm up. Check idle speed and adjust if necessary. Disengage the harness connector and loosen the sensor mounting bolts. Connect a circuit tester to the TP harness, check the closed TP sensor position by closing throttle valve manually. Open the throttle manually and check position. The center point is the correct adjustment. When you are finished, be sure to tighten the TP sensor mounting bolts.

access the pump/sending unit assembly. Do not kink or twist fuel hoses or lines. Use new gasoline fuel hose clamps if possible.

1. Before disconnecting the fuel lines or any of the fuel system components, release the fuel system pressure as described previously in this section. Reducing the fuel pressure a very important step for correct removal of the electric fuel pump/sending unit assembly.

2. Disconnect the negative battery cable.

3. Unfasten the fuel pump/gauge sending unit assembly electrical connector, then remove the fuel tank inspection cover.

➡If the truck has no fuel tank inspection cover, the fuel tank must be lowered or removed to gain access to the in-tank fuel pump.

4. Disconnect the fuel outlet and return hoses. Remove the fuel tank assembly, if necessary.

5. Remove the ring retaining bolts and the O-ring, then lift the fuel pump/sending unit assembly from the fuel tank. Plug the opening with a clean rag to prevent dirt from entering the system.

➡When removing or installing the fuel pump/sending unit assembly, be careful not to damage or deform it. Always install a new O-ring.

To install:

6. Install the fuel pump/sending unit assembly in the fuel tank with a new O-ring, then install the ring retaining bolts.

7. If removed, install the fuel tank. If not, install the fuel tank inspection cover.

8. Reconnect the fuel lines and fasten the electrical connection.

9. Connect the battery cable, then start the engine and check the fuel gauge for proper operation.

➡The "Check Engine Light" may stay on after installation is completed. If so the trouble code stored in the control unit's memory must be erased. To erase the code, disconnect the battery cable for 10 seconds, then reconnect it and verify that the light has extinguished.

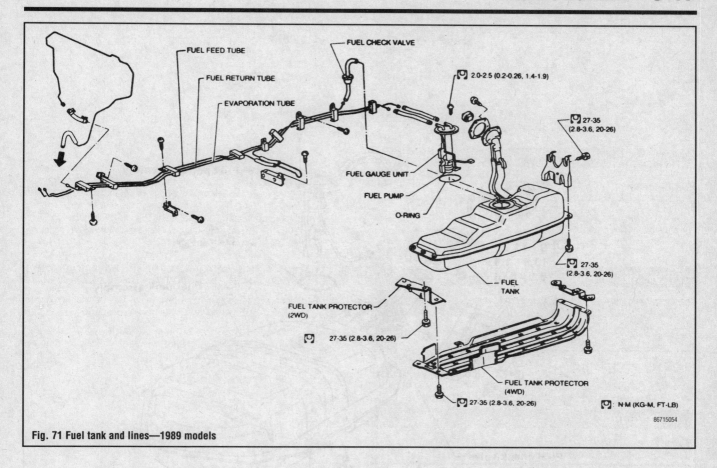

Fig. 71 Fuel tank and lines—1989 models

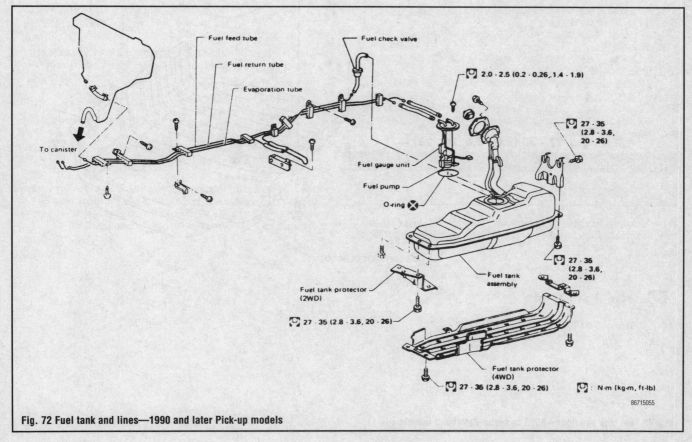

Fig. 72 Fuel tank and lines—1990 and later Pick-up models

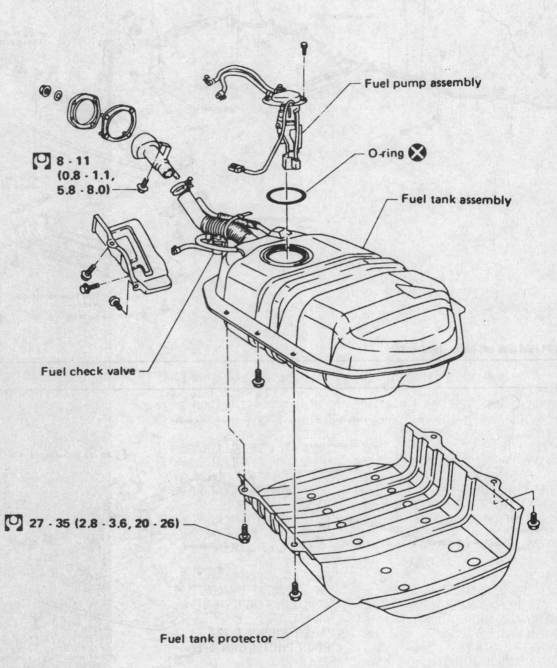

Fuel pump assembly

O-ring

Fuel tank assembly

8 - 11
(0.8 - 1.1,
5.8 - 8.0)

Fuel check valve

27 - 35 (2.8 - 3.6, 20 - 26)

Fuel tank protector

: N·m (kg-m, ft-lb)

86715056

Fig. 73 Fuel tank and lines—1990 and later Pathfinder models

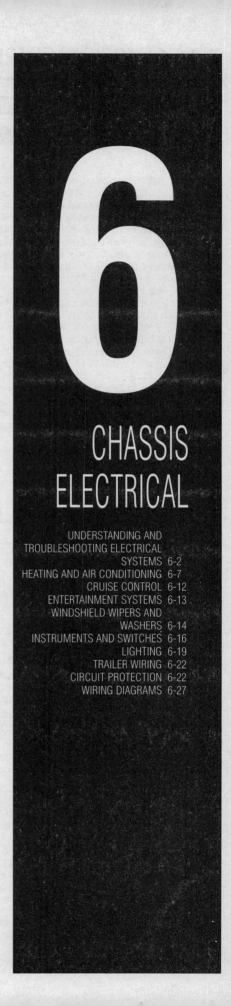

6

CHASSIS ELECTRICAL

UNDERSTANDING AND TROUBLESHOOTING ELECTRICAL SYSTEMS

Basic Electrical Theory

♦ See Figure 1

For any 12 volt, negative ground, electrical system to operate, the electricity must travel in a complete circuit. This simply means that current (power) from the positive (+) terminal of the battery must eventually return to the negative (-) terminal of the battery. Along the way, this current will travel through wires, fuses, switches and components. If, for any reason, the flow of current through the circuit is interrupted, the component fed by that circuit will cease to function properly.

Perhaps the easiest way to visualize a circuit is to think of connecting a light bulb (with two wires attached to it) to the battery—one wire attached to the negative (-) terminal of the battery and the other wire to the positive (+) terminal. With the two wires touching the battery terminals, the circuit would be complete and the light bulb would illuminate. Electricity would follow a path from the battery to the bulb and back to the battery. It's easy to see that with longer wires on our light bulb, it could be mounted anywhere. Further, one wire could be fitted with a switch so that the light could be turned on and off.

The normal automotive circuit differs from this simple example in two ways. First, instead of having a return wire from the bulb to the battery, the current travels through the frame of the vehicle. Since the negative (-) battery cable is attached to the frame (made of electrically conductive metal), the frame of the vehicle can serve as a ground wire to complete the circuit. Secondly, most automotive circuits contain multiple components which receive power from a single circuit. This lessens the amount of wire needed to power components on the vehicle.

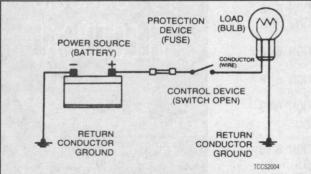

Fig. 1 This example illustrates a simple circuit. When the switch is closed, power from the positive (+) battery terminal flows through the fuse and the switch, and then to the light bulb. The light illuminates and the circuit is completed through the ground wire back to the negative (-) battery terminal. In reality, the two ground points shown in the illustration are attached to the metal frame of the vehicle, which completes the circuit back to the battery

HOW DOES ELECTRICITY WORK: THE WATER ANALOGY

Electricity is the flow of electrons—the subatomic particles that constitute the outer shell of an atom. Electrons spin in an orbit around the center core of an atom. The center core is comprised of protons (positive charge) and neutrons (neutral charge). Electrons have a negative charge and balance out the positive charge of the protons. When an outside force causes the number of electrons to unbalance the charge of the protons, the electrons will split off the atom and look for another atom to balance out. If this imbalance is kept up, electrons will continue to move and an electrical flow will exist.

Many people have been taught electrical theory using an analogy with water. In a comparison with water flowing through a pipe, the electrons would be the water and the wire is the pipe.

The flow of electricity can be measured much like the flow of water through a pipe. The unit of measurement used is amperes, frequently abbreviated as amps (a). You can compare amperage to the volume of water flowing through a pipe. When connected to a circuit, an ammeter will measure the actual amount of current flowing through the circuit. When relatively few electrons flow through a circuit, the amperage is low. When many electrons flow, the amperage is high.

Water pressure is measured in units such as pounds per square inch (psi); The electrical pressure is measured in units called volts (v). When a voltmeter is connected to a circuit, it is measuring the electrical pressure.

The actual flow of electricity depends not only on voltage and amperage, but also on the resistance of the circuit. The higher the resistance, the higher the force necessary to push the current through the circuit. The standard unit for measuring resistance is an ohm. Resistance in a circuit varies depending on the amount and type of components used in the circuit. The main factors which determine resistance are:

• Material—some materials have more resistance than others. Those with high resistance are said to be insulators. Rubber materials (or rubber-like plastics) are some of the most common insulators used in vehicles as they have a very high resistance to electricity. Very low resistance materials are said to be conductors. Copper wire is among the best conductors. Silver is actually a superior conductor to copper and is used in some relay contacts, but its high cost prohibits its use as common wiring. Most automotive wiring is made of copper.

• Size—the larger the wire size being used, the less resistance the wire will have. This is why components which use large amounts of electricity usually have large wires supplying current to them.

• Length—for a given thickness of wire, the longer the wire, the greater the resistance. The shorter the wire, the less the resistance. When determining the proper wire for a circuit, both size and length must be considered to design a circuit that can handle the current needs of the component.

• Temperature—with many materials, the higher the temperature, the greater the resistance (positive temperature coefficient). Some materials exhibit the opposite trait of lower resistance with higher temperatures (negative temperature coefficient). These principles are used in many of the sensors on the engine.

OHM'S LAW

There is a direct relationship between current, voltage and resistance. The relationship between current, voltage and resistance can be summed up by a statement known as Ohm's law.

Voltage (E) is equal to amperage (I) times resistance (R): $E = I \times R$

Other forms of the formula are $R = E/I$ and $I = E/R$

In each of these formulas, E is the voltage in volts, I is the current in amps and R is the resistance in ohms. The basic point to remember is that as the resistance of a circuit goes up, the amount of current that flows in the circuit will go down, if voltage remains the same.

The amount of work that the electricity can perform is expressed as power. The unit of power is the watt (w). The relationship between power, voltage and current is expressed as:

Power (w) is equal to amperage (I) times voltage (E): $W = I \times E$

This is only true for direct current (DC) circuits; The alternating current formula is a tad different, but since the electrical circuits in most vehicles are DC type, we need not get into AC circuit theory.

Electrical Components

POWER SOURCE

Power is supplied to the vehicle by two devices: The battery and the alternator. The battery supplies electrical power during starting or during periods when the current demand of the vehicle's electrical system exceeds the output capacity of the alternator. The alternator supplies electrical current when the engine is running. Just not does the alternator supply the current needs of the vehicle, but it recharges the battery.

The Battery

In most modern vehicles, the battery is a lead/acid electrochemical device consisting of six 2 volt subsections (cells) connected in series, so that the unit is capable of producing approximately 12 volts of electrical pressure. Each subsection consists of a series of positive and negative plates held a short distance apart in a solution of sulfuric acid and water.

The two types of plates are of dissimilar metals. This sets up a chemical reaction, and it is this reaction which produces current flow from the battery when its positive and negative terminals are connected to an electrical load . The power removed from the battery is replaced by the alternator, restoring the battery to its original chemical state.

The Alternator

On some vehicles there isn't an alternator, but a generator. The difference is that an alternator supplies alternating current which is then changed to direct current for use on the vehicle, while a generator produces direct current. Alternators tend to be more efficient and that is why they are used.

Alternators and generators are devices that consist of coils of wires wound together making big electromagnets. One group of coils spins within another set and the interaction of the magnetic fields causes a current to flow. This current is then drawn off the coils and fed into the vehicles electrical system.

GROUND

Two types of grounds are used in automotive electric circuits. Direct ground components are grounded to the frame through their mounting points. All other components use some sort of ground wire which is attached to the frame or chassis of the vehicle. The electrical current runs through the chassis of the vehicle and returns to the battery through the ground (-) cable; if you look, you'll see that the battery ground cable connects between the battery and the frame or chassis of the vehicle.

➡**It should be noted that a good percentage of electrical problems can be traced to bad grounds.**

PROTECTIVE DEVICES

♦ **See Figure 2**

It is possible for large surges of current to pass through the electrical system of your vehicle. If this surge of current were to reach the load in the circuit, the surge could burn it out or severely damage it. It can also overload the wiring, causing the harness to get hot and melt the insulation. To prevent this, fuses, circuit breakers and/or fusible links are connected into the supply wires of the electrical system. These items are nothing more than a built-in weak spot in the system. When an abnormal amount of current flows through the system, these protective devices work as follows to protect the circuit:
- Fuse—when an excessive electrical current passes through a fuse, the fuse "blows" (the conductor melts) and opens the circuit, preventing the passage of current.
- Circuit Breaker—a circuit breaker is basically a self-repairing fuse. It will open the circuit in the same fashion as a fuse, but when the surge subsides, the circuit breaker can be reset and does not need replacement.
- Fusible Link—a fusible link (fuse link or main link) is a short length of special, high temperature insulated wire that acts as a fuse. When an excessive

electrical current passes through a fusible link, the thin gauge wire inside the link melts, creating an intentional open to protect the circuit. To repair the circuit, the link must be replaced. Some newer type fusible links are housed in plug-in modules, which are simply replaced like a fuse, while older type fusible links must be cut and spliced if they melt. Since this link is very early in the electrical path, it's the first place to look if nothing on the vehicle works, yet the battery seems to be charged and is properly connected.

✳✳ CAUTION

Always replace fuses, circuit breakers and fusible links with identically rated components. Under no circumstances should a component of higher or lower amperage rating be substituted.

SWITCHES & RELAYS

♦ **See Figures 3 and 4**

Switches are used in electrical circuits to control the passage of current. The most common use is to open and close circuits between the battery and the various electric devices in the system. Switches are rated according to the amount of amperage they can handle. If a sufficient amperage rated switch is not used in a circuit, the switch could overload and cause damage.

Some electrical components which require a large amount of current to operate use a special switch called a relay. Since these circuits carry a large amount of current, the thickness of the wire in the circuit is also greater. If this large wire were connected from the load to the control switch, the switch would have to carry the high amperage load and the fairing or dash would be twice as large to accommodate the increased size of the wiring harness. To prevent these problems, a relay is used.

Relays are composed of a coil and a set of contacts. When the coil has a current passed though it, a magnetic field is formed and this field causes the contacts to move together, completing the circuit. Most relays are normally open, preventing current from passing through the circuit, but they can take any electrical form depending on the job they are intended to do. Relays can be considered "remote control switches." They allow a smaller current to operate devices that require higher amperages. When a small current operates the coil, a larger current is allowed to pass by the contacts. Some common circuits which may use relays are the horn, headlights, starter, electric fuel pump and other high draw circuits.

LOAD

Every electrical circuit must include a "load" (something to use the electricity coming from the source). Without this load, the battery would attempt to deliver its entire power supply from one pole to another. This is called a "short circuit." All this electricity would take a short cut to ground and cause a great amount of damage to other components in the circuit by developing a tremendous amount of heat. This condition could develop sufficient heat to melt the insulation on all the surrounding wires and reduce a multiple wire cable to a lump of plastic and copper.

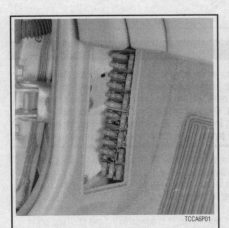

Fig. 2 Most vehicles use one or more fuse panels. This one is located on the driver's side kick panel

TCCA6P01

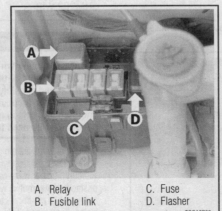

A. Relay
B. Fusible link
C. Fuse
D. Flasher

TCCA6P02

Fig. 3 The underhood fuse and relay panel usually contains fuses, relays, flashers and fusible links

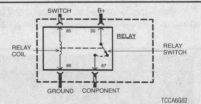

TCCA6G02

Fig. 4 Relays are composed of a coil and a switch. These two components are linked together so that when one operates, the other operates at the same time. The large wires in the circuit are connected from the battery to one side of the relay switch (B+) and from the opposite side of the relay switch to the load (component). Smaller wires are connected from the relay coil to the control switch for the circuit and from the opposite side of the relay coil to ground

WIRING & HARNESSES

The average vehicle contains meters and meters of wiring, with hundreds of individual connections. To protect the many wires from damage and to keep them from becoming a confusing tangle, they are organized into bundles, enclosed in plastic or taped together and called wiring harnesses. Different harnesses serve different parts of the vehicle. Individual wires are color coded to help trace them through a harness where sections are hidden from view.

Automotive wiring or circuit conductors can be either single strand wire, multi-strand wire or printed circuitry. Single strand wire has a solid metal core and is usually used inside such components as alternators, motors, relays and other devices. Multi-strand wire has a core made of many small strands of wire twisted together into a single conductor. Most of the wiring in an automotive electrical system is made up of multi-strand wire, either as a single conductor or grouped together in a harness. All wiring is color coded on the insulator, either as a solid color or as a colored wire with an identification stripe. A printed circuit is a thin film of copper or other conductor that is printed on an insulator backing. Occasionally, a printed circuit is sandwiched between two sheets of plastic for more protection and flexibility. A complete printed circuit, consisting of conductors, insulating material and connectors for lamps or other components is called a printed circuit board. Printed circuitry is used in place of individual wires or harnesses in places where space is limited, such as behind instrument panels.

Since automotive electrical systems are very sensitive to changes in resistance, the selection of properly sized wires is critical when systems are repaired. A loose or corroded connection or a replacement wire that is too small for the circuit will add extra resistance and an additional voltage drop to the circuit.

The wire gauge number is an expression of the cross-section area of the conductor. Vehicles from countries that use the metric system will typically describe the wire size as its cross-sectional area in square millimeters. In this method, the larger the wire, the greater the number. Another common system for expressing wire size is the American Wire Gauge (AWG) system. As gauge number increases, area decreases and the wire becomes smaller. An 18 gauge wire is smaller than a 4 gauge wire. A wire with a higher gauge number will carry less current than a wire with a lower gauge number. Gauge wire size refers to the size of the strands of the conductor, not the size of the complete wire with insulator. It is possible, therefore, to have two wires of the same gauge with different diameters because one may have thicker insulation than the other.

It is essential to understand how a circuit works before trying to figure out why it doesn't. An electrical schematic shows the electrical current paths when a circuit is operating properly. Schematics break the entire electrical system down into individual circuits. In a schematic, usually no attempt is made to represent wiring and components as they physically appear on the vehicle; switches and other components are shown as simply as possible. Face views of harness connectors show the cavity or terminal locations in all multi-pin connectors to help locate test points.

CONNECTORS

▶ See Figures 5 and 6

Three types of connectors are commonly used in automotive applications—weatherproof, molded and hard shell.

• Weatherproof—these connectors are most commonly used where the connector is exposed to the elements. Terminals are protected against moisture

Fig. 5 Hard shell (left) and weatherproof (right) connectors have replaceable terminals

Fig. 6 Weatherproof connectors are most commonly used in the engine compartment or where the connector is exposed to the elements

and dirt by sealing rings which provide a weathertight seal. All repairs require the use of a special terminal and the tool required to service it. Unlike standard blade type terminals, these weatherproof terminals cannot be straightened once they are bent. Make certain that the connectors are properly seated and all of the sealing rings are in place when connecting leads.

• Molded—these connectors require complete replacement of the connector if found to be defective. This means splicing a new connector assembly into the harness. All splices should be soldered to insure proper contact. Use care when probing the connections or replacing terminals in them, as it is possible to create a short circuit between opposite terminals. If this happens to the wrong terminal pair, it is possible to damage certain components. Always use jumper wires between connectors for circuit checking and NEVER probe through weatherproof seals.

• Hard Shell—unlike molded connectors, the terminal contacts in hard-shell connectors can be replaced. Replacement usually involves the use of a special terminal removal tool that depresses the locking tangs (barbs) on the connector terminal and allows the connector to be removed from the rear of the shell. The connector shell should be replaced if it shows any evidence of burning, melting, cracks, or breaks. Replace individual terminals that are burnt, corroded, distorted or loose.

Test Equipment

Pinpointing the exact cause of trouble in an electrical circuit is most times accomplished by the use of special test equipment. The following describes different types of commonly used test equipment and briefly explains how to use them in diagnosis. In addition to the information covered below, the tool manufacturer's instructions booklet (provided with the tester) should be read and clearly understood before attempting any test procedures.

JUMPER WIRES

✳✳ CAUTION

Never use jumper wires made from a thinner gauge wire than the circuit being tested. If the jumper wire is of too small a gauge, it may overheat and possibly melt. Never use jumpers to bypass high resistance loads in a circuit. Bypassing resistances, in effect, creates a short circuit. This may, in turn, cause damage and fire. Jumper wires should only be used to bypass lengths of wire or to simulate switches.

Jumper wires are simple, yet extremely valuable, pieces of test equipment. They are basically test wires which are used to bypass sections of a circuit. Although jumper wires can be purchased, they are usually fabricated from lengths of standard automotive wire and whatever type of connector (alligator clip, spade connector or pin connector) that is required for the particular application being tested. In cramped, hard-to-reach areas, it is advisable to have insulated boots over the jumper wire terminals in order to prevent accidental grounding. It is also advisable to include a standard automotive fuse in any jumper wire. This is commonly referred to as a "fused jumper". By inserting an in-line fuse holder between a set of test leads, a fused jumper wire can be used for bypassing open circuits. Use a 5 amp fuse to provide protection against voltage spikes.

Jumper wires are used primarily to locate open electrical circuits, on either the ground (-) side of the circuit or on the power (+) side. If an electrical component fails to operate, connect the jumper wire between the component and a good ground. If the component operates only with the jumper installed, the ground circuit is open. If the ground circuit is good, but the component does not operate, the circuit between the power feed and component may be open. By moving the jumper wire successively back from the component toward the power source, you can isolate the area of the circuit where the open is located. When the component stops functioning, or the power is cut off, the open is in the segment of wire between the jumper and the point previously tested.

You can sometimes connect the jumper wire directly from the battery to the "hot" terminal of the component, but first make sure the component uses 12 volts in operation. Some electrical components, such as fuel injectors or sensors, are designed to operate on about 4 to 5 volts, and running 12 volts directly to these components will cause damage.

TEST LIGHTS

▶ **See Figure 7**

The test light is used to check circuits and components while electrical current is flowing through them. It is used for voltage and ground tests. To use a 12 volt test light, connect the ground clip to a good ground and probe wherever necessary with the pick. The test light will illuminate when voltage is detected. This does not necessarily mean that 12 volts (or any particular amount of voltage) is present; it only means that some voltage is present. It is advisable before using the test light to touch its ground clip and probe across the battery posts or terminals to make sure the light is operating properly.

✳✳ WARNING

Do not use a test light to probe electronic ignition, spark plug or coil wires. Never use a pick-type test light to probe wiring on computer controlled systems unless specifically instructed to do so. Any wire insulation that is pierced by the test light probe should be taped and sealed with silicone after testing.

Like the jumper wire, the 12 volt test light is used to isolate opens in circuits. But, whereas the jumper wire is used to bypass the open to operate the load, the 12 volt test light is used to locate the presence of voltage in a circuit. If the test light illuminates, there is power up to that point in the circuit; if the test light does not illuminate, there is an open circuit (no power). Move the test light in successive steps back toward the power source until the light in the handle illuminates. The open is between the probe and a point which was previously probed.

The self-powered test light is similar in design to the 12 volt test light, but contains a 1.5 volt penlight battery in the handle. It is most often used in place of a multimeter to check for open or short circuits when power is isolated from the circuit (continuity test).

The battery in a self-powered test light does not provide much current. A weak battery may not provide enough power to illuminate the test light even

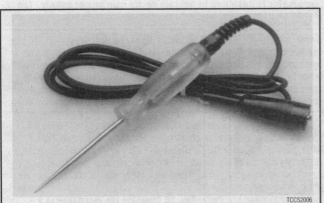

TCCS2006

Fig. 7 A 12 volt test light is used to detect the presence of voltage in a circuit

when a complete circuit is made (especially if there is high resistance in the circuit). Always make sure that the test battery is strong. To check the battery, briefly touch the ground clip to the probe; if the light glows brightly, the battery is strong enough for testing.

➡**A self-powered test light should not be used on any computer controlled system or component. The small amount of electricity transmitted by the test light is enough to damage many electronic automotive components.**

MULTIMETERS

Multimeters are an extremely useful tool for troubleshooting electrical problems. They can be purchased in either analog or digital form and have a price range to suit any budget. A multimeter is a voltmeter, ammeter and ohmmeter (along with other features) combined into one instrument. It is often used when testing solid state circuits because of its high input impedance (usually 10 megaohms or more). A brief description of the multimeter main test functions follows:

• Voltmeter—the voltmeter is used to measure voltage at any point in a circuit, or to measure the voltage drop across any part of a circuit. Voltmeters usually have various scales and a selector switch to allow the reading of different voltage ranges. The voltmeter has a positive and a negative lead. To avoid damage to the meter, always connect the negative lead to the negative (-) side of the circuit (to ground or nearest the ground side of the circuit) and connect the positive lead to the positive (+) side of the circuit (to the power source or the nearest power source). Note that the negative voltmeter lead will always be black and that the positive voltmeter will always be some color other than black (usually red).

• Ohmmeter—the ohmmeter is designed to read resistance (measured in ohms) in a circuit or component. Most ohmmeters will have a selector switch which permits the measurement of different ranges of resistance (usually the selector switch allows the multiplication of the meter reading by 10, 100, 1,000 and 10,000). Some ohmmeters are "auto-ranging" which means the meter itself will determine which scale to use. Since the meters are powered by an internal battery, the ohmmeter can be used like a self-powered test light. When the ohmmeter is connected, current from the ohmmeter flows through the circuit or component being tested. Since the ohmmeter's internal resistance and voltage are known values, the amount of current flow through the meter depends on the resistance of the circuit or component being tested. The ohmmeter can also be used to perform a continuity test for suspected open circuits. In using the meter for making continuity checks, do not be concerned with the actual resistance readings. Zero resistance, or any ohm reading, indicates continuity in the circuit. Infinite resistance indicates an opening in the circuit. A high resistance reading where there should be none indicates a problem in the circuit. Checks for short circuits are made in the same manner as checks for open circuits, except that the circuit must be isolated from both power and normal ground. Infinite resistance indicates no continuity, while zero resistance indicates a dead short.

✳✳ WARNING

Never use an ohmmeter to check the resistance of a component or wire while there is voltage applied to the circuit.

• Ammeter—an ammeter measures the amount of current flowing through a circuit in units called amperes or amps. At normal operating voltage, most circuits have a characteristic amount of amperes, called "current draw" which can be measured using an ammeter. By referring to a specified current draw rating, then measuring the amperes and comparing the two values, one can determine what is happening within the circuit to aid in diagnosis. An open circuit, for example, will not allow any current to flow, so the ammeter reading will be zero. A damaged component or circuit will have an increased current draw, so the reading will be high. The ammeter is always connected in series with the circuit being tested. All of the current that normally flows through the circuit must also flow through the ammeter; if there is any other path for the current to follow, the ammeter reading will not be accurate. The ammeter itself has very little resistance to current flow and, therefore, will not affect the circuit, but it will measure current draw only when the circuit is closed and electricity is flowing. Excessive current draw can blow fuses and drain the battery, while a reduced current draw can cause motors to run slowly, lights to dim and other components to not operate properly.

Troubleshooting Electrical Systems

When diagnosing a specific problem, organized troubleshooting is a must. The complexity of a modern automotive vehicle demands that you approach any problem in a logical, organized manner. There are certain troubleshooting techniques, however, which are standard:

• Establish when the problem occurs. Does the problem appear only under certain conditions? Were there any noises, odors or other unusual symptoms? Isolate the problem area. To do this, make some simple tests and observations, then eliminate the systems that are working properly. Check for obvious problems, such as broken wires and loose or dirty connections. Always check the obvious before assuming something complicated is the cause.

• Test for problems systematically to determine the cause once the problem area is isolated. Are all the components functioning properly? Is there power going to electrical switches and motors? Performing careful, systematic checks will often turn up most causes on the first inspection, without wasting time checking components that have little or no relationship to the problem.

• Test all repairs after the work is done to make sure that the problem is fixed. Some causes can be traced to more than one component, so a careful verification of repair work is important in order to pick up additional malfunctions that may cause a problem to reappear or a different problem to arise. A blown fuse, for example, is a simple problem that may require more than another fuse to repair. If you don't look for a problem that caused a fuse to blow, a shorted wire (for example) may go undetected.

Experience has shown that most problems tend to be the result of a fairly simple and obvious cause, such as loose or corroded connectors, bad grounds or damaged wire insulation which causes a short. This makes careful visual inspection of components during testing essential to quick and accurate troubleshooting.

Testing

OPEN CIRCUITS

▶ See Figure 8

This test already assumes the existence of an open in the circuit and it is used to help locate the open portion.
1. Isolate the circuit from power and ground.
2. Connect the self-powered test light or ohmmeter ground clip to the ground side of the circuit and probe sections of the circuit sequentially.
3. If the light is out or there is infinite resistance, the open is between the probe and the circuit ground.
4. If the light is on or the meter shows continuity, the open is between the probe and the end of the circuit toward the power source.

SHORT CIRCUITS

→Never use a self-powered test light to perform checks for opens or shorts when power is applied to the circuit under test. The test light can be damaged by outside power.

1. Isolate the circuit from power and ground.
2. Connect the self-powered test light or ohmmeter ground clip to a good ground and probe any easy-to-reach point in the circuit.
3. If the light comes on or there is continuity, there is a short somewhere in the circuit.

4. To isolate the short, probe a test point at either end of the isolated circuit (the light should be on or the meter should indicate continuity).
5. Leave the test light probe engaged and sequentially open connectors or switches, remove parts, etc. until the light goes out or continuity is broken.
6. When the light goes out, the short is between the last two circuit components which were opened.

VOLTAGE

This test determines voltage available from the battery and should be the first step in any electrical troubleshooting procedure after visual inspection. Many electrical problems, especially on computer controlled systems, can be caused by a low state of charge in the battery. Excessive corrosion at the battery cable terminals can cause poor contact that will prevent proper charging and full battery current flow.
1. Set the voltmeter selector switch to the 20V position.
2. Connect the multimeter negative lead to the battery's negative (-) post or terminal and the positive lead to the battery's positive (+) post or terminal.
3. Turn the ignition switch **ON** to provide a load.
4. A well charged battery should register over 12 volts. If the meter reads below 11.5 volts, the battery power may be insufficient to operate the electrical system properly.

VOLTAGE DROP

▶ See Figure 9

When current flows through a load, the voltage beyond the load drops. This voltage drop is due to the resistance created by the load and also by small resistances created by corrosion at the connectors and damaged insulation on the wires. The maximum allowable voltage drop under load is critical, especially if there is more than one load in the circuit, since all voltage drops are cumulative.
1. Set the voltmeter selector switch to the 20 volt position.
2. Connect the multimeter negative lead to a good ground.
3. Operate the circuit and check the voltage prior to the first component (load).
4. There should be little or no voltage drop in the circuit prior to the first component. If a voltage drop exists, the wire or connectors in the circuit are suspect.
5. While operating the first component in the circuit, probe the ground side of the component with the positive meter lead and observe the voltage readings. A small voltage drop should be noticed. This voltage drop is caused by the resistance of the component.
6. Repeat the test for each component (load) down the circuit.
7. If a large voltage drop is noticed, the preceding component, wire or connector is suspect.

RESISTANCE

▶ See Figures 10 and 11

❉❉ WARNING

Never use an ohmmeter with power applied to the circuit. The ohmmeter is designed to operate on its own power supply. The

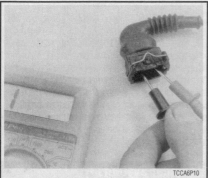

TCCA6P10

Fig. 8 The infinite reading on this multimeter indicates that the circuit is open

TCCA6P07

Fig. 9 This voltage drop test revealed high resistance (low voltage) in the circuit

TCCA6P08

Fig. 10 Checking the resistance of a coolant temperature sensor with an ohmmeter. Reading is 1.04 kilohms

normal 12 volt electrical system voltage and damage the meter!

1. Isolate the circuit from the vehicle's power source.
2. Ensure that the ignition key is **OFF** when disconnecting any components or the battery.
3. Where necessary, also isolate at least one side of the circuit to be checked, in order to avoid reading parallel resistances. Parallel circuit resistances will always give a lower reading than the actual resistance of either of the branches.
4. Connect the meter leads to both sides of the circuit (wire or component) and read the actual measured ohms on the meter scale. Make sure the selector switch is set to the proper ohm scale for the circuit being tested, to avoid misreading the ohmmeter test value.

Wire and Connector Repair

Almost anyone can replace damaged wires, as long as the proper tools and parts are available. Wire and terminals are available to fit almost any need. Even the specialized weatherproof, molded and hard shell connectors are now available from aftermarket suppliers.

Be sure the ends of all the wires are fitted with the proper terminal hardware and connectors. Wrapping a wire around a stud is never a permanent solution and will only cause trouble later. Replace wires one at a time to avoid confusion. Always route wires exactly the same as the factory.

➡**If connector repair is necessary, only attempt it if you have the proper tools. Weatherproof and hard shell connectors require special tools to release the pins inside the connector. Attempting to repair these connectors with conventional hand tools will damage them.**

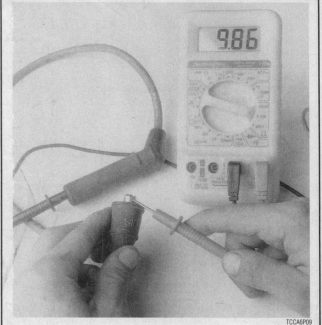

TCCA6P09

Fig. 11 Spark plug wires can be checked for excessive resistance using an ohmmeter

HEATING AND AIR CONDITIONING

Heater Assembly

REMOVAL & INSTALLATION

▶ **See Figure 12**

Nissan offers no factory approved information regarding service to the heating and air conditioning systems. Please utilize this procedures as a general guide, referring to the accompanying figure, as necessary for further clarification.

1. Disconnect the negative battery cable.
2. Drain the cooling system.

✳✳ CAUTION

When draining the coolant, keep in mind that cats and dogs are attracted by ethylene glycol antifreeze, and are quite likely to drink any that is left in an uncovered container or in puddles on the ground. This will prove fatal in sufficient quantity. Always drain the coolant into a sealable container. Coolant should be reused unless it is contaminated or several years old.

3. Remove the heater duct(s) and disconnect the heater hoses at the heater housing assembly.
4. Remove the console box and instrument panel assembly (if necessary).
5. Disconnect the air intake control cable from the housing assembly. Remove all necessary electrical connections.
6. On models equipped with A/C, remove the evaporator unit (do not discharge the A/C system) nuts and bolts, but do not remove the evaporator unit from the vehicle.
7. Remove the heater housing assembly.
To install:
8. Install the heater assembly and tighten the mounting screws.
9. Install the evaporator unit assembly on A/C models.

10. Connect the air intake control cable. Reconnect all necessary electrical connections.
11. Install the instrument panel assembly and console box.
12. Install the heater duct(s).
13. Connect the heater hoses.
14. Connect the negative battery cable and fill the engine with coolant. Adjust the control cable for proper operation. Start the engine and check for any coolant leaks. Check the A/C and heating systems for proper operation.

Blower Motor

REMOVAL & INSTALLATION

▶ **See Figures 13, 14, 15 and 16**

Nissan offers no factory approved information regarding service to the heating and air conditioning systems. Please utilize this procedures as a general guide, referring to the accompanying figures, as necessary for further clarification.

➡**The blower motor assembly is located at the bottom of the intake box which is part of the heater housing. If any control cables must be removed always mark the adjustment for easy installation.**

1. Disconnect the negative battery cable.
2. Remove the heater duct(s).
3. Remove the electrical connector. Remove the blower motor assembly.
To install:
4. Clean the intake box of all dirt, leaves and debris which may have been sucked into the housing. Install the blower motor assembly in the intake box.
5. Reconnect the electrical connection.
6. Install the heater duct(s).
7. Connect the battery cable and check the blower motor for proper operation.

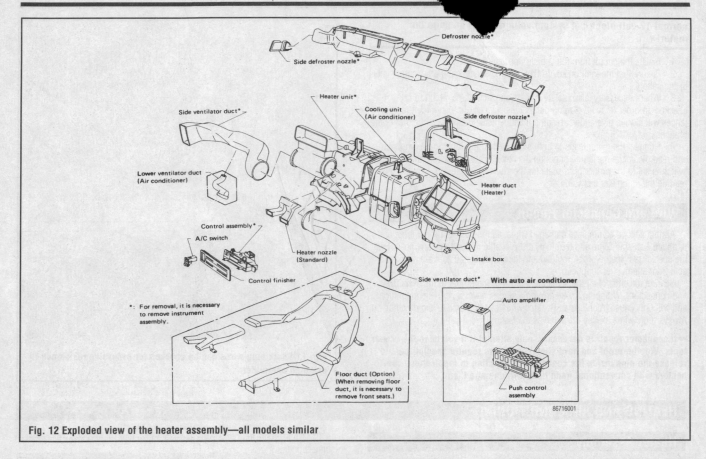

Fig. 12 Exploded view of the heater assembly—all models similar

Fig. 13 First, remove the electrical connection from the blower motor

Fig. 14 Disconnect the blower motor vent tube

Fig. 15 Remove the blower motor retaining screws

Fig. 16 Remove the blower motor from the heater case assembly

Heater Core

REMOVAL & INSTALLATION

▶ See Figures 17, 18, 19, 20 and 21

Nissan offers no factory approved information regarding service to the heating and air conditioning systems. Please utilize this procedures as a general guide, referring to the accompanying figures, as necessary for further clarification.

1. Remove the heater assembly.
2. Remove the screws and clips and separate the heater case halves.
3. Slide out the heater core.

To install:

4. Install the heater core in the heater case and close the two halves. Install the clips.
5. Install the heater assembly.

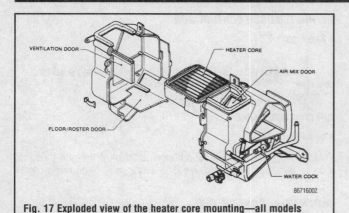

Fig. 17 Exploded view of the heater core mounting—all models

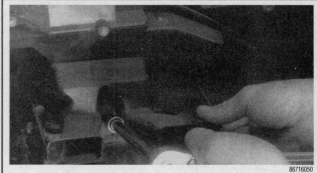

Fig. 18 Remove the lower duct retaining bolt to remove the duct holder assembly

Fig. 19 Remove the duct holder assembly from the vehicle—do not damage the felt seals

Fig. 20 Remove the cooling unit case assembly retaining bolt

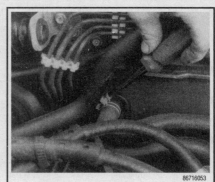

Fig. 21 Always make sure the heater hose clamps are tight

Air Conditioning Components

REMOVAL & INSTALLATION

Repair or service of air conditioning components is not covered by this manual, because of the risk of personal injury or death, and because of the legal ramifications of servicing these components without the proper EPA certification and experience. Cost, personal injury or death, environmental damage, and legal considerations (such as the fact that it is a federal crime to vent refrigerant into the atmosphere), dictate that the A/C components on your vehicle should be serviced only by a Motor Vehicle Air Conditioning (MVAC) trained, and EPA certified automotive technician.

➡**If your vehicle's A/C system uses R-12 refrigerant and is in need of recharging, the A/C system can be converted over to R-134a refrigerant (less environmentally harmful and expensive). Refer to Section 1 for additional information on R-12 to R-134a conversions, and for additional considerations dealing with your vehicle's A/C system.**

Control Head

REMOVAL & INSTALLATION

Nissan offers no factory approved information regarding service to the heating and air conditioning systems. Please utilize this procedures as a general guide, referring to the accompanying figures, as necessary for further clarification.

Manual Control

◗ **See Figures 22, 23 and 24**

1. Disconnect the negative battery cable.
2. Tag and disconnect all control cables at the A/C cooling unit/heater housing assembly and control head.
3. Remove the control knob(s) and slide the panel out through the front of the instrument panel.

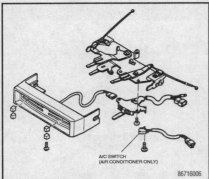

Fig. 22 Exploded view of manual control head

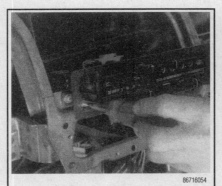

Fig. 23 Remove the retaining screws from the control assembly

Fig. 24 Remove the control cables from the assembly—mark all retaining points for correct installation

4. Installation is the reverse of the removal procedure. Adjust the cables, then check operation of the system.

Auto/Push Button Control

▶ See Figure 25

1. Disconnect the negative battery cable. Remove the center console cluster lid .
2. Remove the radio.
3. Remove the push control unit mounting screws (usually 7) and the bracket.
4. Disconnect the push control unit, the in-vehicle sensor and the harness connectors.
5. Slide out the push control unit.

To install:
6. Install the push control unit.
7. Reengage all sensor and harness connectors.
8. Position the mounting bracket and tighten the screws.
9. Install the radio and then install the center console cluster lid.
10. Connect the negative battery cable.
11. Check system for proper operation.

ADJUSTMENT

Manual Air Conditioner

VENTILATOR DOOR CONTROL ROD

▶ See Figure 26

1. Move the side link.
2. Hold the upper and lower doors and then connect the rods to their respective doors.
3. Verify proper operation.

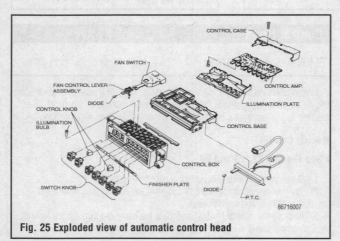

Fig. 25 Exploded view of automatic control head

DEFROSTER DOOR CONTROL ROD

▶ See Figure 27

1. Move the side link.
2. Connect the rod to the side link to the rod while pushing the defroster door lever.
3. Verify proper operation.

AIR CONTROL CABLE

▶ See Figure 28

Move the air control lever to the defroster position. Push the cable sheathing and side link in the correct direction and tighten the clamp. Verify proper operation.

WATER VALVE CONTROL ROD

▶ See Figure 29

➡**When adjusting the water valve control rod, disconnect the temperature control cable at the air mix door lever and then adjust air mix door control cable. Next, adjust the control rod. Reconnect the temperature control cable and then readjust it.**

1. Push the air mix door lever in the correct direction.
2. Pull the control rod in the direction shown (in the accompanying illustration) until there is an 0.08 in. (2mm) clearance between the ends of the rod and link lever. Connect the rod to the door lever.

TEMPERATURE CONTROL CABLE

▶ See Figure 30

Move the temperature control lever to the cold position. Push the cable sheathing and the air mix door lever in the correct and then tighten the clamp. Verify proper operation.

INTAKE DOOR CABLE

▶ See Figure 31

Push the cable sheathing and the intake door lever in the correct direction then tighten the clamp. Verify proper operation.

Auto Air Conditioner

MODE DOOR

▶ See Figure 32

1. Remove the auto amplifier and the relay bracket.
2. Move the side link by hand and hold the mode door in the VENT mode.
3. Install the mode door motor on the heater unit and connect it to the auto A/C harness.
4. Turn the ignition switch to the **ON** position. Move the vent switch to the ON position.
5. Attach the mode door motor rod to the side link rod holder.

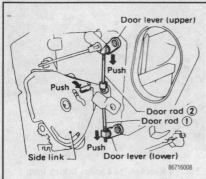

Fig. 26 Ventilator door control rod adjustment—manual control system

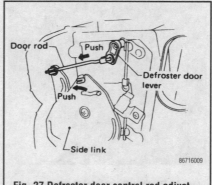

Fig. 27 Defroster door control rod adjustment—manual control system

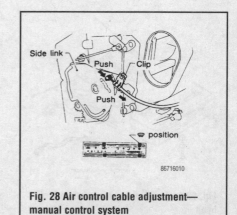

Fig. 28 Air control cable adjustment—manual control system

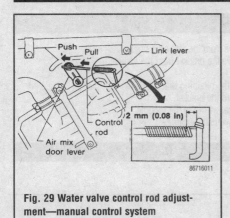

Fig. 29 Water valve control rod adjustment—manual control system

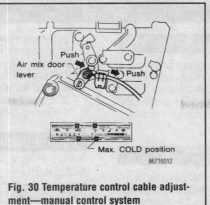
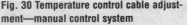

Fig. 30 Temperature control cable adjustment—manual control system

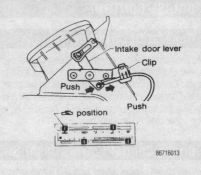

Fig. 31 Intake door control cable adjustment—manual control system

6. Turn the DEF switch ON. Check that the side link operates at the fully open position.

7. Turn the VENT switch ON to check that the side link operates at the fully open position.

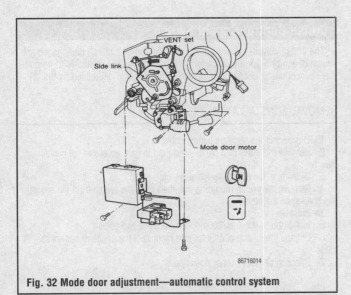

Fig. 32 Mode door adjustment—automatic control system

AIR MIX DOOR

▶ See Figure 33

1. Install the air mix door motor on the heater unit and connect it to the auto A/C harness.

2. Disengage the ambient sensor harness connector, then bridge terminals 5 and 55 with a jumper cable.

3. Set the PTC control at 18°C (65°F) and the air mix door at Full Cold.

4. Move the door lever by hand and hold it at the Full Cold position.

5. Attach the air mix door lever to the rod holder.

6. Check that the air mix door operates properly when the PTC is moved from 65–85°F (18–32°C).

INTAKE DOOR

▶ See Figure 34

1. Engage the intake door motor harness connector and then install the intake door motor.

2. Turn the ignition switch to **ACC**.

3. Turn REC switch OFF.

4. Set the intake door lever in the FRE position and then install the intake door motor on the intake unit.

5. Check the intake door operates properly when the REC switch is turned ON and OFF.

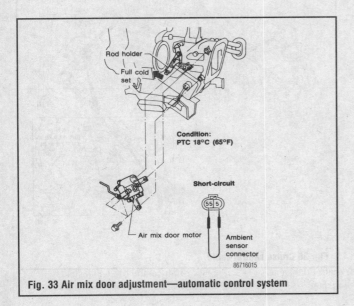

Fig. 33 Air mix door adjustment—automatic control system

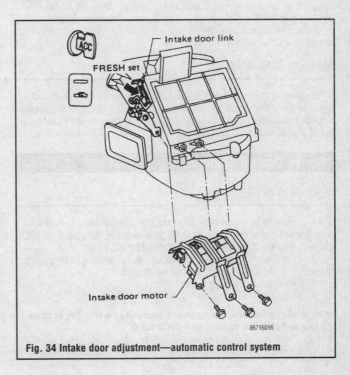

Fig. 34 Intake door adjustment—automatic control system

CRUISE CONTROL

General Description

The cruise control, which is a speed control system, maintains a desired speed of the vehicle under normal driving conditions. The cruise control Electronic Control Unit (ECU) regulates all cruise control functions. The use of the speed control is not recommended when driving conditions do not permit maintaining a constant speed, such as in heavy traffic or on roads that are winding, icy, snow covered or slippery.

Cruise Control Power (Dash) Switch

The cruise control power switch is a rocker-type switch located on the dashboard, to the left of the steering column. When this switch is depressed, power is sent to the control module under the dashboard, and to the speed control switch integrated into the left hand side headlight/turn signal lever (combination switch) on the steering column.

REMOVAL & INSTALLATION

1. Disconnect the negative battery cable.
2. Unfasten the retaining bolts securing the trim panel below the steering column, then place the trim panel aside.
3. Locate the position of the cruise control power switch in the dashboard. Working from behind the dash, push the power switch out with your hand.
4. Once the switch is removed from its mounting position, unplug the wiring harness from the rear of the switch.
   To install:
5. Plug the wiring harness into the rear of the switch.
6. Push the switch into its mounting hole on the dashboard.
7. Position the lower trim panel under the dashboard and secure with the retaining bolts.
8. Connect the negative battery cable.

Cruise Control Speed (Column) Switch

The speed control switch is part of the combination switch assembly found on the steering column. The switch itself is integrated into headlight/turn signal switch lever found on the left-hand side of the column. The speed control switch allows the driver to set the desired cruise speed, in addition to allowing the vehicle to increase the cruising speed, and resume a cruising mode after a cancellation of cruising due to braking or if equipped, clutch engagement.

Because the speed control switch is an integrated part of the column lever, it cannot be replaced by itself.

REMOVAL & INSTALLATION

The cruise control speed switch is an integrated part of the headlight/turn signal switch portion of the combination switch assembly found on the steering column. Please refer to the Combination Switch procedure located in Section 8 of this manual for service information.

Cruise Control Module

REMOVAL & INSTALLATION

1. Locate the control module. To access the control module, remove the panel below the steering column. With the panel removed, the control module is visible to the right of the steering column, above the gas pedal.
2. To remove the module, loosen and remove the retaining bolts securing the module to the bracket next to the steering column.
3. Disconnect the negative battery cable.
4. Disengage the electrical wiring from the module.

➡ On most applications, the module is retained by a clip. Pry back on the clip and slide the module from the bracket.

5. Remove the module from the retaining bracket.
6. If necessary, remove the bracket from the vehicle.
To install:
7. If removed, install the retaining bracket.
8. Install the module to the bracket.
9. Engage the electrical wiring to the module.
10. Connect the negative battery cable.

Control Cable

ADJUSTMENT

▶ **See Figure 35**

Cable Free-play

Measure the cable stroke to where the throttle valve begins to open. If adjustment is necessary. adjust by turning the adjusting nut 1/2 to 1 full turn from the throttle opening position. Securely tighten lock-nut to hold adjusting nut in place.

Cruise Control Cancel Switch

The cruise control system utilizes a brake and/or a clutch disengagement switch depending upon application. The purpose of this switch is to immediately cancel cruise control engagement if the pedal is depressed by the driver.

REMOVAL & INSTALLATION

1. Disconnect the negative battery cable.
2. Remove the lower trim panel if required to gain access to the cancel switch.
3. Disengage the cancel switch connector.
4. Remove the switch mounting nut, then slide the switch from the mounting bracket on the pedal.
   To install:
5. Install the switch into the mounting bracket and adjust.
6. Engage the switch connector and reconnect the negative battery cable.
7. Check system for proper operation.

Fig. 35 Cruise control cable

ENTERTAINMENT SYSTEMS

Radio/Tape player

Always observe the following cautions when working on the radio:
• Always observe the proper polarity of the connections (positive-to-positive and negative-to-negative).
• Never operate the radio without a speaker, to prevent damage to the output transistors. If a new speaker is installed, make sure it has the correct impedance (ohms) for the radio.

REMOVAL & INSTALLATION

▶ **See Figures 36 and 37**

Nissan offers no factory approved information regarding service the radio or entertainment systems. Please utilize this procedures as a general guide, referring to the accompanying figure(s), as necessary for further clarification.
1. Disconnect the negative battery cable.
2. Remove all necessary trim panels.
3. Disconnect the wiring plug at the back of the radio.
4. Remove the mounting screws, and pull the radio from the dash.
5. Disconnect the wiring harness and the antenna.
To install:
6. Reconnect the wiring harness into the rear of the radio and then slide the radio into the instrument panel.
7. Install and tighten the radio mounting screws evenly.
8. Reconnect the antenna and any electrical leads.
9. Install all trim panels. Reconnect the battery and check for proper operation.

AM TRIM ADJUSTMENT

▶ **See Figure 38**

If a new antenna or antenna cable is used, or if poor AM reception is noted, the antenna trimmer on all factory and most aftermarket radios can be adjusted. Turn the radio to a weak station around 1400 kHz. Adjust the trimmer screw until best reception and maximum volume are obtained. The trimmer screw for the factory installed radio is located either above the left station pre-set button or in the lower left corner of the fascia. On some aftermarket units, the trimmer can only be accessed once the case is removed (for more information, contact the aftermarket radio manufacturer).

➡**Never turn or adjust the antenna trimmer more than 1/2 turn!**

For best AM and FM reception, raise the antenna to its full height and make sure the antenna is properly grounded. Weak reception can be caused by loose or corroded antenna connections and fasteners.

Speakers

REMOVAL & INSTALLATION

1. Remove the speaker cover.
2. Remove the attaching screws for the speaker. Note location of speaker wires Remove the speaker.
3. Installation is the reverse of the removal procedure. Make sure that the speaker wires are installed in the correct location. Check radio system for proper operation.

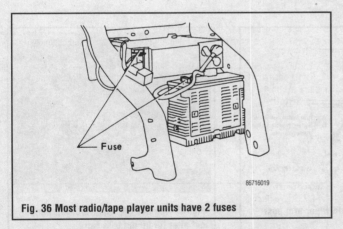

Fig. 36 Most radio/tape player units have 2 fuses

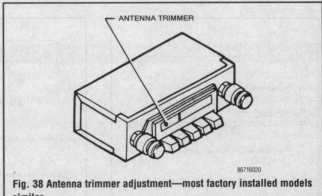

Fig. 38 Antenna trimmer adjustment—most factory installed models similar

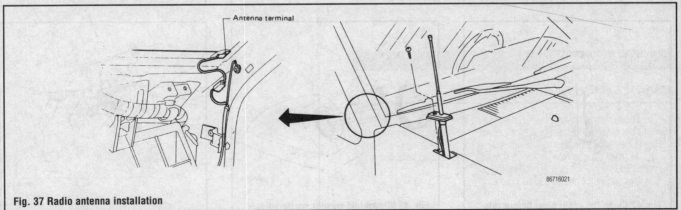

Fig. 37 Radio antenna installation

WINDSHIELD WIPERS AND WASHERS

Blade and Arm

REMOVAL & INSTALLATION

◆ **See Figures 39, 40, 41 and 42**

➥**Wiper blade element replacement is covered in Section 1.**

1. To remove the wiper blades, lift up on the spring release tab located on the wiper blade-to-wiper arm connector.

2. Pull the blade assembly off the wiper arm.

3. There are two types of replacement procedures:

   a. Replace the entire wiper blade as an assembly. Simply snap the replacement into place on the arm.

   b. Press the old wiper blade insert down, away from the blade assembly, to free it from the retaining clips on the blade ends. Slide the insert out of the blade. Slide the new insert into the blade assembly and bend the insert upward slightly to engage the retaining clips.

4. To replace a wiper arm, unscrew the acorn nut which secures it to the pivot, then carefully pull the arm upward and off the pivot.

➥**All models are equipped with a cover over the acorn nut. To expose the nut, remove the cover.**

5. The wiper arms should be installed so that the blades are 0.98 in. (25mm) above, and parallel to, the windshield molding. If the motor has been run, be sure the motor and linkage is in its parked position before installing the wiper arms. To do this, turn the ignition switch **ON**, and cycle the motor three or four times. Shut off the motor with the wiper switch (not the ignition switch), and allow the motor to return to the park position.

Windshield Wiper Motor

REMOVAL & INSTALLATION

◆ **See Figures 43 and 44**

1. Disconnect the negative battery cable.

2. Remove the wiper blades and arms as an assembly from the pivots. The arms are retained to the pivots by nuts. Remove the nuts and pull the arms straight off.

3. Remove the cowl top grille. It is retained by screws at its front edge. Remove the screws and pull the grille forward to disengage the tabs at the rear.

4. Remove the stop ring which connects the wiper motor arm to the connecting rod.

5. Disconnect the wiper motor harness at the connector on the wiper motor body from under the instrument panel.

6. Remove the retaining screws and pull the wiper motor outward and remove the motor from the vehicle.

To install:

7. Install the wiper motor and connect the harness.

8. Connect the linkage to the motor arm and then install the cowling.

9. The wiper arms should be installed so that the blades are 0.98 in. (25mm) above, and parallel to, the windshield molding. If the motor has been run, be sure the motor and linkage is in its parked position before installing the wiper arms. To do this, connect the negative battery cable, then turn the ignition switch **ON** and cycle the motor three or four times. Shut off the motor with the wiper switch (not the ignition switch), and allow the motor to return to the Park position.

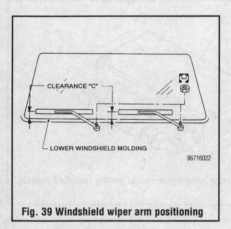

Fig. 39 Windshield wiper arm positioning

Fig. 40 Rear windshield wiper arm positioning

Fig. 41 Remove the wiper arm retaining nut after lift up the trim cap

Fig. 42 Clean the wiper pivot before reinstalling the wiper arm

Fig. 43 Windshield washer nozzle adjustment

Fig. 44 Windshield wiper motor

Wiper Linkage

REMOVAL & INSTALLATION

▶ **See Figures 45 thru 50**

1. Remove the wiper blade and arm from the pivot.
2. Remove the cowl top grille.
3. Remove the two flange nuts retaining the wiper linkage pivot to the cowl top.
4. Remove the stop ring which retains the connecting rod to the wiper motor arm.
5. Remove the wiper motor linkage assembly from the vehicle.
6. Install the linkage in the reverse order of removal.

Rear Wiper and Motor

REMOVAL & INSTALLATION

Pathfinder

1. Disconnect the negative battery cable.
2. Pop up the acorn nut cover, remove the nut and pull off the rear wiper.
3. Remove the pivot nut.
4. Open the rear hatch and remove the plastic trim panel by removing the retaining screws and plastic clips.
5. With the trim panel removed, and accessing the motor from within the hatch panel, pop out the trim clips and remove the wiper motor cover.
6. Disconnect the electrical lead and the washer hose, remove the mounting bolts and lift out the wiper motor.

To install:

7. Position the wiper motor and install the mounting bolts.
8. Connect the lead and the washer hose.

9. Position the wiper motor cover over the opening and press in the retaining clips.
10. Install the pivot nut.
11. Install the wiper arm and tighten the acorn nut. Connect the battery cable.

Windshield Washer Fluid Reservoir

REMOVAL & INSTALLATION

Front and Rear

1. Disconnect the negative battery terminal and fluid reservoir electrical connection.
2. Disconnect the fluid tube from the washer motor.
3. Remove the reservoir retaining bolts and slide out of the bracket.
4. Installation is the reverse of the removal procedure. To make the hose installation easier, apply a thin layer of petroleum jelly to the motor nipple before installing the washer tube. This way the hose will slide over the tube.

Windshield Washer Fluid Motor

REMOVAL & INSTALLATION

Front and Rear

1. Remove the washer reservoir/motor assembly from the vehicle.
2. Remove all connections. Pull the motor from the rubber grommet.
3. Installation is the reverse of the removal procedure. Apply petroleum jelly to the motor tube before installing. The jelly will allow the tube to slide into the grommet with ease. Reconnect all connections.

Fig. 45 First disengage the electrical connection from the wiper motor

Fig. 46 Then, remove the windshield wiper motor retaining bolts

Fig. 47 Remove the windshield wiper motor from the vehicle firewall

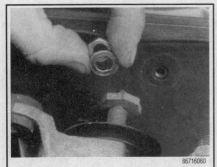

Fig. 48 After lifting the wiper motor from the firewall remove the windshield wiper linkage retaining nut and washer

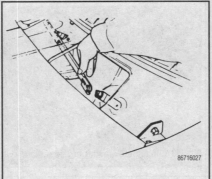

Fig. 49 Disconnecting the windshield wiper linkage

Fig. 50 View of the windshield wiper motor linkage—note the linkage is keyed to the wiper motor assembly

INSTRUMENT AND SWITCHES

➡**For fuel sending unit replacement please refer to Section 5. For instrument panel and console removal and installation please refer to Section 10.**

Instrument Cluster

REMOVAL & INSTALLATION

♦ **See Figures 51 thru 59**

1. Disconnect the negative battery cable.
2. Remove the steering wheel. This is not absolutely necessary, but you'll find it makes cluster removal much easier.
3. Remove the cluster lid mounting screws and lift out the lid.

Fig. 51 Remove the lower trim panel if necessary for instrument panel repairs

4. Remove the cluster assembly mounting screws and then tilt the cluster toward you. Reach behind it to disengage any electrical connections and the speedometer cable. Remove the cluster.

   To install:

5. Position the cluster in the instrument panel, then engage all electrical connections and the speedometer cable.
6. Install the cluster lid.
7. Install the steering wheel if removed. Torque the steering wheel retaining nut to 22—29 ft. lbs. (29—39 Nm).
8. Reconnect the negative battery cable.

Speedometer Cable

REPLACEMENT

♦ **See Figures 54, 55 and 60**

The speedometer cable is connected to the speedometer by means of a press–fit. When you remove the combination meter (cluster), they simply come unplugged.

1. Pull the cable from the cable housing. If the cable is broken, the other half of the cable will have to be removed from the transmission end. Unscrew the retaining knob and remove the cable from the transmission extension housing.
2. Lubricate the cable with graphite powder (sold as speedometer cable lubricant, curiously enough) and feed the cable into the housing. It is best to start at the speedometer end and feed the cable down towards the transmission. It is also usually necessary to unscrew the transmission connection and install the cable end to the gear, then reconnect the housing to the transmission. Slip the cable end into the speedometer, and reconnect the cable housing.
3. The entire cable assembly, including the shield and cable can also be replaced. Although in most cases this is not necessary because only the cable is defective, the following procedure should be used to replace the entire unit:

Fig. 52 Remove the instrument panel trim before removing the cluster assembly

Fig. 53 Remove the instrument cluster assembly—mark all electrical connections

Fig. 54 View of the speedometer cable collar that connects to the cluster assembly

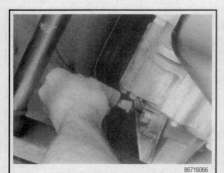

Fig. 55 View of the speedometer cable collar at the transmission end—note the end is keyed for transmission installation

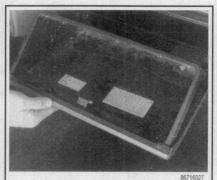

Fig. 56 View of the glove box door installed

Fig. 57 To remove the glove box door remove the door hinge pins

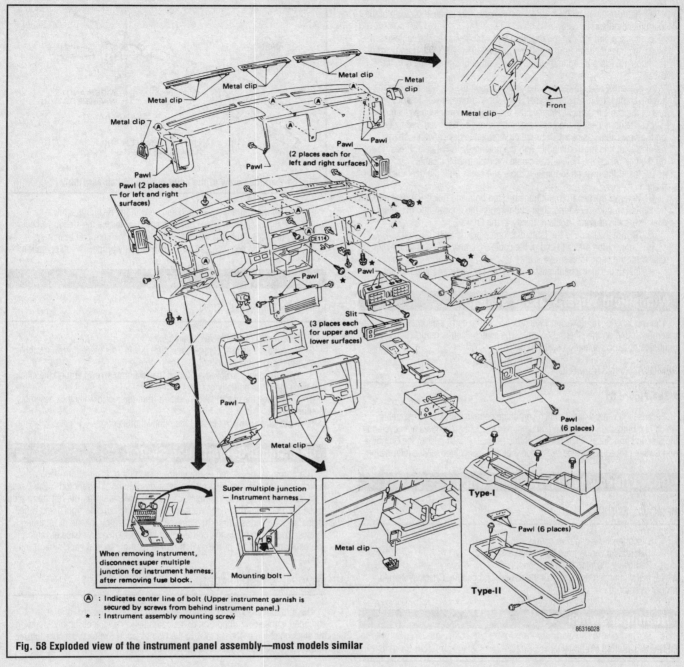

Metal clip

Metal clip

Metal clip

Metal clip

Metal clip

Front

Pawl

Pawl

Pawl (2 places each for left and right surfaces)

Pawl (2 places each for left and right surfaces)

Pawl

CE114

Pawl

Pawl

Pawl

Slit (3 places each for upper and lower surfaces)

Pawl

Metal clip

Pawl (6 places)

Type-I

Pawl (6 places)

Type-II

Super multiple junction — Instrument harness

When removing instrument, disconnect super multiple junction for instrument harness, after removing fuse block.

Mounting bolt

Metal clip

Ⓐ : Indicates center line of bolt (Upper instrument garnish is secured by screws from behind instrument panel.)

★ : Instrument assembly mounting screw

86316028

Fig. 58 Exploded view of the instrument panel assembly—most models similar

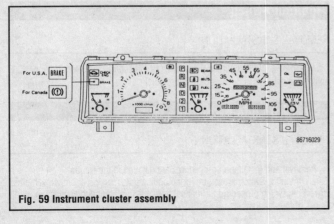

For U.S.A. BRAKE

For Canada

86716029

Fig. 59 Instrument cluster assembly

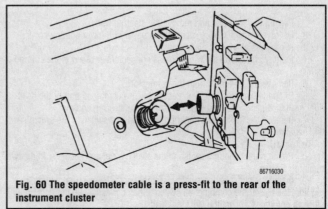

86716030

Fig. 60 The speedometer cable is a press-fit to the rear of the instrument cluster

a. Remove the press-fit connection from the speedometer backing of the instrument cluster.

b. Loosen and remove the retaining bolt which secures the cable assembly to the transmission housing. Carefully pull the cable up and away from the housing. Place a cap in the hole to prevent debris from falling in the case.

c. Carefully and slowly, pull the cable through the fire wall and into the engine compartment. In some cases, the rubber grommet will pop out with the rest of the cable assembly. Remove the assembly and place on a clean table.

d. The drive gear in the cable assembly must be removed and installed on the new cable. Use a small probe other suitable device with a sharp pointed end, and insert the point into the hole in the drive gear. Press down on the clip inside the hole and separate the gear from the cable.

e. Insert the gear on to the new cable and press until the gear clicks into place.

f. Remove the cap from the transmission hole and insert the gear into the transmission body. Feed the other end through the firewall into the interior. Make sure the grommet seats correctly to the firewall.

g. Secure the cable to the transmission using the retaining bolt.

h. Connect the press-fit end of the cable assembly to the speedometer. Listen for the click, to ensure a secure fit.

i. Install the instrument cluster using the procedure outlined earlier.

Windshield Wiper/Washer Switch

The windshield wiper/washer switch is part of the combination switch assembly found on the steering column. The switch itself is mounted to the right side of the combination switch base.

REMOVAL & INSTALLATION

▶ **See Figure 61**

Because the wiper/washer switch part of the combination switch assembly which is mounted on the steering column, replacement procedures are covered in the Steering and Suspension Section of this manual. Please refer to the Combination Switch procedure located in Section 8 of this manual for service information.

Rear Window Wiper/Washer Switch

REMOVAL & INSTALLATION

1. Disconnect the negative battery cable.
2. Disconnect wiring from the switch assembly.
3. Remove the switch from the panel.
4. Installation is the reverse of the removal procedure. Check system for proper operation.

Headlight Switch

REMOVAL & INSTALLATION

1. Disconnect the negative battery cable.
2. Pry out the horn pad and remove the steering wheel.
3. Remove the two screws securing the upper and lower column covers. Pry the two pieces apart, and place aside.
4. Identify and tag all the wire harness connectors encased in the column cover.
5. Remove the terminals from the connector.
6. Slide the combination switch assembly, (a combined unit of the headlight switch, wiper switch and switch case) off the steering column.
7. Remove the two screws securing the headlight switch to the switch case, and separate.

To install:

8. Position the headlight switch to the switch case, and secure with the two retaining screws.
9. Install the combination switch assembly onto the steering column, making sure the tab on the combination switch aligns correctly with the hole on the steering column. Connect the electrical leads.

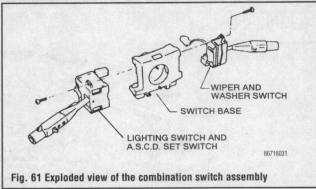

WIPER AND WASHER SWITCH

SWITCH BASE

LIGHTING SWITCH AND A.S.C.D. SET SWITCH

86716031

Fig. 61 Exploded view of the combination switch assembly

10. Install the column covers and secure with the retaining screws.
11. Install the steering wheel onto the column. Torque the steering wheel retaining nut to 22–29 ft. lbs. (29–39 Nm). Install the horn pad assembly.
12. Connect the negative battery cable and verify proper switch operation.

Clock

REMOVAL & INSTALLATION

1. Disconnect the negative battery cable.
2. Remove the central control panel trim piece. This piece surrounds the clock, radio and ventilation control panel.
3. With the panel removed, unfasten the retaining screws around the clock, and slide the clock partially out.
4. Disengage the electrical connection from the rear of the clock assembly, then remove it.
5. Installation is the reverse of the removal procedure.

Turn Signal/Combination Switch

The combination switch is the entire assembly of lever controlled switches which are mounted on the steering column. This includes the headlight, turn signal, and if equipped, cruise control switch on the left-hand side of the column, and the wiper/washer control switch on the right-hand side. These switches are secured to a central switch base by means of retaining screws. You can remove the entire combination switch and base assembly, or you can replace either of the switch housings mounted on each side of the base.

REMOVAL & INSTALLATION

The turn signal switch is an integrated part of the turn signal and, if equipped, cruise control portion of the combination switch assembly found on the steering column. Please refer to the Combination Switch procedure located in Section 8 of this manual for service information.

Ignition Switch

REMOVAL & INSTALLATION

All removal and installation procedures of the column mounted ignition switch are detailed in Section 8 of this manual.

Back-Up Light Switch

REMOVAL & INSTALLATION

Removal and installation procedures are detailed in the Neutral Safety/Inhibitor Switch procedure for automatic transmission equipped vehicles, or reverse switch procedure for manual transmission equipped vehicles in Section 7 of this manual.

LIGHTING

Headlights

REMOVAL & INSTALLATION

▶ See Figures 62, 63, 64 and 65

Sealed Beam Type

1. Disconnect the negative battery cable. Remove the headlight bezel (trim).
2. The sealed beam is held in place by a retainer and either 2 or 4 small screws. Identify these screws before applying any tools.

➡DO NOT confuse the small retaining screws with the larger aiming screws! There will be two aiming screws or adjusters for each lamp. (One adjuster controls the up/down motion and the other controls the left/right motion.) Identify the adjusters and avoid them during removal. If they are not disturbed, the new headlamp should have the same aim as the old one.

3. Using a small screwdriver (preferably magnetic) and a pair of taper-nose pliers if necessary, remove the small screws in the headlamp retainer. DON'T drop the screws.
4. Remove the retainer and the headlamp may be gently pulled free from its mounts. Detach the connector (if the connector is tight wiggle it) from the back of the sealed beam unit and remove the unit from the vehicle.

To install:

5. Place the new headlamp in position (single protrusion on the glass facing upward) and connect the wiring harness. Remember to install the rubber boot on the back of the new lamp—it's a water seal. Make sure the headlight is positioned with the correct side upward.
6. Connect the negative battery cable, then turn on the headlights and check the new lamp for proper function. Remember to check both high and low beams before the final assembly.

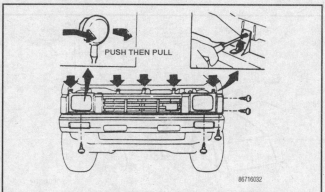

Fig. 62 Remove the grille assembly before removing the headlamp

7. Install the retainer and the small screws that hold it.
8. Reinstall the headlight bezel.

Replaceable Bulb (Semi-Sealed Beam)/Fixed Lens Type

➡This type of light is replace from behind the unit. The lens is not removed or loosened. Do not touch bulb assembly, if possible.

1. Open and support the hood, then disconnect the negative battery cable.
2. Remove the wiring connector from the back of the lamp. Be careful to release the locking tab completely before removal.
3. Grasp the base of the bulb holder, twist it counterclockwise (as viewed from the engine compartment), then carefully remove the bulb holder and bulb from the housing.

✳✳ CAUTION

If replacing a recently burnt out bulb, be careful because the bulb could still be very hot. Use either clean gloves or a clean rag to remove the bulb.

4. Hold the bulb at the base, not at the glass cover portion and unclip the harness from the bulb. Remove the bulb.

➡Because the halogen bulb is sensitive to oils on your fingers, NEVER touch the glass portion of a halogen bulb.

To install:

5. Position the new bulb in the holder and make sure the clip engages firmly.

➡Hold the new bulb with a clean cloth or a piece of paper. DO NOT touch or grasp the bulb with your fingers. The oils from your skin will produce a hot spot on the glass envelope, shortening bulb life. If the bulb is touched accidentally, clean it with alcohol and a clean rag before installation. But remember it is simply safer to avoid handling the bulb by its glass.

6. Install the holder and bulb into the housing. Note that the holder has guides which must align with the housing. When the holder is correctly seated, turn the holder clockwise to lock in place.
7. Connect the wiring harness, then connect the negative battery cable.
8. Turn on the headlights and check the function of the new bulb on both high and low beam.

AIMING THE HEADLIGHTS

▶ See Figures 66, 67, 68 and 69

The headlights must be properly aimed to provide the best, safest road illumination. The lights should be checked for proper aim and adjusted as necessary. Certain state and local authorities have requirements for headlight aiming; these should be checked before adjustment is made.

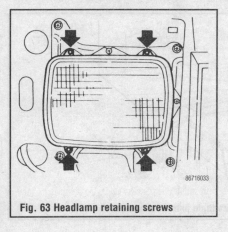

Fig. 63 Headlamp retaining screws

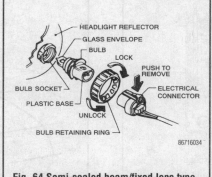
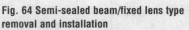

Fig. 64 Semi-sealed beam/fixed lens type removal and installation

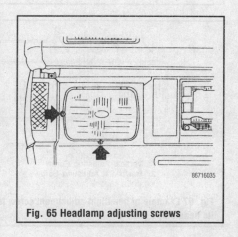

Fig. 65 Headlamp adjusting screws

❊❊ CAUTION

About once a year, when the headlights are replaced or any time front end work is performed on your vehicle, the headlight should be accurately aimed by a reputable repair shop using the proper equipment. Headlights not properly aimed can make it virtually impossible to see and may blind other drivers on the road, possibly causing an accident. Note that the following procedure is a temporary fix, until you can take your vehicle to a repair shop for a proper adjustment.

Headlight adjustment may be temporarily made using a wall, as described below, or on the rear of another vehicle. When adjusted, the lights should not glare in oncoming car or truck windshields, nor should they illuminate the passenger compartment of vehicles driving in front of you. These adjustments are rough and should always be fine-tuned by a repair shop which is equipped with headlight aiming tools. Improper adjustments may be both dangerous and illegal.

For most of the vehicles covered by this manual, horizontal and vertical aiming of each sealed beam unit is provided by two adjusting screws which move the retaining ring and adjusting plate against the tension of a coil spring. There is no adjustment for focus; this is done during headlight manufacturing.

➡Because the composite headlight assembly is bolted into position, no adjustment should be necessary or possible. Some applications, however, may be bolted to an adjuster plate or may be retained by adjusting screws. If so, follow this procedure when adjusting the lights, BUT always have the adjustment checked by a reputable shop.

Before removing the headlight bulb or disturbing the headlamp in any way, note the current settings in order to ease headlight adjustment upon reassembly. If the high or low beam setting of the old lamp still works, this can be done using the wall of a garage or a building:

1. Park the vehicle on a level surface, with the fuel tank about ½ full and with the vehicle empty of all extra cargo (unless normally carried). The vehicle should be facing a wall which is no less than 6 feet (1.8m) high and 12 feet (3.7m) wide. The front of the vehicle should be about 25 feet from the wall.

2. If aiming is to be performed outdoors, it is advisable to wait until dusk in order to properly see the headlight beams on the wall. If done in a garage, darken the area around the wall as much as possible by closing shades or hanging cloth over the windows.

3. Turn the headlights **ON** and mark the wall at the center of each light's low beam, then switch on the brights and mark the center of each light's high beam. A short length of masking tape which is visible from the front of the vehicle may be used. Although marking all four positions is advisable, marking one position from each light should be sufficient.

4. If neither beam on one side is working, and if another like-sized vehicle is available, park the second one in the exact spot where the vehicle was and mark the beams using the same-side light. Then switch the vehicles so the one to be aimed is back in the original spot. It must be parked no closer to or farther away from the wall than the second vehicle.

5. Perform any necessary repairs, but make sure the vehicle is not moved, or is returned to the exact spot from which the lights were marked. Turn the headlights **ON** and adjust the beams to match the marks on the wall.

6. Have the headlight adjustment checked as soon as possible by a reputable repair shop.

Signal and Marker lights

REMOVAL & INSTALLATION

▶ **See Figures 70, 71 and 72**

Front Turn Signal and Parking Lights

1. For access to the bulb. remove the retaining screws and withdraw the turn signal/parking light lens.
2. Depress the bulb slightly while turning counterclockwise to release it.
3. To install the bulb, carefully push downward and turn the bulb clockwise at the same time.
4. Verify that the new bulb is working properly.
5. Install the turn signal/parking light lens using the retaining screws.

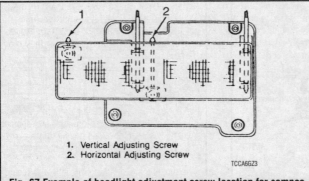

Fig. 66 Location of the aiming screws on most vehicles with sealed beam headlights

1. Vertical Adjusting Screw
2. Horizontal Adjusting Screw

Fig. 67 Example of headlight adjustment screw location for composite headlamps

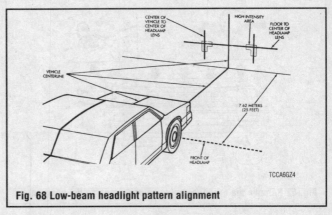

Fig. 68 Low-beam headlight pattern alignment

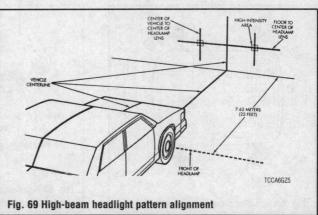

Fig. 69 High-beam headlight pattern alignment

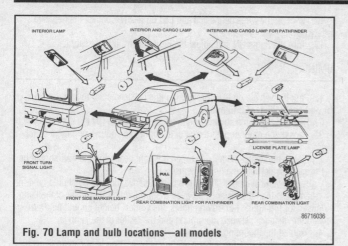

Fig. 70 Lamp and bulb locations—all models

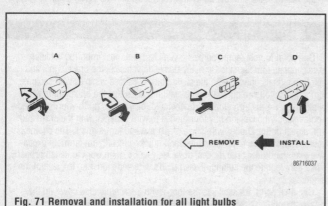

REMOVE → INSTALL

86716037

Fig. 71 Removal and installation for all light bulbs

Item	Wattage (W)	Bulb No.
Front turn signal light	27	1156
Front side marker light	3.8	194
Rear combination light		
Turn signal	27	1156
Stop/Tail	27/8	1157
Back-up	27	1156
License plate light	3.8 or 5	194*
Interior light	10	—

(*: For 3.8 watt lamp)

86716038

Fig. 72 Light bulb installation chart

Side Marker Lights

1. Loosen the retaining screws, then remove the side marker light lens.
2. Turn the bulb socket counterclockwise to release it from lens.
3. Pull the bulb straight outward to remove it from the socket.

To install:

4. Carefully push straight in to seat the bulb in the socket.
5. Insert the bulb and socket assembly into the lens, then turn the socket clockwise to secure it.
6. Position the side marker light lens and secure using the retaining screws.

Rear Turn Signal, Brake and Parking Lights

1. If necessary for access to the bulb socket, remove the rear trim panel, by depressing the clip at the top or the bottom of the panel. Once the clip is depressed, pull the panel away from the surrounding panel.
2. To remove the bulb and socket from the cover housing, grab the socket body and press towards the cover housing slightly, then turn counterclockwise until the bulb and socket are free of the cover body.

3. To remove the bulb, depress the bulb slightly and turn it counterclockwise to release it from the socket.
4. To install the bulb, carefully push down and turn the bulb clockwise at the same time.
5. Insert the bulb and socket into the cover housing opening, and turn the socket body clockwise.
6. Install the trim panel if necessary.

Dome Light

REMOVAL & INSTALLATION

1. Remove the dome light cover, by pressing on the cover at to ends and gently pulling the cover down.
2. Remove the bulb from holder. Use either a clean rag or a pair of gloves because the bulb could be hot. Grasp one end of the bulb and press toward the other end of the bulb, and down towards the floor. This will free the bulb from the mounting clips.
3. Install in the reverse order of the removal procedure.

License Plate Lights

REMOVAL & INSTALLATION

1. Remove the lighting assembly from the bodywork.
2. Disconnect the bulb and socket from the lighting assembly.
3. Remove the bulb from the holder.
4. Reassemble in reverse order of the removal procedure.

Fog Lamps

REMOVAL & INSTALLATION

1. Disconnect the negative battery cable.
2. Disengage the lamp electrical connector.
3. Unscrew the bracket-to-bumper mounting bolts and remove the lamp.
4. Unscrew the two bezel retaining screws and remove the lens retaining bezel.
5. Carefully pull out the lens and disconnect it.
6. Unclip the bulb connector and then unclip the bulb retainer. Remove the bulb.

To install:

7. Install the new bulb and clip it into position. Connect the electrical lead.
8. Reconnect the lens and slide it into the frame.
9. Install the retaining bezel and tighten the two screws.
10. Engage the lamp connector, then install the lamp assembly to the bumper.
11. Connect the negative battery cable and check for proper operation.

INSTALLING AFTERMARKET AUXILIARY LIGHTS

➡**Before installing any aftermarket light, make sure it is legal for road use. Most acceptable lights will have a DOT approval number. Also check your local and regional inspection regulations. In certain areas, aftermarket lights must be installed in a particular manner or they may not be legal for inspection.**

1. Disconnect the negative battery cable.
2. Unpack the contents of the light kit purchased. Place the contents in an open space where you can easily retrieve a piece if needed.
3. Choose a location for the lights. If you are installing fog lights, below the bumper and apart from each other is desirable. Most fog lights are mounted below or very close to the headlights. If you are installing driving lights, above the bumper and close together is desirable. Most driving lights are mounted between the headlights.
4. Drill the needed hole(s) to mount the light. Install the light, and secure using the supplied retainer nut and washer. Tighten the light mounting hardware, but not the light adjustment nut or bolt.

5. Install the relay that came with the light kit in the engine compartment, in a rigid area, such as a fender. Always install the relay with the terminals facing down. This will prevent water from entering the relay assembly.

6. Using the wire supplied, locate the ground terminal on the relay, and connect a length of wire from this terminal to a good ground source. You can drill a hole and screw this wire to an inside piece of metal; just scrape the paint away from the hole to ensure a good connection.

7. Locate the light terminal on the relay; and attach a length of wire between this terminal and the fog/driving lamps.

8. Locate the ignition terminal on the relay, and connect a length of wire between this terminal and the light switch.

9. Find a suitable mounting location for the light switch and install. Some examples of mounting areas are a location close to the main light switch, auxiliary light position in the dash panel, if equipped, or in the center of the dash panel.

10. Depending on local and regional regulations, the other end of the switch can be connected to a constant power source such as the battery, an ignition opening in the fuse panel, or a parking or headlight wire.

11. Locate the power terminal on the relay, and connect a wire with an in-line fuse of at least 10 amperes between the terminal and the battery.

12. With all the wires connected and tied up neatly, connect the negative battery cable.

13. Turn the lights ON and adjust the light pattern, if necessary.

AIMING

1. Park the vehicle on level ground, so it is perpendicular to and, facing a flat wall about 25 ft. (7.6m) away.

2. Remove any stone shields, if equipped, and switch ON the lights.

3. Loosen the mounting hardware of the lights so you can aim them as follows:

a. The horizontal distance between the light beams on the wall should be the same as between the lights themselves.

b. The vertical height of the light beams above the ground should be 4 in. (10cm) less than the distance between the ground and the center of the lamp lenses for fog lights. For driving lights, the vertical height should be even with the distance between the ground and the center of the lamp.

4. Tighten the mounting hardware.

5. Test to make sure the lights work correctly, and the light pattern is even.

TRAILER WIRING

Wiring the vehicle for towing is fairly easy. There are a number of good wiring kits available and these should be used, rather than trying to design your own. All trailers will need brake lights and turn signals as well as tail lights and side marker lights. Most states require extra marker lights for overly wide trailers. Also, most areas require back-up lights for trailers, and most trailer manufacturers have been building trailers with back-up lights for several years.

Additionally, some Class I, most Class II and just about all Class III trailers will have electric brakes. Add to this number an accessories wire, to operate trailer internal equipment or to charge the trailer's battery, and you can have as many as seven wires in the harness.

Determine the equipment on your trailer and buy the wiring kit necessary. The kit will contain all the wires needed, plus a plug adapter set which includes the female plug, mounted on the bumper or hitch, and the male plug, wired into, or plugged into the trailer harness.

When installing the kit, follow the manufacturer's instructions. Though the color coding of the wires should be standard throughout the industry.

One point to note, some domestic vehicles, and most imported vehicles, have separate turn signals. On many domestic vehicles, the brake lights and rear turn signals operate with the same bulb. For those vehicles with separate turn signals, you can purchase an isolation unit so that the brake lights won't blink whenever the turn signals are operated, or, you can go to your local electronics supply house and buy four diodes to wire in series with the brake and turn signal bulbs. Diodes will isolate the brake and turn signals. The choice is yours. The isolation units are simple and quick to install, but far more expensive than the diodes. The diodes, however, require more work to install properly, since they require the cutting of each bulb's wire and soldering in place of the diode.

One final point, the best kits are those with a spring loaded cover on the vehicle mounted socket. This cover prevents dirt and moisture from corroding the terminals. Never let the vehicle socket hang loosely. Always mount it securely to the bumper or hitch.

CIRCUIT PROTECTION

Fuses

REPLACEMENT

▶ **See Figures 73 and 74**

➡**On all models covered in this manual, the fuse box is located in the passenger compartment lower left area next to the steering column. A fuse puller tool is mounted in the fuse box cover for easy replacement of fuses.**

Fuses protect all the major electrical systems in the vehicle. In case of an electrical overload, the fuse melts, breaking the circuit and stopping the flow of electricity.

If a fuse blows, the cause should be investigated and corrected before the installation of a new fuse. This however, is easier to say than to do. Luckily since each fuse protects a limited number of components, your job is narrowed down somewhat. Begin your investigation by looking for obvious fraying, loose connections, breaks in insulation, etc. Use the techniques outlined at the beginning of this section. Electrical problems are almost always a real headache to solve, but patience and persistence, coupled with logic, usually provide a solution.

The amperage of each fuse and the circuit it protects are both marked on the cover of the fuse box, which is located under the instrument panel to the left the steering column.

➡**NEVER USE A FUSE OF HIGHER AMPERAGE RATING THAN THAT SPECIFIED ON THE FUSE BOX COVER.**

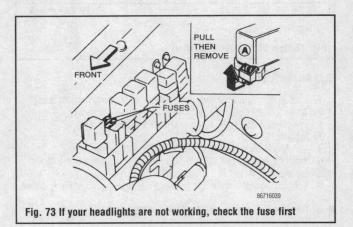

FRONT

PULL THEN REMOVE

FUSES

86716039

Fig. 73 If your headlights are not working, check the fuse first

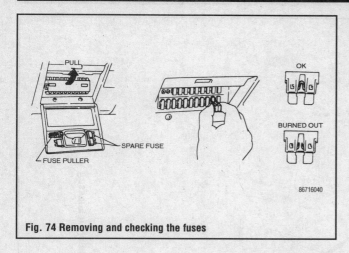

Fig. 74 Removing and checking the fuses

Flashers and Relays

REMOVAL & INSTALLATION

♦ See Figures 75 thru 82

The turn signal and four-way hazard flashers are one combined flasher unit located under the instrument panel to the left of the brake pedal. Replacement is made by unplugging the old flasher unit and plugging in the new one.

Relays are used for horn, air conditioner, blower, fuel pump etc., although obviously not all relays are used on all models. Most other relays are grouped together, and mounted on the right fender in the engine compartment.

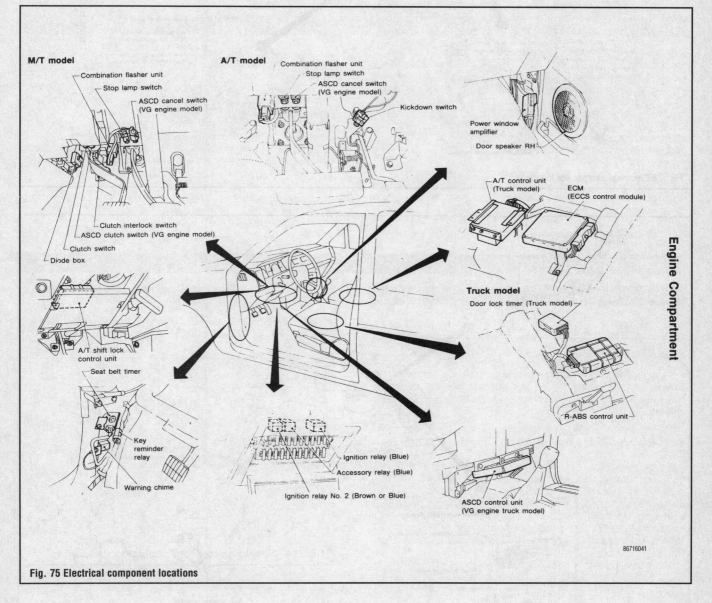

Fig. 75 Electrical component locations

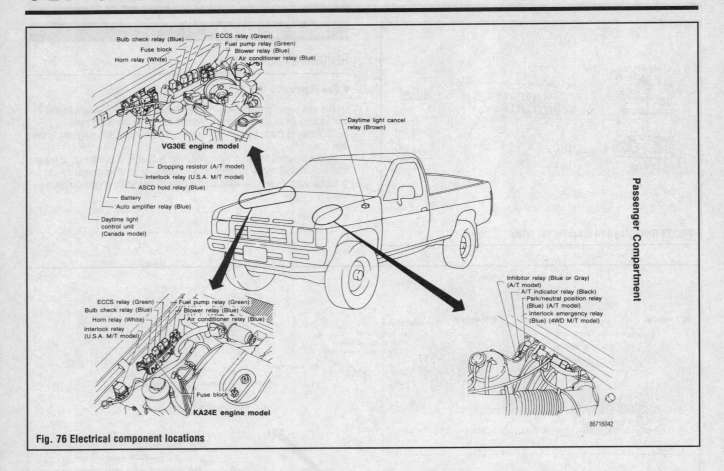

Fig. 76 Electrical component locations

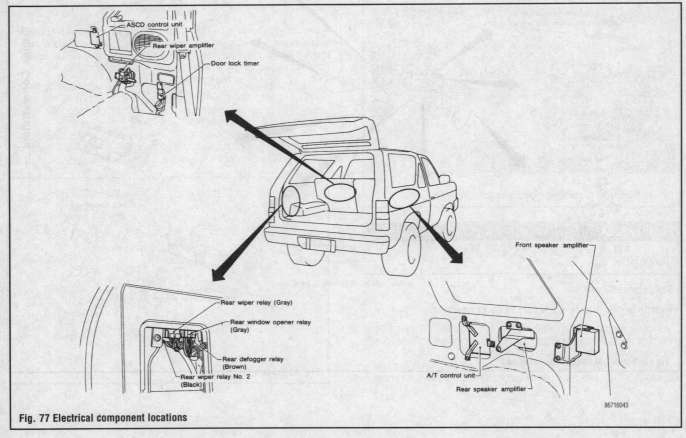

Fig. 77 Electrical component locations

Fig. 78 The engine compartment relay box is clearly marked for correct relay installation

Fig. 79 The fuse box cover under the dash area is also marked

Fig. 80 Remove the fuse box cover holder to gain access to each fuse

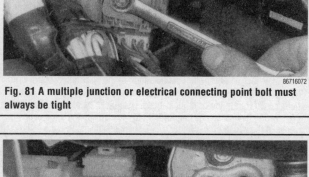

Fig. 81 A multiple junction or electrical connecting point bolt must always be tight

Fig. 82 Removing the multiple junction connection

Fusible Link

REPLACEMENT

▶ See Figures 83 and 84

➡Never wrap the outside of a fusible link with vinyl tape.

All fusible links are located near the battery terminals. Use only replacements of the same electrical capacity as the original. Replacements of a different electrical value will not provide adequate system protection.

The fuse link is a short length of special, Hypalon (high temperature) insulated wire, integral with the engine compartment wiring harness and should not be con-

fused with standard wire. It is several wire gauges smaller than the circuit which it protects. Under no circumstances should a fuse link replacement repair be made using a length of standard wire out from bulk stock or from another wiring harness.

To repair a blown fuse link use the following procedure:

1. Determine which circuit is damaged, its location and the cause of the open fuse link. If the damaged fuse link is one of three fed by a common No. 10 or 12 gauge feed wire, determine the specific affected circuit.

2. Disconnect the negative battery cable.

3. Cut the damaged fuse link from the wiring harness and discard it. If the fuse link is one of three circuits fed by a single feed wire, cut it out of the harness at each splice end and discard it.

4. Identify the proper fuse link and butt connectors for attaching the fuse link to the harness.

5. To repair any fuse link in a 3-link ground with one feed:

a. After cutting the open link out of the harness, cut each of the remaining undamaged fuse links closed to the feed wire weld.

b. Strip approximately ½ in. (13mm) of insulation from the detached ends of the two good fuse links. Then insert two wire ends into one end of a butt connector and carefully push one strip end of the replacement fuse link into the same end of the butt connector and crimp all three firmly together.

➡Care must be taken when fitting the three fuse links into the butt connector as the internal diameter is a snug fit for three wires. Make sure to use a proper crimping tool. Pliers, side cutters, etc., will not apply the proper crimp to retain the wires and withstand a pull test.

c. After crimping the butt connector to the three fuse links, cut the weld portion from the feed wire and strip approximately ½ in. (13mm) of insulation from the end cut. Insert the stripped end into the open end of the butt connector and crimp very firmly.

d. To attach the remaining end of the replacement fuse link, strip approximately ½ in. (13mm) of insulation from the wire end of the circuit from which the blown fuse link was removed, and firmly crimp a butt connector or

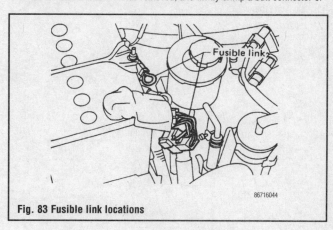

Fig. 83 Fusible link locations

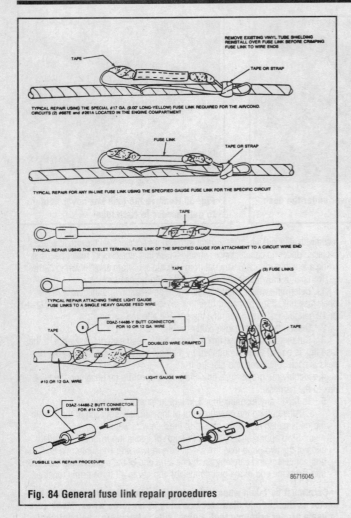

REMOVE EXISTING VINYL TUBE SHIELDING
REINSTALL OVER FUSE LINK BEFORE CRIMPING
FUSE LINK TO WIRE ENDS

TAPE

TAPE OR STRAP

TYPICAL REPAIR USING THE SPECIAL #17 GA. (9.00" LONG-YELLOW) FUSE LINK REQUIRED FOR THE AIR/COND.
CIRCUITS (2) #887E and #261A LOCATED IN THE ENGINE COMPARTMENT

FUSE LINK

TAPE OR STRAP

TYPICAL REPAIR FOR ANY IN-LINE FUSE LINK USING THE SPECIFIED GAUGE FUSE LINK FOR THE SPECIFIC CIRCUIT

TAPE

TYPICAL REPAIR USING THE EYELET TERMINAL FUSE LINK OF THE SPECIFIED GAUGE FOR ATTACHMENT TO A CIRCUIT WIRE END

TAPE

(3) FUSE LINKS

TYPICAL REPAIR ATTACHING THREE LIGHT GAUGE
FUSE LINKS TO A SINGLE HEAVY GAUGE FEED WIRE

TAPE

D3AZ-14488-Y BUTT CONNECTOR
FOR 10 OR 12 GA. WIRE

DOUBLED WIRE CRIMPED

TAPE

#10 OR 12 GA. WIRE

LIGHT GAUGE WIRE

D3AZ-14488-Z BUTT CONNECTOR
FOR #14 OR 18 WIRE

FUSIBLE LINK REPAIR PROCEDURE

86716045

Fig. 84 General fuse link repair procedures

equivalent to the stripped wire. Then, insert the end of the replacement link into the other end of the butt connector and crimp firmly.

e. Using resin core solder with a consistency of 60 percent tin and 40 percent lead, solder the connectors and the wires at the repairs, then insulate with electrical tape.

6. To replace any fuse link on a single circuit in a harness, cut out the damaged portion, strip approximately ½ in. (13mm) of insulation from the two wire ends and attach the appropriate replacement fuse link to the stripped wire ends with two proper size butt connectors. Solder the connectors and wires, then insulate with tape.

7. To repair any fuse link which has an eyelet terminal on one end of such as the charging circuit, cut off the open fuse link behind the weld, strip approximately ½ in. (13mm) of insulation from the cut end and attach the appropriate new eyelet fuse link to the cut stripped wire with an appropriate size butt connector. Solder the connectors and wires at the repair, then insulate with tape.

8. Connect the negative battery cable to the battery and test the system for proper operation.

➡ Do not mistake a resistor wire for a fuse link. The resistor wire is generally longer and has print stating, "resistor—don't cut or splice." When attaching a single No. 16, 17, 18, or 20 gauge fuse link to a heavy gauge wire, always double the stripped wire end of the fuse link before inserting and crimping it into the butt connector for positive wire retention.

Circuit Breakers

Circuit breakers are also located in the fuse box. A circuit breaker is an electrical switch which opens the circuit during an electrical overload. The circuit breaker will remain open until the short or overload condition in the circuit is corrected.

Communication and Additional Electrical Accessories

The electrical system in your vehicle is designed to perform under reasonable operating conditions without interference between components. Before any additional electrical equipment is installed, it is recommended that you consult your Nissan dealer or a reputable repair facility familiar with your vehicle and its systems.

If the vehicle is equipped with mobile radio equipment and/or mobile telephone it may have an effect upon the operation of the Electronic Control Unit (ECU) and Anti-lock Braking System (ABS) control module. Radio Frequency Interference (RFI) from the communications system can be picked up by the vehicle's wiring harnesses and conducted into the ECU, giving it the wrong messages at the wrong time. Although well shielded against RFI, the ECU should be further protected through the following steps:

1. Install the antenna as far as possible from the ECU.

2. Keep the antenna wiring a minimum of eight inches away from any wiring running to the ECU and from the ECU itself. NEVER wind the antenna wire around any other wiring.

3. Mount the equipment as far from the ECU as possible. Be very careful during installation not to drill through any wires or short a wire harness with a mounting screw.

4. Insure that the electrical feed wire(s) to the equipment are properly and tightly connected. Loose connectors can cause interference.

5. Make certain that the equipment is properly grounded to the vehicle. Poor grounding can damage expensive equipment.

6. If possible, make sure the antenna is "trimmed" or adjusted for optimum function.

WIRING DIAGRAMS

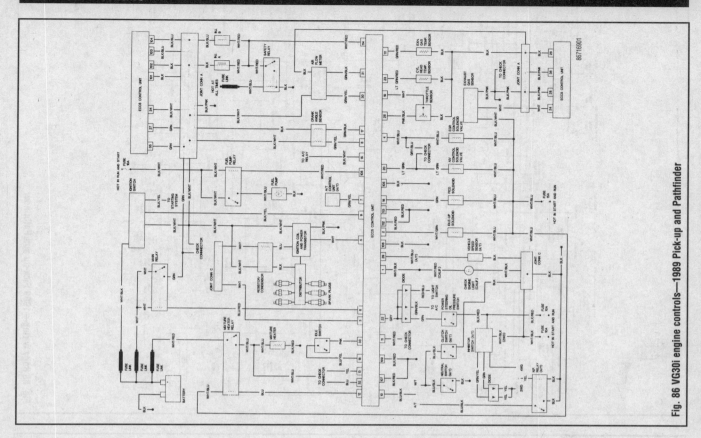

Fig. 86 VG30i engine controls—1989 Pick-up and Pathfinder

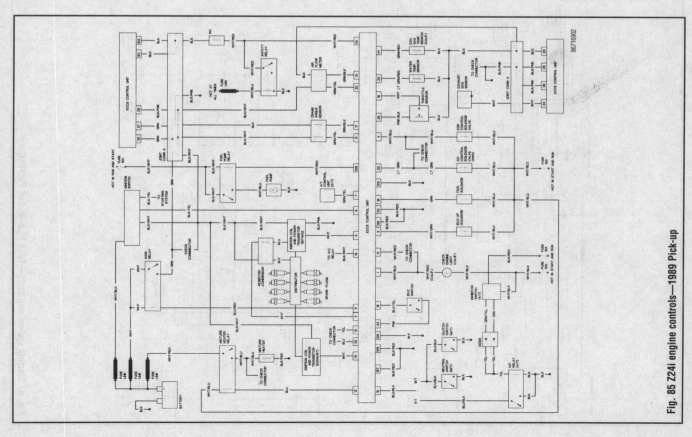

Fig. 85 Z24i engine controls—1989 Pick-up

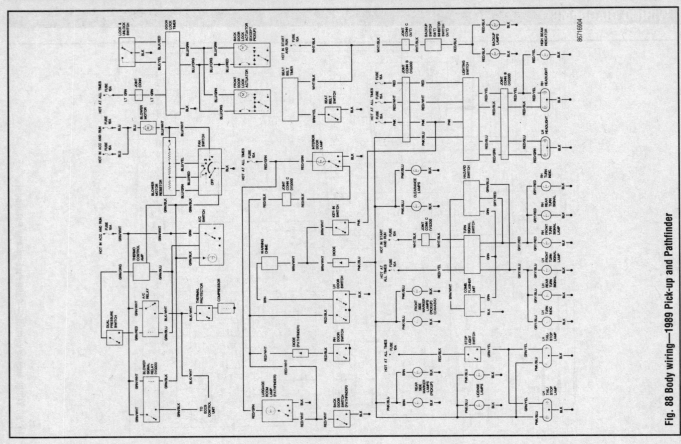

Fig. 88 Body wiring—1989 Pick-up and Pathfinder

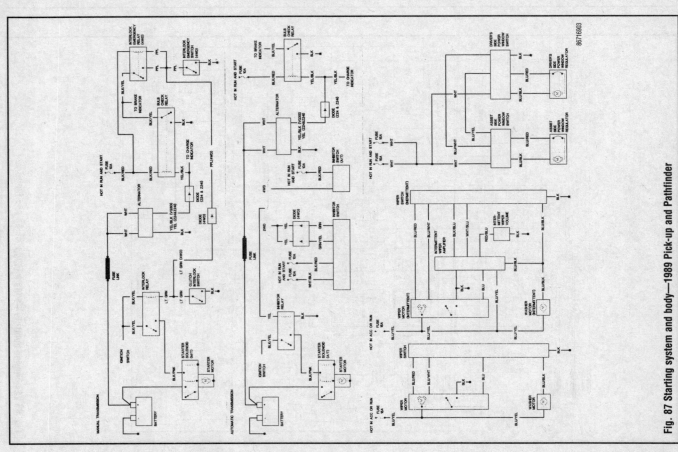

Fig. 87 Starting system and body—1989 Pick-up and Pathfinder

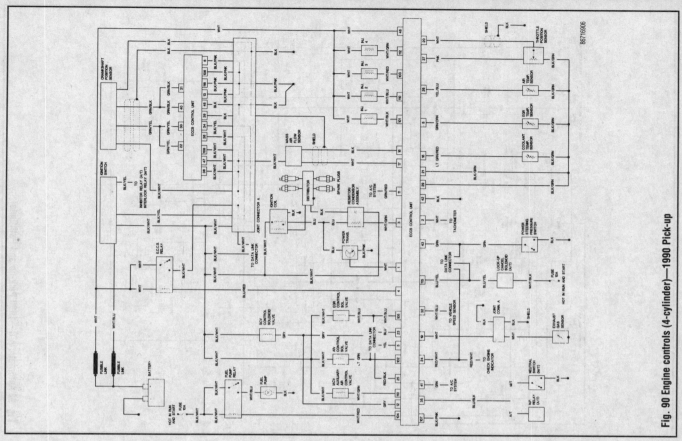

Fig. 90 Engine controls (4-cylinder)—1990 Pick-up

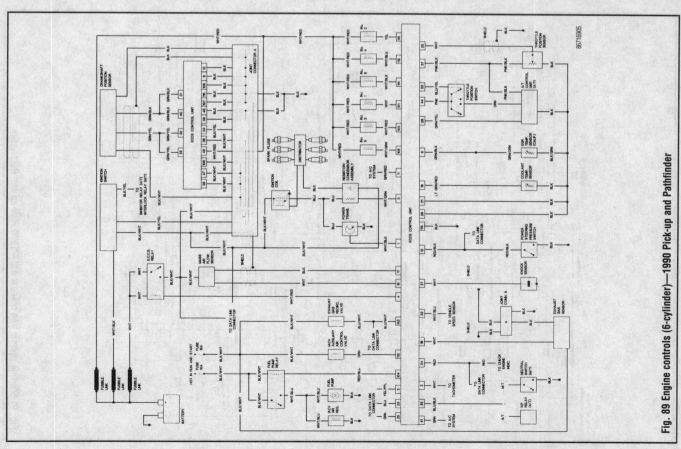

Fig. 89 Engine controls (6-cylinder)—1990 Pick-up and Pathfinder

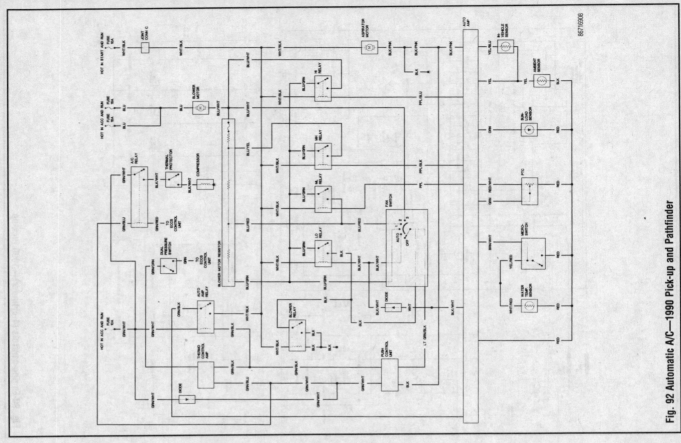

Fig. 92 Automatic A/C—1990 Pick-up and Pathfinder

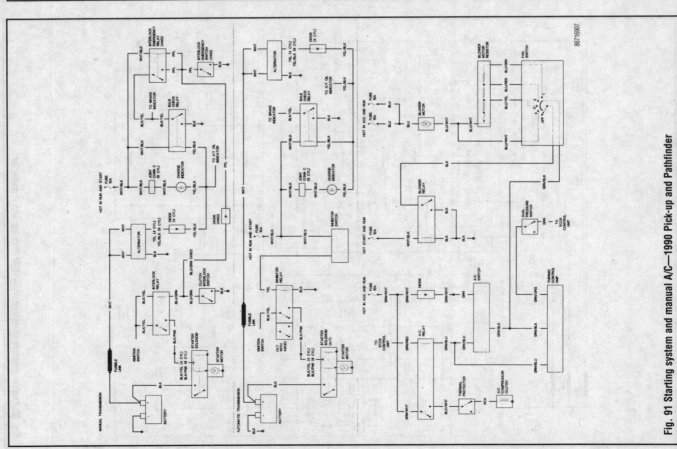

Fig. 91 Starting system and manual A/C—1990 Pick-up and Pathfinder

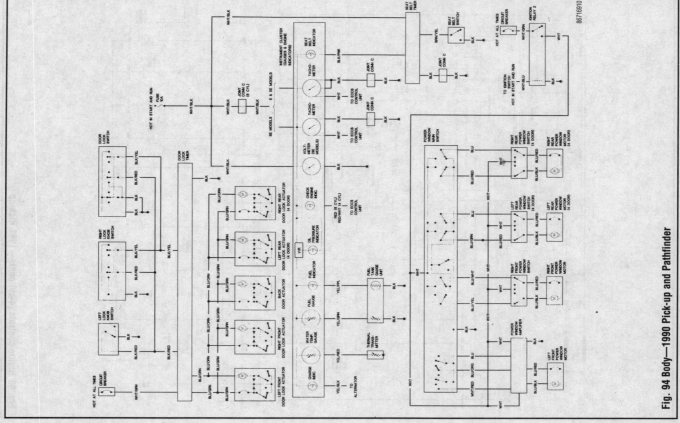

Fig. 94 Body—1990 Pick-up and Pathfinder

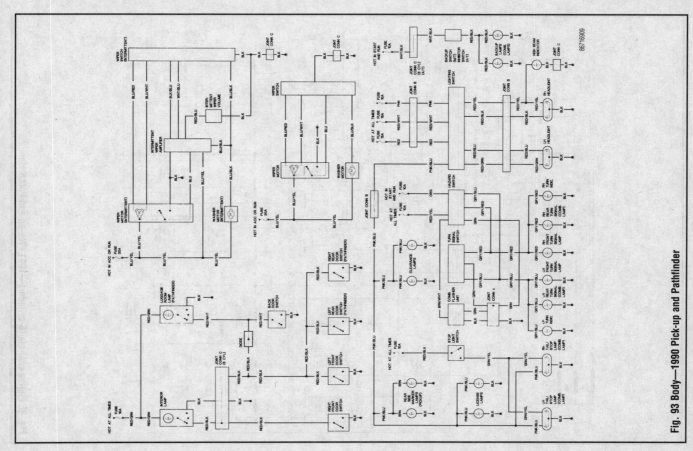

Fig. 93 Body—1990 Pick-up and Pathfinder

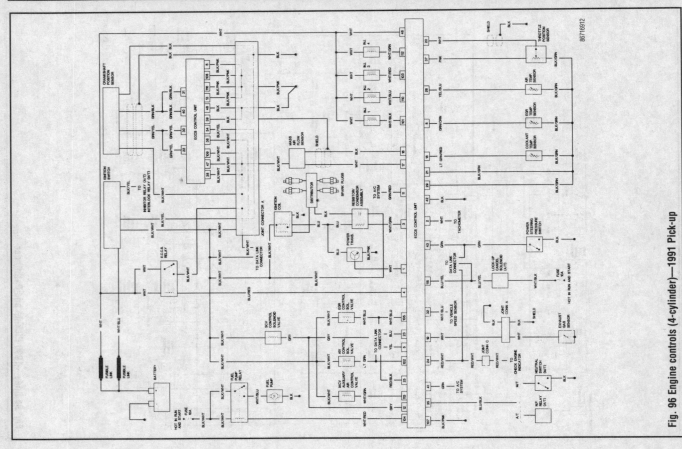

Fig. 96 Engine controls (4-cylinder)—1991 Pick-up

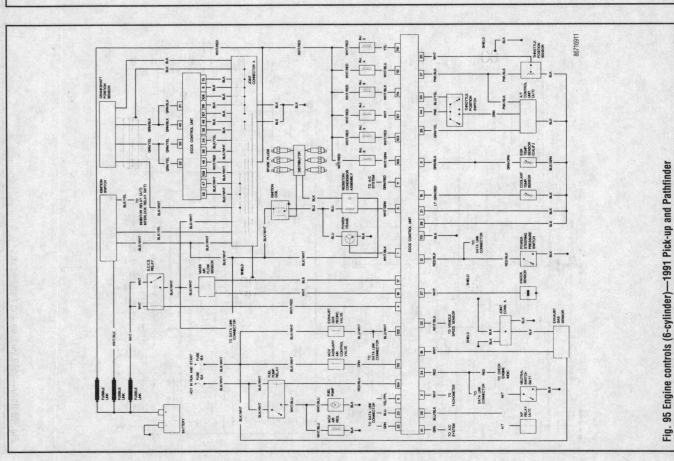

Fig. 95 Engine controls (6-cylinder)—1991 Pick-up and Pathfinder

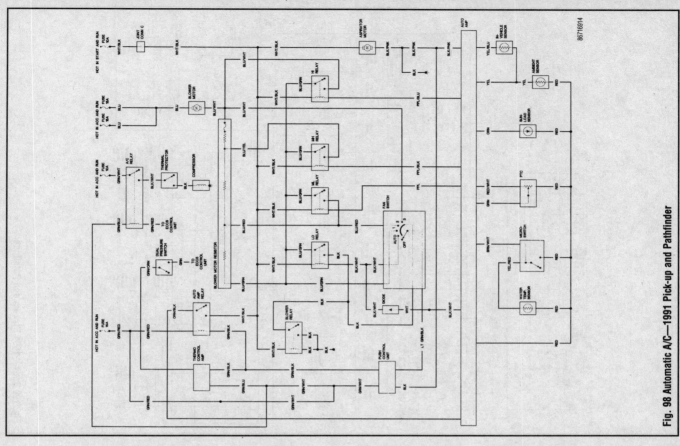

Fig. 98 Automatic A/C—1991 Pick-up and Pathfinder

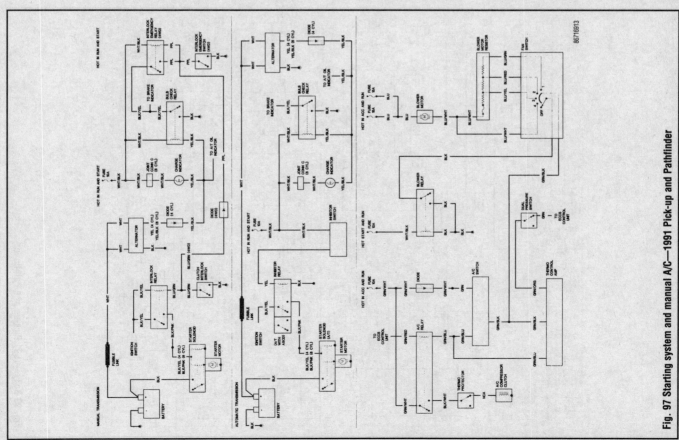

Fig. 97 Starting system and manual A/C—1991 Pick-up and Pathfinder

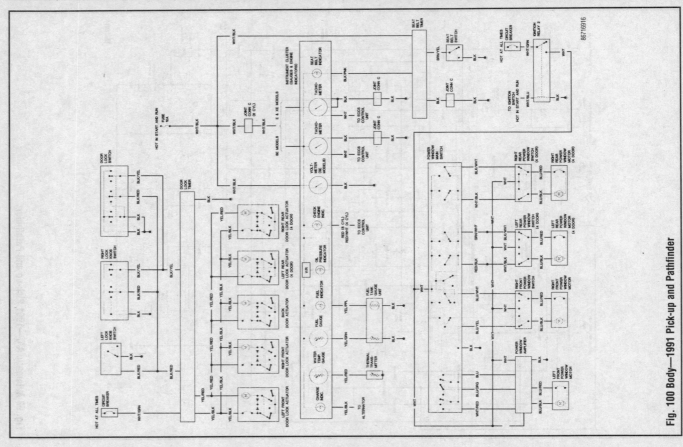

Fig. 100 Body—1991 Pick-up and Pathfinder

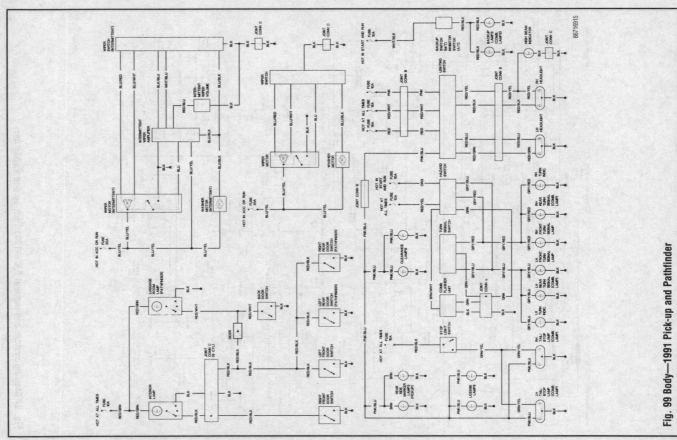

Fig. 99 Body—1991 Pick-up and Pathfinder

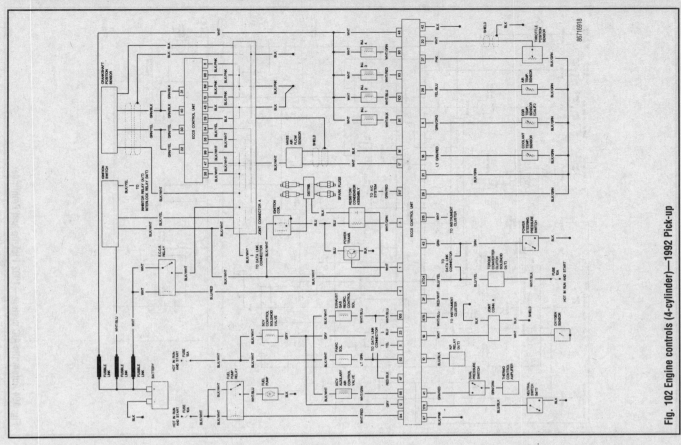

Fig. 102 Engine controls (4-cylinder)—1992 Pick-up

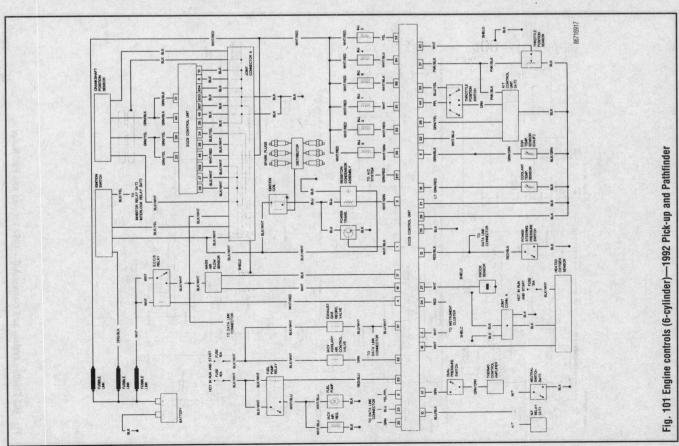

Fig. 101 Engine controls (6-cylinder)—1992 Pick-up and Pathfinder

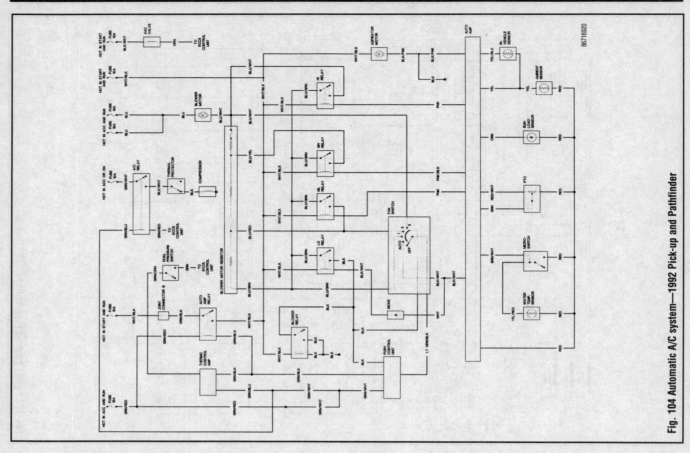

Fig. 104 Automatic A/C system—1992 Pick-up and Pathfinder

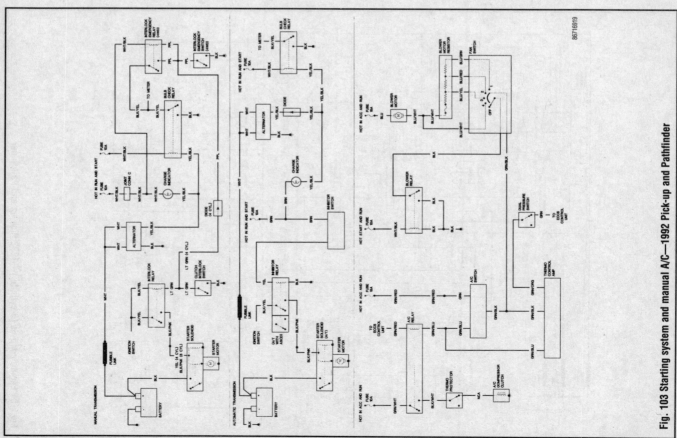

Fig. 103 Starting system and manual A/C—1992 Pick-up and Pathfinder

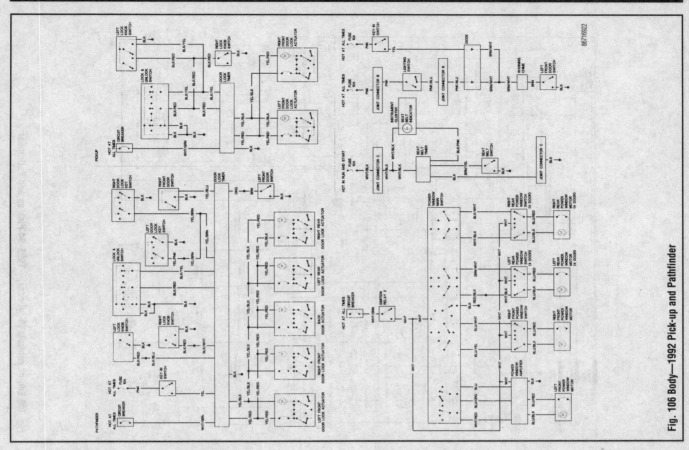

Fig. 106 Body—1992 Pick-up and Pathfinder

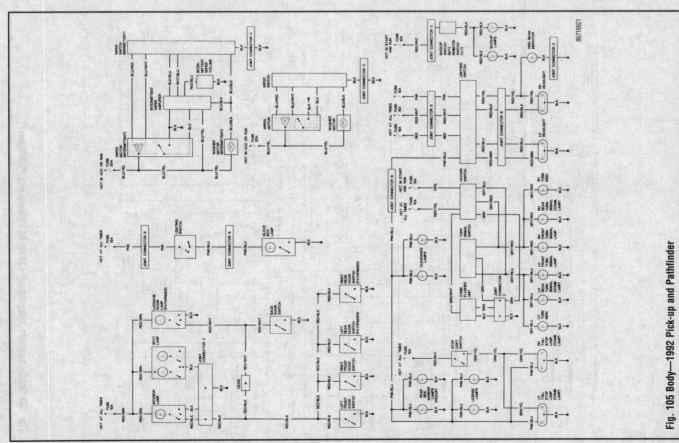

Fig. 105 Body—1992 Pick-up and Pathfinder

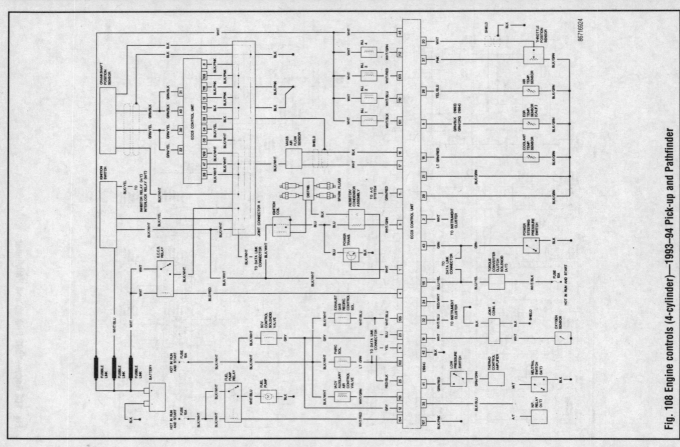

Fig. 108 Engine controls (4-cylinder)—1993–94 Pick-up and Pathfinder

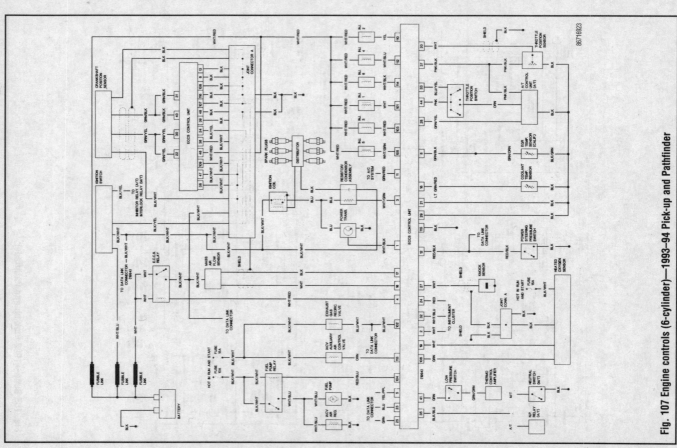

Fig. 107 Engine controls (6-cylinder)—1993–94 Pick-up and Pathfinder

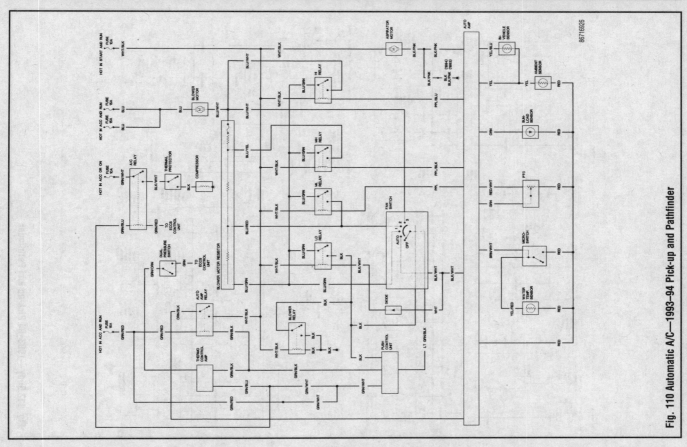

Fig. 110 Automatic A/C—1993–94 Pick-up and Pathfinder

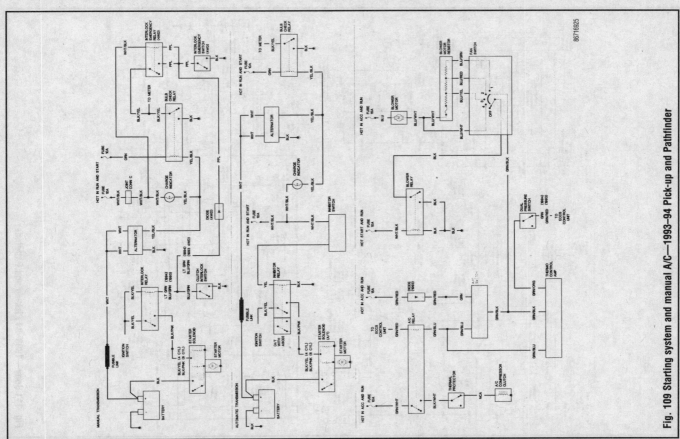

Fig. 109 Starting system and manual A/C—1993–94 Pick-up and Pathfinder

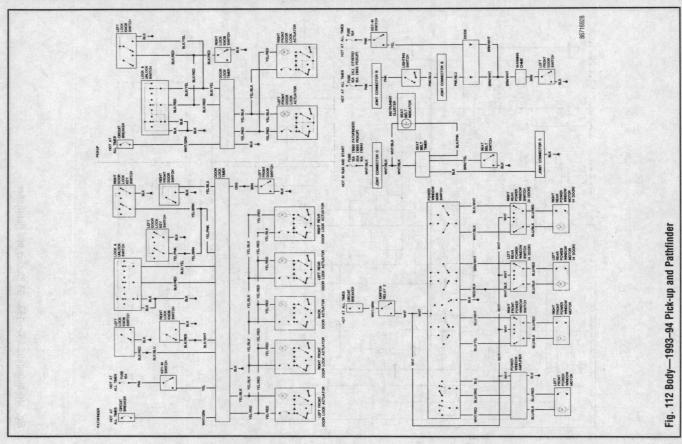

Fig. 112 Body—1993–94 Pick-up and Pathfinder

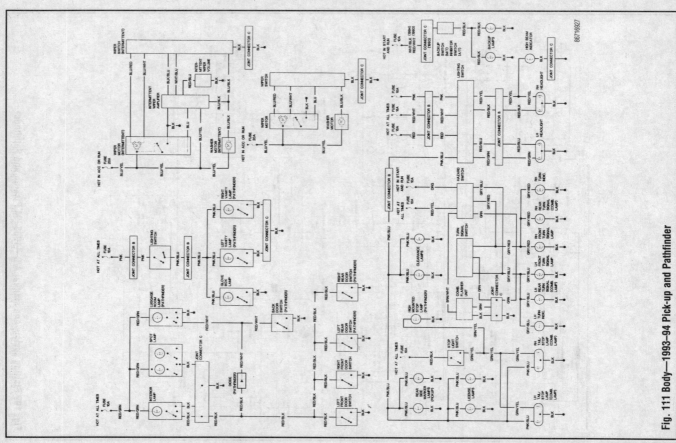

Fig. 111 Body—1993–94 Pick-up and Pathfinder

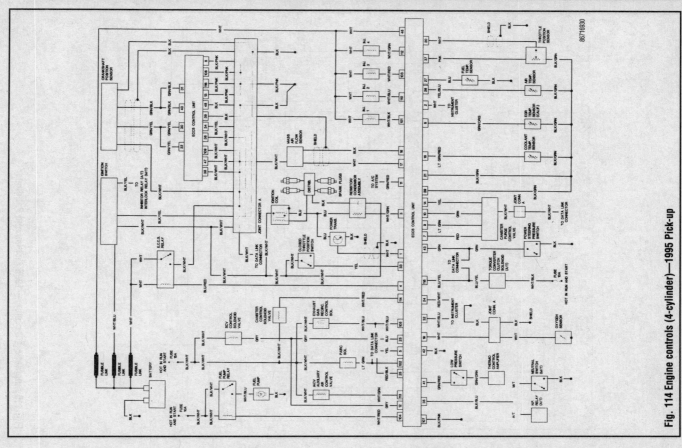

Fig. 114 Engine controls (4-cylinder)—1995 Pick-up

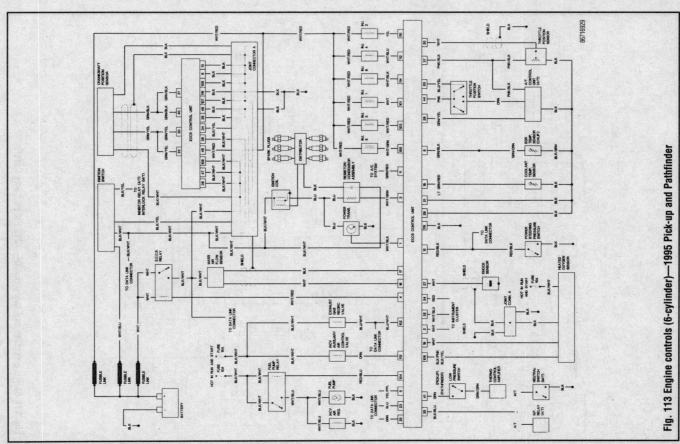

Fig. 113 Engine controls (6-cylinder)—1995 Pick-up and Pathfinder

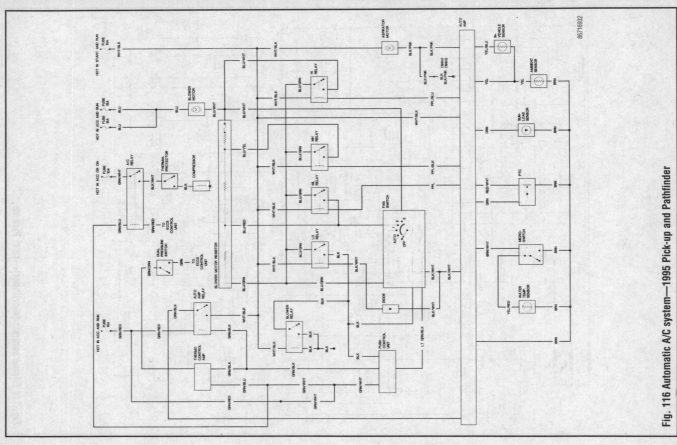

Fig. 116 Automatic A/C system—1995 Pick-up and Pathfinder

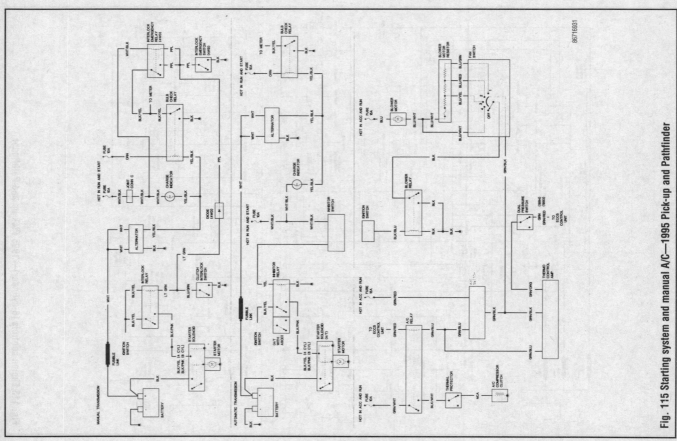

Fig. 115 Starting system and manual A/C—1995 Pick-up and Pathfinder

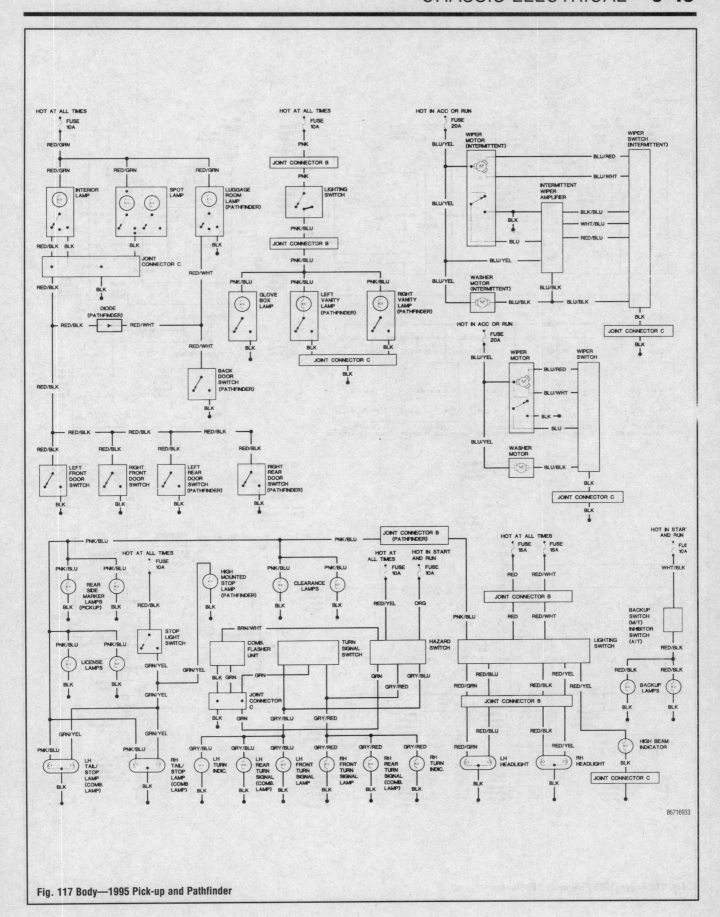

Fig. 117 Body—1995 Pick-up and Pathfinder

86716933

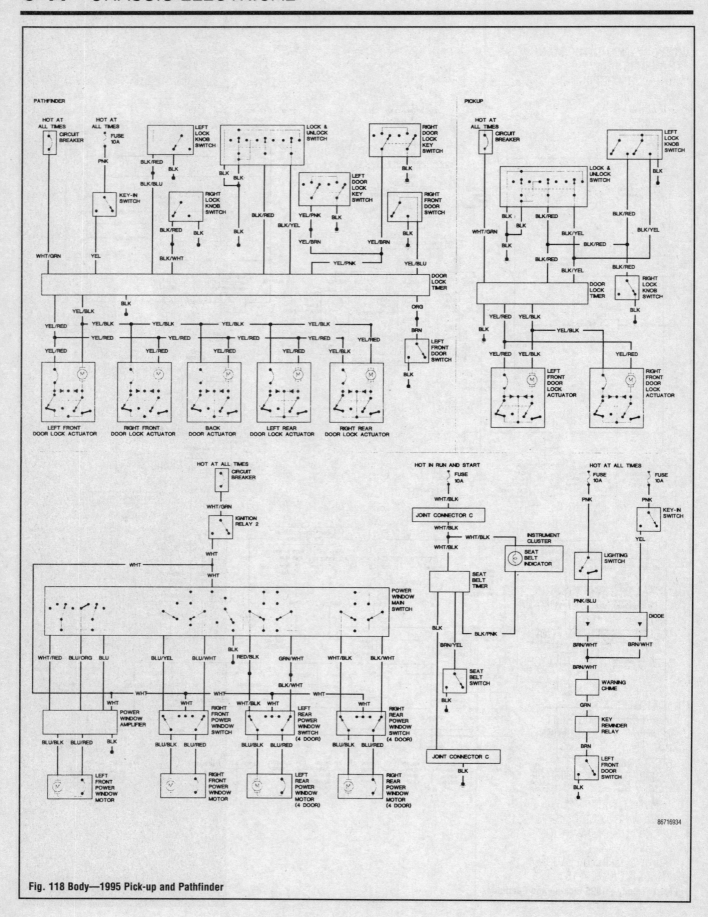

Fig. 118 Body—1995 Pick-up and Pathfinder

86716934

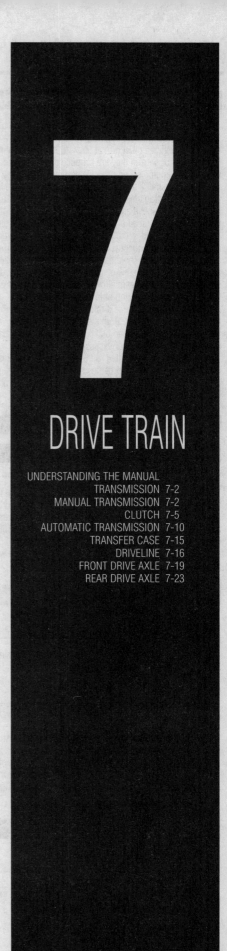

7

DRIVE TRAIN

UNDERSTANDING THE MANUAL TRANSMISSION

Because of the way an internal combustion engine breathes, it can produce torque, or twisting force, only within a narrow speed range. Most modern, overhead valve engines must turn at least 2500 rpm to produce their peak torque. But by 4500 or so rpm they are producing so little torque that continued increases in engine speed produce no power increases. The torque peak on overhead camshaft engines is, generally, much higher, but much narrower.

The manual transmission and clutch are employed to vary the relationship between engine speed and the speed of the wheels so that adequate engine power can be produced under all circumstances. The clutch allows engine torque to be applied to the transmission input shaft gradually, due to mechanical slippage. Consequently, the truck can be started smoothly from a full stop.

The transmission changes the ratio between the rotating speeds of the engine and the wheels by the use of gears; 4-speed or 5-speed transmissions are most common. The lower gears allow full engine power to be applied to the rear wheels during acceleration at low speeds.

The clutch drive plate is a thin disc, the center of which is splined to the transmission input shaft. Both sides of the disc are covered with a layer of material which is similar to brake lining and which is capable of allowing slippage without roughness or excessive noise.

The clutch cover is bolted to the engine flywheel and incorporates a diaphragm spring which provides the pressure to engage the clutch. The cover also houses the pressure plate. The driven disc drive plate is sandwiched between the pressure plate and the smooth surface of the flywheel when the clutch pedal is released, thus forcing it to turn at the same speed as the engine crankshaft.

The transmission contains a mainshaft which passes all the way through the transmission, from the clutch to the driveshaft. This shaft is separated at one point, so that front and rear portions can turn at different speeds.

Power is transmitted by a countershaft in the lower gears and in reverse. The gears of the countershaft mesh with gears on the mainshaft, allowing power to be carried from one to the other. All the countershaft gears are usually integral with that shaft, while several of the mainshaft gears can either rotate independently of the shaft or be locked to it. Shifting from one gear to the next causes one of the gears to be freed from rotating with the shaft and locks another to it. Gears are locked and unlocked by internal dog clutches which slide between the center of the gear and the shaft. The forward gears usually employ synchronizers (friction members which smoothly bring the gear and shaft to the same speed before the toothed dog clutches are engaged).

A clutch pedal free-play adjustment is incorporated in the linkage. Inadequate free-play wears all parts of the clutch releasing mechanisms and may cause slippage. Excessive free-play may cause inadequate release and hard shifting of gears.

Some clutches use a hydraulic system in place of mechanical linkage. If the clutch fails to release, fill the clutch master cylinder with fluid to the proper level and pump the clutch pedal to fill the system. Bleed the system in a similar manner as a brake system. If leaks are located, tighten loose connections and/or overhaul the master or slave cylinder as necessary.

MANUAL TRANSMISSION

Identification

➡ Refer to Section 1, for the manual transmission application chart.

All models covered in this manual have the manual transmission serial number stamped on the front upper face of the transmission case. Models with the Z24i or KA24E engines use an F4W71C 4-speed transmission or the FS5W71C 5-speed transmission. Models with the VG30i or VG30E engines use an FS5R30A 5-speed transmission.

All models have a one piece case, an adapter plate which supports the mainshaft and countershaft, and an extension housing.

Adjustments

LINKAGE AND SHIFTER

All models utilize a floor-mounted shifter and an internally-mounted shift linkage. No external adjustments are either necessary or possible.

CLUTCH INTERLOCK SWITCH

▶ See Figure 1

Adjust the clearance (C) between the clutch pedal stopper bracket and the threaded end of the clutch switch while fully depressing the clutch pedal. There is a lock-nut on the back side of the switch mounting bracket, loosen it and then rotate the nut on the front of the bracket to move the switch assembly in or out. Clearance should be 0.012–0.039 in. (0.3–1.0mm). Tighten the lock-nut to 9–11 ft. lbs. (12–15 Nm).

Shift Linkage

REMOVAL & INSTALLATION

All models utilize and internally-mounted shift linkage. Removal and installation procedures are covered in unit overhaul.

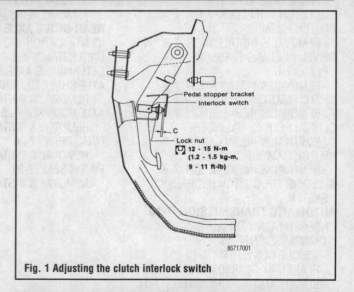

Pedal stopper bracket
Interlock switch

C

Lock nut
12 - 15 N·m
(1.2 - 1.5 kg-m,
9 - 11 ft-lb)

86717001

Fig. 1 Adjusting the clutch interlock switch

Shift Lever

REMOVAL & INSTALLATION

▶ See Figures 2, 3, 4, 5 and 6

All models utilize a floor-mounted shift lever.
1. Unscrew the shifter knob by turning it counterclockwise and then unclip the shifter dust boot where it connects to the console.
2. Slide the boot over the lever. Remove the lower boot retainer clip and slide the lower boot up the lever.
3. Using circlip pliers, remove the retaining circlip and remove the shift lever.
4. When installing the shift lever, use a new circlip and lower dust boot.

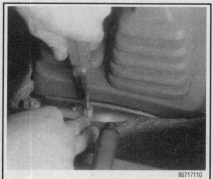

Fig. 2 Remove the shifter boot retaining ring screws

Fig. 3 After removing the screws, lift the retainer ring up

Fig. 4 The boot must be lifted for access to the shifter circlip

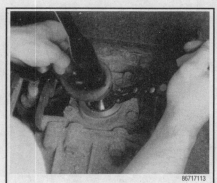

Fig. 5 Remove the circlip to remove the shift lever with a pair of snapring pliers

Fig. 6 Remove the shift lever from the transmission assembly

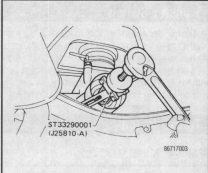

Fig. 7 Removing the extension housing oil seal

Extension Housing Oil Seal

REMOVAL & INSTALLATION

▶ See Figures 7, 8 and 9

1. Raise the truck and support it with jackstands.
2. Disconnect the driveshaft at the rear of the transmission.
3. Install a seal puller (special tool ST33290001/J25810-A) to the extension housing. Put a ratchet on the tool and remove the oil seal.
4. Position a new seal in the extension housing and then mount a seal drift (special tool ST33400001/J26082). Drive the seal into place using the drift and a mallet.

Back-Up Light Switch

REMOVAL & INSTALLATION

1. Raise the vehicle and support it safely with jackstands.
2. Disconnect the electrical connections from the switch (right side of the transmission case).
3. Unscrew the switch and remove it from the transmission housing. When removing, be sure to position a drain pan under the transmission to catch any leaking fluid.
4. Install the switch and connect the electrical lead. Tighten the switch to 14–22 ft. lbs. (20–29 Nm). Lower the truck and check the fluid level.

Neutral Switch

The neutral switch provides feedback on transmission position. It is attached to the front of the transmission and connected to its wiring harness via a square plastic connector which is secured with an integral safety clip.

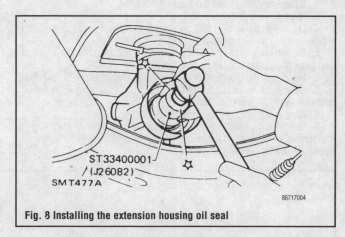

Fig. 8 Installing the extension housing oil seal

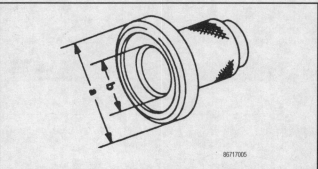

Fig. 9 Special drift tool used to install the oil seal (A) should be 60mm and (B) should be 47mm

Fig. 10 Remove the torsion spring

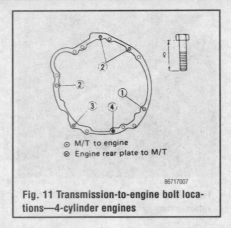

⊙ M/T to engine
⊗ Engine rear plate to M/T

Fig. 11 Transmission-to-engine bolt locations—4-cylinder engines

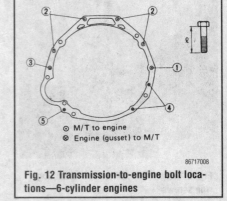

⊙ M/T to engine
⊗ Engine (gusset) to M/T

Fig. 12 Transmission-to-engine bolt locations—6-cylinder engines

Transfer Switch

The transfer switch provides feedback to the transfer case for 4WD models. It is attached to the front of the transmission and connected to its wiring harness via two square plastic connectors. Models with the VG30E engine have safety clips on their connectors that positively engage by snapping into place. Models with the KA24E engine have connectors that simply plug in. The transfer switch is approximately the same position for A/T and M/T models.

Transmission

REMOVAL & INSTALLATION

◆ **See Figures 10 thru 20**

1. Disconnect the negative battery cable.
2. If necessary, disconnect the accelerator linkage.
3. Raise the front of the truck and support it with jackstands.
4. Disconnect the exhaust pipe from the manifold and bracket, if necessary, to gain clearance for transmission removal.
5. Tag and disconnect any switches that are connected to the transmission case (back-up, neutral, top gear or overdrive).
6. Disconnect the speedometer cable where it attaches to the transmission.
7. Remove the driveshaft(s). Don't forget to plug the opening in the rear extension so that oil won't flow out.
8. Remove the clutch slave cylinder.
9. Remove the rubber boot and console box (if so equipped). Place the shift lever in neutral, remove the circlip and then remove the shifter. On 4wd models remove the transfer case shift lever also.

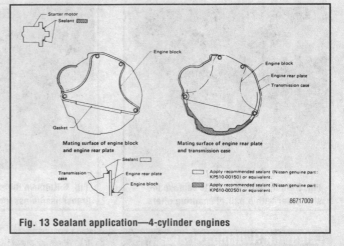

Fig. 13 Sealant application—4-cylinder engines

10. Support the engine by placing a jack under the oil pan with a wooden block used between the jack and the pan.

➡ **Never position the jack directly under the oil pan drain plug.**

11. Support the transmission with a transmission jack.
12. Loosen the rear engine mount securing nuts temporarily and then remove the crossmember. On 4wd models, remove the torsion bar springs.
13. Lower the rear of the engine slightly to allow additional clearance.

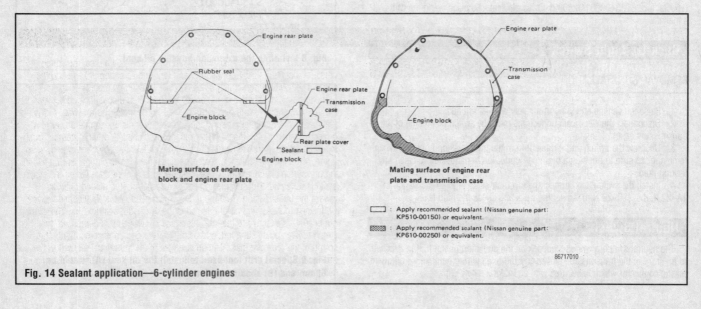

Fig. 14 Sealant application—6-cylinder engines

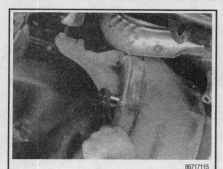

Fig. 15 Remove the bolts from the transmission gussets or brackets before removal of the assembly

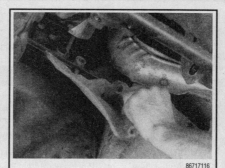

Fig. 16 View of engine-to-transmission supporting bracket—note location for proper installation

Fig. 17 Remove the lower mounting bolt for the transfer case shifter lever

Fig. 18 After removing the hold-down bolt remove, the transfer case lever

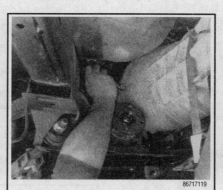

Fig. 19 Remove the transmission retaining bolts with box-type wrench

Fig. 20 Remove the clutch slave cylinder from the transmission assembly

14. Remove the starter electrical connections and the starter motor.

15. Remove the transmission-to-engine mounting bolts, lower the transmission (or transmission and transfer case assembly) and remove it toward the rear.

To install:

16. Install the transmission in the correct position. Tighten all the transmission-to-engine mounting bolts.

   a. On Z24i and KA24E engines, tighten the 4 longest bolts (65mm and 60mm) to 29–36 ft. lbs. (39–49 Nm); tighten the 2 shortest bolts (25mm and 16mm) to 14–18 ft. lbs. (19–25 Nm).

   b. On VG30i and VG30E engines, tighten the 5 longest bolts (65mm and 60mm) to 29–36 ft. lbs. (39–49 Nm); tighten the 4 shortest bolts (55mm, 30mm and 16mm) to 22–29 ft. lbs. (29–39 Nm).

17. Install the starter motor and electrical connections.

18. Install the crossmember assembly and tighten all retaining nuts to crossmember and rear engine mounts. Install the torsion bars on 4wd models.

19. Install the shifter(s). Install the rubber boot and console box if so equipped.

20. Install the clutch slave cylinder.

21. Install the driveshaft(s) and connect the speedometer cable.

22. Connect any switches that are connected to the transmission case (back-up, neutral, transfer switch).

23. Connect the exhaust pipe to the manifold and bracket if necessary.

24. Connect the accelerator linkage.

25. Connect the negative battery cable. Bleed the clutch hydraulic system if necessary. Road test the vehicle for proper operation.

CLUTCH

Understanding the Clutch

The purpose of the clutch is to engage and disengage engine power from the transmission. A vehicle at rest requires a lot of engine torque to get all that weight moving. An internal combustion engine does not develop a high starting torque (unlike steam engines), so it must be allowed to operate without any load until it builds up enough torque to move the vehicle. To an extent, torque increases with engine rpm. The clutch allows the engine to build up torque by physically disconnecting the engine from the transmission, relieving the engine of any load or resistance. The transfer of engine power to the transmission (the load) must be smooth and gradual; if it weren't, drive line components would wear out or break quickly. This power transfer is made possible by gradually releasing the clutch pedal. The clutch disc and pressure plate are the connecting link between the engine and transmission. When the clutch pedal is released, the disc and plate contact each other (clutch engagement), physically joining the engine and transmission. When the pedal is pushed in, the disc and plate separate (the clutch is disengaged), disconnecting the engine from the transmission.

The clutch assembly consists of the flywheel, the clutch disc, the clutch pressure plate, the throw-out bearing and fork, the actuating linkage and the pedal. The flywheel and clutch pressure plate (driving members) are connected to the engine crankshaft and rotate with it. The clutch disc is located between the flywheel and pressure plate; it is splined to the transmission shaft. A driving member is one that is attached to the engine and transfers engine power to a driven member (clutch disc) on the transmission shaft. A driving member (pressure plate) rotates (drives) a driven member (clutch disc) on contact and, in so doing, turns the transmission shaft. There is a circular diaphragm spring within the pressure plate cover (transmission side). In a relaxed state (when the clutch pedal is fully released), this spring is convex; that is, it is dished outward toward the transmission. Pushing in the clutch pedal actuates attached linkage. Connected to the other end of this rod is the throw-out bearing fork. The throw-out bearing is attached to the fork. When the clutch pedal is depressed, the clutch linkage pushes the fork and bearing forward to contact the diaphragm spring of the pressure plate. The outer edges of the spring are secured to the pressure plate and are pivoted on rings so that when the center of the spring is compressed by the throw-out bearing, the outer edges bow outward and, by so doing, pull the pressure plate in the same direction away from the clutch disc. This action separates the disc from the plate, disengaging the clutch and allowing the transmission to be shifted into another gear. A coil type clutch return spring attached to the clutch pedal arm permits full release of the pedal. Releasing the pedal pulls the throw-out bearing away from the diaphragm spring resulting in a reversal of spring position. As bearing pressure is gradually released from the spring center, the outer edges of the spring bow outward, pushing the pressure plate into closer contact with the clutch disc. As the disc and plate move closer together, friction between the two increases and slippage is reduced until, when full spring pressure is applied (by fully releasing the pedal), the speed of the disc and plate are the same. This stops all slipping, creating a direct connection between the plate and disc which results in the transfer of power from the engine to the transmission. The clutch disc is now rotating with the pressure plate at engine speed and, because it is splined to the transmission shaft, the shaft now turns at the same engine speed. Understanding clutch operation can be rather difficult at first; if you're still confused after reading this, consider the following analogy. The action of the diaphragm spring can be compared to that of an oil can bottom. The bottom of an oil can is shaped very much like the clutch diaphragm spring and pushing in on the can bottom and then releasing it produces a similar effect. As mentioned earlier, the clutch pedal return spring permits the full release of the pedal and reduces linkage slack due to wear. As the linkage wears, clutch free-pedal travel will increase and free-travel will decrease as the clutch wears. Free-travel is actually throw-out bearing lash.

The transmission varies the gear ratio between the engine and rear wheels. It can be shifted to change engine speed as driving conditions and loads change. The transmission allows disengaging and reversing power from the engine to the wheels.

Adjustments

PEDAL HEIGHT

▶ **See Figure 21**

The pedal height measurement is gauged from the angle section of the floorboard to the center of the clutch pedal pad as illustrated.

Adjust the pedal height by loosening the lock-nut on the pedal stopper, clutch switch or ASCD switch and turning the adjusting bolt to provide the following specified heights:
- Z24i and KA24E engines: 9.29–9.69 in. (236–246mm)
- VG30i and VG30E engines: 8.94–9.33 in. (227–237mm)

PEDAL FREE-PLAY

▶ **See Figure 22**

The free-play measurement is the total travel of the clutch pedal from the fully released position to where resistance is felt as the pedal is pushed downward.

Adjust the pedal free-play by loosening the pushrod lock-nut and turning the clevis. Free-play should be 0.039–0.059 in. (1.0–1.5mm).

CLUTCH INTERLOCK

Clutch switch adjustment is detailed in the manual transmission section.

Clutch Pedal

REMOVAL & INSTALLATION

▶ **See Figures 23 and 24**

1. Pull out the cotter pin and remove the master cylinder pushrod clevis pin. Pull the pedal from the clevis.
2. Remove the fulcrum pin mounting nut and slide out the pin (be sure to catch the clutch assist spring when it falls off the pin). Remove the pedal from the pedal bracket being careful not to damage the clutch or ASCD switches.
To install:
3. Position the clutch pedal in the pedal bracket and then slide the fulcrum pin through the pedal and the spring. Tighten the mounting nut to 12–16 ft. lbs. (16–22 Nm).
4. Reconnect the master cylinder pushrod and install a new cotter pin into the clevis pin.
5. Check pedal height, free-play and switch adjustments.

Driven Disc and Pressure Plate

The clutch is a hydraulically operated single plate, dry friction disc, diaphragm spring type.

It is operated by a clutch pedal which is mechanically connected to a clutch master cylinder. When the pedal is depressed, the piston in the master cylinder

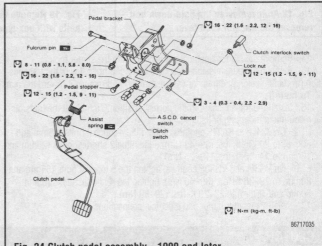

Fig. 24 Clutch pedal assembly—1990 and later

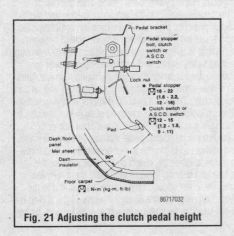

Fig. 21 Adjusting the clutch pedal height

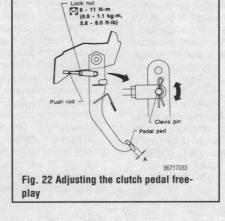

Fig. 22 Adjusting the clutch pedal free-play

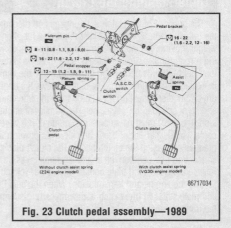

Fig. 23 Clutch pedal assembly—1989

is moved in the master cylinder bore. This movement compresses the hydraulic fluid in the cylinder causing pressure which is transferred through a tube to the slave cylinder.

The slave cylinder is mounted to the clutch housing with its piston connected to the clutch release lever. The hydraulic pressure in the slave cylinder forces the cylinder piston to travel down the cylinder bore and move the clutch release lever, disengaging the clutch.

REMOVAL & INSTALLATION

▶ See Figures 25 thru 38

❈❈ CAUTION

The clutch driven disc contains asbestos, which has been determined to be a cancer causing agent. Never clean clutch surfaces with compressed air! Avoid inhaling any dust from any clutch surface! When cleaning clutch surfaces, use a commercially available brake cleaning fluid.

1. Raise the vehicle and support it with jackstands.
2. Remove the transmission.
3. Mark the clutch assembly-to-flywheel relationship with paint or a center punch so that the clutch assembly can be reassembled in the same position from which it is removed. Insert a clutch aligning tool (dummy shaft) into the hub. This tool is available from your local Nissan dealer or an auto parts store. It is important to support the weight of the clutch while the retaining bolts are being removed.
4. Loosen the clutch cover-to-flywheel attaching bolts, one turn at a time in an alternating sequence, until the spring tension is relieved to avoid distorting or bending the clutch cover. Remove the clutch assembly.

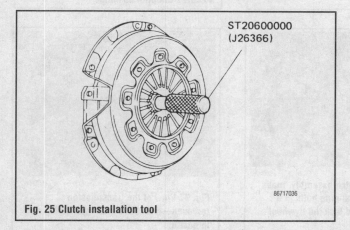

Fig. 25 Clutch installation tool

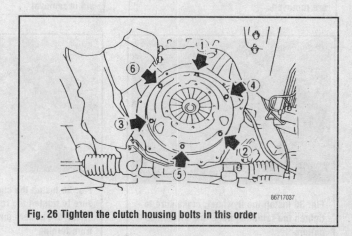

Fig. 26 Tighten the clutch housing bolts in this order

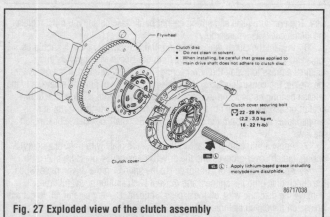

Fig. 27 Exploded view of the clutch assembly

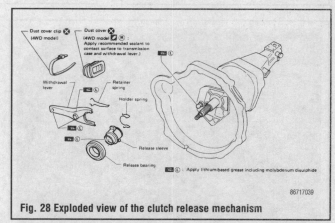

Fig. 28 Exploded view of the clutch release mechanism

Fig. 29 View of the clutch assembly after the transmission is removed

Fig. 30 Install a special aligning tool before removing the clutch assembly

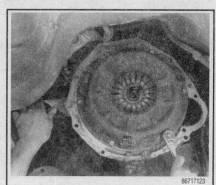

Fig. 31 When removing the clutch assembly lock the flywheel from turning

Fig. 32 View of the clutch pressure plate and disc assembly after the retaining bolts are removed

Fig. 33 When removing the flywheel assembly lock the flywheel from turning to aid in removal

Fig. 34 Remove the flywheel, do not forget to check the pilot bushing

Fig. 35 Install the flywheel, make sure to tighten the retaining bolts in a crisscross pattern

Fig. 36 Install the clutch assembly, make sure to tighten the retaining bolts in a crisscross pattern and lock the flywheel from turning

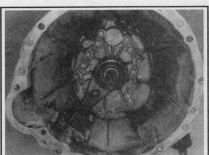

Fig. 37 View of the transmission removed—note the clutch release bearing in position

Fig. 38 Remove the release bearing from the transmission mainshaft

To install:

5. Inspect the flywheel for scoring, roughness, or signs of overheating. Light scoring may be cleaned up with emery cloth, but any deep grooves or scoring warrant replacement or refacing (if possible) of the flywheel. If the clutch facings or flywheel are oily, inspect the transmission front cover oil seal, the pilot bushing, and engine rear seals, etc. for leakage, and correct before replacing the clutch. If the pilot bushing in the crankshaft is worn, replace it. Install it using a soft hammer. The factory supplied part does not have to be oiled, but check the part manufacturer's instructions if you are using an aftermarket part. Inspect the clutch cover for wear or scoring, and replace as neces-

sary. The pressure plate and spring cannot be disassembled; you must replace the clutch cover as an assembly.

6. Inspect the clutch release bearing. If it is rough or noisy, it should be replaced. The bearing can be removed from the sleeve with a puller; this requires a press to install the new bearing. After installation, coat the groove in the sleeve, the contact surfaces of the release lever, pivot pin and sleeve, and the release bearing contact surfaces on the transmission front cover with a light coat of grease. Be careful not to use too much grease, which will run at high temperatures and get onto the clutch facings. Reinstall the release bearing on the lever.

7. Apply a thin coat of grease to the pressure plate wire ring, diaphragm spring, clutch cover grooves and the drive bosses on the pressure plate.

8. Apply a thin coat of Lubriplate® to the splines in the driven plate. Slide the clutch disc onto the splines, and move it back and forth several times. Remove the disc and wipe off the excess lubricant. Be very careful not to get any grease on the clutch facings.

9. Assemble the clutch cover and the clutch plate on the clutch alignment arbor.

10. Align the marks made on the clutch cover and the flywheel (if the old cover is being used) and install the clutch cover-to-flywheel attaching bolts. Three dowels are used to locate the clutch cover on the flywheel properly. Tighten the bolts in an alternating sequence one turn at a time to 16–22 ft. lbs. (22–29 Nm). Remove the aligning arbor (dummy shaft).

11. Install the transmission.

Clutch Master Cylinder

REMOVAL & INSTALLATION

♦ See Figure 39

➡Replace the clutch master cylinder and slave cylinder as a set for added reliability.

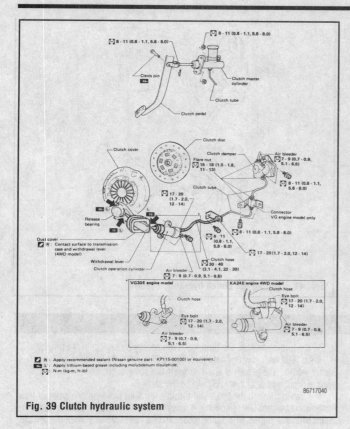

Fig. 39 Clutch hydraulic system

Fig. 40 Bleeding the clutch release cylinder

1. Disconnect the master cylinder pushrod from the clutch pedal.
2. Remove the hydraulic line from the master cylinder being careful not to damage the compression fitting.
3. Remove the two bolts holding the clutch master cylinder to the engine compartment.

✳✳ WARNING

Brake fluid dissolves paint. Do not allow it to drip onto the body when removing the master cylinder. If any does get on the paint, wipe it off immediately.

To install:
4. Install the master cylinder and tighten the mounting bolts to 6–8 ft. lbs. (8–11 Nm). Partially tighten the hydraulic line and then tighten the cylinder mounting bolts.
5. Connect the pushrod to the clutch pedal.
6. Bleed the system and adjust the clutch pedal.

Clutch Release Cylinder

REMOVAL & INSTALLATION

▶ **See Figure 40**

➡ Replace the slave or release cylinder and clutch master cylinder as a set for greater reliability.

1. Raise the front of the truck and support it on jackstands.
2. Remove the tension spring on the clutch fork.
3. Remove the hydraulic line from the release cylinder. Be careful not to damage the fitting.

➡ Cap the line openings immediately to prevent system contamination or excessive fluid loss.

4. Turn the release cylinder pushrod in sufficiently to gain clearance from the fork.

5. Remove the mounting bolts and withdraw the cylinder.
To install:
6. Install the hydraulic line from the master cylinder.
7. Position the cylinder on the clutch housing and install the clamp and retaining screws. Tighten the attaching bolts to 22–30 ft. lbs. (30–40 Nm).

➡ The system must be bled after the cylinder is reinstalled.

Clutch Damper

REMOVAL & INSTALLATION

1. Loosen the union nuts and disconnect the two hydraulic lines at the damper.
2. Remove the mounting bolts and then remove the clutch damper from the firewall.
To install:
3. Install the damper and tighten the bolts to 6–8 ft. lbs. (8–11 Nm).
4. Reconnect the hydraulic lines being careful not to damage the union nuts.
5. Bleed the system.

Bleeding the Clutch Hydraulic System

▶ **See Figure 41**

➡ This procedure may be utilized when either the clutch master or release cylinder has been removed or if any of the hydraulic lines have been disturbed. On all models that incorporate a clutch damper in the hydraulic system, first perform the procedure for the clutch damper and then perform the procedure for the release cylinder.

✳✳ WARNING

Do not spill brake fluid on the body of the vehicle as it will destroy the paint.

1. Fill the master cylinder reservoir with brake fluid and leave the cap removed.

➡ You may have to re-fill the reservoir to prevent sucking in air into the lines, so keep your eye on the fluid level as you perform the bleeding.

2. Attach a clear vinyl tube to the bleeder valve and place the other end into a jar half-full of clean brake fluid.
3. Have an assistant pump the clutch pedal so that the air and/or contaminated fluid in the system can be released.

➡ If the hydraulic lines are empty when beginning this procedure, it may take several pumps at the pedal before any fluid appears at the bleeder valve. In this initial pressurizing stage, you may opt to remove the valve completely and use your finger as a stopper as a stopper to help expedite the process by eliminating repeated opening and closing of the valve. Once fluid appears however, replace the valve and proceed with step 4.

4. With the pedal fully depressed, open the bleeder valve with the correct size open end wrench to release the fluid and then close the valve before the pedal is released.

5. With the valve now closed, release the pedal repeat the process by again depressing the pedal and opening the bleeder valve to let the fluid escape.

➡ Be careful to have the bleeder valve fully closed before your assistant releases the pedal (even part way) or air will be sucked in through the bleeder valve and you will defeat your purpose.

6. Continue to repeat the bleeding process until the fluid coming out is clean and free of any air bubbles.

7. When sure there are no more air bubbles in the system, tighten the plug fully (with the pedal depressed). Replace the plastic cap over the bleeder valve.

8. Fill the master cylinder to the correct level with brake fluid.

9. Check the system for leaks.

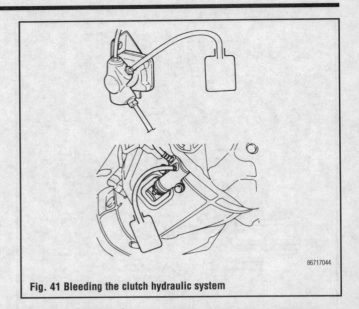

Fig. 41 Bleeding the clutch hydraulic system

86717044

AUTOMATIC TRANSMISSION

Understanding the Automatic Transmission

The automatic transmission allows engine torque and power to be transmitted to the rear wheels within a narrow range of engine operating speeds. It will allow the engine to turn fast enough to produce plenty of power and torque at very low speeds, while keeping it at a sensible rpm at high vehicle speeds (and it does this job without driver assistance). The transmission uses a light fluid as the medium for the transmission of power. This fluid also works in the operation of various hydraulic control circuits and as a lubricant. Because the transmission fluid performs all of these functions, trouble within the unit can easily travel from one part to another. For this reason, and because of the complexity and unusual operating principles of the transmission, a very sound understanding of the basic principles of operation will simplify troubleshooting.

TORQUE CONVERTER

◆ **See Figure 42**

The torque converter replaces the conventional clutch. It has three functions:

1. It allows the engine to idle with the vehicle at a standstill, even with the transmission in gear.

2. It allows the transmission to shift from range-to-range smoothly, without requiring that the driver close the throttle during the shift.

3. It multiplies engine torque to an increasing extent as vehicle speed drops and throttle opening is increased. This has the effect of making the transmission more responsive and reduces the amount of shifting required.

The torque converter is a metal case which is shaped like a sphere that has been flattened on opposite sides. It is bolted to the rear end of the engine's crankshaft. Generally, the entire metal case rotates at engine speed and serves as the engine's flywheel.

The case contains three sets of blades. One set is attached directly to the case. This set forms the torus or pump. Another set is directly connected to the output shaft, and forms the turbine. The third set is mounted on a hub which, in turn, is mounted on a stationary shaft through a one-way clutch. This third set is known as the stator.

A pump, which is driven by the converter hub at engine speed, keeps the torque converter full of transmission fluid at all times. Fluid flows continuously through the unit to provide cooling.

Under low speed acceleration, the torque converter functions as follows:

The torus is turning faster than the turbine. It picks up fluid at the center of the converter and, through centrifugal force, slings it outward. Since the outer edge of the converter moves faster than the portions at the center, the fluid picks up speed.

The fluid then enters the outer edge of the turbine blades. It then travels back toward the center of the converter case along the turbine blades. In impinging

upon the turbine blades, the fluid loses the energy picked up in the torus.

If the fluid was now returned directly into the torus, both halves of the converter would have to turn at approximately the same speed at all times, and torque input and output would both be the same.

In flowing through the torus and turbine, the fluid picks up two types of flow, or flow in two separate directions. It flows through the turbine blades, and it spins with the engine. The stator, whose blades are stationary when the vehicle is being accelerated at low speeds, converts one type of flow into another. Instead of allowing the fluid to flow straight back into the torus, the stator's curved blades turn the fluid almost 90° toward the direction of rotation of the engine. Thus the fluid does not flow as fast toward the torus, but is already spinning when the torus picks it up. This has the effect of allowing the torus to turn much faster than the turbine. This difference in speed may be compared to the difference in speed between the smaller and larger gears in any gear train. The result is that engine power output is higher, and engine torque is multiplied.

As the speed of the turbine increases, the fluid spins faster and faster in the direction of engine rotation. As a result, the ability of the stator to redirect the fluid flow is reduced. Under cruising conditions, the stator is eventually forced to rotate on its one-way clutch in the direction of engine rotation. Under these conditions, the torque converter begins to behave almost like a solid shaft, with the torus and turbine speeds being almost equal.

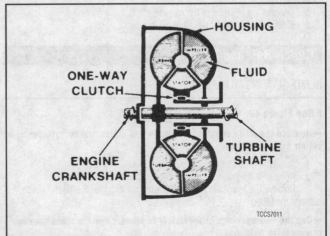

TCCS7011

Fig. 42 The torque converter housing is rotated by the engine's crankshaft, and turns the impeller—The impeller then spins the turbine, which gives motion to the turbine shaft, driving the gears

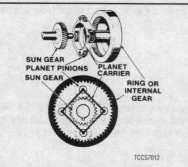

Fig. 43 Planetary gears work in a similar fashion to manual transmission gears, but are composed of three parts

Fig. 44 Planetary gears in the maximum reduction (low) range. The ring gear is held and a lower gear ratio is obtained

Fig. 45 Planetary gears in the minimum reduction (drive) range. The ring gear is allowed to revolve, providing a higher gear ratio

PLANETARY GEARBOX

▶ **See Figures 43, 44 and 45**

The ability of the torque converter to multiply engine torque is limited. Also, the unit tends to be more efficient when the turbine is rotating at relatively high speeds. Therefore, a planetary gearbox is used to carry the power output of the turbine to the driveshaft.

Planetary gears function very similarly to conventional transmission gears. However, their construction is different in that three elements make up one gear system, and, in that all three elements are different from one another. The three elements are: an outer gear that is shaped like a hoop, with teeth cut into the inner surface; a sun gear, mounted on a shaft and located at the very center of the outer gear; and a set of three planet gears, held by pins in a ring-like planet carrier, meshing with both the sun gear and the outer gear. Either the outer gear or the sun gear may be held stationary, providing more than one possible torque multiplication factor for each set of gears. Also, if all three gears are forced to rotate at the same speed, the gearset forms, in effect, a solid shaft.

Most automatics use the planetary gears to provide various reductions ratios. Bands and clutches are used to hold various portions of the gearsets to the transmission case or to the shaft on which they are mounted. Shifting is accomplished, then, by changing the portion of each planetary gearset which is held to the transmission case or to the shaft.

SERVOS AND ACCUMULATORS

▶ **See Figure 46**

The servos are hydraulic pistons and cylinders. They resemble the hydraulic actuators used on many other machines, such as bulldozers. Hydraulic fluid enters the cylinder, under pressure, and forces the piston to move to engage the band or clutches.

The accumulators are used to cushion the engagement of the servos. The transmission fluid must pass through the accumulator on the way to the servo. The accumulator housing contains a thin piston which is sprung away from the

discharge passage of the accumulator. When fluid passes through the accumulator on the way to the servo, it must move the piston against spring pressure, and this action smoothes out the action of the servo.

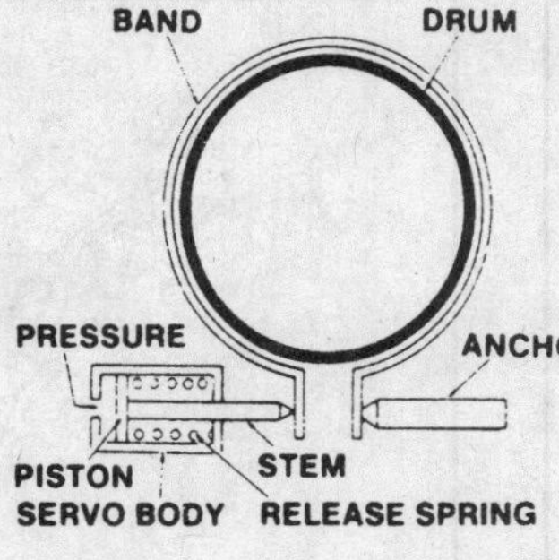

HYDRAULIC CONTROL SYSTEM

The hydraulic pressure used to operate the servos comes from the main transmission oil pump. This fluid is channeled to the various servos through the shift valves. There is generally a manual shift valve which is operated by the transmission selector lever and an automatic shift valve for each automatic upshift the transmission provides.

➡ **Many new transmissions are electronically controlled. On these models, electrical solenoids are used to better control the hydraulic fluid. Usually, the solenoids are regulated by an electronic control module.**

There are two pressures which affect the operation of these valves. One is the governor pressure which is effected by vehicle speed. The other is the modulator pressure which is effected by intake manifold vacuum or throttle position. Governor pressure rises with an increase in vehicle speed, and modulator pressure rises as the throttle is opened wider. By responding to these two pressures, the shift valves cause the upshift points to be delayed with increased throttle opening to make the best use of the engine's power output.

Most transmissions also make use of an auxiliary circuit for downshifting. This circuit may be actuated by the throttle linkage the vacuum line which actuates the modulator, by a cable or by a solenoid. It applies pressure to a special downshift surface on the shift valve or valves.

The transmission modulator also governs the line pressure, used to actuate the servos. In this way, the clutches and bands will be actuated with a force matching the torque output of the engine.

Identification

➡ **Refer to Section 1 for the automatic transmission application chart.**

All illustrations and serial number locations of these models are located in Section 1.

They are fully automatic units, with a three element torque converter and a number of planetary gear sets. The transmission shifts gears in response to signals of both engine speed and manifold vacuum.

While it is unlikely that you will ever disassemble the transmission yourself, there are a few adjustments you can perform which will prolong the transmission's life if performed accurately. The most important thing is to change the fluid regularly, which is covered in Section 1.

Fluid Pan and Filter

REMOVAL & INSTALLATION

Removal and installation of the fluid pan and filter is part of the fluid draining and refilling service which is covered in Section 1 of this manual. Please refer to the procedures in Section 1 for further information.

Fig. 46 Servos, operated by pressure, are used to apply or release the bands, to either hold the ring gear or allow it to rotate

Adjustments

SHIFT LINKAGE

L4N71B, E4N71B and RL4R01A

FLOOR SHIFT MODELS

▶ **See Figure 47**

Move the gear selector lever slowly through the ranges from **P** to **1**. You should be able to feel the detents in each range. If the detents can't be felt, or if the indicator point is out of alignment, the linkage requires adjustment.

1. Position the selector lever in **P**.
2. Loosen the lock-nuts.
3. Tighten the lock-nut (X) until it touches the trunnion, pulling the selector lever toward the **R** side without pushing the button.
4. Back off the lock-nut (X) 1 turn and tighten the lock-nut (Y) to 8–11 ft. lbs. (11–15 Nm).
5. Move the selector lever from the **P** range to the **1** range. Make sure the selector lever moves smoothly.

COLUMN SHIFT MODELS

▶ **See Figure 48**

Move the gear selector lever slowly through the ranges from **P** to **1**. You should be able to feel the detents in each range. If the detents can't be felt, or if the indicator point is out of alignment, the linkage requires adjustment.

1. Position the selector lever in **P**.
2. Loosen the lock-nuts.
3. Tighten the lock-nut (A) until it touches the trunnion, pulling the selector lever toward the **R** side without pushing the button.
4. Back off the lock-nut (A) 2 turns and tighten the lock-nut (B) to 8–11 ft. lbs. (11–15 Nm).

5. Move the selector lever from the **P** range to the **1** range. Make sure the selector lever moves smoothly.

RE4R01A

FLOOR SHIFT MODELS

▶ **See Figures 49 and 50**

Move the gear selector lever slowly through the ranges from **P** to **1**. You should be able to feel the detents in each range. If the detents can't be felt, or if the indicator point is out of alignment, the linkage requires adjustment.

1. Position the selector lever in **P**.
2. Loosen the lock-nuts.
3. Tighten the turnbuckle until it aligns with the inner cable, pulling the selector lever toward the **R** side without pushing the button.
4. Back off the turnbuckle 1 turn and tighten the lock-nuts to 3.3–4.3 ft. lbs. (4.4–5.9 Nm).
5. Move the selector lever from the **P** range to the **1** range. Make sure the selector lever moves smoothly.

NEUTRAL SAFETY/INHIBITOR SWITCH

L4N71B and E4N71B Models

▶ **See Figures 51 and 52**

The switch unit is bolted to the transmission case, behind the transmission shift lever. The switch prevents the engine from being started in any gear position except **P** or **N**. It also controls the back-up lights.

1. Place the transmission selector lever in the **N** position.
2. Remove the screw from the switch.
3. Loosen the attaching bolts. With a 2.0mm aligning pin, move the switch until the pin engages the hole in the rotor.
4. Tighten the attaching bolts equally.

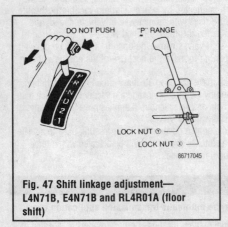

Fig. 47 Shift linkage adjustment— L4N71B, E4N71B and RL4R01A (floor shift)

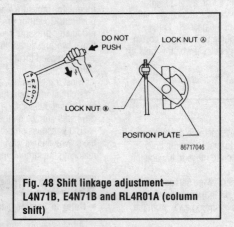

Fig. 48 Shift linkage adjustment— L4N71B, E4N71B and RL4R01A (column shift)

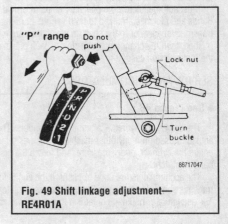

Fig. 49 Shift linkage adjustment— RE4R01A

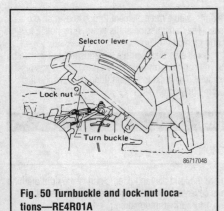

Fig. 50 Turnbuckle and lock-nut locations—RE4R01A

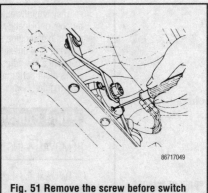
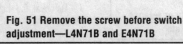

Fig. 51 Remove the screw before switch adjustment—L4N71B and E4N71B

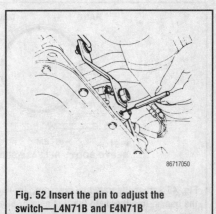

Fig. 52 Insert the pin to adjust the switch—L4N71B and E4N71B

5. Make sure while holding the brakes on, that the engine will start only in **P** or **N**. Check that the back-up lights go on only in **R**.

RL4R01A and RE4R01A Models

♦ See Figures 53 and 54

The switch unit is bolted to the transmission case, behind the transmission shift lever. The switch prevents the engine from being started in any transmission position except **P** or **N**. It also controls the back-up lights.

1. Disconnect the shift linkage at the switch assembly
2. Place the transmission selector lever in the **N** position.
3. Loosen the switch mounting bolts.
4. Insert a 4.0mm aligning pin into the adjusting holes in both the switch and the manual shaft so that it is as vertical as possible.
5. Tighten the mounting bolts equally, connect the shift linkage and remove the pin.
6. Make sure while holding the brakes on, that the engine will start only in **P** or **N**. Check that the back-up lights go on only in **R**.

THROTTLE WIRE

RL4R01A

♦ See Figure 55

1. While pressing on the lock plate, move the adjusting tube in the direction (T). For details, please refer to the accompanying illustration.
2. Release the lock plate.
3. Move the throttle drum quickly from (P2) to (P1)

➡ **Put marks on the throttle wire to facilitate its measurement.**

4. Be sure that the throttle wire stroke (L) is 1.50–1.65 in. (38–42mm) between full throttle and idle.
5. Adjust the throttle wire stroke when the throttle wire/accelerator wire is installed or after the carburetor has been adjusted.

Extension Housing Oil Seal

REMOVAL & INSTALLATION

♦ See Figures 56, 57, 58 and 59

Remove the driveshaft (2wd) or transfer case (4wd) from the transmission and then carefully pry out the oil seal. Install the new oil seal with a drift and a mallet. Install the driveshaft or transfer case.

Transmission

REMOVAL & INSTALLATION

♦ See Figures 60, 61, 62 and 63

1. Disconnect the negative battery cable.
2. Raise the truck and support it safely on jackstands.
3. Disconnect the exhaust pipe from the manifold and discard the gasket. A new gasket must be used upon assembly. Disconnect the exhaust pipe bracket.
4. Remove the fluid charging pipe from the A/T assembly.
5. Remove the oil cooler pipe from the A/T assembly
6. Plug any openings, for example fluid charging pipe hole, etc.
7. Matchmark the U-joint and differential flange and disconnect them. Remove the center bearing mounting bolts and remove the driveshaft. Plug the transmission extension housing.

✵✵ WARNING

Do not damage splines, sleeve yoke or rear oil seal.

8. Disconnect the transfer control linkage from the transfer.

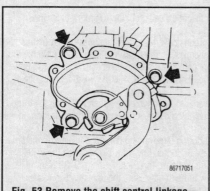

Fig. 53 Remove the shift control linkage—RL4R01A and RE4R01A

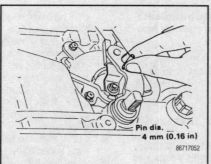

Pin dia. 4 mm (0.16 in)

Fig. 54 Insert the pin through the two adjustment holes—RL4R01A and RE4R01A

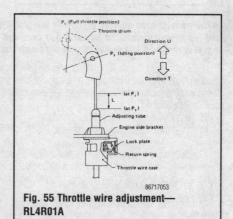

P₁ (Full throttle position)
Throttle drum
Direction U
P₂ (Idling position)
Direction T
(at P₁)
(at P₂)
L
Adjusting tube
Engine side bracket
Lock plate
Return spring
Throttle wire case

Fig. 55 Throttle wire adjustment—RL4R01A

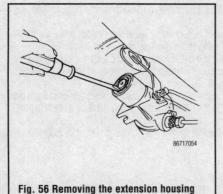

Fig. 56 Removing the extension housing oil seal—2wd models

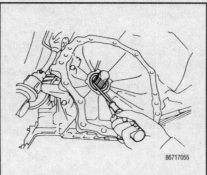

Fig. 57 Removing the extension housing oil seal—4wd models

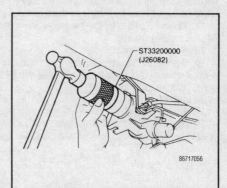

ST33200000 (J26082)

Fig. 58 Installing the extension housing oil seal—2wd models

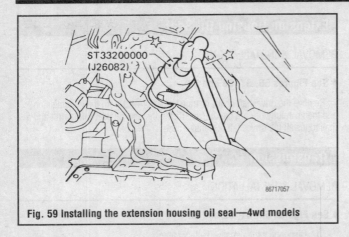

Fig. 59 Installing the extension housing oil seal—4wd models

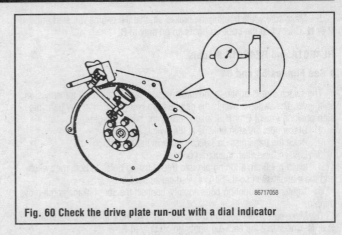

Fig. 60 Check the drive plate run-out with a dial indicator

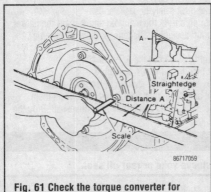

Fig. 61 Check the torque converter for proper installation

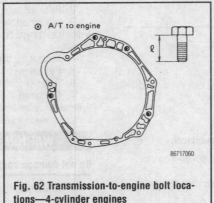

Fig. 62 Transmission-to-engine bolt locations—4-cylinder engines

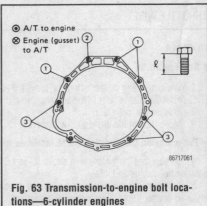

Fig. 63 Transmission-to-engine bolt locations—6-cylinder engines

➥The transfer case on 4WD models is integral with the transmission and fits inline between the transmission case and the extension housing. It is removed and replaced with the transmission.

9. Disconnect the neutral safety (inhibitor) switch wires. Disconnect the vacuum hose from the diaphragm, and the wire from the downshift solenoid. Disconnect the speedometer cable from the extension housing or the transfer case, as applicable.

10. Remove the fluid filler tube.

11. Disconnect the fluid cooler lines at the transmission. Use a flare nut wrench.

12. Support the engine with a jack under the oil pan, placing a wooden block between the pan and the jack as a buffer. Also support the transmission with a jack. For 4-wheel-drive models, support the transfer case with the transmission.

13. Remove the torque converter cover. Matchmark the converter and the drive plate for reassembly; they were balanced as a unit at the factory. Remove the bolts attaching the converter to the drive plate (flywheel). You will have to rotate the engine to do this, using a wrench on the crankshaft pulley bolt.

14. Remove the bolts for the rear engine mount and the crossmember. Remove the crossmember.

15. Remove the starter.

16. Remove the transmission-to-engine bolts. Lower the transmission (on 4-wheel-drive models lower the transfer case with the transmission) back and down, out from under the truck.

To install:

17. Before installing the transmission (or transmission/transfer case for 4WD), check the drive plate run-out with a dial indicator. Turn the crankshaft one full turn. Maximum allowable run-out is 0.020 in. (0.5mm). Replace the

drive plate (and ring gear) if run-out exceeds 0.02 in. (0.5mm); otherwise, reface the drive plate.

18. After connecting the torque converter to the transmission, lay a straightedge across the face of the transmission and measure the distance from the top of the mounting bolt to the straightedge. It should be at least 1.38 in. (35mm) on all transmissions except the RE4R01A and RL4R01A, where it should be at least 1.02 in. (26mm).

19. Install the torque converter to the drive plate. When installing the torque converter, be sure to line up the notch in the converter with the projection on the oil pump.

20. Align the marks made during removal and bolt the converter to the drive plate, tightening the bolts to 29–36 ft. lbs. (39–49 Nm) except on the VG30E where the two shortest bolts are tightened to 22–29 ft. lbs. (29–39 Nm).

21. Rotate the engine a few turns to make sure the transmission rotates freely without binding. The engine-to-transmission bolt torque is 29–36 ft. lbs. (39–49 Nm).

22. Attach any connectors, components and linkage that was detached during the removal.

23. Lower the vehicle, fill the transmission with the proper weight fluid, if necessary.

24. Reconnect the negative battery cable, lower the vehicle, apply the parking brake and start the engine to check the fluid level in the transmission.

25. Shut the engine off and move the gear selector lever through all positions to check for proper operation. Adjust the shift linkage and neutral safety switches.

26. Re-start the engine, allowing it to idle. Shift from gear-to-gear. Each gear engagement should be felt in the selector lever in your hand by a slight "shock" as you shift the transmission.

27. When satisfied the transmission shifts normally, perform a road test.

TRANSFER CASE

Transfer Case

IDENTIFICATION

All 4wd models use a TX10A transfer case.

REMOVAL & INSTALLATION

▶ **See Figures 64, 65 and 66**

1. Disconnect the negative battery cable.
2. Raise the front of the vehicle and support it with jackstands.
3. Drain the fluid from the transmission and transfer cases.
4. Remove the front and rear driveshafts. Be sure to plug the oil seal openings after removal.

➡ **Be very careful not to damage the transfer case spline, yoke or oil seal while removing the driveshafts.**

5. Remove the torsion bar spring.
6. Remove the second crossmember.
7. Disconnect the transfer control lever at the outer shift lever ball joint and position it out of the way.
8. Position a floor jack underneath the transfer case and remove the case-to-transmission mounting bolts. Separate the transfer case from the transmission and slowly lower it out and away from the transmission.

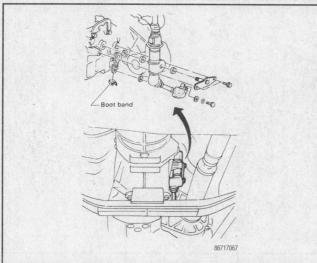

Fig. 64 Removing the transfer control lever from the transfer case

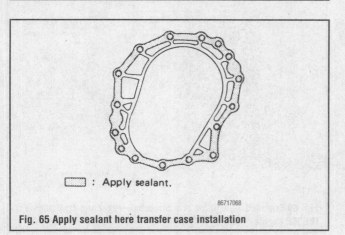

Fig. 65 Apply sealant here transfer case installation

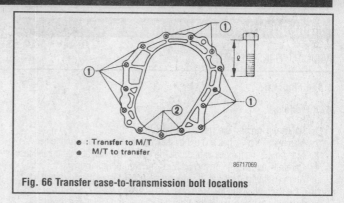

● : Transfer to M/T
● : M/T to transfer

Fig. 66 Transfer case-to-transmission bolt locations

To install:

9. Carefully position the transfer case so that it mates with the transmission and tighten the mounting bolts to 23–30 ft. lbs. (31–41 Nm). On models with manual transmissions, be sure to coat the case mating surface with sealant.
10. Connect the transfer control lever to the outer shift lever and tighten the nut to 18–22 ft. lbs. (25–30 Nm).
11. Install the second crossmember and tighten the bolts to 43–58 ft. lbs. (59–78 Nm). Install the torsion bar spring.
12. Unplug the oil seals and install the two driveshafts.
13. Refill the transmission and transfer case with fluid, then lower the vehicle and connect the battery cable. Road test the truck and check for any leaks or improper operation.

TROUBLESHOOTING

Slips Out of Gear (High-Low)

- Shifting poppet spring weak
- Bearing broken or worn
- Shifting fork bent
- Improper control rod adjustment

Hard Shifting

- Lack of lubricant
- Shift lever binding on shaft
- Shifting poppet ball scored
- Shifting fork bent
- Low tire pressure

Backlash

- Companion yoke loose
- Transfer case loose on mounts
- Internal parts excessively worn

Noisy

- Low lubricant level
- Bearings improperly adjusted or excessively worn
- Gears worn or damaged
- Improper alignment of driveshafts or U-joints

Oil Leakage

- Excessive amount of lubricant in case
- Vent clogged
- Gaskets or seals leaking
- Bearings loose or damaged
- Driveshaft yoke mating surfaces scored

Overheating

- Excessive or insufficient amount of lubricant
- Bearing adjustment too tight

DRIVELINE

Front Driveshaft And U-Joints

REMOVAL & INSTALLATION

▶ **See Figure 67**

4wd Models

1. Raise and support the vehicle on jackstands.
2. Matchmark the flanges and unbolt the front driveshaft at the front differential.
3. Matchmark the flanges and unbolt the front driveshaft at the transfer case.
4. Carefully remove the driveshaft for inspection or replacement.
5. Align the matchmarks at the transfer case and install the driveshaft. Tighten the flange bolts to 29–33 ft. lbs. (39–44 Nm).
6. Align the matchmarks at the front differential and install the driveshaft. Tighten the flange bolts to 29–33 ft. lbs. (39–44 Nm).
7. Lower the vehicle and test for proper operation

U-JOINT OVERHAUL

1. Matchmark the yoke and the driveshaft.
2. Remove the snaprings from the bearings.
3. Position the yoke on vise jaws. Using a bearing remover and a hammer, gently tap the remover until the bearing is driven out of the yoke about 1 inch (25mm).

4. Place the tool in the vise and drive the yoke away from the tool until the bearing is removed.
5. Repeat Steps 3 and 4 for the other bearings.
6. Check for worn or damaged parts. Inspect the bearing journal surfaces for wear.

To assemble:

7. Install the bearing cups, seals, and O-rings in the spider.
8. Grease the spider and the bearings.
9. Position the spider in the yoke.
10. Start the bearings in the yoke, then press them into place, using a vise.
11. If the axial play of the spider is greater than 0.007 in. (0.02mm), select snaprings which will provide the correct play. Be sure that the snaprings are the same size on both sides or driveshaft noise and vibration will result.

Rear Driveshaft and U-Joints

REMOVAL & INSTALLATION

▶ **See Figures 68, 69, 70, 71 and 72**

2wd Models

TWO-PIECE DRIVESHAFT WITH CENTER BEARING

1. Raise the rear of the truck and support the rear axle housing on jackstands.
2. Before you begin to disassemble the driveshaft components, you must

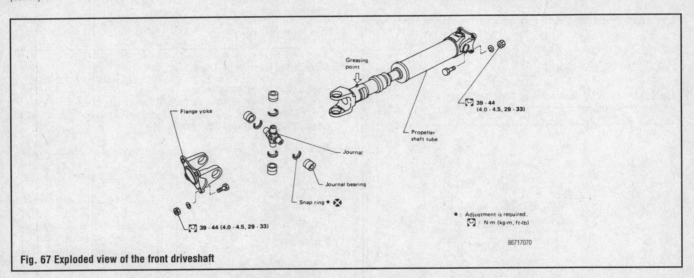

Fig. 67 Exploded view of the front driveshaft

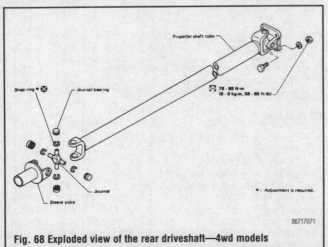

Fig. 68 Exploded view of the rear driveshaft—4wd models

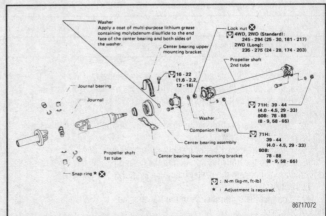

Fig. 69 Exploded view of the rear driveshaft—2wd and 4wd models (VG30E engine)

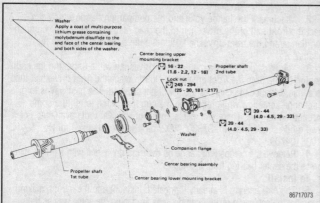

Fig. 70 Exploded view of the rear driveshaft—2wd models (KA24E engine)

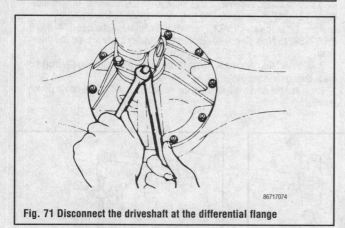

Fig. 71 Disconnect the driveshaft at the differential flange

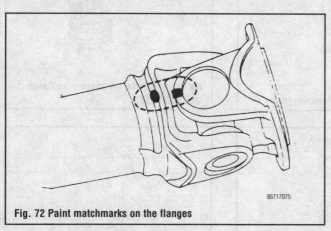

Fig. 72 Paint matchmarks on the flanges

first paint accurate alignment marks on the mating flangers. Do this on the rear universal joint flange, the center flange, and on the transmission flange.

3. Remove the bolts attaching the rear universal joint flange to the drive pinion flange.

4. Drop the rear section of the shaft slightly and pull the unit out of the center bearing sleeve yoke.

5. Remove the center bearing support from the crossmember.

6. Separate the transmission output flange and remove the front half of the driveshaft together with the center bearing assembly.

To install:

7. Connect the output flange of the transmission to the flange on the front half of the shaft.

8. Install the center bearing support to the crossmember, but do not fully tighten the bolts.

9. Install the rear section of the shaft making sure that all mating marks are aligned.

10. Tighten all flange bolts to 29–33 ft. lbs. (39–44 Nm) on Z24i and KA24E engines; or 58–65 ft. lbs. (78–88 Nm) on VG30i and VG30E engines.

11. Tighten the center bearing support bolts to 12–16 ft. lbs. (16–22 Nm).

4wd Models

ONE-PIECE DRIVESHAFT

1. Raise the rear of the truck and support the rear axle housing with jackstands.

2. Paint a mating mark on the two halves of the rear universal joint flange.

3. Remove the bolts which hold the rear flange together.

4. Remove the splined end of the driveshaft from the transmission extension housing. To prevent losing a lot of gear oil, plug the end of the transmission with a rag.

5. Remove the driveshaft from under the truck.

To install:

6. Apply multipurpose grease to the splined end of the shaft.

7. Insert the driveshaft sleeve into the transmission.

➡ **Be careful not to damage the extension housing grease seal.**

8. Align the mating marks on the rear flange and replace the bolts. Tighten to 58–65 ft. lbs. (78–88 Nm).

9. Remove the jackstands and lower the vehicle.

TWO-PIECE DRIVESHAFT WITH CENTER BEARING

1. Raise the rear of the truck and support the rear axle housing on jackstands.

2. Before you begin to disassemble the driveshaft components, you must first paint accurate alignment marks on the mating flangers. Do this on the rear universal joint flange, the center flange, and on the transmission flange.

3. Remove the bolts attaching the rear universal joint flange to the drive pinion flange.

4. Drop the rear section of the shaft slightly and pull the unit out of the center bearing sleeve yoke.

5. Remove the center bearing support from the crossmember.

6. Separate the transmission output flange and remove the front half of the driveshaft together with the center bearing assembly.

To install:

7. Connect the output flange of the transmission to the flange on the front half of the shaft.

8. Install the center bearing support to the crossmember, but do not fully tighten the bolts.

9. Install the rear section of the shaft making sure that all mating marks are aligned.

10. Tighten all flange bolts to 29–33 ft. lbs. (39–44 Nm) on Z24i and KA24E engines; or 58–65 ft. lbs. (78–88 Nm) on VG30i and VG30E engines.

11. Tighten the center bearing support bolts to 12–16 ft. lbs. (16–22 Nm).

U-JOINT OVERHAUL

1. Matchmark the yoke and the driveshaft.

2. Remove the snaprings from the bearings.

3. Position the yoke on vise jaws. Using a bearing remover and a hammer, gently tap the remover until the bearing is driven out of the yoke about 1 inch (25mm).

4. Place the tool in the vise and drive the yoke away from the tool until the bearing is removed.

5. Repeat Steps 3 and 4 for the other bearings.

6. Check for worn or damaged parts. Inspect the bearing journal surfaces for wear.

To assemble:

7. Install the bearing cups, seals, and O-rings in the spider.

8. Grease the spider and the bearings.

9. Position the spider in the yoke.

10. Start the bearings in the yoke, then press them into place, using a vise.

11. If the axial play of the spider is greater than 0.0007 in. (0.02mm), select snaprings which will provide the correct play. Be sure that the snaprings are the same size on both sides or driveshaft noise and vibration will result.

Center Bearing

REMOVAL & INSTALLATION

▶ **See Figures 73 thru 79**

➡The following procedure requires the use of a special lock-nut removal tool, a puller to remove the companion flange, and a press to remove the center bearing. The center bearing is a sealed unit which must be replaced as an assembly if defective.

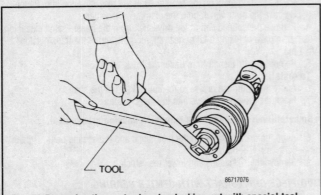

Fig. 73 Removing the center bearing locking nut with special tool

1. Remove the driveshaft.
2. Matchmark the flange yoke and the companion flange which connect the front half of the driveshaft to the rear. Also matchmark the companion flange and the front driveshaft. Remove the bolts and separate the shafts.
3. You must devise a way to hold the driveshaft while unbolting the companion flange from the front driveshaft. Do not place the front driveshaft tube in a vise, because the chances are it will get crushed. The best way is to grip the flange somehow while loosening the nut. It is going to require some strength to remove. There are special lock-nut removal tools available. For 2wd models, use Tool No. ST38060002, on 4wd models use tool No. KV38104700.
4. Remove the companion flange off the front driveshaft with a puller, then press the center bearing from its mount.

To Install:

5. The new bearing is already lubricated. Install it into the mount, making sure that the seals and related components are facing the same way as then removed.
6. Slide the companion flange onto the front driveshaft, aligning the marks made during removal. Install the washer and lock-nut. Tighten the nut to 181–217 ft. lbs. (245–294 Nm) models with Z24i and KA24E engines. On models with VG30i and VG30E engines, tighten to 174–203 ft. lbs. (235–275 Nm). Check that the bearing rotates freely around the driveshaft.
7. Connect the companion flange to the flange yoke, aligning the marks made during disassembly.
8. Install the driveshaft, aligning the marks made at the axle flange during removal.

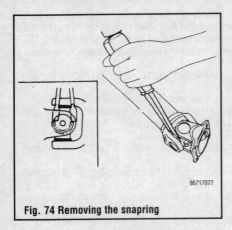

Fig. 74 Removing the snapring

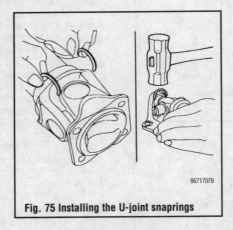

Fig. 75 Installing the U-joint snaprings

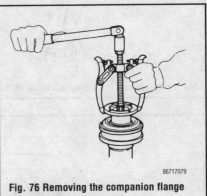

Fig. 76 Removing the companion flange with puller tool

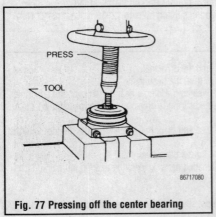

Fig. 77 Pressing off the center bearing

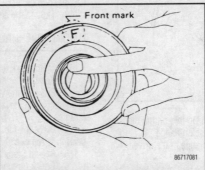

Fig. 78 When installing the center bearing, make sure that the (F) mark faces the front of the truck

Fig. 79 Stake the center bearing nut

FRONT DRIVE AXLE

Identification

➡ **Refer to Section 1, for the front drive axle application chart.**

Front drive axle identification and serial number location illustrations are shown in Section 1.

Free Running Hub

REMOVAL & INSTALLATION

Manual Lock

▸ **See Figures 80, 81 and 82**

1. Raise the front of the vehicle and support the front axle on stands.
2. Remove the wheels.
3. Set the knob of the manual lock to the **free** position.
4. Remove the locking hub cover using a Torx® wrench, while the brake pedal is depressed.
5. Remove the snapring and pull out the drive clutch.

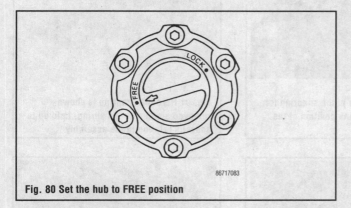

Fig. 80 Set the hub to FREE position

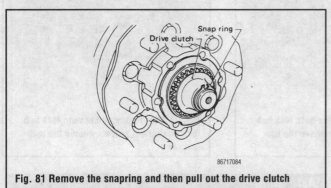

Fig. 81 Remove the snapring and then pull out the drive clutch

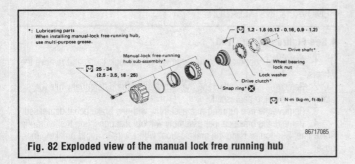

Fig. 82 Exploded view of the manual lock free running hub

To install:

6. Install the drive clutch and snapring. Make sure the hub is in the **free** position.
7. Install the hub cover and tighten the bolts to 18–25 ft. lbs. (25–34 Nm).
8. Install the wheels, remove the stands and lower the vehicle.

Auto Lock

▸ **See Figures 83 thru 96**

1. Raise the front of the vehicle and support the front axle on jackstands.
2. Remove the wheels.

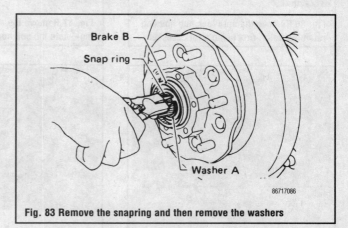

Fig. 83 Remove the snapring and then remove the washers

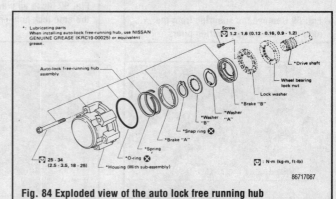

Fig. 84 Exploded view of the auto lock free running hub

Fig. 85 View of the auto lock free running hub installed

Fig. 86 Remove the auto lock hub housing retaining bolts, first using a torx® socket

Fig. 87 Remove the auto lock hub housing—note the sub housing inside the cap

Fig. 88 Remove the auto lock hub housing then remove the O-ring, if necessary

Fig. 89 Remove the snapring from the auto lock hub using snapring pliers

Fig. 90 Close up view of the snapring for the auto lock hub—note position of the tool

Fig. 91 Here the snapring is shown removed along with the spring, held up to show its relation in the assembly

Fig. 92 Remove the washer and brake assembly, keep parts in order for correct installation

Fig. 93 After removing the auto lock hub assembly components remove the lock washer set screw

Fig. 94 After removing the auto lock hub lock washer set screw, remove the lock washer

3. Set the auto-lock free-running hub to the **free** position.

4. Remove the locking hub cover using a Torx® wrench, while the brake pedal is depressed.

5. Remove the spring, brake **A**, the snapring using the appropriate pliers, then remove washer **B**, washer **A** and brake **B**.

6. If wheel bearing removal is desired, after removing the auto lock hub assembly components remove the lock washer set screw. Remove the lock washer for access to the wheel bearing lock-nut, then remove the lock-nut and the wheel bearing is free for removal.

To install:

7. Make sure the hub is in the **free** position and then install washer **B**, washer **A** and brake **B**.

8. Install the snapring.

9. Install the hub cover and tighten the bolts to 18–25 ft. lbs. (25–34 Nm).

10. Install the wheels, remove the stands and then lower the vehicle.

Axle Shaft

REMOVAL & INSTALLATION

◆ **See Figures 97 thru 103**

1. Raise and support the front of the vehicle on jackstands and remove the wheels.

2. Remove the bolts attaching the axle shaft to the differential while the brake pedal is being depressed.

3. Remove the free running hub assembly with the brake pedal depressed.

4. Remove the brake caliper assembly without disconnecting the hydraulic brake line. Support or hang the brake caliper with a wire to avoid breaking the hose.

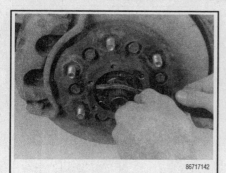

Fig. 95 Loosen the wheel bearing lock-nut—note position of tools used for this job

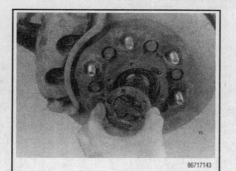

Fig. 96 After loosening the wheel bearing lock-nut remove the lock-nut from the hub assembly

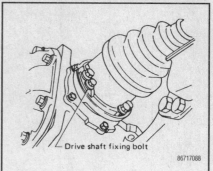

Fig. 97 Disconnect the driveshaft at the final drive unit

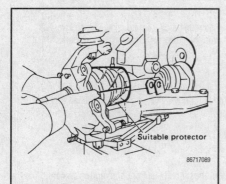

Fig. 98 Remove the driveshaft with the steering knuckle still attached

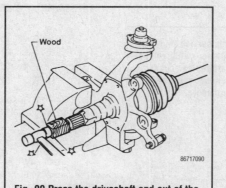

Fig. 99 Press the driveshaft end out of the steering knuckle

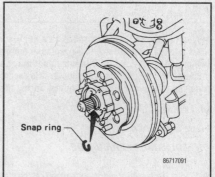

Fig. 100 Don't forget to install the snapring

5. Remove the tie rod ball joint.

6. Support the lower link with a jack and remove the nuts attaching the lower ball joint on the lower link.

7. Remove the upper ball joint attaching bolts.

8. Remove the shock absorber lower attaching bolt.

9. Cover the axle shaft boot with a suitable protector, and then remove the axle shaft with the knuckle still attached.

10. Separate the axle shaft from the knuckle by removing the snapring and lightly tapping the shaft with a rubber mallet.

To install:

11. Install the axle shaft into the knuckle and then install the assembly.

12. When installing the bearing spacer onto the axle shaft, make sure that the bearing spacer is facing in the proper direction. Temporarily install a new snapring on the axle shaft at the same thickness as it was before removal and then measure the axial end-play of the axle shaft with a dial gauge. The axial end-play should be 0.004–0.012 in. (0.1–0.3mm). Select another snapring if not within specifications.

13. Connect the shock absorber and tighten the bolt to 43–58 ft. lbs. (59–78 Nm).

14. Connect the upper ball joint and tighten the bolts to 12–15 ft. lbs. (16–21 Nm).

15. Connect the lower ball joint to the lower link and tighten the nuts to 35–45 ft. lbs. (47–61 Nm).

16. Install the tie rod ball joint and the brake caliper.

17. Install the hub and then connect the axle shaft to the differential and tighten the bolts to 25–33 ft. lbs. (34–44 Nm).

18. Install the wheels, remove the stands and lower the vehicle.

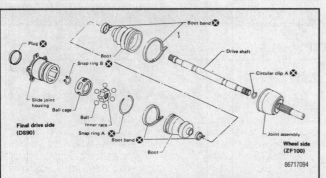

Fig. 101 Exploded view of the front axle driveshaft—6-cylinder engines

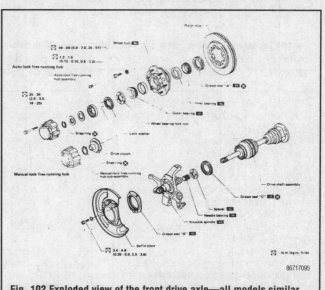

Fig. 102 Exploded view of the front drive axle—all models similar

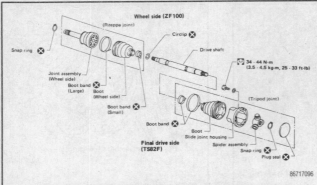

Fig. 103 Exploded view of the front axle driveshaft—4-cylinder engines

JOINT OVERHAUL

→Always refer to the illustrations as a guide for this service repair. Most joint assemblies are to be replaced not overhauled. Although outer (wheel side) boot and joint replacement may sometimes be accomplished with the shaft in the vehicle, it is recommended that the shaft be removed to prevent possible damage during the procedure.

Disassembly

▶ See Figure 104

DIFFERENTIAL CARRIER SIDE

1. Place the axle shaft in a suitable vise and remove the plug seal from the slide joint housing by lightly tapping around the slide joint housing.
2. Remove the boot bands.

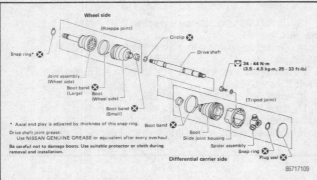

Fig. 104 Exploded view of the front driveshaft assembly—all models similar

3. Move the boot and slide joint housing toward wheel side and put matchmarks.
4. Pry off snaprings. Remove the spider assembly.
5. Remove the boot.

→Clean all parts. Check parts for evidence of wear or damage. Replace the driveshaft if it is twisted or cracked. When replacing boots always replace the boot bands.

WHEEL SIDE

1. Remove the axle and place in a suitable bench vise.
2. Before separating joint assembly, put matchmarks on driveshaft and joint assembly.
3. Remove the boot bands.
4. Separate joint assembly by lightly tapping it. The joint on the wheel side is not to be disassembled.

Assembly

DIFFERENTIAL CARRIER SIDE

1. Install new boot band, boot and side joint housing to the driveshaft.
2. Install spider assembly in the correct position, ensuring marks are properly aligned.
3. Install new snaprings.
4. Pack boot with grease.
5. Set boot length so that it does not swell and deform when it is installed. Make sure that the new boot is properly installed on the driveshaft groove.
6. Lock both boot bands. Install new plug seal (with sealant) to slide joint housing.

WHEEL SIDE

1. Install new boot band on driveshaft.
2. Install joint assembly in the correct position, ensuring marks are properly aligned.
3. Pack boot with grease.
4. Set boot length so that it does not swell and deform when it is installed. Make sure that the new boot is properly installed on the driveshaft groove.
5. Lock both boot bands.

Differential Carrier

REMOVAL & INSTALLATION

▶ See Figures 105, 106 and 107

1. Raise the front of the vehicle and support it with jackstands.
2. Remove the drain plug and drain the differential gear oil.
3. Disconnect the axle shafts at the differential.
4. Remove the front driveshaft.
5. Position a floor jack under the differential and raise it just enough to support the carrier.
6. Loosen all the engine mount bolts, position another floor jack under the engine and raise it just enough to release the pressure on the mounts.

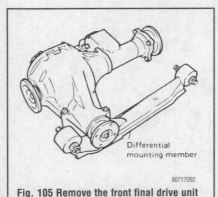

Fig. 105 Remove the front final drive unit with mounting member still attached

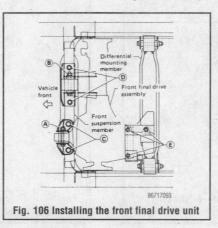

Fig. 106 Installing the front final drive unit

Fig. 107 Removing the front final drive unit using the correct equipment

7. Remove all mounting bolts and lower the differential carrier down and away from the vehicle.

To install:

8. Install the carrier and temporarily tighten nuts **A** and **B**. Tighten bolts **C** and **D**, and nuts **A**, **B** and **E** in order, to 50–64 ft. lbs. (68–87 Nm).

9. Lower the engine and tighten the engine mount bolts.

10. Install the driveshaft and axle shafts.

11. Remove the jackstands, lower the vehicle and fill the differential with gear oil.

Pinion Seal

REMOVAL & INSTALLATION

1. Drain the gear oil from the differential.
2. Raise the front of the vehicle and support it with jackstands.

REAR DRIVE AXLE

Identification

➥Refer to Section 1, for the rear drive axle application chart.

Rear axle identification and serial number locations are illustrated in Section 1.

Understanding Drive Axles

The drive axle is a special type of transmission that reduces the speed of the drive from the engine/transmission and divides the power to the wheels. Power enters the axle from the driveshaft via the companion flange which is mounted on the drive pinion shaft. The drive pinion shaft and gear which carry the power into the differential turn at engine speed. The gear on the end of the pinion shaft drives a large ring gear, of which the axis of rotation is 90 degrees away from that of the pinion. The pinion and gear reduce the gear ratio of the axle, and change the direction of rotation to turn the axle shafts which drive both wheels. The axle gear ratio is found by dividing the number of pinion gear teeth into the number of ring gear teeth.

The ring gear drives the differential case which provides the two mounting points for the ends of a pinion shaft on which are mounted two pinion gears. The pinion gears drive the two side gears, one of which is located on the inner end of each axle shaft.

By driving the axle shafts through the mechanical assembly, the differential allows the outer drive wheel to turn faster than the inner drive wheel in a turn.

The main drive pinion and the side bearings, which bear the weight of the differential case, are shimmed to provide proper bearing preload, and to position the pinion and ring gears properly.

➥The proper adjustment of the relationship of the ring and pinion gears is critical. It should be attempted only by those with extensive equipment and/or experience.

Limited-slip differentials include clutches which tend to link each axle shaft to the differential case. Clutches may be engaged either by spring action or by pressure produced by the torque on the axles during a turn. When turning on dry pavement, the effects of the clutches are overcome, and each wheel turns at the required speed. When slippage occurs at either wheel, however, the clutches will transmit some of the power to the wheel which has the greater amount of traction.

Determining Axle Ratio

The drive axle of a truck is said to have a certain axle ratio. This number (usually a whole number and a decimal fraction) is actually a comparison of the number of gear teeth on the ring gear and the pinion gear. For example, a 4.11 rear means that theoretically, for every 4.11 teeth on the ring gear there is one tooth on the pinion gear or, put another way, the driveshaft must turn 4.11 times to turn the wheels once. Actually, on a 4.11 rear, there might be 37 teeth on the ring gear and 9 teeth on the pinion gear. By dividing the number of teeth on the ring gear, the numerical axle ratio (4.11) is obtained. This also provides a good method of ascertaining exactly the axle ratio with which one is working.

Another method of determining gear ratio is to jack up and support the truck so that both rear wheels are off the ground. Make a chalk mark on the rear wheel and the driveshaft. Put the transmission in neutral. Turn the rear wheel one complete turn and count the number of turns that the driveshaft makes. The number of turns that the driveshaft makes in one complete revolution of the rear wheel is an approximation of the rear axle ratio.

3. Disconnect the front driveshaft at the differential.

4. Using a flange wrench and a 27mm socket, remove the drive pinion nut.

5. Remove the companion flange and then pry out the oil seal.

To install:

6. Coat the cavity between the lips of the oil seal with grease and then install the seal with an oil seal driver tool.

7. Press the companion flange in and install the drive pinion nut. Tighten the nut to 123–145 ft. lbs. (167–196 Nm).

8. Install the driveshaft, remove the stands and lower the vehicle. Refill the differential with gear oil.

Axle Shaft, Bearing and Seal

REMOVAL & INSTALLATION

With Drum Brakes

◆ See Figures 108 thru 113

1. Raise the rear of the vehicle and support it. Remove the rear wheel and tire.

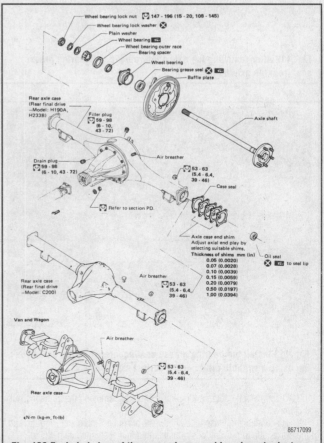

Fig. 108 Exploded view of the rear axle assembly—drum brake type

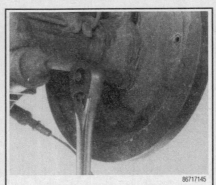

Fig. 109 Remove the nuts securing the wheel bearing cage with the baffle plate

Fig. 110 After unfastening the retainers, remove the backing plate from the axle housing

Fig. 111 View of the axle shaft removed from axle housing—note the splined end of the shaft

Fig. 112 After removing the axle shaft remove the bearing grease seal from the axle housing

Fig. 113 Install the bearing grease seal squarely into the axle housing using a suitable driver or the correct size socket

2. Disconnect the rear parking brake cable by removing the adjusting nut and clamps.

3. Disconnect the brake tube at the rear brake backing plate. Plug the end of the brake tube to prevent loss of brake fluid and system contamination.

4. Remove the brake drum.

5. Remove the nuts securing the wheel bearing cage with the baffle plate.

➡If only removing the axle shaft and the oil seal is good, take care to not damage the seal when pulling the axle. If the wheel bearing and/or seal must be replaced, proceed to step 7.

6. Pull out the axle shaft assembly together with the brake backing plate using a slide hammer.

7. Remove the oil seal in the axle housing if necessary, and discard. It can be pried out with a small pry bar. Oil the lips of the new seal and install it carefully to avoid damage to the lip.

8. To replace the bearing, unbend and discard the lockwasher. Remove the lock-nut with a soft drift and a hammer.

9. Press the old bearing and cage off the shaft.

10. Remove the oil seal in the cage. Use a brass drift to remove the bearing cup after the seal has been removed.

To install:

11. Install a new cup with a brass drift. Install a new oil seal over the bearing cup. Lubricate the area between the seal lips with grease after installation.

12. Place the bearing cage and spacer on the axle shaft, then fit the bearing, tapping it into place with a soft drift and light hammer blows.

13. Place the flat bearing lockwasher over the bearing, then the new nut lockwasher. Install the lock-nut, tightening to 108 ft. lbs. (147 Nm). Continue to tighten after that until the grooves line up with the lockwasher tabs. The nut can be tightened up to 145 ft. lbs. (196 Nm). Bend the lockwasher tabs into place.

14. Lubricate the bearing and recess in the axle housing with wheel bearing grease. Coat the axle splines with gear oil. Coat the seal surface of the shaft with grease.

15. Install the axle shaft and then check the axle end-play. It should be 0.004–0.012 in. (0.1–0.3mm). The end-play is adjusted by adding or removing shims behind the brake backing plate. Tighten the backing plate attaching nuts to 39–46 ft. lbs. (53–63 Nm).

With Disc Brakes

◆ See Figures 114 and 115

1. Raise the rear of the vehicle and support it. Remove the rear wheel and tire.

2. Disconnect the rear parking brake cable by removing the adjusting nut and clamps.

3. Disconnect the brake tube at the rear brake backing plate. Plug the end of the brake tube to prevent loss of brake fluid or system contamination.

4. Remove the brake caliper assembly and rotor.

5. Remove the nuts securing the wheel bearing retainer to the brake backing plate.

6. If replacing the bearing and not just a faulty seal, pull out the axle shaft assembly together with the brake backing plate using a slide hammer.

7. Remove the oil seal in the axle housing if necessary. It can be pried out with a small pry bar.

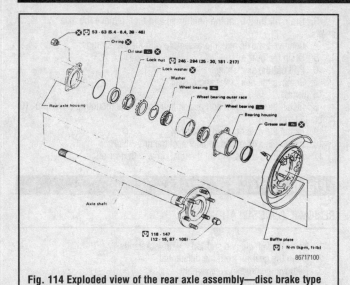

Fig. 114 Exploded view of the rear axle assembly—disc brake type

8. To replace the bearing, unbend and discard the lockwasher. Remove the lock-nut with a spanner wrench.

9. Remove the wheel bearing together with the bearing housing and the backing plate from the axle shaft.

10. Remove the outer wheel bearing inner race from the axle shaft.

11. Pry out the old grease seal from the bearing housing.

12. Press out the wheel bearing outer race.

To install:

13. Using a brass drift, press the new bearing into the housing until it bottoms.

14. Oil the lips of the new seal and install it carefully to avoid damage to the lip. Press on the new seal until it bottoms in the housing.

15. Install the backing plate over the housing and press the axle shaft into the inner bearing race. Be careful not to damage the seal.

16. Grease the seat of the lock-nut and then tighten it to 181–217 ft. lbs. (245–294 Nm).

17. Turn the bearing housing two or three revolutions; it must rotate smoothly. Bend out part of the lock washer in order to lock the nut.

18. Press the new oil seal into the axle housing with a drift and mallet.

19. Lubricate the bearing and recess in the axle housing with wheel bearing grease. Coat the axle splines with gear oil. Coat the seal surface of the shaft with grease.

20. Install the axle shaft and then check the axle end-play. It should be 0.004–0.012 in. (0.1–0.3mm). The end-play is adjusted by adding or removing shims behind the brake backing plate. Tighten the backing plate attaching nuts to 39–46 ft. lbs. (53–63 Nm).

Axle Housing

REMOVAL & INSTALLATION

Pick-up with Leaf Spring Suspension

▶ **See Figure 116**

1. Raise the rear of the vehicle and support it with jackstands. Remove the rear wheels.

2. Remove the driveshaft.

3. Disconnect the parking brake cable and the brake line.

4. Position a floor jack under the center of the axle housing and raise it just enough to support the assembly.

5. Disconnect the lower end of each shock absorber at the spring carrier.

6. Remove the spring carrier U-bolts and let the springs drop down slightly.

7. On 2wd models, carefully maneuver the axle housing out through the springs. This will probably require two floor jacks or another set of jackstands. On 4wd models, the axle housing is below the leaf springs; simply lower the housing and remove it.

To install:

8. Reinstall the axle housing and support it in position. Slide the spring carrier U-bolts over the axle tube (or leaf springs on 4wd models) and tighten the nuts to 65–72 ft. lbs. (88–98 Nm).

9. Reconnect the shock absorbers and tighten the mounting bolts to 22–30 ft. lbs. (30–40 Nm).

10. Connect the parking brake cable and the brake lines.

11. Connect the driveshaft, install the wheels and lower the vehicle.

Pathfinders with 5-Link Suspension

▶ **See Figure 117**

1. Raise the rear of the vehicle and support it with jackstands. Remove the rear wheels.

2. Remove the driveshaft.

3. Disconnect the parking brake cable and the brake line.

4. Position a floor jack under the center of the axle housing and raise it just enough to support the assembly.

5. Remove the stabilizer bar connecting rod-to-body mounting bolts.

6. Disconnect the upper and lower links at the body.

7. Disconnect the panhard rod at the body.

8. Remove the upper shock absorber mounting nuts.

9. Lower the entire axle housing assembly (suspension and all) out and away from the vehicle.

To install:

10. Position the axle housing assembly under the body of the truck and raise it until the upper ends of the shock absorbers can be connected. Tighten the bolts to 22–30 ft. lbs. (30–40 Nm).

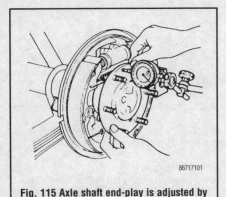

Fig. 115 Axle shaft end-play is adjusted by the addition or subtraction of shims

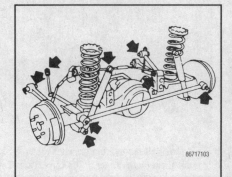

Fig. 116 Slide the axle housing out through the leaf springs

Fig. 117 The axle housing with 5-link type suspension is removed as an assembly

11. Connect the panhard rod and tighten the bolts to 80–108 ft. lbs. (108–147 Nm).

12. Reconnect the upper and lower links and then tighten the bolts to 80–108 ft. lbs. (108–147 Nm).

13. Connect the stabilizer bar connecting rod to the body and tighten the bolts to 19–24 ft. lbs. (25–32 Nm).

14. Connect the parking brake cable and the brake lines.

15. Install the driveshaft. Install the wheels and then lower the vehicle.

Final Drive

REMOVAL & INSTALLATION

Except C200 Models

1. Raise the rear of the truck and support it with jackstands.
2. Disconnect the driveshaft at the final drive unit.
3. Plug the rear oil seal and then remove the axle shafts.
4. Loosen the final drive-to-axle housing mounting bolts and remove the final drive.

To install:

5. Install the final drive and tighten the mounting bolts to 12–18 ft. lbs. (17–25 Nm). Be sure that the gasket on H233B models is installed in the correct position.
6. Install the axle shafts and connect the driveshaft.
7. Lower the vehicle and fill the final drive with gear oil.

C200 Models

1. Raise the rear of the truck and support it with jackstands.
2. Disconnect the driveshaft at the final drive unit.

3. Drain all fluid from the final drive and then remove the axle shafts.
4. Remove the axle housing assembly with the leaf springs.
5. Drain the gear oil.
6. Pull out the axle shafts.
7. Remove the rear cover and gasket.

To Install:

8. Install the rear cover and gasket and tighten the mounting bolts to 8–10 ft. lbs. (11–14 Nm).
9. Install the axle housing assembly.
10. Install the axle shafts and connect the driveshaft.
11. Lower the vehicle and fill the final drive with gear oil.

Pinion Seal

REMOVAL & INSTALLATION

1. Raise the vehicle and support it with jackstands.
2. Drain the gear oil from the differential.
3. Remove the driveshaft assembly.
4. Remove the companion flange retaining nut, while recording the torque necessary to remove the retaining nut. Remove the companion flange and then pry out the oil seal.

To install:

5. Coat the cavity between the lips of the oil seal with grease and then install the oil seal.
6. Press the companion flange in and install the companion flange nut. Tighten the flange retaining nut to the recorded torque specification.
7. Install the driveshaft. Refill the differential with gear oil. Remove the stands and lower the vehicle.

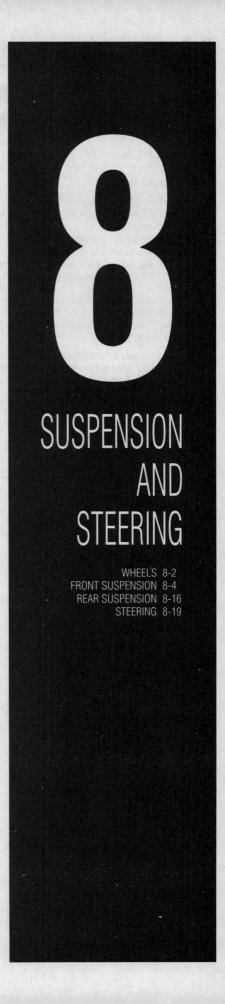

8

SUSPENSION AND STEERING

WHEELS

Wheel Assembly

REMOVAL & INSTALLATION

♦ **See Figures 1 thru 7**

1. Park the vehicle on a level surface.
2. Remove the jack, tire iron and, if necessary, the spare tire from their storage compartments.
3. Check the owner's manual or refer to Section 1 of this manual for the jacking points on your vehicle. Then, place the jack in the proper position.
4. If equipped with lug nut trim caps, remove them by either unscrewing or pulling them off the lug nuts, as appropriate. Consult the owner's manual, if necessary.
5. If equipped with a wheel cover or hub cap, insert the tapered end of the tire iron in the groove and pry off the cover.
6. Apply the parking brake and block the diagonally opposite wheel with a wheel chock or two.

➡Wheel chocks may be purchased at your local auto parts store, or a block of wood cut into wedges may be used. If possible, keep one or two of the chocks in your tire storage compartment, in case any of the tires has to be removed on the side of the road.

7. If equipped with an automatic transmission/transaxle, place the selector lever in **P** or Park; with a manual transmission/transaxle, place the shifter in Reverse.
8. With the tires still on the ground, use the tire iron/wrench to break the lug nuts loose.

➡If a nut is stuck, never use heat to loosen it or damage to the wheel and bearings may occur. If the nuts are seized, one or two heavy ham-

mer blows directly on the end of the bolt usually loosens the rust. Be careful, as continued pounding will likely damage the brake drum or rotor.

9. Using the jack, raise the vehicle until the tire is clear of the ground. Support the vehicle safely using jackstands.
10. Remove the lug nuts, then remove the tire and wheel assembly.

To install:
11. Make sure the wheel and hub mating surfaces, as well as the wheel lug studs, are clean and free of all foreign material. Always remove rust from the wheel mounting surface and the brake rotor or drum. Failure to do so may cause the lug nuts to loosen in service.
12. Install the tire and wheel assembly and hand-tighten the lug nuts.
13. Using the tire wrench, tighten all the lug nuts, in a crisscross pattern, until they are snug.
14. Raise the vehicle and withdraw the jackstand, then lower the vehicle.
15. Using a torque wrench, tighten the lug nuts in a crisscross pattern to ft. lbs. (Nm). Check your owner's manual or refer to Section 1 of this manual for the proper tightening sequence.

❉❉ WARNING

Do not overtighten the lug nuts, as this may cause the wheel studs to stretch or the brake disc (rotor) to warp.

16. If so equipped, install the wheel cover or hub cap. Make sure the valve stem protrudes through the proper opening before tapping the wheel cover into position.
17. If equipped, install the lug nut trim caps by pushing them or screwing them on, as applicable.
18. Remove the jack from under the vehicle, and place the jack and tire iron/wrench in their storage compartments. Remove the wheel chock(s).

Fig. 1 Place the jack at the proper lifting point on your vehicle

Fig. 2 Before jacking the vehicle, block the diagonally opposite wheel with one or, preferably, two chocks

Fig. 3 With the vehicle still on the ground, break the lug nuts loose using the wrench end of the tire iron

Fig. 4 After the lug nuts have been loosened, raise the vehicle using the jack until the tire is clear of the ground

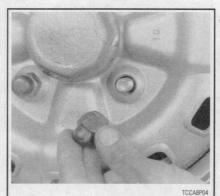

Fig. 5 Remove the lug nuts from the studs

Fig. 6 Remove the wheel and tire assembly from the vehicle

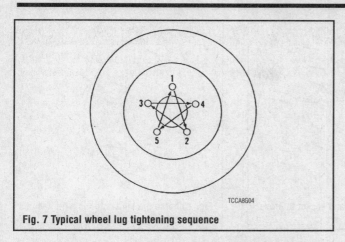

Fig. 7 Typical wheel lug tightening sequence

19. If you have removed a flat or damaged tire, place it in the storage compartment of the vehicle and take it to your local repair station to have it fixed or replaced as soon as possible.

INSPECTION

Inspect the tires for lacerations, puncture marks, nails and other sharp objects. Repair or replace as necessary. Also check the tires for treadwear and air pressure as outlined in Section 1 of this manual.

Check the wheel assemblies for dents, cracks, rust and metal fatigue. Repair or replace as necessary.

Wheel Lug Studs

REMOVAL & INSTALLATION

With Disc Brakes

▶ See Figures 8, 9 and 10

1. Raise and support the appropriate end of the vehicle safely using jackstands, then remove the wheel.

2. Remove the brake pads and caliper. Support the caliper aside using wire or a coat hanger. For details, please refer to Section 9 of this manual.

3. Remove the outer wheel bearing and lift off the rotor. For details on wheel bearing removal, installation and adjustment, please refer to Section 1 of this manual.

4. Properly support the rotor using press bars, then drive the stud out using an arbor press.

➡**If a press is not available, CAREFULLY drive the old stud out using a blunt drift. MAKE SURE the rotor is properly and evenly supported or it may be damaged.**

To install:

5. Clean the stud hole with a wire brush and start the new stud with a hammer and drift pin. Do not use any lubricant or thread sealer.

6. Finish installing the stud with the press.

➡**If a press is not available, start the lug stud through the bore in the hub, then position about 4 flat washers over the stud and thread the lug nut. Hold the hub/rotor while tightening the lug nut, and the stud should be drawn into position. MAKE SURE THE STUD IS FULLY SEATED, then remove the lug nut and washers.**

7. Install the rotor and adjust the wheel bearings.

8. Install the brake caliper and pads.

9. Install the wheel, then remove the jackstands and carefully lower the vehicle.

10. Tighten the lug nuts to the proper torque.

With Drum Brakes

▶ See Figures 11, 12 and 13

1. Raise the vehicle and safely support it with jackstands, then remove the wheel.

2. Remove the brake drum.

3. If necessary to provide clearance, remove the brake shoes, as outlined in Section 9 of this manual.

4. Using a large C-clamp and socket, press the stud from the axle flange.

5. Coat the serrated part of the stud with liquid soap and place it into the hole.

To install:

6. Position about 4 flat washers over the stud and thread the lug nut. Hold the flange while tightening the lug nut, and the stud should be drawn into position. MAKE SURE THE STUD IS FULLY SEATED, then remove the lug nut and washers.

7. If applicable, install the brake shoes.

8. Install the brake drum.

9. Install the wheel, then remove the jackstands and carefully lower the vehicle.

10. Tighten the lug nuts to the proper torque.

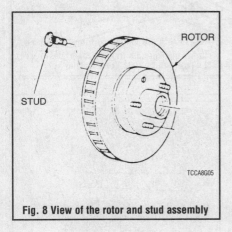

Fig. 8 View of the rotor and stud assembly

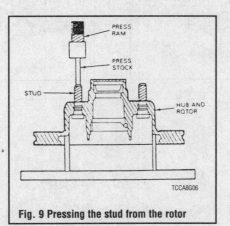

Fig. 9 Pressing the stud from the rotor

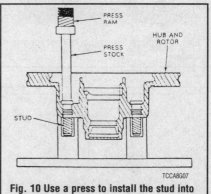

Fig. 10 Use a press to install the stud into the rotor

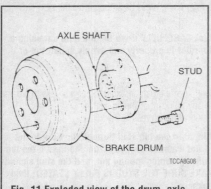

Fig. 11 Exploded view of the drum, axle flange and stud

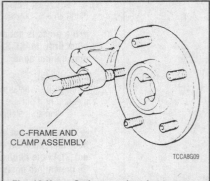

Fig. 12 Use a C-clamp and socket to press out the stud

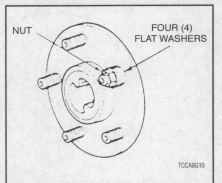

Fig. 13 Force the stud onto the axle flange using washers and a lug nut

FRONT SUSPENSION

Torsion Bars

REMOVAL & INSTALLATION

♦ See Figures 14 thru 22

2wd Models

1. Block the rear wheels and raise and support the front end with jack-stands under the frame rails.
2. Remove the torsion bar spring adjusting nut.
3. Remove the dust cover and remove the snapring from the anchor arm.

4. Pull the anchor arm off toward the rear and then remove the torsion bar spring.
5. Remove the torque arm.

To install:

6. Check the torsion bars for wear, cracks or other damage. Replace them if they are suspect.
7. Install the torque arm on the lower link (control arm) and tighten the bolts to 37–50 ft. lbs. (50–68 Nm).
8. Install the snapring and dust cover on the torsion bar.
9. Coat the splines on the inner end of the torsion bar with chassis lube and install it into the torque arm. The torsion bars are marked **L** and **R** and are not interchangeable.
10. Position a floor jack under the lower link and raise it so that clearance between the link and the rebound bumper is 0.

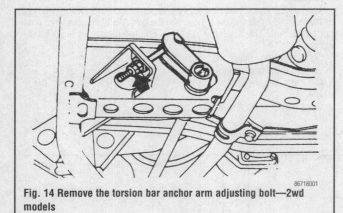

Fig. 14 Remove the torsion bar anchor arm adjusting bolt—2wd models

Fig. 15 Slide back the dust cover and remove the snapring

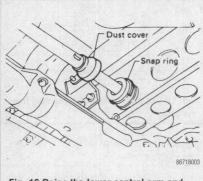
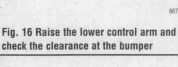

Fig. 16 Raise the lower control arm and check the clearance at the bumper

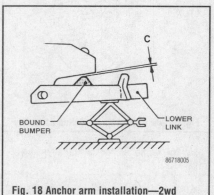

Fig. 17 Torsion bar springs are marked and not interchangeable

Fig. 18 Anchor arm installation—2wd models

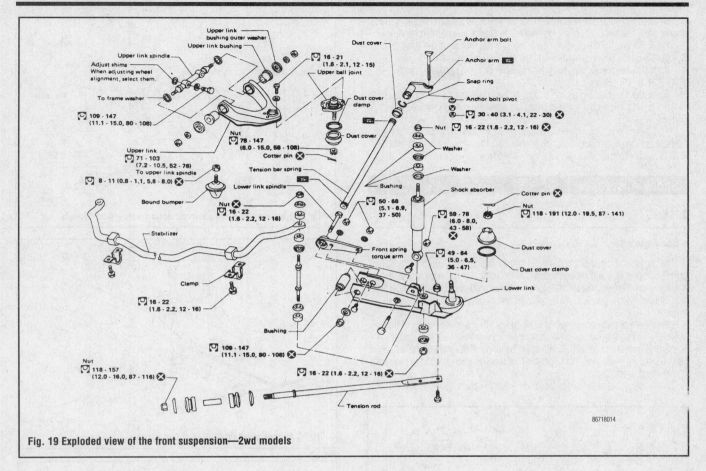

Fig. 19 Exploded view of the front suspension—2wd models

11. Install the anchor arm so that dimension **G** in the illustration is 0.24–0.71 in. (6–18mm).

12. Install the snapring to the anchor arm and dust cover. Make sure that the snapring is properly installed in the groove of the anchor arm.

13. Tighten the anchor arm adjusting nut until dimension **L** is 1.38 in. (35mm) for Heavy Duty, Cab/Chassis and STD models; or 1.93 in. (49mm) for all other models.

14. Lower the truck so that it is resting on its wheels and bounce it several times to set the suspension. Turn the anchor bolt adjusting nut so that dimension **H** in the illustration is 4.25–4.65 in. (108–118mm).

4wd Models

▶ **See Figures 23 thru 34**

1. Block the rear wheels and raise and support the front end with jackstands under the frame rails.

2. Remove the torsion bar spring adjusting nut.

3. Pull back the dust boot and remove the anchor arm snapring.

4. Remove the torque arm attaching nuts, then withdraw the torsion bar spring forward with the torque arm still attached.

To install:

5. Check the torsion bar for wear, cracks or other damage. Replace them if they are suspect.

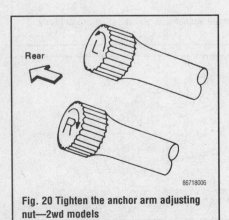

Fig. 20 Tighten the anchor arm adjusting nut—2wd models

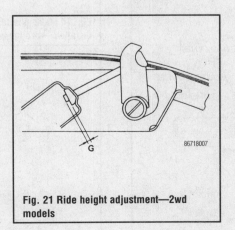

Fig. 21 Ride height adjustment—2wd models

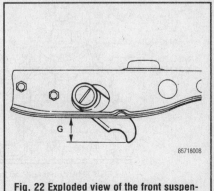

Fig. 22 Exploded view of the front suspension—2wd models

6. Coat the splines on the torsion bar with chassis lube and install it in the anchor arm. The torsion bars are marked **L** and **R** and are not interchangeable.

7. Position a floor jack under the lower link (control arm) and raise it so that the clearance between the link and the rebound bumper is 0.

8. Install the anchor arm so that dimension **G** in the illustration is 1.97–2.36 in. (50–60mm).

9. Install the snapring on the anchor arm and pull the dust boot over it.

10. Tighten the anchor arm adjusting nut until dimension **L** is 3.03 in. (77mm).

11. Lower the truck so that it is resting on its wheels and bounce it several times to set the suspension. Turn the anchor bolt adjusting nut so that dimension **H** in the illustration is 1.61–2.01 in. (41–51mm).

Shock Absorber

TESTING

♦ See Figure 35

The purpose of the shock absorber is simply to limit the motion of the spring during compression and rebound cycles. If the vehicle is not equipped with these motion dampers, the up and down motion would multiply until the vehicle was alternately trying to leap off the ground and to pound itself into the pavement.

Contrary to popular rumor, the shocks do not affect the ride height of the vehicle. This is controlled by other suspension components such as springs and tires. Worn shock absorbers can affect handling; if the front of the vehicle is rising or falling excessively, the "footprint" of the tires changes on the pavement and steering is affected.

The simplest test of the shock absorber is simply push down on one corner

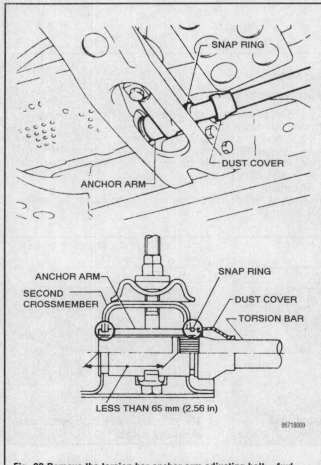

Fig. 23 Remove the torsion bar anchor arm adjusting bolt—4wd models

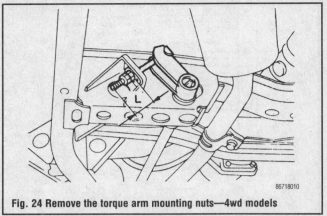

Fig. 24 Remove the torque arm mounting nuts—4wd models

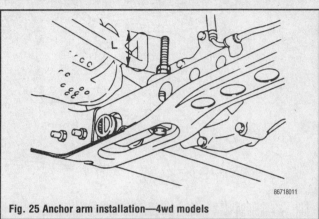

Fig. 25 Anchor arm installation—4wd models

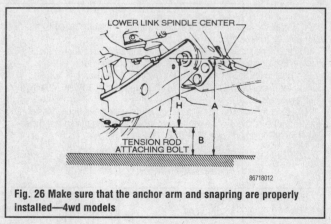

Fig. 26 Make sure that the anchor arm and snapring are properly installed—4wd models

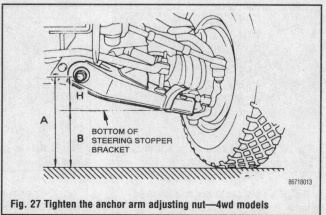

Fig. 27 Tighten the anchor arm adjusting nut—4wd models

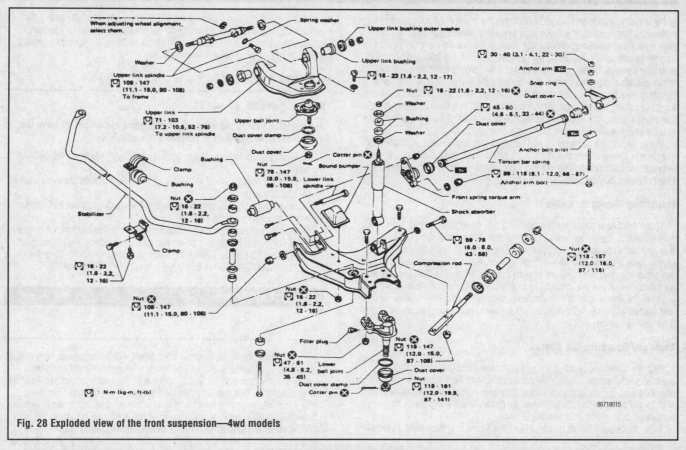

Fig. 28 Exploded view of the front suspension—4wd models

Fig. 29 Remove the torsion bar spring nut—4wd models

Fig. 30 Pull back the dust boot and remove the snapring

Fig. 31 Remove the torque arm attaching nuts

Fig. 32 View of the torque arm attaching point

Fig. 33 Removing the anchor arm and torsion bar assembly

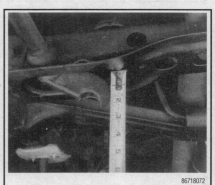

Fig. 34 Correct measurement of the anchor arm assembly is between

of the unladen vehicle and release it. Observe the motion of the body as it is released. In most cases, it will come up beyond it original rest position, dip back below it and settle quickly to rest. This shows that the damper is controlling the spring action. Any tendency to excessive pitch (up-and-down) motion or failure to return to rest within 2-3 cycles is a sign of poor function within the shock absorber. Oil-filled shocks may have a light film of oil around the seal, resulting from normal breathing and air exchange. This should NOT be taken as a sign of failure, but any sign of thick or running oil definitely indicates failure. Gas filled shocks may also show some film at the shaft; if the gas has leaked out, the shock will have almost no resistance to motion.

While each shock absorber can be replaced individually, it is recommended that they be changed as a pair (both front or both rear) to maintain equal response on both sides of the vehicle. Chances are quite good that if one has failed, its mate is weak also.

Inspecting Shocks for Leaks

Disconnect each shock lower mount and pull down on the shock until it is fully extended. inspect for leaks in the seal area. Shock absorber fluid is very thin and has a characteristic odor and dark brown color. Don't confuse the glossy paint on some shocks with leaking fluid. A slight trace of fluid is a normal condition; they are designed to seep a certain amount of fluid past the seals for lubrication. If you are in doubt as to whether the fluid on the shock is coming from the shock itself or from some other source, wipe the seal area clean and manually operate the shock (see the following procedure). Fluid will appear if the unit is leaking.

Manually Operating the Shocks

Grip the lower end of the shock and pull down (rebound stroke) and then push up (compression stroke). The control arms will limit the movement of front shocks during the compression stroke. Compare the rebound resistance of both shocks and compare the compression resistance. Usually any shock showing a noticeable difference will be the one at fault.

If the shock has internal noises, extend the shock fully then exert an extra

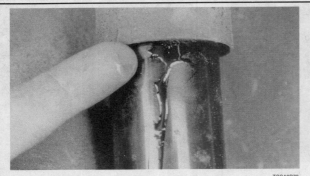

Fig. 35 When fluid is seeping out of the shock absorber, it's time to replace it

pull. If a small additional movement is felt, this usually means a loose piston and the shock should be replaced. Other noises that are cause for replacing shocks are a squeal after a full stroke in both directions, a clicking noise on fast reverse and a lag at reversal near mid-stroke.

REMOVAL & INSTALLATION

◆ See Figures 36, 37 and 38

➡**If vehicle is equipped with adjustable shock absorbers, remove the electrical connection before removing the assembly.**

1. Raise the front of the vehicle and support it with safety stands. Remove the wheel.
2. Hold the upper stem of the shock absorber and remove the nuts, washer, and rubber bushing.
3. Remove the bolt from the lower end of the shock absorber and remove the shock absorber from the vehicle.
4. Install the shock absorber. Replace all of the rubber bushings with new ones if a new shock absorber is being installed. Install the lower retaining bolt from the front of the truck. Tighten the upper attaching nut to 12–16 ft. lbs. (16–22 Nm) and the lower nut to 43–58 ft. lbs. (59–68 Nm).

Upper Ball Joint

INSPECTION

The ball joint should be replaced when play becomes excessive. Nissan does not publish specifications on just what constitutes excessive play, relying instead on a method of determining the force (in inch lbs.) required to keep the ball joint turning. This method is not very helpful to the backyard mechanic since it involves removing the ball joint, which is what we are trying to avoid in the first place. An effective way to determine ball joint play is to raise the truck until the wheel is just a couple of inches off the ground and the ball joint is unloaded, which means that you can't jack directly under the ball joint. Place a long bar under the tire and move the wheel and tire assembly up and down. Keep one hand on top of the tire while doing this. If there is over ¼ in. (6mm) of play at the top of the tire, the ball joint is probably bad. This assuming that the wheel bearings are in good shape and properly adjusted. As a double check, have someone watch the ball joint while you move the tire up and down with the bar. If considerable play is seen, besides feeling play at the top of the wheel, the ball joints need to be replaced.

REMOVAL & INSTALLATION

◆ See Figures 39, 40 and 41

1. Raise and support the front end with jackstands under the frame rails.
2. Remove the front wheels.
3. Support the lower control arm with a floor jack (this service step is very important) and remove the upper ball joint-to-knuckle nut.
4. Using a ball joint separator or gear arm puller, such as tool ST29020001 (2wd) or HT72520000 (4wd), remove the ball joint from the knuckle.

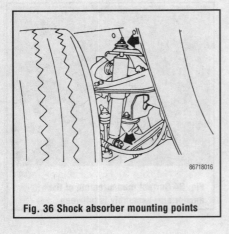

Fig. 36 Shock absorber mounting points

Fig. 37 Removing the upper shock mounting nut

Fig. 38 Removing the lower shock mounting bolt

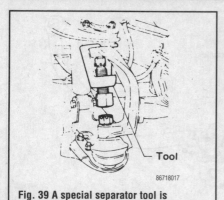

Fig. 39 A special separator tool is required to remove the upper ball joint

Fig. 40 With the lower control arm assembly properly supported, remove the retaining bolts from the upper control arm

Fig. 41 View of the upper ball joint still attached to the steering knuckle—lower control arm must be supported

5. Unbolt the ball joint from the upper arm.

To install:

6. Install the ball joint in the upper control arm and tighten the bolts to 12–17 ft. lbs. (16–23 Nm).

7. Press the ball stud into the steering knuckle and tighten the nut to 58–108 ft. lbs. (78–147 Nm). Be sure to use a new cotter pin.

8. Install the wheels and then lower the vehicle.

9. Check the front end alignment.

Lower Ball Joint

INSPECTION

The ball joint should be replaced when play becomes excessive. Nissan does not publish specifications on just what constitutes excessive play, relying instead on a method of determining the force (in inch lbs.) required to keep the ball joint turning. This method is not very helpful to the backyard mechanic since it involves removing the ball joint, which is what we are trying to avoid in the first place. An effective way to determine ball joint play is to raise the truck until the wheel is just a couple of inches off the ground and the ball joint is unloaded, which means that you can't jack directly under the ball joint. Place a long bar under the tire and move the wheel and tire assembly up and down. Keep one hand on top of the tire while doing this. If there is over ¼ in. (6mm) of play at the top of the tire, the ball joint is probably bad. This assuming that the wheel bearings are properly adjusted. As a double check, have someone watch the ball joint while you move the tire up and down with the bar. If considerable play is seen, besides feeling play at the top of the wheel, the ball joints need to be replaced.

REMOVAL & INSTALLATION

➡The lower ball joint on 2wd models is integral with the lower control arm. They are removed and replaced as a unit; please refer to the Lower Control Arm procedures for more details.

4wd Models Only

▶ See Figures 42, 43, 44, 45 and 46

1. Raise and support the front of the vehicle on jackstands under the frame rails.

2. Support the lower control arm with a floor jack (this service step is very important).

3. Remove the front wheels.

4. Unbolt the shock absorber from the lower arm.

5. Remove the ball joint nut.

6. Using a ball joint separator or gear arm puller, such as tool ST29020001 (2wd) or HT72520000 (4wd), remove the ball joint from the knuckle.

7. Unbolt the ball joint from the lower arm.

To install:

8. Install the ball joint to the lower arm and tighten the nuts to 35–45 ft. lbs. (47–61 Nm).

9. Press the ball stud into the knuckle and tighten the nut to 87–141 ft. lbs. (118–191 Nm). Make sure you use a new cotter pin.

10. Connect the lower end of the shock absorber.

11. Install the wheels and lower the vehicle.

12. Check the front end alignment.

Tension Rod and Stabilizer Bar

REMOVAL & INSTALLATION

▶ See Figures 47, 48 and 49

2wd Models Only

1. With the truck resting on its wheels, remove the underpan.

2. If the tension rod installation is correct, the white painted marks on the stabilizer bar, at the bushings, should be visible.

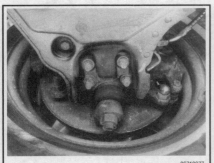

Fig. 42 View of the lower control arm and lower ball joint attached to steering knuckle

Fig. 43 View of the lower control arm attached to the frame of the vehicle

Fig. 44 Remove the lower ball joint retaining bolts—only when the lower control arm is supported

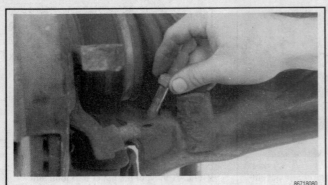

Fig. 45 Remove the lower ball joint-to-control arm bolts—note the bolt is installed with the head upward

Fig. 46 Removing the lower ball joint assembly from the lower control arm—note jack under the lower control arm for support

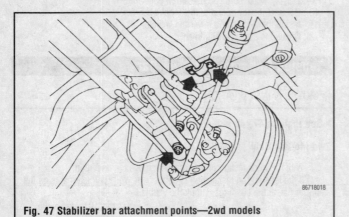

Fig. 47 Stabilizer bar attachment points—2wd models

3. The tension bar and stabilizer bar can be unbolted and removed with the vehicle supported on jackstands.

4. To install, simply position the component and tighten the nuts and bolts. Tighten the stabilizer bar through-bolt and the bar bushing clamp bolts to 12–16 ft. lbs. (16–22 Nm). Tighten the tension rod-to-lower link bolts to 36–47 ft. lbs. (49–64 Nm); and the tension rod-to-frame anchor nut to 87–116 ft. lbs. (118–157 Nm). Replace the bushings whenever the parts are changed. Replace any bushing that appears dry, cracked or compressed.

5. Check the stabilizer bar with the truck on its wheels to see if both white painted marks on the stabilizer bar are visible at the bushings.

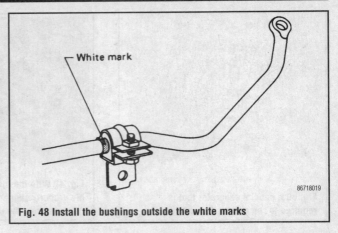

Fig. 48 Install the bushings outside the white marks

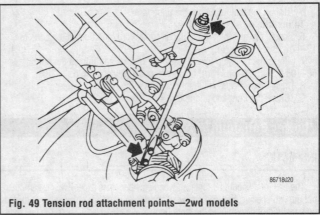

Fig. 49 Tension rod attachment points—2wd models

Compression Rod and Stabilizer Bar

REMOVAL & INSTALLATION

▶ See Figures 50, 51, 52 and 53

4wd Models Only

1. With the truck resting on its wheels, remove the underpan.

2. If the compression rod installation is correct, the white painted marks on the stabilizer bar, at the bushings, should be visible.

3. The compression rod and stabilizer bar can be unbolted and removed with the vehicle supported on jackstands.

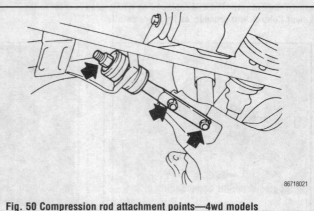

Fig. 50 Compression rod attachment points—4wd models

Fig. 51 View of the compression rod with bushings installed in the vehicle—4wd models

Fig. 52 Removing the stabilizer bar bushing bracket

Fig. 53 Removing the stabilizer bar bushing—note position of bushing upon installation

4. To install, simply position the component and tighten the nuts and bolts. Tighten the stabilizer bar through-bolt and the bar bushing clamp bolts to 12–16 ft. lbs. (16–22 Nm). Tighten the compression rod-to-lower link bolts to 87–108 ft. lbs. (118–147 Nm); and the compression rod-to-frame anchor nut to 87–116 ft. lbs. (118–157 Nm). Replace the bushings whenever the parts are changed. Replace any bushing that appears dry, cracked or compressed.

5. Check the stabilizer bar with the truck on its wheels to see if both white painted marks on the stabilizer bar are visible at the bushings.

Upper Control Arm

REMOVAL & INSTALLATION

▶ See Figures 54, 55 and 56

1. Separate the upper ball joint from the knuckle as previously described.
2. Disconnect the shock absorber at the upper end.
3. Unbolt the control arm spindle. Lift out the upper control arm.

To install:

4. The bushings may now be pressed out from both sides of the control arm.
5. Apply a soapy solution to new bushings and press them into position in one end of the arm, so that the flange on the bushing firmly contacts the end surface of the upper link collar.
6. Install the spindle and press in the remaining bushings.

➡The inner washers are installed with the rounded edges facing inward.

7. Temporarily tighten the spindle end nuts.
8. Install the upper ball joint.
9. Bolt the control arm to the frame. Tighten the bolts to 80–108 ft. lbs. (109–147 Nrn).

10. Tighten the spindle end nut with camber adjusting shims. Tighten the nuts to 52–76 ft. lbs. (71–83 Nm). Check the dimensions **A** and **B** in the illustration. Dimension **A** should be 4.33 in. (110mm). Dimension **B** should be 1.26 in. (32mm).

11. Install the ball joint to the knuckle and check the front end alignment.

Lower Control Arm

REMOVAL & INSTALLATION

▶ See Figures 57, 58, 59, 60 and 61

➡The lower ball joint on 2wd models is integral with the lower control arm. They are removed and replaced as a unit.

1. Make matching marks on the anchor arm crossmember when loosening the adjusting nut until there is no tension on the torsion bar and remove the torsion bar.
2. Separate the lower ball joint from the knuckle spindle on 2wd models. On 4wd models, separate it from the control arm.
3. Remove the front lower control arm attaching nut.
4. If necessary, remove the bushing of the lower control arm spindle from the frame using a suitable bushing press tool.

To install:

5. Coat the control arm bushing with soapy water and then install the arm to the frame. Tighten the bolt to 80–108 ft. lbs. (109–147 Nm).
6. Connect the ball joint to the knuckle on 2wd models or to the control arm on 4wd models.
7. Install the torsion bar and lower the vehicle.
8. Check the front end alignment.

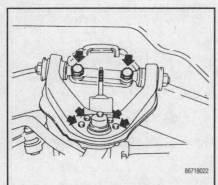

Fig. 54 Removing the upper control arm assembly

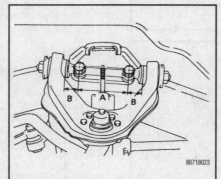

Fig. 55 Upper control arm measuring points—all models similar

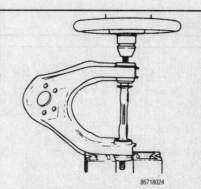

Fig. 56 Press out the spindle and upper control bushings

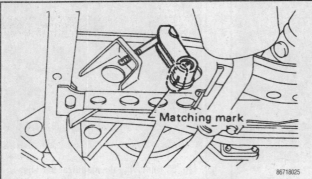

Fig. 57 Matchmark the anchor arm to the crossmember when removing the lower control arm—2wd models

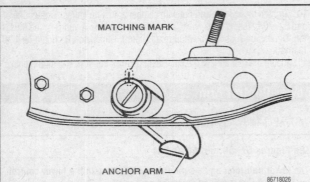

Fig. 58 Matchmark the anchor arm to the crossmember when removing the lower control arm—4wd models

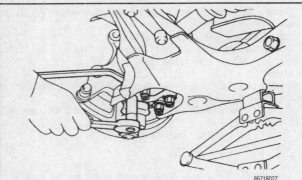

Fig. 59 Disconnect the lower ball joint from the lower arm—4wd models

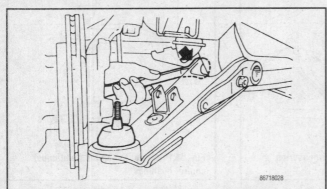

Fig. 60 Disconnect the lower ball joint from the lower arm—2wd models

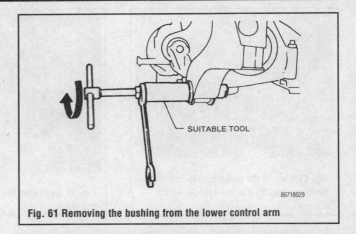

Fig. 61 Removing the bushing from the lower control arm

Steering Knuckle And Spindle

REMOVAL & INSTALLATION

2wd Models

1. Raise the front of the vehicle and support it safely with jackstands.
2. Remove the front wheels.
3. Disconnect the brake hose from the knuckle at the bracket.
4. Remove the brake caliper.
5. Remove the dust cap, and then remove the cotter pin, adjusting cap and spindle nut from the knuckle spindle.
6. Remove the wheel hub and rotor assembly.
7. Remove the hub from the rotor assembly.
8. Remove the outer bearing cone with fingers and remove the inner bearing cone by prying out the grease seal. Discard the grease seal.
9. If it is necessary to replace the bearing outer race, drive it out from the hub with a brass drift and mallet. Evenly tap the bearing outer race through the hole inside the hub.
10. Remove the baffle plate.
11. Loosen but do not remove the upper and lower ball joint tightening nut.
12. Separate the upper and lower ball joint from the knuckle spindle.
13. Jack up the lower control arm (link), then remove the ball joint tightening nut.
14. Separate the knuckle spindle from the upper and lower control arms (links).
15. When installing, please note the following exceptions:
    a. While jacking up the lower link, install the knuckle spindle to the upper and lower ball joints.
    b. When installing the knuckle arm, tighten the retaining bolts to 53–72 ft. lbs. (72–97 Nm).
    c. Install the front hub wheel bearings as outlined in Section 1.
    d. When attaching the disc rotor to the hub, tighten the bolts to 36–51 ft. lbs. (49–69 Nm).

4wd Models

▶ See Figures 62 and 63

1. Remove the Auto-lock or Manual-lock free running hub assembly as detailed in Section 7.
2. Separate the axle shaft from the knuckle spindle by slightly tapping the axle shaft end.
3. Loosen, but do not remove the upper and lower ball joint-to-spindle nuts.
4. Separate the knuckle spindle from the upper and lower ball joint studs with Tool HT72520000, or other equivalent separating tool.
5. Support the lower control arm with a floor jack and remove the ball joint tightening nuts.
6. Remove the knuckle spindle from the control arms.
7. When installing, follow these notes:
    a. When installing the needle bearing into the knuckle, apply grease and make sure the bearing is in the proper direction.

Fig. 62 Tapping the axle shaft from the spindle—always use a wooden block to protect the axle shaft

Fig. 63 Removing the knuckle spindle from the axle shaft—note axle shaft is removed from the vehicle for illustration purposes only

b. With the lower control arm jacked up, install the knuckle spindle to the upper and lower ball joints.

c. Adjust the wheel bearing preload.

d. When installing the axle shaft, never reuse the snapring, and check axial end-play. Refer to Section 7.

Front Axle Hub and Wheel Bearing

REMOVAL & INSTALLATION

2wd Models

▶ **See Figures 64, 65, 66 and 67**

➡ Refer to wheel bearing service and bearing preload adjustment procedures found in Section 1.

1. Raise the front of the truck and support it with safety stands. Remove the wheels.

2. Remove the brake caliper and suspend it with wire, out of the way. Remove the caliper torque plate if equipped.

3. Remove the dust cap and then remove the cotter pin, lock washer (if equipped) nut lock and nut.

4. Pull the hub/disc assembly off the spindle with the outer bearing. Don't let the bearing fall out.

5. Pry the inner oil seal out and remove the inner bearing.

To install:

6. Clean and inspect the bearings and outer races.

7. Using a brass drift and a hammer, drive out the bearing outer race. Press a new one into position.

8. Pack the bearings with grease until it oozes out the other side. Coat the inside of the hub and cap with grease.

9. Position the inner bearing into the hub, coat the oil seal with grease and press it into the hub.

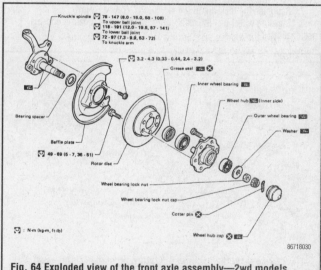

Fig. 64 Exploded view of the front axle assembly—2wd models

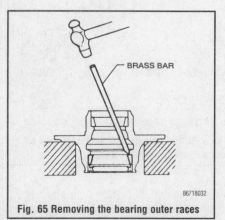

Fig. 65 Removing the bearing outer races

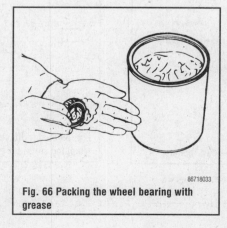

Fig. 66 Packing the wheel bearing with grease

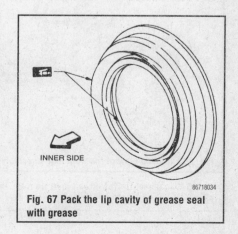

Fig. 67 Pack the lip cavity of grease seal with grease

10. Press the hub assembly onto the spindle and install the outer bearing and thrust washer.

11. Install the hub nut. Turn the hub a few times to seat the bearings and then loosen the nut until there is 0mm axial play. Using a spring tension gauge, check that the preload (with new grease seal installed) is 2.2–6.4 lbs. (9.8–28.4N)

12. Install the lock-nut, new cotter pin and hub grease cap.

13. Install the brake torque plate. Install the brake caliper.

14. Install the wheels and lower the truck.

4wd Models

♦ **See Figure 68**

The hub and bearing service procedures for a 4wd models are basically the same as those for a 2wd version, with the exception of removing the free running hub assembly and the bearing preload adjustment. Refer to Sections 1 and 7 for additional information. Adjust the preload after the wheel bearing is replaced or the front axle assembly is reassembled.

BEARING PRELOAD ADJUSTMENT

1. Thoroughly clean all parts and pack the wheel bearings.

2. Apply grease to threaded portions of the spindle, grease seal lip and wheel hub.

3. Tighten the wheel bearing lock-nut with a socket and torque wrench to 58–72 ft. lbs. (78–98 Nm).

4. Rotate the hub in both directions a few times to seat the bearings. Loosen wheel bearing lock-nut.

5. Retighten the lock-nut to 0.4–1.1 ft. lbs. (0.5–1.5 Nm).

6. Turn wheel hub several times in both directions.

7. Retighten the lock-nut to 0.4–1.1 ft. lbs. (0.5–1.5 Nm).

8. Measure wheel bearing axial end-play. The wheel bearing end-play specification is 0.

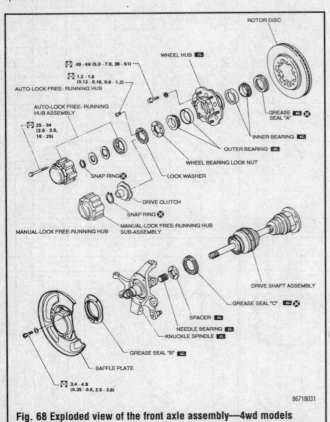

Fig. 68 Exploded view of the front axle assembly—4wd models

9. Install lock washer by tightening the lock-nut within 15–30 degrees.

10. Turn wheel hub several times in both directions. Wheel bearing should be seated correctly.

11. If necessary, measure wheel bearing preload.

➡**Measure wheel bearing preload with a spring-type gauge; measure at wheel hub bolt, with tire removed. The hub assembly should rotate with 1.6–4.7 lbs. (0.73–2.13 kg) of pressure.**

Wheel Alignment

If the tires are worn unevenly, if the vehicle is not stable on the highway or if the handling seems uneven in spirited driving, the wheel alignment should be checked. If an alignment problem is suspected, first check for improper tire inflation and other possible causes. These can be worn suspension or steering components, accident damage or even unmatched tires. If any worn or damaged components are found, they must be replaced before the wheels can be properly aligned. Wheel alignment requires very expensive equipment and involves minute adjustments which must be accurate; it should only be performed by a trained technician. Take your vehicle to a properly equipped shop.

Following is a description of the alignment angles which are adjustable on most vehicles and how they affect vehicle handling. Although these angles can apply to both the front and rear wheels, usually only the front suspension is adjustable.

CASTER

♦ **See Figure 69**

Looking at a vehicle from the side, caster angle describes the steering axis rather than a wheel angle. The steering knuckle is attached to a control arm or strut at the top and a control arm at the bottom. The wheel pivots around the line between these points to steer the vehicle. When the upper point is tilted back, this is described as positive caster. Having a positive caster tends to make the wheels self-centering, increasing directional stability. Excessive positive caster makes the wheels hard to steer, while an uneven caster will cause a pull to one side. Overloading the vehicle or sagging rear springs will affect caster, as will raising the rear of the vehicle. If the rear of the vehicle is lower than normal, the caster becomes more positive.

CAMBER

♦ **See Figure 70**

Looking from the front of the vehicle, camber is the inward or outward tilt of the top of wheels. When the tops of the wheels are tilted in, this is negative camber; if they are tilted out, it is positive. In a turn, a slight amount of negative camber helps maximize contact of the tire with the road. However, too much negative camber compromises straight-line stability, increases bump steer and torque steer.

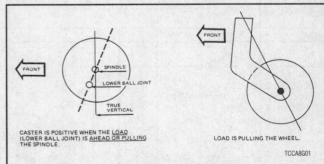

Fig. 69 Caster affects straight-line stability. Caster wheels used on shopping carts, for example, employ positive caster

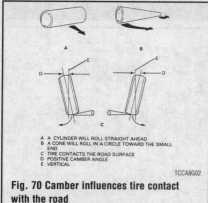

Fig. 70 Camber influences tire contact with the road

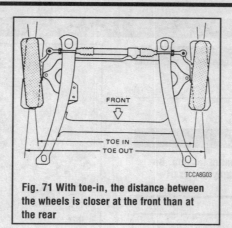

Fig. 71 With toe-in, the distance between the wheels is closer at the front than at the rear

Fig. 72 Steering angle adjustment

TOE

▶ **See Figure 71**

Looking down at the wheels from above the vehicle, toe angle is the distance between the front of the wheels, relative to the distance between the back of the wheels. If the wheels are closer at the front, they are said to be toed-in or to have negative toe. A small amount of negative toe enhances directional stability and provides a smoother ride on the highway.

STEERING ANGLE ADJUSTMENT

▶ **See Figure 72**

The maximum steering angle is adjusted by stopper bolts located on the inside of the steering knuckle/spindle. Loosen the lock-nut on the stopper bolt, turn the stopper bolt in or out as required to obtain the proper maximum steering angle and retighten the lock-nut.

WHEEL ALIGNMENT SPECIFICATIONS

Year	Models	Caster (deg.) Range	Pref.	Camber (deg.) Range	Pref.	Toe-in (in.)	Steering Axis Inclination (deg.)
1989	2WD	$\frac{5}{16}$N–$1\frac{3}{16}$P	$\frac{7}{16}$P	$\frac{3}{8}$N–$1\frac{1}{8}$P	$\frac{3}{8}$P	0.04–0.20	$8\frac{5}{8}$–$9\frac{13}{16}$
	4WD	$\frac{1}{16}$N–$1\frac{7}{16}$P	$\frac{11}{16}$P	$\frac{9}{16}$P–$2\frac{1}{16}$P	$1\frac{5}{16}$P	0.08–0.24①	$7\frac{3}{8}$–$8\frac{7}{8}$
1990	2WD	$\frac{5}{16}$N–$1\frac{3}{16}$P	$\frac{7}{16}$P	$\frac{3}{8}$N–$1\frac{1}{8}$P	$\frac{3}{8}$P	②	$8\frac{5}{8}$–$9\frac{13}{16}$
	4WD	$\frac{1}{16}$N–$1\frac{7}{16}$P	$\frac{11}{16}$P	$\frac{9}{16}$P–$2\frac{1}{16}$P	$1\frac{5}{16}$P	③	$7\frac{3}{8}$–$8\frac{7}{8}$
1991	2WD	$\frac{5}{16}$N–$1\frac{3}{16}$P	$\frac{7}{16}$P	$\frac{3}{8}$N–$1\frac{1}{8}$P	$\frac{3}{8}$P	②	$8\frac{5}{8}$–$9\frac{13}{16}$
	4WD	$\frac{1}{16}$N–$1\frac{7}{16}$P	$\frac{11}{16}$P	$\frac{9}{16}$P–$2\frac{1}{16}$P	$1\frac{5}{16}$P	③	$7\frac{3}{8}$–$8\frac{7}{8}$
1992	2WD	$\frac{5}{16}$N–$1\frac{3}{16}$P	$\frac{7}{16}$P	$\frac{3}{8}$N–$1\frac{1}{8}$P	$\frac{3}{8}$P	②	$8\frac{5}{8}$–$9\frac{13}{16}$
	4WD	$\frac{1}{16}$N–$1\frac{7}{16}$P	$\frac{11}{16}$P	$\frac{9}{16}$P–$2\frac{1}{16}$P	$1\frac{5}{16}$P	③	$7\frac{3}{8}$–$8\frac{7}{8}$
1993	2WD	$\frac{5}{16}$N–$1\frac{3}{16}$P	$\frac{7}{16}$P	$\frac{3}{8}$N–$1\frac{1}{8}$P	$\frac{3}{8}$P	②	$8\frac{5}{8}$–$9\frac{13}{16}$
	4WD	$\frac{1}{16}$N–$1\frac{7}{16}$P	$\frac{11}{16}$P	$\frac{9}{16}$P–$2\frac{1}{16}$P	$1\frac{5}{16}$P	③	$7\frac{3}{8}$–$8\frac{7}{8}$
1994	2WD	$\frac{5}{16}$N–$1\frac{3}{16}$P	$\frac{7}{16}$P	$\frac{3}{8}$N–$1\frac{1}{8}$P	$\frac{3}{8}$P	②	$8\frac{5}{8}$–$9\frac{13}{16}$
	4WD	$\frac{1}{16}$N–$1\frac{7}{16}$P	$\frac{11}{16}$P	$\frac{9}{16}$P–$2\frac{1}{16}$P	$1\frac{5}{16}$P	③	$7\frac{3}{8}$–$8\frac{7}{8}$
1995	2WD	$\frac{5}{16}$N–$1\frac{3}{16}$P	$\frac{7}{16}$P	$\frac{3}{8}$N–$1\frac{1}{8}$P	$\frac{3}{8}$P	②	$8\frac{5}{8}$–$9\frac{13}{16}$
	4WD	$\frac{1}{16}$N–$1\frac{7}{16}$P	$\frac{11}{16}$P	$\frac{9}{16}$P–$2\frac{1}{16}$P	$1\frac{5}{16}$P	③	$7\frac{3}{8}$–$8\frac{7}{8}$

① Pathfinder: 0.0–0.16 in.
② Bias tire: 0.12–0.28 in.
Radial tire: 0.04–0.20 in.
③ Bias tire: 0.12–0.28 in.
Radial tire: 0.08–0.24 in.

86718C01

REAR SUSPENSION

Coil Springs

REMOVAL & INSTALLATION

▶ See Figures 73, 74, 75 and 76

✳✳ CAUTION

The coil springs are under a considerable amount of tension. Be very careful when removing or installing them; they can exert enough force to cause serious injuries.

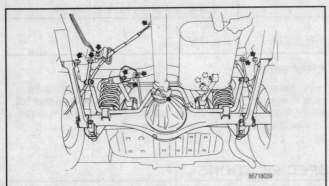

Fig. 73 Remove the rear axle assembly before lifting out the coil springs—Pathfinder

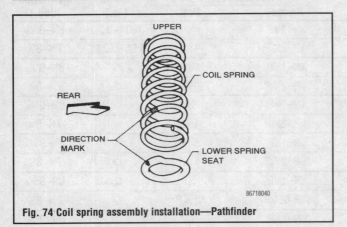

Fig. 74 Coil spring assembly installation—Pathfinder

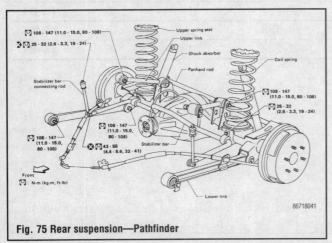

Fig. 75 Rear suspension—Pathfinder

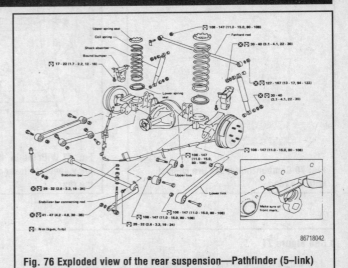

Fig. 76 Exploded view of the rear suspension—Pathfinder (5–link)

Pathfinder Only

1. Raise the rear of the truck and remove the rear axle as detailed in Section 7 under Rear Axle 5-Link.
2. Remove the coil springs and their spring seats. Be careful to keep all components in their proper order.
3. Install the spring seats on the rear axle in the proper directions and then raise the axle housing until the springs can be inserted.
4. Install the rear axle housing.

Leaf Springs

REMOVAL & INSTALLATION

▶ See Figures 77, 78, 79, 80 and 81

✳✳ CAUTION

The leaf springs are under a considerable amount of tension. Be very careful when removing or installing them; they can exert enough force to cause serious injuries.

Pick-up Only

1. Raise the rear of the truck and support it with jackstands placed under the frame.

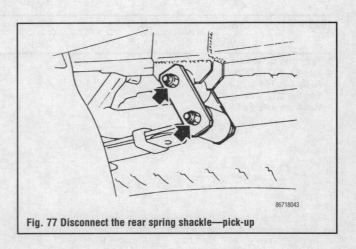

Fig. 77 Disconnect the rear spring shackle—pick-up

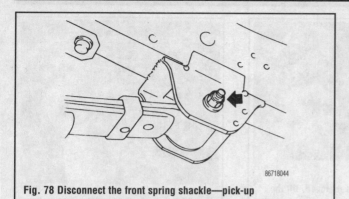

86718044

Fig. 78 Disconnect the front spring shackle—pick-up

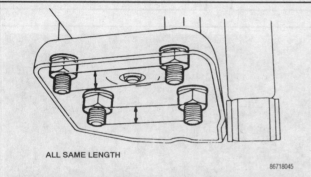

ALL SAME LENGTH

86718045

Fig. 79 When installing the U-bolts, make sure that all exposed bolt ends are the same length

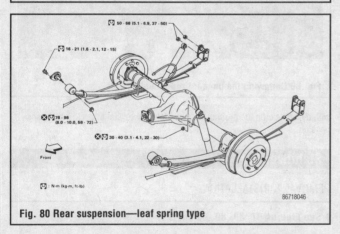

86718046

Fig. 80 Rear suspension—leaf spring type

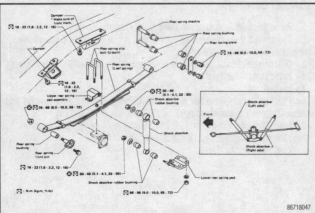

86718047

Fig. 81 Exploded view of the rear suspension—leaf spring type

2. Disconnect the shock absorbers at their lower end. Disconnect the parking brake cables from the springs.

3. Remove the nuts securing the U-bolts around the axle housing.

4. Place a jack under the rear axle housing and raise the housing just enough to remove the weight from the springs.

5. Remove the nuts from the spring shackles, drive out the shackle pins and remove the spring from the vehicle.

To install:

6. Install the springs. The weight of the truck must be on the rear wheels before tightening the front pin, shackle, and shock absorber attaching nuts.

7. Bounce the truck several times to set the suspension and then tighten the front pin and shackle nuts to 58–72 ft. lbs. (78–98 Nm). Tighten the U-bolt nuts to 65–72 ft. lbs. (88–98 Nm). Tighten the shock absorber lower end nut 22–30 ft. lbs. (30–40 Nm).

Shock Absorbers

TESTING

♦ See Figure 82

The purpose of the shock absorber is simply to limit the motion of the spring during compression and rebound cycles. If the vehicle is not equipped with these motion dampers, the up and down motion would multiply until the vehicle was alternately trying to leap off the ground and to pound itself into the pavement.

Contrary to popular rumor, the shocks do not affect the ride height of the vehicle. This is controlled by other suspension components such as springs and tires. Worn shock absorbers can affect handling; if the front of the vehicle is rising or falling excessively, the "footprint" of the tires changes on the pavement and steering is affected.

The simplest test of the shock absorber is simply push down on one corner of the unladen vehicle and release it. Observe the motion of the body as it is released. In most cases, it will come up beyond it original rest position, dip back below it and settle quickly to rest. This shows that the damper is controlling the spring action. Any tendency to excessive pitch (up-and-down) motion or failure to return to rest within 2-3 cycles is a sign of poor function within the shock absorber. Oil-filled shocks may have a light film of oil around the seal, resulting from normal breathing and air exchange. This should NOT be taken as a sign of failure, but any sign of thick or running oil definitely indicates failure. Gas filled shocks may also show some film at the shaft; if the gas has leaked out, the shock will have almost no resistance to motion.

While each shock absorber can be replaced individually, it is recommended that they be changed as a pair (both front or both rear) to maintain equal response on both sides of the vehicle. Chances are quite good that if one has failed, its mate is weak also.

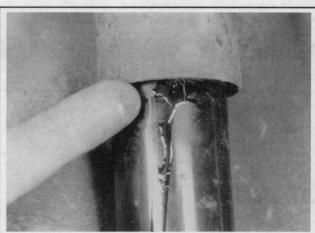

TCCA8P73

Fig. 82 When fluid is seeping out of the shock absorber, it's time to replace it

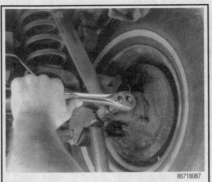

Fig. 83 Removing the lower mount retaining nut on the rear shock absorber

Fig. 84 Once the nut is removed, lift the washer from the shock lower mount—note position of washer

Fig. 85 Removing the rear shock absorber from the lower mounting

REMOVAL & INSTALLATION

▶ **See Figures 83, 84 and 85**

➡ **If vehicle is equipped with adjustable shock absorbers, remove the electrical connection before removing the assembly.**

1. Raise the rear of the vehicle.
2. Support the rear axle housing with jackstands.
3. Unfasten the upper shock absorber retaining nuts and/or bolts from the upper frame member.
4. Depending upon the type of rear spring used, either disconnect the lower end of the shock absorber from the spring seat, or the rear axle housing, by removing its cotter pins, nuts and/or bolts.
5. Remove the shock absorber. Inspect the shock for wear, leaks, or other signs of damage.
6. Install the shock absorber and tighten the upper bolts to 22–30 ft. lbs. (30–40 Nm). Tighten the shock absorber lower bolt to 22–30 ft. lbs. (30–40 Nm).

Control Arms/Links

REMOVAL & INSTALLATION

Pathfinder Only

Control arm removal and installation is fairly simple; raise the vehicle and support the rear axle housing and then unbolt the control arms. Always install the bolts in the same direction that they were removed. All bolts should be tightened to 80–108 ft. lbs. (108–147 Nm) with the vehicle on the ground. Bounce the truck several times to set the suspension.

Panhard Rod

REMOVAL & INSTALLATION

▶ **See Figure 86**

Pathfinder Only

1. Raise the vehicle and support the rear axle housing.
2. Unbolt the rod.
3. Installation is the reverse of removal. Tighten the right side bolt to 80–108 ft. lbs. (108–147 Nm) and the left side bolt to 36–51 ft. lbs. (49–69 Nm) on 1989 models or 94–123 ft. lbs. (127–167 Nm) on 1990–95 models

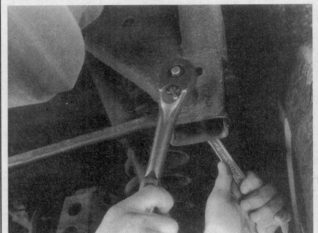

Fig. 86 Removing the panhard rod mounting bolt

with the vehicle on the ground. Bounce the truck several times to set the suspension.

Stabilizer Bar

REMOVAL & INSTALLATION

▶ **See Figures 87, 88, 89, 90 and 91**

Pathfinder Only

1. Raise the truck and support it with safety stands.
2. Disconnect the stabilizer bar connecting rod at the body. Remove the retainer and cushion from the link.
3. Disconnect the stabilizer bar bracket and cushion from the axle housing.
4. Remove the stabilizer bar.
   To install:
5. Position the stabilizer bar at the axle housing and install the bracket and cushion. Tighten the mounting bolts to 19–24 ft. lbs. (25–32 Nm).
6. Install the connecting rod to the body with the retainers and cushion. Tighten the mounting bolts to 19–24 ft. lbs. (25–32 Nm).
7. Lower the truck.

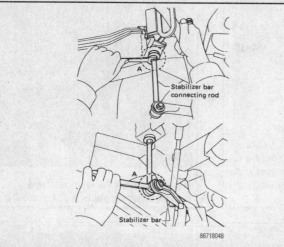

Fig. 87 When removing and installing the stabilizer bar, secure portion A—Pathfinder

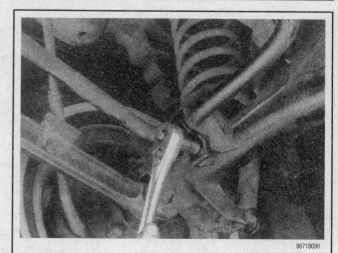

Fig. 88 Removing the stabilizer bar-to-rear axle housing mounting bolt

Fig. 89 View of the stabilizer bar-to-rear axle housing mounting—note position of rubber bushing

Fig. 90 Removing the stabilizer bar-to-connecting rod link nut

Fig. 91 View of the stabilizer bar-to-connecting rod link hardware

STEERING

Steering Wheel

REMOVAL & INSTALLATION

1. Position the wheels in the straight ahead position.
2. Disconnect the negative battery cable.
3. Remove the horn pad by unscrewing the two screws from the rear side of the steering wheel crossbar.
4. Punchmark the top of the steering column shaft and the steering wheel flange.
5. Remove the attaching nut and remove the steering wheel with a puller tool.

➡Do not strike the shaft with a hammer, which may cause the column to collapse.

To install:
6. Install the steering wheel so that the punchmarks are aligned.
7. Tighten the steering wheel attaching nut to 22–29 ft. lbs. (29–39 Nm).
8. Install the horn pad.

Combination Switch

The combination switch is the entire assembly of lever controlled switches which are mounted on the steering column. This includes the headlight, turn signal, and if equipped, cruise control switch on the left-hand side of the column, and the wiper/washer control switch on the right-hand side. These switches are secured to a central switch base by means of retaining screws. Using this procedure you may remove the entire combination switch and base assembly, or you can replace either of the individual switches.

REMOVAL & INSTALLATION

♦ See Figures 92 thru 103

1. Disconnect the negative battery cable.
2. Remove the steering wheel as outlined earlier.
3. From under the steering column, unthread the two retaining screws securing the lower portion of the column cover. Once the screws are removed, carefully separate and remove the upper and lower column cover portions.
4. Trace the switch wiring harness to the multi-connector(s). Mark and tag the individual harnesses. Once the tagging is complete, push in the lock levers and pull apart the connectors. If only one of the switches is being replaced, then only the wiring on that side of the column must be disconnected.
5. If the entire switch assembly is being removed, first check behind the assembly for any retaining screw(s). It may be necessary to rotate or tilt the base slightly to free the alignment tab, then carefully pull the switch and base assembly from the steering column. BE very careful not to break the alignment tab on the switch base.
6. If one or more of the switches are being replaced, unfasten the mounting screws, then remove the switch from the base assembly.
To install:
7. Position the switch to the switch base, and secure using the mounting screws tightened evenly.

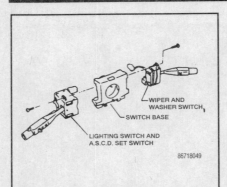

Fig. 92 Switches can be removed without removing the switch base

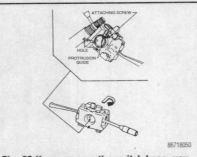

Fig. 93 If you remove the switch base, you must align the tab on the switch base with the hole in the steering column upon installation

Fig. 94 Unthread the lower retaining screws to remove the horn pad assembly

Fig. 95 After the retaining screws are removed, lift off the horn pad assembly

Fig. 96 Remove the steering wheel retaining nut and note steering wheel alignment

Fig. 97 Install a steering wheel puller onto the wheel—the puller must be on straight

Fig. 98 Remove the steering wheel after the puller is threaded down about 5 turns

Fig. 99 Loosen and remove the retainers from the steering column covers

Fig. 100 Remove the column covers to gain access to the combination switch assembly

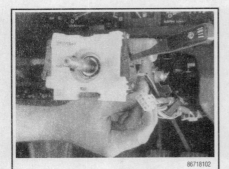

Fig. 101 Mark and tag all electrical connections to the combination switch before unplugging the harnesses

Fig. 102 If necessary, remove the switch retaining screws (in this case the wiper/washer switch)

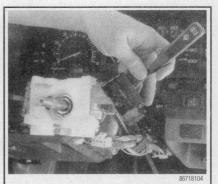

Fig. 103 Remove the lever switch from the combination switch base assembly

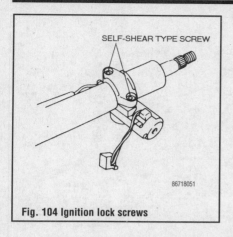

Fig. 104 Ignition lock screws

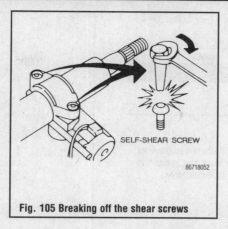

Fig. 105 Breaking off the shear screws

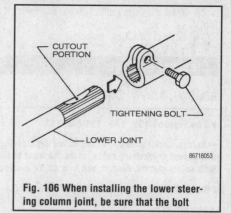

Fig. 106 When installing the lower steering column joint, be sure that the bolt

8. If removed, install the switch base assembly to the steering column. Be sure to align the tab on the switch body with the hole in the steering column. Make sure the base is secured in position, if applicable, install the retaining screw(s).

9. Connect the switch harnesses.

10. Install the steering wheel column covers, making sure the tabs connect correctly. Secure from under the steering wheel using the retaining screws tightened evenly. Position the steering wheel on the column and secure as outlined earlier.

11. Connect the negative battery cable.

Ignition Lock/Switch

REMOVAL & INSTALLATION

▶ **See Figures 104 and 105**

1. Disconnect the battery ground cable.
2. Remove the steering wheel and the column covers.
3. Drill out the shear bolts holding the lock assembly in place and remove the conventional bolts.
4. Disconnect the wiring from the switch and remove the assembly.
5. Unscrew the retaining bolts in the lock cylinder and separate the switch from the lock.

To install:

6. Connect the switch to the lock cylinder and tighten the retaining screws evenly.
7. Make sure that the hole in the column and the mating part of the lock cylinder are aligned. Install new shear bolts and break off their heads.
8. Connect the electrical lead to the switch and then install the column covers.
9. Install the steering wheel and connect the battery cable.

Steering Column

REMOVAL & INSTALLATION

▶ **See Figures 106, 107 and 108**

➡Nissan offers no factory approved service procedures for the steering column removal and installation on the trucks covered by this manual. Please use the following procedures as a guide.

1. Disconnect the negative battery cable.
2. Remove the pinch bolt securing the worm shaft to the steering coupling.
3. Remove the steering wheel.
4. Remove the steering column shell covers.
5. Remove the combination switch.
6. Remove the driver's side heater duct.
7. Remove the jacket tube bracket plate from the firewall behind the pedals.
8. Remove the column mounting bracket and remove the steering column assembly.

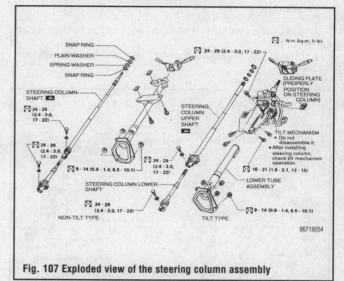

Fig. 107 Exploded view of the steering column assembly

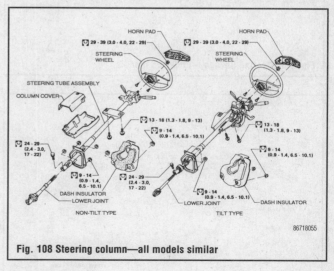

Fig. 108 Steering column—all models similar

To install:

9. Set the front wheels in the straight-ahead position and make sure that the punchmark on the upper end surface of the steering column is at the center of the upper side (its facing upward) and then install the column.

10. Tighten the column mounting bracket and jacket tube bracket plate mounting bolts.

11. Connect the heater duct and install the combination switch.

12. Install the shell covers and the steering wheel.

13. Install the worm shaft pinch bolt and tighten it to 17–22 ft. lbs. (24–29 Nm).

14. Connect the battery cable.

Steering Linkage

REMOVAL & INSTALLATION

♦ See Figures 109, 110, 111 and 112

➡Before working on any of the following steering linkage components, disconnect the battery cable, raise the front of the truck and support it with safety stands. Always use new cotter pins upon installation.

Pitman Arm

1989 MODELS

1. Remove the strut bar.
2. Loosen the pitman arm nut.
3. Using a tie rod end puller or equivalent, disconnect the pitman arm from the sector shaft.
4. Using a tie rod end puller or equivalent, disconnect the pitman arm from the cross rod.

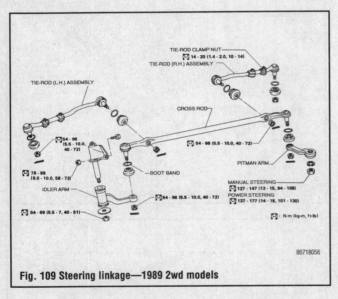

Fig. 109 Steering linkage—1989 2wd models

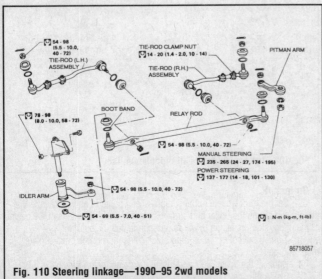

Fig. 110 Steering linkage—1990–95 2wd models

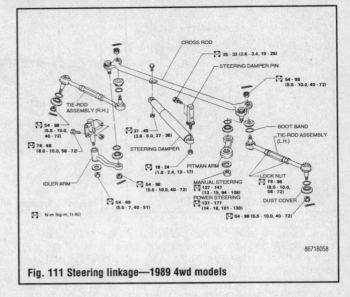

Fig. 111 Steering linkage—1989 4wd models

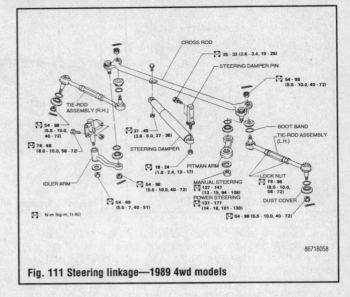

Fig. 112 Steering linkage—1990–95 4wd models

To install:

5. Align the marks on the pitman arm and sector shaft and connect them. Tighten the nut to 94–108 ft. lbs. (127–147 Nm) on models with manual steering; or 101–130 ft. lbs. (137–177 Nm) on models with power steering.

6. Connect the arm to the cross rod and tighten the nut. Install a new cotter pin.

7. Install the strut bar.

1990–95 MODELS

♦ See Figures 113 and 114

1. Remove the strut bar.
2. Loosen the pitman arm nut.
3. Using a tie rod end puller or equivalent, disconnect the pitman arm from the sector shaft.
4. Using a tie rod end puller or equivalent, disconnect the pitman arm from the relay rod.

To install:

5. Align the marks on the pitman arm and sector shaft and connect them. Tighten the nut to 174–195 ft. lbs. (235–265 Nm) on 2wd models with manual steering and all 4wd models; or 101–130 ft. lbs. (137–177 Nm) on 2wd models with power steering.

6. Connect the arm to the relay rod and tighten the nut. Install a new cotter pin.

7. Install the strut bar.

Fig. 113 Install a pitman arm/tie rod puller on the sector shaft

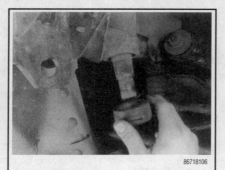

Fig. 114 Removing the pitman arm from the sector shaft—note arm is keyed for proper installation

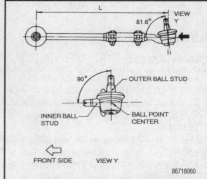

Fig. 115 Measuring the tie rod length and angle—2wd models

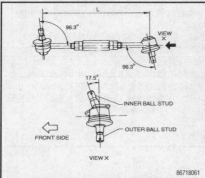

Fig. 116 Measuring the tie rod length and angle—4wd models

Fig. 117 Remove the cotter pin from the tie rod assembly—always replace the cotter pin with a new one upon installation

Fig. 118 Removing the tie rod assembly nut

Fig. 119 Install the tie rod puller to remove the tie rod

Fig. 120 After installing the puller, thread it down a few turns to loosen the tie rod, then remove the rod end from the spindle

Fig. 121 Loosen the tie rod lock-nut after installing the tie rod into the spindle

Tie Rod

ALL MODELS

▶ See Figures 115 thru 121

1. Using a tie rod end puller, disconnect the tie rod from the cross rod.
2. Using a tie rod end puller, disconnect the tie rod from the knuckle arm.
3. Remove the tie rod and remove the tie rod ends.

To install:

4. Screw the tie rod ends onto the tie rod. The tie rod length should be 13.54 in. (344mm) for 2wd models and 11.06 in. (281mm) on 4wd models.
The remaining length of threads on both ends should always be equal. The tie rod ends should always be screwed on at least 1.38 in. (35mm).
5. Turn the tie rod ends so they cross at about 90° on 2wd models or 17.5° on 4wd models. Tighten the clamp nuts to 10–14 ft. lbs (14–20 Nm) on 2wd models. Tighten the lock-nuts to 58–72 ft. lbs. (78–98 Nm) on all 4wd models.

6. Connect the tie rod to the knuckle arm and cross rod and tighten the mounting nuts to 40–72 ft. lbs. (54–98 Nm).

Cross Rod

1989 MODELS

1. Disconnect the tie rod ends from the cross rod.
2. Using a tie rod end puller, disconnect the pitman arm from the cross rod.
3. Using a tie rod end puller, disconnect the idler arm from the cross rod.
4. Remove the rod and inspect it for cracks or other damage.

To install:

5. Connect the cross rod to the idler arm and tighten the nut 40–72 ft. lbs. (54–98 Nm).
6. Connect the cross rod to the pitman arm and tighten the nut to 40–72 ft. lbs. (54–98 Nm).

7. Connect the tie rod ends to the cross rod and tighten the nuts to 40–72 ft. lbs. (54–98 Nm).

Relay Rod

1990–95 MODELS

1. Disconnect the tie rod ends from the relay rod.
2. Using a tie rod end puller, disconnect the pitman arm from the relay rod.
3. Using a tie rod end puller, disconnect the idler arm from the relay rod.
4. Remove the rod and inspect it for cracks or other damage.
To install:
5. Connect the relay rod to the idler arm and tighten the nut 40–72 ft. lbs. (54–98 Nm).
6. Connect the relay rod to the pitman arm and tighten the nut to 40–72 ft. lbs. (54–98 Nm).
7. Connect the tie rod ends to the relay rod and tighten the nuts to 40–72 ft. lbs. (54–98 Nm).

Steering Damper

1989 MODELS

1. Disconnect the steering damper at the cross rod.
2. Disconnect the damper at the frame and remove the damper with all washers and cushions.
3. Install the damper to the frame bracket and tighten the nut to 13–17 ft. lbs. (18–24 Nm).
4. Connect the other end of the steering damper to the cross rod and tighten the nut to 27–36 ft. lbs. (37–49 Nm).

1990–95 MODELS

1. Disconnect the steering damper at the relay rod.
2. Disconnect the damper at the frame and remove the damper with all washers and cushions.
3. Install the damper to the frame bracket and tighten the nut to 13–17 ft. lbs. (18–24 Nm).
4. Connect the other end of the steering damper to the relay rod and tighten the nut to 27–36 ft. lbs. (37–49 Nm).

Idler Arm Bracket

1989 MODELS

1. Disconnect the cross rod from the idler arm.
2. Remove the mounting bolts and remove the idler arm bracket with the arm attached.
3. Position the bracket and arm on the frame and tighten the bolts to 58–72 ft. lbs. (78–98 Nm).
4. Connect the idler arm to the cross rod and tighten the nut to 40–72 ft. lbs. (54–98 Nm). Install a new cotter pin.

1990–95 MODELS

1. Disconnect the relay rod from the idler arm.

2. Remove the mounting bolts and remove the idler arm bracket with the arm attached.
3. Position the bracket and arm on the frame and tighten the bolts to 58–72 ft. lbs. (78–98 Nm).
4. Connect the idler arm to the relay rod and tighten the nut to 40–72 ft. lbs. (54–98 Nm). Install a new cotter pin.

Manual Steering Gear

ADJUSTMENTS

Adjustments to the manual steering gear are not necessary during normal service. Adjustments are performed only as part of overhaul.

Worm Bearing Preload

1. Mount the gear in a vise.
2. Using an inch lbs. torque wrench and spanner KV48101400, or its equivalent, rotate the worm shaft a few turns in each direction to settle the bearing and measure the existing preload.
3. If preload is not 1.7–5.2 inch lbs. on 1989 models or 6.1–7.8 inch lbs. 1990–95 models loosen the lock-nut and turn the adjusting plug with the spanner, in a clockwise rotation ONLY. Never adjust preload by turning the adjusting plug counterclockwise. If preload cannot be obtained in this manner, rebuild the gear.
4. Apply liquid sealer on the shaft threads and tighten the lock-nut to 181–231 ft. lbs. (245–314 Nm) on 1989 models, or 166–188 ft. lbs. (226–255 Nm) on 1990–95 models.

REMOVAL & INSTALLATION

▶ **See Figure 122**

1. Raise and support the truck on jackstands.
2. Unbolt the wormshaft pinch bolt at the rubber coupling.
3. Matchmark the pitman arm and sector shaft, and with the wheels in a straight ahead position, remove the pitman arm with a puller.
4. Unbolt and remove the gear from the frame.
To install:
5. Install the gear and tighten the bolts to 62–71 ft. lbs. (84–96 Nm).
6. Press the pitman arm onto the sector shaft so that the marks are aligned and then tighten the nut to 94–108 ft. lbs. (127–147 Nm) on 1989 models, or 174–195 ft. lbs. (235–265 Nm) on 1990–95 models.
7. Slide the worm shaft into the coupling pinch bolt and tighten the bolt to 17–22 ft. lbs. (24–29 Nm).

Power Steering Gear

TURNING TORQUE ADJUSTMENT

1. Mount the gear on a holding fixture in a vise.
2. Turn the stub shaft (the shaft that connects with the steering column) several turns in either direction.
3. Mount an inch lbs. torque wrench on the stub shaft and turn it lock-to-lock, counting the total number of turns. Divide that number by 2 and position the torque wrench and shaft at the mid-point.
4. Measure the amount of force needed to turn the shaft past the midpoint in both directions. The force should be 3.5 inch lbs. on 1989 models and 11.7 inch lbs. on the 1990–95 models.
5. To correct the adjustment, loosen the lock-nut on the adjusting screw and turn the screw to give the correct torque. Tighten the lock-nut to 25–29 ft. lbs. (34–39 Nm).

REMOVAL & INSTALLATION

▶ **See Figure 123**

1. Matchmark and remove the pitman arm from the sector shaft, using a puller tool.
2. Matchmark and disconnect the steering stub shaft from the gear at the coupling.

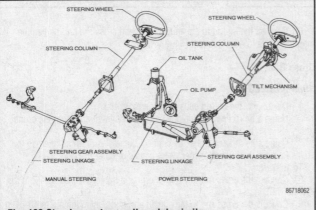

Fig. 122 Steering system—all models similar

86718062

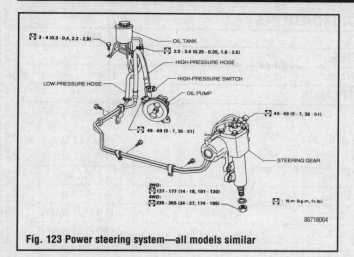

Fig. 123 Power steering system—all models similar

3. Disconnect the fluid lines from the gear and cap the lines and openings in the gear.

4. Unbolt and remove the gear assembly from the frame.

5. Installation is the reverse of the removal. When installing, observe the following torque specifications:

- Gear housing-to-frame: 62–71 ft. lbs. (84–96 Nm).
- Steering stub shaft-to-coupling: 17–22 ft. lbs. (24–29 Nm).
- Pitman arm-to-sector shaft (refer to the service procedures above).

Power Steering Pump

REMOVAL & INSTALLATION

1. Remove the fan shroud.
2. Unfasten the nut from the center of the pump pulley.

➥**Use the drive belt as a brake to keep the pulley from rotating.**

3. Remove the drive belt.
4. Remove the pulley and the bracket from the pump shaft.
5. Detach the intake and outlet hoses from the pump reservoir.

➥**Tie the hose ends up high so the fluid cannot flow out of them. Drain or plug the pump to prevent fluid leakage.**

6. Remove the bolt from the rear mounting brace.
7. Remove the bracket bolts and then remove the pump.

To install:

8. Install the pump and tighten the pump pulley mounting bolt to 23–31 ft. lbs. (31–42 Nm) on Z24i engines and 40–50 ft. lbs. (54–68 Nm) on all other engines.

9. Adjust the pump drive belt tension. Refer to procedures in Section 1.

10. Fill the reservoir with Dexron®II automatic transmission fluid. Bleed the air from the system.

BLEEDING

1. Raise the front of the truck and support it securely with jackstands.
2. Fill the pump reservoir with Dexron®II automatic transmission fluid.
3. Rotate the steering wheel from lock-to-lock several times. Add fluid as necessary.

➥**Never hold the steering wheel in the lock position for more than 15 seconds.**

4. Repeat Step 3 until the fluid level in the reservoir remains the same.
5. Start the engine. With the engine idling, turn the steering wheel from lock-to-lock several times.
6. Lower the front of the truck and repeat Step 5.
7. Center the wheel at the midpoint of its travel. Stop the engine.
8. The fluid level should not have risen more than 5mm.
9. Check for fluid leakage.

TORQUE SPECIFICATIONS

Component	U.S.	Metric
WHEELS		
All wheels	87–108 ft. lbs.	118–147 Nm
FRONT SUSPENSION		
Compression rod		
4WD models		
Rod-to-lower link bolts	87–108 ft. lbs.	118–147 Nm
Rod-to-frame anchor nut	87–116 ft. lbs.	118–157 Nm
Knuckle arm-to-knuckle bolts	53–72 ft. lbs.	72–97 Nm
Lower ball joint-to-control arm	35–45 ft. lbs.	47–61 Nm
Lower ball stud-to-knuckle	87–141 ft. lbs.	118–191 Nm
Lower control arm-to-frame bolt	80–108 ft. lbs.	109–147 Nm
Rotor-to-hub bolts	36–51 ft. lbs.	49–69 Nm
Shock absorber		
Upper attaching nut	12–16 ft. lbs.	16–22 Nm
Lower nut	43–58 ft. lbs.	59–68 Nm
Stabilizer bar		
Through-bolt	12–16 ft. lbs.	16–22 Nm
Bushing clamp bolts	12–16 ft. lbs.	16–22 Nm
Tension rod		
2WD models		
Rod-to-lower link bolts	36–47 ft. lbs.	49–64 Nm
Rod-to-frame anchor nut	87–116 ft. lbs.	118–157 Nm
Torque arm-to-lower control arm	37–50 ft. lbs.	50–68 Nm
Upper ball joint-to-control arm	12–17 ft. lbs.	16–23 Nm
Upper ball stud-to-steering knuckle	58–108 ft. lbs.	78–147 Nm
Upper control arm-to-frame bolts	80–108 ft. lbs.	109–147 Nm
Upper control arm-to-spindle nut	52–76 ft. lbs.	71–83 Nm
REAR SUSPENSION		
Control arms		
Pathfinder only		
All bolts	80–108 ft. lbs.	108–147 Nm
Leaf springs		
Front pin and shackle nuts		
Exc. 1989 2WD models	58–72 ft. lbs.	78–98 Nm
1989 2WD models	37–50 ft. lbs.	50–68 Nm
U-bolt nuts	65–72 ft. lbs.	88–98 Nm
Panhard rod		
Pathfinder only		
Right-side bolt	80–108 ft. lbs.	108–147 Nm
Left-side bolt		
1989	36–51 ft. lbs.	49–69 Nm
1990–95	94–123 ft. lbs.	127–167 Nm
Shock absorber upper and lower ends	22–30 ft. lbs.	30–40 Nm
Stabilizer bar		
Pathfinder only		
All bolts	19–24 ft. lbs.	25–32 Nm

86718C02

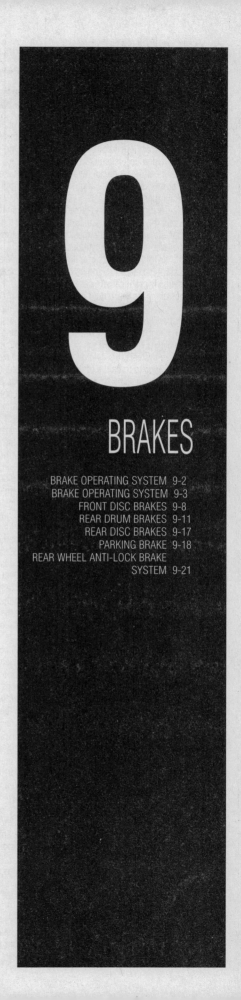

9

BRAKES

BASIC OPERATING PRINCIPLES

Hydraulic systems are used to actuate the brakes of all automobiles and most trucks. The system transports the power required to force the frictional surfaces of the braking system together from the pedal to the individual brake units at each wheel. A hydraulic system is used for two reasons.

First, fluid under pressure can be carried to all locations of an automobile by small pipes and flexible hoses without taking up a significant amount of room or posing routing problems.

Second, a great mechanical advantage can be given to the brake pedal end of the system, and the foot pressure required to actuate the brakes can be reduced by making the surface area of the master cylinder pistons smaller than that of any of the pistons in the wheel cylinders or calipers.

The master cylinder consists of a fluid reservoir and a double cylinder/piston assembly. Dual-type master cylinders are designed to separate the front and rear braking systems hydraulically in case of a leak.

Steel lines carry the brake fluid to a point on the vehicle's frame near each of the vehicle's wheels. The fluid is then carried to the calipers and wheel cylinders by flexible tubes, in order to allow for suspension and steering movements.

In drum brake systems, each wheel cylinder contains two pistons, one at either end, which push outward in opposite directions.

In disc brake systems, the cylinders are part of the calipers. One cylinder in each caliper is used to force the brake pads against the disc.

All pistons employ some type of seal, usually made of rubber, to minimize fluid leakage. A rubber dust boot seals the outer end of the cylinder against dust and dirt. The boot fits around the outer end of the piston on disc brake calipers, and around the brake actuating rod on wheel cylinders.

The hydraulic system operates as follows: When at rest, the entire system, from the piston(s) in the master cylinder to those in the wheel cylinders and/or calipers, is full of brake fluid. Upon application of the brake pedal, fluid trapped in front of the master cylinder piston(s) is forced through the lines to the wheel cylinders and/or calipers. There, the fluid forces the pistons outward (in the case of drum brakes) and/or inward toward the disc (in the case of disc brakes). The motion of the pistons is opposed by return springs mounted outside the cylinders in drum brakes, and by spring seals, in disc brakes.

Upon release of the brake pedal, a spring located inside the master cylinder immediately returns the master cylinder pistons to the normal position. The pistons contain check valves and the master cylinder has compensating ports drilled in it. These are uncovered as the pistons reach their normal position. The piston check valves allow fluid to flow toward the wheel cylinders or calipers as the pistons withdraw. Then, as the return springs force the brake pads or shoes into the released position, the excess fluid returns to the reservoir through the compensating ports. Any fluid that has leaked out of the system will be replaced through the compensating ports during the time that the pedal is in the released position.

Dual circuit master cylinders employ two pistons, located one behind the other, in the same cylinder. The primary piston is actuated directly by mechanical linkage from the brake pedal through the power booster. The secondary piston is actuated by fluid trapped between the two pistons. If a leak develops in front of the secondary piston, it moves forward until it bottoms against the front of the master cylinder, and the fluid trapped between the pistons will operate the rear brakes. If the rear brakes develop a leak, the primary piston will move forward until direct contact with the secondary piston takes place, and it will force the secondary piston to actuate the front brakes. In either case, the brake pedal moves farther when the brakes are applied, and less braking power is available.

All dual circuit systems use a switch to warn the driver when only half of the brake system is operational. This switch is located in a valve body which is mounted on the firewall or the frame below the master cylinder. A hydraulic piston receives pressure from both circuits, each circuit's pressure being applied to one end of the piston. When the pressures are in balance, the piston remains stationary. When one circuit has a leak, however, the greater pressure in that circuit during application of the brakes will push the piston to one side, closing the switch and activating the brake warning light.

In disc brake systems, this valve body also contains a metering valve and, in some cases, a proportioning valve. The metering valve keeps pressure from traveling to the disc brakes on the front wheels until the brake shoes on the rear wheels have contacted the drums, ensuring that the front brakes will never be used alone. The proportioning valve controls the pressure to the rear brakes to lessen the chance of rear wheel lock-up during very hard braking.

Warning lights may be tested by depressing the brake pedal and holding it while opening one of the wheel cylinder bleeder screws. If this does not cause the light to go on, substitute a new lamp, then make continuity checks; replace the switch as necessary.

The hydraulic system may be checked for leaks by applying pressure to the pedal gradually and steadily. If the pedal sinks very slowly to the floor, the system has a leak. This is not to be confused with a springy or spongy feel due to the compression of air within the lines. If the system leaks, there will be a gradual change in the position of the pedal with a constant pressure.

Check for leaks along all lines and at wheel cylinders/calipers. If no external leaks are apparent, the problem is inside the master cylinder.

Disc Brakes

Instead of the traditional expanding brakes that press outward against a circular drum, disc brake systems utilize a disc (rotor) with brake pads positioned on either side of it. Braking effect is achieved in a manner similar to the way you would squeeze a spinning phonograph record between your fingers. The disc (rotor) is a casting with cooling fins between the two braking surfaces. This enables air to circulate between the braking surfaces, making them less sensitive to heat buildup and more resistant to fade. Dirt and water do not affect braking action since contaminants are thrown off by the centrifugal action of the rotor or scraped off by the pads. Also, the equal clamping action of the two brake pads tends to ensure uniform, straight-line stops. Disc brakes are inherently self-adjusting.

There are three general types of disc brake:
- Fixed caliper
- Floating caliper
- Sliding caliper

The fixed caliper design uses two pistons mounted on either side of the rotor (in each side of the caliper). The caliper is mounted rigidly and does not move.

The sliding and floating caliper designs are quite similar. In fact, these two types are often lumped together. In both designs, the pad on the inside of the rotor is moved into contact with the rotor by hydraulic force. The caliper, which is not held in a fixed position, moves slightly, bringing the outside pad into contact with the rotor. There are various methods of attaching floating calipers. Some pivot at the bottom or top, and some slide on mounting bolts. In any event, the end result is the same.

Drum Brakes

Drum brakes employ two brake shoes mounted on a stationary backing plate. These shoes are positioned inside a circular drum which rotates with the wheel assembly. The shoes are held in place by springs. This allows them to slide toward the drums (when they are applied) while keeping the linings and drums in alignment. The shoes are actuated by a wheel cylinder which is mounted at the top of the backing plate. When the brakes are applied, hydraulic pressure forces the wheel cylinder's actuating links outward. Since these links bear directly against the top of the brake shoes, the tops of the shoes are then forced against the inner side of the drum. This action forces the bottoms of the two shoes to contact the brake drum by rotating the entire assembly slightly (known as servo action). When pressure within the wheel cylinder is relaxed, return springs pull the shoes back away from the drum.

Most modern drum brakes are designed to self-adjust themselves during application when the vehicle is moving in reverse. This motion causes both shoes to rotate very slightly with the drum, rocking an adjusting lever, thereby causing rotation of the adjusting screw.

Power Brake Booster

Power brakes operate just as non-power brake systems except in the actuation of the master cylinder pistons. A vacuum diaphragm is located on the front of the master cylinder and assists the driver in applying the brakes, reducing both the effort and travel he must put into moving the brake pedal.

The vacuum diaphragm housing is connected to the intake manifold by a vacuum hose. A check valve is placed at the point where the hose enters the diaphragm housing, so that during periods of low manifold vacuum brake assist vacuum will not be lost.

Depressing the brake pedal closes off the vacuum source and allows atmospheric pressure to enter on one side of the diaphragm. This causes the master cylinder pistons to move and apply the brakes. When the brake pedal is released, vacuum is applied to both sides of the diaphragm, and return springs return the diaphragm and master cylinder pistons to the released position. If the vacuum fails, the brake pedal rod will butt against the end of the master cylinder actuating rod, and direct mechanical application will occur as the pedal is depressed.

The hydraulic and mechanical problems that apply to conventional brake systems also apply to power brakes, and should be checked if the following tests do not reveal the problem.

Test for a system vacuum leak as follows:

1. Operate the engine at idle without touching the brake pedal for at least one minute.
2. Turn off the engine, then wait one minute.
3. Test for the presence of assist vacuum by depressing the brake pedal and

releasing it several times. If vacuum is present, light application will produce less and less pedal travel. If there is no vacuum, air is leaking into the system somewhere.

Test for system operation as follows:

1. Pump the brake pedal (with engine off) until the supply vacuum is entirely gone.
2. Put a light, steady pressure on the pedal.
3. Start the engine, and operate it at idle. If the system is operating, the brake pedal should move toward the floor when constant pressure is maintained on the pedal.

Power brake systems may be tested for hydraulic leaks just as ordinary systems are tested.

BRAKE OPERATING SYSTEM

✳✳ CAUTION

Brake shoes may contain asbestos, which has been determined to be a cancer causing agent. Never clean the brake surfaces with compressed air! Avoid inhaling any dust from any brake surface! When cleaning brake surfaces, use a commercially available brake cleaning fluid.

Adjustments

DISC BRAKES

All disc brakes are inherently self-adjusting. No periodic adjustment is either necessary or possible.

On models with rear disc brakes, the parking brake is actuated by means of conventional drum brake shoes. For adjustment of these shoes, please refer to the Parking Brake portion of this section.

DRUM BRAKES

▶ **See Figure 1**

➡**All models, utilize self-adjusting rear brakes. The following procedure is necessary only after the brake shoes have been changed.**

1. Raise and safely support the rear of the vehicle until the wheel to be adjusted completely clears the ground.
2. Make sure that the parking brake is completely released.
3. Remove the rubber boot from the rear of the brake backing plate.
4. Lightly tap the adjuster housing forward with a hammer and screwdriver.
5. Turn the adjuster wheel downward with a screwdriver to spread the brake shoes. Stop turning the adjuster wheel when the brake drum is locked and the wheel cannot be turned by hand.
6. Turn the adjuster wheel upward, backing off the shoes from the brake drum about 12 notches, to obtain the correct clearance between the brake shoes

and drum. Turn the wheel to make sure that the brake drum will turn without dragging.

7. Install the rubber boot.
8. Adjust the other wheel in the same manner. Before lowering the vehicle, make sure that the rear wheels spin free.
9. Lower the vehicle and check the brake fluid level.

BRAKE PEDAL

▶ **See Figures 2 and 3**

Pedal Height

1. Measure the distance between the center (upper surface) of the pedal pad and the floor pad.

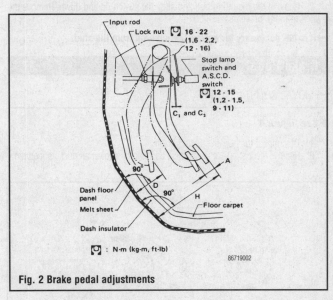

Fig. 2 Brake pedal adjustments

Fig. 1 Adjusting the rear drum brakes

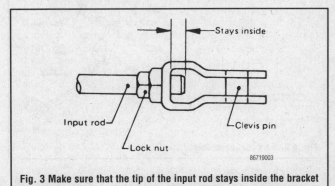

Fig. 3 Make sure that the tip of the input rod stays inside the bracket

2. If out of specifications, loosen the brake light switch.

3. Turn the pedal pushrod (input rod) until the pedal height is within specifications. Pedal height should be 8.35–8.75 in. (212–222mm) on models with an automatic transmission; or 8.23–8.62 in. (209–219mm) on models with a manual transmission.

4. Move the brake light switch until clearance between the plunger and the pedal is 0.012–0.039 in. (0.3–1.0mm). Tighten the switch.

5. Check the brake pedal free-play.

Free-Play

1. With the engine **OFF**, depress the brake pedal several times until there is no vacuum left in the brake booster.

2. Push the pedal down until resistance is first felt. Measure this distance; it should be 0.04–0.12 in. (1–3mm).

3. Adjust the free-play by turning the pedal pushrod.

4. Start the engine and recheck the free-play.

5. Recheck the pedal height.

Reserve Distance

Depress the brake pedal to the bottom of the pedal travel and measure the distance from the center (upper surface) of the pedal pad to the floor mat. If the distance is out of specifications, recheck the other pedal adjustments and the master cylinder. Pedal depressed height should be at least 4.72 in. (12cm).

Brake Light Switch

REMOVAL & INSTALLATION

1. Disconnect the electrical harness at the switch.

2. Remove the mounting bolt and slide the switch up and down. Remove the switch from the brake pedal.

➡It is not necessary to remove the pushrod from the stud.

Brake Pedal

REMOVAL & INSTALLATION

◆ See Figure 4

1. Disconnect the negative battery cable.

2. Remove the instrument lower finish panel and the lower air duct, as required.

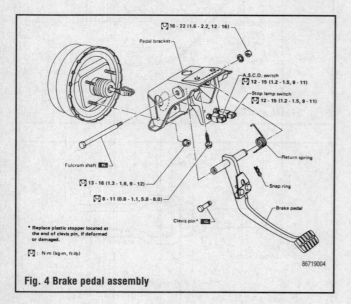

* Replace plastic stopper located at the end of clevis pin, if deformed or damaged.

⊡ : N·m (kg-m, ft-lb)

86719004

Fig. 4 Brake pedal assembly

3. Remove the brake pedal return spring. Disconnect and remove the brake light switch.

4. Remove the clip and clevis pin.

5. Unbolt and remove the brake pedal assembly from the vehicle.

6. Installation is the reverse of the removal procedure. Check and adjust the brake pedal as required. Assure that the brake lights are fully functional.

Master Cylinder

REMOVAL & INSTALLATION

➡Be careful not to spill brake fluid on the painted surfaces of the vehicle, as it will damage the paint.

1. Unfasten the hydraulic lines from the master cylinder.

2. Disconnect the hydraulic fluid pressure differential switch wiring. On models with fluid level sensors, also disconnect the fluid level sensor wiring.

3. Loosen the master cylinder reservoir mounting bolts.

4. On models with manual brakes, unfasten the master cylinder securing bolts and the clevis pin from the brake pedal, then remove the master cylinder. On models with power brakes, unfasten the nuts and remove the master cylinder assembly from the power brake unit.

To install:

5. Install the master cylinder in reverse order of removal and note the following:

• Many models have an **UP** mark on the cylinder boot; make sure it is in the correct position.

• Before tightening the master cylinder mounting nuts or bolts, screw the hydraulic lines into the cylinder body a few turns.

• After installation is completed, bleed the master cylinder and the brake system.

• Check and adjust the brake pedal as necessary.

➡When replacing the master cylinder, it is best to BENCH BLEED the master cylinder before installing it to the vehicle. Mount the master cylinder into a soft-jawed vise or suitable equivalent, so as not to damage the cylinder. Fill the cylinder to the correct level with new DOT 3 type brake fluid. Block off all the outer brake line holes but one, then position a long wooden dowel in the bore to actuate the brake master cylinder. Pump the brake master cylinder 3 or 4 times (push in and out with the dowel) until brake fluid is released and no air is in the brake fluid. Repeat this procedure until all brake fluid is released from every hole and no air is expelled.

OVERHAUL

◆ See Figure 5

➡Because of the importance of the master cylinder, replacement (rather than overhaul) is recommended if it is worn or damaged.

1. Place the cylinder securely in a soft-jawed vise or suitable equivalent. Remove the reservoir caps and floats. Unscrew the bolts which secure the reservoir(s) to the main body.

2. Remove the pressure differential warning switch assembly. Working from the rear of the cylinder, remove the boot, snapring, stop washer, primary piston, spacer, cylinder cup, spring retainer, and spring, in that order.

3. Remove the end plug and gasket from the front of the cylinder (if equipped), then remove the front piston stop bolt from underneath. Pull out the spring, retainer, secondary piston, spacer, and cylinder cup.

4. Remove the two outlet fittings, washers, check valves and springs.

5. Remove the piston cups from their seats only if they are to be replaced.

6. Wash all parts in clean brake fluid, then dry them with compressed air (if available). Do not dry parts with a shop rag, as this can deposit lint and dirt particles inside the assembled master cylinder. Inspect the cylinder bore for wear, scuff marks, or nicks. Cylinders may be honed slightly, but the limit is 0.006 in. (0.15mm).

7. Replace any worn or damaged parts. Coat all parts with clean brake fluid, then reassemble the master cylinder.

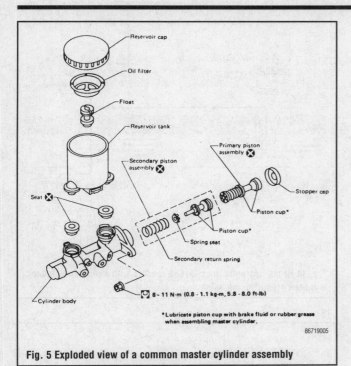

Fig. 5 Exploded view of a common master cylinder assembly

➡**Absolute cleanliness is essential!**

8. Install the master cylinder.
9. Bleed the hydraulic system after the master cylinder is installed.

Power Brake Booster

➡**Vacuum boosters are found only on models equipped with power brakes.**

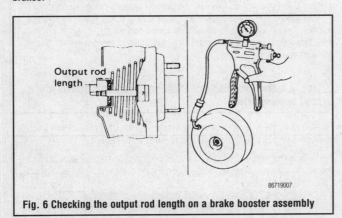

Fig. 6 Checking the output rod length on a brake booster assembly

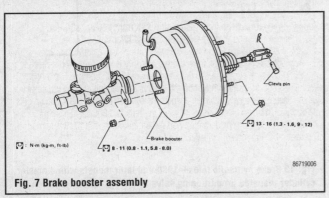

Fig. 7 Brake booster assembly

REMOVAL & INSTALLATION

▶ **See Figures 6 and 7**

1. Remove the master cylinder as previously detailed.
2. Locate the clevis rod where it attaches to the brake pedal. Pull out the clip and then remove the clevis pin.
3. Disconnect the vacuum hose from the booster.
4. Loosen the four nuts, then pull out the vacuum booster, the bracket and the gasket.

➡**Some 4wd models may have two extra brackets that must be removed when removing the brake booster.**

To install:

5. Install the booster and tighten the mounting bolts to 6–8 ft. lbs. (0.8–1.1 Nm) on 1989 models; or 9–12 ft. lbs. (13–16 Nm) on 1990–95 models. Attach the vacuum hose.
6. Connect the clevis rod to the brake pedal.
7. Install the master cylinder. Check the brake pedal adjustment and bleed the brakes.

➡**If necessary, check the output rod length by attaching a vacuum pump to the vacuum nipple on the booster. At 19.69 in. Hg (66.49 kPa), the length should be about 0.4045–0.4144 in. (10.275–10.525mm).**

Load Sensing Valve (LSV)

The purpose of this valve is to control the fluid pressure applied to the brakes to prevent rear wheel lock-up during weight transfer at high speed stops. This valve should be replaced and a system inspection performed, if system trouble is suspected.

REMOVAL & INSTALLATION

▶ **See Figures 8 and 9**

1. Disconnect the brake lines going to the valve.
2. If applicable, unfasten the mounting bolts, then remove the valve.

➡**This valve cannot be rebuilt; it must be replaced as an assembly.**

3. Installation is the reverse of removal.
4. Bleed the brake system.

Brake Hoses and Lines

INSPECTION

▶ **See Figures 10 thru 15**

Inspect the hydraulic brake lines at the recommended intervals in the maintenance schedule. Check the flexible brake hoses that connect the steel tubing to

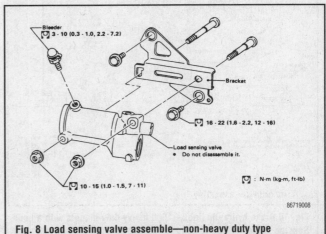

Fig. 8 Load sensing valve assemble—non-heavy duty type

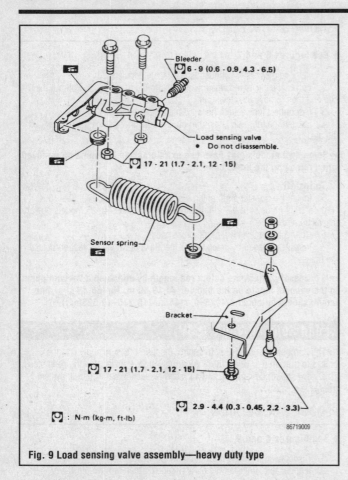

Fig. 9 Load sensing valve assembly—heavy duty type

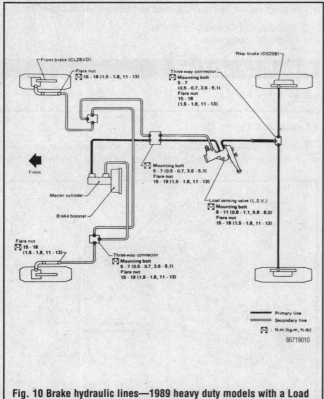

Fig. 10 Brake hydraulic lines—1989 heavy duty models with a Load Sensing Valve

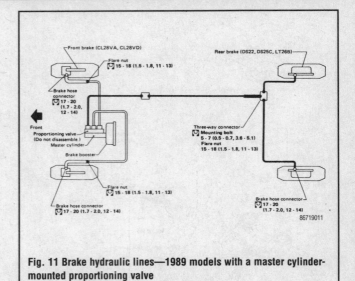

Fig. 11 Brake hydraulic lines—1989 models with a master cylinder-mounted proportioning valve

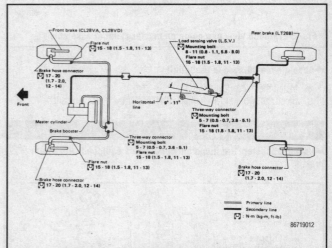

Fig. 12 Brake hydraulic lines—1989 non-heavy duty models with a Load Sensing Valve

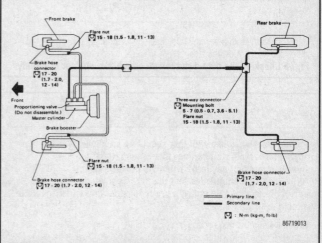

Fig. 13 Brake hydraulic lines—1990 and later models with a master cylinder-mounted proportioning valve

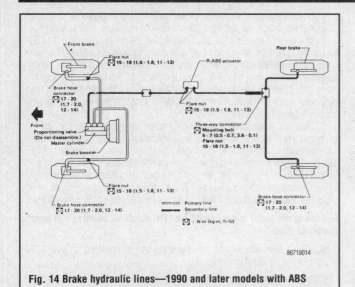

Fig. 14 Brake hydraulic lines—1990 and later models with ABS

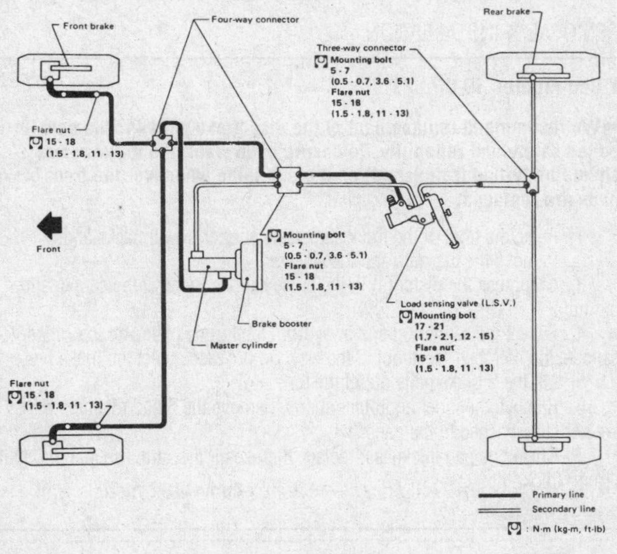

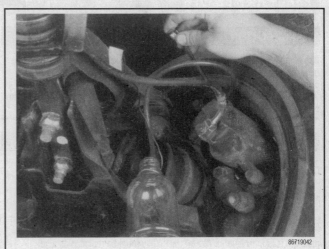

86719015

Fig. 15 Brake hydraulic lines—1990 and later models with a Load Sensing Valve

When installing a new front brake hose, position the hose to avoid contact with other chassis parts. Place a new copper gasket over the hose fitting and thread the hose assembly into the front wheel cylinder. A new rear brake hose must be positioned clear of the exhaust pipe or shock absorber. Thread the hose into the rear brake tube connector. When installing either a new front or rear brake hose, engage the opposite end of the hose to the bracket on the frame. Install the horseshoe type retaining clip and connect the tube to the hose with the tube fitting nut.

Always bleed the system after hose or line replacement. Before and during bleeding, make sure that the master cylinder is kept full of the specified clean brake fluid.

Bleeding Brake System

▶ See Figures 16 and 17

The purpose of bleeding the brakes is to expel air trapped in the hydraulic system. The system should be bled whenever the pedal feels spongy, indicating that compressable air has entered the system. It should also be bled whenever the system has been opened or repaired. You will need a helper for this job.

➡ **In order to ease access to the bleeder screws, it may be helpful to raise the vehicle and safely support it while bleeding the brakes.**

86719042

Fig. 16 Bleeding the front caliper—note position of the bleeder bottle and hose

each wheel cylinder. Replace any hose that shows signs of softening, cracking, or other damage. Follow the steel tubing from the master cylinder to the flexible hose fitting at each wheel. If a section of the tubing is found to be damaged, replace the entire section with tubing of the same type (steel, not copper), size, shape, and length.

REMOVAL & INSTALLATION

➡ **Flaring steel lines is a skill that should be practiced before it is performed on a vehicle's brake line. It is essential that the flare be made uniformly to prevent any leaks when the brake system is under pressure. It is also recommended that the flare be a double flare. With the supply of parts available today, a preflared steel brake line should be available to fit your needs.**

When installing a new section of brake tubing, flush clean brake fluid or denatured alcohol through to remove any dirt or foreign material from the line. Be sure to double flare both ends to provide sound, leak-proof connections. When bending the tubing to fit the underbody contours, be careful not to kink or crack the line. Tighten all hydraulic connections to 10–15 ft. lbs. (15–18 Nm).

86719043

Fig. 17 Bleeding the rear wheel cylinder—do not let the master cylinder run dry during the bleeding operation

1. Clean all the bleeder screws; since seizure is a common problem with bleeder screws, you may want to give each one a shot of a penetrating lubricant. In the event that one or more bleeder screws break off, it may be necessary to replace the attached part(s).

➡**Brake fluid picks up moisture from the air. Don't leave the master cylinder or the fluid container uncovered any longer than necessary. Be careful! Brake fluid damages paint. Check the level of the fluid often when bleeding, and refill the reservoirs as necessary. Don't let them run dry, or you will have to repeat the process.**

2. Fill the master cylinder with clean, unused DOT 3 brake fluid.

➡**Never reuse brake fluid which has been bled from the brake system.**

3. The sequence for bleeding is as follows:
• Models equipped with a Load Sensing Valve (LSV): LSV air bleeder, left rear wheel cylinder, right rear wheel cylinder, left front caliper, right front caliper.
• Models not equipped with a Load Sensing Valve (LSV): left rear wheel cylinder, right rear wheel cylinder, left front caliper, right front caliper.

➡**On models with ABS, be sure to turn the ignition OFF and detach the actuator connector. For additional information and service procedures, refer to the ABS section.**

• Models equipped with ABS: left rear caliper or wheel cylinder, right rear caliper or wheel cylinder, left front caliper, right front caliper, ABS actuator.

4. If equipped with an LSV, attach a length of clear vinyl tubing to the LSV air bleeder. Insert the other end of the tube into a clear, clean jar half filled with brake fluid. Have your helper slowly depress the brake pedal. As this is done, open the bleeder screw 1/3–1/2 of a turn, and allow the fluid to run through the tube. Then close the bleeder screw before the pedal reaches the end of its travel. Have your assistant slowly release the pedal. Repeat this process until no air bubbles appear in the expelled fluid.

5. Attach a length of clear vinyl tubing to the bleeder screw on the first caliper or wheel cylinder in the bleeding sequence. Insert the other end of the tube into a clear, clean jar half filled with brake fluid. Have your helper slowly depress the brake pedal. As this is done, open the bleeder screw 1/3–1/2 of a turn, and allow the fluid to run through the tube. Then close the bleeder screw before the pedal reaches the end of its travel. Have your assistant slowly release the pedal. Repeat this process until no air bubbles appear in the expelled fluid.

➡**If the brake pedal is depressed too fast, small air bubbles will form in the brake fluid.**

6. Repeat the procedure on the other three brakes, checking the level of fluid in the cylinder reservoirs often.

FRONT DISC BRAKES

✴✴ CAUTION

Brake shoes may contain asbestos, which has been determined to be a cancer causing agent. Never clean the brake surfaces with compressed air! Avoid inhaling any dust from any brake surface! When cleaning brake surfaces, use a commercially available brake cleaning fluid.

Brake Pads

INSPECTION

▸ **See Figure 18**

The pads should be removed so that the thickness of the remaining friction material (dimension **A** in the illustration) can be measured. If either or both pads are less than 0.08 in. (2mm) thick, they must be replaced as a set.

➡**This measurement may disagree with your state inspection laws; if your state law requires a thicker minimum, be sure to heed the applicable standard.**

REMOVAL & INSTALLATION

▸ **See Figures 19 thru 27**

➡**We recommend replacement of the disc brake pads in axle sets for added safety and reliability. To ensure even wear, the brake rotors should be turned (refinished) on a brake lathe whenever the front brake pads are replaced.**

1. Raise the front of the truck and safely support it with jackstands.
2. Remove the lug nuts and the wheels.
3. Compress the piston(s) in the brake caliper. Remove the caliper slide pin bolt.
4. Swivel the caliper up and away from the torque plate. Tie the caliper to a suspension member so it's out of the way. Do not disconnect the brake line.
5. Lift the 2 brake pads out of the torque plate.
6. Remove the inner and outer shims. Remove the 2 pad retainers if they are not still attached to the pads.
7. Check the pad thickness; replace the pads if they are less than 0.039 in. (1mm) thick.

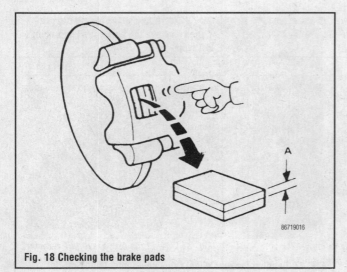

Fig. 18 Checking the brake pads

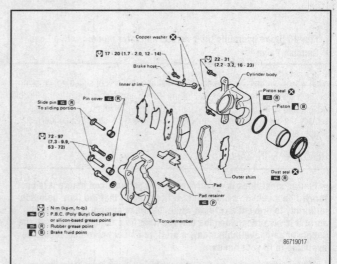

Fig. 19 Exploded view of the front disc brake—single piston type caliper

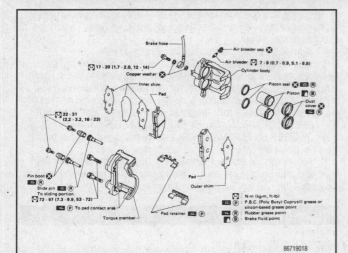

Fig. 20 Exploded view of the front disc brake—double piston type caliper

➡This minimum thickness measurement may disagree with your state inspection laws.

To install:
8. Install the inner and outer shims into the torque plate.
9. Install a pad retainer to the bottom of each pad.
10. Install the pads into the torque plate.

➡When installing new brake pads, make sure your hands are clean. Do not allow any grease or oil to touch the contact face of the pads, or the brakes will not stop the truck properly.

11. Using a C-clamp or hammer handle, press the caliper piston back into the housing.

➡Never press the piston into the caliper when the pads are out on both sides of the truck.

12. Untie the caliper and swivel it back into position over the torque plate so that the dust boot is not pinched. Install the slide pin and tighten it to 53–72 ft. lbs. (72–97 Nm).
13. Check the condition of the cylinder side bushing boots.
14. If applicable, repeat Steps 3–13 for the other side of the vehicle.
15. Install the wheels and lower the truck. Bleed the brakes and road test the vehicle.

Fig. 21 Compress the front pistons in the brake caliper slowly and evenly

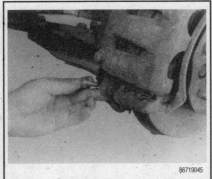

Fig. 22 Remove the caliper slide pin bolt—all models similar

Fig. 23 Swivel the caliper up and away from the torque plate to remove the brake pads

Fig. 24 After the caliper is properly positioned, remove the brake pad inner shim hardware

Fig. 25 Remove the inner disc brake pad—note the position of all related hardware

Fig. 26 Remove the outer disc brake pad—note the position of all related hardware

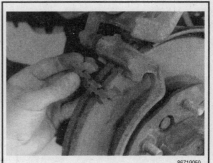

Fig. 27 View of the disc brake pad retainer hardware—if damaged or worn, replace it upon installation

Brake Caliper

REMOVAL & INSTALLATION

➥We recommend replacement of the disc brake caliper in axle sets for added safety and reliability.

1. Raise the front of the truck and safely support it with jackstands.
2. Remove the lug nuts and the wheel.
3. Attach a clear vinyl tube to the bleeder plug on the brake caliper, and insert the other end into a jar half filled with brake fluid. Bleed off a small amount of brake fluid.
4. Disconnect and plug the brake line.
5. Remove both caliper slide pin bolts and lift out the caliper. If necessary, compress the piston(s) in the caliper's cylinder body before removing the caliper.

To install:

6. Press the caliper piston(s) back into the housing until they are flush, then install the caliper. Tighten the mounting bolts to 53–72 ft. lbs. (72–97 Nm).
7. Reconnect the brake line.
8. Install the wheel and lower the truck. Bleed the brakes and road test the vehicle.

OVERHAUL

◆ See Figures 28, 29, 30 and 31

➥If the overhaul condition of this brake system part is in doubt, replace with a complete assembly.

1. Remove the caliper assembly.
2. Remove the dust cover.
3. Using compressed air from a portable compressor or other source, place the air nozzle in the brake line hole and force the piston out of the caliper's cylinder body. It's a good idea to place a piece of wood in the cylinder body to cushion the piston as it leaves the cylinder. Wear safety goggles, as some brake fluid may be sprayed out.
4. Remove the piston seal from its groove in the cylinder.
5. Rinse all parts in clean brake fluid. Check the cylinder bore and piston for wear, scratches and scoring. Minor rust and scratches in the cylinder bore may be removed with fine emery cloth. Any other damage will necessitate the replacement of the affected cylinder body. Any cracks in the torque member will require replacement of the part. The piston sliding surface is plated. DO NOT USE EMERY CLOTH OR ANY OTHER POLISHING MATERIAL TO REMOVE RUST OR OTHER FOREIGN MATTER! Replace the piston seal and dust boot. If the support pins are damaged at all, replace them.
6. Assembly is the reverse of disassembly. Coat all metal parts with clean brake fluid prior to assembly. Apply a thin coating of silicone brake lubricant to the support pins and bushings. Tighten the pin bolts.

Brake Disc (Rotor)

REMOVAL & INSTALLATION

◆ See Figures 32 thru 37

➥We recommend replacement of the brake rotor in axle sets for added safety and reliability.

1. Raise the front of the truck and safely support it with jackstands.
2. Remove the lug nuts and the wheel.
3. Remove the brake pads, caliper and torque member, as detailed earlier in this section.
4. Check the disc run-out.
5. Remove the grease cap from the hub. Remove the cotter pin and the castellated nut.
6. Remove the wheel hub with the brake disc attached.
7. Perform the disc inspection procedure, as outlined later in this section.

Fig. 28 Force the piston out from the caliper assembly with compressed air— note wood block protects the pistons from damage

Fig. 29 Removing the pistons from the caliper assembly

Fig. 30 View of the caliper dust cover (or dust seal)

Fig. 31 Removing the disc brake piston seal—always use a new piston seal upon installation

Fig. 32 Removing the torque member mounting bolts

Fig. 33 Removing the torque member from the vehicle

Fig. 34 Remove the automatic hub cover to gain access to the wheel bearing assembly

Fig. 35 After removing the wheel bearing lock-nut, remove the outer wheel bearing

Fig. 36 After the wheel bearing is removed, the brake hub/disc assembly can be pulled from the vehicle

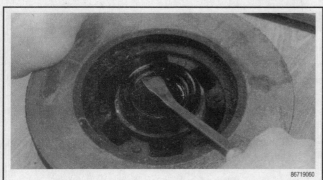

Fig. 37 With the brake hub/disc assembly removed, pry out the grease seal—be sure to use a new seal upon installation

To install:

8. Coat the hub oil seal lip with multipurpose grease and install the disc/hub assembly.

9. Check and adjust the wheel bearing preload, as described in Sections 1 (2wd) or 8 (4wd).

10. Measure the disc run-out. Check it against the figures in the Brake Specifications chart and against the figures noted during removal.

➥If the wheel bearing nut is improperly tightened, disc run-out will be affected.

11. Install the castellated nut with a new cotter pin, then install the grease cap.

12. Install the torque member, caliper and brake pads.

13. Bleed the brake system.

14. Lower the vehicle, then road test the truck.

INSPECTION

Examine the disc. If it is worn, warped or scored, it must be replaced. Check the thickness of the disc against the figures given in the Brake Specifications chart. If it is below specifications, replace it. Use a micrometer to measure the thickness.

Disc run-out should be measured before the disc is removed and again, after the disc is installed. Use a dial indicator mounted on a stand to determine run-out. If run-out exceeds 0.0028 in. (0.07mm), replace the disc.

➥Be sure that the wheel bearing nut is properly tightened. If it is not, an inaccurate run-out reading may be obtained. If a different run-out reading is obtained after installation of the same disc, an improperly tightened wheel bearing nut may be the cause.

For wheel bearing removal, installation and adjustment, please refer to Sections 1 and 8.

REAR DRUM BRAKES

Brake Drums

✳✳ CAUTION

Brake shoes may contain asbestos, which has been determined to be a cancer causing agent. Never clean the brake surfaces with compressed air! Avoid inhaling any dust from any brake surface! When cleaning brake surfaces, use a commercially available brake cleaning fluid.

REMOVAL & INSTALLATION

▶ See Figures 38, 39, 40 and 41

➥We recommend replacement of the brake drum in axle sets for added safety and reliability.

1. Remove the hub cap and loosen the lug nuts.

2. Raise the rear of the vehicle and safely support it on jackstands.

3. Remove the lug nuts, tire and wheel.

4. Loosen the brake adjustment, if necessary, then remove the brake drum. Inspect the brake drum, as described below.

Fig. 38 View of the brake drum installed on the vehicle—note the two holes in the drum between the wheel studs

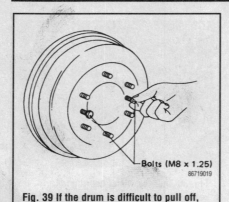

Fig. 39 If the drum is difficult to pull off, try threading two bolts into the holes . . .

Fig. 40 . . . and tighten them until the drum comes free

Fig. 41 View of the brake drum removed from the vehicle—note that brake dust often contains asbestos

➡ Do not depress the brake pedal with the brake drum removed.

5. Installation is the reverse of the removal procedure. Adjust the brakes, if necessary.

INSPECTION

▶ **See Figure 42**

1. Clean the drum with a rag and a little paint thinner.

※※ CAUTION

Do not blow the brake dust out of the drum with compressed air or lung power. Brake linings may contain asbestos, a known cancer causing agent.

2. Inspect the drum for cracks, grooves, scoring and out-of-roundness.
3. Light scoring may be removed with fine emery paper; heavy scores or grooves will require turning the drum on a lathe. This can be done at many automotive machine shops and some service stations.
4. If turning the drum is indicated, it must first be measured to determine whether or not the inside dimension of the drum will be within limitations after removing the score marks. The service limits of the brake drums are detailed in the Brake Specifications chart.
5. Check the drum for concentricity. An inside micrometer is necessary for an exact measurement; unless this tool is available, the drum should be taken to a machine shop to be checked. Any drum which measures more than 0.006 in. (0.15mm) out-of-round will likely result in an inaccurate brake adjustment or other problems, and should be refinished or replaced.

➡ **Make all measurements at right angles to each other, and at the open and closed edges of the drum machined surface.**

Brake Shoes

INSPECTION

▶ **See Figure 43**

Measure the lining thickness, dimension **A** in the illustration. The wear limit is 0.059 in. (1.5mm); brake shoes which do not meet this standard should be replaced. Also, inspect the shoes for cracked linings or abnormal wear.

➡ **It is not unusual for the primary and secondary brake shoes to wear at different rates. Always replace both shoes, even if only one fails inspection.**

REMOVAL & INSTALLATION

▶ **See Figures 44 thru 57**

➡ **We recommend replacement of brake shoes in axle sets for added safety and reliability. To ensure even wear, out-of-round drums should be turned (refinished) on a brake lathe whenever the shoes are replaced.**

1. Remove the hub cap and loosen the lug nuts.
2. Raise and support the rear of the vehicle safely.
3. Remove the lug nuts, tire and wheel.
4. Remove the brake drum.
5. With a brake tool, remove the shoe hold-down anti-rattle spring retainers. Depress the retainer while rotating it 90 degrees to align the retainer slot with the pin flanged end. Remove the retainers, springs, spring seats, and pins.
6. Open the brake shoes outward against the return springs, then remove the parking brake extension link.
7. Disconnect the brake shoe return springs.
8. Remove the shoes from the backing plate. The secondary shoe must be disconnected from the parking brake toggle lever after withdrawing the clevis pin.

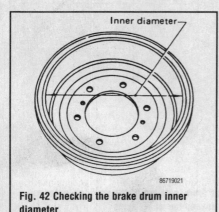

Fig. 42 Checking the brake drum inner diameter

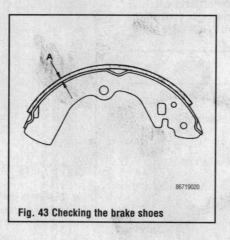

Fig. 43 Checking the brake shoes

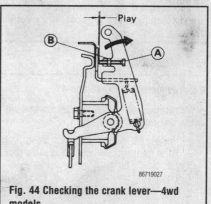

Fig. 44 Checking the crank lever—4wd models

Fig. 45 View of the rear drum brake—all models similar

Fig. 46 Remove the right brake hold-down spring—note the special brake tool used for this job

Fig. 47 Remove the brake lower return spring—make sure the spring is in the hole

Fig. 48 Remove the brake upper return spring—make sure the spring is in the hole

Fig. 49 Remove the brake adjuster assembly—note the location of the assembly

Fig. 50 Remove the left brake hold-down spring—note the special brake tool used for this job

Fig. 51 Remove the parking brake spring from the brake shoe

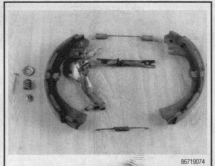

Fig. 52 View of the rear brake assembly—note the location of all springs and hardware

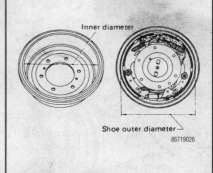

Fig. 53 Measure the brake shoe outer diameter and brake drum inner diameter

9. Remove the rubber boot from behind the backing plate then slide the adjuster shim, lockplate, and adjuster springs off the back of the assembly. Remove the adjuster assembly from the backing plate.

To install:

10. Clean the backing plate and adjuster assembly so they are free of all dust and dirt.

11. Check the wheel cylinders. Replace or overhaul, as needed.

12. Apply brake grease to the adjuster assembly housing bore, adjuster wheel, and adjuster screw. Assemble the adjuster mechanism with its screw turned all the way in. Apply brake grease to the sliding surfaces of the adjuster assembly, brake backing plate, and the retaining spring. Install the adjuster assembly to the backing plate.

13. On 4wd models, make sure that after installation there is no play between the crank lever and backing plate when pulling on the lever. If play exists, adjust bolt **A** and lock-nut **B**.

14. Assemble the secondary brake shoe to the parking brake toggle lever, then adjust the clearance.

15. Before assembling the brake shoes to the backing plate, apply brake grease to the following areas: the brake shoe grooves in the parking brake extension link, the inside surfaces of the anti-rattle (retaining) spring seats, and the contact surfaces between the brake backing plate and the brake shoes.

16. Assemble the brake shoes to the backing plate. Measure the inner diameter of the brake, then measure the outer diameter of the shoes (at the center). The shoe outer diameter should be 0.0098–0.0157 in. (0.25–0.40mm) less than the drum measurement; if not, adjust by rotating the star wheel adjuster.

17. Install the brake drum and the wheel.

18. Adjust and bleed the brakes.

➡Adjust the shoe-to-drum clearance by operating the parking brake lever several times.

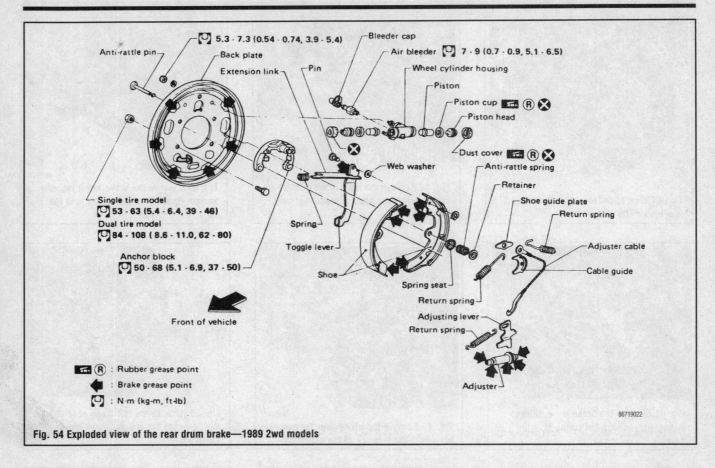

Fig. 54 Exploded view of the rear drum brake—1989 2wd models

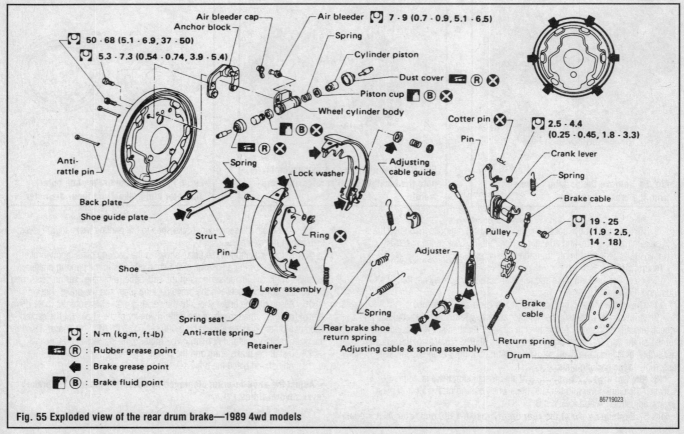

Fig. 55 Exploded view of the rear drum brake—1989 4wd models

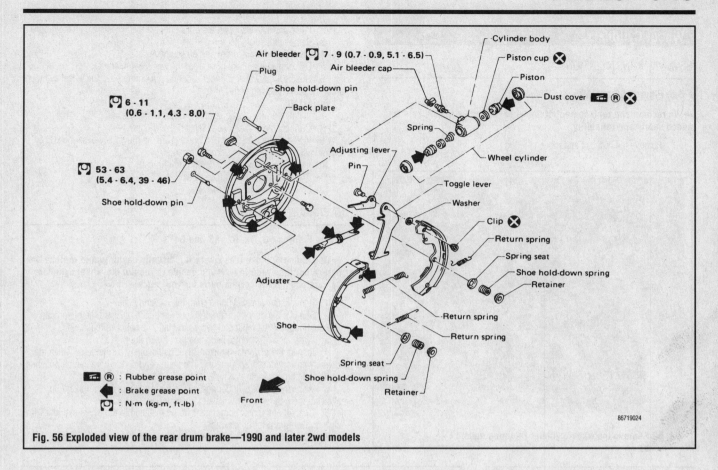

Fig. 56 Exploded view of the rear drum brake—1990 and later 2wd models

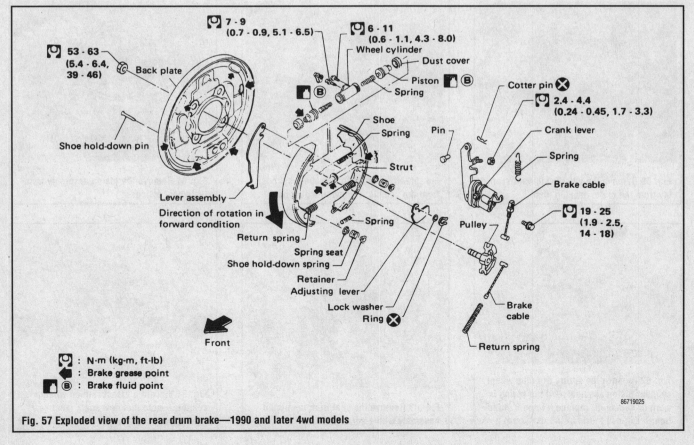

Fig. 57 Exploded view of the rear drum brake—1990 and later 4wd models

Wheel Cylinders

REMOVAL & INSTALLATION

▶ **See Figures 58 and 59**

➡**We recommend replacement of the wheel cylinders in axle sets for added safety and reliability.**

1. Remove the hub cap and loosen the lug nuts.

Fig. 58 Remove the wheel cylinder retaining bolts

2. Raise and safely support the truck until the rear wheels are off the ground.
3. Remove the lug nuts, tire and wheel.
4. Remove the brake drum and brake shoes.
5. Disconnect the brake hose from the wheel cylinder.
6. Unscrew the wheel cylinder securing nut and remove the wheel cylinder from the brake backing plate.

To install:

7. Install the wheel cylinder to the brake backing plate.
8. Connect the brake hose to the wheel cylinder.
9. Install the brake shoes and brake drum, as previously described. Properly adjust the brake shoe-to-drum clearance.
10. Install the tire/wheel assembly and hub cap.
11. Bleed the brake hydraulic system.
12. Lower the vehicle and road test.

OVERHAUL

▶ **See Figures 60, 61, 62, 63 and 64**

➡**This is one of those jobs where it is usually easier just to replace the part rather than rebuild it. If you decide to rebuild the wheel cylinders, be sure you get the correct parts for your truck.**

1. Remove the wheel cylinder from the backing plate.
2. Remove the dust boot and take out the piston. Discard the piston cup. The dust boot can be reused, if necessary, but it is better to replace it.
3. Wash all of the components in clean brake fluid.
4. Inspect the piston and piston bore. Replace any components which are severely corroded, scored, or worn. The piston and piston bore can be polished lightly with crocus cloth.
5. Wash the wheel cylinder and piston thoroughly in clean brake fluid, allowing them to remain lubricated for assembly.
6. Coat all of the new components to be installed in the wheel cylinder with clean brake fluid prior to assembly.
7. Assemble the wheel cylinder and install it to the backing plate.

Fig. 59 Remove the wheel cylinder assembly from the brake backing plate

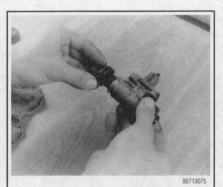

Fig. 60 After removing the wheel cylinder from the vehicle, remove the dust boot

Fig. 61 Remove the piston assembly from the wheel cylinder

Fig. 62 Remove the spring from the wheel cylinder piston assembly—if the spring is worn or damaged, replace it upon installation

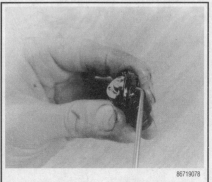

Fig. 63 Remove the seal from the piston assembly with a small pick

Fig. 64 View of a disassembled wheel cylinder—note that new seals must be used upon installation

REAR DISC BRAKES

Brake Pads

INSPECTION

The pads should be removed so that the thickness of the remaining friction material can be measured. If the pads are less than 0.08 in. (2mm) thick, they must be replaced. This measurement may disagree with your state inspection laws; if your state's law requires a thicker minimum, be sure to heed those standards.

➡**Always replace all pads on both wheels. The factory kit includes four pads, clips, pins, and springs; all parts should be installed.**

REMOVAL & INSTALLATION

◆ **See Figures 65, 66 and 67**

➡**We recommend replacement of the disc brake pads in axle sets for added safety and reliability. To ensure even wear, warped brake rotors should be turned (refinished) on a brake lathe, whenever the rear brake pads are replaced.**

1. Remove the hub cap and loosen the lug nuts.
2. Raise the rear of the truck and safely support it with jackstands.
3. Remove the lug nuts and the wheel.
4. Attach a clear vinyl tube to the bleeder plug on the caliper's cylinder body, then insert the other end into a jar half filled with brake fluid. Bleed off a small amount of brake fluid.
5. Compress the piston(s) in the brake caliper. Remove the caliper guide pin on the lower side.
6. Swivel the caliper up and away from the torque plate. Tie the caliper to a suspension member so it is out of the way. Do not disconnect the brake line.
7. Lift the 2 brake pads out of the torque plate.
8. Remove the inner and outer shims and cover. Remove the pad retainer if it is not still attached to the pads.
9. Check the pad thickness and replace the pads if they are less than 0.039 in. (1mm) thick.

➡**This minimum thickness measurement may disagree with your state or other jurisdiction's inspection laws; if so, heed your local requirements.**

To install:

10. Install the inner and outer shims into the torque plate.

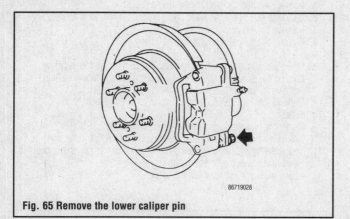

Fig. 65 Remove the lower caliper pin

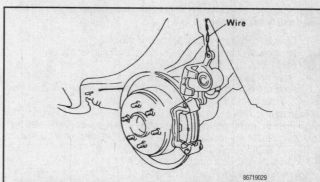

Fig. 66 Swivel the caliper upward for removal of the rear disc brake pads

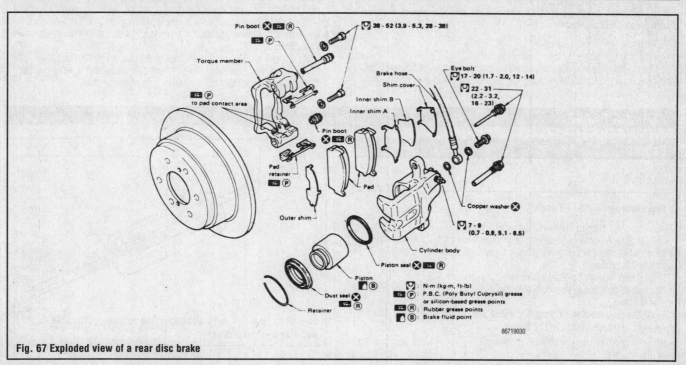

Fig. 67 Exploded view of a rear disc brake

11. Install the pad retainer.
12. Install the pads into the torque plate.

➡**When installing new brake pads, make sure your hands are clean. Do not allow any grease or oil to touch the contact face of the pads or the brakes will not stop the truck properly!**

13. Using a C-clamp or hammer handle, press the caliper piston back into the housing.

➡**Never press the piston into the caliper when the pads are out on both sides of the truck.**

14. Untie the caliper and swivel it back into position over the torque plate so that the dust boot is not pinched. Install the guide pin and tighten it to 23–30 ft. lbs. (31–41 Nm) on 1989 models; or 28–38 ft. lbs. (38–52 Nm) on 1990–95 models.
15. Check the condition of the cylinder side bushing boots.
16. Install the wheel and bleed the brakes.
17. Lower the truck and road test the vehicle.

Brake Caliper

REMOVAL & INSTALLATION

➡**We recommend replacement of the disc brake caliper in axle sets for added safety and reliability.**

1. Remove the hub cap and loosen the lug nuts.
2. Raise the rear of the truck and safely support it with jackstands.
3. Remove the lug nuts and the wheel.
4. Disconnect and plug the brake line.
5. Remove the caliper slide pin bolts and lift out the caliper. Compress the piston(s) in the brake caliper, if necessary.

To install:
6. Press the caliper piston into the housing until it is flush, then install the caliper. Tighten the mounting bolts 23–30 ft. lbs. (31–41 Nm) on 1989 models; or 28–38 ft. lbs. (38–52 Nm) on 1990–95 models.
7. Install the wheel and bleed the brakes.
8. Lower the truck and road test the vehicle.

OVERHAUL

➡**If the overhaul condition of this brake system part is in doubt, replace it with a complete assembly.**

1. Remove the caliper assembly.
2. Remove the retainer snapring and dust seal.
3. Using compressed air from a portable compressor or other source, place the air nozzle in the brake line hole and force the piston out of the cylinder body.

It's a good idea to place a piece of wood in the cylinder body to cushion the piston as it leaves the cylinder. Wear safety goggles, as some brake fluid may be sprayed out.
4. Remove the piston seal from its groove in the cylinder.
5. Rinse all parts in clean brake fluid. Check the cylinder bore and piston for wear, scratches and scoring. Minor rust and scratches in the cylinder bore may be removed with fine emery cloth. Any other damage will necessitate the replacement of the affected cylinder body. Any cracks in the torque member will require replacement of the part. The piston sliding surface is plated. DO NOT USE EMERY CLOTH OR ANY OTHER POLISHING MATERIAL TO REMOVE RUST OR OTHER FOREIGN MATTER! Replace the piston seal and dust boot. If the support pins are damaged at all, replace them.
6. Assemble parts in the reverse order of their disassembly. Be sure to coat all metal parts with clean brake fluid prior to assembly. Apply a thin coating of silicone brake lubricant to the support pins and bushings. Tighten the pin bolts.

Brake Disc (Rotor)

REMOVAL & INSTALLATION

➡**We recommend replacement of the brake rotor in axle sets for added safety and reliability.**

1. Remove the hub cap and loosen the lug nuts.
2. Raise the rear of the truck and safely support it with jackstands.
3. Remove the lug nuts and the wheel.
4. Remove the caliper, brake pads and torque member as previously detailed.
5. Using a dial indicator, check the disc run-out, as described below.
6. Loosen the parking brake shoes by rotating the star wheel upward.
7. Remove the brake disc/parking brake drum assembly.
8. Perform the disc inspection procedure, as outlined below.

To install:
9. Install the brake disc/parking brake drum assembly.
10. Adjust the parking brake shoes, as described later in this section.
11. Install the torque member, brake pads and caliper as previously detailed.
12. Bleed and adjust the brake system.
13. Lower the truck and road test the vehicle.

INSPECTION

Examine the disc. If it is worn, warped or scored, it must be replaced. Check the thickness of the disc against the specifications given in the Brake Specifications chart. If it is below specifications, replace it. Use a micrometer to measure the thickness.

Disc run-out should be measured before the disc is removed and again, after the disc is installed. Use a dial indicator mounted on a stand to determine run-out. If run-out exceeds 0.0028 in. (0.07mm), replace the disc.

PARKING BRAKE

Cables

ADJUSTMENT

▸ **See Figures 68, 69, 70 and 71**

1. Raise and support the rear of the vehicle safely.
2. On vehicles equipped with rear drum brakes, check the brake adjustment and correct as necessary. The drum brake adjustment procedure is described earlier in this section.
3. Loosen the brake cable adjuster assembly lock-nut.
4. Rotate the adjuster assembly until the parking brake control lever operating stroke is as follows:
• center lever (except Pathfinder) and 2wd with stick lever—10–12 notches
• 4wd with stick lever—9–11 notches
• Pathfinder with a center lever—7–9 notches

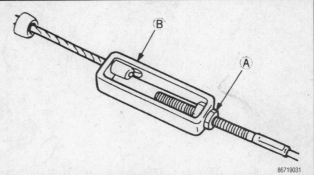

86719031

Fig. 68 Loosen lock-nut A before turning parking brake cable adjuster B—4wd pickup

Fig. 69 Grasp the unthreaded portion of the parking brake cable adjuster with locking pliers, while turning the adjusting nut—Pathfinder

Fig. 70 View of the brake warning lamp switch—note that the console assembly must be removed

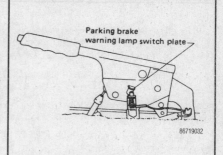

Fig. 71 If necessary, bend the brake warning lamp switch plate to adjust the lamp's activation

➡Notches are measured from the rest position (in or down) to the full-on position (out or up).

5. Release the parking brake and make sure that the rear wheels turn freely with no drag.

6. On 1989 models, the brake light should come on after 1 notch (pickup w/ center lever) or 2 notches (pickup w/ stick lever and Pathfinders w/ center lever). On 1990–95 models, it should come on after 1 notch (stick lever) or 2 notches (center lever). If not, adjust the switch by bending the plate.

7. Tighten the lock-nut at the parking brake cable adjuster assembly, then lower and road test the vehicle.

REMOVAL & INSTALLATION

▶ **See Figures 72, 73 and 74**

1. Fully release the parking brake control lever.
2. Raise and support the rear of the vehicle safely.
3. Loosen the cable lever adjusting nut at the frame crossmember.
4. Disconnect the cable from the control lever.
5. Remove the rear drums, then disconnect the brake cables from the parking brake toggle levers.
6. Remove the lockplate, spring and clip, then pull the parking brake cable out toward the cable lever.
7. Remove the lever cotter pin and disconnect the cable.
8. Install the cables in the reverse order of removal. Be sure to use new cotter pins. Apply a light coat of grease to the cables to make sure that they slide properly. Adjust the parking brakes.
9. Lower the truck and test the parking brake operation.

Parking Brake Shoes

➡Vehicles equipped with rear disc brakes utilize separate drum-type brake shoes for parking brakes.

ADJUSTMENT

➡Vehicles equipped with rear drum brakes do not contain separate parking brake shoes, so no separate parking brake shoe adjustment is required.

Vehicles With Rear Disc Brakes

▶ **See Figure 75**

1. Raise and support the rear of the truck safely.
2. Remove the adjuster hole plug at the rear of the brake backing plate.
3. Make sure that the parking brake is fully released, then rotate the star wheel adjuster downward with a brake adjusting tool until the shoes are touching the brake drum.
4. Back off the star wheel 7–8 notches.
5. Install the hole plug and rotate the wheel a few times to ensure that the shoes are not dragging on the drums.
6. Lower the truck and test the parking brake operation.

REMOVAL & INSTALLATION

➡Vehicles equipped with rear drum brakes do not contain separate parking brake shoes, so no separate parking brake shoe procedure is required.

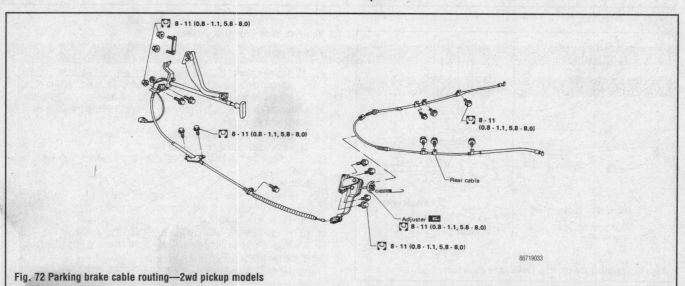

Fig. 72 Parking brake cable routing—2wd pickup models

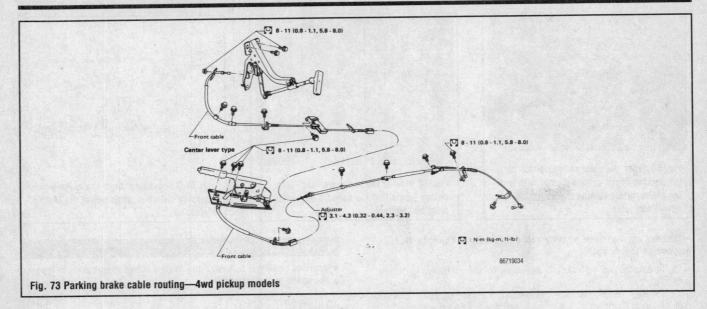

Fig. 73 Parking brake cable routing—4wd pickup models

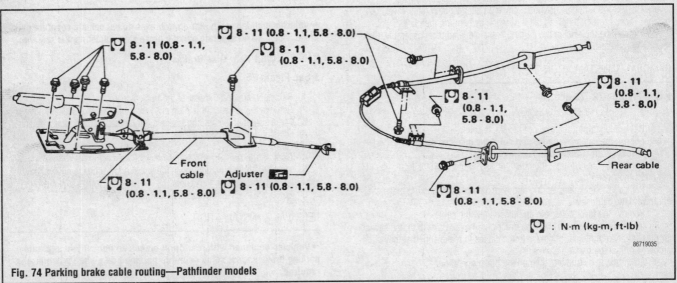

Fig. 74 Parking brake cable routing—Pathfinder models

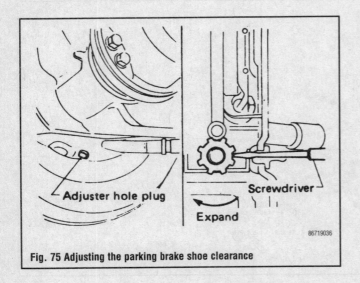

Fig. 75 Adjusting the parking brake shoe clearance

Vehicles With Rear Disc Brakes

♦ See Figure 76

1. Raise the rear of the truck and support it with safety stands.
2. Remove the adjuster hole plug at the rear of the brake backing plate.
3. Make sure that the parking brake is fully released and rotate the star wheel adjuster downward with a brake adjusting tool so that the shoes come out of contact with the drum.
4. Remove the brake disc/parking brake drum assembly.
5. Remove the spring retainer and springs.
6. Unhook the brake return and adjusting screw springs, then swivel out the brake shoes.

To install:

7. Position the brake shoes on the backing plate.
8. Install the return and adjusting screw springs.
9. Position the brake strut, then install the guide plate.
10. Position the anti-rattle springs, then install the retainers.
11. Install the brake disc/parking brake drum assembly, then adjust the parking brake shoes.
12. Lower the truck and test the parking brake operation.

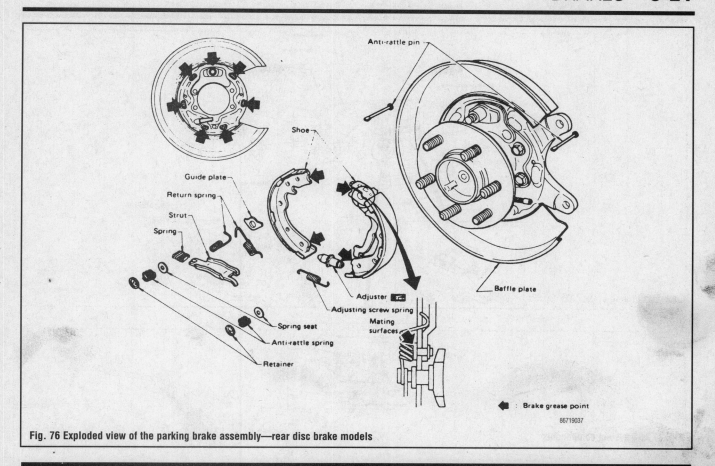

Fig. 76 Exploded view of the parking brake assembly—rear disc brake models

REAR WHEEL ANTI-LOCK BRAKE SYSTEM

System Description and Operation

The Rear Anti-lock Brake System (R-ABS) found on Nissan pickup trucks and Pathfinders is designed to prevent or reduce locking of the rear wheels under heavy braking. Because of the vehicle's load carrying capacity, the handling and braking characteristics will change significantly as the weight increases. The R-ABS system senses impending lock-up at the rear wheels under all operating conditions and modulates brake line pressures to allow the wheels maximum braking without locking. This increases vehicle stability under hard braking.

When the brake pedal is applied, the R-ABS module senses the drop in rear wheel speed based on signals from the rear wheel speed sensor. If the rate of deceleration is too great (based on pre-programmed values), the module determines that wheel lock will occur.

The module energizes the isolation solenoid, an electro-hydraulic valve, to isolate the wheel cylinders from the master cylinder line pressure. With this valve actuated, line pressure is held constant and cannot increase. Additional pedal pressure has no effect. If the rate of deceleration is still seen to be too great, the module pulses the dump solenoid momentarily.

The dump solenoid releases fluid trapped between the isolation solenoid and the wheel, reducing line pressure. The excess fluid is temporarily routed to an accumulator where it is stored until the isolation valve is de-energized. Reducing the line pressure allows the wheel to roll more freely. The module sees the increase in wheel speed and releases the isolation solenoid.

When the isolation solenoid is de-energized, the pressure from the brake pedal is allowed to act directly on the brakes. The module senses the wheel speed reduction and the cycle repeats until the brake pedal is no longer applied or braking force does not threaten to lock the wheels. The module is capable of repeating the control cycle several times per second.

R-ABS Control Unit (Module)

◆ See Figures 77 and 78

The R-ABS control module is the electronic heart of the system. It is located below the right-side dashboard and is connected to the R-ABS control harness.

The control module receives inputs from the ignition, the brake lamp switch, the wheel speed sensor, and the brake fluid level switch. It controls output to the hydraulic unit solenoid valves and the amber dash warning lamp.

The R-ABS module performs system tests and self-tests during start-up and normal operation. The solenoid valve, fluid level and speed sensor are monitored for correct operation. If a fault is found, the module will immediately disable the anti-lock function and light the amber ANTI-LOCK dash warning lamp.

The module will assign a fault code and store it in memory. The code may be retrieved by placing the system into diagnostic mode. Codes will only be displayed when the dash warning lamp is lit. A stored code will be erased when the ignition is switched OFF. If the problem exists when the engine is restarted, the self-check will note the fault and again set the code.

REMOVAL & INSTALLATION

1. Turn the ignition switch OFF.
2. Remove the bolts holding the module to its bracket.
3. Carefully disconnect the multi-pin harness from the module, then remove the module.
4. Reassemble in the reverse order, making certain the multi-pin connector is firmly engaged and the connector lock is secured.

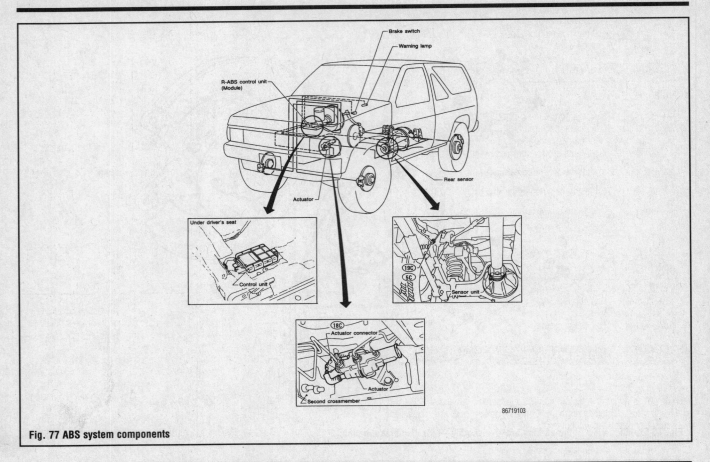

Fig. 77 ABS system components

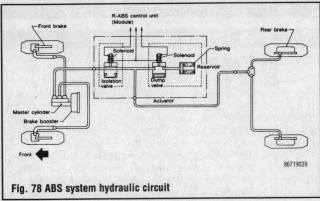

Fig. 78 ABS system hydraulic circuit

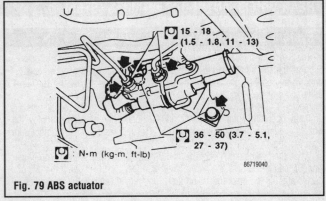

Fig. 79 ABS actuator

Hydraulic Actuator

The actuator contains the electric isolation and dump solenoids. It also contains the small accumulator into which released brake fluid is routed and stored. The accumulator only retains fluid under pressure when the R-ABS is in operation.

The hydraulic actuator unit is mounted on the frame rail ahead of the right rear wheel.

REMOVAL & INSTALLATION

♦ **See Figure 79**

1. Disconnect the negative battery cable.
2. Drain the brake fluid.
3. Raise and safely support the vehicle.
4. Locate the actuator under the right side of the vehicle. Detach the brake lines and the electrical connectors.

5. Unfasten the mounting bolts and remove the actuator.
To install:
6. Install the actuator and tighten the mounting bolts to 27–37 ft. lbs. (36–50 Nm).
7. Fasten the brake lines and electrical connectors.
8. Refill the master cylinder with new brake fluid and bleed the brake system.
9. Lower the vehicle and connect the battery cable.

Rear Wheel Speed Sensor

The speed of the rear wheels is monitored by a sensor located in the rear differential housing. A toothed wheel or rotor rotates with the drive line, passing in front of the sensor. As the teeth of the ring pass the sensor, the peaks and valleys generate a small AC voltage which is transmitted to the R-ABS module. The module compares the signals and reacts to rapid loss of wheel speed at a particular wheel by engaging the R-ABS system.

The sensor may be removed for testing or replacement, but the companion flange on the differential must be removed for access. Removing the flange also allows access to the toothed rotor.

REMOVAL & INSTALLATION

▶ **See Figure 80**

1. Elevate and safely support the rear of the vehicle.
2. Matchmark and remove the rear driveshaft from the rear differential.
3. Detach the sensor harness at the connector.
4. Remove the nut holding the companion flange to the differential.

➡**This nut should be tight and may be difficult to remove.**

5. Remove the companion flange with the rotor from the differential housing.
6. Remove the 3 retaining bolts holding the speed sensor, then remove the sensor.

To install:

7. Fit the sensor into place and install the 3 bolts. Tighten the bolts to 7 ft. lbs. (10 Nm).
8. Place the companion flange in position and start the retaining nut. Tighten the nut to 175 ft. lbs. (236 Nm).
9. Attach the sensor connector to the wire harness.
10. Install the driveshaft.
11. Lower the vehicle to the ground.

Dashboard Warning Lamps

The R-ABS system uses an amber ANTI-LOCK warning lamp to advise the operator of faults. The lamp should come on briefly during engine start-up and then go out. If the lamp lights during vehicle operation, a fault has been found and the anti-lock system is disabled. If only the amber lamp is lit, the vehicle may be safely driven but without the benefit of the anti-lock function.

The conventional brake system uses the familiar red BRAKE warning lamp. Should the BRAKE warning lamp come on, it will usually trigger the ANTI-LOCK lamp as well. Any time the red lamp is lit, the conventional braking system may be impaired. Great care must be used when operating the vehicle.

Diagnosis and Testing

SYSTEM PRECAUTIONS

• Certain components within the ABS system are not intended to be serviced or repaired. Only those components with service procedures should be repaired.
• Do not use rubber hoses or other parts not specifically specified for the ABS system. When using repair kits, install all parts included in the kit. Partial or incorrect repair may lead to functional problems and require the replacement of components.

• Lubricate rubber parts with clean, fresh brake fluid to ease assembly. Do not use lubricated shop air to clean parts; damage to rubber components may result.
• Use only DOT 3 brake fluid from an unopened container.
• If any hydraulic component or line is removed or replaced, it may be necessary to bleed the entire system.
• A clean repair area is essential. Always clean the reservoir and cap thoroughly before removing the cap. The slightest amount of dirt in the fluid may plug an orifice and impair the system function. Use denatured alcohol to clean components.
• Do not allow ABS components to come into contact with any substance containing mineral oil; this includes used shop rags.
• The anti-lock brake controller is a microprocessor similar to other computer units in the vehicle. Ensure that the ignition switch is **OFF** before removing or installing controller harnesses. Avoid static electricity discharge at or near the controller.
• If any arc welding is to be done on the vehicle, the ABS controller should be disconnected before welding operations begin.
• If the vehicle is to be baked after painting, disconnect and remove the ABS controller from the vehicle.

INITIAL CHECKS

Before diagnosing an apparent ABS problem, check the battery condition; approximately 12 volts are required to operate the system. Turn the ignition switch **ON** and check that the ABS dashboard warning lamp comes on for 3–4 seconds. If the lamp does not come on, repair the fuse, bulb or wiring.

Also, make absolutely certain that the normal braking system is in correct working order. Many common brake problems (dragging parking brake, seepage, etc.) will affect the ABS system. A visual check of specific system components may reveal problems creating an apparent ABS malfunction. Performing this inspection may reveal a simple failure, thus eliminating extended diagnostic time. Perform the following checks before assuming an ABS problem:

1. Check the tire pressures; they must be approximately equal for the system to operate correctly.
2. Check the wheels and tires on the vehicle. They must be of the same size and type to generate accurate speed signals.
3. Inspect the brake fluid level in the reservoir.
4. Inspect the brake lines, hoses, master cylinder, brake calipers and cylinders for leakage.
5. Check the brake lines and hoses for excessive wear, heat damage, punctures, contact with other parts, missing clips or holders, blockage or crimping.
6. Inspect the calipers or wheel cylinders for rust or corrosion. Check for proper sliding action, if applicable.
7. Check the caliper and wheel cylinder pistons for freedom of motion during application and release.
8. Inspect the rear speed sensor for proper mounting and connections.
9. Confirm an ABS fault occurrence. Certain driver induced faults, such as not releasing the parking brake fully, will set a fault code and trigger the dash warning light(s). Excessive wheel spin on low-traction surfaces, high speed acceleration or riding the brake pedal may also set fault codes and trigger a

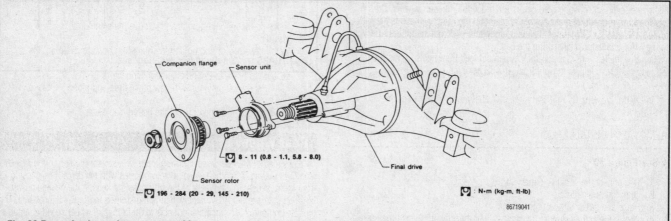

Fig. 80 Rear wheel speed sensor assembly

warning lamp. These induced faults are not system failures, but examples of vehicle performance outside the parameters of the control unit.

10. Many system shutdowns are due to loss of sensor signals to or from the controller. The most common cause is not a failed sensor but a loose, corroded or dirty connector. Check harness and component connectors carefully.

DIAGNOSTIC CODES

▶ See Figure 81

➡ To obtain satisfactory self-diagnosing results, the vehicle must be driven in 2wd above 25 mph (40 km/h) for at least 1 minute. After the vehicle is stopped, the number of warning flashes is counted by grounding the check terminal, with the engine running.

If a malfunction occurs, the system will identify the problem, and the computer will assign and store a fault code for the fault(s). The dashboard warning lamp will be illuminated to inform the driver that a fault has been found.

During diagnostics, the system will transmit the stored code(s) by flashing the dashboard warning lamp. If two or more codes are stored, repair the first fault. After the first fault part or unit has been repaired, the warning lamp will then flash to indicate that the other part or unit is malfunctioning.

READING CODES

To obtain satisfactory self-diagnosing results, the vehicle must be driven in 2wd above 25 mph (40 km/h) for at least 1 minute. After the vehicle is stopped, the number of warning flashes is counted by grounding the check terminal (lower right corner of the check connector terminal to a body ground), with the engine running. The check connector is located under the dashboard to the left of the brake pedal. Refer to the following circuit diagram and diagnostic charts.

CLEARING CODES

A stored code will be erased when the ignition is switched **OFF**. If the problem exists when the engine is restarted, the self-check will note the fault and again set the code.

Filling and Bleeding

The brake fluid reservoir is located on top of the master cylinder. While no special procedures are needed to fill the fluid, the reservoir cap and surrounding area must be wiped clean of all dirt and debris before removing the cap. The slightest amount of dirt in the fluid can cause a system malfunction. Use only fresh DOT 3 fluid from a sealed container. Use of old, polluted or non-approved fluid can seriously impair the function of the system.

Bleeding is performed using the 2-person manual method with the battery cable disconnected. The system or any wheel must be bled with the ignition **OFF** and the connector at the hydraulic actuator disengaged. After all wheels have been bled, bleed the hydraulic actuator using the same procedure as the wheels. Tighten each wheel bleeder plug to 6 ft. lbs. (8 Nm).

If the master cylinder has been repaired or if the reservoir has been emptied, the master cylinder must be bled before the individual lines or wheels. During any bleeding procedure, make certain to maintain the fluid level above the MIN line on the reservoir. When the bleeding procedure is complete, fill the reservoir to the MAX line before reinstalling the cap.

For all vehicles with rear anti-lock systems, bleed the wheels in this order: left rear, right rear, left front, right front, R-ABS actuator.

PROCEDURE		SYMPTOM	Pedal vibration & noise	Long stopping distance	Brake pedal stroke	R-ABS doesn't work	R-ABS works frequently
Electrical Components Inspection		Sensor Unit and Actuator				○	
Diagnostic Procedure (Select inspection with LED flashing No.)		Warning flashing 5	○	○	○	○	○
		Warning flashing 13,14 or 15	○	○	○	○	
		Warning flashing 6	○	○	○	○	
		Warning flashing 9 or 10	○	○	○	○	
		Warning flashing 3 or 8	○	○	○	○	
		Warning flashing 4	○	○	○		
		Warning flashing 2 or 7	○	○	○		
Diagnostic Procedure		Diagnostic Procedure 6					○
		Diagnostic Procedure 5					
		Diagnostic Procedure 4				○	
		Diagnostic Procedure 3			○		
		Diagnostic Procedure 2		○			
		Diagnostic Procedure 1	○				
Preliminary Check		Preliminary Check 2				○	
		Preliminary Check 1				○	

86719100

Fig. 81 ABS trouble diagnosis symptom chart

CHECKING THE NUMBER OF WARNING LAMP FLASHES

When a problem occurs in the R-ABS, the warning lamp on the instrument panel comes on. As shown in the table, the control unit performs self-diagnosis.

To obtain satisfactory self-diagnosing results, the vehicle must be driven in 2WD above 40 km/h (25 MPH) for at least one minute before the self-diagnosis is performed. After the vehicle has been stopped, the number of warning flashes is counted by grounding the check terminal, with the engine running, there be identifying a malfunctioning part or unit by the number of flashes.

If more than two parts or units malfunction at the same time, the warning lamp will flash to indicate one of the malfunctioning parts or units. After the part or unit has been repaired, the warning lamp will then flash to indicate that the other part or unit is malfunctioning.

No. of warning flashes	Detected items	Malfunctioning cause or part			Diagnostic Procedure
2	Actuator	ISO solenoid		Open	Diagnostic Procedure 7
7				Shorted	Diagnostic Procedure 7
4				Blocked	Diagnostic Procedure 8
3		DUMP solenoid		Open	Diagnostic Procedure 9
8			Short circuit		Diagnostic Procedure 9
9	Sensor		Open		Diagnostic Procedure 10
10			Short circuit		Diagnostic Procedure 10
6	Control Unit		Erratic		Diagnostic Procedure 11
13, 14 or 15			—		Diagnostic Procedure 12
5	Other				Diagnostic Procedure 13

CAUTION:

When driving in 4WD, the rear anti-lock brake system is not effective in most cases. The rear wheels will lock if the front wheels lock as the transfer mechanically couples the front and rear axles together. If this happens, the rear anti-lock brake system may not function but the ordinary brakes will operate normally. The "ANTI-LOCK" brake warning light will then come on. The above condition is not a malfunction and the rear anti-lock brake system can be re-activated by starting the engine again. The "Anti-Lock" brake warning light will then go off.

8671910Z

Preliminary Check 1

A
1) Turn ignition switch on.
2) Check warning lamp activation. When ignition switch is turned on, warning lamp should turn on.

— No → Go to "Diagnostic Procedure 6". If OK, replace control unit.

— Yes ↓

B Check warning lamp deactivates within a few seconds.

— No → Go to Preliminary Check 2 below.

— Yes ↓

C Check warning lamp reactivation.

— Yes → Go to Preliminary Check 2 below.

— No ↓

D
1) Drive vehicle with 2WD for 1 minute or more at 40 km/h (25 MPH) or more.
2) Check warning lamp reactivation.

— Yes → Go to Preliminary Check 2 below.

— No ↓

1) Stop engine.
2) Turn ignition switch on again. Check actuator clicking noise, when warning lamp turns off.

— OK → Self-operating function is OK.

— NG ↓

Check actuator.
Refer to "Electrical Components Inspection".

Located behind second cross member:
Listen for actuator clicking noise in a quiet area.

Preliminary Check 2

1) Start engine.
2) Ground the check terminal of check connector.
3) Check the warning lamp flashing.

— No → Check brake fluid level. Go to "Diagnostic Procedure 6".

— OK → Replace control unit.

— Yes ↓

Count the number of flashes. Go to "Self-diagnosis".

8671910I

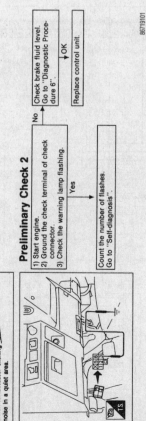

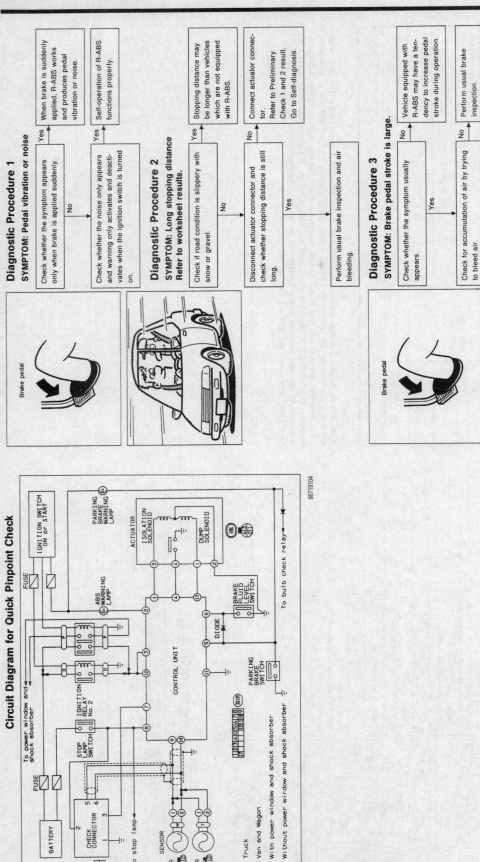

Diagnostic Procedure 1
SYMPTOM: Pedal vibration or noise

Check whether the symptom appears only when brake is applied suddenly.
— Yes → When brake is suddenly applied, R-ABS works and produces pedal vibration or noise.
— No →

Check whether the noise only appears and warning only activates and deactivates when the ignition switch is turned on.
— Yes → Self-operation of R-ABS functions properly.

Diagnostic Procedure 2
SYMPTOM: Long stopping distance
Refer to worksheet results.

Check if road condition is slippery with snow or gravel.
— Yes → Stopping distance may be longer than vehicles which are not equipped with R-ABS.
— No →

Disconnect actuator connector and check whether stopping distance is still long.
— No → Connect actuator connector. Refer to Preliminary Check 1 and 2 result. Go to Self-diagnosis.
— Yes →

Perform usual brake inspection and air bleeding.

Diagnostic Procedure 3
SYMPTOM: Brake pedal stroke is large.

Check whether the symptom usually appears.
— No → Vehicle equipped with R-ABS may have a tendency to increase pedal stroke during operation.
— Yes →

Check for accumulation of air by trying to bleed air.
— No → Perform usual brake inspection.

Brake pedal

Circuit Diagram for Quick Pinpoint Check

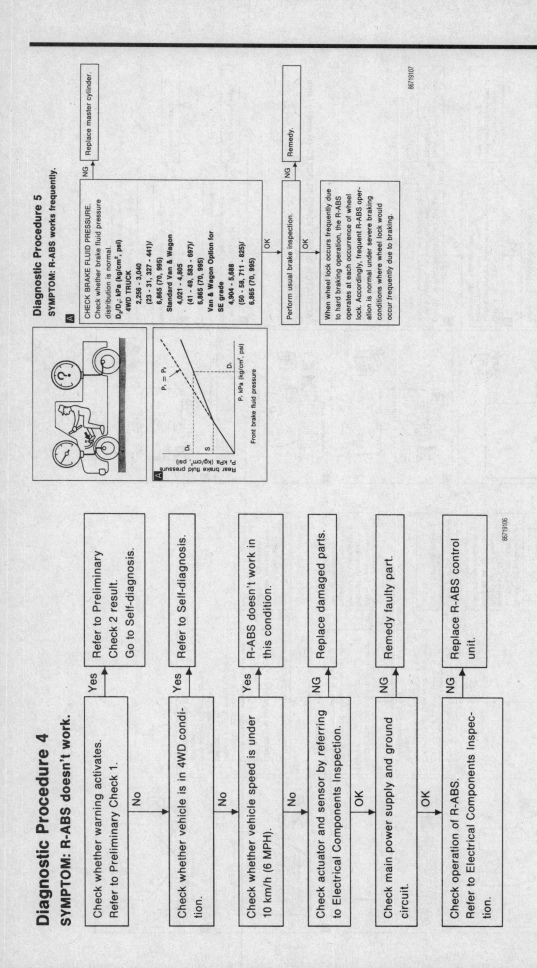

Diagnostic Procedure 4
SYMPTOM: R-ABS doesn't work.

Check whether warning activates. Refer to Preliminary Check 1.
— Yes → Refer to Preliminary Check 2 result. Go to Self-diagnosis.
— No →

Check whether vehicle is in 4WD condition.
— Yes → Refer to Self-diagnosis.
— No →

Check whether vehicle speed is under 10 km/h (6 MPH).
— Yes → R-ABS doesn't work in this condition.
— No →

Check actuator and sensor by referring to Electrical Components Inspection.
— NG → Replace damaged parts.
— OK →

Check main power supply and ground circuit.
— NG → Remedy faulty part.
— OK →

Check operation of R-ABS. Refer to Electrical Components Inspection.
— NG → Replace R-ABS control unit.

86719106

Diagnostic Procedure 5
SYMPTOM: R-ABS works frequently.

CHECK BRAKE FLUID PRESSURE. Check whether brake fluid pressure distribution is normal.
— NG → Replace master cylinder.
— OK →

D_2/D_1: kPa (kg/cm², psi)

4WD TRUCK
2,256 - 3,040
(23 - 31, 327 - 441)/
6,865 (70, 995)

Standard Van & Wagon
4,021 - 4,805
(41 - 49, 583 - 697)/
6,865 (70, 995)

Van & Wagon Option for SE grade
4,904 - 5,688
(50 - 58, 711 - 825)/
6,865 (70, 995)

$P_1 = P_2$
D_2
D_1
S
P_2, kPa (kg/cm², psi)
Rear brake fluid pressure
Front brake fluid pressure
P_1 kPa (kg/cm², psi)

Perform usual brake inspection.
— NG → Remedy.
— OK →

When wheel lock occurs frequently due to hard braking operation, the R-ABS operates at each occurrence of wheel lock. Accordingly, frequent R-ABS operation is normal under severe braking conditions where wheel lock would occur frequently due to braking.

86719107

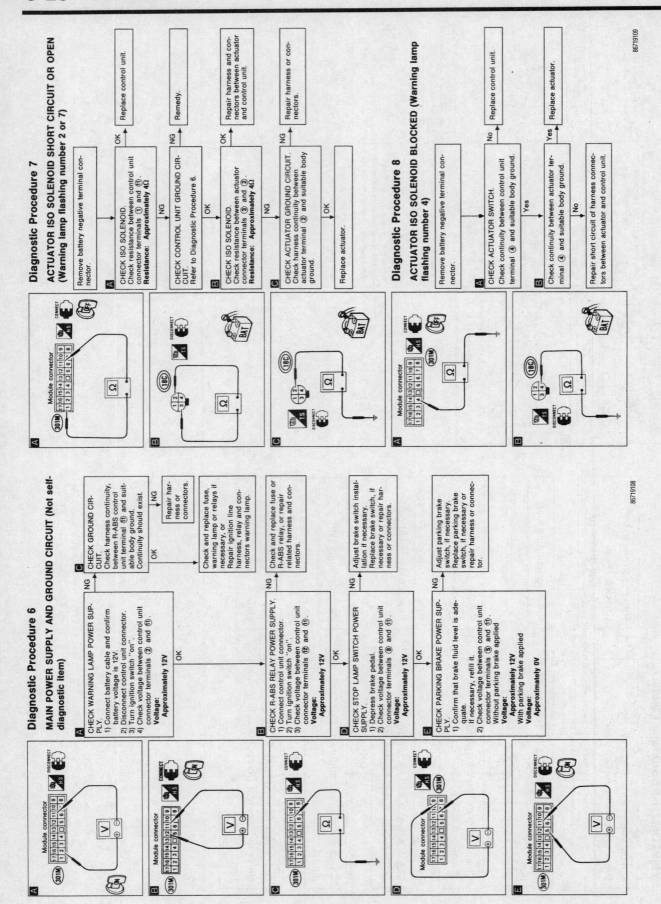

Diagnostic Procedure 7

ACTUATOR ISO SOLENOID SHORT CIRCUIT OR OPEN (Warning lamp flashing number 2 or 7)

Remove battery negative terminal connector.

A. CHECK ISO SOLENOID.
Check resistance between control unit connector terminals ① and ①.
Resistance: Approximately 4Ω

— OK → Replace control unit.
— NG →

B. CHECK CONTROL UNIT GROUND CIRCUIT.
Refer to Diagnostic Procedure 6.

— OK →
— NG → Remedy.

CHECK ISO SOLENOID.
Check resistance between actuator connector terminals ③ and ②.
Resistance: Approximately 4Ω

— OK → Repair harness and connectors between actuator and control unit.
— NG →

C. CHECK ACTUATOR GROUND CIRCUIT.
Check harness continuity between actuator terminal ② and suitable body ground.

— OK → Replace actuator.
— NG → Repair harness or connectors.

Diagnostic Procedure 8

ACTUATOR ISO SOLENOID BLOCKED (Warning lamp flashing number 4)

Remove battery negative terminal connector.

A. CHECK ACTUATOR SWITCH.
Check continuity between control unit terminal ④ and suitable body ground.

— No → Replace control unit.
— Yes →

B. Check continuity between actuator terminal ④ and suitable body ground.

— Yes → Replace actuator.
— No → Repair short circuit of harness connectors between actuator and control unit.

Diagnostic Procedure 6

MAIN POWER SUPPLY AND GROUND CIRCUIT (Not self-diagnostic item)

A. CHECK WARNING LAMP POWER SUPPLY.
1) Connect battery cable and confirm battery voltage is 12V.
2) Disconnect control unit connector.
3) Turn ignition switch "on".
4) Check voltage between control unit connector terminals ② and ①.
Voltage: Approximately 12V

— NG →
C. CHECK GROUND CIRCUIT.
Check harness continuity, between R-ABS control unit terminal ① and suitable body ground. Continuity should exist.

— NG → Repair harness or connectors.
— OK → Check and replace fuse, warning lamp or relays if necessary, or Repair ignition line harness, relay and connectors warning lamp.

— OK →

B. CHECK R-ABS RELAY POWER SUPPLY.
1) Connect control unit connector.
2) Turn ignition switch "on".
3) Check voltage between control unit terminals ⑫ and ①.
Voltage: Approximately 12V

— NG → Check and replace fuse or R-ABS relay, or repair related harness and connectors.
— OK →

D. CHECK STOP LAMP SWITCH POWER SUPPLY.
1) Depress brake pedal.
2) Check voltage between control unit terminals ⑧ and ①.
Voltage: Approximately 12V

— NG → Adjust brake switch installation if necessary. Replace brake switch, if necessary or repair harness or connectors.
— OK →

E. CHECK PARKING BRAKE POWER SUPPLY.
1) Confirm that brake fluid level is adequate.
If necessary, refill it.
2) Check voltage between control unit terminals ⑤ and ①.
Without parking brake applied
Voltage: Approximately 12V
With parking brake applied
Voltage: Approximately 0V

— NG → Adjust parking brake switch, if necessary. Replace parking brake switch, if necessary or repair harness or connector.

86719109

86719108

Diagnostic Procedure 10

SENSOR OPEN OR SHORT CIRCUIT (Warning lamp flashing number 9 or 10)

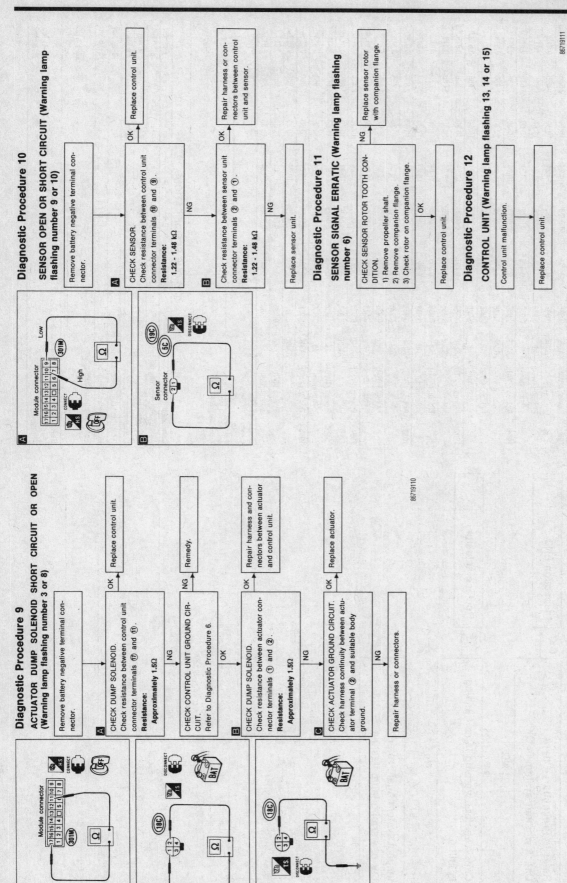

Remove battery negative terminal connector.

↓

A CHECK SENSOR.
Check resistance between control unit connector terminals ⑩ and ⑨.
Resistance:
1.22 - 1.48 kΩ → OK → Replace control unit.

↓ NG

B Check resistance between sensor unit connector terminals ② and ①.
Resistance:
1.22 - 1.48 kΩ → OK → Repair harness or connectors between control unit and sensor.

↓ NG

Replace sensor unit.

Diagnostic Procedure 11

SENSOR SIGNAL ERRATIC (Warning lamp flashing number 6)

CHECK SENSOR ROTOR TOOTH CONDITION.
1) Remove propeller shaft.
2) Remove companion flange.
3) Check rotor on companion flange. → NG → Replace sensor rotor with companion flange.

↓ OK

Replace control unit.

Diagnostic Procedure 12

CONTROL UNIT (Warning lamp flashing 13, 14 or 15)

Control unit malfunction. → Replace control unit.

86719111

Diagnostic Procedure 9

ACTUATOR DUMP SOLENOID SHORT CIRCUIT OR OPEN (Warning lamp flashing number 3 or 8)

Remove battery negative terminal connector.

↓

A CHECK DUMP SOLENOID.
Check resistance between control unit connector terminals ⑦ and ⑪.
Resistance:
Approximately 1.5Ω → OK → Replace control unit.

↓ NG

CHECK CONTROL UNIT GROUND CIRCUIT.
Refer to Diagnostic Procedure 6. → NG → Remedy.

↓ OK

B CHECK DUMP SOLENOID.
Check resistance between actuator connector terminals ① and ②.
Resistance:
Approximately 1.5Ω → OK → Repair harness and connectors between actuator and control unit.

↓ NG

C CHECK ACTUATOR GROUND CIRCUIT.
Check harness continuity between actuator terminal ② and suitable body ground. → OK → Replace actuator.

↓ NG

Repair harness or connectors.

86719110

BRAKE SPECIFICATIONS

All specifications in inches

Year	Model	Engine	Master Cyl. Bore	Brake Disc		Brake Drum		Wheel Cyl. or Caliper Bore	
				Minimum Thickness	Maximum Run-out	Orig. Inside Dia.	Max. Wear Limit	Front	Rear
1989	Pick-up (2WD)	Z24i	0.938	0.787	0.0028	10.24	10.30	2.386	0.875
		VG30i	1.000①	0.945	0.0028	10.24②	10.30③	1.685	0.938④
	Pick-up (4WD)	All	0.938	0.945	0.0028	10.00	10.06	1.685	0.688
	Pathfinder	All	0.938	0.945⑤	0.0028	10.24	10.30	1.685	0.813
1990	Pick-up (2WD)	KA24E	0.938	0.787	0.0028	10.24	10.30	2.386	0.875
		VG30E	0.938	0.945	0.0028	10.24	10.30	1.685	0.813
	Pick-up (4WD)	All	0.938	0.945	0.0028	11.61	11.67	1.685	0.813
	Pathfinder	All	0.938	0.945⑥	0.0028	10.24	10.30	1.685	0.813⑥
1991	Pick-up (2WD)	KA24E	0.938	0.787	0.0028	10.24	10.30	2.386	0.875
		VG30E	0.938	0.945	0.0028	10.24	10.30	1.685	0.813
	Pick-up (4WD)	All	0.938	0.945	0.0028	11.61	11.67	1.685	0.813
	Pathfinder	All	0.938	0.945⑥	0.0028	10.24	10.30	1.685	0.813⑥
1992	Pick-up (2WD)	KA24E	0.938	0.787	0.0028	10.24	10.30	2.386	0.875
		VG30E	0.938	0.945	0.0028	10.24	10.30	1.685	0.813
	Pick-up (4WD)	All	0.938	0.945	0.0028	11.61	11.67	1.685	0.813
	Pathfinder	All	0.938	0.945⑥	0.0028	10.24	10.30	1.685	0.813⑥
1993	Pick-up (2WD)	KA24E	0.938	0.787	0.0028	10.24	10.30	2.386	0.875
		VG30E	0.938	0.945	0.0028	10.24	10.30	1.685	0.813
	Pick-up (4WD)	All	0.938	0.945	0.0028	11.61	11.67	1.685	0.813
	Pathfinder	All	0.938	0.945⑥	0.0028	10.24	10.30	1.685	0.813⑥
1994	Pick-up (2WD)	KA24E	0.938	0.787	0.0028	10.24	10.30	2.386	0.875
		VG30E	0.938	0.945	0.0028	10.24	10.30	1.685	0.813
	Pick-up (4WD)	All	0.938	0.945	0.0028	11.61	11.67	1.685	0.813
	Pathfinder	All	0.938	0.945⑥	0.0028	10.24	10.30	1.685	0.813⑥
1995	Pick-up (2WD)	KA24E	0.938	0.787	0.0028	10.24	10.30	2.386	0.875
		VG30E	0.938	0.945	0.0028	10.24	10.30	1.685	0.813
	Pick-up (4WD)	All	0.938	0.945	0.0028	11.61	11.67	1.685	0.813
	Pathfinder	All	0.938	0.945⑤	0.0028	10.24	10.30	1.685	0.813⑥

① Heavy duty: 0.938
② Heavy duty: 10.00
③ Heavy duty: 10.06
④ Heavy duty: 0.688
⑤ Rear disc: 0.630
⑥ Rear disc: 1.686

86719C01

TORQUE SPECIFICATIONS

Component	U.S.	Metric
ABS actuator mounting bolts	27–37 ft. lbs.	36–50 Nm
ABS sensor bolts	7 ft. lbs.	10 Nm
Bleeder plugs	6 ft. lbs.	8 Nm
Front disc brake caliper-to-torque plate	53–72 ft. lbs.	72–97 Nm
Hydraulic line connections	10–15 ft. lbs.	15–18 Nm
Power booster mounting bolts		
1989	6–8 ft. lbs.	0.8–1.1 Nm
1990–95	9–12 ft. lbs.	13–16 Nm
Rear disc brake caliper-to-torque plate		
1989	23–30 ft. lbs.	31–41 Nm
1990–95	28–38 ft. lbs.	38–52 Nm

86719C02

Diagnostic Procedure 13
Other (Warning lamp flashing 5)

Overhaul both rear brakes.

↓

Refer to Preliminary Check 1.
Check whether system is OK.

— OK → Inspection END

— NG ↓

Check whether warning lamp flashing is still 5.

— Yes → Replace actuator.

— No ↓

Inspect system again referring to number of warning lamp flashes.

86719112

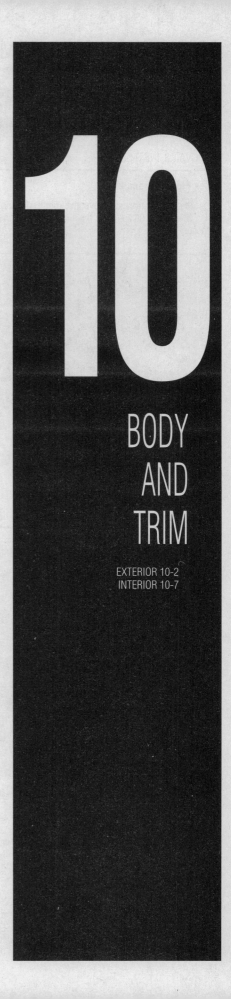

10

BODY
AND
TRIM

EXTERIOR 10-2
INTERIOR 10-7

EXTERIOR

Hood

REMOVAL & INSTALLATION

▶ **See Figures 1 and 2**

1. Place protective covers over the front fender and cowl top grille.
2. Open the hood and mark the hinge locations on the hood for installation purposes.

Fig. 1 Mark the hood hinge for correct installation

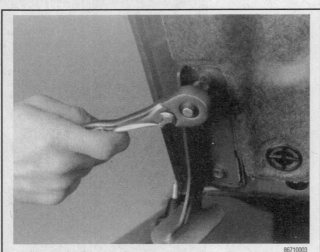

Fig. 2 Remove the hood hinge retaining bolt—but be sure to support the hood before loosening them

3. Remove the hood hinge-to-hood retaining bolts and carefully lift the hood from the vehicle.
4. Installation is the reverse of the removal procedure. Adjust the hood for proper alignment.

ADJUSTMENT

1. Loosen the hinge-to-hood bolts attaching the hood hinge(s).
2. Adjust the hood back-and-forth or side-to-side until it is in the proper position.

3. Loosen the bolts attaching the hood lock and adjust the hood lock back-and-forth or side-to-side until it is in the proper position. Make sure it opens and closes smoothly.
4. Loosen the lock-nut on the dovetail bolt (part of the hood latch assembly) and turn the dovetail bolt in or out as necessary to obtain the correct height.
5. Tighten the lock-nut firmly while holding the dovetail bolt with a screwdriver to secure the adjustment. Torque the lock-nut to 14–19 ft. lbs. (19–26 Nm).

➡**Make sure that the safety catch hooks the hood properly when the hood latch has been disengaged.**

Doors

REMOVAL & INSTALLATION

1. With the door in the full open position, place a jack or stand under the door to support its weight when the bolts are removed. Place a rag between the door and the jack or stand to avoid damaging the painted surface.
2. While supporting the door remove the upper and lower hinge attaching bolts and remove the door.
3. Installation is the reverse of the removal procedure. Adjust the door for proper alignment.

ADJUSTMENT

▶ **See Figure 3**

To adjust the door alignment, loosen the door hinge and door lock striker bolts, then move the door to the desired position. Once the door is properly aligned, tighten the hinge and/or striker bolts.

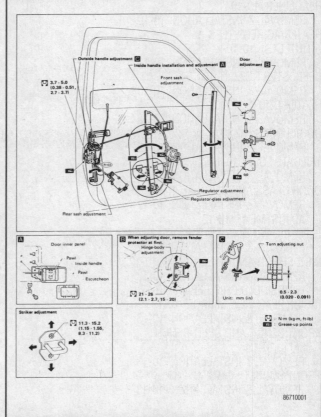

Fig. 3 Door components and adjustment procedures

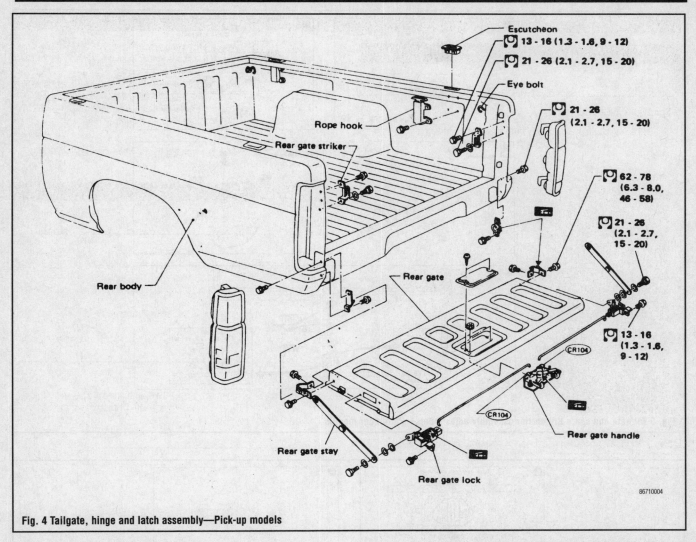

Fig. 4 Tailgate, hinge and latch assembly—Pick-up models

➡Make sure the weatherstrip contacts the body opening evenly to prevent the entry of water.

Tailgate

REMOVAL & INSTALLATION

▶ **See Figures 4 and 5**

1. Open the rear gate.
2. For the pick-up, have an assistant support the gate while you remove the gate hinge stay attaching bolts, then remove the rear gate from the truck.
3. For the Pathfinder, prop the gate open, mark the bolts by scribing around them, then disconnect the prop struts. Have an assistant support the gate, then remove the nuts and lift the gate from the vehicle.
4. Installation is the reverse of the removal procedure. Adjust the rear gate for proper alignment.

ADJUSTMENT

▶ **See Figures 6 and 7**

The rear gate may be adjusted by loosening the hinge attaching bolts and moving the gate as required. The height may be adjusted by adding or removing shims at the rear gate hinge.

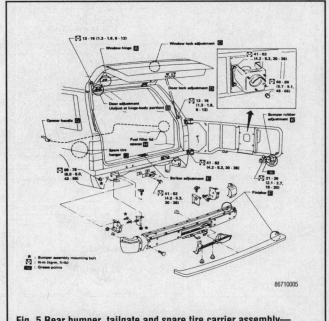

Fig. 5 Rear bumper, tailgate and spare tire carrier assembly—Pathfinder models

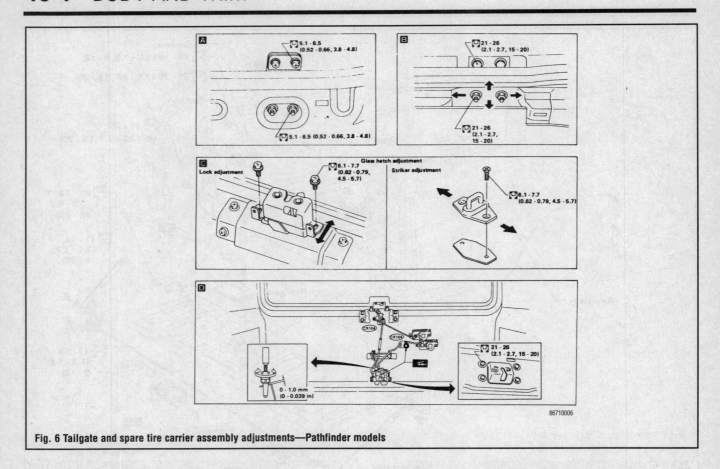

Fig. 6 Tailgate and spare tire carrier assembly adjustments—Pathfinder models

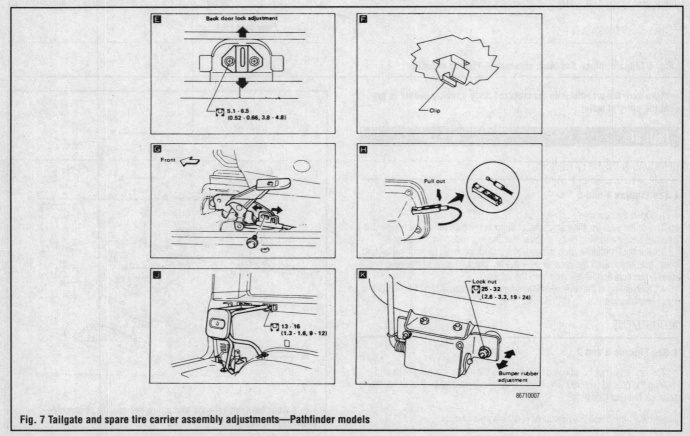

Fig. 7 Tailgate and spare tire carrier assembly adjustments—Pathfinder models

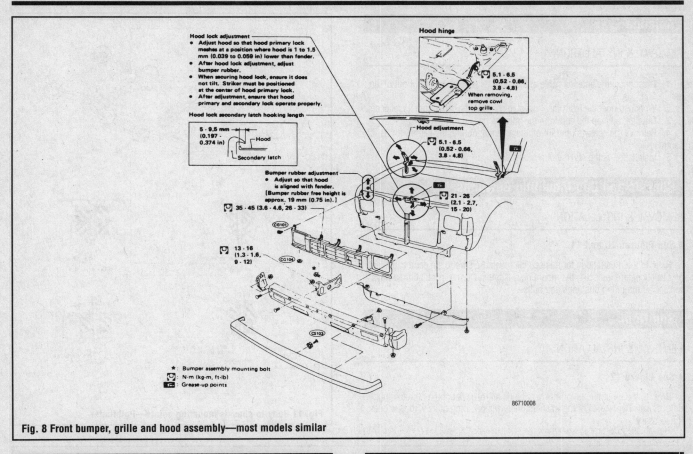

Fig. 8 Front bumper, grille and hood assembly—most models similar

Front or Rear Bumper

REMOVAL & INSTALLATION

▶ **See Figure 8**

1. Support the bumper.
2. If necessary, remove any finish panel, or covers impeding bumper removal.
3. Remove the bumper retaining nuts and bolts, then remove the bumper from the vehicle.
4. Installation is the reverse of removal.

Outside Mirrors

REMOVAL & INSTALLATION

▶ **See Figure 9**

All mirrors are removed by removing the mounting screws and lifting off the mirror and gasket. If necessary, you may have to remove the trim panel, located in the corner of the window to gain access to the mirror mounting screws. On electric type application, disconnect the electrical connection before removing the assembly.

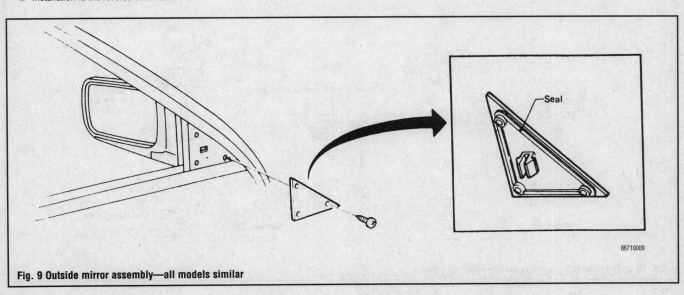

Fig. 9 Outside mirror assembly—all models similar

Antenna

REMOVAL & INSTALLATION

1. Disconnect the antenna cable at the radio by pulling it straight out of the set.
2. Working under the instrument panel, disengage the cable from its retainers.
3. Outside, unsnap the cap from the antenna base.
4. Remove the screw(s) and lift off the antenna, pulling the cable with it, carefully.
5. Installation is the reverse of removal.

Chassis and Cab Mounting Bushings

REMOVAL & INSTALLATION

▶ **See Figures 10 and 11**

Refer to the illustrations for this service repair. Be sure to suspend cab evenly and safely before replacing the mounting bushings. During installation, always replace all mounting bushings and bolts.

Sun Roof

REMOVAL & INSTALLATION

▶ **See Figure 12**

Refer to the illustrations for this service repair. Always tighten all retaining bolts evenly. Replace all of the washers under the retaining bolts with new ones, if necessary.

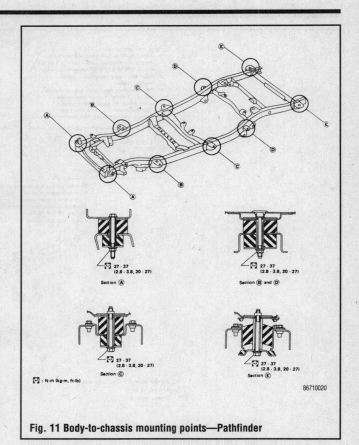

Fig. 11 Body-to-chassis mounting points—Pathfinder

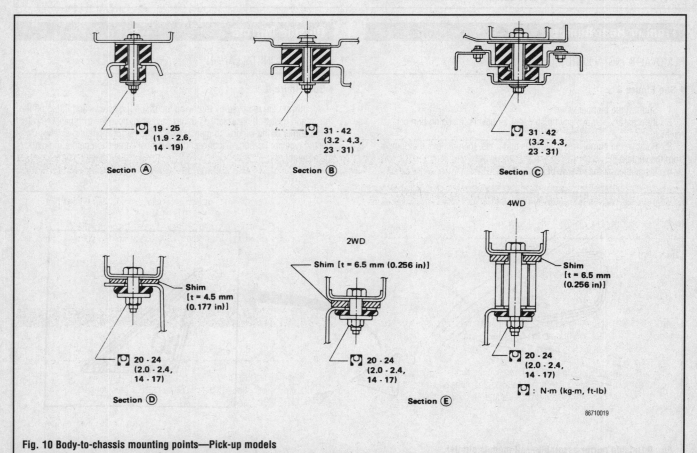

Fig. 10 Body-to-chassis mounting points—Pick-up models

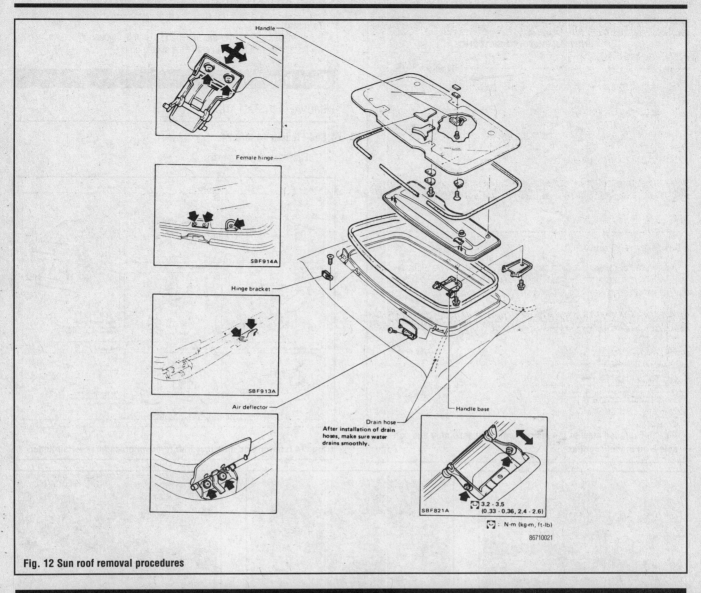

Fig. 12 Sun roof removal procedures

Instrument Panel and Pad

REMOVAL & INSTALLATION

▶ **See Figure 13**

1. Disconnect the negative battery cable.
2. Remove the radio.
3. Remove the ashtray.
4. Remove the control head.
5. Remove the mounting screws and pull out the center console. Disconnect the cigarette lighter and remove the console.
6. Press in the connecting pawls, then remove the left and right side window defroster outlets.
7. Press in the connecting pawls and remove the two fresh air ducts.
8. Carefully press in the connecting clips and remove the three defroster ducts.
9. Remove the assembly retaining screws and lift out the panel and pad assembly.

To install:

10. Position the instrument panel and pad assembly, then tighten the mounting screws.
11. Position the three defroster ducts and press them into place.
12. Position the two fresh air ducts and the side window defroster ducts, then press them into position.
13. Connect the cigarette lighter and install the center console.
14. Install the control head, ashtray and radio.
15. Reconnect the negative battery cable.

Console

REMOVAL & INSTALLATION

1. Remove the shifter knobs and pull out the dust boot(s).
2. Remove the mounting screws and carefully lift the console out over the shift lever and brake handle.

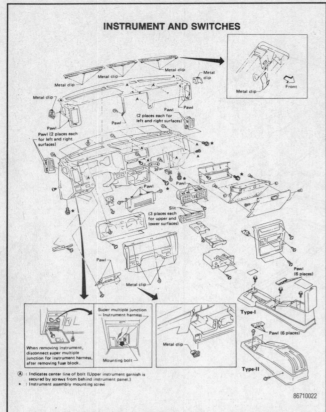

INSTRUMENT AND SWITCHES

Fig. 13 Exploded view of the instrument panel assembly and console—all models similar

To install:
3. Slide the console over the shifter and install the mounting screws.
4. Install the dust boot and screw the shift knob on.

Door Trim Panels

REMOVAL & INSTALLATION

▶ See Figures 14 thru 24

1. Fully lower the door glass.

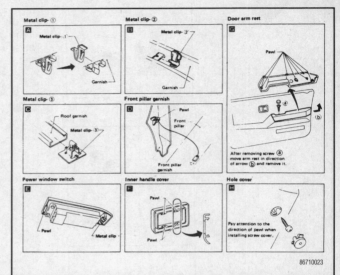

Fig. 14 Interior side and floor trim removal procedures—Pathfinder

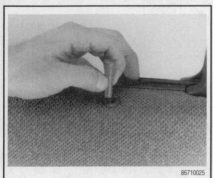

Fig. 15 Remove the lock button first before removing the door panel

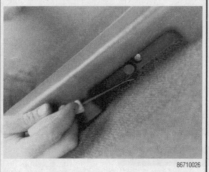

Fig. 16 Remove the plug to gain access to door panel retaining screws

Fig. 17 Remove the trim cover

Fig. 18 Remove the door handle trim

Fig. 19 Remove the power window switch trim panel

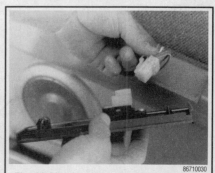

Fig. 20 After loosening the power window switch trim panel, disengage the electrical connection

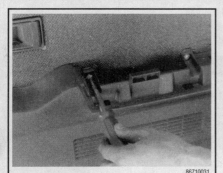

Fig. 21 Remove all the necessary trim panels before removing the door panel clips

Fig. 22 View of the door panel retaining clip—clip must be installed in the hole straight

Fig. 23 Make sure the watershield plastic is in place before installing the door panel

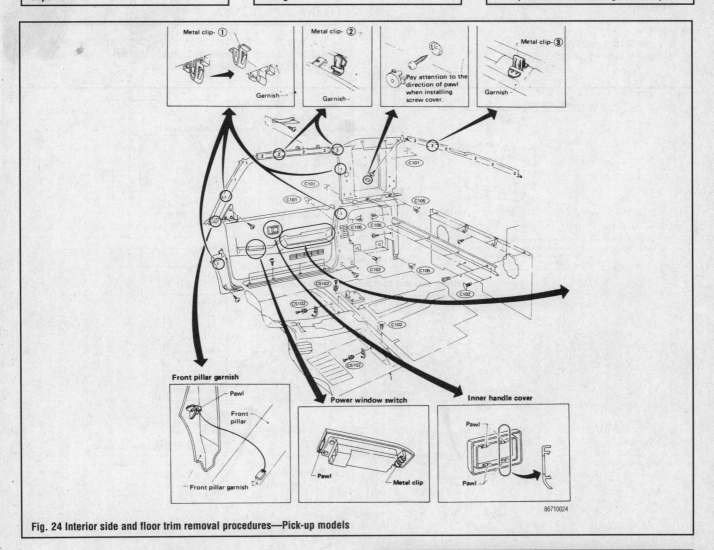

Fig. 24 Interior side and floor trim removal procedures—Pick-up models

2. Remove the arm rest, door lock knob and inside door handle escutcheon.

3. For vehicles with manual windows, remove the regulator handle which is retained by a spring clip.

4. Gently pry the door panel away from the door.

5. Installation is the reverse of removal. For vehicles with manual windows, install the regulator handle (correct position) by aligning it with the one on the opposite door, them push it onto its shaft until the spring clips into place.

Interior Trim Panels

REMOVAL & INSTALLATION

The interior trim panels are generally retained by screws, push type or spring loaded fasteners. To remove the spring type fasteners, apply light hand pressure to separate the trim. To remove the push type fasteners, insert a clip remover tool or the blade of a screwdriver that has been wrapped in tape (to protect the surfaces from damage) between the trim panel and the fastener to be removed, then pry the retainer upward.

Headliner

REMOVAL & INSTALLATION

◆ **See Figures 25, 26 and 27**

1. Disconnect the negative battery cable.
2. Remove the sunvisors and the inner rear view mirror.
3. Remove both front pillar garnish moldings.
4. Remove the side and rear trim.
5. Remove the side assist grips and interior light.
6. Remove the headliner from the vehicle taking care not to bend or distort the liner.

To install:

7. Install the headliner into the vehicle taking care not to bend or distort the liner.
8. Install the side assist grips and interior light.
9. Install both front pillar garnish moldings.

10. Install the side and rear trim.
11. Install the sunvisors and the inner rear view mirror.
12. Connect the negative battery cable.

Heater/AC Registers (Outlets)

REMOVAL & INSTALLATION

1. Disconnect the negative battery cable.
2. If necessary, remove the trim panel.
3. Remove the mounting screws and remove the register.
4. The installation is the reverse of the removal procedure.

Defroster Nozzle

REMOVAL & INSTALLATION

To remove the nozzle, remove all retaining screws then tape the end of a screwdriver and insert it between the defroster nozzle and the panel. Gently pry the nozzle out. To install, push into place by hand.

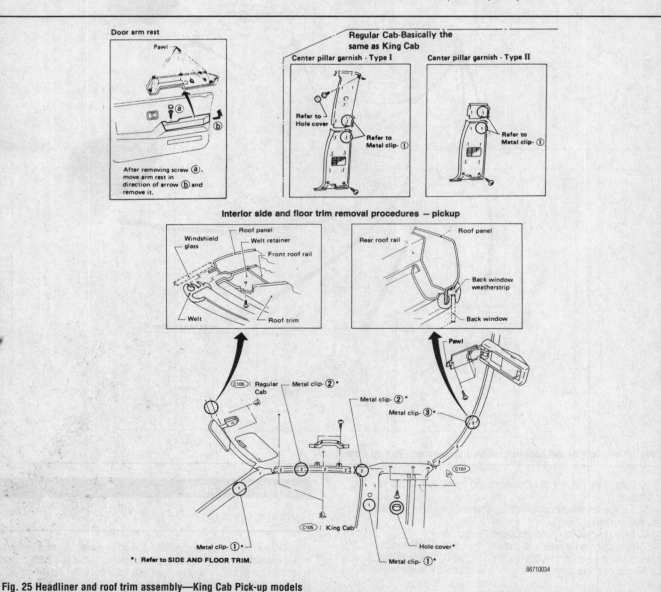

Fig. 25 Headliner and roof trim assembly—King Cab Pick-up models

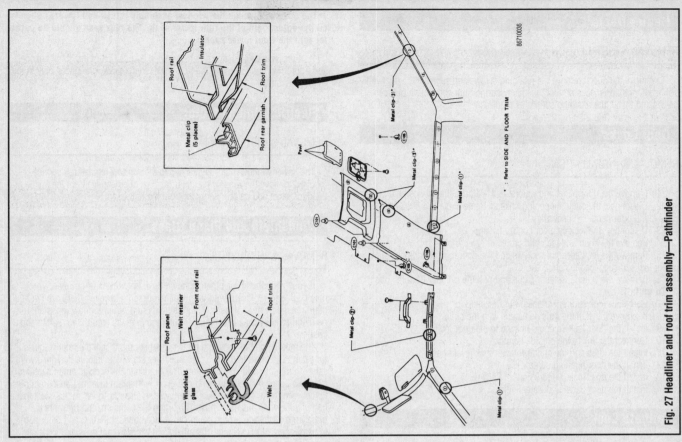

Fig. 27 Headliner and roof trim assembly—Pathfinder

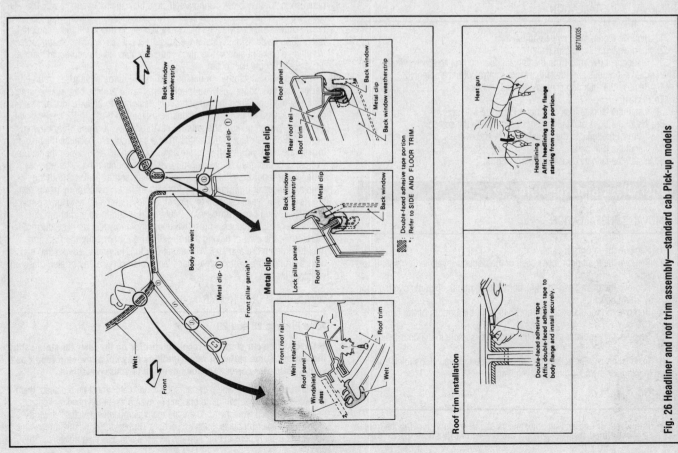

Fig. 26 Headliner and roof trim assembly—standard cab Pick-up models

Heater Ducts

REMOVAL & INSTALLATION

To remove the ducts, remove the retaining screws and separate the ductwork. To install, position pieces of duct together assuring tight connection between pieces and install the retaining screws as required.

Door Locks

REMOVAL & INSTALLATION

1. Remove the door panel and watershield. Remove the service hole cover.
2. Disconnect the outside opening linkage. Remove the two bolts and remove the door handle, if necessary.
3. Disconnect the lock cylinder control linkage.
4. Remove the knob and the child protector lever knob.
5. Remove the lock assembly screws and the door lock. If equipped with power locks, disengage the connector.
6. Remove the cylinder retaining clip and pull the cylinder from the door.

To install:

7. Coat door lock sliding surfaces with grease.
8. If removed, install the outside handle with the bolts.
9. Install the door lock solenoid linkage to the door lock.
10. Connect the link to the outside handle.
11. Install the knob and the child protector lock lever knob.
12. Install the door opening control link.
13. Install the door lock cylinder control linkage.
14. Install the door panel and watershield.

Tailgate Lock

REMOVAL & INSTALLATION

1. Remove the tailgate inside garnish trim.
2. Remove the tailgate trim panel.
3. Disconnect the links from the tailgate door control and lock cylinder. Then remove the bolts and the tailgate lock control with the solenoid.
4. Remove the retaining screws and the cylinder.

To install:

5. Install the tailgate lock cylinder and secure with screws.
6. Install the bolts and tailgate lock control with the solenoid.
7. Connect the links to the tailgate control and cylinder.
8. Install the trim panel.
9. Install the tailgate door inner garnish trim.

Door Glass and Regulator

REMOVAL & INSTALLATION

1. Remove the door trim panel.
2. Remove the front door lower sash or the front door ventilator frame, if so equipped.
3. Remove the door glass-to-regulator attaching bolts, then remove the door glass by lifting upwards.
4. Remove the regulator attaching bolts from the bottom of the regulator.
5. Remove the regulator through the large access hole in the door inside panel.
6. Installation is the reverse of removal. Grease the regulator sliding surfaces, then adjust the door glass and regulator.

ADJUSTMENT

1. In-and-out or fore-and-aft adjustments can be made by moving the front or rear sash and guide channel as required.

➡ The ease with which the window assembly raises and lowers depends on the adjustment of the rear lower sash. The rear sash should be parallel with the front lower sash.

2. Fore-and-aft adjustment is determined by position of the guide channel and front lower sash. Moving the front lower sash backward reduces play in the window assembly.

Electric Window Motor

REMOVAL & INSTALLATION

The power window motor is attached to the window regulator. If service is required, remove the window regulator (as described earlier) from the inside of the door panel and detach the motor from the regulator.

Windshield and Fixed Glass

REMOVAL & INSTALLATION

If your windshield, or other fixed window, is cracked or chipped, you may decide to replace it with a new one yourself. However, there are two main reasons why replacement windshields and other window glass should be installed only by a professional automotive glass technician: safety and cost.

The most important reason a professional should install automotive glass is for safety. The glass in the vehicle, especially the windshield, is designed with safety in mind in case of a collision. The windshield is specially manufactured from two panes of specially-tempered glass with a thin layer of transparent plastic between them. This construction allows the glass to "give" in the event that a part of your body hits the windshield during the collision, and prevents the glass from shattering, which could cause lacerations, blinding and other harm to passengers of the vehicle. The other fixed windows are designed to be tempered so that if they break during a collision, they shatter in such a way that there are no large pointed glass pieces. The professional automotive glass technician knows how to install the glass in a vehicle so that it will function optimally during a collision. Without the proper experience, knowledge and tools, installing a piece of automotive glass yourself could lead to additional harm if an accident should ever occur.

Cost is also a factor when deciding to install automotive glass yourself. Performing this could cost you much more than a professional may charge for the same job. Since the windshield is designed to break under stress, an often life saving characteristic, windshields tend to break VERY easily when an inexperienced person attempts to install one. Do-it-yourselfers buying two, three or even four windshields from a salvage yard because they have broken them during installation are common stories. Also, since the automotive glass is designed to prevent the outside elements from entering your vehicle, improper installation can lead to water and air leaks. Annoying whining noises at highway speeds from air leaks or inside body panel rusting from water leaks can add to your stress level and subtract from your wallet. After buying two or three windshields, installing them and ending up with a leak that produces a noise while driving and water damage during rainstorms, the cost of having a professional do it correctly the first time may be much more alluring. We here at Chilton, therefore, advise that you have a professional automotive glass technician service any broken glass on your vehicle.

WINDSHIELD CHIP REPAIR

▶ **See Figures 28 and 29**

➡ **Check with your state and local authorities on the laws for state safety inspection. Some states or municipalities may not allow chip repair as a viable option for correcting stone damage to your windshield.**

Although severely cracked or damaged windshields must be replaced, there is something that you can do to prolong or even prevent the need for replacement of a chipped windshield. There are many companies which offer windshield chip repair products, such as Loctite's® Bullseye™ windshield repair kit. These kits usually consist of a syringe, pedestal and a sealing adhesive. The

TCCA0P00

Fig. 28 Small chips on your windshield can be fixed with an after-market repair kit, such as the one from Loctite®

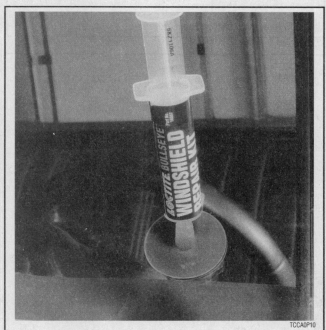

TCCA0P10

Fig. 29 Most kits use a self-stick applicator and syringe to inject the adhesive into the chip or crack

syringe is mounted on the pedestal and is used to create a vacuum which pulls the plastic layer against the glass. This helps make the chip transparent. The adhesive is then injected which seals the chip and helps to prevent further stress cracks from developing

➡ **Always follow the specific manufacturer's instructions.**

Inside Rear View Mirror

REMOVAL & INSTALLATION

➡ **The inside rear view mirror is attached to a base which is secured to the windshield with a special type of glue. If the base should happen to loosen or come off of the windshield, purchase a base glue kit (available at an auto supply store) and follow the manufacturer's instructions carefully to ensure proper bonding of the base to the windshield.**

Remove the inner rear view mirror by loosening the set screw on the mirror stem (remove the cover) and lifting mirror off of the base, which is glued onto the windshield. The installation is the reverse of the removal procedure.

Front Bench and Split-Bench Seats

➡ **See Figure 30**

REMOVAL & INSTALLATION

1. If equipped with power seats, disconnect the negative battery cable.
2. Remove the seat track-to-floor pan bolts and lift out the seat. If applicable, disconnect any necessary wiring.
3. Place the seat on a work bench, then remove the track-to-seat retaining bolts and remove the track from the seat.
4. Position the track to the seat, then install the retaining bolts.
5. If necessary, engage the electrical connector(s). Apply sealer to the hole areas and install the seat. Tighten the bolts.
6. If applicable, connect the negative battery cable.

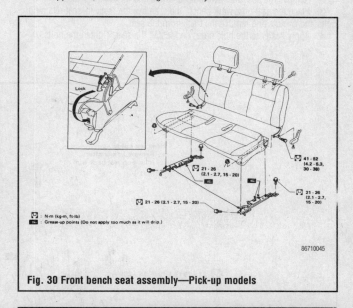

86710045

Fig. 30 Front bench seat assembly—Pick-up models

Front Bucket Seats

REMOVAL & INSTALLATION

➡ **See Figures 31 and 32**

1. If equipped with power seats, disconnect the negative battery cable.
2. Remove the seat track-to-floor pan bolts and lift out the seat. If applicable, disconnect any necessary wiring.
3. Place the seat on a work bench, then remove the track-to-seat retaining bolts and/or nuts and remove the track from the seat.
4. Repeat Steps 1–3 for the other seat.

86710048

Fig. 31 Remove the cover trim cap to gain access to seat track retaining bolts—all models similar

5. Position the track to the seat, then install the retaining bolts.

6. If necessary, engage the electrical connector(s). Apply sealer to the hole areas and install the seat. Tighten the bolts.

7. If applicable, connect the negative battery cable.

Rear Bench Seat

REMOVAL & INSTALLATION

♦ **See Figures 33 and 34**

Pathfinder Only

1. Release the seat back locks on each side of the seat.
2. Remove the seat track-to-floor pan bolts and lift out the seat.
3. Place the seat on a work bench, then remove the track-to-seat retaining bolts and/or nuts and remove the track from the seat.
4. Apply sealer to the hole areas and install the seat. Tighten the bolts.

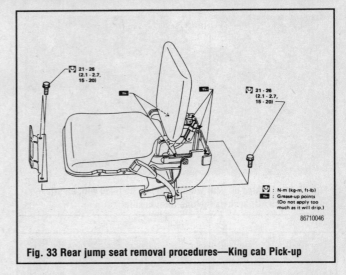

Fig. 33 Rear jump seat removal procedures—King cab Pick-up

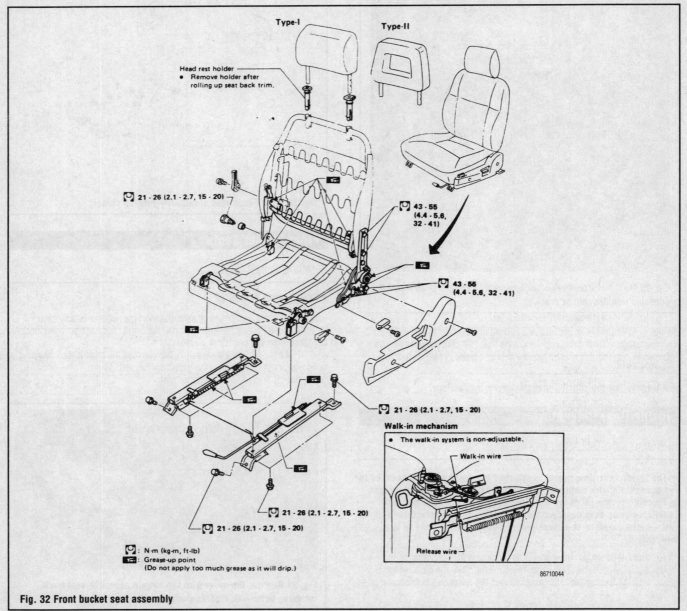

Fig. 32 Front bucket seat assembly

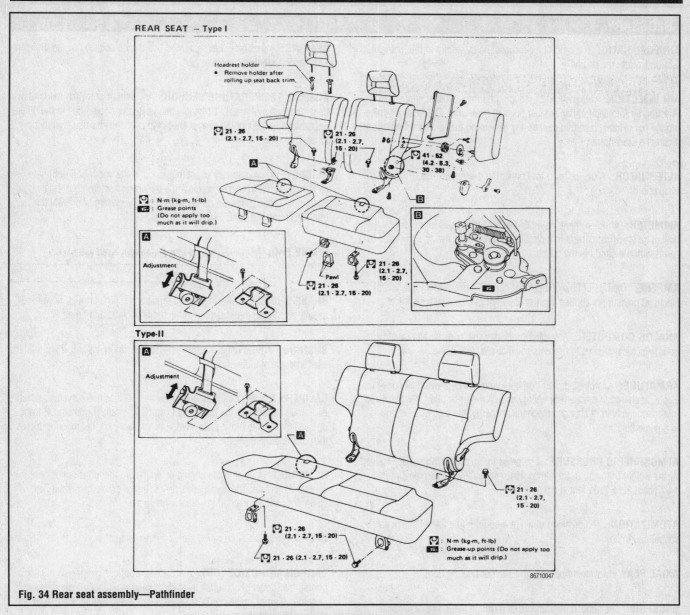

Fig. 34 Rear seat assembly—Pathfinder

TORQUE SPECIFICATIONS

Component	U.S.	Metric
Door stricker adjustment bolt	8–11 ft. lbs.	11–15 Nm
Power door lock actuator	90–125 inch lbs.	10–14 Nm
Front door hinge bolts	20 ft. lbs.	26 Nm
Rear door hinge bolts	20 ft. lbs.	26 Nm
Window channel retainer	90–125 inch lbs.	10–14 Nm
Window-to-regulator sash bolts	60 inch lbs.	7 Nm
Seat adjuster-to-seat bottom frame	21 ft. lbs.	28 Nm
Seat adjuster-to-floor pan	24 ft. lbs.	32 Nm
Seat belt retractor bolt	35 ft. lbs.	48 Nm
Seat belt anchor bolt	35 ft. lbs.	48 Nm
Bumper bolts	20 ft. lbs.	26 Nm

86710C01

GLOSSARY

AIR/FUEL RATIO: The ratio of air-to-gasoline by weight in the fuel mixture drawn into the engine.

AIR INJECTION: One method of reducing harmful exhaust emissions by injecting air into each of the exhaust ports of an engine. The fresh air entering the hot exhaust manifold causes any remaining fuel to be burned before it can exit the tailpipe.

ALTERNATOR: A device used for converting mechanical energy into electrical energy.

AMMETER: An instrument, calibrated in amperes, used to measure the flow of an electrical current in a circuit. Ammeters are always connected in series with the circuit being tested.

AMPERE: The rate of flow of electrical current present when one volt of electrical pressure is applied against one ohm of electrical resistance.

ANALOG COMPUTER: Any microprocessor that uses similar (analogous) electrical signals to make its calculations.

ARMATURE: A laminated, soft iron core wrapped by a wire that converts electrical energy to mechanical energy as in a motor or relay. When rotated in a magnetic field, it changes mechanical energy into electrical energy as in a generator.

ATMOSPHERIC PRESSURE: The pressure on the Earth's surface caused by the weight of the air in the atmosphere. At sea level, this pressure is 14.7 psi at 32°F (101 kPa at 0°C).

ATOMIZATION: The breaking down of a liquid into a fine mist that can be suspended in air.

AXIAL PLAY: Movement parallel to a shaft or bearing bore.

BACKFIRE: The sudden combustion of gases in the intake or exhaust system that results in a loud explosion.

BACKLASH: The clearance or play between two parts, such as meshed gears.

BACKPRESSURE: Restrictions in the exhaust system that slow the exit of exhaust gases from the combustion chamber.

BAKELITE: A heat resistant, plastic insulator material commonly used in printed circuit boards and transistorized components.

BALL BEARING: A bearing made up of hardened inner and outer races between which hardened steel balls roll.

BALLAST RESISTOR: A resistor in the primary ignition circuit that lowers voltage after the engine is started to reduce wear on ignition components.

BEARING: A friction reducing, supportive device usually located between a stationary part and a moving part.

BIMETAL TEMPERATURE SENSOR: Any sensor or switch made of two dissimilar types of metal that bend when heated or cooled due to the different expansion rates of the alloys. These types of sensors usually function as an on/off switch.

BLOWBY: Combustion gases, composed of water vapor and unburned fuel, that leak past the piston rings into the crankcase during normal engine operation. These gases are removed by the PCV system to prevent the buildup of harmful acids in the crankcase.

BRAKE PAD: A brake shoe and lining assembly used with disc brakes.

BRAKE SHOE: The backing for the brake lining. The term is, however, usually applied to the assembly of the brake backing and lining.

BUSHING: A liner, usually removable, for a bearing; an anti-friction liner used in place of a bearing.

CALIPER: A hydraulically activated device in a disc brake system, which is mounted straddling the brake rotor (disc). The caliper contains at least one piston and two brake pads. Hydraulic pressure on the piston(s) forces the pads against the rotor.

CAMSHAFT: A shaft in the engine on which are the lobes (cams) which operate the valves. The camshaft is driven by the crankshaft, via a belt, chain or gears, at one half the crankshaft speed.

CAPACITOR: A device which stores an electrical charge.

CARBON MONOXIDE (CO): A colorless, odorless gas given off as a normal byproduct of combustion. It is poisonous and extremely dangerous in confined areas, building up slowly to toxic levels without warning if adequate ventilation is not available.

CARBURETOR: A device, usually mounted on the intake manifold of an engine, which mixes the air and fuel in the proper proportion to allow even combustion.

CATALYTIC CONVERTER: A device installed in the exhaust system, like a muffler, that converts harmful byproducts of combustion into carbon dioxide and water vapor by means of a heat-producing chemical reaction.

CENTRIFUGAL ADVANCE: A mechanical method of advancing the spark timing by using flyweights in the distributor that react to centrifugal force generated by the distributor shaft rotation.

CHECK VALVE: Any one-way valve installed to permit the flow of air, fuel or vacuum in one direction only.

CHOKE: A device, usually a moveable valve, placed in the intake path of a carburetor to restrict the flow of air.

CIRCUIT: Any unbroken path through which an electrical current can flow. Also used to describe fuel flow in some instances.

CIRCUIT BREAKER: A switch which protects an electrical circuit from overload by opening the circuit when the current flow exceeds a predetermined level. Some circuit breakers must be reset manually, while most reset automatically.

COIL (IGNITION): A transformer in the ignition circuit which steps up the voltage provided to the spark plugs.

COMBINATION MANIFOLD: An assembly which includes both the intake and exhaust manifolds in one casting.

COMBINATION VALVE: A device used in some fuel systems that routes fuel vapors to a charcoal storage canister instead of venting them into the atmosphere. The valve relieves fuel tank pressure and allows fresh air into the tank as the fuel level drops to prevent a vapor lock situation.

COMPRESSION RATIO: The comparison of the total volume of the cylinder and combustion chamber with the piston at BDC and the piston at TDC.

CONDENSER: 1. An electrical device which acts to store an electrical charge, preventing voltage surges. 2. A radiator-like device in the air conditioning system in which refrigerant gas condenses into a liquid, giving off heat.

CONDUCTOR: Any material through which an electrical current can be transmitted easily.

CONTINUITY: Continuous or complete circuit. Can be checked with an ohmmeter.

COUNTERSHAFT: An intermediate shaft which is rotated by a mainshaft and transmits, in turn, that rotation to a working part.

CRANKCASE: The lower part of an engine in which the crankshaft and related parts operate.

CRANKSHAFT: The main driving shaft of an engine which receives reciprocating motion from the pistons and converts it to rotary motion.

CYLINDER: In an engine, the round hole in the engine block in which the piston(s) ride.

CYLINDER BLOCK: The main structural member of an engine in which is found the cylinders, crankshaft and other principal parts.

CYLINDER HEAD: The detachable portion of the engine, usually fastened to the top of the cylinder block and containing all or most of the combustion chambers. On overhead valve engines, it contains the valves and their operating parts. On overhead cam engines, it contains the camshaft as well.

DEAD CENTER: The extreme top or bottom of the piston stroke.

DETONATION: An unwanted explosion of the air/fuel mixture in the combustion chamber caused by excess heat and compression, advanced timing, or an overly lean mixture. Also referred to as "ping".

DIAPHRAGM: A thin, flexible wall separating two cavities, such as in a vacuum advance unit.

DIESELING: A condition in which hot spots in the combustion chamber cause the engine to run on after the key is turned off.

DIFFERENTIAL: A geared assembly which allows the transmission of motion between drive axles, giving one axle the ability to turn faster than the other.

DIODE: An electrical device that will allow current to flow in one direction only.

DISC BRAKE: A hydraulic braking assembly consisting of a brake disc, or rotor, mounted on an axle, and a caliper assembly containing, usually two brake pads which are activated by hydraulic pressure. The pads are forced against the sides of the disc, creating friction which slows the vehicle.

DISTRIBUTOR: A mechanically driven device on an engine which is responsible for electrically firing the spark plug at a predetermined point of the piston stroke.

DOWEL PIN: A pin, inserted in mating holes in two different parts allowing those parts to maintain a fixed relationship.

DRUM BRAKE: A braking system which consists of two brake shoes and one or two wheel cylinders, mounted on a fixed backing plate, and a brake drum, mounted on an axle, which revolves around the assembly.

DWELL: The rate, measured in degrees of shaft rotation, at which an electrical circuit cycles on and off.

ELECTRONIC CONTROL UNIT (ECU): Ignition module, module, amplifier or igniter. See Module for definition.

ELECTRONIC IGNITION: A system in which the timing and firing of the spark plugs is controlled by an electronic control unit, usually called a module. These systems have no points or condenser.

END-PLAY: The measured amount of axial movement in a shaft.

ENGINE: A device that converts heat into mechanical energy.

EXHAUST MANIFOLD: A set of cast passages or pipes which conduct exhaust gases from the engine.

FEELER GAUGE: A blade, usually metal, or precisely predetermined thickness, used to measure the clearance between two parts.

FIRING ORDER: The order in which combustion occurs in the cylinders of an engine. Also the order in which spark is distributed to the plugs by the distributor.

FLOODING: The presence of too much fuel in the intake manifold and combustion chamber which prevents the air/fuel mixture from firing, thereby causing a no-start situation.

FLYWHEEL: A disc shaped part bolted to the rear end of the crankshaft. Around the outer perimeter is affixed the ring gear. The starter drive engages the ring gear, turning the flywheel, which rotates the crankshaft, imparting the initial starting motion to the engine.

FOOT POUND (ft. lbs. or sometimes, ft.lb.): The amount of energy or work needed to raise an item weighing one pound, a distance of one foot.

FUSE: A protective device in a circuit which prevents circuit overload by breaking the circuit when a specific amperage is present. The device is constructed around a strip or wire of a lower amperage rating than the circuit it is designed to protect. When an amperage higher than that stamped on the fuse is present in the circuit, the strip or wire melts, opening the circuit.

GEAR RATIO: The ratio between the number of teeth on meshing gears.

GENERATOR: A device which converts mechanical energy into electrical energy.

HEAT RANGE: The measure of a spark plug's ability to dissipate heat from its firing end. The higher the heat range, the hotter the plug fires.

HUB: The center part of a wheel or gear.

HYDROCARBON (HC): Any chemical compound made up of hydrogen and carbon. A major pollutant formed by the engine as a byproduct of combustion.

HYDROMETER: An instrument used to measure the specific gravity of a solution.

INCH POUND (inch lbs.; sometimes in.lb. or in. lbs.): One twelfth of a foot pound.

INDUCTION: A means of transferring electrical energy in the form of a magnetic field. Principle used in the ignition coil to increase voltage.

INJECTOR: A device which receives metered fuel under relatively low pressure and is activated to inject the fuel into the engine under relatively high pressure at a predetermined time.

INPUT SHAFT: The shaft to which torque is applied, usually carrying the driving gear or gears.

INTAKE MANIFOLD: A casting of passages or pipes used to conduct air or a fuel/air mixture to the cylinders.

JOURNAL: The bearing surface within which a shaft operates.

KEY: A small block usually fitted in a notch between a shaft and a hub to prevent slippage of the two parts.

MANIFOLD: A casting of passages or set of pipes which connect the cylinders to an inlet or outlet source.

MANIFOLD VACUUM: Low pressure in an engine intake manifold formed just below the throttle plates. Manifold vacuum is highest at idle and drops under acceleration.

MASTER CYLINDER: The primary fluid pressurizing device in a hydraulic system. In automotive use, it is found in brake and hydraulic clutch systems and is pedal activated, either directly or, in a power brake system, through the power booster.

MODULE: Electronic control unit, amplifier or igniter of solid state or integrated design which controls the current flow in the ignition primary circuit based on input from the pick-up coil. When the module opens the primary circuit, high secondary voltage is induced in the coil.

NEEDLE BEARING: A bearing which consists of a number (usually a large number) of long, thin rollers.

OHM: (Ω) The unit used to measure the resistance of conductor-to-electrical flow. One ohm is the amount of resistance that limits current flow to one ampere in a circuit with one volt of pressure.

OHMMETER: An instrument used for measuring the resistance, in ohms, in an electrical circuit.

OUTPUT SHAFT: The shaft which transmits torque from a device, such as a transmission.

OVERDRIVE: A gear assembly which produces more shaft revolutions than that transmitted to it.

OVERHEAD CAMSHAFT (OHC): An engine configuration in which the camshaft is mounted on top of the cylinder head and operates the valve either directly or by means of rocker arms.

OVERHEAD VALVE (OHV): An engine configuration in which all of the valves are located in the cylinder head and the camshaft is located in the cylinder block. The camshaft operates the valves via lifters and pushrods.

OXIDES OF NITROGEN (NOx): Chemical compounds of nitrogen produced as a byproduct of combustion. They combine with hydrocarbons to produce smog.

OXYGEN SENSOR: Use with the feedback system to sense the presence of oxygen in the exhaust gas and signal the computer which can reference the voltage signal to an air/fuel ratio.

PINION: The smaller of two meshing gears.

PISTON RING: An open-ended ring with fits into a groove on the outer diameter of the piston. Its chief function is to form a seal between the piston and cylinder wall. Most automotive pistons have three rings: two for compression sealing; one for oil sealing.

PRELOAD: A predetermined load placed on a bearing during assembly or by adjustment.

PRIMARY CIRCUIT: the low voltage side of the ignition system which consists of the ignition switch, ballast resistor or resistance wire, bypass, coil, electronic control unit and pick-up coil as well as the connecting wires and harnesses.

PRESS FIT: The mating of two parts under pressure, due to the inner diameter of one being smaller than the outer diameter of the other, or vice versa; an interference fit.

RACE: The surface on the inner or outer ring of a bearing on which the balls, needles or rollers move.

REGULATOR: A device which maintains the amperage and/or voltage levels of a circuit at predetermined values.

RELAY: A switch which automatically opens and/or closes a circuit.

RESISTANCE: The opposition to the flow of current through a circuit or electrical device, and is measured in ohms. Resistance is equal to the voltage divided by the amperage.

RESISTOR: A device, usually made of wire, which offers a preset amount of resistance in an electrical circuit.

RING GEAR: The name given to a ring-shaped gear attached to a differential case, or affixed to a flywheel or as part of a planetary gear set.

ROLLER BEARING: A bearing made up of hardened inner and outer races between which hardened steel rollers move.

ROTOR: 1. The disc-shaped part of a disc brake assembly, upon which the brake pads bear; also called, brake disc. 2. The device mounted atop the distributor shaft, which passes current to the distributor cap tower contacts.

SECONDARY CIRCUIT: The high voltage side of the ignition system, usually above 20,000 volts. The secondary includes the ignition coil, coil wire, distributor cap and rotor, spark plug wires and spark plugs.

SENDING UNIT: A mechanical, electrical, hydraulic or electro-magnetic device which transmits information to a gauge.

SENSOR: Any device designed to measure engine operating conditions or ambient pressures and temperatures. Usually electronic in nature and designed to send a voltage signal to an on-board computer, some sensors may operate as a simple on/off switch or they may provide a variable voltage signal (like a potentiometer) as conditions or measured parameters change.

SHIM: Spacers of precise, predetermined thickness used between parts to establish a proper working relationship.

SLAVE CYLINDER: In automotive use, a device in the hydraulic clutch system which is activated by hydraulic force, disengaging the clutch.

SOLENOID: A coil used to produce a magnetic field, the effect of which is to produce work.

SPARK PLUG: A device screwed into the combustion chamber of a spark ignition engine. The basic construction is a conductive core inside of a ceramic insulator, mounted in an outer conductive base. An electrical charge from the spark plug wire travels along the conductive core and jumps a preset air gap to a grounding point or points at the end of the conductive base. The resultant spark ignites the fuel/air mixture in the combustion chamber.

SPLINES: Ridges machined or cast onto the outer diameter of a shaft or inner diameter of a bore to enable parts to mate without rotation.

TACHOMETER: A device used to measure the rotary speed of an engine, shaft, gear, etc., usually in rotations per minute.

THERMOSTAT: A valve, located in the cooling system of an engine, which is closed when cold and opens gradually in response to engine heating, controlling the temperature of the coolant and rate of coolant flow.

TOP DEAD CENTER (TDC): The point at which the piston reaches the top of its travel on the compression stroke.

TORQUE: The twisting force applied to an object.

TORQUE CONVERTER: A turbine used to transmit power from a driving member to a driven member via hydraulic action, providing changes in drive ratio and torque. In automotive use, it links the driveplate at the rear of the engine to the automatic transmission.

TRANSDUCER: A device used to change a force into an electrical signal.

TRANSISTOR: A semi-conductor component which can be actuated by a small voltage to perform an electrical switching function.

TUNE-UP: A regular maintenance function, usually associated with the replacement and adjustment of parts and components in the electrical and fuel systems of a vehicle for the purpose of attaining optimum performance.

TURBOCHARGER: An exhaust driven pump which compresses intake air and forces it into the combustion chambers at higher than atmospheric pressures. The increased air pressure allows more fuel to be burned and results in increased horsepower being produced.

VACUUM ADVANCE: A device which advances the ignition timing in response to increased engine vacuum.

VACUUM GAUGE: An instrument used to measure the presence of vacuum in a chamber.

VALVE: A device which control the pressure, direction of flow or rate of flow of a liquid or gas.

VALVE CLEARANCE: The measured gap between the end of the valve stem and the rocker arm, cam lobe or follower that activates the valve.

VISCOSITY: The rating of a liquid's internal resistance to flow.

VOLTMETER: An instrument used for measuring electrical force in units called volts. Voltmeters are always connected parallel with the circuit being tested.

WHEEL CYLINDER: Found in the automotive drum brake assembly, it is a device, actuated by hydraulic pressure, which, through internal pistons, pushes the brake shoes outward against the drums.

MASTER INDEX